The Financial Marketplace

S. Kerry Cooper
Donald R. Fraser
Texas A & M University

Addison-Wesley Publishing Company   Reading, Massachusetts
Menlo Park, California • London • Amsterdam • Don Mills, Ontario • Sydney

Library of Congress Cataloging in Publication Data

Cooper, S Kerry.
  The financial marketplace.

  Includes index.
  1. Finance. 2. Finance—United States. I. Fraser,
Donald R., joint author. II. Title.
HG173.C675   332.1   80-28495
ISBN 0-201-00196-9

Reprinted with corrections, March 1983

ISBN 0-201-00196-9
  BCDEFGHIJ-DO-89876543

For our wives
Maryvonne
Lyn
and kids
Chris and Danielle
Eleanor

Preface

This book is designed primarily for use in those courses dealing with the macrofinancial environment. Such courses generally stress the importance of financial markets, the nature and role of the financial system and the significance of money and banking in the economy. In these types of courses, the book is designed to "stand alone" as the principal source of reference material. However, the book is also suitable for use as supplemental material in courses primarily concerned with microfinancial decision-making such as traditional financial management, bank management, and financial institutions management courses. The structure and nature of the book reflect the authors' conviction that effective microfinancial decision-making requires an understanding of the macrofinancial environment. This conviction has been reinforced by our observation of the scope and pace of change in the macrofinancial environment in recent years.

The book covers the full range of financial markets, financial instruments, and the major financial and nonfinancial participants in financial markets. Emphasis is given to some of the major innovations in financial markets, with a complete chapter devoted to the financial futures markets. In addition, since developments in the financial markets are closely intertwined with monetary policy, considerable attention is paid to the structure and role of the Federal Reserve System and the goals and methods of monetary control.

The sequence of chapter coverage can be easily adapted to suit the background of students and the emphasis and orientation of the instructor and the course in which the book is used. For example, coverage of Chapter 6 (Money and the Financial System) and Chapter 7 (The Structure and Role of the Federal Reserve System) may be of marginal value for students with a strong background in economics. Also, instructors wishing to devote maximum attention to private-sector financial markets, instruments, and institutions (and less to monetary policy and other macroeconomic influences) may choose to omit or minimize coverage of Chapters 6, 7, 21 (Monetary Policy: Implementation and Impact), and 22 (Fiscal Policy and Federal Debt Management) and perhaps one or more chapters in Part III as well. Finally, some instructors may consider the degree of coverage of the international financial system offered by Chapter 19 (The International Monetary System) to be adequate, and thus choose to omit Chapter 20 (International Financial Markets and Institutions), which presents a more detailed discussion of topics surveyed in Chapter 19.

The text material is presented with a minimum amount of mathematical treatment and only limited integration with the original literature. Technical terms are carefully defined when introduced and, on occasion, redefined when employed in a subsequent chapter. (This facilitates altering the chapter sequence and also helps the student develop a thorough grasp of the terminology of the financial marketplace.) A careful balance of description and analysis has been attempted for all subjects. It is intended that students using this text will find the descriptive content complete and the analytical aspect useful in analyzing, interpreting, and understanding the financial marketplace.

The text material is supplemented by a number of appendixes, which are of two basic varieties. Some provide discusssion of certain current controversies in the operation and regulation of the financial system, such as the issue of interstate banking (the appendix to Chapter 5). Though important, these controversies do not merit complete treatment in the chapters themselves. The other type of appendix provides an extension of a topic discussed briefly in the body of the chapter it follows. For example, Chapter 3 (The Flow of Funds Accounts in the U.S. Economy) is followed by an appendix that describes how funds-flow analysis can be used in forecasting. The appendix to Chapter 9 provides an exensive analysis of the empirical literature that has evaluated the different explanations of the yield curve. These appendixes can be useful to an interested student who seeks to obtain more in-depth knowledge of some important topics than it was possible or necessary to include within the chapters themselves.

Finally, this book is as up-to-date as the authors and publishers could possibly make it. Full treatment is included, for example, of the Depository Institutions Deregulation and Monetary Control Act of 1980, the current measures of monetary aggregates, and the Federal Reserve System's present approach to monetary control.

We are extremely grateful to the many individuals who reviewed portions of earlier drafts of the manuscript. We hope they will see the benefits of their constructive comments. In particular, we are deeply indebted to five individuals who reviewed in detail the entire manuscript: Doug Austin, University of Toledo; Paul Horvitz, University of Houston; Tim Koch, Texas Tech University; Morgan Lynge, University of Illinois; and James Verbrugge, University of Georgia. Their comments and suggestions were consistently valuable. They are not, of course, responsible for any errors or oversights contained herein.

Finally, we wish to thank the staff at Addison-Wesley Publishing Company, especially our editors Bill Hamilton, Margaret Cassidy, and Mary Clare McEwing, who have worked so hard to bring this text into print.

We welcome suggestions and comments on this text from both students and faculty.

College Station, Texas   S.K.C.
September, 1981   D.R.F.

Contents

PART 1 THE STRUCTURE AND ROLE OF THE FINANCIAL SYSTEM   **1**

Chapter 1   An Overview of the Financial System   **3**

The role of the financial system 4 ◻ Financial intermediaries and instruments 7 ◻ Plan of the book 11 ◻ Summary 12 ◻ Questions 12 ◻ References 12

Chapter 2   The Role of Financial Markets: Saving, Investment, and Financial Intermediation   **15**

Saving, investment, and financial markets 15 ◻ Financial intermediation 17 ◻ Types of financial markets 21 ◻ The efficiency of the financial system 23 ◻ Summary 26 ◻ Questions 27 ◻ References 27

Chapter 3   The Flow of Funds Accounts in the U.S. Economy   **29**

Concept of the flow of funds 29 ◻ The flow of funds accounts as published by the Federal Reserve 34 ◻ Summary 40 ◻ Questions 40 ◻ References 41 ◻ Appendix: Using the flow of funds to forecast financial market pressures 42

Chapter 4   Financial Intermediaries: Banking and Nonbanking Financial Institutions   **49**

Banks versus nonbanks: A comparison 49 ◻ The bank as a firm: Sources and uses of funds 50 ◻ Types of financial institutions 57 ◻ Growing competition among financial institutions 67 ◻ The Depository Institutions Deregulation and Monetary Control Act of 1980 69 ◻ Summary 71 ◻ Questions 71 ◻ References 72 ◻ Appendix: Electronic funds transfer systems and the role of financial intermediaries 73

Chapter 5   The Regulatory Environment: The Role of Government in the Financial System   **77**

Regulatory influences of government 78 ◻ The functions of regulatory agencies 84 ◻ Limits on borrowing and lending behavior of individual institutions 86 ◻ Securities and Exchange Commission 90 ◻ Government as a financial intermediary 91 ◻ Summary 93 ◻ Questions 93 ◻ References 94 ◻ Appendix: The question of interstate banking 95

PART II   THE FEDERAL RESERVE AND MONETARY CONTROL   **101**

Chapter 6   Money and the Financial System   **103**

The nature of money 103 □ Measurement of the money supply 106 □ The economic significance of money 108 □ Money creation: Demand deposit expansion 112 □ The quantity of bank reserves 116 □ The monetary base and the monetary multiplier 120 □ Summary 122 □ Questions 123 □ References 123 □ Appendix: How much does money matter? 125

Chapter 7   The Structure and Role of the Federal Reserve System   **129**

The founding of the Federal Reserve 130 □ Structure of the Federal Reserve System 132 □ Instruments of monetary and credit policy 138 □ Problems of monetary control 146 □ The Fed as fiscal agent 147 □ Regulation and supervision of member banks 147 □ Summary 148 □ Questions 149 □ References 150

PART III   THE DETERMINATION, STRUCTURE, AND SIGNIFICANCE OF INTEREST RATES   **151**

Chapter 8   The Level of Interest Rates   **153**

The interest rate as an allocating device 154 □ Yields and prices 154 □ The loanable funds theory 159 □ Explaining an interest rate cycle using the loanable funds theory 168 □ Summary 170 □ Questions 171 □ References 171 □ Appendix: The liquidity preference theory of interest rate determination □ 172

Chapter 9   The Term Structure of Interest Rates   **177**

Maturity and yield 178 □ Explaining the yield curve 183 □ Maturity versus duration 190 □ Uses of the yield curve 192 □ Summary 196 □ Questions 197 □ References 198 □ Appendix: Empirical Evidence on the term structure 199

Chapter 10   Inflation and Other Influences on the Structure of Interest Rates   **203**

Inflation 203 □ Default risk 211 □ Taxability 214 □ Callability 217 □ Marketability 218 □ Summary 218 □ Questions 219 □ References 220

PART IV   FINANCIAL MARKETS   **221**

Chapter 11   Risk, Return, and the Efficiency of Financial Markets   **223**

Part 1: Asset Pricing in Financial Markets 224 □ Portfolio selection and diversification 224 □ The capital-asset-pricing model 230 □ Financial market efficiency 234 □ Part 2:

Types of Financial Markets 235 □ Summary 239 □ Questions 240 □ References 241

Chapter 12 Operations of Financial Institutions in the Financial Markets   **243**

The basic role of financial institutions 244 □ Maturity management 248 □ Credit-risk management 254 □ Maturity management, credit-risk management, and the basic functions of financial institutions: A synthesis 256 □ Summary 257 □ Questions 257 □ References 258

Chapter 13 The Money Market: Part 1   **259**

The money market: An overview 259 □ Security dealers 261 □ Federal funds 262 □ Certificates of Deposit 267 □ Eurodollars 271 □ Bankers acceptances 271 □ Summary 275 □ Questions 276 □ References 276

Chapter 14 The Money Market: Part 2   **277**

U.S. government securities 277 □ U.S. government agency securities 282 □ Commercial paper 287 □ Summary 292 □ Questions 293 □ References 293

Chapter 15 The Capital Market: Bonds   **295**

Dimensions of the capital market 296 □ Corporate bonds 297 □ State and local government bonds 302 □ U.S. government and government agency securities 306 □ Summary 308 □ Questions 309 □ References 310

Chapter 16 The Capital Market: Mortgage Instruments   **311**

Characteristics of mortgages 312 □ The demand for mortgage funds 315 □ The supply of mortgage funds 315 □ The troubled mortgage market 320 □ Summary 321 □ Questions 321 □ References 322

Chapter 17 The Capital Market: Equity Securities   **323**

Business corporation equity financing 325 □ Characteristics of equity securities 328 □ Ownership of equity securities 329 □ The primary market for equities 330 □ The secondary market for equity securities 332 □ Valuation of equity securities 334 □ The record of equity returns 337 □ Summary 337 □ Questions 338 □ References 338 □ Appendix: The options market 339

Chapter 18 Financial Futures Markets   **343**

The nature of financial futures markets 344 □ Buying and selling financial futures contracts 348 □ Uses of the financial futures markets: Interest-bearing securities 349 □ Uses of the financial futures markets: Foreign currencies 355 □ Issues raised by the growth of financial futures markets 357 □ Summary 359 □ Questions 359 □ References 360

PART V   THE INTERNATIONAL FINANCIAL SYSTEM   361

Chapter 19   The International Monetary System   363

Fundamentals of the international payments system 364 □ Modern exchange rate systems 372 □ The role of commercial banks in international payments 375 □ Interest rate and exchange rate relationships 378 □ International financial markets 381 □ A fragile international monetary system? 383 □ Summary 388 □ Questions 389 □ References 390

Chapter 20   International Financial Markets and Institutions   391

International money markets 392 □ The international capital market 400 □ U.S. commercial banking abroad 407 □ Foreign banks in the United States 409 □ International banking and financial markets: A need for controls? 411 □ Summary 413 □ Questions 414 □ References 414

PART VI   MONETARY, FISCAL, AND DEBT MANAGEMENT POLICIES   417

Chapter 21   Monetary Policy: Implementation and Impact   419

Economic policy and economic activity 419 □ Goals of economic policy 423 □ Effects of monetary policy 430 □ Unsettled issues of monetary policy 434 □ Monetary policy targets 436 □ The future of monetary policy 440 □ Summary 441 □ Questions 442 □ References 442 □ Appendix: Expectations, economic policy, and the Phillips curve 444

Chapter 22   Fiscal Policy and Federal Debt Management: Taxing, Spending, and Borrowing   449

Fiscal management activities of the U.S. Treasury 450 □ Fiscal policy 453 □ "Automatic" and discretionary fiscal effects 461 □ Debt management as a tool of economic policy 463 □ Summary 465 □ Questions 466 □ References 466

Index   469

Part I

The Structure and Role of the Financial System

Chapter 1

An Overview of the Financial System

The financial system of the United States and other developed nations performs a number of functions that are essential for a modern private-enterprise economy. Two of the most important of these functions consist of providing the means by which payments for transactions are accomplished and savings are accumulated and channeled into investment uses. Paying for goods and services, saving, lending, borrowing, and investing are all activities that are carried out in the framework of instruments, institutions, and markets that constitute the financial system. Included in this framework are the financial agents of the central government, which in this country include the U.S. Treasury and the Federal Reserve System, as well as numerous private institutions and agents. A complex and sophisticated financial system is an integral and essential component of the economic system of any advanced, industrialized society.

The financial system's components can be defined as follows: *financial instruments* are documentary evidences of obligations underlying the exchange of resources among contracting parties; *financial markets* are the arenas or mechanisms by which financial instruments are traded; and *financial institutions* create and trade financial instruments and otherwise facilitate the flows of resources among market participants. Financial instruments include bank deposits, debt securities, and shares of stock issued by corporations. Financial markets are the stock market, bond market, mortgage market, and what is called the "money market" (in which short-term debt securities are traded). Financial institutions include commercial banks, savings and loan associations, insurance companies, and brokerage firms.

Knowledge of the nature and significance of the financial system is best attained by gaining an understanding of these various instruments, markets, and institutions and of the ways the financial requirements of a modern economy are satisfied by their interaction. This book focuses primarily on financial markets, for it is in these markets that financial institutions, savers, and investors "come together" to effect exchanges of financial instruments. The financial marketplace is the core of the financial system.

The purpose of this chapter is to develop an overview of the role, structure, and operation of the financial system. In addition, a brief discussion of this book's organization and content is included.

THE ROLE OF THE FINANCIAL SYSTEM

The Economic Significance of the Financial System

Economic activity is characterized by a great many exchange transactions—the buying and selling of goods, services, and productive resources. Economists often find useful a distinction between the "real" and "financial" aspects of these transactions. In a sales transaction, for example, a buyer takes physical possession of goods in exchange for his payment of money or his promise to pay in the future. The former aspect of the transaction is "real"; the latter is "financial." The goods are "real assets"; the payment is with a "financial asset." In a barter system, goods are exchanged for goods; the introduction of money as a medium of exchange adds the "financial" element to economic transactions.

As the "real" aspects of transactions become more complex, involving exchanges over time as well as at a point in time, their "financial" aspects necessarily become more involved. The "real" aspect of a loan, for example, is the postponement by the lender of the opportunity to consume now (buy something with the funds instead of lending them) with the expectation of consuming more in the future. The "financial" aspect of a loan involves the creation of a financial instrument, which may range from an IOU between friends through the execution of a bank note indicating due date, interest, etc., to the rather complex process of the issuing by a corporation of debt securities.

There are very important relationships between the financial system of a nation (and, indeed, the world) and the enormously varied and complex activities of people working, buying, and selling as part of the ordinary course of human affairs. The financial system includes both markets for financial instruments and those institutions concerned with financial transactions, just as the "real" component of the economic system includes both markets for goods and services and those institutions that bring together people and resources to produce goods and services. The financial system is a vital component of the total economic system, greatly increasing its capacity to satisfy the needs and wants of people for goods.

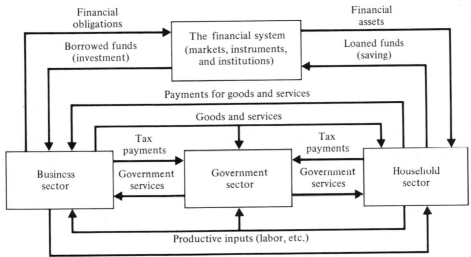

Fig. 1.1 Exchange flows in an economic system

To a large degree, the economic role of the financial system can be characterized as one of facilitating real and financial transactions. Figure 1.1 depicts the relationship between the financial system and the various real and financial flows in the economy. In this simplified view, the economic system consists of a *business* sector, a *household* sector, and a *government* sector. In terms of *real flows,* the business sector produces goods and services, which are purchased by the household sector for consumption purposes. The household sector provides labor and other necessary productive inputs to the business sector in exchange for wages, salaries, and other compensation. (We shall say more about these ''other'' inputs and compensation shortly.) The government sector collects tax payments from the household and business sectors and uses these receipts to buy goods, services, and productive inputs, which are then utilized to supply government services (roads, law enforcement, etc.) to the other sectors.[1]

Turning to the role of the financial system (other than the payments function) in this simple model of the economy, we may note that the financial system is interposed between flows of saving, investment, and financial instruments (financial assets of savers and financial obligations of investors). We may note further that these flows reflect *exchanges of resource use over time,* rather than exchanges of real resources at points in time (''spot'' exchanges). Exchanges of resource use over time (lending and borrowing) is made possible

---

1. For the sake of simplicity, Fig. 1.1 assumes a ''balanced budget'' in the government sector. Actually, of course, the government sector is a frequent participant in financial markets—borrowing funds by issuing financial obligations.

by economic participants' forgoing current consumption in favor of future consumption. This postponement of consumption—*saving*—is encouraged by the prospect that future consumption opportunities will be enlarged as the result of the productive use of the resources presently made available for *investment* purposes.[2]

The existence of saving in an economic system provides an opportunity for the business sector to expand the means of production. In a private-enterprise economy, households can use saved receipts to lend to business firms or to purchase ownership shares in business firms. Such transfers of purchasing power supply the business sector with *money capital,* the financial resources that enable firms to gather and utilize real resources for investment and thereby increase output of goods and services. The investment of these funds in turn provides the means of paying a return on savings—*interest* in the case of loaned funds and *dividends* in the case of purchases of ownership shares. The flow of saved resources to the business and government sectors from the household sector is a productive input into these sectors, just as is labor. Interest and dividends are the compensation for this flow of saved resources, just as wages are the compensation for labor provided. (These are the "other" inputs and compensation mentioned previously.)

Economic units, whether in the household, business, or government sector, that spend less than their net receipts are called *surplus economic units.* This excess of net receipts over expenditures for a period of time is called *saving* when it occurs in the household sector, *retained earnings* in the business sector, and a *budget surplus* in the government sector. (The term "saving" is used for all instances of surplus receipts in the following discussion.) An economic unit in any of the economy's sectors may also elect (voluntarily or involuntarily) to spend *more* than its net receipts by drawing on past savings (dissaving) or by borrowing. These economic units are called *deficit* economic units. *Dissaving* is made possible by the conversion of past saved funds into presently spendable funds.

The financial system—the framework of instruments, markets, and institutions—facilitates the transfer of saved funds from surplus (savers) to deficit spending units (borrowers).[3] A deficit spending unit may borrow from a surplus unit by exchanging a financial instrument (a promise to make future payments) for the latter's saved funds. The issuer of the instrument (the borrower) thus incurs a *financial obligation.* The recipient of the instrument (the lender) obtains a *financial asset.* Such exchanges of saved funds for financial assets are readily and efficiently accomplished in financial markets. The important contribution to this process made by the third component of the financial system—financial institutions— is made through their role as *intermediaries* between lenders and borrowers. The financial intermediation process is of great significance for the channeling of saved funds into investment uses. Financial intermediation involves financial instrument creation and

---

2. *Saving* is a *flow,* an amount for some *period of time* equal to the difference between two other flows for that period—income and consumption spending. *Savings* is a *stock,* the accumulated quantity of saved funds at a *point in time.*

3. A deficit spending unit need not be a borrower if it has saved resources from prior periods. In this case, dissaving is possible by expending these saved resources. If, as is likely, the saved resources are held in the form of financial instruments, they can be readily converted into money for spending purposes.

acquisition and financial market activities, as well as financial institutions, and warrants some additional introductory discussion.

Financial Intermediation

Financial intermediation greatly facilitates the process by which the savings of surplus economic units are exchanged for financial obligations (promises to pay) of deficit economic units. Financial intermediation involves the purchase by financial intermediaries of financial obligations of borrowing economic units in the various sectors of the economy with funds obtained from savers who, in turn, acquire financial obligations of these intermediaries. The financial obligations of intermediaries, called *indirect securities,* include deposits with commercial banks, savings and loan associations, and other "depository institutions," as well as claims against pension funds and insurance companies arising from contributions and premiums. These obligations are "indirect" in the sense that, unlike the *direct (or primary) securities* issued by deficit spending units in the economy to obtain funds for investment or consumption, the funds obtained from their issuance are utilized primarily to acquire other (primary) securities. For reasons discussed at length in the next chapter, indirect securities have a number of significant advantages (relative to primary securities) for many savers—a fact that accounts for the large and significant economic role played by financial intermediaries.

The flow of funds related to the saving-investment process depicted at the top of Fig. 1.1 may thus be intermediated or nonintermediated. Nonintermediated flows occur when households acquire the financial obligations of the business sector directly, for example, when households purchase corporate bonds or shares of stock in financial markets. Intermediated flows occur when households acquire financial claims against intermediaries, and the latter purchase primary securities issued by business firms. A common example of this indirect flow is the loan to a business firm of household savings on deposit with a financial institution.

Succeeding chapters contain a great deal of detailed discussion about the major financial intermediaries and the financial instruments in which they deal.[4] The next section of this chapter includes a sketch of the principal types of intermediaries, along with a brief description of the most important financial instruments traded in financial markets. A corresponding description of financial markets is included in the next chapter.

FINANCIAL INTERMEDIARIES AND INSTRUMENTS

Types of Financial Intermediaries

Commercial Banks. Commercial banks, perhaps the most familiar type of intermediary, issue "indirect securities" in the form of demand deposits (checking accounts) and time

---

4. Participants in the financial markets include financial institutions that do *not* play a financial intermediation role but serve rather as brokers between buyers and sellers of financial instruments. This group includes dealers in financial securities and investment banking firms.

deposits (savings accounts). Time deposits called *certificates of deposit* (CDs) have become increasingly important in recent years. Demand deposits are payable to the depositor (or *for* the depositor) on demand, but time certificates have a stipulated time to maturity (ranging from 14 days to several years, with interest rates generally increasing with maturity). "Passbook" savings accounts are generally paid on demand, although banks can legally require a notice-of-withdrawal period.

Commercial banks acquire direct securities by lending to business firms and consumers and by purchasing various types of securities (mostly federal, state, and local government securities) in the securities markets.

Operating distinctions between commercial banks and other depository institutions have been narrowed and blurred in recent years by the rapid pace of financial innovation and legal change. In particular, the fact that banks no longer have a "monopoly" on their liabilities (demand deposits) as a means of payment has had a considerable impact. The pressures of rapid inflation on all depository institutions has also had the effect of reducing operating differences.

Savings and Loan Associations.   Like commercial banks, savings and loan associations are depository institutions, and the indirect securities they issue have essentially the same characteristics as the time deposits of commercial banks. In the case of *mutual* savings and loan associations, depositors are technically owners, and deposit claims are often called *shares,* but the distinction has no operational significance. Savings and loan associations' principal holdings of direct securities are mortgages on residential dwellings.

Mutual Savings Banks.   Mutual savings banks are very similar to savings and loan associations in terms of the types of indirect securities issued and direct securities acquired. However, they are much less numerous (only about 500 are in operation) and are geographically concentrated in the northeastern United States.

Credit Unions.   Credit unions are cooperatively owned associations, usually with membership exhibiting some particular institutional or professional affiliation. Their indirect securities are member deposits (shares), and their direct securities are generally loans to members (consumer loans).

Insurance Companies.   Insurance companies are nondepository intermediaries of considerable significance. The "indirect securities" issued by insurance firms are various types of life, asset protection, and annuity policies. The premium payments on these policies are utilized to acquire a wide variety of direct securities, including corporate stocks and bonds, real estate mortgages, and government securities.

Mutual Funds.   While nondepository in nature, mutual funds constitute a form of "pure" intermediation. Investors buy ownership shares (indirect securities) of the mutual fund, which in turn purchases direct securities. Mutual funds differ somewhat in organization form and vary quite widely in terms of the type of direct securities purchased. Mutual funds serve to provide investors with considerable diversification, liquidity, and professional security analysis and selection, irrespective of the magnitude of the sum invested.

Pension Funds.   The indirect securities issued by pension funds are the obligations to the covered employees for retirement pensions. The contributions to the fund—by either employers or employees or both—are used to purchase various types of direct securities, including corporate stocks and bonds, government securities, and real estate mortgages.

The list above is not exhaustive, but it does include the most important privately owned financial intermediaries. There are a number of government agencies that serve a significant financial intermediation function, but discussion of their nature and role will be deferred to a later chapter.

Types of Financial Instruments

A financial instrument is generally defined as an obligation, in money terms, of a borrower of funds (the issuer of the instrument) to the holder of the instrument. For the holder of the financial instrument, it is a financial asset. To the issuer of the financial instrument, it is a financial obligation. Financial instruments may be issued by economic units within the private sector or the public sector (federal, state, or local governments). In the case of the private sector, financial instruments may be either *debt* instruments or *equity* instruments. Debt instruments in turn may be either *short-term* (all payments of interest and principal occur within one year) or *long-term* (all other obligations). This one-year distinction is obviously arbitrary, but it is commonly employed.

Government Debt Instruments.   The U.S. Treasury issues enormous amounts of *Treasury bills* with maturities (period to payment) ranging up to one year. Various other U.S. government agencies also issue short-term debt instruments. The federal government is also a principal supplier of longer-term debt securities—*Treasury notes* (one to ten years in maturity), *Treasury bonds,* and issues of various agencies with maturities up to 25 years.

State and local governments are not major issuers of short-term debt instruments, but they borrow large sums via the issuance of long-term *municipal bonds*.

Private Debt Instruments.   The business sector's extensive borrowing is accomplished by a large variety of debt instruments. Firms with strong credit ratings issue short-term *commercial paper,* unsecured notes with maturities of nine months and less. The negotiable *certificates of deposits* issued by commercial banks are also a notable short-term financial instrument. *Bankers acceptances,* which usually originate in the financing of international trade and obtain their name from the guarantee of payment by a bank, are another important short-term debt instrument.

Long-term private debt instruments include *corporate bonds,* of which there are a great many varieties. In general, corporate bonds are issued in denominations of $1000 per bond, have fixed maturity dates, and pay a stated amount of interest per bond at designated dates. *Mortgages,* loans secured by real property, represent another major long-term financial instrument.

Equity Instruments.   In addition to bond issues, corporations obtain external long-term capital by issuing shares of stock. Stockholders have ownership rights, including a claim to dividends, rather than creditor status. Corporations must always have shares of *common stock* outstanding, which represent the ultimate (residual) ownership of the firm. *Preferred stock* may also be issued. The "preferences" of preferred stock include priority as to dividend payment and claims to assets in the event of liquidation. The dividends on preferred stock are usually "cumulative"; that is, any dividends "passed" (not paid) in any period must be paid before any dividends can be paid to the common stockholders. Unlike debt instruments, equity instruments do not have a date of maturity. A stockholder can generally recover his investment only by selling shares.

Succeeding chapters will develop descriptions of the various characteristics of these financial instruments in detail. A discussion of the role and nature of the *financial markets* in which financial instruments are traded is the subject of the next chapter. As previously indicated, this component of the financial system receives principal attention in this book.

PLAN OF THE BOOK

This book consists of six interrelated parts. Part I develops an overview of the financial system—its structure, components, and role. The nature and significance of financial intermediation is discussed in detail and is related to an overall description of the flow of funds in the U.S. economy. Description and comparative analysis of banking and nonbanking institutions are included, along with an examination of the sources and uses of funds of the principal financial institutions. In this part and at various subsequent points in the book, attention is given to the effect of recent financial innovations and regulatory changes on competition and other aspects of the operations of financial institutions and the financial markets. The financial system is characterized by considerable government regulation, and this part of the book concludes with an overview and assessment of the regulatory environment.

Part II is concerned with the nature and significance of money, money creation, and the structure and role of the monetary authority—the Federal Reserve System. The fundamentals of the relationship between the money supply and Federal Reserve policy measures are included. However, detailed description and analysis of the economic effects of Federal Reserve monetary policy tools and operations are deferred to Part VI.

Part III focuses on interest rates, an economic variable of considerable significance to the financial system. Examined first are the principal factors determining the *level* of interest rates (and cyclical changes in rate levels), with the discussion focusing primarily on the supply and demand for loanable funds. Considered next are the various causal factors and operational implications of the term structure of interest rates. The concluding chapter in this section assesses the influence of inflation, taxation, and various other factors on both the level and structure of rates.

Part IV is the longest and most important section of the book. It offers a detailed description and analysis of the operating characteristics of the money and capital markets. This discussion is linked to a corresponding description and analysis of the major financial instruments traded in financial markets, and the operations of financial institutions in these markets. This part notably includes treatment of the financial futures market and the elements of portfolio selection theory.

Part V offers an overview of the international financial system and its linkages with the domestic system, including the fundamentals of foreign exchange markets, the characteristics and instruments of the Eurocurrency and Eurobond markets, and a brief discussion of the international aspects of commercial banking.

Part VI considers the macroeconomic policy dimensions of the financial system—the monetary, fiscal, and debt management policies of the federal government. The nature and significance of the implementation and impact of these policies and the problems associated with their use to pursue economic progress and stability are discussed.

SUMMARY

The financial system is a vital component of a modern economy. It is the framework of instruments, markets, and institutions in which exchanges of resources at points in time and over time are accomplished. More specifically, the financial system facilitates payments for goods, services, and productive resources (the exchange of real assets) and provides the means for the efficient accumulation of saved funds and their allocation into investment uses. The financial system includes such private *institutions* as commercial banks, savings and loan associations, and insurance companies, as well as such government institutions as the U.S. Treasury and the Federal Reserve System. Financial markets include the stock market, bond market, money market, and mortgage market. Financial *instruments* utilized in the financial system (other than money) include such financial obligations as shares of stocks, debt securities, and mortgages.

Saving and investment are essential for economic growth, and facilitating the process by which the savings of surplus economic units (savers) are channeled to deficit economic units (investors) for investment purposes is a vital role of the financial system. In addition to the instruments, markets, and institutions that the financial system provides to accomplish the efficient transfer of saved funds, the financial system facilitates the saving-investment process through financial intermediation. Financial intermediaries acquire the financial obligations of deficit spending units (primary securities) and issue their own financial obligations to surplus spending units (indirect securities). Such intermediated flows of funds are predominant in the financing of investment spending.

QUESTIONS

1. Define the term "financial system." What economic functions are performed by the financial system?

2. Name and define the major components of the financial system, and give examples of each.

3. What is the distinction between "real" assets and "financial" assets? Why are financial assets so important to the exchange of the use of real resources over time (borrowing and lending)?

4. Define financial intermediation, primary securities, and indirect securities, and describe their relationships.

REFERENCES

Jones, Frank J., *Macrofinance: The Financial System and the Economy* (Cambridge, Mass.: Winthrop, 1978), Chs. 1, 2.

Ray, Marvin E., and David L. Scott, *Finance* (Cambridge, Mass.: Winthrop, 1978), Chs. 1, 2, 4, 5.

Welshans, Merle T., *Finance: An Introduction to Financial Markets and Institutions,* 5th ed. (Cincinnati, Ohio: Southwestern, 1980), Chs. 1, 6.

Chapter 2

The Role of Financial Markets: Saving, Investment, and Financial Intermediation

This book is primarily concerned with financial transactions—the lending and borrowing of money, the purchase and sale of securities, the purchase and sale of foreign currencies in the international financial markets, and other similar types of financial activities. Yet these financial transactions represent a superstructure that is built over a group of nonfinancial activities. Indeed, it is the nature of these nonfinancial decisions made by consumers and businesses that creates the need for financial markets. The present chapter sketches these basic nonfinancial decisions and their impact on financial markets. In particular, this chapter is concerned with the roles of saving and investment and their significance for financial markets.

SAVING, INVESTMENT, AND FINANCIAL MARKETS

Fundamental to understanding the role of financial markets in the economy is some understanding of saving and investment. Decisions to save and invest strongly influence the level of employment, production, and income. Moreover, to a considerable extent the long-term economic growth of a society depends on the saving and investment habits of its population.

Saving

Saving refers to the act of postponing current consumption; as such, saving is sometimes referred to as abstinence—abstaining from using all of one's current income to purchase goods and services. Saving releases resources for the consumption of other economic units or for *investment* by the saver or others. It is in the use of savings for investment purposes that the act of saving has its paramount economic significance. Through investment an economy both broadens and deepens its productive capacity. Investment is necessary for the business sector to expand its equipment and other productive facilities and to finance inventories as production expands.

It should be noted that the decision to save—to postpone current consumption—and the decision as to where to place these savings—a savings account, Treasury securities, stocks, or other types of financial assets—are quite distinct and fundamentally different decisions. The decision to save is essentially nonfinancial in nature and depends on the individual's preference for present consumption as compared with future consumption, as well as on various other factors (see Chapter 8 for a more complete discussion). In contrast, the decision whether to open or add to a savings account, buy stocks, or purchase other types of financial assets is a financial transaction determined by the relative return/risk characteristics of the different assets.[1] It is the former decision—to postpone current consumption—that makes resources available for investment purposes and thus is essential for economic growth. As emphasized in Chapter 1, the role played by the financial system in facilitating the saving-investment process is of paramount importance.

Investment

Investment (in the present context) refers to the acquisition of new productive equipment, buildings, and inventory, i.e., the purchase of real assets. Such increases in capital are one means of expanding the productive capacity of an economy. Economic growth is fundamentally dependent on investment. It is important to distinguish between this type of investment—the acquisition of real productive assets—and the acquisition of financial assets, such as stocks and bonds. Increases in real productive assets add to the output capacity of the economy, and they can be achieved only in conjunction with the act of saving. Real resources can be used to expand the capital base of the economy only if those real resources are not being used to produce consumer goods. In contrast, investment in common stock or in bonds—financial investment—does not add directly to the productive base of the economy. When one person buys a share of stock and some other person sells that share, from society's perspective there has been no net investment.

The foregoing discussion is not meant to imply that transactions in the financial markets are unimportant. Indeed, much of this book is devoted to explaining why these financial transactions are important to economic stability and growth. But it is necessary to note the

---

1. The saving habits of individuals tend to be relatively stable, but the particular type of financial outlet for that saving shifts substantially as relative rates on different financial instruments change.

crucial distinction between real investment and financial investment. Throughout this chapter, unless otherwise noted, the term *investment* will be used to refer to investment in real capital assets.

The Importance of Saving and Investment

The volume of saving and investment is important from at least two perspectives. First, the amount of saving and investment has a profound impact on the *economic growth* potential of an economy. Although economic growth is a complex issue involving social, political, and cultural characteristics of nations, as well as the availability of natural resources and various other economic factors, one of the most significant influences is investment. Additions to plant and equipment incorporating new technology and other types of investment are at the base of an expanding economy. It is no accident that nations that devote a large proportion of their resources to investment also have had rapid economic growth. And of course, such large amounts of investment cannot occur without substantial saving. Resources cannot be devoted to investment unless those resources are released from the production of consumer goods through the act of saving. Many observers view the relatively slow growth in productivity in the United States in recent years as attributable to policies that have encouraged consumption at the expense of saving and discouraged productivity-expanding investment.

A second way in which the volume of saving and investment is significant is through their influences on *economic stability* and the business cycle. The total volume of saving and investment is one of the determining factors in affecting the long-run growth rate of an economy, but the *balance between* the amount that people desire to save and invest is a basic factor in affecting the short-run economic stability of the economy. If the volume of *desired* saving exceeds the volume of *desired* investment, there will be insufficient demand for the total output of the economy. As a result, production will be cut, income and employment will fall, and indeed, actual saving will decline. To a considerable extent the Great Depression of the 1930s can be explained as resulting from an excess of desired saving as compared with desired investment. In contrast, if desired investment exceeds desired saving, there will be an excessive amount of demand for the current level of output. At output levels where substantial amounts of unused labor and capital resources are available, the result of the imbalance of desired investment over desired saving is an expansion in total output. As the economy comes closer to full employment of resources, however, the result is increases in prices for goods and services. Ultimately, at the point where no further resources are available, the excess of desired investment simply results in higher prices for a constant quantity of goods and services.

FINANCIAL INTERMEDIATION

To this point, our discussion has focused on the nature of saving and investment and why they are important. The relationship of financial markets to the saving-investment process stems from an important aspect of this process: saving and investing in most advanced economies are done by different groups. Most saving is done by individuals (households), and most investing is done by business.[2] As a result, individuals have extra funds to provide to business to hire labor and capital and expand the productive capacity of the economy. But there must be some mechanism by which saved funds (which represent released real resources) are made available to those who need the funds (command over real resources) in order to accomplish their investment goals. This mechanism is provided by the financial marketplace.

Figure 2.1 provides lists of the major participants and instruments in the saving-investment process. At the core of the process are the basic economic sectors of our economy—business, government (federal, state, and local), and households. These economic sectors are connected with one another, and saving is channeled to investment through the financial system, often through the intermediating function of financial institutions. For example, households may deposit saved funds with a commercial bank, saving and loan association, or other similar type of financial institution. The command over real resources that these funds represent is thus transferred to the financial institution, and the individual receives a financial asset—a savings account—which is commonly referred to as an indirect security. As the second step in this process, the financial institution may loan funds to a business to expand its plant and obtain a mortgage on the plant. The mortgage itself is usually referred to as a *primary* (direct) security, since it is issued by one of the nonfinancial spending units of the economy—households, businesses, or governments. This process is illustrated in more detail in Fig. 2.2. In step 1 the individual exchanges a real resource claim for a savings account, and the financial institution obtains the real resource claim. In step 2 the real resource claim is transferred to the business, and the financial institution acquires an interest-yielding mortgage. Therefore, through the use of the financial institution and the securities market, the claim on real resources has been transferred from an economic unit with surplus resources to a unit with deficient resources.

This illustration of the role of financial markets in the saving-investment process is the typical case in which the flow of funds from saver to investor is intermediated; that is, a financial intermediary has been interposed between the saver and the investor. It would of course have been possible for funds to be transferred from the household sector to the business sector without the intervention of the financial intermediary. This possibility, illustrated in Fig. 2.3, is often referred to as *direct finance* (as opposed to *indirect finance* when a financial intermediary is involved). In this instance, the claim on real resources is transferred from the household to the business sector directly, and the mortgage is transferred from the business sector to the household sector. The household sector holds the mortgage (a primary, or direct, security), an asset in Fig. 2.3 rather than the savings account (an indirect security) in Fig. 2.2.

---

2. This does not mean that business does not save, nor does it mean that individuals do not invest. Obviously, business through the act of retaining earnings saves a great deal, and individuals through their purchase of homes and other real assets invest a great deal. But on balance, households save more than they invest, and businesses invest more than they save. Furthermore, the government sector must be included. However, over a long period government varies from being a net saver to a net investor.

Fundamental (nonfinancial) participants	Financial institutions	Financial instruments
Businesses	Commercial banks	Checking accounts
Government	Savings and loan associations	Savings accounts
Households	Mutual savings banks	Certificates of deposit
	Credit unions	Loans
	Life insurance companies	Government bonds
	Property and casualty insurance companies	Mortgages
	Mutual funds	Corporate bonds
	Pension funds	Stocks

Fig. 2.1   Participants and instruments in the financial markets

Business		Financial institution		Household
(2)	(2)	(1)	(1)	(1)
+Real resource claim	+Mortgage	+Real resource claim	+Savings account	+Savings account
		(2) −Real resource claim		−Real resource claim
		(2) +Mortgage		

Fig. 2.2   Saving/investment with financial institution

Business		Household
(1)	(1)	(1)
+Real resource claim	+Mortgage	+Mortgage
		(2) −Real resource claim

Fig. 2.3   Saving/investment without financial institution

Figures 2.2 and 2.3 look fairly similar from the perspective of the business and household sectors. The question might be raised as to whether one funds transfer procedure is preferable to the other. If not, we would expect to find direct finance to be at least as prevalent as indirect finance. In fact, however, the overwhelming proportion of the flow of funds in the United States and other advanced economies is *indirect* in nature and involves the interposition of financial intermediaries between savers and investors. This suggests that there are some significant advantages to the indirect transfer of funds, especially since these advantages must be sufficient to offset the costs involved in the intermediation by financial institutions.

The very fact that financial intermediaries exist in such large numbers and varieties and have such a high degree of economic significance is *prima facie* evidence that the indirect securities they issue are greatly desired by households and other owners of savings. Surplus economic units always have the option of acquiring primary securities and, indeed, do purchase and hold large amounts of these obligations. The purchase of primary securities, however, has certain disadvantages—particularly to the individuals and entities whose savings tend to be relatively small in amount.

Disadvantages of Primary Securities

One disadvantage of primary securities is "search costs"—the costs in time and out-of-pocket outlays of identifying and analyzing securities that are candidates for possible acquisition. Households, for example, can be expected to have limited information about the availability of borrowers and little expertise in evaluating risk and return characteristics of primary securities. Another disadvantage of primary securities is "transactional costs"—brokerage commissions and other costs of buying and selling securities. An example is the cost of "odd-lot" purchases of corporate stock (less than 100 shares). Further, trades of large blocks of shares that involve many round lots are subject to substantially lower commission costs per share traded than a single round lot. Still another disadvantage for the "small" saver is that it requires a large amount of funds to reduce the overall risk of holding primary securities by *diversification* (holding various types of securities, the fortunes of which are not likely to be affected in the same way by economic events). Finally, the desired degree of *liquidity* (ease of converting assets to cash quickly without appreciable losses) is difficult to achieve with holdings of primary securities unless, again, a relatively large sum is involved.

These various disadvantages of direct securities do not generally hold for indirect securities, and therein lie the advantages of the latter. With a minimum of search and transactions costs, a saver can find a financial institution that will accept a deposit (issue an indirect security). The indirect securities thus obtained are likely to be quite low-risk and to be as liquid as the depositor desires. The advantages of indirect securities relative to primary securities (and thus of indirect finance relative to direct finance) can be summed up in terms of their relative *denomination, risk,* and *liquidity* aspects. Indirect securities, such as savings accounts, are available in *small denominations* (the saver may have only a small amount of funds) whereas primary securities (such as a mortgage) are available only in relatively large denominations. This *denomination* advantage for indirect securities has been especially important in recent years with the large growth in the number of savers of relatively modest means. Second, the perceived *risk* to the household sector is likely to be less with an indirect security as compared with a primary security. With such indirect securities as savings accounts, the household sector is acquiring the liability of a financial institution that is able to *reduce risk* through skilled management and diversification among a larger number of assets. Moreover, in some financial institutions, government has further reduced risk to the saver through deposit insurance.[3] Third, indirect securities have attractive *liquidity* features. The saver may obtain the return of principal at virtually any time without concern about receiving less than was invested. On the other hand, a primary security such as a mortgage may be impossible to sell prior to its maturity and then perhaps only at a substantial loss.

The financial intermediary itself is an *acquirer of direct securities.* By pooling relatively small individual amounts of funds obtained by the issue of indirect securities, the intermediary marshals a large aggregate sum that effectively serves to minimize the disadvantages of direct security acquisition. Enjoying what are called *economies of scale,* financial intermediaries are able to spread search, analysis, and transactions costs over a large volume of diverse security purchases and sales. Because of their large holdings of direct securities, financial intermediaries are able to achieve the desired degree of diversification and liquidity at low unit costs. These various economies in the holding of direct securities and the advantages they entail for the management of liquidity make it possible for financial institutions to issue indirect securities tailored to the needs of their customers. In a sense, *depository intermediaries transform relatively illiquid direct securities into highly liquid indirect securities.*

The motive of financial intermediaries in performing the intermediation function is, of course, profit. These institutions anticipate that the net returns on the financial obligations they acquire will exceed the net costs of the obligations they issue by a satisfactory margin. The fact that returns on the former type of obligations (direct securities) are likely to be higher than returns on the latter (indirect securities) is due to the relatively greater risk and lesser liquidity associated with direct securities.

TYPES OF FINANCIAL MARKETS

Although all financial markets involve the process of transferring funds from savers (lenders) to borrowers, the precise role played by different financial markets varies widely. These differences may be characterized by classifying the financial markets in a variety of ways. Perhaps the most common classification is the distinction often made between *money* and *capital* markets. This distinction, though arbitrary to a considerable extent, is based on the maturity of the financial assets purchased and sold in the market. By this classification, short-term financial assets (usually with a maturity of one year or less) are involved in the money market. Examples are Treasury bills, commercial paper, bankers acceptances, and other short-maturity financial assets. These types of financial instruments are used by individuals, business, and governments primarily as a means to adjust *liquidity*. (See

---

3. Deposit insurance is limited to commercial banks, savings and loan associations, credit unions, and mutual savings banks—the so-called *depository* institutions.

Chapter 13 for a more complete discussion of the role of money market instruments.) In contrast, longer-term instruments traded in the capital markets include corporate bonds and stocks, mortgages, and U.S. government and municipal bonds.

It is helpful in understanding the role of financial markets to distinguish also between *intermediated* and *nonintermediated financial markets.* Intermediated financial markets include the financial instruments that are created by financial intermediaries (so-called indirect securities). For example, the federal funds market is a market in which the reserves held by member banks at the Federal Reserve are bought and sold by financial intermediaries. Similarly, the market for large certificates of deposit is an intermediated market, since the asset bought and sold is the liability of a financial institution. Nonintermediated financial markets involve exchanges of primary, or direct, securities. For example, the market for corporate bonds (a primary security) is essentially a nonintermediated market, since most corporate bonds are issued by nonfinancial as opposed to financial institutions. The function of financial intermediaries is to transfer funds from savers to investors. In this process, financial intermediaries not only transfer funds but also transform primary into indirect securities. Financial intermediation thus results in the creation of new financial assets.

A third way in which the financial markets may be classified is in terms of the legal obligation of the issuer of a security. The fundamental difference here is between *debt* and *equity* securities. Debt represents a promise to pay a specified amount at a specified time; equity represents an ownership interest in a business. The money market is entirely a market for debt instruments, whereas the capital market includes trading in both debt and equity instruments. The intermediated financial markets are primarily (though not exclusively) debt markets, but the nonintermediated financial markets include both debt and equity securities.

A fourth distinction that is especially important in understanding the use made by market participants of the different financial markets is that between the *primary market* and the *secondary market.* The primary market is the market for new securities.[4] For example, when General Motors sells additional stock, the relevant market is the primary market. Similarly, when a large bank borrows by issuing a certificate of deposit, the relevant market is the primary market. It is, of course, through the primary market that the financial markets play their essential role of transferring funds from savers to investors. Yet the secondary markets, in which existing securities are bought and sold, also play an important role in the funds transfer process. Without an adequate secondary market providing liquidity for the financial instruments, investors would be less willing to purchase stocks and bonds in the primary market. Funds would be less available to investors, and the price of such funds would be higher.

---

4. The "primary market" should not be confused with "primary securities." A primary security, such as a share of stock, remains a primary security even when traded in the secondary market.

THE EFFICIENCY OF THE FINANCIAL SYSTEM

It has been asserted that the financial system serves to make the functioning of the economic system—the production and distribution of goods and services—more *efficient*. To better assess this contribution to economic efficiency, it is useful to recognize two types of efficiency—operational (or transactions) efficiency and allocational efficiency. *Operational efficiency* is attained by the minimization of the amount of resources required for the performance of the volume of exchange transactions (trading of goods, services, and productive resources) necessary for allocational efficiency. *Allocational efficiency* is attained when the maximum quantity of output of goods and services, in the optimal composition, is achieved from a given level of available productive resources (an achievement that in turn implies an optimal combination of these resources). These two types of efficiency are obviously interrelated, and their attainment requires a ''joint solution.'' Allocational efficiency requires some optimal volume and pattern of exchange, which is in turn governed by the amount of search and transactions costs required for exchanges to take place. Correspondingly, the gains available from potential exchanges (the reallocation of resources), in conjunction with the costs of these exchanges, will determine the volume of exchanges that will be effected. As long as gains from exchange exceed the costs of exchange, exchange will occur. The minimization of exchange costs thus implies the maximization of exchange gains, subject to the condition that resources devoted to the consummation of exhanges are made unavailable for other productive purposes. Exchange transactions do, of course, consume resources in the form of the time and efforts of the individuals involved in trading activities, the real assets (land, equipment, etc.) devoted to trading activities, and the materials and supplies utilized in identifying, analyzing, monitoring, and recording exchanges.

As noted in Chapter 1, the financial system contributes to operational efficiency by providing a payments mechanism for effecting exchanges. Sellers of goods, services, and productive resources can exchange them for money, a means of ''generalized purchasing power'' that enables these sellers, in turn, to buy the particular goods, services, and productive resources they most desire. Buyers and sellers are spared the onerous search and transactions costs that a barter system entails. Producers and suppliers of productive resources are able to specialize, and specialization and division of labor contribute both to operational efficiency and allocational efficiency (by increasing the amount of output that can be attained with a given amount of resources). The payments mechanism embodied in the financial system facilitates the establishment of *markets* for goods, services, and productive resources and the formation of *prices,* which serve a ''signaling'' function in the allocation process. The information conveyed by relative prices (and other market information) is an operationally efficient means of achieving allocational efficiency.

The payments mechanism also facilitates the transfer of resources from surplus to deficit economic units, an aspect of the financial system that contributes to operational efficiency and is essential to allocational efficiency. Further, just as the payments mechanism facilitates the formation of markets for the exchange of goods, services, and productive resources (and the establishment of prices for them), it makes possible the development of *financial markets* for the exchange of resource use *over time* (borrowing and lending). Financial markets serve to establish relative "prices" for the financial obligations (financial instruments) that are used to effect such exchanges and thus channel the savings of surplus economic units to those deficit economic units that are the "highest bidders." This ensures the flow of available funds into the most productive uses, consistent with the wants and needs of society. In other words, those deficit units willing to pay the highest returns to units forgoing consumption (and thus making resources available for other purposes) are the units expecting to realize the highest returns from the investment of these resources. Thus it is possible for productive resources made available for investment by savers to be efficiently allocated among competing possibilities.

The intermediation function of the financial system further facilitates the transfer of funds from surplus to deficit economic units. Financial intermediaries, by issuing indirect securities to savers, pool the savings of many economic units into an aggregate sum sufficiently large to realize many economies of scale in the purchase of direct securities by these intermediaries. The effect of intermediation is to enhance operational efficiency via these economies and to improve allocational efficiency by channeling savings into appropriate investment uses.

The saving-investment process, whether direct or intermediated, is an exchange of the use of resources over time and, as an exchange, is subject to the test of operational efficiency. The contribution of financial intermediaries to the operational efficiency of these exchanges is apparent from our previous discussion of their role, since they serve to offer saving units an efficient alternative to the acquisition of direct securities. The financial markets in which saving units, borrowing units, and intermediaries exchange financial obligations constitute an operationally efficient process of the allocation of saved funds.

Risk, Returns, and Financial Markets Efficiency

Prices of a good, service, productive resource, or security are a form of information that, in a market economy, affects myriad decisions concerning the future pattern of utilization of these goods, services, resources, and claims to resources. Prices are themselves a product of information about numerous aspects of the commodities being priced—to name a few, the available quantity (supply), quality (and other aspects bearing on overall desirability), and forecast patterns of future supply and demand for the commodity. As new information becomes available about a commodity and its value to society, the price of the commodity is likely to change. In an *efficient market,* such price adjustment to new information occurs in a rapid (virtually immediate) and unbiased fashion.

If the financial system is to make its maximum potential contribution to the attainment of operational efficiency of exchanges and the efficient allocation of resources, financial markets must be efficient. In other words, the prices of the financial instruments that are traded in financial markets must reflect all available information. In a common (and useful) simplification, prices of financial claims are viewed as being determined by their *expected returns* and related *risk*. These terms warrant an introductory discussion. (More detailed examination is offered in Chapter 11.)

The concept of a "return" on saved funds is a familiar one. Such "rewards" for saving may take the form of, for example, interest on a savings account in a commercial bank, dividends on corporate stock, or increases in the market price of securities. The term "expected return," in its technical application, may be less familiar. The concept of an "expected return" links a possible return (or outcome) from the acquisition of a financial instrument and the likelihood (or probability) of realizing that return. An expected return is calculated mathematically by multiplying each possible return by its probability of occurrence and summing the results. For example, if the amounts of the only two possible dollar returns on a financial asset are $500 and $0, and if the probability of the $500 return is 0.25 and the probability of the $0 return is 0.75, the expected dollar return is

$$0.25(\$500) + 0.75(\$0) = \$125.$$

The concept of assigning a probability to the occurrence of a future event is familiar to anyone who pays attention to weather forecasts. Weather forecasts are made on the basis of information about patterns of current weather conditions and knowledge of past associations of given weather conditions to subsequent weather conditions. In other words, a statement that "there is a 30 percent chance of rain tomorrow" means (roughly interpreted) that today's weather conditions are followed by rain the next day about 30 days out of 100.

Weather forecasts have improved greatly in recent years because of improved methods for gathering and interpreting information. The same is true of forecasting financial events. Financial predictions are also based on information of current developments and knowledge of the association between given conditions and subsequent conditions. As methods for gathering and interpreting financial information have improved, and as knowledge of financial phenomena has accumulated, the capacity of the financial community to assess future financial trends has improved considerably (although it would still be unwise to overestimate one's capacity to forecast financial developments).

Informed predictions can be made, but the future remains unknowable. Associations among economic and financial variables are often difficult to identify and disentangle, and causes and effects are frequently interwined. Further, many events bearing heavily on financial developments are *random* and thus unpredictable by definition. Whenever knowledge about future events is imperfect (as it is most of the time), *risk* exists. Thus when a financial asset has an *expected* return, risk exists unless the return is *certain,* in which case there is only one possible return, and its probability of occurrence is 100 percent. As the number of possible returns increases (and the probability of any given return diminishes), risk increases.[5]

---

5. A common measure of risk is the *variance* of the probability distribution of possible returns. Mathematically, the variance is the sum of the squares of the arithmetic differences between all possible returns and the expected return of the distribution.

Economic behavior of individuals and institutions is characterized by *risk aversion,* the desire to avoid risk. The degree of risk aversion varies among individuals (and some people are "risk-neutral" or even "risk-loving"), but in general, insofar as acquisition of financial assets is concerned, additional risk will be accepted only if it is accompanied by an increase in expected return. The prices established in the financial markets for the various financial instruments being traded will thus reflect perceptions of their risk and expected returns. For example, if security A offers the same expected return as security B, but security B is perceived to be riskier (the realization of the expected return is less likely), security A will have a higher price than security B. (In terms of relative returns, security B must offer a higher return than security A in order to compensate for the additional risk.) Indeed, if the financial markets are to be allocationally efficient, it is essential that prices of all financial assets reflect their expected returns and risk.

Expectations as to future returns and the risk attached to the realization of those returns are, of course, perceptions of financial market participants. These market participants constantly search for new information and analyze all existing information as it may bear on the risk and returns of securities. A financial market (like any market) thus becomes more efficient as the number of participants increases, as the means of gathering and communicating information becomes more rapid, and as the tools of analyzing information become more sophisticated.

In a modern, advanced market economy such as that of the United States, the number of knowledgeable participants in financial markets is very large, and the communications and analysis network for financial information operates with remarkable speed. Market efficiency is inherently an empirical question, and various segments of the financial markets have been the focus of empirical investigations of efficiency by researchers. Although the conceptual and methodological frameworks of these studies have been criticized, their results generally indicate that the securities markets operate with a high degree of efficiency in the processing and assimilating of relevant information. This issue, together with the various factors underlying it, is addressed in more detail in Chapter 11.

SUMMARY

Saving and investment are processes of critical importance for economic growth. The act of saving releases productive resources (which would otherwise be used for consumption) that can be invested to expand the productive capacity of the economy. The saving and investment process is greatly facilitated by the existence of financial markets. Financial markets provide a means of efficiently channeling funds from savers to investors.

The transfer of funds from savers to investors in financial markets may be direct or intermediated. In a direct transfer, a saver receives a primary security from one of the nonfinancial economic units of the economy—households, businesses, or governments—in exchange for the use of saved funds. In an intermediated transfer, the saver receives an indirect security from a financial intermediary, and the funds flow to nonfinancial spending units when the intermediary acquires primary securities. The operations of financial inter-mediaries are of great importance in financial markets because of the ability of these institutions to "manufacture" liquidity and reduce risk for savers.

QUESTIONS

1. What are the principal components of the financial system? How are they linked together to facilitate saving and investment?

2. What process is described by the phrase "exchange of resource use over time"? What is the relationship of this process to economic growth?

3. Define the term "financial intermediation." How and why is the saving-investment process facilitated by intermediation?

4. Why do savers often prefer indirect to primary securities? How does this preference relate to the economic function performed by financial intermediaries?

5. Name and describe four possible classifications of types of financial markets.

6. Describe the relationship between "allocational" and "operational" efficiency, ex-plaining each of these terms in your description.

7. What is meant by the phrase "financial market efficiency"? How is financial market efficiency related to information about the risk and potential returns offered by financial instruments?

REFERENCES

Gurley, John, and Edward Shaw, *Money in a Theory of Finance* (Washington, D.C.: Brookings Institution, 1960).

Moore, Basil J., *An Introduction to the Theory of Finance* (New York: Free Press, 1968).

Smith, Paul F., *Economics of Financial Institutions and Markets* (Homewood, Ill.: Irwin, 1971).

Chapter 3

The Flow of Funds Accounts in the U.S. Economy

One of the most useful techniques for the analysis of financial markets is the flow of funds accounts. These accounts, which are published quarterly by the Federal Reserve System, are to a considerable extent a companion to the National Income Accounts published by the United States Department of Commerce. But whereas the National Income Accounts focus on the "real" or nonfinancial side of the economy by providing information on the Gross National Product and other measures of production, the flow of funds accounts focus on the financial side of the economy by providing information on lending and borrowing and other such financial transactions. Our treatment of the flow of funds is divided into two sections. First, we discuss the concept of the flow of funds accounts in considerable detail, not only to present a basis for understanding the flow of funds accounts as published by the Federal Reserve, but also to provide further illustration of the role of financial markets. Second, we discuss some examples of actual flow of funds accounts.

CONCEPT OF THE FLOW OF FUNDS

The flow of funds accounts in concept are quite simple: the economy is divided into a number of sectors that are thought to be similar in terms of basic economic behavior; statements of sources and uses of funds for each sector are created; and an interlocking matrix of the sectors for the entire economy is constructed. The basic sectors encompass business, household, and government components of the economy, as discussed earlier. In addition, a sector statement for financial institutions is prepared. For each sector a balance sheet of assets, liabilities, and net worth at a moment in time is constructed, as in Table 3.1.

Table 3.1 Sector balance sheet, December 31, 1980

Real assets		10	Short-term liabilities	5
Financial assets		20	Long-term liabilities	5
Money	10		Net worth	20
Other	10			
Total assets		30	Total liabilities and net worth	30

Assets

The assets are divided into two categories: *real assets* and *financial assets*. The financial assets, in turn, are divided into two components: *money* and *other financial assets*. These distinctions are of substantial importance in our understanding of the role of financial markets. Real assets appear on the balance sheet of only one economic unit. Examples are inventory, land, and plant and equipment. In contrast, financial assets—since they are obligations of their issuers—appear on the balance sheet of more than one economic unit. For example, the accounts receivable held by one business as an asset appear on the books of another business as a liability—accounts payable. Similarly, a corporate bond held by an individual as an asset also appears on the balance sheet of the issuing corporation as a liability.[1] It is important to note that the summation of real and financial assets across economic units produces fundamentally different results. Adding together the balance sheets of all economic units produces a total for real assets that is the sum of the parts. But adding together the balance sheet of all economic units will not have a similar result for financial assets, since every financial asset will have a corresponding financial liability. In the process of summing the balance sheets of all economic units, the financial assets are canceled out by the liabilities. This fundamental difference between real assets and financial assets is frequently used to illustrate the fact that a society's wealth is embodied in its real assets, not in its financial assets. Increasing the stock of real assets increases the productive capacity of an economy, but an increase in society's holdings of financial assets—money, for example—has no effect on the real wealth of the society (although increases in financial assets may mirror increases in real assets).

The distinction drawn between money and other financial assets is also of substantial importance. The term "money" refers to demand deposits at banks and other depository financial institutions, as well as to currency and coin. Other financial assets include

---

1. Money is an asset to the holder but a liability to the issuer. If the money is checkbook money—demand deposits—it is a liability of the issuing bank. If it is government money—currency and coin—it is a liability of the government. In either case it appears on the books of two economic units, the holder and the issuer.

corporate bonds, U.S. government bonds, municipal bonds, mortgages, common stock, preferred stock, and other types of financial instruments. These "other financial assets" could be money market or capital market instruments, debt or equity, primary (direct) or indirect securities, intermediated or nonintermediated instruments, and acquired in either primary or secondary markets. When an economic unit acquires one of these types of financial assets, funds are provided to another economic unit. In contrast, when money is acquired, no funds are provided on a net basis to the basic economic units of the economy.

Liabilities and Net Worth

On the right-hand side of the balance sheet the two basic components are *liabilities* and *net worth* (both of which are financial in nature). The liabilities represent the funds that this economic unit or sector owes to other economic units. It is conventional to divide these debts into short-term (or current) and long-term liabilities. The liabilities of this sector, of course, are the financial assets of some other sector. The net worth account represents the difference between the value of the assets and the value of the liabilities. For a business firm *net worth* is usually referred to as *book value*.

Fundamental Equalities

The balance sheet for a sector or for an individual economic unit must balance. The sum of the assets must equal the sum of the liabilities and net worth. In Table 3.1, the assets (30) do indeed equal the liabilities (10) plus the net worth (20). However, for a sector (or for an individual economic unit) the amount of net worth need not equal the amount of real assets, and the amount of liabilities need not equal the amount of financial assets. In the example in Table 3.1, net worth (20) exceeds real assets (10), and liabilities (10) are less than financial assets (20). The balance of net worth, as compared with real assets, and the amount of financial assets, as compared with liabilities, are very important magnitudes. Algebraically, the fundamental equalities for a sector are as follows: Real Assets (A_R) + Financial Assets (A_F) = Liabilities (L) + Net Worth (NW), or

$$A_R + A_F = L + NW.$$

However, for a sector,

$$A_R \neq NW \text{ and } A_F \neq L.$$

Of course, for the *entire* economy,

$$A_R \equiv NW \text{ and } A_F \equiv L.$$

More will be said of the significance of these relationships below.

To this point, we have a sector balance sheet at a moment of time, *not* a flow of funds statement. The balance sheet is static in concept. In contrast, the flow of funds statement is dynamic in concept. The flow of funds measures the sources and uses of funds for a sector over some time period. The transition from the static to the dynamic is accomplished by constructing a second balance sheet for the same sector at a different moment of time (see Table 3.2). The determination of the sources and uses of funds from the first to the second point in time is accomplished by comparing the two balance sheets (Table 3.3).

In measuring the sources and uses of funds as they appear in Table 3.3, we must stay within the fundamental accounting identity, in which sources of funds are

1. increases in liabilities,
2. increases in net worth,
3. decreases in assets,

and uses of funds are

1. decreases in liabilities,
2. decreases in net worth,
3. increases in assets.

In comparing Tables 3.1 and 3.2, we note that real assets rose by 10 and financial assets rose by 20, both increases representing a use of funds. These uses of funds were financed by an increase in liabilities of 10 and an increase in net worth of 20, both representing a source of funds. It should be noted, of course, that since the two balance sheets (Tables 3.1 and 3.2) must balance, the "Changes in Sector Balance Sheet" (Table 3.3) must also balance. Total sources of funds must equal total uses of funds.

Activities

Each of the sources and uses of funds presented in Table 3.3 has been labeled to represent the nature of the activity. Hence the increase in real assets is termed *investment*, the increase in money balances is referred to as *hoarding*, and the increase in other financial assets is called *lending*. The distinction between hoarding and lending is an important one, since hoarding does not provide funds to financial markets but lending does. On the sources side of the statement, an increase in liabilities is referred to as borrowing, and an increase in net worth is termed saving. If desired, the last account—saving—can be broken down further into income and consumption for an individual, or profit after taxes and cash dividends for a business.

In order both to construct a more meaningful flow of funds statement and to explain more completely the role of financial markets, we can divide the sources and uses of funds into real and financial accounts, as in Table 3.4. By this division, saving represents a "real" source, and investment represents a "real" use. In contrast, borrowing represents a financial source, and hoarding and lending represent financial uses. For example, in Table 3.4, the sector we have been discussing has saving of 20 and investment of 10. Any sector such as this one with more saving than investment is referred to as a *surplus unit*. If saving were less than investment, the sector would be called a *deficit unit*. Looking now at financial transactions, we see that total financial sources are 10 and total financial uses are 20. This

Table 3.2   Sector balance sheet, December 31, 1981

Real assets		20	Short-term liabilities	5
Financial assets		40	Long-term liabilities	15
Money	15		Net worth	40
Other	25			
Total assets		60	Total liabilities and net worth	60

Table 3.3   Changes in sector balance sheet, December 31, 1980, to December 31, 1981

Uses of funds			Sources of Funds	
Real assets (investment)		+10	Liabilities	+10
			Short-term 0	
			Long-term +10 (borrowing)	
Financial assets		+20	Net worth (saving)	+20
Money (hoarding)	+ 5			
Other (lending)	+15			
Total uses		+30	Total sources	+30

Table 3.4   Real and financial sources and uses of funds, December 31, 1980 to December 31, 1981

Real uses			Real sources	
Investment		+10	Saving	+20
Financial uses			Financial sources	
Hoarding	+ 5		Borrowing	+10
Lending	+15			
Total uses		+30	Total sources	+30

sector is described as a *net creditor*. In contrast, if total financial sources were more than total financial uses, the sector would be described as a net borrower or *net debtor*.

We are now in a position to explain more fully the fundamental relationships applicable to the flow of funds accounts. As we do so, we must carefully distinguish what must be true for a sector from what must be true for the entire economy. From the perspective of a sector, saving need not equal investment. *Indeed, it is the fact that saving and investment are not equal for individual sectors that creates the role of financial markets.* Some sectors, such as households, are surplus sectors; others, such as businesses, are deficit sectors. Similarly, from the perspective of the sector, financial sources and financial uses need not be equal—the sector may be a net debtor or a net creditor. Yet since total sources must equal total uses, there is a fundamental relationship between real sources and uses and financial sources and uses:

1. *A surplus sector (with saving greater than investment) must dispose of that surplus by hoarding, lending, or repaying debt.* The surplus sector must be a net creditor in the same amount as the amount of the surplus. In Table 3.4, the sector has a surplus of 10 (saving of 20 and investment of 10). It also has a net creditor position of 10 (hoarding of 5, lending of 15, and borrowing of 10). Hence the surplus sector is a supplier of funds to financial markets.

2. *A deficit sector (with saving less than investment) must finance that deficit by dishoarding, selling nonmonetary financial assets (dislending?), or borrowing,* where dishoarding is a reduction in holdings of money balances, selling nonmonetary financial assets (calling in loans) is a reduction in these assets, and borrowing represents an increase in liabilities. (The reader may wish to change the numbers in Table 3.4 to prove the truth of this statement.) Hence the deficit sector is a demander of funds in financial markets.

From the perspective of the entire economy, the relationships are quite different: investment must equal saving (the fundamental identity of realized saving and investment). Furthermore, from the perspective of the entire economy, financial sources must equal financial uses. Yet it is not these equalities that are of interest to the student of financial markets. It is the basic inequalities at the sector level that are of interest, since it is these inequalities that create the need for intermediation and a role for financial markets. We now turn our attention to illustrations of these basic concepts and to a discussion of the nature of various financial markets through a discussion of the flow of funds tables published by the Federal Reserve.

THE FLOW OF FUNDS ACCOUNTS AS PUBLISHED BY THE FEDERAL RESERVE

The flow of funds accounts, as published by the Federal Reserve, are based on the concepts discussed above. However, in application, the published flow of funds accounts differ somewhat from the illustrations employed above. We present below some abbreviated flow of funds accounts from Federal Reserve publications, with emphasis on the data that illustrate the concepts of saving, investment, and the role of financial markets. Our interest centers primarily in the household sector—the principal surplus sector—and the business sector—the principal deficit sector.

Household Sector

Table 3.5 presents the sources and uses of funds for the *household sector*—actually the sector is composed of households, personal trusts, and nonprofit organizations—for the third quarter of 1980.[2] Gross saving (prior to considering the depreciation of real capital assets held by the sector) amounted to $389.0 billion. Borrowing, which is represented by the net increase in liabilities (total borrowing minus repayment of existing debt), amounted

---

2. It is important to note that the flow of funds provides no data on subsections of each sector (types of businesses, for example) or on the gross changes in assets and liabilities. For example, borrowing is the net increase in liabilities between two time periods, which is the amount of new borrowing minus the volume of debt repayments.

Table 3.5 Flow of funds account for household sector, 3rd quarter, 1980 (billions of dollars)

Capital investment	$287.0	Net increase in liabilities	$109.6
Net acquisition of		Gross saving	$389.0
financial assets	275.7		
Money $27.6			
Other financial			
assets $248.1			
Statistical discrepancy	−$ 64.1		
Total uses	$498.6	Total sources	$498.6

Source: Board of Governors of the Federal Reserve System, *Flow of Funds Accounts 3rd Quarter 1980*, p. 7.

to $109.6 billion, so total sources of funds for the sector amounted to $498.6 billion. On the uses side of the balance sheet, capital investment—principally homes and household durable goods—was $287.0 billion, and the acquisition of financial assets on a net basis was $275.7 billion. Since the sources and uses of funds for the sector must balance by definition, and since the data in Table 3.5, which are gathered by the Federal Reserve from a variety of sources, do not balance, it is necessary to add a separate item, called "Statistical Discrepancy," which is always a use of funds and which takes a magnitude and sign that are just sufficient to balance the sources and uses.

As revealed by Table 3.5, the household sector, as usual, was a *net surplus sector* in the third quarter of 1980; that is, its gross saving exceeded its gross investment in real assets. In fact, gross saving exceeded gross investment by more than $100 billion. Necessarily, then, the household sector had to dispose of this surplus as a net creditor in financial markets and did so both by hoarding (an increase in money holdings) and lending (acquisition of other financial assets). Hoarding amounted to $27.6 billion, and lending was $248.1 billion. Furthermore, as shown in Table 3.6, the household sector's lending was principally concentrated in the acquisition of intermediated or indirect securities. For example, the two largest categories of lending—acquisition of time and saving accounts at commercial banks and savings institutions ($122.8 billion) and the buildup of pension fund reserves ($78.4 billion)—involved the acquisition of indirect securities issued by depository financial institutions on the one hand and pension funds on the other. In contrast, the acquisition of primary securities directly from the issuer was concentrated in debt securities (principally U.S. government securities), and holdings of equities actually declined.

Business Sector

In contrast to the household sector, which is a surplus sector and a lender, the *business sector* is a *deficit sector* and a borrower. As shown in Table 3.7, gross saving for the business sector ($220.0 billion), is substantially less than capital investment ($264.1 billion), which is composed of plant and equipment and changes in inventory holdings. This deficit in "real terms" of $44.1 billion, which is common for the business sector, must be

Table 3.6   Distribution of net acquisition of financial assets by the household sector, 3rd quarter, 1980 (billions of dollars)

Total net acquisition of financial assets	$275.7
Demand deposits and currency	27.6
Time and savings accounts at commercial banks and savings institutions	122.8
U.S. government securities	38.4
State and local obligations	−0.3
Corporate and foreign bonds	6.5
Mortgages	13.6
Open market paper	−0.5
Money market fund shares	5.1
Investment company shares	−4.2
Other corporate equities	−4.9
Life insurance reserves	11.4
Pension fund reserves	78.4
Other	−18.2

Source: Board of Governors of the Federal Reserve System, *Flow of Funds Accounts, 3rd Quarter 1980*, p.7

Table 3.7   Flow of funds account for business sector, 3rd quarter 1980 (billions of dollars)

Capital expenditure	$264.1	Net increase in liabilities	$97.5
Net acquisition of financial assets	37.4	Gross saving	222.0
Statistical discrepancy	18.0		
Total uses	$319.5	Total sources	$319.5

Source: Board of Governors of the Federal Reserve System, *Flow of Funds Accounts, 3rd Quarter 1980*, p. 9.

Table 3.8   Distribution of the net increase in liabilities for the business sector, 3rd quarter 1980 (billions of dollars)

Net increase in liabilities	$97.5
Corporate equities	4.9
Bonds	35.7
Mortgages	42.6
Bank loans	52.4
Other loans	3.9
Trade debt	−9.0
Other liabilities	−33.0

Source: Board of Governors of the Federal Reserve System, *Flow of Funds Accounts, 3rd Quarter 1980*, p. 9.

financed; thus the business sector is a net borrower and a demander of funds in the financial market. In fact, borrowing exceeded lending by $60.1 billion. As shown in Table 3.8, most of the borrowing was done through the issuance of debt securities.[3] Because of the relatively high cost of equity capital in recent years, most external funds have come through debt issues. In fact, new corporate equities were only $4.9 billion, whereas bonds, mortgages, bank loans, and other borrowed funds were much greater (see Table 3.8).

As discussed above, the financial markets exist to channel funds from the saving surplus sectors, principally households, to deficit sectors, principally businesses. This flow of funds may either be direct from surplus to deficit sector or indirect through financial intermediaries. In the former case, the saving surplus sector acquires a primary, or direct, security. In the latter case, the saving surplus sector acquires an indirect, or intermediated, security. We now illustrate these conduits for saving by describing two types of financial markets—corporate bonds and home mortgages—and two types of financial institutions—commercial banks and private nonbank financial institutions.

Illustrations

The corporate bond market is one of the major financial markets in the United States. The supply of corporate bonds is dominated by nonfinancial corporate business. However, both finance companies and foreign issues (rest of the world) account for a substantial part of the supply of new corporate bonds. Viewing the corporate bond market from a demand perspective (see Table 3.9), one can see that most corporate bonds are sold to insurance companies and pension funds (both those of private companies and those of state and local governments). The insurance companies and pension funds, in turn, obtain their funds by selling securities to the saving surplus sectors.

Table 3.9   Sources and uses of funds in the corporate bond market, 3rd quarter 1980 (billions of dollars)

Net issues	$38.3	Net purchases	$38.3
Nonfinancial corporate business	33.6	Life insurance companies	4.4
Finance companies	3.9	Private pension funds	9.4
Rest of the world	−0.1	State and local government	
Other	0.9	Retirement funds	8.0
		Other insurance companies	4.3
		Household	6.5
		Other	5.7

Source: Board of Governors of the Federal Reserve System, *Flow of Funds Accounts, 3rd quarter 1980*, p. 35.

---

3. New equity securities are treated as liabilities within the flow of funds framework.

The mortgage market is an especially large component of the domestic financial market. Spurred by rising prices for homes and other real property, as well as the traditional heavy use of borrowed funds to purchase these types of assets, the increase in mortgages has developed at a very rapid rate. Total mortgages increased by $126.5 billion (see Table 3.10), which is almost four times the increase in corporate bonds outstanding. Most ($83.9) of the mortgages were for the purchase of homes, and most ($77.2) were originated by households. In terms of the acquirers or purchasers of mortgages, an examination of Table 3.10 reveals that, as with most financial instruments, most purchasers are financial institutions. In fact, almost one half of the mortgages were purchased by savings institutions and commercial banks. Savings institutions generally concentrate in home mortgages, whereas commercial banks are more active in the acquisition of commercial mortgages. Very few mortgages, as a percentage of the total increase in mortgages, are acquired directly by households or other basic nonfinancial sectors of the economy, with the exception of government-sponsored mortgage pools.

Table 3.10   Sources and uses of funds in the mortgage market, 3rd quarter 1980 (billions of dollars)

Net change in mortgages	
Home mortgages	$83.9
Multifamily residential	10.4
Commercial	20.4
Farm	11.8
Total	$126.5
Borrowed by:	
Households	$77.2
Nonprofit institutions	0.9
Nonfinancial business	42.6
Other	5.8
Total	$126.5
Acquired by:	
Households	$13.6
Savings institutions	40.7
Commercial banking	11.8
Insurance	15.7
Agricultural credit agencies	8.7
Mortgage pools	25.4
Other	10.6
Total	$126.5

Source: Board of Governors of the Federal Reserve System, *Flow of Funds Accounts 3rd Quarter 1980*, p. 37.

Table 3.11   Sector statement of sources and uses of funds for commercial banks, 3rd quarter 1980 (billions of dollars)

Plant and equipment	$6.5	Net increase in liabilities	$92.2
Net acquisition of financial		Gross savings	2.7
assets	95.7		
Statistical discrepancy	−7.3		
Total uses	$94.9	Total sources	$94.9

Source: Board of Governors of the Federal Reserve System, *Flow of Funds Accounts, 3rd Quarter 1980*, p. 19.

Table 3.12   Sector statement of sources and uses of funds for private nonbank financial institutions, 3rd quarter 1980 (billions of dollars)

Physical investment	$1.9	Net increase in liabilities	$190.1
Net acquisition of financial		Gross savings	12.4
assets	200.5		
Discrepancy	0.1		
Total sources	$202.5	Total sources	$202.5

Source: Board of Governors of the Federal Reserve System, *Flow of Funds Accounts, 3rd Quarter 1980*, p. 21.

Information on the sources and uses of funds for commercial banks and also for all private nonbank financial institutions is contained in Tables 3.11 and 3.12. Note that the volume of saving and investment (see "Plant and Equipment") is quite low for these sectors, as compared with their financial activities of borrowing and lending. In contrast, for the household sector and for the business sector, saving and investment are large in relation to their net financial transactions. This reflects the basic differences in the functions performed by these sectors. Households and businesses are essentially engaged in production, consumption, investment, and saving. Financial transactions stem from these basic "real" activities. In contrast, financial institutions exist to intermediate between surplus (saving) and deficit (investing) sectors. Their role in saving and investment is primarily as intermediary.

Commercial banks obtain their funds by borrowing from households, businesses, governments, and others. These borrowings are reflected in the creation of intermediated (indirect) securities, such as demand deposits and time and savings deposits. Nonbank financial institutions also obtain their funds by borrowing. However, their sources traditionally have not included demand deposits but have been limited to time and savings accounts, insurance and premium reserves, and other types of borrowing. On the other side of the statement, commercial banks utilize these funds, and this use serves as a conduit for channeling savings to investment by acquiring primary or direct securities from their borrowers. Most securities acquired by commercial banks are fixed-income in nature; they include issues of business, households, and governments. Similarly, private nonbank financial institutions acquire primary, or direct, securities from borrowers, although they include both debt and equity securities. Moreover, securities acquired by private nonbank financial institutions tend to be longer-term in maturity. More detail on the different behavior characteristics of these various financial institutions is provided in the next chapter.

SUMMARY

The flow of funds accounts in concept are quite simple. The economy is divided into sectors that are relatively similar in terms of economic behavior. Balance sheets are constructed for each sector at particular points of time. Changes in these balance sheets between different points of time are then calculated. These balance sheet changes then become the raw material for a statement of sources of funds for a sector and a statement of uses of funds for a sector. These statements must conform to certain basic identities for a sector, such as: investment need not equal saving nor lending equal borrowing, but total sources must equal total uses. Yet, although the basic concept of the flow of funds is relatively simple, the flow of funds data, as published by the Federal Reserve, are both complex and exceedingly useful.

Because the economy is divided into basic and similar sectors and sources and uses of funds are constructed, it becomes possible to determine the surplus or deficit nature of the sectors, their principal financial liabilities as additional sources of funds, and their principal financial assets as other uses of funds. Moreover, by placing the sectors side by side and examining the interlocking nature of the flow of funds accounts, one can determine the role played in financial markets by different participants. It is not surprising that many analysts of financial market developments view the flow of funds data provided by the Federal Reserve as indispensable to this work.

QUESTIONS

1. Under what conditions might the business sector not be a deficit sector? What would be the implications for interest rate movements if business was a surplus sector?

2. If buying and selling of existing bonds and stock is not investment from a social perspective, of what importance is it?

3. What are the basic factors that account for the domination of financial institutions in the total flow of funds? Under what economic conditions may the share of funds that flows through financial institutions diminish?

4. Make a list of "real" assets, and compare that list with another list of financial assets. Why is it that society's wealth is the sum of its real assets, not of its financial assets?

5. If you were an analyst of financial markets, what information in addition to that provided by the Federal Reserve would you want?

6. Comment on the validity of each of the following:
   a) saving must equal investment both for a sector and for the economy.
   b) lending plus hoarding must equal borrowing for the sector but not for the economy.

REFERENCES

Board of Governors of the Federal Reserve System, *Introduction to Flow of Funds,* February 1975.

Flow of Funds Accounts: 1946–1975, Annual Total Flows and Year-End Assets and Liabilities, December 1976.

Copeland, M.A., *A Study of Moneyflows in the United States* (New York: National Bureau of Economic Research, 1952).

The Flow of Funds Approach to Social Accounting (New York: National Bureau of Economic Research, 1962).

Ritter, Lawrence S., *The Flow of Funds Accounts: A Framework for Financial Analysis* (New York: Institute of Finance, New York University, 1968).

Taylor, Stephen, "Uses of Flow-of-Funds Accounts in the Federal Reserve System," *Journal of Finance,* May 1963, pp. 249–258.

APPENDIX

USING THE FLOW OF FUNDS TO FORECAST FINANCIAL MARKET PRESSURES

As discussed in Chapter 3, the flow of funds accounts are historical in nature; that is, they record what has happened in the financial system during some specified past period. Although this information is useful in providing perspective and understanding of trends in financial markets, there are limits to the practical usefulness of historical data. Reflecting these limitations is the fact that a number of financial market participants have developed models that forecast future flows of funds in the financial markets. These forecasts of future flows of funds are then used to identify potential pressures in financial markets, such as a shortage of funds in the mortgage market or a particularly large supply of municipal securities relative to the anticipated demand for municipals. Moreover, these forecasts of future flows of funds can be used to explain changes in the general level of interest rates, as well as changes in interest rate levels in one market (municipals, for example) as compared with changes in interest rate levels in another market (corporate bonds as another example).

Most forecasts of future flow of funds movements begin with forecasts for the entire economy, including the strength of expenditures in the business sector for plant expansion and inventory building, as well as consumer purchases of houses and such durable goods as automobiles. Moreover, the strength of the economy is a prime determinant of budget balance of the government sector, especially the federal government. Once expenditure patterns are anticipated, these expenditures are translated into predicted borrowing behavior. For example, a prediction of a large expansion in business plant and equipment expenditures would imply a large demand for business borrowing, especially for long-term funds in the bond market. Moreover, a prediction of a large increase in household demand for home ownership would imply a large demand for single-family mortgage credit. Increasingly, financial analysts have also had to contend with the impact of inflation on credit demands. For example, if household demand for homes remains the same but the price of houses rises by 15 percent, then household demand for credit to finance house purchases would increase by 15 percent.

Forecasts of the demand for credit must then be combined with forecasts of the supply of credit in order to anticipate financial market pressures. The supply of credit ultimately reflects the volume of saving of the household, business, and government sectors. However, since most saving is done by individuals, the focus of analysis is frequently on the saving behavior of the household sector. These saving-pattern forecasts are then turned into supply-of-funds estimates by making assumptions about the disposition of saving. For example, the financial markets would be affected differently if households chose to dispose of their saving by acquiring savings deposits at savings and loan associations, as contrasted with increasing their contributions to pension funds, given the different investment patterns of these institutions. Moreover, since most saving is used to acquire indirect securities issued by financial institutions (an intermediated flow of funds) rather than to acquire primary securities directly, it is important to forecast the portfolio management practices of the major financial institutions. Finally, and particularly important in explaining the supply of funds available from commercial banks and other depository financial institutions, one should include some expectation regarding the posture of Federal Reserve monetary policy. For example, the anticipation of a stimulative monetary policy would imply a large supply of funds available from financial institutions, especially commercial banks. In contrast, the anticipation of a restrictive monetary policy would imply a smaller supply of funds available from commercial banks and other financial institutions.

Once these forecasts of supply and demand for funds in financial markets are prepared, it is then necessary to put them together in order to predict financial market pressures. Of course, after the fact, supply and demand must balance. However, the financial analyst can use these individual estimates in order to predict financial market pressures in individual markets and the changes in the flows of funds and in interest rates that will be necessary to make the total supply of and demand for funds balance.

There are a number of businesses, mostly financial institutions, that prepare forecasts of the flow of funds. They include the investment banking firm of Salomon Brothers, the large commercial bank Bankers Trust Company, and the Life Insurance Association of America. Our analysis concentrates on the funds flow forecasts made by Salomon Brothers for the year 1980, forecasts that were made and published in the fall of 1979.[4]

Table 3A.1 presents a summary of the Salomon Brothers forecast for financial markets for 1980. The economic forecast on which the 1980 outlook for financial markets was prepared included two conflicting factors. First, it was anticipated that the economy would experience a recession in 1980, beginning in the first half of the year and continuing throughout the year. Real gross national product (gross national product adjusted for price changes) was forecasted to fall 1.5 percent, in contrast to the 2.7 percent increase in 1979. However, the declines in the various sectors of the economy were not expected to be uniform. Housing starts were expected to fall from 1.75 million units in 1979 to 1.47 million units in 1980. In contrast, plant and equipment expenditures by businesses were expected to fall by a much smaller quantity in real terms. Although the decline in expenditures in real terms for housing and plant and equipment expenditures would normally have been expected to sharply reduce the demand for credit, the persistence of rapid inflation partially offset these factors. Moreover, the forecasted recession would have sharply increased the size of the federal deficit. As a result, with a forecasted increase in prices of about 10 percent, the increase in total credit demand of 10.5 percent for 1980 was not much less than the 12.5 percent increase experienced in 1979.

The household sector was forecasted to continue its relatively low saving rate behavior. In contrast, saving by the business sector was expected to decline as corporate profits fell with the recession, and saving by the government sector (actually state and local governments since the federal government has virtually always had a deficit in recent years) was

---

4. For details of this forecast, see *1980 Prospects For Financial Markets,* Bond Market Research, Salomon Brothers, New York.

Table 3A.1 Summary of Supply and Demand for Credit (billions of dollars)

| | Annual Net Increases in Amounts Outstanding | | | | | | | Amt. Out. |
	1974	1975	1976	1977	1978	1979	1980	31Dec79
Net Demand								
Privately held mortgages	42.2	42.0	70.4	109.0	116.5	118.5	100.7	1,102.9
Corporate and foreign bonds	29.1	39.1	39.1	37.4	33.5	32.8	42.7	475.6
Subtotal long-term private	71.3	81.1	109.5	146.4	150.0	151.3	143.4	1,578.5
Short-term business borrowing	50.4	−16.0	9.8	47.0	78.5	112.9	81.5	577.3
Short-term other borrowing	16.3	14.4	40.7	49.6	66.0	62.3	43.9	486.6
Subtotal short-term private	66.7	−1.6	50.5	96.6	144.5	175.2	125.4	1,063.9
Privately held federal debt	28.4	82.6	71.8	73.3	83.8	66.9	96.5	760.0
Tax-exempt notes and bonds	14.5	16.3	17.1	31.1	32.9	22.0	27.0	328.0
Subtotal government debt	42.9	98.9	88.9	104.4	116.7	88.9	123.5	1,088.0
Total Net Demand for Credit	180.9	178.4	248.9	347.4	411.2	415.4	392.3	3,730.4
Net Supply[1]								
Thrift institutions	25.8	53.7	70.0	81.8	80.2	66.7	58.8	738.1
Insurance, pensions, endowments	29.0	40.9	53.1	67.3	70.2	75.1	81.4	690.6
Investment companies	1.7	3.7	4.6	6.7	8.3	23.2	20.7	57.4
Other nonbank finance	3.9	−4.3	8.7	17.6	15.9	25.6	19.5	185.6
Subtotal nonbank finance	60.4	94.0	136.4	173.4	174.6	190.6	180.4	1,671.7
Commercial banks[2]	52.6	29.9	59.6	83.5	107.0	124.3	100.0	1,091.9
Business corporations	8.8	11.6	7.7	4.9	4.5	10.3	12.2	121.4
State and local government	1.1	2.4	4.9	11.3	14.7	5.2	3.0	72.5
Foreign[3]	18.5	7.1	19.6	44.1	57.4	21.7	34.6	249.0

| | Annual Net Increases in Amounts Outstanding | | | | | | | Amt. Out. |
	1974	1975	1976	1977	1978	1979	1980	31Dec79
Subtotal	141.4	145.0	228.2	317.2	358.2	352.1	330.2	3,206.5
Residual (mostly household direct)	39.5	33.4	20.7	30.2	53.0	63.3	62.1	523.9
Total Net Supply of Credit	180.9	178.4	248.9	347.4	411.2	415.4	392.3	3,730.4
Percentage Growth in Outstandings								
Total credit	9.3	8.4	10.8	13.6	14.2	12.5	10.5	
Government	7.8	16.8	12.9	13.4	13.2	8.9	11.4	
Household	7.0	6.3	11.6	14.9	14.9	12.8	9.1	
Corporate	14.2	3.6	7.4	11.9	14.1	16.1	11.8	
Long-term	8.2	8.0	10.7	12.9	11.7	10.6	9.1	
Short-term	12.5	-0.3	8.5	14.9	19.4	19.7	11.8	
Held by nonbank finance	7.2	10.4	13.7	15.3	13.4	12.9	10.8	
Commercial banks	8.3	4.3	8.3	10.7	12.4	12.8	9.2	
Foreign	23.0	7.2	18.5	35.1	33.8	9.5	13.9	
Household direct	13.9	10.3	5.8	8.0	13.0	13.7	11.9	
Economic correlations								
Growth in real GNP	-1.4	-1.3	5.9	5.3	4.4	2.7	-1.5	
Nominal GNP	8.1	8.2	11.3	11.6	12.0	11.8	9.5	

1. Excludes funds for equities, cash, and miscellaneous demands not tabulated above.
2. Includes loans transferred to books of nonoperating holding and other bank-related companies.
3. Includes U.S. branches of foreign banks.

Source: Salomon Brothers, *1980 Prospects for Financial Markets* (New York: Bond Market Research), p. 19. Reprinted by permission.

forecasted to fall because of declining tax revenues relative to rising expenditures. Moreover, the forecast for 1980 assumed a tax cut by the federal government in order to stimulate the depressed economy. Furthermore, with the anticipated persistence of high inflation, it was not expected that the Federal Reserve would be able to substantially loosen monetary policy.

The net result of these supply and demand factors is presented in Table 3A.1. The net demand for funds is divided into three components: long-term private, short-term private, and government debt. Although the net demand for credit was forecasted to decline slightly, from $415.4 billion in 1979 to an anticipated $392.3 billion in 1980, it was anticipated that different sectors of the market would respond differently to the recession. Demand for credit through issuing mortgages was expected to fall moderately, reducing pressures on the mortgage market. In contrast, the demand for credit through bond issues was expected to rise moderately, placing pressures on the bond market. However, short-term borrowing by businesses and others was expected to fall sharply, as businesses curtailed their inventory holdings because of the recession and as consumers reduced their credit demand to finance purchases of autos and other goods. This sharp reduction in short-term credit demands might be expected to reduce pressures on lenders, such as commercial banks, who are involved primarily in short-term credit demands. In contrast, privately held federal debt was expected to increase markedly as the federal government faced a large deficit due to the combined influence of the recession and the anticipated tax cuts. Of course, to the extent that the federal deficit was financed by short-term borrowings, it would partially or fully offset the reduced pressure on short-term lenders resulting from diminished short-term private borrowings.

Turning to the supply of funds in the financial markets, the Salomon Brothers approach divides the total supply of funds into the following components: nonbank finance, commercial banks, business corporations, state and local governments, foreign, and residual (mostly household direct). The distinction between nonbank finance and commercial banks apparently reflects the traditional though decreasingly relevant distinction between commercial banks as institutions that create money and nonbank financial institutions as institutions that do not. However, it is also important to note that the supply of credit from nonbank financial institutions is much more stable than from commercial banks.

The Salomon Brothers forecast for 1980 projected a small decline in the volume of funds provided by nonbank financial institutions. Declines were anticipated for thrift institutions (savings and loan associations, mutual savings banks, and credit unions), as well as for investment companies and other nonbank financial institutions. Partially, at least, these declines in funds provided reflect the expectation of high interest rates for the projected period, which is in turn a conclusion of the forecast. This mixing of conclusion and forecast reflects the necessity of adjusting the supply and demand forecasts through an iterative process that seeks to determine simultaneously the supply and demand for funds and the interest rate.

Other sources of supply reflect a number of different factors. Commercial bank supplies of funds were forecasted to decline from $124.3 billion to $100.0 billion, reflecting the anticipated monetary stringency of the period, a result that would place pressure on short-term financial markets. Business corporation supply of funds was forecasted to decline as profits fell with the recession, and state and local government supply was expected to diminish as the recession caused tax revenues to fall. In contrast, foreign supply was expected to increase substantially as at least some portion of the huge OPEC surplus was invested in the U.S. financial markets.

The residual figure, the difference between the total demand for credit and the supply of credit previously accounted for, is an especially important number in forecasting the degree of pressure in financial markets. This number represents the amount of credit that must be supplied by households directly through the acquisition of primary securities. Keep in mind, however, that households generally prefer to acquire indirect financial instruments with their funds. In order to induce households to devote a greater portion of their funds to primary securities, it is necessary to offer them a higher return. Hence an increase in the residual generally implies rising rates, whereas a decline in the residual generally represents falling rates. As Table 3A.1 shows, the residual (which normally declines during a recession) did not show any forecasted reduction. Reflecting this factor as well as other components of the supply and demand for credit, Salomon Brothers did not foresee any marked reduction in interest rates in 1980, a very unusual expectation in a recessionary period. In fact, they forecasted new postwar highs for rates in the first half of 1980, a forecast that subsequently proved accurate.

Chapter 4

Financial Intermediaries: Banking and Nonbanking Financial Institutions

The purpose of this chapter is to discuss the major financial institutions that dominate the flow of funds. Initially we present a basic discussion and comparison of the commercial banking industry and contrast banks with nonbanking firms. We then present a more detailed description of the major financial institutions—viewing the bank as a business organization with emphasis on the sources and uses of bank funds—and then a detailed treatment of the different types of nonbank financial institutions (savings and loan associations, mutual savings banks, credit unions, insurance companies, pension funds, and others). The chapter closes with a discussion of the changing competitive environment and the Depository Institutions Deregulation and Monetary Control Act of 1980, which has substantially altered the functions of depository financial institutions. The nature of this nation's financial insitutions is undergoing a dramatic change, the nature of which we hope to convey by the discussion in this chapter.

BANKS VERSUS NONBANKS: A COMPARISON

A sharp distinction has traditionally been drawn between the *commercial bank* on the one hand and all other financial institutions on the other—life insurance companies, property and casualty insurance companies, savings and loan associations, credit unions, mutual savings banks, mutual funds, and other types of *nonbank* financial institutions. This distinction is usually based on the fact that—in past years, at least—commercial banks created money in the process of lending, whereas nonbank financial institutions did not.

Banks add to the money supply and to the volume of total demand when they acquire financial assets. In contrast, savings and loan associations, life insurance companies, and other nonbank financial institutions only lend the funds left with them, thereby affecting the turnover of money (its velocity) but not the total quantity of money. Hence indirect securities of commercial banks are usually referred to as *monetary indirect securities,* but indirect securities of other financial institutions are *nonmonetary indirect securities.* Moreover, in accordance with the view that the total quantity of money is an important variable for economic growth and stability, *and* that the turnover of money is relatively constant, it becomes necessary for the central bank—the Federal Reserve in the United States—to control the ability of commercial banks to expand credit and thereby create money. In contrast, the nonbank financial institutions, in terms of this logic, need not be subject to the same type of macroeconomic controls.

This traditional distinction between banks and nonbanks is losing much of its validity. As we will discuss more fully below, with the passage of the Depository Institutions Deregulation and Monetary Control Act of 1980, savings and loan associations, mutual savings banks, and credit unions are now able to offer transactions accounts that are functionally equivalent to demand deposits. In addition, many observers emphasize credit and velocity rather than money only. Yet there still remain many significant differences between these types of organizations. Commercial banks continue to draw funds from relatively short-maturity sources—demand deposits and short-term certificates of deposit. Most nonbank financial institutions draw their funds from longer-term sources, which have also been traditionally more stable sources. Moreover, commercial bank *uses of funds* still remain relatively short-term; the maturity structure of bank assets is quite short. In contrast, the maturity structure of the assets of most nonbank financial institutions is usually quite long, often three or four times or more as long as the maturity structure of a commercial bank's assets. As a generalization, though with growing exceptions, commercial banks serve different types of financial markets than do nonbank financial institutions.

THE BANK AS A FIRM: SOURCES AND USES OF FUNDS

Bank Functions

The sources and uses of funds for commercial banks reflect the functions banks perform in our economy. For instance, the importance of demand deposits as a source of funds reflects the fact that commercial banks remain the dominant financial institution in administering the means of payment. If an individual or a business writes a check, the probability is high that this check will be drawn on a demand deposit in a commercial bank and collected through the banking system.[1] However, as the prevailing level of interest rates has risen in recent

---

1. The traditional monopoly of the demand deposit service by commercial banks was broken in the 1970s by the development of Negotiable Orders of Withdrawal (N.O.W.) accounts and share drafts. Still, banks continue to dominate the payments system. These as well as other significant changes in the financial system are treated later in this chapter.

years, individuals and businesses have economized on their cash balances. Moreover, the development of such new technology as electronic funds transfer systems has further reduced the desired cash balances of economic units. As a result, although demand deposits remain an important source of funds to commercial banks, their growth has been quite slow, and their relative importance as a source of bank funds has diminished. In addition to offering demand deposit services, commercial banks also offer an outlet for savings by providing a variety of savings accounts and different types of certificates of deposit. Most commercial banks offer passbook savings accounts and small (consumer) certificates of deposit featuring longer maturity and higher rates than those of savings accounts. Moreover, a number of commercial banks (principally the large banks) obtain a substantial quantity of funds from offering large ($100,000 and over) business-type certificates of deposit.

Turning to the asset side of the balance sheet (i.e., uses of funds), we note that commercial banks provide credit to the community. Indeed, it may be argued that the provision of credit to the local community is the principal function performed by commercial banks. This credit encompasses loans to individuals, businesses, and governments for a number of different purposes and for a variety of maturities. Given the importance of credit creation, it is not surprising to find that the asset position of commercial banks is dominated by loans or that interest payments on loans are the principal source of bank revenue. In addition to their basic roles of administering the payments mechanism, providing an outlet for individual and business savings, and making credit available to different sectors of the economy, commercial banks also provide a number of services that do not show up directly on their balance sheets. For example, commercial banks offer trust services to individuals and businesses. For a fee, many banks will manage the portfolio of a corporate pension program, manage funds for a minor, and provide other trust services. The assets managed by the bank's trust department, however, do not show up in the bank's balance sheet, since they are not owned by the bank. Banks also provide safekeeping services for a fee, of which the safe deposit box is perhaps the most widely known. Furthermore, commercial banks increasingly are generating income by offering advice on a fee basis to their individual and business customers. Again, this service need not directly influence the asset and liability structure of the bank's balance sheet, though it often does have a substantial impact on the revenue, expenses, and profitability of the banking organization.

Assets and Liabilities

Table 4.1 presents the major assets and liabilities of the commercial banking industry as of November 1980. This table in conjunction with attention to the various functions performed by commercial banks will serve as a vehicle for our discussion of the sources and uses of bank funds. As discussed above, one of the principal functions of the commercial banking industry is to offer demand deposit services—transactions accounts—to the public and to administer the payments system. This basic function is reflected in the large amount of

Table 4.1   Assets and liabilities of commercial banks, November 1980 (billions of dollars)

Assets	
Loans and investments	
Loans	$906.0
Investments	317.5
U.S. Treasury securities	106.0
Other	211.5
Cash assets	
Total	$175.7
Currency and coin	17.0
Reserves with Federal Reserve Banks	30.3
Balances with depository institutions	56.2
Cash items in process of collection	72.2
Other assets	76.0
Liabilities and capital	
Deposits	
Demand	$393.4
Savings	210.0
Time	520.9
Borrowings	$238.0
Capital	$112.9
Total assets/liabilities and capital	$1475.2

Source: Federal Reserve *Bulletin*, December 1980, A17.

demand deposits at commercial banks, almost $400 billion, which represents almost 30 percent of all bank funds. Moreover, in order to offer these services, individual banks must cooperate with other banks on the clearing and processing of checks. This cooperation among banks leads to a large volume of interbank deposits (deposits from one bank held at another bank). In addition, as a part of its vital role in the payments system, commercial banks provide individuals and businesses with currency and coins. This function is reflected in the balance sheet of commercial banks as a $17 billion holding of currency and coin.

The role of commercial banks as an outlet for the savings of individuals and businesses also is reflected in the balance sheet of the industry. Time and savings deposits at commercial banks amounted to more than $700 billion in late 1980, substantially more than the volume of demand deposits. These deposits encompassed the passbook savings account,

Table 4.2   Percentage distribution of loans at commercial banks, September 1980

	Percentage of total loans
Commercial and industrial loans	35.1
Real estate loans	28.9
Loans to individuals	19.6
Security loans	1.8
Loans to nonbank financial institutions	3.3
Agricultural loans	3.8
Lease-financing receivables	1.2
All other loans	6.3
	100.0

Source: Federal Reserve *Bulletin,* November 1980, A15.

various types of consumer certificates of deposit, and the large ($100,000 and over) certificate of deposit offered primarily to business firms. Vigorous commercial bank competition for time deposits dates back only a few decades. Yet the impact of their competition has been strongly felt in that market, and this competition has greatly affected the balance sheet of the nation's commercial banks. However, the role of savings accounts has diminished markedly in recent years as banks have relied on six-month money market certificates and 30-month certificate accounts in order to attract the deposits of individuals.

The credit-creation function is reflected on the asset side of the balance sheet. By far the greatest part of bank assets is in the loan portfolio. Total loans approached $1 trillion in November 1980. These loans included credit extensions to households, businesses, and government for a wide variety of purposes. In fact, commercial banks are probably the most diversified lenders among the nation's financial institutions. This diversification is illustrated by Table 4.2, which provides information on the loan portfolio at commercial banks.

Reflecting the traditional orientation of commercial banks toward businesses, the greatest portion of credit extension (35.1 percent of total loans) at these banks is in the form of commercial and industrial loans—loans to businesses for acquiring inventory, carrying accounts receivable, purchasing new equipment, and other similar purposes. Moreover, substantial amounts of credit (3.3 percent of total loans) are extended from commercial banks to other financial institutions, principally to securities dealers to finance their inventories of securities and to sales and personal finance companies. Indeed, most small sales and personal finance companies obtain the bulk of their funds from commercial banks. Another rapidly growing type of bank lending is the real estate loan, both for acquisition of single-family houses and for the purchase of income-producing property, such as apartments and office buildings. The expansion in real estate lending is in part attributable to the growth in time deposits at commercial banks, which has allowed the acquisition of longer-maturity, less-liquid assets. It is also attributable somewhat to a change in the attitude of bankers about the appropriateness of different kinds of lending. As of September

1980, real estate loans constituted 28.9 percent of the total loan portfolio. The third major type of credit at commercial banks is in the form of loans to individuals—consumer loans for the purchase of consumer durable goods, consolidation of debts, vacations, and other purposes. At one time commercial banks discouraged consumer loans as unproductive, but in recent years consumer loans have expanded rapidly, particularly in the form of credit extensions under credit card arrangements.

One should bear in mind, of course, that the allocation of loans varies widely among banks of different sizes and locations. The credit distribution of smaller banks, especially those located outside urban areas, tends to favor agricultural production. Moreover, consumer loans and real estate loans often account for a larger fraction of the total loan portfolio at the smaller banks. Large banks tend to be more oriented to nonagricultural business lending.

A number of other observations should also be made about the assets, liabilities, and capital at commercial banks. Commercial banks generally hold substantial amounts of liquid assets. For example, cash and short-term securities usually comprise much larger fractions of total assets at commercial banks than at nonbank financial institutions. In Table 4.1, cash assets alone are equal to more than 10 percent of total assets. Moreover, a large fraction of the investment portfolio of commercial banks is held in the form of short-term securities, especially the holdings of U.S. Treasury securities. The substantial holdings of cash assets is attributable to the large volume of unstable demand deposits, as well as the role played by commercial banks in administering the nation's payments system. In addition, commercial banks play an important role in assisting the United States government in financing the government's activities. Banks serve as a depository of the U.S. government (tax and loan accounts) as well as for state and local government securities.[2] Tax collections of the U.S. government are deposited at commercial banks, and banks play an important role in the sale of savings bonds.

To this point we have not mentioned two important sources of bank funds: borrowings and capital. Borrowings not only represent a significant present source of funds but are also a growing source. These nondeposit sources of funds are used for a variety of purposes. For *short-term liquidity adjustments,* commercial banks frequently borrow through the federal funds market, through the use of repurchase agreements, or through the Eurodollar market. Federal funds borrowings represent short-term (usually one-day) loans from one bank to another bank. Repurchase agreements represent a type of borrowing whereby a bank sells a security to someone with the commitment to repurchase it (usually within a short period). Eurodollar borrowings represent the lending of dollar deposits from banks outside the United States. *Longer-term borrowings* are used to allow the bank to expand beyond the size made possible through local deposit funds.

---

2. Holdings of state and local government securities (municipals) are included in Table 4.1 as "other" securities. These securities, which have become the dominant type of security held in the portfolio of most banks, are purchased because their income is exempt from the federal income tax and because the commercial bank generally needs to shelter taxable income. Further, governments often require that their deposits be secured by the posting of collateral by the depository banks, and security holdings serve this purpose.

The capital account at commercial banks—common stock, surplus, and retained earnings—plays a quantitatively small but vital role. This owner's equity must provide the original funds for a new bank to acquire its facilities. Moreover, for an existing bank, capital provides a cushion to protect depositors and other creditors against loss from bad loans, security defaults, theft, and other hazards. Yet the capital account is very small, representing generally no more than 7 or 8 percent of total bank assets. Therefore banks should not take great risk in their loan or investment portfolios.

Changes in Sources and Uses of Funds

Sharp changes in recent years in the sources and uses of funds at commercial banks have reflected substantial changes in the functions performed by commercial banks, as well as increasing competition from other financial institutions. Commercial banks have relied more on time and savings deposits and less on demand deposits for funds, they have increasingly relied on borrowed, nondeposit sources of funds as compared with traditional deposits, and they have substituted long-term debt securities for equity in the capital base. On the uses side of the balance sheet, cash assets have been reduced as a percentage of total assets, short-term securities held for liquidity purposes have been reduced, the loan portfolio has been expanded to account for a greater fraction of the total uses of bank funds, the nature and maturity of bank loans have changed, and the composition of the long-term securities portfolio has been altered. There has indeed been a marked revolution in the sources and uses of bank funds in the post–World War II era. This revolution has taken the commercial banking industry into direct competition with many nonbank financial institutions and has fundamentally altered the nature of this country's financial system.

Sources of Funds

The decline in non-interest-bearing demand deposits relative to time and savings accounts reflects a number of interrelated factors. Individuals and businesses have been reluctant to leave large amounts of funds idle in non-interest-earning demand deposits in a high-interest environment. At the same time, commercial banks have been much more aggressive in offering a variety of savings and time accounts that would appeal to different customers. And of course, the development of the large business certificate of deposit in the early 1960s opened up new sources of funds for the banking industry.[3] Moreover, the Federal Reserve has raised the maximum permissible ceilings on the rates banks can pay to obtain funds (Regulation Q) and has even eliminated the ceilings on some types of accounts (the large CD and the money market CD).[4]

---

3. The First National City Bank of New York first began to offer in the early 1960s large, negotiable certificates of deposit in which a secondary market existed. For a more detailed discussion of this money market instrument, see Chapter 13.

4. Rates paid by commercial banks for deposits are governed by the Federal Reserve's Regulation Q. However, the Fed has increasingly liberalized this regulation by raising the maximum permissible rates and also by allowing banks to offer some deposits with no rate ceilings or with floating rate ceilings. For example, in the late 1970s banks were permitted to offer the "money market" CD—a six-month, $10,000-minimum CD—in which the rate was tied to the market rate on Treasury bills.

The growing reliance on nondeposit, borrowed funds is somewhat more complex to understand. As already noted, these borrowed funds encompass purchases of federal funds, the use of repurchase agreements, and borrowing in the Eurodollar market. For many banks that desire to expand their assets beyond the size made possible through local deposits (mostly large banks), the use of borrowed funds provides one possibility—and frequently the least costly possibility. Funds can be borrowed in the federal funds or Eurodollar markets and used to support a larger loan portfolio. Funds can also be borrowed through selling large certificates of deposit, but the nondeposit borrowings are frequently less costly because of the traditional absence of reserve requirements and F.D.I.C. assessment.[5] However, although this strategy of funding the loan portfolio with short-term borrowings may increase the profits of commercial banks, it also increases risk. The increased risk includes both availability risk—the risk that borrowed funds will not be available when needed—and price risk—the risk that the funds, though available, will carry an excessively high cost. Some observers have commented that the more aggressive use of borrowed funds at the nation's large banks in recent years is one of the major factors associated with the failures among large banks in the early and mid-1970s.

A third major change in the sources of bank funds is the change in the capital account. Although there has been some reduction in the amount of capital relative to total assets at the nation's commercial banks, particularly at the large banks, the most significant change has occurred in the composition of total capital. Banks have increasingly substituted long-term borrowed funds for equity capital. This substitution principally reflects the attempt by bank management to stabilize the return on equity at a time of diminishing profit margins by using the less costly borrowed funds. It also reflects the generally depressed market for equity securities in recent years, a development that has caused firms in other industries as well to increase their debt-to-equity ratio. Banks have sold large amounts of long-term debt in recent decades, but their offerings of new equity securities have been relatively small.

Uses of Funds

Turning to the uses side of the balance sheet, we note that the general trend has been toward a less-liquid, longer-maturity asset structure. Cash assets have been squeezed in response to the higher opportunity cost associated with rising interest rates. Short-term security holdings, which provide liquidity, have been reduced in response to the smaller need for liquidity associated with the change in the composition of deposits. Moreover, the needed liquidity has been increasingly provided by *liability management*—borrowing funds when liquidity is needed—as a substitute for *asset management*—liquidating an asset to provide the required funds. At least a portion of the growth in nondeposit liabilities at commercial banks reflects the use of liability management to provide liquidity. Furthermore, banks practice liability management through the sale of large certificates of deposit.

---

5. Insured commercial banks must pay an annual assessment to the Federal Deposit Insurance Corporation (F.D.I.C.) based on the size of their deposits. Federal funds and Eurodollar borrowings are not classified as deposits; therefore they are not insured, but they also carry no F.D.I.C. assessment.

Perhaps the most significant change in the asset portfolio at commercial banks has been the increased size of the loan portfolio and the change in the composition of that portfolio. In line with the longer maturity of bank deposits, as well as with greater willingness on the part of bank management to take risks, the fraction of the total portfolio devoted to loans has expanded. The nature of the loans in the loan portfolio, as well as the maturity of those loans, has also changed. At one time, banks were principally interested in making short-term loans to business. Increasingly banks are interested in *any* legal and credit-worthy loan that serves their customers. Further, the acceptable maturity of these loans has increased substantially. As discussed above, the principal impact of this change in attitude has been in the real estate and consumer areas, and as a result, bank competition with other financial institutions for loans has increased significantly. In many areas, for example, banks are now in direct competition with savings and loan associations for single-family home loans.

Not only have bank loan portfolios changed, but bank investment portfolios have also lengthened in maturity and changed in composition. The most notable impact of this development has been on the mix between Treasury and municipal securities. As banks have sought to shelter their income from taxes, they have increasingly substituted municipal securities (securities issued by states and local governments), whose interest income is exempt from the federal income tax, for Treasury securities, whose interest income is taxable by the federal government. In fact, banks have moved into the municipal market so aggressively in recent decades that they have become the dominant buyer of these types of securities.

TYPES OF FINANCIAL INSTITUTIONS

Financial institutions other than commercial banks comprise a diverse group performing a variety of financial services. To name a few types, nonbank financial institutions include savings and loan associations, mutual savings banks, credit unions, property and casualty insurance companies, life insurance companies, pension funds, finance companies, and mutual funds. There are a number of similarities, however, among these institutions, so groupings by common purpose are often made. These groupings include *depository* financial institutions (sometimes referred to as thrift institutions), *contractual* institutions, and other financial institutions. We now turn our attention to each of these broad categories and the specific institutions in each group.

Depository Financial Institutions

The depository financial institutions encompass savings and loan associations, mutual savings banks, and credit unions. They are grouped together as "thrift" institutions because they all offer an interest-bearing outlet for the savings of individuals and others and because these deposits are highly substitutable and therefore highly competitive with one another in the portfolio of savers. Moreover, these nonbank depository financial institutions are becoming more alike, and they are also, as a group, becoming more like commercial banks.

Along with the commercial banks, which are also depository financial institutions, these nonbank depository financial institutions provide a common outlet for savings funds. However, the total assets of all three thrift institutions are considerably *smaller* than the total assets of the commercial banking industry. Moreover, though similar in many respects, these nonbank depository institutions do have substantial differences, which require a separate discussion of each individual institution.

Savings and Loan Associations.   Savings and loan associations were first formed in the early nineteenth century to provide a source of funds so that individuals could own their own homes. At that time, credit for the purchase of a house was difficult to obtain, and installment terms were short. The associations were formed as mutuals; that is, each member or owner placed funds into a pool, the borrowers drew funds from the pool when they needed money, and gradually they paid back the funds so that others could borrow and buy or build a house.

Reflecting this tradition, the primary use of funds at savings and loan associations was from the beginning and is today the making of loans on single-family dwellings. As indicated in Table 4.3, the result is that the dominant asset in the portfolio of savings and loan associations is the mortgage—primarily, though not exclusively, the single-family home mortgage. For example, as of the end of 1979, mortgages constituted about 80 percent of the financial assets of savings and loans. The savings and loan association is a highly specialized financial institution. All other uses of funds are minor in comparison with this concentration in mortgages. Some highly liquid assets are held in the form of time deposits and short-term securities. However, the need for liquidity at savings and loans is slight, since their sources of funds have traditionally been relatively stable. Savings and loans usually have held small amounts of municipal securities, because their effective tax rate has been quite low. One interesting use of funds revealed in Table 4.3 is the $14.3 billion in consumer credit. In recent years, savings and loans have sought and in many states have received authorization to offer consumer loans on the same basis as banks and other consumer lenders. Their use of this power is reflected in a sharp growth in the proportion of assets devoted to consumer credit extensions. Moreover, effective at the end of 1980, savings and loans received the authority nationally to sharply expand their holdings of consumer loans and other nontraditional uses of funds.

Table 4.3   Financial assets and liabilities of savings and loan associations, 1979 (billions of dollars)

Total financial assets	$579.1	Liabilities	$546.6
Mortgages	475.7	Savings shares	470.1
Consumer credit	14.3	FHLB advances	41.8
Time deposits	6.0	Other liabilities	34.7
U.S. Treasury securities	4.7		
Agency securities	32.1		
State and local government securities	1.2		
Other assets	45.1		

Source: Board of Governors of the Federal Reserve System, *Flow of Funds Accounts, Assets and Liabilities Outstanding, 1969–1979*, p. 552.

As indicated also in Table 4.3, savings and loan associations have three basic sources of funds: savings shares, Federal Home Loan Bank (FHLB) advances, and other liabilities. By far the dominant source of funds is the savings accounts of individuals and others. In fact, at the end of 1979, savings shares totaled $470.1 billion, or almost 90 percent of total borrowed funds. These savings shares included ordinary passbook accounts, as well as many types of certificates of deposit. Increasingly, however, the growth in savings shares at savings and loans is in certificate accounts, particularly money market certificates. In addition, savings and loan associations borrow funds from their supervisory authority—the Federal Home Loan Bank Board. Some of this borrowing occurs for reasons of interest rate differentials, for example, when the advances from the Federal Home Loan Bank are lower-cost funds than savings shares. FHLB advances are thus generally large when interest rates are high and in periods when savings and loans find it difficult to obtain funds from savings shares. During these periods of *disintermediation,* when the flow of funds bypasses the financial intermediaries and goes directly to primary securities, savings and loan associations make heavy use of borrowings from the Federal Home Loan Bank. As a third and nontraditional source of funds, many savings and loans have tried to develop access to the open capital market. One way—which shows up in the balance sheet as "other liabilities"—is to sell bonds backed by the mortgages in the portfolio of the savings and loan (so-called mortgage-backed bonds). With increasing competition for funds in recent years, there has been a strong trend among savings and loans, especially at the larger institutions, to find such nontraditional sources. And with the recently granted authority to offer interest-bearing transactions accounts in the form of negotiable orders of withdrawal (N.O.W.) accounts, there will undoubtedly be a substantial change in the mix of sources of funds at savings and loan associations.

Mutual Savings Banks.   Mutual savings banks are a type of financial institution that is common in only a few states of the nation. Originating in the northeastern states in the latter part of the nineteenth century, mutual savings banks were formed to offer an outlet for the savings of the "new" immigrants at a time when other financial institutions did not seek small savings accounts. Operating under state charter and with authorization in only a few states—principally the Northeast, middle Atlantic states, and the Pacific Northwest— mutual savings banks did not grow very extensively. As the population of the nation has shifted westward, mutual savings banks have been unable to follow. To a considerable extent, the savings and loan association has filled that role in states that do not provide for the chartering of mutual savings banks. Hence total assets of mutual savings banks are only about one third of the total assets of savings and loan associations.

As revealed in Table 4.4, sources of funds at mutual savings banks are limited to various kinds of savings accounts, including passbook savings accounts, and a variety of types of certificates of deposit. In attracting funds, mutual savings banks are in direct competition with other nonbank depository institutions—savings and loan associations and credit unions—as well as with commercial banks. This emphasis on thrift deposits as the basic source of funds is consistent with the history and tradition of the industry. But even

Table 4.4   Financial assets and liabilities of mutual savings banks, 1979 (billions of dollars)

Total financial assets	$165.0	Liabilities	$152.8
Mortgages	98.7	Savings deposits	145.6
Corporate bonds	20.8	Other	7.2
U.S. Treasury securities	4.3		
U.S. government agency securities	15.5		
State and local obligations	3.2		
Consumer credit	3.6		
Other assets	18.9		

Source: Board of Governors of the Federal Reserve System, *Flow of Funds Accounts, Assets and Liabilities Outstanding, 1969–1979, p. 552.*

though their sources of funds are quite similar to those of savings and loans and credit unions, their uses of funds are much more diversified than those of either of the other nonbank thrift institutions— a fact that partially reflects less regulatory restriction on portfolio management. Given their relatively stable sources of funds, mutual savings banks have emphasized long-term investment—principally in mortgages and corporate bonds. Unlike the savings and loan associations, however, which hold primarily conventional (noninsured) mortgages, mutual savings banks invest principally in Federal Housing Administration (FHA) and Veterans Administration (VA) insured and guaranteed mortgages. This emphasis on government-guaranteed mortgages reflects the fact that many mortgages acquired by mutual savings banks are originated outside the market area of the mutual savings bank; there is relatively small demand for mortgages in the areas where mutual savings banks are located.[6] Beyond the concentration in mortgages, mutual savings banks buy large quantities of high-quality corporate bonds. Indeed, the relative amount of new funds committed to mortgages versus corporate bonds in any one year will vary markedly as yields on the two financial instruments change. Other uses of funds by mutual savings banks include U.S. government and government agency securities, which are held primarily for liquidity, and some consumer credit. And as with savings and loan associations, the available sources and uses of funds have been changed greatly by the Depository Institutions Deregulation and Monetary Control Act of 1980, which broadens the sources and uses of funds at these institutions.

Credit Unions.   The smallest but the most rapidly growing of the nonbank thrift institutions is the credit union. Established as cooperative institutions—with membership comprising both borrowers and depositors—credit unions are among the newest of the nation's financial institutions. Tracing their roots back only to the 1920s in the United States, credit unions were established to provide consumer credit at reasonable rates to the "laboring classes" at a time when commercial banks viewed such credit extensions as "unproductive." Credit union membership was limited to individuals with a "common bond," either a

---

6. Most of the funds of mutual savings banks are obtained in the northeastern part of the United States, which is a capital surplus area, but most of the demand for the funds comes from the West and South, which are capital deficit areas.

common employer or membership in a common organization, such as a fraternal club. The growth of credit unions formed by employees of a common employer has been further encouraged by frequent donations of space and other facilities by the employer.

Credit unions have traditionally obtained their funds by offering members one type of account—a share in the credit union. Legally this share represents an ownership interest in the credit union, and there is no return guaranteed. Functionally, however, the share is equivalent to a deposit. As Table 4.5 shows, $56.2 billion of the total of $62.3 billion in financial assets held by credit unions in 1979 were financed with the sale of credit union shares. In recent years, however, there has been some diversification of sources of funds. Many credit unions now offer different returns on different instruments of different maturities. Moreover, a number of credit unions offer share drafts, which are functionally equivalent to demand deposits but which *pay interest* on the average balance of the account, and which were authorized nationwide under the Depository Institutions Deregulation and Monetary Control Act of 1980.

The principal use of credit union funds is to make loans to members for nonbusiness purposes. As Table 4.5 shows, consumer credit is the dominant financial asset held by credit unions. These loans are for a wide variety of purposes: purchases of automobiles and other durable goods, vacations, and consolidation of debts. Recently credit unions have received the additional authority to offer long-term mortgage loans. However, there are numerous restrictions on the loan portfolio of credit unions, including limitations on rates charged. Maturity of the loan portfolio is also restricted. With the exception of home mortgage loans, credit unions are limited to relatively short-term loans. In addition to these consumer loans, credit unions hold as assets a large amount of investment securities, primarily in the form of U.S. government securities and deposits at savings and loan associations. These assets are generally held for liquidity purposes, but they may also be held for income by credit unions when loan demand from members is relatively weak.[7] Since credit unions do not pay any federal income taxes, they have no incentive to hold state and local government securities.

Table 4.5 Financial assets and liabilities of credit unions, 1979 (billions of dollars)

Total financial assets	$62.3	Credit union shares	$56.2
Consumer credit	48.2		
U.S. government securities	4.7		
Savings and loan shares	3.6		
Home mortgages	3.8		
Other	2.0		

Source: Board of Governors of the Federal Reserve System, *Flow of Funds Accounts, Assets and Liabilities Outstanding, 1969–1979*, p. 552.

7. Some credit unions have large inflows of savings with weak loan demand, and other credit unions have strong credit demand but weak savings inflows. Since the owners of the credit union are *both* the depositors and the borrowers—unlike the mutual savings banks and mutual savings and loans, where only the depositors are owners—the management of the credit unions often have a difficult task balancing the conflicting interests of these two groups.

Contractual Financial Institutions

Just as we can group the depository financial institutions together by a common element, so can we place together for discussion four financial institutions that share one element in common—obtaining their funds under some form of contract. These so-called contractual financial institutions include insurance companies, both life insurance and property and casualty forms, and pension funds, both private and public. The common element—contractually determined sources of funds—is a very important factor in influencing the behavior of these institutions. With a relatively assured, predictable, and stable source of funds, each of the contractual financial institutions has great flexibility in investment policy. As a general rule, the contractual financial institutions hold very small quantities of liquid assets and invest in long-maturity assets, which often have very limited liquidity. Moreover, the contractual financial institutions are the major purchasers of equity securities.

Insurance Companies.   The insurance industry is divided into two groups according to the function performed by the individual firms: life insurance companies and property and casualty insurance companies. Life insurance companies sell protection against premature death (term life), as well as long-term savings through a buildup of cash value in a whole life policy. Moreover, many life insurance companies actively compete for the management of pension funds for both private and public firms. All three of these functions provide funds to the life insurance companies, although the great bulk of assets under management is attributable to the last two activities. In contrast, property and casualty insurance companies are more specialized in function, selling protection on property through auto, fire, and other types of insurance.

The liabilities of life insurance companies, as presented in Table 4.6, reflect the basic functions of the industry. Life insurance reserves represent the claims on the firms from life insurance policyholders. Similarly, pension fund reserves represent the claims of pension fund beneficiaries. Given the long-term, stable sources of funds from premium payments,

Table 4.6   Financial assets and liabilities of life insurance companies, 1979 (billions of dollars)

Total financial assets	$420.5	Total liabilities	$396.6
Demand deposits and currency	2.0	Life insurance reserves	201.6
Corporate equities	40.1	Pension fund reserves	138.8
Corporate bonds	173.1	Other liabilities	56.2
Mortgages	119.2		
Policy loans	34.4		
Treasury issues	4.8		
Agency issues	8.8		
State and local obligations	6.4		
Open-market paper	7.3		
Other assets	24.4		

Source: Board of Governors of the Federal Reserve System, *Flow of Funds Accounts, Assets and Liabilities Outstanding, 1969–1979*, p. 553.

life insurance company investments are also long-term. The two largest commitments of funds are to corporate bonds ($173.1 billion) and mortgages ($119.2 billion). The corporate bonds are usually medium-to-high quality issues acquired by direct negotiation with the issuer, and the mortgages are usually on income-producing properties, such as apartment houses and office buildings, and on farm land. Corporate equities represent only about 10 percent of the total financial assets of life insurance companies, but the fraction has been growing as insurance companies have penetrated the pension fund market and invested many of these funds in equities. In contrast, short-term investments held for liquidity purposes represent a very small fraction of total financial assets because the need for liquidity is minimal. Moreover, holdings of state and local government issues are less than 2 percent of total financial assets, reflecting the low tax exposure of the industry.[8]

The portfolio of property and casualty insurance companies is quite different from the asset structure at life insurance companies. Property and casualty insurance companies have heavy investments in municipal bonds—indeed, they are the second largest buyer of municipals in many years—and in corporate equities. The investments in municipals reflect the relatively high tax exposure of these firms, and the equity holdings are intended to offer some hedge against the rising costs of claims in an inflationary environment. Remember that a life insurance company knows precisely its liability on any claim, but the property and casualty insurance company knows only the maximum amount of the claim. Consequently, as revealed in Table 4.7, other insurance companies (primarily property and casualty insurance companies) hold a larger fraction of their assets in liquid investment securities than do life insurance companies.

Pension Funds. Pension funds represent the other type of contractual financial institution. Not only are the assets of pension funds large, but they are growing rapidly as life expectancy increases and as concern increases about providing for financial security during

Table 4.7 Financial assets and liabilities of other insurance companies, 1979 (billions of dollars)

Total financial assets	$156.7	Total liabilities	$111.6
Demand deposits and currency	2.3	Policy payables	110.6
Corporate equities	25.6	Other	1.0
Treasury issues	11.9		
Agency issues	6.8		
State and local obligations	74.7		
Corporate bonds	22.2		
Other assets	13.2		

Source: Board of Governors of the Federal Reserve System, *Flow of Funds Accounts, Assets and Liabilities Outstanding, 1969–1979*, p. 552.

8. A substantial amount of funds ($34.4 billion in 1979) at life insurance companies is devoted to policy loans. These are loans to policyholders at fixed rates (usually 5 percent) specified in the policy and in amounts based on the cash value of the policy. When interest rates increase, policy loans generally rise as policyholders borrow the relatively cheap money available from this source.

retirement years. Some of the retirement funds—so-called insured plans—are held by life insurance companies and are reflected in Table 4.6. However, most pension plans are noninsured (not administered by a life insurance company). These noninsured pension plans, many of which are administered by trust departments of commercial banks, are in turn divided into private pension funds (funds of private firms) and state and local government employee retirement funds.[9] This distinction is significant, since the investment policies of the two types of funds differ markedly.

As revealed in Table 4.8, a large part (almost 60 percent) of the assets of private pension funds is invested in equities. The heavy concentration in equities is made possible by the long time horizon of the pension program whereby benefits are payable some years in the future. Over an extended period, the return on equities *should* exceed the return on debt securities for such investors as pension funds that can afford to ride out the large fluctuations that occur in the value of equity securities. Corporate bond holdings are the second largest investment holdings of private pension funds. Highly liquid short-term investment securities do not play a major role in the asset structure of private pension funds. The need for liquidity by pension funds is virtually nil, at least as compared with other financial institutions. Moreover, since pension funds are not subject to tax (the tax is paid by the beneficiary at the time benefits are paid), there is no incentive for them to hold tax-free state and local government issues.

The asset portfolios of state and local government pension funds are quite different from the portfolios of private funds. Reflecting the greater restrictions on investment policies that have traditionally been applied to state and local government plans, corporate bonds and other debt securities are the dominant investment. As shown in Table 4.9,

Table 4.8   Financial assets of private pension funds, 1979 (billions of dollars)

Total financial assets	$236.8
Demand deposits and currency	1.9
Time deposits	8.7
Corporate equities	136.4
Treasury issues	18.4
Agency issues	7.0
Corporate bonds	55.2
Mortgages	3.5
Miscellaneous assets	5.7

Source: Board of Governors of the Federal Reserve System, *Flow of Funds Accounts, Assets and Liabilities Outstanding, 1969–1979*, p. 553.

---

9. There are, of course, other retirement programs, including the massive social security system. However, social security payments are made primarily from current social security taxes, not from the social security trust fund. Moreover, the federal government also has a variety of retirement programs for employees, but they have few assets set aside to provide future benefits.

corporate bonds totaled $86.2 billion in 1979, whereas corporate equities totaled only $43.6 billion. However, state and local government pension funds have increased the proportion of their assets devoted to equities in recent years as regulations governing their portfolio have been liberalized. In contrast, the private pension funds have reduced their relative commitment to equities because the performance of the stock market in the decade of the 1970s was quite poor. As a result, the portfolios of the two types of financial institutions are growing more alike.

Table 4.9 Financial assets of state and local government employee retirement funds, 1979 (billions of dollars)

Total financial assets	$178.9
Demand deposits and currency	3.7
Corporate equities	43.6
Treasury issues	15.0
Agency issues	17.1
Corporate bonds	86.2
Mortgages	9.4
Other assets	3.9

Source: Board of Governors of the Federal Reserve System, *Flow of Funds Accounts, Assets and Liabilities Outstanding, 1969–1979*, p. 553.

Table 4.10 Financial assets and liabilities of finance companies, 1979 (billions of dollars)

Total financial assets	$168.9	Total liabilities	$161.5
Demand deposits and currency	4.6	Corporate bonds	57.0
Mortgages	11.4	Bank loans	20.8
Consumer credit	82.6	Open-market paper	61.2
Other loans (to business)	70.3	Other	22.5

Source: Board of Governors of the Federal Reserve System, *Flow of Funds Accounts, Assets and Liabilities Outstanding, 1969–1979*, p. 554.

Other Financial Institutions

There are various other financial institutions that serve specialized parts of the financial system in addition to the depository and contractual institutions discussed above, but we will concentrate on two: *finance companies* and *investment companies*. Finance companies provide credit to consumers to purchase consumer durable goods, such as automobiles, and to business to buy inventory and other assets. In contrast, investment companies (or mutual funds, as they are more commonly called) pool the funds of many individuals and invest in a variety of financial assets but primarily in equities.

Finance Companies.   Finance companies raise funds by both short- and long-term borrowing (see Table 4.10). Short-term borrowing is done both through banks and by sale of

Table 4.11   Financial assets of open-end
investment companies, 1979 (billions of dollars)

Total financial assets	46.2
Demand deposits and currency	0.7
Corporate equities	33.7
U.S. government securities	1.4
Corporate bonds	6.5
Other	3.9

Note: Excludes assets of money market funds.

Source: Board of Governors of the Federal Reserve
System, *Flow of Funds Accounts, Assets and Liabilities
Outstanding,* 1969–1979, p. 554.

open-market paper (commercial paper). Small finance companies tend to rely more on bank credit, but the larger finance companies depend almost entirely on open-market paper for their short-term funds. In addition, finance companies sell bonds to raise long-term funds. Investments are primarily in consumer credit ($82.6 billion) and loans to business ($70.3 billion). At one time, finance companies tended to specialize in either consumer or business credit. However, these firms have become increasingly involved in providing both types of credit.

Investment Companies.   The final type of financial institution we will discuss in this chapter is the investment company or mutual fund (Table 4.11). This type of financial institution pools the funds of investors, generally small investors, and purchases a diversified portfolio of securities. It offers to the small investor the opportunity to obtain a diversified portfolio of securities that would be impossible to obtain through direct investment in direct securities. Although investment companies have existed for many decades, the industry as we know it today is principally a post–World War II phenomenon. During the early postwar period when stock prices were increasing, the industry offered a way for the small investor to obtain high returns. With the poor performance of equities in the decade of the 1970s, however, the growth of the mutual fund industry slowed dramatically. As a result, the industry has increasingly turned to the offering of funds that specialize in corporate bonds and other fixed income securities (such as corporate and municipal bonds), so the proportion of equities in total fund assets has diminished.

The most striking and significant development in the investment company industry in recent years has been the development of the money market fund. Money market funds, established in the early 1970s to allow investors to obtain the high yields available from money market instruments, grew explosively in 1979 and 1980. Indeed, by late 1980, total money market fund assets exceeded $80 billion, larger than the total assets of the rest of the mutual fund industry combined. This growth was one of the principal factors behind the passage of the Depository Institutions Deregulation and Monetary Control Act of 1980.

GROWING COMPETITION AMONG FINANCIAL INSTITUTIONS

As discussed above, each of the nation's financial institutions has evolved a specialized role in the money and capital markets. Yet this historical specialization is diminishing (and competition is increasing) rapidly as the sources and uses of funds at individual financial institutions change and as the functions of different financial institutions broaden and overlap. Partially, the increased competition represents the reaction of financial institutions to changing demands by their customers and to changing technology. To a considerable degree, the greater competition reflects the relaxation of various regulatory restrictions that were originally designed to cope with the economic distress of the 1930s. These factors (and others) have resulted in a financial system that in the decade of the 1980s is considerably different from that of the 1950s and 1960s. We discuss below some of the more important aspects of the growing competition among financial institutions.

Perhaps the most significant expansion in competition is among the nation's *depository financial institutions*—commercial banks, savings and loan associations, mutual savings banks, and credit unions. At one time their functions were quite specialized, with only a limited degree of overlap. Banks obtained funds from demand deposits and made loans to businesses for short-term working capital needs, and nonbank depository institutions obtained funds from savings accounts and made relatively long-term loans to consumers. Today, however, the degree of overlap in function is substantial. Commercial banks obtain more and more of their funds from time and savings accounts in direct competition with savings and loans, mutual savings banks, and credit unions. And nonbank depository institutions have developed a variety of devices to "invade" the demand deposit market dominated by commercial banks. Nonbank financial institutions (as well as commercial banks) now offer Negotiable Orders of Withdrawal (N.O.W. accounts), which are functionally equivalent to checking accounts but which have the added feature of paying interest. In fact, it appears increasingly likely that all deposits at depository financial institutions will pay interest in the near future.

Evidence of increased competition is also pronounced on the asset side of the balance sheet. Commercial banks have invaded the consumer loan market in force. Many commercial banks have begun to make long-term mortgage loans in large volume in direct competition with savings and loan associations. Savings and loan associations have increased their commitment to consumer loans, and credit unions have begun to make long-term mortgage loans to their members. The maturity of bank loans has increased, placing banks in direct competition with such long-term lenders as life insurance companies and pension funds. In short, no longer are services to consumers and businesses available from only one type of financial institution. Borrowers and depositors increasingly have a wide variety of choices.

Another example of growing competition stems from that new type of financial institution just discussed—the *money market fund.* A type of open-end investment company, the money market fund invests in the major money market instruments, such as commercial paper, certificates of deposit, and Treasury bills. It obtains funds to make these investments by selling shares to consumers and businesses. In periods of high interest rates, the yield on these shares can be very attractive as compared with the yield on savings accounts at depository financial institutions. Moreover, the fact that customers of money market funds may write checks on their accounts creates, in effect, high-interest–paying demand deposits. In early 1980, for example, when money market rates were quite high—money market funds were paying about 14 percent—more than $50 billion was moved into money market funds. To judge the comparative significance of this development, the reader should note that the total financial assets of credit unions at the end of 1979 (see Table 4.5) were only $62.3 billion.

A further example of the expansion in competition among the nation's financial institutions is the growth of *bank holding companies*. A bank holding company is a corporation that holds stock in one or more commercial banks. Through the holding company device, commercial banks have been able to expand geographically in areas where such expansion through branching was difficult or impossible. The competitive implications of holding company growth through acquisition of commercial banks is important, but the most significant aspect of this movement for our discussion is the impact on competition among nonbank financial institutions. Bank holding companies are allowed to enter a number of nonbank financial industries through either the acquisition of existing firms or the establishment of new ones. These include consumer credit companies, leasing companies, and mortgage banking firms, as well as other financial institutions. Throughout the decade of the 1970s, bank holding companies expanded rapidly into these nonbanking areas and dramatically changed the nature of competition in these industries.

Another development that has raised profound issues of national policy is the movement toward electronic transfer of funds. That movement could, if not properly controlled, create a great advantage for commercial banks, as administrators of the nation's payments system, over nonbank depository institutions. Conversely, the N.O.W. account has provided the nonbank depository institutions with an entrance into the demand deposit market at the expense of the commercial banks, though at considerable interest-cost burden to the issuers of the accounts.

The payments mechanism in the United States has been and remains today primarily a checking account system. Checks are written for the purchase of goods and services and to obtain currency, and the checks are processed through the banking system. Indeed, the volume of checks necessary to handle the transaction needs of the public is staggering. In 1980, for example, Americans wrote an estimated 80 billion checks. It is becoming increasingly obvious that a substitute for checks must be found to effectively transfer ownership of demand deposits.

To this point, there are three basic forms to short-circuit the paper involved in the check clearing process: automated clearinghouses, automated teller machines, and point-of-sale terminals. Automated clearinghouses encompass direct deposit of checks, as well as preauthorized bill payments. As might be suspected, the thrift institutions are very concerned about the potential advantages given to the commercial banking industry by direct deposit if such mechanisms are limited to commercial banks. In addition to the automated clearinghouse, the electronic funds transfer movement so far includes automated teller machines, or money machines that allow the automatic withdrawal of cash and the movement of funds from one type of account to another. The savings and loan associations have been quite active in the use of this type of equipment, which, if conveniently placed, allows the customer to use a savings account as a demand deposit. From the long-term perspective, however, the innovation that probably has the greatest potential for altering the competitive balance among the nation's financial institutions is the point-of-sale terminal. Such a terminal, placed in a retail firm, allows direct transfer at the point of sale from the buyer to the seller. Naturally, savings and loans and other thrift institutions want to have their computers connected to the point-of-sale system.

In contrast to the developments in electronic funds transfer systems, which are made possible by changes in technology, the N.O.W. account movement stems from the desire of nonbank financial institutions to capture new customers by offering services that are, in function if not in label, equivalent to demand deposits. These third-party payments systems are similar to checking accounts, but interest is paid on the average balance in an account, and the N.O.W. is not legally a demand instrument since payment may be delayed by the financial institution. Begun in Massachusetts by the Savings Bank of Worcester, N.O.W. accounts have spread throughout New England and New York. The impact of N.O.W.'s on the competitive structure and earnings of financial institutions has been substantial.

THE DEPOSITORY INSTITUTIONS DEREGULATION AND MONETARY CONTROL ACT OF 1980

Passage of the Depository Institutions Deregulation and Monetary Control Act of 1980 has substantially altered the ground rules under which financial institutions compete. The trend toward greater similarity among the nation's depository financial institutions was accelerated by the passage of this act. The competitive overlap among commercial banks, savings and loan associations, mutual savings banks, and credit unions was sharply increased by it. The act contains too many provisions to cover in depth, but it is important for our discussion in this chapter to note the following.

1. Permitted nationwide Negotiable Order of Withdrawal accounts. Effective December 31, 1980, all depository financial institutions were allowed to offer N.O.W. accounts to individuals and nonprofit organizations. The act also allows banks to provide automatic transfer services from savings accounts to checking accounts and authorizes all federally insured credit unions to offer share drafts.

2. Phased out ceilings on deposit interest rates. Reflecting the growing view that interest-rate ceilings on deposits discourage saving and create inequities for depositors, especially by discriminating against savers of relatively modest means, the act provides for a gradual phaseout of interest-rate ceilings over a six-year period from the date of passage of the act.

3. Required reserves on all transactions accounts at depository institutions. For the first time, all depository institutions will be subject to the same reserve requirements. Specifically, the act states that any reserve requirement will now be uniformly applied to all accounts at all depository institutions. The act provides for an eight-year phasein of reserve requirements for depository institutions that are not Federal Reserve members and a four-year phasedown of previous reserve requirements for member banks.

4. Expanded power of thrift institutions. Federally chartered savings and loan associations were authorized to invest up to 20 percent of their assets in consumer loans, commercial paper, and corporate debt securities. The authority to make real estate loans was expanded by the removal of any geographical lending restrictions, provision for a 90-percent loan-to-asset limit in place of the existing $75,000 limit, and removal of the first-lien restrictions on residential real estate loans. Federally chartered savings and loan associations were also authorized to offer credit-card services and to exercise trust and fiduciary services. Mutual savings banks were authorized to make commercial, corporate, and business loans up to 5 percent of their total assets. Mutual savings banks were also authorized to accept demand deposits in connection with commercial, corporate, or business loan relationships.

5. Eliminated usury ceilings. State usury ceilings on first residential mortgage loans were eliminated unless a state adopts a new ceiling before April 1, 1983. Credit unions may increase their loan-rate ceiling from 12 percent to 15 percent and may raise the ceiling higher for periods up to 18 months. The act also preempted state usury ceilings on business and agricultural loans above $25,000 and permitted an interest rate of not more than 5 percent above the Federal Reserve discount rate, including any surcharge. This provision expires April 1, 1983, or at an earlier date if the state expressly reinstates a usury ceiling. To prevent discrimination on other loans, a rate ceiling was established at one percentage point above the Federal Reserve discount rate.

This act is broad in scope and fundamental in effect. Its intent is clearly to reduce the differences in regulation and function among the nation's depository institutions. Although these depository institutions will not be identical after the act is fully implemented, they will be quite similar, especially in their sources of funds. As a result, the traditional distinctions among financial institutions, which were discussed earlier in this chapter, will blur further during the decade of the 1980s. Indeed, perhaps the distinctions may cease to exist entirely at some point in the future.

It is still too early to know what the long-run implications of the act will be. The phaseout of Regulation Q ceilings should reduce the incidence of disintermediation. Now, in periods of high interest rates, financial institutions should be better able to offer competitive rates of return on deposit accounts. As a result, the flow of funds to depository institutions should be more stable over the business cycle. Yet these funds may be more costly, particularly as interest is paid on transactions accounts. It is therefore expected that financial institutions will make portfolio adjustments in response to their higher costs. This raises important questions about the availability of credit to certain sectors of the economy, especially housing, if the traditional lender—the savings and loan—does indeed diversify its portfolio substantially. Other questions may be raised about the impact of the act on the viability of different financial institutions. In a more competitive financial environment, failures may be more common, particularly among the smaller financial institutions. As a result, many observers have forecast a drastic reduction in the number of independent financial institutions.

SUMMARY

The United States has evolved over more than two centuries a financial system in which the role of individual financial institutions has been highly specialized. Commercial banks have dominated the payments mechanism and served the needs of business. Other depository financial institutions have served as outlets for consumer savings and provided loans for housing and other types of credit to individuals. And other types of financial institutions have provided specialized financial services.

This specialized-role financial system is changing dramatically. Technology, through electronic funds transfer and other developments, is altering the financial system. Moreover, in a world of high and unstable interest rates, the nature of financial institutions is likely to be altered further. Under the Depository Institutions Deregulation and Monetary Control Act of 1980, the arena for competition has broadened, and the degree of specialization is further diminishing.

QUESTIONS

1. Carefully compare the characteristics of commercial banks on the one hand with those of nonbank financial institutions on the other. Have their roles become more alike or more different? Why? Explain.

2. Banks perform a number of functions. What are the functions and how are they reflected on the financial statements of the banking industry?

3. What are the major changes in the sources and uses of funds at commercial banks in recent years? What reasons can you give for these changes?

4. What are the similarities and differences among savings and loan associations, mutual savings banks, and credit unions?

5. What are contractual financial institutions? How do they differ from depository financial institutions?

6. What are the similarities and differences among the different types of contractual financial institutions?

7. Make a list of the areas in which there has been growing competition among depository financial institutions. What are the reasons for this increased competition?

8. How might the development of electronic funds transfer systems affect the nature of competition among financial institutions?

9. Discuss the provisions of the Depository Institutions Deregulation and Monetary Control act of 1980. How might the act affect the sources and uses of funds at depository financial institutions?

REFERENCES

"The Depository Institutions Deregulation and Monetary Control Act of 1980," *Federal Reserve Bulletin,* June 1980, pp. 444–452.

Dougall, Herbert E., and Jack E. Gaumnitz, *Capital Markets and Institutions,* 4th ed. (Englewood Cliffs, N.J.: Prentice-Hall, 1980).

Farwell, Loring, *et al., Financial Institutions* (Homewood, Ill.: Irwin, 1966).

Kroos, Herman E., and Martin R. Blyn, *A History of Financial Intermediaries* (New York: Random House, 1971).

Light, J.O., and William L. White, *The Financial System* (Homewood, Ill.: Irwin, 1979).

Polakoff, Murray E., *et al., Financial Institutions and Markets* (Boston: Houghton Mifflin, 1981).

Reed, Edward, *et al., Commercial Banking* (Englewood Cliffs, N.J.: Prentice-Hall, 1980).

Rose, Peter S., and Donald R. Fraser, *Financial Institutions* (Dallas: Business Publications, 1980).

APPENDIX

ELECTRONIC FUNDS TRANSFER SYSTEMS AND THE ROLE OF FINANCIAL INTERMEDIARIES

As discussed throughout Chapter 4, the nature of financial institutions, as well as the structure of the entire financial system, has been undergoing rapid change in recent years. This change reflects a number of interrelated factors: the attempt by managers of financial institutions to avoid regulatory restrictions on the behavior of individual financial institutions, pressures of rising costs, high and volatile interest rates, and enormous changes in the technology applicable to financial services. The last factor, changing technology, may over time substantially alter the nature of the financial system. An important part of this development is known as electronic funds transfer systems (EFTS).

It is perhaps appropriate to begin by discussing the nature of electronic funds transfer systems. As we will see, the subject covers a number of different functions within the financial system, each with different implications for the future of financial institutions. Moreover, electronic funds transfer systems are not new, though their importance has grown enormously in the past few years and promises to grow even more in the near future.

Electronic funds transfer systems may be defined as mechanisms for the electronic movement of funds among economic units. The economic units may be individuals, businesses, governments, or financial institutions. Electronic funds transfer systems may be contrasted with the paper funds transfer systems (such as the use of checks) that have dominated the payments system in recent decades. Electronic funds transfer systems are generally defined to include bank wire systems, automated clearinghouses, automated teller machines, and point-of-sale systems. Each of these has the goal of reducing the flow of paper in the financial system by substituting electronic impulses for paper-based systems. (See the articles by Niblack and by Grandstaff and Smaistrla in the references section of this appendix for useful discussions of the nature of electronic funds transfer systems.)

Types of Electronic Funds Transfer Systems

Bank Wire Systems.   The beginnings of the electronic funds transfer movement may be traced to the bank wire system established by the Federal Reserve in 1918. Under this system as currently constituted, the Federal Reserve Banks and their branches, the Board of Governors, the U.S. Treasury, and more than 200 commercial banks (mostly large banks that engage in substantial transactions in the money market) are linked together by electronic means. This bank wire system principally functions as a device to transfer member bank reserve balances among different banks in the Federal Reserve System. For example, when one bank sells federal funds to another bank, it may instruct the Federal Reserve to transfer reserve balances from its account to the account of the bank that has purchased federal funds, and this transfer can be made over the Fed's bank wire. In addition, the Fed's bank wire system also assists in the "book entry" transfer of U.S. government securities, by which the accounts of commercial banks are adjusted electronically to reflect their securities transactions. A further wire system has been established in the past few years by major commercial banks so that payments can be sent electronically among themselves. At last count, this private bank wire system included well over 100 banks.

Automated Clearinghouses.   One of the most significant aspects in the electronic funds transfer development is the automated clearinghouse. Of course, local clearinghouses at which commercial banks physically exchange checks and "settle up" their balances have been common for decades. Yet the handling of large amounts of paper items is time-consuming and costly. In an automated clearinghouse, the transfer of funds occurs electronically by means of computer tapes, a mechanism that offers large potential cost savings. These potential cost savings are particularly significant in recurring transactions, such as the deposit of payroll funds by an employer.

In contrast to the Federal Reserve bank wire system, which is many decades old, automated clearinghouses date back only to the late 1960s. California bankers in 1968 formed a special group to investigate the feasibility of using magnetic tapes in the clearing function. Later the Committee on Paperless Entries built on the experience of the California group, leading in 1973 to the formation of the Georgia Automated Clearinghouse Association. In 1974 the National Automated Clearinghouse Association was formed in order to tie together regionally the developing local automated clearinghouses. By the mid-1970s there were more than 30 members processing well over one million payments per month. Many of these automated clearinghouses are operated by the Federal Reserve, reflecting its traditional role in the payments system.

Teller Machines.   Another important dimension of the electronic funds transfer movement is the growth of teller machines, referred to as customer bank communications terminals (CBCT) by the Comptroller of the Currency and remote service units (RSU) by the Federal Home Loan Bank Board. These teller machines vary widely in function; some are completely automatic and tied directly into the computer of the individual financial institution offering the service. Some teller machines are located on the premises of the financial institution, but others are located at a distance from the financial institution; however, off-premises teller machines have been restricted in many states by court rulings that they constituted branch banks.

The automated teller machines (ATM) generally perform a variety of services. They include receiving deposits, providing currency, transferring funds between accounts, making credit card advances, and receiving payments. The customer gains access to the teller machine usually by a magnetic strip card in association with a personal identification number (P.I.N.) number).

Point-of-Sale Systems.   Perhaps the most significant component of the electronic funds transfer system as far as the future of financial intermediaries is concerned is the point-of-sale system. Such an on-line system allows a customer to immediately transfer funds to the seller at the time of sale. In order to implement a point-of-sale system, there are on-line terminals located at the place at which the sale is consummated. The buyer has his or her "debit" card inserted into a terminal, which immediately debits the customer's bank account and credits the merchant's bank account. If the customer and the merchant use the same bank, the procedure is relatively simple. However, if the customer and the merchant use a different bank, then the computers of the two banks are connected through a switching and processing center (SPC). The potential for cost savings through point-of-sale systems is substantial. It has been estimated that about 30 percent of personal checks are written to grocery stores or other retail establishments. Thus substitution of point-of-sale systems for checks in retail transactions would markedly reduce the flow of paper in the payments system.

Implications of Electronic Funds Transfer Systems

The spread of electronic funds transfer systems has been less rapid than many had originally anticipated. In part this slower development of EFTS has resulted from consumer reluctance to adopt the new technology, problems of adapting the technology to a system of substantial regulations and restrictions on the behavior of individual financial institutions, and the existence of higher costs of purchase and operation of EFTS than many had originally anticipated. Yet EFTS is spreading and promises to become very commonplace in the future. When that occurs, the implications for financial market participants, including financial institutions, will be substantial.

It must be recognized initially that the development of EFTS involves the substitution of capital for labor and to a considerable extent the substitution of fixed costs for variable costs. Moreover, the equipment needed to operate an EFTS efficiently involves substantial capital outlays. Consequently, questions have been raised as to whether small financial institutions—bank and nonbank alike—can afford to commit the resources to acquire the equipment, whether they have the technical expertise to operate the systems, and whether they have the necessary volume of operations to make efficient use of the systems. The growth of EFTS may so increase the economies of scale among depository financial institutions that it will make small financial institutions uncompetitive. If so, EFTS will further contribute to the consolidation of resources in the financial system.

A related issue is that of ownership of and access to the equipment that is integral to EFTS. This is particularly important for automated clearinghouses, but it is also significant for automated teller machines and point-of-sale terminals. For example, should automated clearinghouses be viewed as natural monopolies and as such be subject to government regulation or ownership? Some have argued that the Federal Reserve should operate all automated clearinghouses as a part of its traditional role in the payments mechanism. Others have argued that over time and as the volume of transactions expands, private industry can play an important part in providing this service. And there is the significant question of access to the EFTS system. This is of particular concern to nonbank financial institutions and smaller commercial banks, which fear that unless they are guaranteed equal access, they will not be able to compete in the changed financial environment.

Regardless of how these issues are settled, the EFTS development is likely to have a major impact on the way in which financial transactions are handled by individuals, businesses, financial intermediaries, and governments. For individuals, the replacement of currency with credit and debit cards will become more common. Moreover, the cards will provide instant access to credit from a depository financial institution. However, the time delay between writing a check and the debit of that check against the customer's account will either cease to exist or be markedly reduced. Similar developments will permeate the business sector. Payments for labor and other inputs into the production process will be made with direct deposit to the appropriate financial institution or by electronic transfer to the seller's account. Active management of cash balances through the money market will become common. For financial institutions, all deposits will pay interest, and the interest may be paid over very short intervals. Service charges will be carefully levied for each service provided. Reserve management will be instantaneous. For government, daily cash management will be done electronically, and government debt will cease to have a paper representation. Moreover, there is likely to be a major impact on monetary policy. The development of EFTS is likely to reduce the demand for money by the public and further blur the distinction among different kinds of liquid assets used as money. The development of EFTS systems may thus make management of the economy more difficult for the Federal Reserve.

It is not likely that all these effects will occur in the immediate future. Indeed, some of them may never occur. Yet it seems likely that the pace of change will accelerate and EFT systems will become more common in the future. As this change occurs, the existing set of regulations of financial institutions will have to be altered markedly, and the entire nature of financial institutions may change dramatically.

REFERENCES

Dingle, James F., "The Public Policy Implications of Electronic Funds Transfer Systems," *Journal of Bank Research,* Spring 1976, pp. 30–36.

EFT and the Public Interest, a report of the National Commission on Electronic Funds Transfers, Washington, D.C., February 1977.

Flanneny, Mark J., and Dwight M. Jaffee, *The Economic Implications of an Electronic Monetary Transfer System* (Lexington, Mass.: D.C. Heath, 1973).

Grandstaff, Mary C., and Charles J. Smaistrla, "A Primer on Electronic Funds Transfer," Federal Reserve Bank of Dallas *Business Review,* September 1976, pp. 7–14.

Niblack, William C., "Development of Electronic Funds Transfer Systems," Federal Reserve Bank of St. Louis *Monthly Review,* September 1976, pp. 10–18.

Smaistrla, Charles J., "Current Issues in Electronic Funds Transfer," Federal Reserve Bank of Dallas *Business Review,* February 1977, pp. 1–7.

Chapter 5

The Regulatory Environment: The Role of Government in the Financial System

As discussed in the previous chapter, the pace of change in the financial system has been rapid in recent years. The financial system in the early 1980s is quite different from that in the early 1970s and even further removed from that of the early 1960s. And the financial system of the 1990s will undoubtedly differ considerably from the financial system of today. In part, the continuous evolution of the financial system reflects changing demands for financial services by households, businesses, and governments, changing economic and financial conditions, cost pressures on individual financial institutions and markets, and advances in technology. Throughout this book, as we cover the various financial markets and institutions, we will integrate into the discussion the major economic factors that are producing change in the financial system.

One major influence on the financial system that we have not yet discussed in depth is government regulation. Not only is the effect of *government regulations* on the overall financial system pervasive, but the influence of government on the *allocation of credit* has grown markedly in recent years. This influence reflects the enormous importance of the financial system to the efficient functioning of the economy and the increasing attempt to use government to achieve some socially desired allocation of resources. As an example of regulation, the types of securities sold in financial markets are strongly affected by government policy. In addition, the scope and nature of the operations of financial institutions, which acquire most of the direct securities issued by households, businesses, and governments, are strongly influenced by government. Further, the interest rates paid for funds by financial institutions and the rates they charge for loans reflect government policy.

Some of this government regulation obviously stems from the desire to achieve specific improvements in the functioning of the financial system, such as greater availability of credit to minority groups. However, many types of government regulation originated as responses to financial crises during periods of failure at banks and other financial institutions. And it is specially interesting to note that many types of government regulations of the financial system actually conflict in their objectives. For example, one type of government regulation may seek to increase the flow of credit to housing while at the same time another type is producing (inadvertently) the opposite impact. Indeed, government has attempted in numerous ways to increase the flow of credit to housing, but that it has succeeded is not at all clear. In any case, it is apparent that an understanding of the financial system requires an examination of the role of government.

We attempt in this chapter to present in a concise form a discussion of the major types of regulation that apply to the financial system. Excluded from this chapter, however, is any treatment of the role of monetary and fiscal policy, both of which impact on the overall supply and cost of credit. They will be discussed in Chapters 6, 7, 21, and 22. In addition, some of the dimensions of regulation were covered in Chapter 4. Our concern in this chapter is with those government policies that affect the *allocation of credit to particular sectors of the economy and the relative cost of credit to individual parts of the economy, rather than the overall supply and cost of credit.* [1] Obviously, we can present only the highlights of these policies and their effects. However, we will provide a further discussion of the influence of government regulation where appropriate in the remaining chapters of the book.

The chapter is divided into two basic parts. The first part, concerned with the *regulatory influences of government,* deals with the individual regulations that affect financial markets and institutions. The focus is on the regulatory influences relating to financial institutions, the limits on rates that financial institutions may pay to obtain funds, usury laws, consumer protection laws, and other types of government regulation. In the second part of the chapter, we examine the government sector from the vantage point of a *financial intermediary* that affects the allocation of funds. In particular, we look at those programs that have sought to provide a greater quantity and lower cost of funds to two sectors of the economy: *housing and agriculture.* Naturally, these influences overlap. Yet the distinction is useful for explanatory purposes.

REGULATORY INFLUENCES OF GOVERNMENT

As mentioned earlier, the structure of the financial system as it exists today reflects a complex interaction over a period of decades both of fundamental economic factors and of

---

1. For example, the Federal Reserve, through its monetary policy actions, has traditionally been concerned with the total supply of credit and not with its allocation. The Federal Reserve's position has been that it would create the "appropriate" amount of credit and allow the market to make the allocation. Our discussion in this chapter deals mainly with the ways in which other government policies do influence this allocation of credit.

government regulations. This interaction has produced a financial system composed of *specialized* financial institutions subject to regulation by *specialized* regulatory agencies. Moreover, these regulatory agencies have imposed considerable restrictions on the entry of new financial firms into the financial services industry—particularly among depository financial institutions—and on the extent of competition among various types of financial institutions within the financial system. Both such controls attempt to affect the risk characteristics of the securities offered to the public by financial institutions. Government regulations affect and to a degree determine the rates financial institutions can pay on the indirect securities they offer to the public (under Regulation Q) and also the rates they can charge on their extensions of credit (under various usury laws). When financial institutions acquire direct securities issued by the public, these financial institutions are subject to a wide variety of limitations on their behavior under various consumer protection laws. In addition, the various securities laws administered by the Securities and Exchange Commission require extensive disclosure of information by those seeking to sell securities in the public marketplace. We attempt to explain briefly in the next few pages each one of these regulatory influences of government.

Regulation and Its Influence on the Role of Individual Institutions

As discussed earlier, the various financial institutions in the United States have traditionally been quite specialized in function. Commercial banks have traditionally obtained their funds from demand deposit accounts and have concentrated on short-term lending. Savings and loan associations have traditionally offered various forms of savings vehicles to households and have concentrated their lending in single-family residential mortgages. And a similar (though less narrow) form of specialization occurs for nondepository financial institutions, such as consumer and business finance companies. Although the degree of specialization has diminished somewhat, and although the degree of overlap among the functions of different financial institutions has expanded considerably (thereby increasing competition among the different institutions), it remains true that most financial institutions play a rather specialized role in the financial system.

The degree of specialization observable today among the nation's financial institutions reflects the joint influence of historical and regulatory factors. Many financial institutions were founded in order to serve one particular need within the financial system. For example, savings and loan associations were originally formed in order to provide mortgage credit to individuals at a time when commercial banks and other lenders would not extend lengthy mortgage loans. Similarly, credit unions were formed in order to provide consumer loans at reasonable rates at a time when commercial banks considered consumer lending to be an unproductive use of funds. Beyond these historical antecedents, however, the role played by each institution and the basic nature of each institution today reflect the substantial amount of government regulations that limit the behavior of the institution both in raising and using funds.

The nature of government regulation of the place of individual financial institutions within the financial system is characterized by two interrelated constraints: limitations on *function* and limitations on *risk*.

Function

To some extent limitations on function have as their purpose limitations on risk. There has always been substantial concern about the failure of individual financial institutions, especially of commercial banks, which dominate the payments mechanism. Yet there are other factors involved in this limitation of function besides risk reduction.

The commercial banking industry offers numerous examples of limitations on function. Regulation has sought to prevent financial interlocks between the commercial banking industry and the various types of nonfinancial business, such as manufacturing, wholesaling, and retailing. This goal is embodied in the prohibition (with but a few limited exceptions) of commercial bank ownership of stock in nonfinancial businesses. In the United States, commercial banks by law are *lenders* rather than *owners*. In contrast, in most of western Europe and in Japan a long tradition of interconnection exists between banking and nonfinancial firms through stock ownership. Moreover, statutes in the United States prevent commercial banks from performing investment banking functions, such as underwriting securities.[2]

Savings and loan associations provide another example of regulations that limit the functions of a financial institution. Originally, of course, savings and loans were created to invest in single-family mortgages. Yet in order to encourage existing savings and loans to continue such policies and to subsidize the mortgage market (more will be said about this type of subsidy later in the chapter), savings and loan associations were given special tax breaks if they concentrated their assets in mortgage loans. These special tax reductions took the form of tax-free additions to bad-debt reserves out of taxable income—which had the result of sharply reducing the effective tax rate of the savings and loan industry. However, this tax-avoidance device is only available to savings and loans that keep at least 85 percent of their earning assets in mortgage loans.

Risk

Perhaps the most substantial regulations on the behavior of U.S. financial institutions relate to risk. Extensive provisions of law and regulation limit the degree of risk that a financial institution may take in the assets it acquires and thus in the securities it offers to the public in order to raise funds. These limitations are most severe for the depository financial institutions—commercial banks, savings and loans, mutual savings banks, and credit unions—but they also apply to many nondepository financial institutions. Although there have always been regulatory limitations on the degree of risk that can be assumed by financial institutions, the restrictions became much more severe following the financial crisis (and numerous bank failures) of the early 1930s. In recent decades, when failures

---

2. Prior to the early 1930s, commercial banks were allowed to perform investment banking functions. However, following a number of abuses of their investment banking powers in the early 1930s, commercial bank underwriting of securities was limited to U.S. Government and general-obligation municipal securities.

among the nation's financial institutions have been infrequent, many of these limitations on the risk exposure of individual institutions have been relaxed to some extent.

A few examples may be useful in explaining the limitations on risk produced by the regulation of different financial institutions. Commercial banks may extend credit only through acquiring financial assets that are "nonspeculative" in nature. If municipal securities in the portfolio are rated by one of the rating agencies (such as Moody's or Standard and Poor's), they must be at least of "investment grade."[3] And if financial assets in the portfolio are not rated, then management is responsible for maintaining adequate credit files to demonstrate to the regulatory authorities that their credit extensions represent "sound credit." Not only are there limitations on the quality of individual financial assets held within the portfolio of the financial institution, but there are also restrictions on the fraction of the portfolio devoted to any borrower. For example, national banks may not lend more than 10 percent of their capital to any one borrower. In addition, national banks may not have real estate loans that exceed their total capital position or 70 percent of their time and savings deposits, whichever is larger.

From a broader perspective, the bank regulatory agencies periodically evaluate the liquidity position of the bank, the adequacy of the capital base it has available to offset losses, the quality of its management, and other dimensions of the bank that bear on the risk of default and thereby on the riskiness of the securities offered to the public by these financial institutions.[4] Indeed, a bank or savings and loan association cannot even receive a charter unless it meets minimum capital standards established by the regulatory authorities. Similar types of restrictions on risk-bearing at commercial banks also apply to other financial institutions.

Examinations

Related to risk reduction is the tradition of outside examination. Periodic and unannounced inspections or examinations by officials of the regulatory agencies (examiners) occur at many types of financial institutions. The purpose of these examinations is to appraise the "quality of management" of the organization in both its financial and its nonfinancial dimensions. More specifically, the purpose of the examinations is to identify problem areas within the organization and eliminate the problems before they threaten the viability of the organization. The adequacy of internal controls to prevent the theft of assets is evaluated. The extent to which the institution is conforming to the detailed regulations designed to reduce risk and achieve other objectives is examined, and the quality of the asset portfolio is scrutinized. Loans are evaluated as good, substandard, doubtful, and loss. If any asset is of unsatisfactory quality ("loss"), the institution is forced to "write off" the asset against its

---

3. Investment-grade securities are those in the top four categories according to the Moody's and Standard and Poor's rating systems.

4. The riskiness of the indirect securities of depository financial institutions is, of course, also greatly affected by the existence of deposit insurance.

capital account. And if the capital account proves inadequate, the institution is forced to raise additional capital through the sale of stock or through other means, such as greater retention of earnings (as opposed to the payment of cash dividends to stockholders).

Structure of the Industry

Risk of failure, as well as the overall performance of firms, is also affected by the number and size distribution of financial institutions (frequently referred to as the *structure of the industry)*. As a result, the structure of the financial services industry, especially for commercial banks and other depository financial institutions, is subject to regulation. This regulation principally impacts through control of *mergers, branching,* and *the entry of new firms.* In evaluating requests by existing firms to merge or establish branches and by organizers of new firms to establish additional competitors, the regulatory authorities must evaluate the impact of these developments on the safety and stability of other firms in the industry. Limitations on branching and attitudes toward mergers affect the degree of concentration (the share of the market controlled by a few firms) and thereby the stability of individual institutions. The restriction of entry into the financial marketplace by new competitors has been one of the principal means to control risk. For example, to obtain a bank charter (a permit to operate commercial banking functions) an applicant must, among other things, establish that: (1) there is a need for a new bank; (2) the bank will be profitable within a reasonable time; and (3) the chartering of the new bank *will not cause substantial harm to existing banks in the market areas.*

The last requirement appears to be very peculiar in a competitive system. Not only must those who wish to start a new bank show that there is a need for a new firm (for most industries such need is demonstrated after the fact by the market test), but they must also show that no harm will be done to their competitors (in most industries the *objective* is to harm competitors). The result of such restrictions on entry is of course to limit competition and also to reduce the efficiency of operation of the financial system. Although this reduction in number of competing firms does limit the extent and significance of failures, the limitations on entry provide existing firms with the opportunity to earn a higher risk-adjusted return than would be possible with fewer restrictions on entry. In effect, restrictions on entry allow inefficient firms to earn ''normal'' profits and efficient firms to earn above-''normal'' profits.

Nondepository Financial Institutions

Nondepository financial institutions are also subject to regulations with risk reduction as their purpose. However, limitations on risk-bearing by these types of institutions are generally less severe than at depository institutions. In the case of life insurance companies, for example, the types of securities that may be acquired are usually restricted by state law. Pension funds which—at least in their asset management—have traditionally been among the least regulated of all financial institutions, must be managed according to the ''prudent man'' rule; that is, management must be able to show that in its investment decisions it operates as a prudent man would.[5]

Risk versus Performance?

The preoccupation of the regulatory system with risk limitations stems from the financial crisis of the early 1930s. In that period, literally thousands of banks and other financial institutions failed, and thousands of individuals lost their savings. The legislative reaction to this financial disaster was to encumber the financial system with a host of regulations designed to reduce risk, some of which we have discussed above. However, the post–World War II era has been characterized by a more stable economic and social environment, and therefore questions have been raised about the desirability of a regulatory system that concentrates on risk reduction. Obviously any type of regulation that affects the risk structure of the nation's financial institutions also affects other aspects of the behavior of the financial system. In fact, currently existing financial regulations reduce competition through the encouragement of specialization among financial institutions and through individual regulations designed to reduce risk. And with the reduction in competition there is almost certainly a reduction in the efficiency with which individual financial institutions perform their basic functions and in the overall performance of the financial system. Risk, competition, and performance should all be related.

This relationship of competition, risk, and performance is illustrated in Fig. 5.1. At the left of the figure is a situation in which there are substantial limitations on risk levels at individual financial institutions, competition is stifled, and the performance of the financial system is far below optimal. At the other extreme, regulatory restrictions on risk-taking are reduced, competition is encouraged, and the financial system operates more efficiently. Of course, at the left-hand side of Fig. 5.1 the number of failures among financial institutions would be small, whereas at the right-hand side the number of failures would be much higher.

The U.S. financial system immediately after the end of World War II might have been viewed as very close to the left-hand side of Fig. 5.1. In more recent years, however, the degree of specialization among financial institutions has diminished, resulting in increased competition. Regulatory restrictions have also been reduced, further intensifying competition. As a result, the U.S. financial system has moved closer to the middle of the spectrum depicted in Fig. 5.1. Major studies of the financial system in the postwar era have recommended further reductions in restrictions on competition among the individual finan-

Low Competition	High Competition
Low Risk	High Risk
Low Performance	High Performance

Fig. 5.1   A spectrum of competition, risk, and performance for the financial system

5. The relative freedom from restrictions on assets held is much more valid for private than for public pension funds.

cial institutions. And as discussed in the previous chapter, the passage in 1980 of the Depository Institutions Deregulation and Monetary Control Act moved the financial system further toward the right-hand side of Fig. 5.1. Changing technology, as well as changes in regulation, are continuing to move the financial system in that direction.

THE FUNCTIONS OF REGULATORY AGENCIES

The substantial amount of detailed regulation of the behavior of individual financial institutions and markets creates a need for appropriate organizations to police and enforce the regulations. In the United States, a variety of government regulatory agencies perform these functions. These agencies, frequently specialized along the same lines as the institutions they regulate, exist at both federal and state levels. Moreover, there is considerable overlap among the functions of the regulatory agencies. Indeed, there is overlapping of function not only between federal and state government agencies but also between various federal agencies themselves.

   Figure 5.2 serves to indicate both the specialized nature of the regulatory agencies, especially of those that regulate commercial banks, and the degree of overlapping regulation. Note that the degree of regulation is greatest for the depository financial institutions, reflecting concern for the safety and liquidity of the public's deposits. The overlapping nature of regulation is also most prevalent for the depository financial institutions. However, the amount of regulation is substantial for all financial institutions.

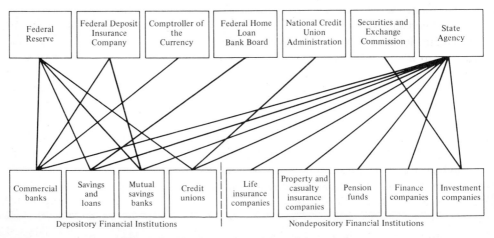

Fig. 5.2   The framework of financial regulation

Depository Financial Institutions

Government regulatory agencies that affect the behavior of depository financial institutions exist at both federal and state government levels. At the federal level, there are three agencies concerned with regulation of commercial banks: the Federal Reserve System, the

Comptroller of the Currency, and the Federal Deposit Insurance Corporation (F.D.I.C.). Each state has some agency concerned with bank regulation, usually referred to as the State Banking Commission. As discussed earlier, the Federal Reserve is the nation's central bank and has sole control over monetary policy. However, the Fed also has substantial supervisory authority over commercial banks (which it shares with other bank regulatory authorities) and sole control over bank holding companies. The Comptroller of the Currency, the oldest of the federal bank regulatory authorities, was established in 1863, when the U.S. Congress passed legislation permitting federal chartering of national banks. The Comptroller has varying supervisory powers with regard to these federally chartered banks. The Federal Deposit Insurance Corporation was established in 1933 in order to provide deposit insurance for commercial and mutual savings banks. As a part of that function, the F.D.I.C. has developed extensive regulations applicable to the activities of banks under its supervision.

The overlapping of supervision at state and federal levels of government reflects the fact that a new bank may be chartered by either the federal or a state government. This procedure—known as the *dual banking* system—immensely complicates the regulation of commercial banking in the United States. If chartered by the federal government, the bank is referred to as a *national* bank, and it must conform to the regulations governing national banks. If the bank is chartered by one of the state governments, it is referred to as a *state* bank, and it must conform to the regulations governing state banks in the state in which the charter was granted. The degree of overlap also reflects the historical evolution of regulation by which three different regulatory agencies were created at different periods of time with different functions—the Comptroller, Federal Reserve, and F.D.I.C.

A state-chartered bank is always subject to the regulation of and examination by the appropriate state bank regulating authority. If the state bank is insured (as almost all are), the bank is further subject to the supervision of the Federal Deposit Insurance Corporation. If the state bank is a member of the Federal Reserve (as many are), the bank is also subject to the supervision of the Federal Reserve. The situation can be equally complex for a national bank. The principal supervising agency for a national bank is the Comptroller of the Currency. However, every nationally chartered bank must be insured (hence subject to the supervision of the Federal Deposit Insurance Corporation) and must be a member of the Federal Reserve (hence subject to the supervision of the Federal Reserve System).

Similar though less extensive overlapping of regulatory authority occurs for the other depository financial institutions. Savings and loan associations are chartered and regulated at both state and federal levels, although there is only one relevant federal regulatory agency, the Federal Home Loan Bank Board and its subsidiary, the Federal Savings and Loan Insurance Corporation. Credit unions are chartered and regulated at both state and federal levels.

Nondepository Financial Institutions

The various types of nondepository financial institutions are chartered only at the state level, and they are regulated principally by state government, as illustrated in Fig. 5.2. This regulation encompasses specific types of statutory law, such as the "legal list," which limits the types of securities insurance companies may acquire, and case law, such as the "prudent man" rule, which for decades has influenced the behavior of financial institutions. Since the early 1930s, the federally created Securities and Exchange Commission (SEC) has exerted considerable influence on the behavior of financial institutions and markets. The influence on individual institutions is most direct for investment companies (mutual funds), but the SEC affects the behavior of both depository and nondepository financial institutions through affecting their ability to raise funds by offering securities to the public.

LIMITS ON BORROWING AND LENDING BEHAVIOR OF INDIVIDUAL INSTITUTIONS

There are also a substantial number of limitations on the ability of individual financial institutions to acquire and use funds. The most severe limitations apply to depository financial institutions, although many restrictions apply also to nondepository financial institutions. Many of these limitations, which seek to reduce the risk of institutional failure, have been discussed earlier in this chapter. We concentrate here on three of them:

1. Limitations on the rates paid by financial institutions to acquire funds—commonly referred to as Regulation Q limitations
2. Limitations on the rates charged on loans by financial institutions (usury laws)
3. Limitations on the behavior of financial institutions under various consumer protection laws

Deposit Rate Ceilings (Regulation Q)

Regulatory agencies sharply limit the rates that depository financial institutions may pay on their deposits.[6] Beginning in 1933, commercial banks were prohibited from paying explicit interest on demand deposits (implicit interest has been paid through offering "free" checking accounts, radios, and other devices to attract accounts). In addition, rates paid by banks and nonbank depository financial institutions for savings and time deposits have been restricted by rate ceilings.[7] Historically these limitations reflect a desire to reduce the risk of failure. It was believed (incorrectly, as studies have shown) in the early 1930s, when the current legislation governing depository financial institutions was enacted, that the payment of high rates for funds increased the likelihood of failure by forcing institutions to seek higher-yielding and more risky assets. However, increasingly the use of Regulation Q ceilings has involved two other goals. Regulation Q has been employed to protect savings and loans and other "thrift" institutions from competition from banks and from financial

---

6. Rates on nondeposit liabilities are usually not subject to the same ceilings.

7. Ceilings on rates paid by savings and loans and mutual savings banks were not imposed until 1966.

instruments offered in the open marketplace. This protection has been sought through establishing a differential and higher ceiling on rates paid by savings and loans as compared with commercial banks. For example, savings and loans in the 1970s were allowed to offer ¼ of one percentage point more interest on comparable thrift accounts than commercial banks were allowed to offer. In addition, Regulation Q has been used as a tool of monetary control by the Federal Reserve. For example, in periods of high interest rates, the Fed has sought to curtail the availability of credit from the depository financial institutions by not raising the Q ceilings. As market rates increase, the securities (deposits) offered by these institutions become less competitive. As a result, the borrowing *and lending* of the institutions is curtailed. The first example of this use of Regulation Q occurred in 1966, when the Fed did not raise Q ceilings as open-market interest rates increased. As a result, the first "credit crunch" developed.

Changing competitive pressures in a high-interest, inflationary environment have gradually diminished the significance of Regulation Q. After all, such limitations on the rates paid by financial institutions substantially reduce the income available to savers and result in a subsidy to borrowers by savers. The marketplace has found ways to circumvent restrictions on the payment of explicit interest on demand deposits. Perhaps the most significant innovation is the Negotiable Order of Withdrawal (N.O.W.) account. Originated by a mutual savings bank in Massachusetts in the early 1970s (after that bank had observed a loophole in the state law), the N.O.W. account is a savings account which pays interest and against which drafts (negotiable orders) may be drawn. Though not legally a checking account, the N.O.W. account is *functionally* a checking account. After spreading throughout New England in the latter part of the 1970s (and being restricted from other states by congressional legislation) the N.O.W. account became nationwide in 1981 following the passage of the Depository Institutions Deregulation and Monetary Control Act.[8]

A reduced role for Regulation Q has not been limited to demand deposits. Gradually through the decade of the 1970s the ceiling rates on deposit accounts at banks and other depository financial institutions have been increased or in some cases eliminated. Increases in the ceiling rates have occurred more frequently than in the past in order to preserve the competitiveness of the depository institutions with the marketplace in a period of rising rates. Indeed, the phenomenal growth of money market mutual funds in the late 1970s forced a relaxation of the Q ceilings. For some types of deposits (those of $100,000 or more) the ceilings have been removed entirely or related to the openly competitive marketplace (for example, the so-called money market CD's, in which the rate is tied to the Treasury bill rate). Moreover, the interest differential allowed between banks and savings and loan associations has been narrowed and for some types of funds eliminated entirely. And once the Depository Instititions Deregulation and Monetary Control Act of 1980 has been fully implemented, all interest rate ceilings on time and savings accounts at depository financial institutions will cease to exist.

---

8. Credit unions also may offer an interest-bearing third-party payment device, referred to as a share draft.

Usury Laws

Usury laws are limitations on the maximum rates charged for loans. Stemming from medieval church doctrine concerning the undesirability of charging interest and from the populist concern in the United States with excessive interest, usury statutes exist in almost every state of the nation. It is often argued that the existence of usury laws results in a greater volume of credit to borrowers at lower rates than would be so in the absence of such laws. These usury ceilings have been most significant in consumer and mortgage lending, although they have also applied to business lending, even to lending to corporate entities.

Prior to the mid-1960s, usury laws were of little practical significance, since effective rates on loans were generally lower than the ceilings established under various state laws. Beginning in 1966 and continuing through the decade of the 1970s with rising inflation and rising interest rates, however, the usury laws became much more important. At times of peak interest rates, usury laws in many states substantially distorted the flow of funds. In fact, usury laws have resulted in screening out access to credit by higher-risk borrowers as financial institutions ration credit by quality of borrower rather than price. Moreover, usury laws have substantially distorted the geographic distribution of credit in periods of high interest rates. It also appears that usury laws have reduced the total quantity of credit available, as financial institutions have reallocated their portfolio toward assets not subject to the usury statutes. The distortion was greatest in the housing sector; individuals in states with low usury law ceilings found that mortgage funds were unavailable. Fortunately, however, over time state usury law ceilings have been raised or abolished in many states. Since usury laws, when effective as restraints, seriously distort the flow of funds and do not provide credit to those they are designed to help, it would be preferable that all states abolish these usury statutes. And as discussed in the previous chapter, the Depository Institutions Deregulation and Monetary Control Act of 1980 substantially reduced the applicability of state usury laws.

Consumer Protection Laws

One of the outgrowths of the consumer movement of the 1960s and 1970s was the enactment of a variety of laws that restrict the flexibility of financial institutions in extending consumer credit. Some of them were enacted at the state levels, but most such laws were passed by the United States Congress. The first, passed in 1969, was the Truth-in-Lending Act. Designed more for disclosure than for specific regulatory purposes, the truth-in-lending concept required each consumer lender to furnish the borrower with an accurate statement of the cost of credit. This cost of credit—expressed as the annual percentage rate (APR)—includes both the interest rate and any fees charged. Under the Truth-in-Lending Act, the lender must disclose: (1) the total finance charge, which encompasses virtually all the costs to which the borrower is subject in obtaining the loan; (2) the annual percentage rate (APR), which provides a standard and comparable method of computing the "true" interest rate on the loan from different lenders; (3) other terms and conditions of the loan.

The Fair Credit Billing Act is a part of the federal Consumer Protection Act, which establishes procedures for resolving in an expeditious manner any billing errors or disputes and relates particularly to credit cards, which are very important to commercial banks. In particular, the Fair Credit Billing provision requires that credit cards be issued only in response to applications (bans the unsolicited mailing of credit cards) and establishes a maximum liability of the cardholder for unauthorized use of a credit card.

The Equal Credit Opportunity Act, the Real Estate Settlement Procedures Act, the Fair Housing Act, the Home Mortgage Disclosure Act, and the Community Reinvestment Act are all important regulatory acts. Passed in 1974, the *Equal Credit Opportunity Act* forbids discrimination by consumer lenders on the basis of race, sex, marital status, color, religion, national origin, age, or receipt of income from public programs. The *Real Estate Settlement Procedures Act* requires lending institutions to provide real estate loan applicants with: (1) a booklet that provides information on settlement costs and borrower's rights; (2) a written estimate of the settlement costs; and (3) a copy of a uniform settlement statement that conforms to the disclosure requirements of the Truth-in-Lending Act. The *Fair Housing Act* prohibits discrimination by a lender in its credit extension on the basis of age, sex, race, national origin, or marital status. These antidiscrimination provisions are basically similar to the ones contained in the Equal Credit Opportunity Act. *The Home Mortgage Disclosure Act* requires that mortgage lenders disclose the geographic area of their mortgage lending. Finally, the *Community Reinvestment Act* requires the regulatory authorities to take into account the degree to which the institution is meeting the credit needs of its community when evaluating applications from depository financial institutions to branch or merge.

Despite the proliferation of these consumer credit regulations, there is very little information available on either their costs or benefits. The costs, while conceptually quantifiable, have been virtually ignored in the process of enacting these regulations into law. Yet one study estimated that the cost to financial institutions of the Equal Credit Opportunity Act alone was almost $300 million.[9] Although there are undoubtedly benefits associated with these acts, there has been little attempt to quantify their magnitude. The attitude of the United States Congress appears to have been that these types of protection are desirable, and their benefits, whatever they may be, exceed their costs, whatever they may be.

Unlike Regulation Q restrictions or usury law ceilings, both of which have been liberalized considerably in recent years and which appear likely to be liberalized further in the future, the various types of restrictions on credit extensions by financial institutions appear to be growing in significance. This is especially true for depository institutions. As society becomes more concerned with equal access to credit, it is likely to place additional restrictions on the lending behavior of financial institutions. And as concern grows about the proper allocation of credit—meeting the needs of the population for housing and meeting

---

9. James F. Smith, "The Equal Credit Opportunity Act of 1974: A Cost/Benefit Analysis," *The Journal of Finance,* May 1977, pp. 609–621.

the credit needs of minority individuals, for example—it seems increasingly likely that some form of credit allocation may be imposed on the lending behavior of the major financial institutions.

SECURITIES AND EXCHANGE COMMISSION

One of the most significant of the regulatory bodies of the United States financial system is the Securities and Exchange Commission. Established in the early 1930s, the SEC was created in order to ensure the full disclosure of information to investors prior to their acquisition of securities. In essence, the SEC requires that all securities sold interstate in the United States (with the exception of securities of certain specified types and securities that raise less than a specified amount of funds) be registered with the commission. In this registration, the issuer of the proposed securities must provide relevant financial and nonfinancial data, including potential conflict of interest by insiders and a description of the risk elements involved in the purchase of the securities. Until the registration has become effective (during the period when the SEC staff is reviewing the material), the securities may not be sold. After the registration becomes effective, securities may be sold only after a prospectus containing the relevant information from the registration statement is provided to the purchasers. After the sale, moreover, purchasers may sue the issuers for any misrepresentations contained in the prospectus. The goal of the SEC is not to reduce or eliminate risky securities, however; it is only to see that full disclosure of risk is provided prior to the purchase of the securities.[10]

In addition to its control over the issuance of new securities, the SEC has a variety of controls over the trading of existing securities in the secondary market. For example, the SEC may dictate the rules of trading for regional and national securities markets. To a considerable extent, the SEC has relied on self-policing by the individual exchanges. However, in a number of issues the SEC has dictated important changes in the operations of the security exchanges. For example, prior to 1976 all members of the New York Stock Exchange were required by exchange policy to charge uniform commissions for trading securities. The SEC then forced the exchange to adopt a negotiated rate structure whereby each member would set its own rates in negotiation with its customers.[11] By doing so, the SEC hoped to increase the operational efficiency of the financial markets. In addition, the SEC has taken the lead in recent years in integrating the regional securities markets into one national market system. Additional discussion of the SEC and securities regulation in general is included in Chapter 17.

---

10. One controversial aspect of the disclosure goal of the SEC relates to accounting standards. In some cases, the SEC has required the use of accounting procedures for public companies that differ considerably from those generally accepted by the accounting profession.

11. The goal of this action was to reduce commission rates through encouraging price competition. Unfortunately, the goal has been only partly successful. Rates charged on large block transactions with institutions have fallen, but rates on smaller transactions with individuals have increased.

GOVERNMENT AS A FINANCIAL INTERMEDIARY

We now turn our attention to the various government programs that have been a more indirect influence on the flow of financial resources. These include programs of both state and local governments and of the federal government. They involve government guarantees of loans made by private lenders, such as through the FHA and VA in the mortgage market, through the Small Business Administration for loans made to small businesses, and through a number of programs designed to increase the flow of credit to education by means of guarantees of loans to students for higher education expenses or outright government loans for these purposes. Moreover, state and local governments are heavily involved in the sale of tax-exempt securities for the purpose of providing credit to industry in order to install pollution control equipment and also to provide credit to individuals to purchase homes. In many of these programs the government unit acts as a financial intermediary. The explosive growth of these programs in recent years has raised important questions about the appropriateness of government entry into these areas and, to some extent, about the success of the programs themselves.

The two programs that have had the greatest influence relate to agriculture and housing. The United States government has adopted a policy for the past five decades of providing funds for those two purposes at lower cost than would be available if funds were provided strictly on a risk return basis. Partly this subsidy reflects a favorable attitude toward the "yeoman" farmer, as well as the attitude that home ownership is an "unalienable American right." Partly also, however, it reflects the pressures of various interest groups, particularly in agriculture.

Agriculture

Subsidization of agriculture is done primarily through the Farm Credit System. This system is composed of three constituent parts: The Banks for Cooperatives (BC), the Federal Intermediate Credit Banks (FICB), and the Federal Land Banks (FLB). Each of these organizations provides credit to various portions of the agricultural sector. Each obtains its funds through public borrowings. Though legally not a part of the federal government—since ownership is in the hands of the borrowing farmers and ranchers—the farm credit agencies are able to borrow at rates very similar to those for direct government debt because of the implicit assumption by the marketplace that the United States government would "bail out" the farm credit agencies in the event of impending default.

Table 5.1 provides information on the net loans of the farm credit agencies in the years from 1976 through 1980. To some degree, credit provided by the farm credit agencies is supplemental to credit provided by the private sector, rising in periods of high interest rates when the availability of credit from the private sector is reduced and falling in periods when interest rates are declining and credit availability is ample. Yet in all periods the supply of credit to agriculture by these federally sponsored agencies is large. For example, in 1979, the farm credit agencies provided $10 billion to agriculture, which represents almost 50 percent of the funds raised by the farm sector through borrowing.

Table 5.1 Loans to agriculture by farm credit agencies, (billions of dollars)

	1976	1977	1978	1979	1980
Total loans	$4.8	$5.0	$5.4	$10.5	$10.0
Farm mortgages	2.5	2.9	3.2	5.0	5.0
Loans to coops (BC)	1.0	0.6	0.7	2.2	4.1
Loans to farmers (FICB)	1.3	1.5	1.5	3.3	0.9

Note: Data for 1980 are for the third quarter, annual rate, seasonally adjusted.

Source: Board of Governors of the Federal Reserve System, *Flow of Funds Accounts, 3rd Quarter 1980*, p. 15.

Table 5.2 Housing credit by government-sponsored credit agencies 1974–1980 (billions of dollars)

	1974	1975	1976	1977	1978	1979	1980
Housing credit	28.0	−1.2	−1.6	4.9	21.5	18.5	8.1
Residential mortgages	14.6	2.8	0.4	0.5	9.0	9.4	3.7
FHLB loans to savings							
and loan associations	13.4	−4.0	−2.0	4.4	12.5	9.1	4.4
Federally sponsored							
mortgage pools	9.8	10.3	15.7	20.5	18.3	28.1	25.4
Home mortgages	9.1	9.9	14.6	19.0	15.8	24.0	24.1
Multifamily mortgages	0.3	0.5	0.6	1.2	1.9	2.1	0.7
Farm mortgages	0.4	−0.1	0.5	0.3	0.6	2.0	0.6

Note: Data for 1980 are for the third quarter, annual rate, seasonally adjusted.

Source: Board of Governors of the Federal Reserve System, *Flow of Funds Accounts, 3rd Quarter 1980*, p.15.

Housing

Subsidization of housing is done through a variety of devices. Originally the federal government sought to expand the flow of credit to housing and lower the cost of funds by insuring the lender against default risk through FHA and VA programs, and by establishing the Federal National Mortgage Association (FNMA) to create a secondary market in government-insured and -guaranteed mortgages. Recently, however, government has played a more active role in providing credit for housing. This action has taken the form of loans from federally sponsored credit agencies, such as the Government National Mortgage Association (GNMA) and loans to the important single-family mortgage lenders—the savings and loan associations—by the Federal Home Loan Bank (FHLB) Board. In addition, however, the federal government through its Government National Mortgage Association has sponsored government-guaranteed mortgage pools by which mortgage bankers and other traditional mortgage lenders could gain access to the open-credit markets. By this device, a mortgage lender assembles a pool of mortgages and sells certificates, which represent an interest in the pool. These pass-through certificates are then guaranteed as to timely payment of interest and principal by the Government National Mortgage Association.

Table 5.2 provides information on the impact of these various federal programs on the flow of mortgage credit. As the data in this table show, the role of government-sponsored agencies is highly cyclical. In periods of high and rising interest rates, such as 1974, government substantially supplements the private flow of funds whereas in periods of falling interest rates and greater credit availability, as in 1976, the role of government-sponsored agencies is smaller. For example, in 1974, the government-sponsored agencies and the mortgage pools together provided more than one third of all funds advanced for home mortgages. And the growth of federally sponsored mortgage pools has been phenomenal. By 1978, federally sponsored mortgage pools alone provided about 15 percent of all funds advanced for home mortgages.

SUMMARY

Government influence on the financial markets reflects a complex set of factors: desires to protect the public against loss of their deposits stemming from the failure of major financial institutions; desires to increase the flow of credit (and lower its cost) for specific sectors of the economy that are thought to be especially worthy (agriculture and housing); desires to ensure equal access to credit for selected segments of the population, such as certain minority groups; and a variety of other reasons as well. Some of these factors reflect conscious and careful study over a number of years; others reflect government response to an actual or presumed crisis; still others reflect historical accident. Whatever the causes, it is impossible to understand the functioning of the financial system without an understanding of the influence of government policy. To a considerable extent, the functions of individual financial institutions reflect the role of government regulations. And increasingly government is acting in many ways as a financial intermediary—particularly in housing and agricultural finance—by borrowing funds and lending those funds to particular types of borrowers. Throughout the remainder of this book we will inject a discussion of the role of government into our treatment of the various financial markets and institutions wherever necessary.

QUESTIONS

1. Make a list of the major types of securities offered by depository financial institutions. In what ways are the characteristics of these securities affected by government?

2. Why are the major U.S. financial institutions specialized in their functions? Does this relate in any way to government regulation?

3. In what way is control over entry related to the risk of the failure of financial institutions? Should we allow free entry into the financial services industry? What would be the advantages and disadvantages of such a policy?

4. What is meant by the "prudent man" rule? How does it affect the behavior of financial institutions?

5. Why is there overlap among the bank regulatory agencies? What are the advantages and disadvantages of such overlap?

6. What is Regulation Q? What are some of the consequences of this regulation?

7. Make a list of the major consumer credit laws as they affect financial institutions. What impact might these regulations have on the behavior of financial institutions?

8. What is the Securities and Exchange Commission? What are its functions?

9. What are the arguments for providing indirect subsidies to agriculture and housing? What are some of the consequences?

REFERENCES

Cargill, Thomas F., *Money, the Financial System, and Monetary Policy* (Englewood Cliffs, N.J.: Prentice-Hall 1979), Ch. 8.

Fand, D., "Financial Regulation and the Allocative Efficiency of Our Capital Markets," *National Banking Review,* September 1965.

Nathan, Harold C., "Economic Analysis of Usury Laws," *Journal of Bank Research,* Winter 1980, pp. 200–211.

Pyle, David, "The Losses on Savings Deposits from Interest Rate Regulation," *Bell Journal of Economics and Management,* Autumn 1974, pp. 614–622.

Report of the President's Commission on Financial Structure and Regulation (Hunt Commission) (Washington, D.C.: U.S. Government Printing Office, December 1971).

Robinson, Roland I., "The Hunt Commission Report," *Journal of Finance,* September 1972.

Smith, James F., "The Equal Credit Opportunity Act of 1974: A Cost/Benefit Analysis," *Journal of Finance,* May 1977, pp. 609–621.

APPENDIX

THE QUESTION OF INTERSTATE BANKING

Commercial banking organizations have traditionally faced substantial regulatory limitations in their attempts to expand geographically in order to meet the financial needs of existing customers and also to penetrate new market areas. Under the McFadden Act of 1927, expansion by national banks through branching has been subject to the branching laws of individual states. These branching laws have ranged from complete prohibition of branching (unit banking states) through the allowance of branching within designated portions of a state (limited branching) to branching throughout an entire state (statewide branching). With exception only for preexisting branching, which has been allowed under "grandfather" legislation, interstate branching has been prohibited. Similar regulations govern expansion by banking organizations through the holding company device. Limitations on the existence and importance of bank holding companies (corporations that hold control in one or more banks) have been imposed by many states. Some states prohibit bank holding companies entirely, others limit holding companies to one bank, and still others limit them to ownership of a fixed number of banks or a fixed percentage of the total deposits of all banks in the state. Interstate acquisition of commercial banks by bank holding companies has been prohibited except in states that establish reciprocal arrangements.

The net result of these limitations has been a highly fragmented banking system, composed of large numbers of small banking organizations. In contrast, most industrial nations have a highly concentrated banking system, composed of a small number of large banking organizations spread throughout the nation. In Great Britain, for example, four "clearing banks" (Barclays, National Westminster, Lloyds, and Midland) control 95 percent of all bank deposits and have a network of about 12,000 branches.

Despite these substantial restrictions, banking organizations have found ways to engage in some forms of interstate operations, but not those that directly accept deposits and make loans. Various devices have been used by banking organizations to expand the geographical scope of their business. For example, domestic banks have established loan production offices in many areas of the nation, especially in those that are growing rapidly and are generating substantial commercial loan demand. These loan production offices solicit loan business throughout the nation, even though for legal reasons the loans are "booked" in the home state of the banking organization. Moreover, many large banking organizations have established subsidiaries that are limited to financing international business (referred to as Edge Act subsidiaries), although the definition of what constitutes international business has broadened over time. There has also been extensive interstate banking by foreign banking organizations. By 1980, the banking assets of foreign banking organizations exceeded $100 billion, and almost a hundred foreign banks have offices in more than one state. The International Banking Act of 1978, however, did limit the interstate expansion of foreign banking organizations.

But perhaps the most significant example of the interstate operations of banking organizations is the nonbank activities of bank holding companies. Under the 1970 amendments to the Bank Holding Company Act, the Board of Governors of the Federal Reserve System has established permissible nonbank activities for bank holding companies in which a holding company may engage nationwide either by purchasing an existing firm or starting a new firm (*de novo* entry). The Board approved 19 such activities during the 1970s, including mortgage banking, consumer and commercial finance, factoring, insurance agencies, insurance underwriting, trust activities, leasing, data processing, and other similar financial activities closely related to banking. Of these, the principal activities of bank holding companies have been in mortgage banking and consumer and commercial finance. For example, in the period from 1971 through 1977, the Board approved 499 applications to acquire consumer and commercial finance companies and 108 applications to acquire mortgage banking firms.

The importance of these nonbank activities in making some banking organizations national in scope was pointed out in a recent article in the *Federal Reserve Bulletin*.[12] According to that article, Citicorp (the parent holding company for Citibank of New York) has 229 consumer finance and mortgage lending offices in 55 cities. If loan production offices and Edge Act subsidiaries are included, Citicorp has roughly 400 offices, Bank of America has more than 300 offices in 41 states, and Manufacturers Hanover Trust has about 200 offices.

These developments, along with technological changes, such as the growth of electronic funds transfer systems, and rising costs associated with the spread of negotiable order of withdrawal accounts, have intensified the long-standing debate on the advantages and disadvantages of limitations on the geographical scope of banking organizations. Throughout the post–World War II era, there has been a movement toward reducing the restrictions on banking organizations, particularly allowing greater intrastate branching, but the debate now centers on the desirability of interstate banking. In a review of the interstate banking controversy itself, however, it is important to begin by examining the pros and cons of branching and holding company expansion.

The Branch Banking Controversy

The controversy over the proper geographical scope of branching by commercial banks has been so intense and so lengthy that it has been called "the perennial issue." Stemming from interpretations of the National Bank Act of 1863, the controversy has existed for more than a century, and it has frequently been noted more for emotionalism than for rational analysis. Yet an extensive literature exists dealing with the impact of branch banking on individual banks and the banking system. This literature concentrates on the impact of branch banking on the operating efficiency of commercial banks, on the price and quantity of banking services, and on competition.

---

12. Stephen A. Rhoades, "The Competitive Effects of Interstate Banking," *Federal Reserve Bulletin,* January 1980, pp. 1–8.

An important question about branching concerns its impact on operating efficiency. For example, those who favor relaxation of branching restrictions often argue that greater branching would allow banks to operate with higher degrees of operating efficiency. A number of studies have examined this issue by relating branching to the cost of providing specific services, such as demand deposits, time deposits, and various types of loans (see in particular the studies of Bell and Murphy, Benston, Longbrake, and Mullineaux, referenced at the end of this appendix). The studies are mixed in their results, but they provide only limited evidence for the existence of economies of scale in banking. The economies of scale that do appear to exist seem to be exhausted rather quickly, at least by the time a bank reaches $100 million in size. These results thus suggest that large banks have no great operating efficiency advantages over smaller banks. They also imply that if branching restrictions were relaxed, large banks would not necessarily drive small banks out of existence.

Another important issue in the branching controversy focuses on the impact of branching on the prices and quantities of bank services. The concern is that branch expansion will increase the concentration of economic resources, resulting in less competition, higher prices for banking services, and a reduced quantity of credit. However, if increased branching were to reduce the costs of commercial bank operations, this reduction in costs could partially or totally offset the impact of higher concentration. Studies have examined the relationship of branching to the rates charged on various types of loans—commercial, mortgage, and consumer installment—as well as the relationship of branching to interest rates paid on time deposits and to bank service charges on demand deposits. The evidence of these numerous studies is by no means definitive. Some have found that branching leads to reduced loan rates, and others have found that branching is associated with higher loan rates. For example, Horvitz found that unit banks charged lower rates than branch banks in the same market, whereas Kohn found that branch banks charged lower rates. Similar conflicting evidence has been found with regard to the relationship between branching and other dimensions of bank performance, but virtually all studies found that branch banks had higher loan-to-deposit ratios than unit banks. However, differences in the prices and quantity of financial services offered by branch banks do not appear to be substantial.

Analysis has also focused on the impact of branching on concentration and competition. Indeed, much of the opposition to branching stems from concern over excessive concentration of economic resources associated with liberalized branching. This concern is usually based on observations that concentration of banking resources is higher in statewide branching states than in states that prohibit or limit branching. Yet it does not necessarily follow that concentration increases in a state following liberalization of branching statutes. For example, relaxation of branching limitations in New York and Virginia in the early 1960s did not markedly increase the degree of local market concentration (see Shull).

The Holding Company Controversy

Since interstate banking may occur through the holding company device as well as through relaxation of branching restrictions, it is also important to investigate the evidence dealing with the impact of holding company expansion. Here also the literature is extensive. Studies have investigated the potential impact of holding company acquisitions on the price and quantity of bank services, the risk level of banking organizations, economies of scale, the concentration of bank resources, and the risk of bank failures (see the literature reviews by Rose and Fraser and by Chase and Mingo).

It has been argued that the acquisition of a bank by a holding company will have a substantial impact on the behavior of the acquired bank. In particular, the argument goes, banks affiliated with bank holding companies can, because of pooling of risk, adopt a more aggressive portfolio management policy, reducing cash and liquid asset holdings and increasing the proportion of assets devoted to the loan portfolio. If there are economies of scale associated with holding company acquisitions, the acquired bank may be able to offer services at lower prices and/or pay higher rates for its time and savings deposits. Results of a number of research projects do suggest that holding company–affiliated banks operate with somewhat smaller cash asset positions, less investment in securities (primarily municipal securities), and greater investments in loans. In contrast, however, most other financial ratios for banks affiliated with bank holding companies do not appear to differ from independent banks. And the evidence on the impact of holding company acquisitions on the prices of bank services is mixed and contradictory, perhaps reflecting the lack of any evidence of substantial economies of scale for a bank affiliated with a holding company.

There appear to be some limited benefits associated with holding company expansion, but there are also some apparent, potentially significant social costs. In particular, holding company expansion, like branch expansion, may lead to greater concentration of bank resources. The expansion of banking organizations through the holding company device (as through additional branches) raises the general question of concentration of economic resources. Growth of holding companies may increase the risk of failure, particularly if the banks operated by holding companies engage in more aggressive portfolio management practices, as they seem to do. In addition, the impact of financial problems at the holding company, perhaps associated with difficulties in the nonbank subsidiaries of the holding company, may "spill over" and cause financial problems for the bank subsidiaries of the holding company.

Interstate Banking

As discussed above, a number of banking organizations have already positioned themselves for interstate operations. Technological changes in the form of electronic funds transfer systems, as well as growing competition fostered by the Depository Institutions Deregulation and Monetary Control Act of 1980, have increased pressure for wider limits on the geographic expansion of commercial banks, both intra- and interstate.

What can be said about the potential impact of interstate banking? All types of forecasts are obviously subject to a wide margin of error, but the information presented above on the impact of branching and holding company affiliation, as well as other relevant studies, provides some important insights. It seems reasonable to believe that the impact of interstate banking will differ, depending on whether the expansion takes place through allowing banks to branch outside their states' borders, either regionally or nationally, or through allowing holding company to expand by acquiring banks regionally or nationally. These two alternatives are of course not mutually exclusive; both could be allowed simultaneously. Further, although economic theory would generally find reductions of barriers to entry into banking markets desirable because of the potential for greater competition, the ultimate impact obviously depends on the manner in which entry occurs. For example, entry by acquisition of existing banks rather than *de novo* entry (either new branches or new banks) is less likely to produce positive effects on competition and bank performance. Yet entry by acquisition, which has been the most common form of expansion for banks and bank holding companies within an individual state, will lead to increases in concentration at the national level. Thus it is clear that public policy must carefully guide the development of interstate banking if it is to produce significant social benefits.

REFERENCES

Bell, Frederick, and Neil B. Murphy, *Costs in Commercial Banking,* Research Report Number 41, Federal Reserve Bank of Boston, 1968.

Benston, George, Jr., "Branch Banking and Economies of Scale," *Journal of Finance,* May 1965, pp. 312–331.

Chase, Samuel, and John J. Mingo, "The Regulation of Bank Holding Companies," *Journal of Finance,* May 1975, pp. 281–292.

Horvitz, Paul M., *Concentration and Competition in New England Banking,* Research Report Number 2, Federal Reserve Bank of Boston, 1958.

Kohn, Ernest, *Branch Banking, Bank Mergers, and the Public Interest,* New York State Banking Department, 1964.

Longbrake, William A., *Productive Efficiency in Commercial Banking,* Working Paper 72-10 (Washington, D.C.: Federal Deposit Insurance Corporation, 1972).

Mote, Larry R., "The Perennial Issue: Branch Banking," Federal Reserve Bank of Chicago *Business Conditions,* February 1974, pp. 3–23.

Mullineaux, Donald J., "Branch Versus Unit Banking—An Analysis of Relative Costs," in *Changing Pennsylvania's Branching Laws,* Federal Reserve Bank of Philadelphia, 1973.

Rhoades, Stephen, "The Competitive Effects of Interstate Banking," *Federal Reserve Bulletin,* January 1980, pp. 1–8.

Rose, Peter S., and Donald R. Fraser, "The Impact of Holding Company Acquisitions on Bank Performance," *The Bankers Magazine,* Spring 1973, pp. 85–91.

Savage, Donald T., and Elinor H. Solomon, "Branch Banking—The Competitive Issues," *Journal of Bank Research,* Summer 1980, pp. 110–121.

Shull, Bernard, "Multiple-Office Banking and the Structure of Banking Markets: The New York and Virginia Experience," *Proceedings of a Conference on Bank Structure and Competition,* Federal Reserve Bank of Chicago, 1973.

Part II

The Federal Reserve and Monetary Control

Chapter 6

Money and the Financial System

Money is an integral and essential part of the financial system of any country. Whether called dollars, pesos, pounds, or francs, money is necessary to serve as a means of payment, a store of value, and a unit of account in all but the most elemental economic systems. This chapter is concerned with the nature of money, its economic significance, the process by which it is created, and the factors that determine its quantity (supply).

Increases and decreases in the supply of money are both cause and effect of events in the "real" sector of the economy. Because money is the means by which spending is accomplished, the quantity of money is of great significance for the level of prices, interest rates, and the employment of productive resources to produce goods and services.

Thus the institutions and process involved in money creation and the control of its quantity are vital elements of the financial system. Banks continue to play the principal role in the creation (and destruction) of money, and we will examine banking with regard to this aspect of its activities. Actions of the public, the U.S. government, and the Federal Reserve System also impact on the quantity of money, and these aspects of change in the potential money supply also receive attention.

THE NATURE OF MONEY

Money is anything that is generally accepted as payment for goods, services, and debts. Money is a *medium of exchange;* people accept money in exchange for the goods or services they provide in the expectation that they can subsequently exchange the money for goods and services they wish to acquire. Without such a medium of exchange, people must resort to *barter*—the direct exchange of goods and services for other goods and services—and barter is a very inefficient means of effecting exchanges. Barter involves finding another party who has what you want and wants what you have to exchange. It requires searching out all the possible exchange partners necessary to supply one's needs and wants for goods and services, and then reaching agreement on the terms of the exchange. Barter thus results in very high *search and transactions costs*—as the costs of effecting exchanges are called. In other words, bartering obliges people to spend a great deal of time searching, negotiating, and otherwise incurring considerable costs in their trading activities.

Money also serves as a *unit of account,* or a "standard of value." Money's role as a "measuring rod" allows the use of established prices for transactions. Money's unit-of-account function allows the measurement of economic values to be accomplished in a universally (almost) understood fashion. In addition to serving as a medium of exchange and a unit of account, money is both a convenient way to save (a *store of value*) and a convenient way to borrow (a *standard of deferred payment*). In its store-of-value function, money facilitates saving by providing a means of securing future purchasing power from present income. In its standard-of-deferred-payment function, money facilitates borrowing (and lending) by providing a measure of the purchasing power that is being borrowed and lent. Money is unique in its immediacy as a means of making payment for goods and services; it is the most liquid of assets.

A great many things have served as money throughout history. Shells, animal skins, and tobacco were acceptable as money at early points in the colonial history of the United States. Metals of various types have been used as money over the ages. Until humans developed methods to produce such metals as copper, bronze, and iron in quantity, these metals were used as money. Gold and silver have the longest history of all money items; their relative scarcity has made them "precious" since their discovery many centuries ago. Scarcity is an essential characteristic for any item to serve as money; durability and high value per unit of weight are other important characteristics. Unlike such things as furs, metals, and tobacco, which have a value in use separate and apart from their use as money (*commodity* money), modern money (both currency and coin) is essentially valuable only as money. Such money is *fiat* money; it is money because the government has declared it to be money.

Money Standards

The adoption by a nation of a particular type of money as a standard of value is termed a *money standard.* The first money standards were based on gold and silver. The *gold standard* originated in England in the seventeenth century with the coinage of a gold coin called the guinea, valued at £1 (one pound). The value of a pound was thus defined in terms of gold. It was not until 1816, however, that England officially adopted gold as the sole standard of value. Gold thus became "legal tender," with government-mandated acceptability for payment of public and private debts.

Other European countries and the United States employed silver or bimetallic monetary standards until the latter part of the nineteenth century. The United States officially went on the gold standard in 1900, although it had been on a *de facto* gold standard since 1879, when U.S. Treasury paper currency ("greenbacks") was made redeemable in gold. Most European nations had also gone on the gold standard by that time.

Paper money came into widespread use in the eighteenth century, being issued by both banks and governments. The basis of its acceptability was the promise of eventual convertibility into gold or silver. Such promises were broken often enough to cause paper money to be viewed with suspicion. The expression, "not worth a continental" relates to paper money issued by the Continental Congress in 1775 at the beginning of the Revolutionary War. These "bills of credit" were pledged to be redeemed eventually in Spanish silver dollars (or the equivalent value in gold or silver). Drastically overissued, the continental bills were virtually worthless by 1779. France's experience with paper money after the French Revolution was similar.

The various failures of paper money standards due to overissuance by governments made clear the importance of *scarcity* in the acceptability of any item as money. Whereas the quantity of, say, gold in existence is a function of a costly search and production process, the quantity of paper currency (fiat money) is subject only to the capacity of the government's printing presses. The amount of money—the *money supply*—is an economic variable of great significance. Sadly enough, it is by no means firmly established that the world's various governments possess the will or wisdom to control the supply of money in a manner conducive to optimal economic performance.

Modern Money

The United States abandoned the conventional gold standard in 1933. From 1933–1968, the monetary use of gold was limited to international payments and the "backing" of the principal U.S. paper currency, Federal Reserve notes, which are obligations of the Federal Reserve Banks. This "gold cover" was never more than a fraction of the total amount of Federal Reserve notes and member bank reserve deposits, and it was removed completely in 1968. In 1971, the other major monetary use of gold—settling of international financial obligations—was also terminated; the U.S. Treasury will no longer redeem foreign-held dollars in gold.[1]

There are three major types of money in present use in the United States and most of the world's nations—metal coins, paper money, and bank demand deposits (checking ac-

---

1. The worldwide "demonetization" of gold has had a dramatic effect on its price. When the United States was swapping gold for foreign dollar holdings, the price was long "pegged" at $35 an ounce. Since 1973 there has been only a free market price of gold, and it has climbed steadily, reaching more than $800 an ounce at one point.

counts) plus other "checkable" deposits with financial institutions. Note that checks, which are used as payment in many transactions, are not money. *Checkable deposits* are money; checks serve to transfer ownership of these deposits, which are claims against the issuing financial institutions, from one party to another.

Now that the United States is no longer on a gold or "gold exchange" standard, its monetary standard is perhaps best described as a *credit standard*. Coins and currency are obligations of the U.S. government. Checkable deposits are obligations of commercial banks and other depository institutions. This credit standard "works" for this nation and others because people are willing to accept coins, currency, and checkable deposits as payment, not because these items have any intrinsic value in use.

The Depository Institutions Deregulation and Monetary Control Act of 1980 had considerable impact on the payments system of the United States. As previously indicated, this legislation also had considerable effects on the nation's financial markets and institutions and on the conduct of monetary policy by the Federal Reserve System. As discussed in Chapters 4 and 5, the act provided for the phased elimination of many restrictions that had existed in the U.S. financial system since the 1930s, such as interest rate ceilings and prohibition of payment of interest on checking accounts, and it broadened the scope of permissible activities and services by nonbank depository institutions.[2] In terms of the payments mechanism, the major impact of the legislation was the broadening of the means of payment. Negotiable orders of withdrawal (N.O.W.) accounts, hitherto limited to eight states in the Northeast, were permitted nationwide. Savings-to-checking-account transfers, the use of share drafts by credit unions, and electronic payments systems (through remote service units) of savings and loan associations were also permitted by this law. The act marked the end of the prohibition of payment of interest on checkable deposits and altered the components of "money" in this country—previously limited to coins, currency, and demand deposits in banks.

MEASUREMENT OF THE MONEY SUPPLY

Money is ordinarily defined as a generalized means of purchasing power that is acceptable as payment for goods and services. Currency, coin, and all checkable deposits obviously qualify as "money," since they serve as an immediate means of payment. *Noncheckable* deposits and similar liquid assets are not money in terms of this definition, since they must first be converted into checkable deposits or currency before being used for payment. Such highly liquid assets, because of the ease with which they can be converted into money, are often referred to as "near monies."

Measurement of the amounts of money and liquid assets ("monetary aggregates") is important for economic policy purposes. Monitoring of these various quantities is accomplished by the Federal Reserve. Table 6.1 indicates the measures of money and liquid assets employed by the Fed and the amounts of these monetary aggregates as of June 1980.

---

2. Chapter 7 discusses the impact of the act on the Federal Reserve System's tools of monetary control.

Table 6.1   Measures of money and liquid assets, June 1980 (Billions of dollars, averages of daily figures, not seasonally adjusted)

Aggregates and components	Component amount	Aggregate amount
Currency	111.1	
Demand deposits	259.0	
Other checkable deposits	19.6	
M-1		389.7
Small-denomination time deposits	720.6	
Savings deposits	382.8	
Money market mutual fund shares	74.2	
Overnight repurchase agreements of commercial banks and overnight Eurodollar deposits of U.S. residents	22.6	
M-1	389.7	
M-2		1,587.0
Large-denomination time deposits	228.3	
Term repurchase agreements at depository institutions	28.0	
M-2	1,587.0	
M-3		1,843.3
Various liquid assets, such as U.S. Treasury bills and other liquid Treasury securities, U.S. savings bonds, bankers acceptances, commercial paper, and term Eurodollars held by nonbank U.S. residents	385.1	
M-3	1,843.3	
L		2,228.4

Source: Board of Governors of the Federal Reserve System, *Federal Reserve Bulletin,* September 1980.

The Federal Reserve's measures of monetary aggregates are labeled M-1, M-2, M-3, and L. M-1 is a measure of money as conventionally defined—a means of payment used in effecting transactions. M-1 consists of currency and coins in circulation, demand deposits (except those of foreign commercial banks and official institutions), and other checkable deposits. "Other checkable deposits" include negotiable orders of withdrawal (N.O.W.) accounts and automatic transfer from savings (A.T.S.) accounts with depository institutions, and credit union share draft accounts. Thus the components of M-1 are financial assets that are acceptable as a means of payment and are held for the purpose of making payments. For this reason, holdings of M-1 are often referred to as "transactions balances." M-1 is subdivided into M-1A, currency plus bank demand deposits, and M-1B, which is M-1A plus other checkable deposits.

The use of monetary measures other than M-1 (M-2, M-3, and L) reflects the fact that spending units in the economy hold large amounts of "near-money" liquid assets, which can quickly be converted to M-1 and then used to make payments. Indeed, some liquid asset holdings often represent temporarily "parked" money, which is not presently required for payments purposes, but which will soon be returned to the spending stream. As indicated in Table 6.1, certain liquid asset items are included with M-1 to develop these broader monetary aggregates. The characteristic that distinguishes M-2, M-3, and L from one another is that each successive measure includes less liquid assets; the incremental components of M-3 are less liquid than those of M-2, and the incremental components of L are in turn less liquid than those of M-3. The concept underlying the definitional boundaries of these various measures is that M-2 is more nearly "money" than M-3, and M-3 is closer to being "money" than L. The choice of liquid assets to be included in a given monetary aggregate is, of course, necessarily a matter of judgment and arbitrary to some degree.

One component of M-2, money market mutual fund shares, deserves special note. Shares in money market funds are not issued by depository institutions and thus, unlike the other components of M-2, do not constitute a claim against a bank or thrift institution. Further, many of these funds offer check-writing privileges and thus could be viewed as M-1 items. Such checking privileges, however, are generally characterized by high minimum amounts per check. Money market fund balances are thus used infrequently for direct payments purposes. For this reason, money market mutual fund shares are included with savings accounts and other "store-of-value" deposits, which are highly liquid non-transactions balances, in M-2.

M-3 is essentially a measure of M-2 plus the amounts of certain less liquid variants of items included in M-2. M-2 includes *small* time deposits; M-3 includes *large* (denominations of $100,000 or more) time deposits. M-2 includes *overnight* RPs (repurchase agreements) and M-3 includes *longer-term* RPs.

The aggregate L—liquid assets—consists of M-3 plus longer-term Eurodollars held by U.S. nonbank residents, bankers acceptances (bank-guaranteed promissory notes), commercial paper, savings bonds, and various liquid obligations of the U.S. Treasury. Liquid Treasury obligations include all bills with an original maturity of less than one year and all Treasury notes and bonds maturing within the ensuing 18 months. (As with M-1, M-2, and M-3, each component of L is measured net of holdings by financial institutions whose liabilities are elsewhere included in the measures of monetary aggregates.) As indicated in Table 6.1, L is a huge aggregate amount; it is meant to be a measure of aggregate short-term credit in the economy—a measure of liquidity rather than money.

The importance of these various measures of monetary aggregates is due to the great significance of money in the economy. Indeed, the degree of refinement of any particular monetary measurement scheme is a function of how closely changes in the monetary aggregates are related to changes in economic variables. We turn now to a discussion of the role that the quantity of money plays in the performance of the economy.

THE ECONOMIC SIGNIFICANCE OF MONEY

The linkage of money to prices is inherent in money's role as a medium of exchange and a unit of account. It follows that the *quantity* of money is closely related to the *level* of prices, a relationship that has been recognized for centuries. Less apparent but equally real is the impact of the quantity of money on the employment of resources to produce goods and services.

The "circulation" of money in a market economy occurs in two channels. The producers of goods and services make payments to the suppliers of the resources necessary for production. Such payments include wages, salaries, interest, rents, and dividends. Payments for the factors of production thus constitute one channel of money flows in the economy. The other channel is the flow of payments *to* producers as goods and services are purchased from them. These receipts of producers supply the means of payment for factors of production to produce additional goods and services, and so on. This "circular flow" of money receipts and payments constitutes the aggregate money income stream for an economy.

The Velocity of Money

Money units can be used over and over again in the circular flow of income. The more often money units are used for payments in a given period—the faster money "turns over"—the smaller the required size of the supply of money for a given volume of real income at a fixed price level.[3] This rate of turnover of the money stock is called the *velocity* of money, since it amounts to the rate at which money is spent on goods and services within a given time period. Monetary velocity is thus a measure of the frequency with which the average dollar is utilized to effect transactions during a given span of time.

Monetary velocity depends largely on established habits of payments. In our society, for example, workers are likely to be paid weekly, biweekly, or monthly, but not daily or annually. The frequency of wage and salary collection affects the amount of money workers hold from one payday to the next; their *average money holdings* will decrease as the frequency of their collection of wages and salaries increases, and vice versa. This inverse relationship between average money holdings and the frequency of receipts is true for other household income sources and for business firms' income as well. Thus, for a given level of income, the smaller the average money holdings by the various economic units of an economy are, the larger monetary velocity will be, and vice versa.

Conventional patterns of receipts and payments largely determine the amount of average money holdings and thus the velocity of the money stock. Historically, such transaction patterns have tended to change rather slowly. In recent decades, however, a combination of relatively rapidly occurring social, economic, and technological developments has impacted significantly on the payments process, and the effect has been to reduce average cash balances in the economy (as measured by M-1). For example, the effects of electronic funds transfers in speeding up payments and the various procedures employed by

---

3. The distinction between "real" and "nominal" income is important to an understanding of the economic role of *money*. The concept of *real income* is the physical quantity of goods and services, independent of its monetary measurement. *Nominal income* is determined by both the level of real income and the level of prices. For a given level of real income, nominal income is a function of the price level. For example, if the price level doubles when real income is unchanged, nominal income will also double.

business firms in speeding up collections have served to greatly reduce the amount of M-1 required for a given transactions volume. The emergence of mass use of credit cards has had a similar effect.

Although conventional patterns of receipts and payments largely determine average cash holdings (and thus monetary velocity), certain economic variables also influence the average amount of money balances held by households and business firms. *Income and wealth* of economic units have an effect—holdings of cash balances tend to increase as income and total wealth increase. *Interest rates* also affect money holdings (and thus money velocity). The higher the rate of interest, the more expensive idle cash balances become, and vice versa. Thus we may expect velocity to increase (average holdings of cash balances to decrease) as interest rates rise and to decline as interest rates fall. The magnitude of the so-called interest-elasticity of the demand for money (the degree of sensitivity of the desired size of average money holdings to interest rate changes) is an unsettled issue, however.

Another significant factor regarding the amount of money balances people choose to hold is *expectations* regarding the future course of economic events. If a high rate of inflation is expected, for example, individuals will tend to hold less cash, since the purchasing power of money is eroded by price increases.[4] On the other hand, expectations of declining prices and/or employment tend to result in increased money holdings. Expectations regarding the future course of interest rates may also affect desired cash balances. When interest rates are expected to rise, individuals may choose to *wait* to lend until higher rates are available and thus hold larger cash balances.

The Equation of Exchange

In a monetary economy, it is obvious that all money *payments* spent for goods and services in a given time period must equal all money *receipts* of sellers of those goods and services during that time period. This is a useful notion when expressed as "the equation of exchange":

$$MV = PQ.$$

In this version, M is the total money stock, V is the income velocity of money, P is the weighted average price of all goods and services sold, and Q is the physical quantity of those goods and services. Thus MV is total money payments to suppliers of goods and services, PQ is the total money receipts of these suppliers, and their equality is apparent.[5]

---

4. An extreme case of this phenomenon occurred in Germany during the "hyperinflation" of the 1920s. It is reported that workers paid once or more daily would hurry home and distribute the money to all family members with instructions to go out and buy any items they could find available for sale—before prices rose further.

5. As formulated here, PQ is total income for an economy for a time period—the gross (or net) national product—and V is *income* velocity of money. An alternative formulation is to consider all exchanges of money (total transactions) rather than only spending on final goods and services. In this case, sales of intermediate goods, used items, and financial assets are also included. When *all* spending is thus considered, V is the *transactions* velocity of money and is clearly much larger than income velocity.

Although true by definition, the equation of exchange is a useful means of assessing the economic significance of money. It serves as a springboard for economic theorizing about the relationship of the money supply to the price level and real income. For example, in its earliest (and simplest) version, the Quantity Theory of Money is an extension of the equation of exchange. As originally formulated, the Quantity Theory of Money holds that the money supply determines the price level; changes in the level of prices (P) are directly proportional to changes in the quantity of money (M). This result follows from the postulation of a constant V and a constant Q by the quantity theorists. We may note that a constant V is plausible only if habits and conventions of payment are the principal determinants of V and are very slow to change or, if other factors affect V, those factors are also constant.[6] A constant Q is plausible if the equilibrating mechanisms of a market economy ensure full employment of all available resources (as the quantity theorists presumed), or if a wise, perhaps omniscient, central government pursues economic policies that result in full resource employment (as modern economists may fondly hope).

The Quantity Theory is only one possible scenario. Another is that changes in the money supply are matched by exact inverse changes in the velocity of money; i.e., P and Q are constant. (This is the extreme "money does not matter" approach.) It could also be postulated that changes in M have a corresponding direct effect on Q, with V and P constant except when Q is at its maximum (at full employment of resources).

The most plausible scenario is that changes in M will generally impact on V, P, and Q, and the magnitude of the relative effects on each will be a function of the present levels of V and Q (which, unlike P, have practical maximums in the short run); expectations; and the present level of interest rates (since rates of interest affect spending). For example, an increase in the money supply during a severe economic depression would be likely to impact primarily on Q. With large quantities of unemployed resources, increases in Q resulting from increased M should not generate significant upward pressure on P. On the other hand, increases in M when the economy is enjoying full employment of available resources will almost certainly result in higher P (and probably a somewhat lower V).

Chapter 21 of this book examines the principal issues relating to the impact of changes in the money supply on the economy. Monetary policy—the attempt by the government to pursue economic objectives by engineering deliberate changes in the money stock—is a major tool of economic policy. The role of the money supply in interest rate determination is an important element of monetary policy, and this role is discussed in Chapter 8. For our purposes in this chapter and in Chapter 7, we need only recognize that the quantity of money has considerable economic significance. We turn our attention now to the process by which money is created, and the ways in which the supply of money can be controlled. Our discussion focuses initially on the process of demand deposit expansion in the commercial banking system.

---

6. The modern version of the Quantity Theory of Money—monetarism—is discussed in Chapters 21 and 22 of this book.

MONEY CREATION: DEMAND DEPOSIT EXPANSION

As indicated in Table 6.1, demand deposits in commercial banks are the predominant component of modern money in the U.S. financial system. These deposits are liabilities (debts) of the banks that issue them. Banks accept these deposits (and thus incur an obligation to the depositor for the amount deposited) in order to obtain the means of acquiring interest-earning assets—loans to individuals and business firms and interest-bearing securities. A restriction of this use of deposits by banks to obtain assets is the *reserve requirement* set by the Federal Reserve System that limits use of deposits for bank lending and investing purposes to a specified fraction of total deposits.[7]

The reader is probably aware that what a single bank cannot do—create money by expanding demand deposits in the process of acquiring interest-earning assets—the banking system as a whole can do. Because money creation by demand deposit expansion is so fundamental to an understanding of the financial system, a review of this process is warranted.

The Commercial Bank Balance Sheet

Under the double-entry system of accounting, the financial position of an economic entity is depicted in a "balance sheet." The fundamental balance sheet equation for any business entity (including banks) is

$$\text{Assets} = \text{Liabilities} + \text{Capital.}$$

Assets are things of value belonging to the entity for which the balance sheet is prepared. For a bank, assets typically include such items as vault cash, loans (receivables), securities, and the bank's deposits with its Federal Reserve Bank (to satisfy reserve requirements). *Liabilities* are debts, and the principal obligations of banks are to its depositors. In addition to demand deposits, a bank is likely to have sizable amounts of time and savings deposits among its deposit liabilities. *Capital* is the sum of the owners' funds that have been paid into the entity (contributed capital) and past earnings that have been retained in the business instead of being paid to owners as dividends (retained earnings).

In the double-entry accounting model, asset accounts are *increased* with *debits* and *decreased* with *credits*. Liability and capital accounts are *increased* with *credits* and *decreased* with *debits*. These debit-credit rules, in conjunction with the requirement that all changes in assets, liabilities, and capital be recorded so that debits = credits, serve to keep the balance sheet "in balance."

A typical condensed balance sheet for a commercial bank in "T-account form" is shown in Fig. 6.1. Note that deposits with the Federal Reserve consist of "required reserves" and "excess reserves." The amount of required reserves is determined by the

---

7. The Federal Reserve sets reserve requirements at a specified percentage of customer deposits. Reserves are held in the form of vault cash and deposits at the Federal Reserve Banks. Since 1980, the Fed's reserve requirements have applied to all depository institutions, as discussed in the next chapter.

amount of deposit liabilities of the bank and the magnitude (a percentage of deposits) of the reserve requirements.

Balance sheet

Assets		Liabilities and capital	
Cash in vault	$ X	Demand deposits	$ X
Deposits at Federal		Time and savings deposits	X
Reserve Bank:		Other liabilities	X
Required reserves	X	Capital	X
Excess reserves	X		
Loans	X		$XX
Securities	X		
Building and equipment	X		
Other assets	X		
	$XX		

Figure 6.1

Nature of Deposit Expansion.   To review the process of demand deposit expansion by the banking system, it is useful to assume the following simplified situation.

1. Only loans, securities, and reserves are considered on the asset side, and only demand deposits on the liabilities side. Effects of currency in circulation, time deposits, etc., are ignored.
2. The legal reserve requirement for demand deposits is assumed to be 20 percent. All bank reserves, including those necessary to meet the legal requirement (legal reserves) and any "excess reserves" are held in a Federal Reserve Bank. (In practice, a bank's vault cash is part of its legal reserves.)
3. The banking system initially has zero excess reserves.

We will consider for all banks in this example only *changes* in their balance sheets, not total amounts. We begin with Bank A. Suppose the Federal Reserve purchases $1000 of securities from Bank A. (At a later point in this chapter, we will examine the motivation for such a purchase.) The Fed pays for the securities by crediting Bank A's account with a Federal Reserve Bank. The effect on Bank A's balance sheet is:

Bank A

Securities	−1000
Excess reserves	+1000

Bank A now has $1000 of excess reserves on deposit with the Federal Reserve, which can be used to acquire interest-earning assets. Unless Bank A uses some or all of these new excess reserves for this purpose, there will be no change in the money supply as a result of this purchase of securities by the Federal Reserve. Banks do not generally hold significant amounts of excess reserves, however, and we may assume that Bank A will use its new reserves of $1000 by lending that amount to a customer, Mr. One. It accomplishes this by increasing Mr. One's account by $1000 and recording a new asset (a loan) on its books:

Bank A			
Loans	+1000	Demand deposits	+1000
Excess reserves	−200		
Required reserves	+200		

When Bank A creates the demand deposit of $1000 by using its excess reserves in that amount, the money supply increases by $1000. The bank's excess reserves shrink (and required reserves expand) by $0.20 \times \$1000 = \$200$. Immediately after the loan is made, Bank A has $800 of excess reserves ($1000 − $200). Should Bank A use this amount of excess reserves to acquire assets? The answer is *No*, for the following reasons.

1. Mr. One borrowed the $1000 in order to buy something, and he will write a check on his account at Bank A to make the purchase. In a system of numerous banks, the recipient of the check from Mr. One (let's call him Mr. Two) is unlikely to redeposit the check with Bank A.

2. When Mr. Two deposits the $1000 check at his bank (Bank B), Bank A loses the excess reserves of $800 to Bank B.

The balance sheet effects of (1) and (2) above are as follows:

Bank A			
Excess reserves	−800	Demand deposits	−1000
Required reserves	−200		

Bank B			
Excess reserves	+800	Demand deposits	+1000
Required reserves	+200		

At this point, Bank A has no more excess reserves, and Bank B has $800 of excess reserves. (Note that if Bank A had loaned more than its initial increase in excess reserves of $1000, it would now have a deficiency in its required reserves.) Bank B can now make new loans in the amount of its excess reserves, and we may assume that it lends $800 to Mr. Three, one of its customers. As before, the balance sheet effect of the loan is:

	Bank B		
Loans	+800	Demand deposits	+800
Excess reserves	−160		
Required reserves	+160		

Mr. Three subsequently writes a check to Mr. Four, who banks at Bank C and deposits the check there. Bank C thus acquires excess reserves of $640, which is $(1 − 0.20)$ $800, and Bank B loses reserves in that amount:

	Bank B		
Excess reserves	−640	Demand deposits	−800
Required reserves	−160		

	Bank C		
Excess reserves	+640	Demand deposits	+800
Required reserves	+160		

Bank C will now be in a position to lend $640, the amount of its excess reserves. Such lending will result in new excess reserves of $(1 − 0.20)$ $640, or $512, being supplied to Bank D, which can then lend that amount. This process will continue, with the amount of excess reserves being transferred from bank to bank diminishing by 20% (the reserve requirement ratio) each time. Each individual bank lends (creates demand deposits) only in the amount of its excess reserves. But all the banks taken together have created demand deposits in an amount that is a multiple of the original increase in excess reserves of $1000. If the new demand deposits are summed, we add $1000, $800, $640, $512, etc., approaching at the limit of the process a sum of $5000. Matching this increase in demand deposits of $5000 is an increase in required reserves of $1000. Thus all of the original injection of excess reserves has become required reserves.

In this simplified system, the multiplier for this multiple expansion of deposits is the reciprocal of the reserve requirement ratio; that is, 1/0.20, or 5, in the example above. Stated as an equation,

$$\Delta D = \Delta R/r_d,$$

where ΔD is the total potential change in demand deposits resulting from an injection of new reserves, ΔR is the dollar amount of such an injection, and r_d is the reserve requirement for demand deposits.

THE QUANTITY OF BANK RESERVES

As described above, the elements of money creation are simple. When a bank obtains new excess reserves, it can make loans (or buy securities) simply by increasing the borrower's (or seller's) demand deposits. As these funds are spent, they become excess reserves for other banks, and the process is repeated. Though simple, the process involves an apparent paradox: banks create deposits in the act of lending, but they can lend only if they have deposits in sufficient amount. Reconciling this paradox is best accomplished by identifying two different types of deposits—*primary* and *derivative.*

Primary deposits supply reserves to banks and thus make new lending possible. They generally arise from deposits of currency or checks drawn on other banks. As excess reserves resulting from primary deposits are used to make loans, *derivative deposits* are created. For instance, in the example in the preceding section, Bank B received a primary deposit of $1000 (a check drawn on Bank A) and subsequently created a derivative deposit of $800, which in turn became a primary deposit for Bank C. Derivative deposits, both in existence and magnitude, are a function of primary deposits.

Note that when a bank obtains primary deposits (and thus gains excess reserves) from some other bank, the reserves of the banking system have not changed. An expansion of the money supply can occur when new reserves are supplied to the banking system by a nonbank source. By the same token, a contraction of the money supply is likely to occur when the reserves of the banking system contract. There are three possible sources of change in the quantity of bank reserves—the public, the Federal Reserve, and the Treasury.

The Public

The public's demand for the amount of currency it wishes to hold (relative to deposits) may change. If the public *increases* its holdings of currency, the banking system will lose reserves. Since bank reserves support a multiple of demand deposits, this occurrence (if not offset by other changes in reserves) reduces the money supply. The reverse holds for *decreases* in the amount of currency in circulation. If more currency is deposited in banks by the public, the banking system gains reserves, thus making possible an expansion of demand deposits.

Changes in the public's desired holdings of other types of assets can also affect the relative amounts of required and excess reserves that constitute the total quantity of reserves held by the banking system. This is true essentially because of different reserve requirements for noncheckable deposits as compared with demand deposits. Since reserve requirements for noncheckable deposits are lower than those for demand deposits, increased holdings of the former relative to the latter supply excess reserves to banks. On the other hand, a shift in the public's portfolio preference toward demand deposits and out of noncheckable deposits will result in a reduction of excess reserves held by the banking system.

The Federal Reserve

The central role of the Federal Reserve Banks in the financial system warrants the detailed discussion of the organization and functions of the Federal Reserve System, which are the subjects of the next chapter. We need note here only that the Federal Reserve System is this nation's central bank and thus exercises control of the money supply and exerts regulatory authority over those commercial banks that are its members. Further description in this chapter is limited to those aspects of the Federal Reserve's role relating to the quantity and composition of the money supply.

The following condensed balance sheet for the Federal Reserve Banks shows the major categories of the Fed's assets and liabilities.

<table>
<tr><td colspan="2" align="center">Federal Reserve Banks</td></tr>
<tr><td>Cash</td><td>Federal Reserve notes</td></tr>
<tr><td>Gold certificates</td><td>Deposits of financial institutions</td></tr>
<tr><td>Loans to member banks</td><td>(reserves)</td></tr>
<tr><td>U.S. government securities</td><td>U.S. Treasury deposits</td></tr>
<tr><td>Cash items in process</td><td>Foreign deposits</td></tr>
<tr><td>of collection</td><td>Deferred availability</td></tr>
<tr><td>Other assets</td><td>cash items</td></tr>
<tr><td></td><td>Other liabilities</td></tr>
<tr><td></td><td>Capital</td></tr>
</table>

Cash is principally currency (mostly coins) issued by the Treasury and held by the Federal Reserve. The Federal Reserve's role in the distribution of Treasury currency will be discussed later.

Monetary gold holdings of the federal government are the responsibility of the U.S. Treasury, but the Federal Reserve has ownership claims on the gold stock via *gold certificates*. The dollar amount for these gold certificates is quite large, but their significance for the money supply is minor.

Cash items in process of collection (shown as an asset) and *deferred-availability cash items* (shown as a liability) relate to *float,* which is the monetary effect of time lags in the clearing of checks. For example, suppose that a check drawn on Bank X is deposited with Bank Y, and Bank Y sends the check to a Federal Reserve Bank for clearing. On receipt of the check, the Federal Reserve Bank debits (increases) "cash items in process of collection" and credits (increases) "deferred-availability cash items." The check proceeds will be credited to Bank Y's account within two days, at which point the "deferred-availability cash items" account is debited (reduced) for that amount. The corresponding "cash items in process of collection" account is not credited (reduced), however, until Bank X receives the check for payment. During this time lag, both Bank X and Bank Y have the check amount in their deposit account with the Federal Reserve. In terms of the balance sheet, reserve deposits of financial institutions will always be greater by the amount that the balance of "cash items in process of collection" exceeds the balance of "deferred-availability cash items," which is *Federal Reserve float*. Federal Reserve float thus constitutes a net source of reserves for member banks. Its magnitude for any time period is a function of how efficiently the transportation and communication systems normally employed in check-clearing are functioning during that time span. The Fed is presently attempting to greatly reduce float.

As discussed in more detail in the next chapter, financial institutions subject to the Fed's reserve requirements can borrow funds from the Federal Reserve. The so-called federal funds market, in which banks lend reserves to other banks, has supplanted this function of the Federal Reserve to a large degree, but borrowing from the Federal Reserve remains a significant source of reserves in its aggregate amount.

The U.S. government securities held by the Federal Reserve are an asset item of special importance. These security holdings make possible the "open-market operations" of the Federal Reserve—the buying and selling of government securities in the marketplace. Such purchases and sales of securities by the Federal Reserve impact directly on reserves. For example, when the Federal Reserve *buys* securities, it pays with a check drawn on itself, which is credited to the reserves of the depositor when that depositor sends it to the Federal Reserve Bank. The effect on the Federal Reserve's balance sheet of a $1000 purchase of securities is:

Federal Reserve Banks			
U.S. government securities	+1000	Deposits of financial institutions (reserves)	+1000

If the purchase of securities is *from a bank,* excess reserves increase by the entire amount of the purchase. If the Fed purchases securities *from a nonbank depositor,* the increase in excess reserves is (1 − reserve requirement ratio) $1000, since a $1000 deposit is created by the seller of the securities. If the Federal Reserve *sells* securities, the seller's check for the amount of the sale will result in a decrease in member bank deposits at the Federal Reserve:

Federal Reserve Banks			
U.S. government securities	−1000	Deposits of financial institutions (reserves)	−1000

Again, the change in the amount of excess reserves depends on what the reserve requirement ratio is and whether the purchaser of the securities is a bank or a nonbank party. Open-market operations are the principal tool of the Federal Reserve in pursuing its policy objectives. This important instrument of monetary policy will be the subject of detailed discussion in Chapters 7 and 21.

The Federal Reserve serves as the principal bank of the U.S. Treasury, and Treasury deposits are a major component of Federal Reserve liabilities. The Treasury also maintains accounts, called Tax and Loan Accounts, in thousands of commercial banks across the country. These accounts serve as "collection points" for payments of federal taxes by individuals and business firms. They are often the source of funds for purchases of Treasury securities by banks for themselves or for their customers (thus the "Loan" part of their name). Tax and Loan Accounts are periodically transferred to the Treasury's balance with the Federal Reserve for purposes of federal disbursements. The transfer of funds from "T & L" accounts to the Federal Reserve account drains reserves from the banking system, but their subsequent disbursement by the Treasury restores the reserves (as recipients of government payments deposit the funds in their banks). Nonetheless, time lags between such transfers, collections in the T & L accounts, and Treasury expenditures frequently impact sharply on individual bank reserves and can create a degree of disturbance for the banking system as a whole.[8]

Although the U.S. Treasury continues to produce the coin component of currency in circulation, the Federal Reserve is now the sole issuer of all new paper currency. *Federal Reserve notes* account for more than 90 percent of all paper currency.[9] The Federal Reserve supplies Federal Reserve notes to banks on demand, reducing their deposits at the Federal Reserve Banks by the amount of currency sent. For example, a $100,000 transfer would have this effect:

Federal Reserve Bank

Federal Reserve notes	+100,000
Deposits of financial institutions (reserves)	−100,000

As long as the currency provided to the banks remains in bank vaults, it remains part of bank reserves. As discussed previously, an increase in the amount of currency in circulation *outside* banks will reduce bank reserves.

When banks find themselves holding excessive amounts of currency, they return the undesired amount to the Federal Reserve for deposit credit, an action that in itself does not

---

8. The purpose of Tax and Loan Accounts is to minimize fluctuations in bank reserves of Treasury receipts and payments. By keeping receipts in the general location of their collection (in T & L Accounts) until needed for Treasury disbursement, the Treasury avoids draining reserves from banks every time tax payments are made. See Chapter 22 for additional discussion of T & L accounts.

9. New coins are minted at the Treasury's Bureau of the Mint facilities in Philadelphia, Denver, and San Francisco. Federal Reserve notes are printed for the Federal Reserve by the Treasury's Bureau of Printing and Engraving in Washington, D.C.

affect total reserves. If the amount of currency in circulation outside banks decreases, however, the reserves of the banking system are increased as currency flows into deposit accounts.

The Treasury

Although its primary role is to serve as paying and collecting agent for the federal government, the U.S. Treasury also has a part to play in the monetary system. In the past, the Treasury was a significant issuer of paper currency (particularly so-called silver certificates), but at the present time its currency production is limited to coins. The Federal Reserve ''buys'' coins from the Treasury by crediting (increasing) the Treasury's account with the Federal Reserve Bank and then provides coins to depository financial institutions on request, reducing the deposit account in the amount of coin provided. The effect on the balance sheet of the Federal Reserve is:

	Federal Reserve Banks		
Treasury currency	+5000	Treasury deposits	+5000
Treasury currency	−5000	Deposits of financial institutions	−5000

As with paper currency (Federal Reserve notes), banks will return any undesired amount of coins to the Federal Reserve for deposit credit.

This concludes our sketch of various *direct* effects on the composition and quantity of the money supply (M-1) of actions of the public, the Federal Reserve Banks, and the Treasury. However, there are numerous *indirect* effects on monetary aggregates of the behavior of these entities, which we will discuss in subsequent chapters.

THE MONETARY BASE AND THE MONETARY MULTIPLIER

The deposit expansion process described above for demand deposits in commercial banks holds generally for checkable deposits. The existence of reserve requirements on these deposits creates a limit to the expansion process, as indicated in the foregoing discussion. This limit is the reciprocal of the reserve requirement ratio (the fraction of deposits that must be held as reserves). For example, a reserve requirement of 10 percent, 1/10, suggests that an increase in reserves can generate 10 times the amount of the increase in new deposits and a reserve requirement of 20 percent, 1/5, can generate 5 times the amount. In practice, the multiplier effect will be less than this limit because of ''leakages'' into assets other than checkable deposits—currency holdings, noncheckable deposits, government deposits, and holdings of excess reserves by financial institutions. Thus a measure of the *monetary multiplier*—the number of times an injection of new reserves will reproduce itself as new money—must reflect these various other influences.

A useful way to develop and view the monetary multiplier is in terms of the *monetary base*, defined as the reserves of financial institutions that issue checkable deposits plus currency in circulation outside banks. The money supply is determined by the amount of the monetary base, the relative proportions of reserves and currency in the monetary base, and the size of the monetary multiplier. Clearly, all else being equal, the greater the amount of the monetary base, the greater the amount of potential money creation. The composition of the monetary base—the amount of reserves relative to currency—is a factor because reserves permit deposit expansion, but currency in circulation does not. Finally, for a given amount and composition of the monetary base, the quantity of money is determined by the size of the monetary multiplier. The size of the monetary multiplier, in turn, is determined by the magnitude of the reserve requirement on deposits and the degree of "leakage" of money into noncheckable deposits, currency, and government deposits. (To the extent that reserves are "lost" by these leakages, further deposit expansion cannot occur.)

The monetary multiplier can be formulated in a number of ways. One of the more manageable approaches can be developed as follows:

1. Variables:
   R = reserves held by financial institutions that issue checkable deposits
   C = currency in circulation
   D = checkable deposits (other than U.S. government)
   T = noncheckable time and savings deposits in depository institutions
   G = deposits of the U.S. government
   M = money supply (M-1)

2. Relationships (ratios):
   a) Ratio of reserves to total deposits, r:
   $$r = \frac{R}{D + T + G} \quad \text{and thus } R = r(D + T + G).$$
   b) Ratio of currency to checkable deposits, k:
   $$k = \frac{C}{D} \quad \text{and thus } C = kD.$$
   c) Ratio of noncheckable deposits to checkable deposits, t:
   $$t = \frac{T}{D} \quad \text{and thus } T = tD.$$
   d) Ratio of government deposits to checkable deposits, g:
   $$g = \frac{G}{D} \quad \text{and thus } G = gD.$$

3. Definition of money (checkable deposits plus currency in circulation outside banks):
   $M = D + C$.

4. Definition of monetary base, X (reserves plus currency in circulation):
   $X = R + C$.

5. Algebraic development of money multiplier, Z:
   a) $M = Z(X)$,
      and by substitution,
   b) $D + C = Z(R + C)$,
      or $Z = \dfrac{D + C}{R + C}$.
   c) Recalling that $C = kD$ and $R = R(D + T + G)$, and substituting,
      $$Z = \frac{D + kD}{r(D + T + G) + kD} = \frac{D(1 + k)}{D[r(1 + t + g) + k]},$$
      or $Z = \dfrac{1 + k}{r(1 + t + g) + k}$.
      The money supply is thus determined to be
      $$M = \left(\frac{1 + k}{r(1 + t + g) + k} \right)(R + C).$$

This formulation reflects the composite decision model for the public, the Treasury, and the Federal Reserve, which will determine how much money will exist. The decisions and actions of these economic units jointly determine the amount of reserves and currency in circulation (the monetary base) and the size of the monetary multiplier. The magnitude of reserve requirements (on both checkable and noncheckable deposits), the demand of the public for currency, and the Treasury's operations all impound on the value of Z, the money multiplier. Changes in reserve requirements, in the demand for currency relative to deposits, and in the ratios of checkable to noncheckable deposits and U.S. government deposits to other deposits will result in shifts in the magnitude of the money multiplier. There are other (and more complex) approaches to developing the money multiplier, but this formulation serves our purpose of summarizing how decisions of the public, the U.S. Treasury, and the Federal Reserve impact on the money supply.

Although the public, the Treasury, and commercial banks can all have a significant impact on the money supply, the Federal Reserve System is our economy's ultimate arbiter concerning the amount of money in existence. The Federal Reserve has the ability to impact critically on both the money multiplier (via reserve requirements) and bank reserves (via open-market operations) and, more important, the mandate to control the supply of money. The next chapter traces the historical development of this role for the Federal Reserve, describes its organization and operating procedures, and discusses in more detail its tools for monetary control.

SUMMARY

Money is essential to a modern economy, and its quantity is of great significance to the level of prices and the degree of resource employment in an economy. Money serves as a *medium of exchange,* a *unit of account,* a *store of value,* and a *standard of deferred payment,* thus making possible the exchange of goods and services via a means of generalized purchasing power and the saving, lending, and borrowing of such purchasing power.

A variety of items have served as money over the centuries, but modern money consists of currency and checkable deposits in depository institutions. "Near monies" include time and savings deposits with commercial banks and other financial institutions. The operations of institutions holding checkable deposits create money, because their lending activities result in the expansion of demand deposits. Actions by the public and the government also affect the quantity of money.

The money supply is determined by the size of the *monetary base*—currency in circulation plus bank reserves—and the size of the *money multiplier*. In the United States, the Federal Reserve System controls the size of the money supply largely by controlling the amount of bank reserves via its open-market sales and purchases of securities. The Federal Reserve also affects the size of the money multiplier by its power to set reserve requirements. Other influences on the magnitude of the money multiplier include the amount of currency in circulation, relative demand for noncheckable and checkable deposits, and the amount of Treasury deposits with commercial banks. Ultimately the Federal Reserve System can determine the size of the money stock, although its control may be less timely and precise than desired.

QUESTIONS

1. What are four basic functions of money? Describe the contribution of each to the economic system.

2. What is a "monetary standard"? Describe this nation's present monetary standard. Why does it "work"?

3. Explain "monetary velocity." What are the principal determinants of the velocity of money?

4. How are demand deposits created by the banking system? Can an individual bank create money? Use the concepts of "primary" and "derivative" bank deposits in your answer.

5. What is the "monetary base"? How is it related to the magnitude of the money supply?

6. Give an example of an action by each of the following that will change the amount of reserves held by commercial banks.
   a) The public
   b) The Federal Reserve
   c) The U.S. Treasury

7. Name the principal determinants of the "monetary multiplier."

REFERENCES

Crick, W.F., "The Genesis of Bank Deposits," *Economica*, 1927. Reprinted in American Economic Association, *Readings in Monetary Theory* (Homewood, Ill.: Irwin, 1951), pp. 41–53.

Horvitz, Paul M., *Monetary Policy and the Financial System* (Englewood Cliffs, N.J.: Prentice-Hall, 1979).

Laidler, David, ''The Definitions of Money,'' *Journal of Money, Credit, and Banking,* August 1969.

Lombra, Raymond, James B. Herendeen, and Raymond G. Torto, *Money and the Financial System* (New York: McGraw-Hill, 1980).

APPENDIX

HOW MUCH DOES MONEY MATTER?

What is the degree of influence that changes in the money supply have on the level of employment and the stability of prices? Depending on which economist you believe, you may conclude that the rate of growth of the money supply has minor influence on both, is the essential determinant of both, or affects only the level of prices whereas "real" (nonmonetary) forces determine the level of output and employment. If the reader considers this to be a rather disappointing state of affairs, perhaps the balance of this appendix (and Chapter 21 as well) may serve to engender some sympathy for the many economists who have grappled with this issue. (However, the authors, will *not* seek to settle the issue once and for all.)

The economists who formulated the equation of exchange and the Quantity Theory of Money believed that the quantity of money *in the long run* determined only the level of prices. The so-called Cambridge equation, an alternative expression of the equation of exchange, makes this evident. The Cambridge equation amounts to taking the equation of exchange,

$$MV = PQ,$$

dividing PQ by V, or

$$M = PQ/V,$$

and labeling $1/V$ as k; thus

$$M = kPQ.$$

So what? The significance lies in the behavioral connotation of k. It serves to express the demand for money (how much money the public wishes to hold) as a fraction of money income. This formulation substitutes a *behavioral* variable, k, for V, which *in appearance* (in reality, V is only $1/k$) is a mechanical one. Since the purpose of money is to make payments, the value of k can be viewed as determined by the pattern of payments in an economy, a pattern that tends to be both highly regularized and slow to change. The demand for money is thus tightly—even totally—linked to the volume of payments, or the level of money income, PQ. A constant k means that the public persists in holding only the amount of money equal to kPQ. Money supplied in excess of kPQ will quickly be spent on goods and services, driving up the level of prices until the new kPQ equals the money supply, and vice versa. If changes in the money supply were to be perceived as having an impact on Q (output and employment), the case had to be made that k was not a constant magnitude.

Until the Great Depression of the 1930s, there was little demand for such a case to be made. The quantity theorists believed in the equilibrating capacity of the "real" marketplace to maintain full employment and maximum output. Until the 1930s, the periods of interruption of this condition were either of such short duration or so obviously related to such disturbances as war and famine that most economists were comfortable with the notion. Worldwide economic collapse engendered a demand for some new notions about the economic order.

What is called Keynesianism resulted. John Maynard Keynes's 1936 book, *The General Theory of Employment, Interest, and Money* is generally recognized as having launched a new era of economic interventionism by governments and caused the emergence of fiscal policy (the deliberate use of government spending and taxing powers to affect economic conditions) as a principal tool of such government "management" of the economy. Much less recognized is the contribution of Keynesian thought to the emergence of discretionary monetary policy as a means of government attempts at economic stabilization. (If the reader does not already know how Keynes gave *fiscal policy* intellectual respectability, Chapter 22 offers a succinct account. Attention here is limited to Keynes's contribution to monetary policy.)

Aside from his contribution to making the management of aggregate spending ("effective demand") by government an accepted aspect of modern economies, Keynes opened the door to discretionary monetary policy by developing a plausible case for a variable k (or V) in the Cambridge equation. Keynes argued that money holdings were sensitive to the rate of interest. The value of k would fall (V would rise) as interest rates rose, and vice versa; the public would choose to hold smaller cash balances when yields on financial assets increased. A variable k expands the potential impact of changes in the money supply to Q as well as P. The management of the quantity of money could now be viewed as a potential stimulant for output and employment, as well as a means of controlling the price level.

In their fascination with the now-intellectually-respectable tool of fiscal policy, many of Keynes's disciples (Keynes died in 1946) neglected monetary policy. As Keynesianism was generally practiced and preached in the 1940s and 1950s, little significance was attached to the money supply. (Keynes himself would doubtless have disapproved.) To a large degree, Keynesianism became synonymous with "fiscalism"—the belief that fiscal policy, not monetary policy, was the most effective way to "manage" the economy.

Emerging as the opponents of fiscalism (and, more in appearance than in reality, of Keynesian thought) were the latter-day quantity theorists—"monetarists"—led by Milton Friedman. The monetarists' attack on fiscal policy (as well as the touting of monetary policy) was primarily an empirical effort. In a plethora of studies, the quantity of money was repeatedly shown to be of considerable economic significance, with fiscal variables showing poorly, if at all. The ascendancy of monetarism in the late 1960s and 1970s, however, was probably more due to the replacement of unemployment by inflation as the principal economic bugaboo than to the labors of the monetarists. The fiscal remedy for inflation is increased taxes and/or reduced government spending (the reverse is true for unemployment)—actions likely to give even the hardiest of politicians pause. The monetary remedy, tightening the money supply, is more politically palatable because it is less visible, less understood, and can always be blamed on the central bankers.

On the intellectual front, recent years have seen a rediscovery of Keynes as a *monetary* economist and the growing acceptance by Keynesians of monetary policy as an equal partner of fiscal policy. Ironically, some monetarists were having no part of such detente and rapprochement in the realm of economic theory. Instead, the old Quantity Theory notion that money can affect only the level of prices, not output, was resurrected. One limb of this new branch of monetarism is the notion, advanced most notably by Milton Friedman, that employment is determined by the ''natural rate of unemployment.'' This natural rate is the fraction of the labor force that will be jobless even when the real wage rate is in equilibrium. At this level of unemployment, the demand for labor is in line with the supply of labor, the real wage rate will not decline to permit any expansion of employment, and efforts to trigger such expansion (whether by monetary or fiscal policy) will result only in inflation.

Still another offshoot of monetarist theorizing holds that monetary or fiscal policy cannot affect output and employment (but only prices) because such measures are fully anticipated by business and consumers and are fully offset by their anticipatory responses. This ''rational expectations'' hypothesis is discussed (in simplified fashion) in the appendix to Chapter 21.

How much does money matter for the economy's health and well-being? The foregoing discussion serves to make the point that we really don't know just how or to what degree variations in the rate of growth in the money supply affect output, employment, and prices. We *do* know that the quantity of money is of great importance in the financial system, and that the actions of the Federal Reserve System in controlling the money supply do, indeed, matter to a very significant degree for the financial marketplace.

REFERENCES

Friedman, Milton, ''A Restatement of the Quantity Theory of Money,'' in M. Friedman (ed.), *Studies in the Quantity Theory of Money* (Chicago: University of Chicago Press, 1956), pp. 3–21.

Gordon, Robert (ed.), *Milton Friedman's Monetary Framework* (Chicago: University of Chicago Press, 1974).

Leijonhufvud, Axel, *On Keynesian Economics* and *the Economics of Keynes* (New York: Oxford University Press, 1968).

Ritter, Lawrence S., ''The Role of Money in Keynesian Theory,'' in Deane Carson (ed.), *Banking and Monetary Studies* (Homewood, Ill.: Irwin, 1963) pp. 134–150.

Chapter 7

The Structure and Role of the Federal Reserve System

The preceding chapter discussed the nature of money, its economic significance, and the contemporary framework for its creation and control. The unique role of the commercial banking system in money creation was described, and the factors that determine the limits of deposit expansion by banks were identified and discussed. The importance of the money supply in an economy and the role that financial institutions and markets play in determining the quantity of money and credit make it inevitable that the central governments of modern nations will seek to control the money stock and will regulate the private institutions that, in their role as financial intermediaries, have such an enormous economic influence.

Most nations have institutions called *central banks,* which are instruments of governmental policy regarding money and credit conditions, and which exercise regulatory authority over financial institutions and markets. In England the Bank of England, established in the late seventeenth century, performs these functions. In France it is the Bank of France (established in 1800) and in Canada the Bank of Canada (established in 1935). In this country it is the Federal Reserve System (the Fed), established by an act of Congress in 1913.

In this chapter we trace the origins and development of the Federal Reserve System, its organization and operating characteristics, and we focus primarily on its roles as ultimate arbiter of the money supply and as principal regulator of financial institutions and markets. We describe and discuss the policy instruments of the Federal Reserve in exercising its powers of monetary control. There are certain technical difficulties confronted by the Federal Reserve in controlling money and credit, and there are political difficulties with which monetary policy is involved, but detailed discussion of these matters is deferred until Chapter 21.

THE FOUNDING OF THE FEDERAL RESERVE

In 1791, at the urging of the Secretary of the Treasury, Alexander Hamilton, the U.S. Congress established a national bank. The First Bank of the United States, as it was called, was this nation's first central bank. Working closely with the Treasury, the Bank did much to stabilize the money and banking system of the new republic. For a variety of reasons, however, intense political opposition to the Bank developed, and it failed in its bid for rechartering in 1811.

The nation's second experiment with a central bank began in 1816, with congressional chartering (for 20 years) of the Second Bank of the United States. Although most economic historians give it high marks for its performance, the Second Bank, like its predecessor, was a victim of political and special-interest-group maneuvering and was not rechartered. For the next three decades, until the establishment of the *National Banking System,* bank chartering was solely the province of the states. And for a full three quarters of a century, until the founding of the Federal Reserve System in 1913, the United States had no central bank.

The National Banking System

The era of virtually unrestricted state banking, from about 1836 to 1863, was a generally chaotic one. Growth in the number of state banks was rapid, despite frequent failures. In 1834 there were 506 state banks, and in 1860 there were 1562, with more than $200 million of state bank notes in circulation in the latter year.[1]

The establishment of the National Banking System in 1863 resulted in some measure of order for the U.S. banking system, but that was not the primary reason for its creation. Its principal purpose was to provide a market for U.S. bonds in view of the pressing financing needs created by the Civil War. Since the National Bank Act of 1863 required that one third of the capital of each bank securing a national charter be secured by U.S. bonds deposited with the Comptroller of the Currency and tied the issuing of bank notes to holdings of U.S. government securities, it was hoped that a new market for federal bonds would be created.

To "encourage" state banks to become national banks, the Congress in 1864 levied a 2 percent tax on state bank notes, and the tax was soon thereafter raised to 10 percent. As a

---

1. During this early period of U.S. banking history, the use of checking accounts was generally limited to major cities. Thus when banks made loans, they usually gave the borrower paper currency printed for that particular bank. These banks' notes amounted to a promise to pay in gold or silver when presented for "redemption in specie" ("specie" means minted gold or silver). If state banks overissued these notes, as they frequently did, failure resulted when the banks could not meet redemption demands.

result, there were 1644 national banks by 1866. A decade later, however, the growing use of checking accounts (rather than bank notes) had sparked a resurgence of state banking, and there were more than 1500 state banks by 1888. This country's present dual system of both national and state banks thus became an important feature of the American economic system.

The overall effect of the national banking system was positive. Compared with their predecessor state banks, most of the national banks were financially healthy, and the standardized national bank notes held their value better than those of the pre–Civil War state banks. One reason was the reserve requirements imposed by Congress on national banks (25 percent of deposits for large city banks and 15 percent for smaller banks). Another reason was the requirement that national bank notes be backed by U.S. Treasury bonds. (If a bank failed, the Treasury could sell the collateral bonds to redeem the notes.)

However, the national banking system did not solve the problem of ensuring that the quantity of money would be appropriate for the economy's needs. As under the state banking system, the money supply was "inelastic"; the system did not provide a mechanism by which available funds could expand and contract with the needs of commerce and industry. Since note issue was based on government securities, the quantity of national bank notes was related to the size of the federal debt, which was generally shrinking during the latter part of the nineteenth century. The quantity of "specie" (and of paper currency backed by it) was a function of the fortunes of domestic and foreign miners.

Another problem with the national banking system was the so-called pyramiding of reserves. This phenomenon resulted from the fact that *legal* reserves of national banks were held at other (larger) national banks; "country" banks held their reserves with "reserve city" banks, and the latter held their reserves with "central reserve city" banks. However, the banks had to use their vault cash to redeem deposit liabilities. The pyramiding provided reserves to reserve city and central reserve city banks, which permitted loans (and deposits) to expand but without a corresponding increase in vault cash.

The financial "panics" of 1873, 1884, 1893, and 1907 were largely the result of pyramided reserves in conjunction with the general inelasticity of the monetary system. Business expansion tended to trigger both deposit expansion and a drain on vault cash in banks. Country banks, running low on vault cash, would call on their reserve city bank depositories for cash, and the latter would then do the same with their central reserve city depositories. With all the banks in the chain scrambling for cash, loans were called and lending was curtailed. As banks began to suspend specie payment, the "panic" spread and fed on itself. There was no "lender of last resort" to ease the situation.

Establishment of the Federal Reserve System

The panic of 1907 triggered a demand for money and banking reform, manifested initially by the creation of a National Monetary Commission to study the problem and propose alternatives. Its 1910 report called for a central bank for the United States, the operations of which would serve to provide an "elastic currency" and eliminate the problems associated with "pyramided reserves."

The Federal Reserve System was established by the Federal Reserve Act of 1913. It was formulated as a uniquely American institution—its organization reflecting much of what the American people of the day believed to be appropriate in terms of decentralization versus centralization, private versus public enterprise, and small versus large institutions. Instead of establishing a single central bank (as most European nations had previously established), the act established the Federal Reserve System as an organization of *twelve* regional Federal Reserve Banks with a Board of Governors in Washington, D.C. All national banks were required to join the system (become "member banks"), and state banks were permitted to join, but they were not forced to do so. Ownership of the various Federal Reserve Banks was vested in the member banks.

The present role and functions of the Federal Reserve System are quite different from those envisioned by its founders. Some of the changes are the result of the Banking Acts of 1933 and 1935, which were in turn enacted as a consequence of the economic depression of the 1930s and the weaknesses in the country's financial system that it exposed. Other changes have come about as an evolutionary consequence of economic change and as a product of shifting American attitudes regarding centralization and government intervention in the economy.

For our purposes, the *present* structure, function, and operating characteristics of the Federal Reserve System are most relevant. In the following sections of this chapter, therefore, we will focus on the modern framework, making reference to discarded past arrangements only when such discussion is useful for understanding the present system.

STRUCTURE OF THE FEDERAL RESERVE SYSTEM

The major components of the Federal Reserve System are member banks, the twelve Federal Reserve Banks, the Board of Governors, and the Federal Open Market Committee. Figure 7.1 offers a schematic representation of the system's organization.

Member Banks

National banks but not state banks are required to be members of the Federal Reserve System. As of December 31, 1978, there were 5591 member banks in the system, of which about 83 percent were nationally chartered and 17 percent were state-chartered. Federal Reserve member banks thus comprised less than 40 percent of all commercial banks. However, since larger banks are more likely to be members than smaller banks (partly because larger banks are likely to be national banks), member banks held more than 70 percent of total deposits in 1978.

Prior to enactment of the Depository Institutions Deregulation and Monetary Control Act of 1980 (D.I.D.M.C.A.), the relative costs and benefits of Fed membership versus nonmembership were rather sharply defined for a bank. Fed membership entitled a bank to such Fed services as access to the check-clearing, wire-transfer, and securities-safekeeping facilities of the system. Further, membership provided a ready source of currency and coin and—of particular importance—entitled a bank to request loans from the Fed. Along with

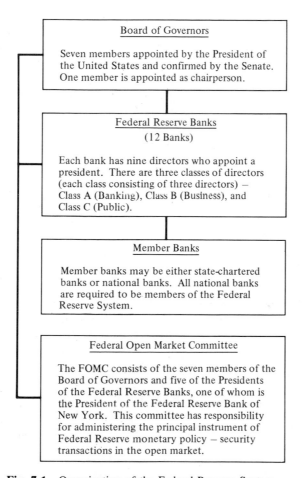

Fig. 7.1 Organization of the Federal Reserve System

these various privileges, membership entailed (and still entails) a number of obligations. These obligations include subscribing to capital stock of the bank's district Federal Reserve Bank, complying with Federal Reserve rules and regulations, paying checks presented at par (face value), and, in the case of state member banks, being examined and supervised by the Federal Reserve Banks. The most significant obligation (and cost) of membership, however, was adherence to the Fed's reserve requirement. Until D.I.D.M.C.A. mandated uniform reserve requirement for all banks, this obligation often resulted in member banks' bearing heavier costs from holding reserves than were borne by nonmember banks, whose reserve requirements were then established by the various states of charter.

The fact that Federal Reserve System membership declined steadily after World War II until 1980 indicates that, for many banks, the pre-D.I.D.M.C.A. costs and benefits of membership favored nonmembership.[2] During this period, the percentage of all banks holding system membership fell from more than 50 percent to less than 40 percent. The percentage of bank deposits held by members dropped from almost 90 to less than 75. In the 1970s, the Federal Reserve Board of Governors became quite concerned about this decline in membership because of the implications it then held for the effectiveness of monetary policy. Since the Fed had no control over reserve requirements of nonmember banks, declining membership implied declining ability of the Fed to control the money supply.

Indeed, the principal reason for the decline in bank membership between 1945 and 1980 was the magnitude and nature of the Fed's reserve requirements relative to those imposed by the various states on nonmember banks. Not only was the Fed's reserve requirement ratio frequently higher than those of many states, but it also immobilized that percentage of member bank deposits in nonearning form, since the Fed mandates that reserves be held either as vault cash or as deposits with the district Federal Reserve Bank. Some states had reserve requirements for nonmember banks that allowed correspondent accounts (interbank deposits) to be counted as reserves, and a number of states allowed reserves to be held in some interest-earning asset. These differences between Fed and state reserve requirements amounted to the imposition of a significant cost for membership in the Federal Reserve System.

At the urging of the Fed, the U.S. Congress mandated in 1980 the elimination of differential reserve requirements between member and nonmember banks. This provision was part of the wide-ranging, watershed banking legislation that the Depository Institutions Deregulation and Monetary Control Act of 1980 constituted. The act called for the phased establishment of uniform reserve requirements for all depository institutions. These reserve requirements were initially set at 3 percent of transactions balances (checkable deposits) up to $25 million and 12 percent of transactions balances over $25 million at all depository institutions. Reserves on nonpersonal time deposits with original maturities of less than four years were set at 3 percent of such deposits.[3] The Fed was empowered to alter the reserve requirement ratio on checkable deposits above $25 million within a range of 8 to 14 percent, and on nonpersonal time deposits from 0 to 9 percent. The Fed could also require additional reserves equal to as much as 4 percent of checkable deposits, but interest would be paid on these reserves. The act provided that these requirements would be phased in for nonmember depository institutions over an eight-year period.[4] Member bank reserve requirements were to be reduced to the new levels over a four-year period.

D.I.D.M.C.A. also made the various services of the Fed available to nonmember depository institutions as well as member banks. Beginning in 1981, these services were to

---

2. Further, nonmember banks were frequently able to secure the same types of service offered by the Fed from their large city correspondent banks and some services *not* offered by the Fed, such as loan participation and investment assistance.

3. A reserve requirement of 3 percent for Eurodollar liabilities was also set by the act.

4. Nonmember institutions were allowed to hold reserves directly with the Fed *or* indirectly through "pass-through" arrangements with a correspondent bank, a Federal Home Loan Bank, or the National Credit Union Administration Central Liquidity Facility.

be provided on an explicit-fee basis rather than as a privilege of Fed membership. And of particular significance, all depository institutions subject to reserve requirements were made immediately eligible by the act to request loans from the Fed.

It is apparent that this highly significant banking legislation greatly narrowed the difference between being a member and not being a member of the Federal Reserve System. The act will amost certainly check the decline in Fed membership, but the proportionate size of such membership is no longer of great significance for the financial system.

The Federal Reserve Banks

The 12 regional Federal Reserve Banks, each of which has a "district," are located in the cities of Boston, New York, Philadelphia, Cleveland, Richmond, Atlanta, Chicago, St. Louis, Minneapolis, Kansas City, Dallas, and San Francisco. Each bank has a president and nine directors, six of whom are elected by the member banks (three bankers and three nonbankers) and three of whom are appointed by the Board of Governors.

The various reserve banks are "owned" by member banks in the sense that each member bank must subscribe to stock in its district bank in the amount of 3 percent of its total capital. Member banks are paid dividends at a rate of 6 percent per annum on their stock "purchase." This arrangement is an artifact of the 1913 Federal Reserve Act (the Fed's architects were opposed to government ownership of banks) and has no real significance; the stock ownership carries no private property rights. If a member bank relinquishes its membership, the Federal Reserve stock must be returned; it cannot be sold.

When the Fed was founded, it was intended that the regional reserve banks would have a great deal of autonomy and influence in the system's operations. And, indeed, they did play such a role in the early years of the Fed's existence. Today, however, most policy powers are centralized in the Board of Governors, and the regional banks are largely extensions of the Board. A great deal of economic analysis and policy discussion takes place at the regional banks, but it amounts only to a conduit for channeling information and advice to the Board of Governors. The regional reserve banks are primarily involved in providing various operating services to member banks, such as check clearing and the shipment of currency and coin.

The principal source of revenues for the Federal Reserve System is interest earnings on holdings of securities and on loans to member banks. These revenues are used to pay operating expenses and the statutory 6 percent dividend on Federal Reserve stock held by member banks. The remainder (less any required additions to Federal Reserve Bank capital) is paid to the Treasury. This remittance to the Treasury, which has amounted to more than 80 percent of system's revenues since the Fed was established, has averaged between five and six billion dollars a year in recent years.

Board of Governors

The Board of Governors consists of seven members appointed for 14-year terms by the President of the United States. The appointments, which must be approved by the U.S.

Senate, are "staggered" so that one governor's term expires every two years. A governor who serves a full term cannot be reappointed. A chairman and vice-chairman of the Board are designated by the President for four-year terms, and they can serve in this capacity for an additional term, subject to the general limitation on time in service on the Board.

The Board of Governors is located in Washington, D.C. Its functions, broadly stated, are formulating and executing monetary policy, overseeing the operations of the Federal Reserve Banks, and exercising various regulatory and supervisory powers over member banks. A more specific listing of major responsibilities follows:

1. Setting reserve requirements on depository institution transactions balances within the limits mandated by Congress (as discussed previously, uniform reserve requirements now apply to all depository institutions).

2. Determining the rate of interest (discount rate) to be charged for borrowings from the Federal Reserve Banks.[5]

3. Participating in planning the nature and magnitude of Federal Reserve open-market operations (the buying and selling of securities by the Fed) via membership of the seven governors on the Federal Open Market Committee.

4. Appointing three directors on each Federal Reserve Bank board of directors and approving the appointment of the president of each regional bank.

5. Providing for periodic audit of regional Federal Reserve Banks.

6. Reviewing and approving or disapproving applications by bank holding companies to acquire banks and other firms.

7. Reviewing (for possible approval) applications for merger of two or more banks into a state member bank.

8. Providing for supervision and examination policies and procedures for state-chartered member banks. (Bank examinations are actually conducted by the staffs of the various Federal Reserve Banks.)

The Board of Governors has considerable economic power, and since its chairman generally dominates the Board, the chairman of the Board of Governors has come to be viewed as a principal figure in the formulation of U.S. economic policy. This development is attributable to a number of factors, including the great increase in the perceived importance of monetary policy (relative to fiscal policy) in recent years, the personalities of recent chairmen, and a number of political factors relating to the degree of power that can be effectively wielded by the President and by congressional leaders in economic matters.

---

5. Technically, the discount rate is determined by the various reserve banks, subject to review and approval by the Board. In fact, the Board has now assumed the power to determine the discount rate for all Federal Reserve Banks.

The Federal Open Market Committee

The chairman of the Board of Governors is also chairman of the Federal Open Market Committee (FOMC). The voting members of the FOMC are the seven Board governors and five of the twelve Federal Reserve Bank presidents. The president of the New York Fed is a permanent voting member (and also vice-chairman), but the other four reserve bank positions on the FOMC (one-year terms) are rotated among the other presidents. The seven other Federal Reserve Bank presidents also generally attend the meetings of the committee along with a number of senior staff personnel.

Meetings generally consume an entire day and occur about once a month. FOMC members are briefed on a wide range of domestic and international economic developments. Policy options and potential strategies in the conduct of open-market operations are discussed. The committee then agrees on policy guidelines for open-market operations to be conducted over the period before the next meeting of the group. A policy statement incorporating these guidelines is then drafted and presented to the Manager of the System Open Market Account, an officer of the Federal Reserve Bank of New York who is responsible for the execution of open-market operations. The statement serves as the directive for the day-to-day implementation of the Federal Reserve's operations in the securities markets.

The directives, which are not made public until about a month after each meeting, indicate the Fed's general monetary objective over the period until the next meeting. The directives typically include a brief review of economic developments, a summary of the committee's economic objectives, and instructions to the account manager for conducting open-market operations. The policy statements may seem rather vague to an outsider—policy direction is couched in phrases like "actions to moderate pressures on financial markets," "moderate growth in monetary aggregates," and "fostering financial conditions that will encourage economic recovery while resisting inflationary pressures," and so forth. Further, such guides are interspersed with highly technical discussions of current economic conditions. However, the Manager of the System Open Market Account always sits in on the FOMC meetings that produce these directives and is thus likely to know more about what the Fed wants than the statements actually say. Moreover, there is daily communication between the manager and the Board in the normal course of implementing the general policy directives.[6] The directives issued by the FOMC, along with a summary justification of the committee's actions, is made public after the *next* FOMC meeting. The "Record of Policy Actions of the Federal Open Market Committee" is published in the *Federal Reserve Bulletin* soon after its public release.

Open-market operations constitute the Fed's principal tool of monetary policy. Thus the FOMC is an important component of the Federal Reserve System. We turn now to a

---

6. In addition to its regular meetings, the FOMC occasionally holds telephone consultations between the dates of scheduled meetings. Such sessions may result in revised instructions to the manager.

discussion of the Fed's various policy instruments and the means of their employment in the Fed's pursuit of monetary goals.

INSTRUMENTS OF MONETARY AND CREDIT POLICY

The means by which the Federal Reserve can affect the monetary base, the money multiplier, and thus the supply of money were discussed briefly in the previous chapter. The Fed can expand or contract reserves by buying or selling securities (open-market operations) and by varying the volume of its lending to depository institutions. The Fed can increase or decrease the magnitude of the money multiplier by lowering or raising the reserve requirement ratio, an action that also changes the proportions of required and excess reserves (which constitute total reserves). When the Fed wishes to stimulate economic activity, it will take action to increase the quantity of excess reserves held by banks and other depository institutions. When excess reserves increase, these institutions have the means and incentive to acquire additional interest-earning assets (make loans and acquire securities), and as a result, there is an expansion of deposits and currency in circulation. If the Fed instead seeks to restrain economic activity, its policy actions will be aimed at reducing reserves. A reduction in reserves is likely to force depository institutions to cut back on lending and investing; the result is a decrease in deposits and cash outside banks. The Fed can thus affect the availability of credit, the money supply, and interest rates by its policy actions. Changes in these variables in turn impact considerably on economic activity. The Fed also has a considerable degree of influence with depository institutions, and it employs "moral suasion" to steer these institutions toward behavior consistent with Fed policy. We will now look at each of the Fed's major policy instruments.

Open-Market Operations

Open-market operations are by far the most frequently used policy tool of the Fed because of their flexibility and effectiveness. Open-market operations impact directly on reserves; reserves increase when the Fed buys securities and decrease when the Fed sells securities. Most of the uses of this technique are "defensive" in nature—designed to offset undesired temporary changes in reserves due to some of the factors discussed in the preceding chapter. For example, currency in circulation outside depository financial institutions tends to increase greatly during the period immediately before Christmas. This occurrence drains reserves, and it would result in a multiple contraction of demand deposits if reserves were not injected into the financial system by the Fed to offset it. Such injection is accomplished by Fed purchases of Treasury securities in its open-market operations. When Christmas is over and currency flows back, the Fed reverses its field, selling securities to avoid an undesired expansion of reserves. Other short-run disturbances that call for such *defensive* open-market operations include cyclical changes in Federal Reserve "float" (as defined in Chapter 6), new Treasury issues of securities, seasonal variations in the demand for credit, and changes in the Treasury's balance with the Fed.

The Fed employs so-called *dynamic* open-market operations in its pursuit of longer-run objectives. When inflation is the foremost economic problem, the Fed is likely to be pursuing a policy of monetary stringency—slowing money supply growth and allowing interest rates to rise. In this case, the Fed's dynamic open-market operations amount to net sales of securities and the corresponding reduction in reserves. On the other hand, depressed economic activity is likely to result in open-market operations that inject reserves into the financial system in order to permit monetary expansion and an easing of interest rates. To some extent, dynamic operations can be augmented by *not* using the usual defensive operations to offset an extraneous reserve change in the desired direction. On the other hand, the Fed must often employ defensive measures in the course of conducting dynamic operations in order for the latter to proceed smoothly.

Open-market operations are conducted by the Open Market Trading Desk of the Federal Reserve Bank of New York under the direction of the Manager of the System Open Market Account. The Fed conducts open market operations virtually every business day, and the Open Market Trading Desk is a very busy place. In addition to trading activities, the account manager and his staff must continuously monitor a wide range of information about conditions in the financial markets, Treasury activities, and the reserve positions of depository institutions. The staff is in constant contact with the dozen or so large government-bond dealers with whom the trading desk does most of its business. Daily contact is also generally maintained between the trading desk and the Board of Governors and the various presidents of the Federal Reserve Banks. Such contact is generally accomplished by telephone discussions between trading-desk officers and senior members of the Board's staff (and sometimes the governors themselves) and the bank presidents. These discussions focus primarily on developments in the securities markets, the reserve positions of depository institutions, and the actions taken and to be taken by the trading desk.

Most of the Fed's security trading is done in Treasury bills, which are short-term U.S. government securities. (The Fed also trades occasionally in "bankers acceptances," a short-term note used in the financing of foreign trade that bears a bank's promise to pay.) The New York dealers with whom the Fed trades (about half of these major dealers are banks) hold large inventories of Treasury bills. The dollar volume of Fed trading is enormous. Table 7.1 indicates the amount, by major type of financial instrument, of Federal Reserve purchases and sales in recent years.

Two items in Table 7.1 warrant explanation: "repurchase agreements" and "matched sale-purchase transactions." A *repurchase agreement* ("RP") involves an agreement between the Open Market Trading Desk and a security dealer that the Fed will *buy* securities from the dealer subject to dealer repurchase at the end of a specified time period (perhaps as short as a single day). Similarly, a *matched sale-purchase transaction* ("reverse RP") is accomplished by a *sale* of securities to a dealer concurrent with Fed agreement to buy them back at the end of the agreed period. The trading desk utilizes repurchase agreements to *supply* reserves to the market for a short time period and reverse RPs to *withdraw* reserves for a limited time. RPs and reverse RPs are convenient instruments for defensive open-market operations. Both the Fed's frequent use of repurchase agreements and matched sale-purchase transactions and the significance of day-to-day "defensive operations" are evidenced by the fact, as shown in Table 7.1, that the dollar amount of these transactions is about ten times that of outright purchases and sales of securities by the Fed.

Table 7.1   Federal Reserve open market transactions, 1976–1979, (millions of dollars)

Type of transaction	1976	1977	1978	1979
U.S. Government securities				
Outright transactions (excluding matched sale-purchase transactions)				
Treasury bills:				
Gross purchases	14,343	13,738	16,628	16,623
Gross sales	8,462	7,241	13,725	7,480
Redemptions	5,017	2,136	2,033	2,900
Others within 1 year:				
Gross purchases	472	3,017	1,184	3,203
Gross sales	0	0	0	0
Exchange, or maturity shift	792	4,499	−5,170	6,031
Redemptions	0	2,500	0	2,600
1 to 5 years:				
Gross purchases	3,202	2,833	4,188	2,148
Gross sales	177	0	0	0
Exchange, or maturity shift	−2,588	−6,649	−178	−5,185
5 to 10 years:				
Gross purchases	1,048	758	1,526	523
Gross sales	0	0	0	0
Exchange, or maturity shift	1,572	548	2,803	−2465
Over 10 years:				
Gross purchases	642	553	1,063	454
Gross sales	0	0	0	0
Exchange, or maturity shift	225	1,565	2,545	1,619
All maturities:				
Gross purchases	19,707	20,898	24,591	22,950
Gross sales	8,639	7,241	13,725	7,480
Redemptions	5,017	4,636	2,033	5,500
Matched sale-purchase transactions				
Gross sales	196,078	425,214	511,126	626,403
Gross purchases	196,579	423,841	510,854	623,245
Repurchase agreements				
Gross purchases	232,891	178,683	151,618	107,374
Gross sales	230,355	180,535	152,436	107,291
Net change in U.S. government securities	9,087	5,798	7,743	6,896

Type of transaction	1976	1977	1978	1979
Federal agency obligations				
Outright transactions				
Gross purchases	891	1,433	301	853
Gross sales	0	0	173	399
Redemptions	169	223	235	134
Repurchase agreements:				
Gross purchases	10,520	13,811	40,567	37,321
Gross sales	10,360	13,638	40,885	36,960
Net change in federal agency obligations	882	1,383	−426	681
Bankers acceptances				
Outright transactions, net	−545	−196	0	0
Repurchase agreements, net	410	159	−366	116
Net change in bankers acceptances	−135	−37	−366	116
Total net change in System Open				
Market Account	9,833	7,143	6,951	7,693

Source: Board of Governors of the Federal Reserve System, *Federal Reserve Bulletin*, December 1979, A 11.

Table 7.1 also shows, as indicated above, that the Fed deals primarily in Treasury bills and does comparatively little trading in longer-term securities. The market for short-term securities (the money market) has greater breadth and depth than the capital market (the market for securities having a maturity of more than one year). This fact, along with the nature of the role of time-to-maturity to the security price–interest rate relationship that is described in Chapter 9, makes the money market an attractive arena for Fed opportunities. By primarily confining its trading to Treasury bills, the Fed reduces the likelihood of undue disturbances in the bond market and minimizes interest rate fluctuations related to its operations.

Finally, note in Table 7.1 that the net change in the Fed's holdings of securities was positive—the Fed increased the amount of its holdings of U.S. government securities and federal agency obligations—over this time period. This is hardly surprising, for as the economy expands, the money supply is likely to expand also. Monetary expansion in turn requires an expansion of the monetary base—currency in circulation and reserves. Such long-term expansion in reserves can be accomplished in whole or in part by growth in the Fed's holdings of securities. Chapter 21 discusses the process by which the Fed establishes monetary growth goals for given time periods, which in turn determine the nature and scope of its policy actions during those periods.

Federal Reserve Lending

When the Federal Reserve System was established, its role as lender to member banks was considered to be one of its principal functions, and indeed, this was so during its early years of operation. The provision of facilities for the "discounting" (selling) of "commercial paper" (written instruments pertaining to business loans) to the Federal Reserve by member banks was regarded as the key element of the Fed's perceived role in supplying an "elastic currency." The theory ("real bills" doctrine) was that as business loan demand mounted during an economic upswing, banks would have more commercial paper to discount in order to obtain more loanable funds. As loan demand abated and outstanding business loans were paid, commercial banks would repay their indebtedness to the Fed. Thus the volume of outstanding Fed loans would expand and contract with the level of business activity, and so would the money supply. This notion of "elasticity" in the money supply has largely been discarded. Instead, a phrase such as "leaning against the wind" (checking inflationary booms and deflationary slides) better characterizes modern-day Fed objectives than does the idea of automatic accommodation of the business cycle. The notion of an "elastic currency" has thus been supplanted by more direct and purposeful management of money and credit conditions by the Fed, and open-market operations have made Fed lending very much a secondary instrument of Federal Reserve policy.

In the early years of the Fed's existence, bankers actually appeared at a reserve bank teller window to request loans from the Fed, and this gave the Fed's credit-granting role the figurative label of "discount window." The interest rate charged on member bank borrowing from the Fed is still called the "discount rate," and the Fed's lending facilities are still referred to as the "discount window," but only a small portion of Fed loans to member banks are presently accomplished by the discounting of commercial paper. (And bankers are unlikely to appear at a reserve bank teller window!) The general practice at present is for banks to post government securities as collateral for direct advances from the Fed. Further, the Depository Institutions Deregulation and Monetary Control Act of 1980 made the privilege of requesting loans from the Fed available to *all* depository institutions required to hold reserves against deposits, not just member banks.[7] At the time of D.I.D.M.C.A.'s enactment (1980), this amounted to extending the discount privilege to 15,000 additional institutions.

As presently conceived, the purpose of the discount window is to help depository institutions adjust to short-run reserve needs when they encounter difficulty securing needed reserves elsewhere.[8] The Federal Reserve frowns on continuous borrowings by institutions and invokes "administrative counseling" for those borrowers that are judged to be inappropriately using the discount window privilege. From the perspective of a depository institution considering use of the discount window, this attitude of the Fed constitutes a qualitative cost factor that must be weighed along with the discount rate of Fed loans for purposes of

---

7. Nonmember depository institutions, however, are expected to turn first to special industry lenders (such as the Federal Home Loan Banks) for funds rather than to the discount window.

8. The development of the so-called federal funds market, in which depository institutions with excess reserves lend (sell) them to institutions that need additional reserves, has greatly reduced their need to use the Fed's discount window. The Fed prefers that depository institutions turn first to the federal funds market to borrow reserves, partly because interinstitution loans of reserves, unlike its own, do not change the aggregate amount of reserves.

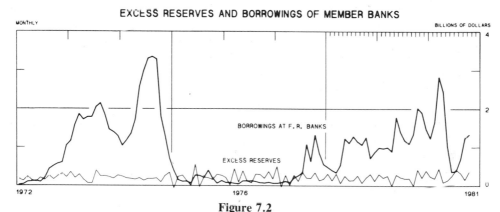

Figure 7.2

(Source: Board of Governors of the Federal Reserve System, *Historical Chart Book.*)

comparing the costs of this source with the costs of alternative reserve sources (federal funds, selling off securities, etc.).

Despite the Fed's rather stern view of the discount mechanism, depository institution borrowing has been generally high, but it does fluctuate very widely over the business cycle. Figure 7.2 indicates the magnitudes of member bank borrowings (and excess reserve positions) in recent years. As one might expect, when the Fed allows the discount rate to lag behind movements in money market rates, as it has frequently done, borrowing rises when interest rates rise and falls when credit conditions ease. When the Fed follows a practice of infrequent revision of the discount rate, it is almost ensured that both average borrowing and the range of magnitudes of borrowing would be much greater if the Fed did not exercise administrative restraint on use of the discount window.

It can be argued that the discount window, though to some extent it may be an outmoded mechanism, is useful on grounds of equity, since its availability is of importance to many smaller institutions that lack the range and quantity of resources available to larger ones. Further, the discount window can be (and has been) a stabilizing factor during periods of financial disturbances. Two examples are the 1966 "credit crunch" and the 1970 collapse of the Penn Central Railroad, which sent off shock waves in the commercial paper market. Thus the "lender of last resort" function continues to be of importance. It has also been argued that the Fed's power to set the discount rate is a useful "signaling" device for its monetary policy objectives (so-called announcement effects). It has been rightly pointed out, however, that many other means of communication are available to the Fed, none of which represent a source of disturbance in the level of bank reserves.

On balance, the discount window is probably best viewed not as a tool of monetary policy but as an "escape valve" to ease the pressures on banks and the economy while adjustment to more stringent credit conditions is being accomplished, or as a "rapid rescue" mechanism when financial crisis threatens for individual banks or for the entire banking system. In recent years, when the borrowing privilege was limited to member banks, borrowing from the Federal Reserve, on the average, constituted less than 2 percent of total bank reserves—hardly providing the Fed with a significant degree of leverage in influencing monetary variables. This may change, of course, with the expansion of the number of eligible institutions. Nonetheless, since changes in the discount rate are unlikely to have a major effect on the magnitude of borrowings, and unless the amount of reserves that exist because of the discount window increases significantly, the monetary effect of such changes is likely to remain small. The Fed has continued to make occasional *symbolic* use of discount rate changes in recent years, but its periodic alteration is usually aimed only at keeping it in line with the money market rate structure. Such changes must be coordinated with other policy actions, for the quantity of reserves supplied via the discount window must be taken into account in the Fed's task of managing total reserves.

Reserve Requirements

As policy tools, changes in reserve requirements have been likened to an axe and open-market operations to a rapier. Changes in the reserve requirement ratio impact immediately on both the legal reserve positions of depository institutions and the money multiplier, thus changing both the amount of reserves required against existing deposits and the quantity of deposits that a given level of reserves can support. *Decreases* in the reserve requirement ratio free reserves and increase the monetary multiplier, and increases in the volume of credit and the money supply are likely to follow. The reverse holds for *increases* in the reserve requirement. Though an extremely powerful tool, reserve requirement changes can hardly be employed on a day-to-day basis (as can open-market operations), unless very small changes in reserve requirement ratios are to be used.[9] Nonetheless, the Federal Reserve has changed the reserve requirement ratio on the average of once a year in the past two decades. Most of these changes, however, were quite small, and some were related to a major structural overhaul of reserve requirements by the Fed in 1972. As discussed earlier, in 1980 the D.I.D.M.C.A. mandated a new structure of reserve requirements applicable to all depository institutions, to be phased in over a period of several years.

Whether reserve requirements are *increased* (to tighten the supply of money and credit when inflationary pressures exist) or *decreased* (to ease credit and expand the money supply as a counter to recessionary developments in the economy), the impact on depository institutions is immediate and universal. The effects of open-market operations, on the other hand, work their way through the economy more slowly, initially impacting on institutions in money market centers and then being transmitted, with a lag, through financial markets to financial institutions around the country. The immediacy and magnitude of the effects of reserve requirement changes can be helpful to a stabilization program of the Fed. The same lack of subtlety, relative to open-market operations, that makes this policy instrument unsuitable for the mere smoothing of economic fluctuations renders it more effective when the Fed desires "announcement effects" to speed up the impact of its actions.

---

9. In 1975, for example, a *decrease* in reserve requirements of one half of one percent for the first $400 million of a bank's demand deposits and one percent of demand deposits in excess of that amount created more than a billion dollars of new excess reserves. (And this change applied only to *member* banks.)

In any event, the Fed must coordinate reserve requirement changes with open-market and discount-window operations to cushion and smooth the adjustment to the new level of required reserves. When reserve requirements are increased, the Fed may temporarily ease its discount-window posture and use open-market operations to supply reserves to depository institutions until an adjustment by the depository system is substantially accomplished. Such adjustment will involve depository institutions in the selling of securities, in bidding more aggressively for "federal funds," and in the curbing of lending. These actions serve to put upward pressure on market interest rates, spread reserve pressures throughout the financial system, and slow the growth of the money supply. All of these results, of course, are the Fed's objectives when it raises reserve requirements, unless a "structural change," rather than economic policy, is the impetus.

Credit Controls

The various "quantitative" instruments of Fed monetary policy—open-market operations, reserve requirements, and discount-window policy—are intended to affect the *aggregate amount* of money and credit. At various times in the past, the Fed has had the power to regulate the terms of credit-granting in the economy, such as repayment periods and the minimum amount of down payments. One such direct credit control available to the Fed since the 1930s is the margin for stock purchases, which amounts to a minimum down payment for securities purchased on credit. This control is intended as a means of countering the use of credit to finance speculative booms in the stock market—a reaction to the excesses of the 1920s prior to the stock market's famous "crash" in 1929.

The Credit Control Act of 1969 permits the President to authorize the Federal Reserve to "regulate and control any and all extensions of credit" when deemed necessary to control inflation. The Fed received such "authorization" under the act in 1979 and 1980 and took various actions under its authority to curb lending. (These actions were not universally popular, and they resulted in a significant degree of sentiment in the U.S. Congress for repeal of the act.)

Interest Rate Ceilings

The Fed's power, acquired in the 1930s, to set interest rate ceilings on savings and time deposits of member banks is a minor policy instrument that is currently being phased out as a result of the gradual elimination of interest rate controls mandated by the Depository Institutions Deregulation and Monetary Control Act of 1980. Before D.I.D.M.C.A., the Fed specified these ceiling rates for member banks in the Board's Regulation Q. The rates were set in consultation with the Federal Deposit Insurance Corporation, which exercised this power for nonmember insured banks, and the Federal Home Loan Bank Board, which set the ceiling rate on dividends paid by member and insured savings and loan associations. D.I.D.M.C.A. established a Depository Institutions Deregulation Commission to assume these scattered powers for all depository institutions and to proceed with phased elimination of interest rate ceilings on savings and time deposit accounts by April 1986.

Few observers will mourn the elimination of interest rate ceilings. These controls are of little policy value, they introduce various distortions in the economy, and they are inequitable for the "small" saver. Decontrol was resisted by savings and loan associations, however, because the old control structure allowed them to offer deposit rates of one quarter of a percent higher than commercial banks. D.I.D.M.C.A. placated the savings and loans by permitting them to expand their lending powers into areas previously dominated by commercial banks, as well as allowing them to issue checkable deposits. Moreover, savings and loan associations, like all depository institutions, will benefit from at least one aspect of the demise of rate ceilings—elimination of the tendency for "disintermediation" to occur when market interest rates surpass the ceiling rates by significant margins, and savers withdraw (and withhold) funds from intermediaries in favor of direct security or mutual fund purchases.

PROBLEMS OF MONETARY CONTROL

The Federal Reserve System attempts to control money and credit in such a way as to achieve certain ultimate economic goals: an increase in the rate of economic growth, increase in employment, reduction in the rate of inflation, etc. These are not easy tasks for a number of reasons. One is that the "linkage" between changes in monetary and credit aggregates and "real" economic variables is only imperfectly understood. And there is an inevitable lag between Fed action and ultimate impact. These difficulties will be discussed in Chapter 21.

The Fed also has the problem of identifying an immediate target for its operations. Given the time lag before monetary changes affect the price level, employment, etc., the Fed must aim at some rate of growth of monetary and credit aggregates and/or some level of interest rates. Even the proper money supply measure is unsettled, as indicated in the previous chapter. Further, the direction of changes in the money supply, amount of bank credit, and interest rates do not always signal the same economic message, a fact that continues to fuel a debate of long duration about which of these financial variables is most intimately related to "real" economic variables. The Fed's long-standing emphasis on such money market variables as the federal funds rate as targets (and indicators) of policy actions was the subject of severe criticism by "monetarist" economists, who urged an emphasis on monetary aggregates. In recent years, as Chapter 21 will show, the Fed has shifted its emphasis from money market variables to monetary aggregates. The Fed presently focuses its primary attention on the achievement of targeted growth paths for reserves—targets chosen in order to achieve growth of the monetary aggregates within a desired range. Further discussion of the Fed's approach to monetary control is best deferred to Chapter 21. For the purpose of the ensuing chapters, however, it will be important to recall the Fed's pervasive and highly significant presence in financial markets.

THE FED AS FISCAL AGENT

Like most central banks, the Federal Reserve System acts as the principal fiscal agent for the national government. The Fed is the federal government's main bank, since the Treasury keeps its "checking account" with the Fed. The Fed also handles new issues of Treasury securities. The reserve banks process applications from would-be purchasers of Treasury securities, allocate the securities among bidders, deliver the securities, and collect the purchase price from security buyers. The Fed also redeems Treasury securities, transfers securities by wire to other locations, pays interest on securities, and assists the Treasury and other government agencies in a number of other ways.

The Federal Reserve Bank of New York acts as the Treasury's agent in the latter's foreign exchange operations. The Fed also conducts such operations on its own in pursuit of the government's foreign economic policy objectives. Such operations include "dollar support" actions—the purchase of dollars (the selling of foreign currencies for dollars) in foreign exchange markets in order to increase or maintain the dollar's value in these markets. The Fed maintains close relations with foreign central banks in pursuit of common goals of international financial order.

REGULATION AND SUPERVISION OF MEMBER BANKS

The Fed performs important regulatory and supervisory functions regarding the structure of the banking system in the United States and its domestic and foreign operations. The regulatory function includes formulating and promulgating rules and regulations for the conduct of banking. The Fed's responsibilities also encompass the overseeing of measures to ensure the soundness of individual banks and the monitoring of actions that affect the structure of the banking system, specifically bank mergers and acquisitions.

The regulatory and supervisory structure of the U.S. banking system is unique in the world. There are three federal bodies and 50 state agencies concerned with the functioning of this system. At the federal level, in addition to the Federal Reserve System, the Federal Deposit Insurance Corporation (F.D.I.C.) and the Comptroller of the Currency have some measures of responsibility for supervising and regulating commercial banks. The obvious potential for inefficiency that such overlapping responsibilities creates has been handled by various cooperative arrangements among the federal and state agencies. Thus the Comptroller has primary responsibility for national banks, the Fed focuses on state member banks, and the F.D.I.C. has the principal supervisory responsibility for insured nonmember state banks. The examining function is allocated in this fashion among the federal agencies, with the Fed and F.D.I.C. coordinating examinations of state-chartered banks with the various state banking authorities.

The Fed and Banking Structure

The Federal Reserve Board of Governors has responsibility for reviewing and approving (or disapproving) certain bank merger proposals and all bank holding company acquisitions.

For proposed mergers, jurisdiction is established by the charter status of the resulting banks: if a national bank, the Comptroller of the Currency; if a state-chartered member bank, the Fed; and if a nonmember insured state bank, the F.D.I.C. Merger review policy and procedures, as well as jurisdiction, are dictated by the Bank Merger Act of 1960.

The Fed's responsibility for bank holding companies is worthy of special note. In a 1970 amendment of the statute that gave the Fed this responsibility (the Bank Holding Company Act of 1956), a bank holding company was defined as any company that (1) directly or indirectly controls 25 percent of the voting shares of a bank; (2) controls the election of a majority of a bank's directors; or (3) controls the management or policies of a bank. This amendment limited bank holding company activities to those "closely related to banking" and gave the Fed authority to define the range of such activities.

Bank holding companies must register with the Fed and file periodic reports with the Board of Governors. Board approval must be obtained to acquire more than 5 percent of the shares of either additional banks or nonbanking companies. In the case of nonbanking companies, only certain types of companies, those involved in designated banking-related activities, are eligible for acquisition by bank holding companies. In reviewing such requests, the Board considers the potential effect of the acquisition on present and future competition, the financial condition of the banks controlled by the holding company, and the impact on availability of banking and bank-related services to the public.

The Board also has statutory responsibilities relating to international operations of member banks. The Fed must approve the establishment of foreign branches and subsidiaries, and it regulates their operations. International activities of U.S. banks will be discussed in Chapters 19 and 20.

SUMMARY

The Federal Reserve System performs functions of vital importance to the American economy. As this nation's central bank, it has the basic responsibility for maintaining money and credit conditions that are consistent with sustainable economic growth, price stability, and a strong dollar in the foreign exchange markets. The Fed controls monetary and credit aggregates by means of open-market operations and changes in reserve requirement ratios, and by controlling the cost and volume of its lending to depository institutions. The Fed also exercises various regulatory and supervisory powers over member banks with the objective of maintaining a sound and competitive banking system.

The major components of the Fed are the member banks (which technically "own" the Federal Reserve Banks), the 12 Federal Reserve Banks, the Board of Governors, and the Federal Open Market Committee (FOMC). Fewer than two out of five U.S. banks are presently members of the system, but member banks account for about 70 percent of total bank deposits. All national banks must belong to the Federal Reserve System, but many state banks have not chosen to join because membership long entailed holding a significant portion of their assets in nonearning required reserves. The Depository Institutions Deregulation and Monetary Control Act of 1980 greatly changed the cost-benefit equation of membership versus nonmembership in the Fed. This law mandated uniform reserve requirements for all depository institutions while also making Fed services and the discount window available to nonmember institutions.

The Board of Governors, rather than the regional banks, is the seat of power in the Fed. The various banks in the system essentially carry out Board policy, perform various operating functions, and serve as centers of economic information and research. The FOMC is also a highly significant entity in the Federal Reserve System because of the status of open-market operations as the principal tool of monetary policy.

The Fed makes extensive use of *open-market operations* to offset undesired temporary changes in the level of depository institution reserves. These so-called defensive operations serve to minimize the effects on reserves of such disturbances as seasonal shifts in the demand for credit and the amount of currency in circulation, cyclical changes in Federal Reserve float, and U.S. Treasury operations. *Dynamic* open-market operations, on the other hand, are the manifestation of an economic policy goal of the Fed: to restrict growth in money and credit aggregates when inflation is the target, and to ease them when the objective is economic expansion.

Changes in reserve requirements (aside from "structural" changes, as in the 1972 and 1980 revisions) are used only in the "dynamic" sense. Increases in reserve requirements serve to tighten money and credit, both by increasing the amount of bank reserves that are immobilized as required reserves and by lowering the ratio. This is an extremely powerful policy tool, which is used sparingly and the implementation of which is eased by appropriate use of open-market operations.

The *discount window* is something of an anachronism, but it still provides the Fed with a ready and convenient means of serving as "lender of last resort" during periods of financial stress for individual institutions and the financial system. In general, institutions are discouraged from using Fed borrowings as a continuing source of funds.

In its policy operations, the Fed has employed a variety of "targets" at different times. It has recently shifted from a focus on the Federal funds rate to reserves as "operating targets." In recent years, the FOMC has increasingly emphasized the rates of growth in monetary and credit aggregates as policy goals.

In addition to its function of monetary control, the Fed has the responsibility for monitoring the financial health of member banks (with the Comptroller of the Currency actually assuming this role for national banks), administering various regulations governing the financial system, and reviewing applications for bank mergers and for acquisitions by bank holding companies.

QUESTIONS

1. How did this nation's dual system of both national and state banks evolve? What is the relationship of this banking structure to membership in the Federal Reserve system?

2. What is meant by the term "an elastic money supply"? Is the provision of an "elastic" money supply an objective of Federal Reserve policy today?

3. What problems of the money and banking system of the United States led to the establishment of the Federal Reserve System?

4. Describe the organization and structure of the Federal Reserve System.

5. Why have many state banks chosen not to be members of the Federal Reserve System?

6. What are the principal responsibilities of the Board of Governors of the Federal Reserve System?

7. What are "open-market operations"? Describe their nature and purpose.

8. Why does the Fed exercise "administrative restraint" on the use of the discount window?

9. Evaluate and discuss the following statement: "Open market operations have emerged as the Fed's principal monetary policy tool, because the discount mechanism is too weak and changes in reserve requirements are too powerful."

10. Describe how the responsibility for bank regulation and supervision is assigned in the United States.

REFERENCES

Board of Governors of the Federal Reserve System, *Federal Reserve System: Purposes and Functions,* Washington, D.C.

————, "Monetary Aggregates and Money Market Conditions in Open Market Policy," *Federal Reserve Bulletin,* February 1971, pp. 79–104.

————, "The Depository Institutions Deregulation and Monetary Control Act of 1980," *Federal Reserve Bulletin,* September 1980, pp. 444–453.

Cacy, J.A., "Reserve Requirements and Monetary Control," Federal Reserve Bank of Kansas City, *Monthly Review,* May 1976, pp. 3–13.

Laidler, David, "The Definition of Money," *Journal of Money, Credit, and Banking,* August 1969, pp. 508–525.

Pierce, James L., and Thomas D. Thompson, "Some Issues in Controlling the Stock of Money," *Controlling Monetary Aggregates II: The Implementation,* Federal Reserve Bank of Boston, 1972.

Part III

The Determination, Structure, and Significance of Interest Rates

Chapter 8

The Level of Interest Rates

This chapter discusses the factors that influence the "pure" or basic interest rate. This "pure" or basic interest rate may be thought of as only the cost of "renting" money, without consideration of the default risk incurred by the lender, the administrative and processing costs involved in the lending process, or any of the many other factors influencing interest rates, which are discussed in Chapters 9 and 10. Although there is no such thing as "the" interest rate, and in fact, there are thousands of different rates that exist at the same time in financial markets, the concept is useful in understanding the role of interest rates in an economy. And even though there *are* thousands of different interest rates, these rates do tend to rise and fall together.

In the present chapter we discuss initially the role of "the" interest rate as an allocator of financial resources. We then present a discussion of the relationship between the interest rate on a fixed-income security (bond, mortgage, etc.) and the price of that security. This very simple relationship is a frequent source of confusion among students of financial markets. We then discuss the underlying economic factors that determine the "pure" rate, using the "loanable funds" explanation of the interest rate. Finally, we trace through an interest rate cycle, again using the loanable funds explanation.

THE INTEREST RATE AS AN ALLOCATING DEVICE

The interest rate is the price of money: the price of renting the use of the resources that money commands for a specified period of time. As with any price determined by the free interplay of supply and demand in a market economy, the price of money—the interest rate—plays a vital role in the allocation of resources and in the decision-making of consumers and businesses. For example, an increase in the interest rate provides additional incentives for individuals and others to postpone current consumption (save) and thereby free resources for investment. Government policies intended to expand the volume of saving should aim at increasing the attractiveness of saving by increasing the return to saving—the interest rate.[1]

The significant role of interest rates as an allocating device is particularly evident when we recognize the large number of different rates that exist in the financial marketplace. In this environment, *relative* interest rates become vital in affecting the allocation of financial resources. For example, if one sector of the economy has exceptionally profitable investment opportunities, it will be able to offer higher returns on its securities in order to attract funds. These higher returns will serve as a signal to the marketplace. Investors will divert funds from other, lower-return investments into the area that now offers the higher returns. Financial resources (and thus command over real resources) will flow from low- to high-return investment projects. Individual borrowers and lenders acting in their own self-interest—borrowers seeking to attract funds to invest in high-profit opportunities and investors seeking the highest return possible consistent with an acceptable risk level—produce a funds allocation that is consistent with the community interest. Funds are allocated from low- to high-priority areas not by any government bureaucracy but by the impersonal market mechanism acting through relative differences in the price of money (the interest rate).

YIELDS AND PRICES

It is important to understand the fundamental *inverse* relationship between the price of a fixed-income instrument and the yield on that instrument. It is also important to understand how the prices of fixed-income instruments change as yields change and how the relationship between price changes and yield changes is affected by the maturity of the fixed-income instrument. Before we discuss these relationships, however, it will be useful to define a few terms. For illustration we choose a bond, but the illustration would be equally valid for any fixed-income instrument.

A bond is defined as a fixed-income instrument because it offers the investor a fixed cash flow—payment of interest in a specified amount at a specified time and repayment of

---

1. The return that is relevant to the choice between present and future consumption is the return net of taxes and after adjustment for any loss of purchasing power due to inflation. We should also note that many factors other than the net return on savings influence the amount individuals choose to save.

principal at maturity. Most bonds are offered in $1000 denominations (par) and carry a fixed cash payment that is determined by multiplying the rate of interest stated on the bond itself, known as the *coupon rate* or stated rate, by the $1000 principal amount.[2] For example, a bond quoted as a 5 due in 1993 is a 5-percent bond (coupon rate), will mature in 1993 (the investor will be repaid the principal amount of $1000 in 1993), and will pay the investor $50 annually (5 percent times $1000) for the life of the bond. The coupon rate and hence the cash flow to the bondholder is specified at the time of the initial sale of the bond in the primary market and remains unchanged during the life of the bond.

Current Yield and Yield to Maturity

There are a number of ways of describing the yield on a bond. The two most common designations are the *current yield* (CY) and the *yield to maturity* (YTM). The current yield is simply the cash flow each year received by the investor (interest payment) divided by the current market price of the bond. Mathematically, the current yield is given by Eq. (8.1),

$$\text{Current yield (CY)} = \text{Interest/Price,} \qquad (8.1)$$

and the current yield on the 5 due in 1993 is 10 percent *if the price of the bond in the secondary market is 500.*[3] In this case, the bond is known as a *discount bond,* that is, a bond that sells below its par or principal value ($1000 in this and most other cases). Conversely, if the bond sells above its par value, it is known as a *premium bond.*

Though useful in some instances, the current yield is inadequate in describing the return to the investor since it ignores the return associated with the difference between the purchase price and the par or principal value of the bond at maturity. For example, in the situation illustrated above, the investor would have purchased the bond at $500 and yet would receive $1000 at maturity. In this case the investor's "true" yield would clearly exceed the current yield. Conversely, if the price of the bond in the secondary market exceeded par ($1100, for example), then the investor would pay $1100 today but would receive only $1000 at maturity. The difference between the investment ($1100) and par ($1000) would reduce the "true" yield to the investor.

A more accurate measure of the return on a bond is the yield to maturity, which takes into account the periodic interest payments, the price paid for the bond, *and* the gain or loss to the investor at the maturity of the bond. This measure is called the yield to maturity because *it assumes that the purchased bond is held until maturity.* It is the rate of return that equates the present value of the cash flows from the bond (interest and principal) with the current price of the bond. Mathematically, the yield to maturity on a bond is given by Eq. (8.2),

---

2. Most corporate and U.S. government bonds are offered in $1000 units, but most issues of state and local governments are in $5000 minimum denominations.

3. Since we are discussing the rate of interest independent of default-risk characteristics of a financial instrument, the rise in the current yield above the coupon rate might be due to a rise in the general level of interest rates since the time the bond was brought to market initially.

$$P' = I_1/(1 + r)^1 + I_2/(1 + r)^2 + \cdots + I_n/(1 + r)^n + P''_n/1 + r)^n, \qquad (8.2)$$

where P' = price of the bond, I = interest payments, P''_n = par or principal value, n = number of periods until maturity, and r = yield to maturity.

In the situation discussed above—the 5 due in 1993—if we assume that the bond was purchased in 1982 at a price of $500, the yield to maturity would approximate 14 percent.[4] We should note here that the current yield of 10 percent was raised to 14 percent by the gain to the investor resulting from purchasing the bond below par (at a discount of $500) and yet receiving par value of $1000 at maturity.

The yield to maturity may be obtained without these calculations by the use of bond tables, which list the yield to maturity for any bonds, given the coupon rate, price, and maturity of the bond. For example, in Table 8.1, the yield to maturity for 6-percent coupon rate bonds maturing in 30, 31, and 32 years is given for different prices. Hence a 6-percent coupon bond that matures in 32 years and sells at a price of $83.99 per 100 bond would carry a yield to maturity of 7.30 percent. However, if one needs only an approximation, Eq. 8.3 will generally provide a useable estimate of the yield to maturity on a bond.

$$\text{YTM} = \frac{I \pm \dfrac{(\text{Par}) - (\text{Price})}{n}}{\dfrac{(\text{Par}) + (\text{Price})}{2}}, \qquad (8.3)$$

where YTM = yield to maturity, I = the interest payment, Par = par or principal value of the bond, Price = market price of the bond, and n = number of years to maturity.

In our illustration, the yield to maturity in 1982 on the 5 due in 1993 with a market price of 500 is approximately:

$$\text{YTM} = \frac{50 + \dfrac{(1000 - 500)}{11}}{\dfrac{(1000 + 500)}{2}} = \frac{50 + 45.45}{750} = 12.7 \text{ percent.}$$

We should point out that the yield to maturity as calculated here is often referred to as the *promised* rate. It is the promised rate because it is the rate the borrower implicitly promises to pay to the lender, given the coupon rate, price, and maturity of the financial instrument. Since in this discussion we are assuming that there is no default risk (that all promises will be kept), the investor who purchases the bond and holds it until maturity is assured of actually realizing the promised rate (i.e., the realized rate and the promised rate will be the same). In the real world, of course, where default risk actually exists and where promises are not always kept, the investor might realize less than the promised yield.[5]

---

4. For simplicity, we have assumed that the interest payments are made annually. In fact, interest payments on most bonds are made semiannually. There will be then twice as many *interest periods* (n) as years to maturity, and interest payments (I) for each six-month period will be used in the formula.

5. Much more will be said in Chapter 10 about the influence of default risk on the interest rate on a fixed-income instrument.

However, if the security is held until maturity, the investor can never achieve a return higher than the promised yield.[6]

Table 8.1   Yield to maturity for 6-percent-coupon, 30-, 31-, and 32-year bonds at different prices

	Price, $		
Yield to maturity, %	30-year bond	31-year bond	32-year bond
4.75	119.88	120.18	120.46
5.05	114.60	114.80	115.00
5.30	110.46	110.60	110.73
6.00	100.00	100.00	100.00
6.20	97.29	97.26	97.23
6.45	94.06	94.00	93.94
6.75	90.41	90.31	90.22
6.95	88.09	87.98	87.87
7.30	84.26	84.12	83.99
7.75	79.73	79.56	79.40

Source: *Comprehensive Bond Value Tables*, (Boston: Financial Publishing Company, 1958).

Relationship Between Yield and Price

Most bonds are originally sold at par. Over time, however, the market price of the bond may rise above or fall below par for a variety of reasons. One especially important reason concerns changes in interest rate levels. It should be clear from Eq. (8.2) that the price of a bond and the yield to maturity on the bond move inversely. In fact, they are mirror images of each other. Since I is fixed for the life of the bond, once r is known, P is known, and conversely, once P is known, r is known. This mathematical truism may seem simple enough, but the *inverse* relationship between interest rates and bond prices is frequently confusing. Yet it forms the basis of two important observations about the behavior of bond prices and yields:

1. *Bond prices and yields move inversely—when the general level of interest rates rises, the prices of existing bonds fall. Conversely, when the general level of interest rates falls, the prices of existing bonds rise.* Hence investors in existing bonds are likely to suffer capital losses from depreciating prices in periods of rising interest rates. On the other hand, investors are likely to realize capital gains from the appreciation of their bond portfolios in periods of falling rates. This relationship, often referred to as "interest rate" risk, is quite evident in Table 8.2, which illustrates the price of a 32-year bond with a 6-percent coupon but with different yield-to-maturity assumptions. At a yield to maturity of 6 percent, which

6. If the investor does not hold the security until maturity, but instead sells it at a price exceeding par value—perhaps due to generally declining interest rates—the realized yield may exceed the promised yield.

Table 8.2   Price of 6-percent-coupon, 32-year-maturity bond at different interest rates

Yield to maturity, %	Price, $
8.5	727.20
8	770.30
7	872.90
6	1000.00
5	1158.80
4.75	1204.60

Source: *Comprehensive Bond Value Tables* (Boston: Financial Publishing Company, 1958).

is equal to the coupon rate, the bond would sell at a price of $1000. However, at an 8.5-percent yield to maturity, the price of the bond would be only $727.20. Hence an investor who purchased the bond at par when interest rates were 6 percent would stand to lose more than 25 percent of the total investment if interest rates rose above 8 percent. Of course, if interest rates fell to 4.75 percent in this case, the investor would have an opportunity for a capital gain of about $204.60. Again, we emphasize that this price change has nothing to do with changes in the credit quality of the bond (likelihood of payment of interest and principal); it is solely attributable to changes in the general level of interest rates.

2. *For a given change in interest rates, the prices of long-term bonds will change more than the prices of short-term bonds.* If the general *level* of interest rates rises, the prices of all bonds will fall, but the prices of long-term bonds will fall more than the prices of short-term bonds. Conversely, if the general level of interest rates falls, the prices of all bonds will rise, but the prices of long-term bonds will rise more than the prices of short term bonds. Perhaps the best way to understand this relationship is to examine Eq. (8.3). In that equation, it is apparent that raising or lowering the yield to maturity (YTM) by a given amount requires a greater change in price for a longer-term than a shorter-term bond. This generalization implies greater price variability for longer-term bonds and hence greater risk to the investor that these bonds will have to be sold at a loss if they are sold prior to maturity; that is, interest rate risk is greater for longer-term than for shorter-term bonds.

The significance of this generalization is reduced to some degree by the observed fact that when overall interest rates rise, short-term rates usually rise more than long-term rates, and when overall rates fall, short-term rates usually fall more than long-term rates. Yet it remains true that price variability on long-term bonds is considerably greater than on short-term bonds.

The differential impact of interest rate movements on the prices of bonds with varying maturities is shown in Table 8.3. This table provides the prices of a 6-percent coupon bond with 8-, 16-, and 32-year maturities under different interest rate assumptions. At a 6-percent yield to maturity, all bonds sell at par. As the required interest rate demanded in the market

Table 8.3 Price of 6-percent-coupon, 32-year-maturity, 16-year-maturity, and 8-year-maturity bonds at different interest rates

Yield to maturity	Price of 32-year bond, $	Price of 16-year bond, $	Price of 8-year bond, $
7.5	819.7	861.6	911.0
7	872.9	904.7	939.5
6	1000.0	1000.0	1000.0
5	1158.8	1109.2	1065.3
4	1359.2	1234.7	1135.8

Source: *Comprehensive Bond Value Tables* (Boston: Financial Publishing Company, 1958).

increases, the prices of all the bonds fall as expected, but for given increases in rates, the prices of the longer-term bonds fall more than the prices of the shorter-term bonds. For example, if the required yield to maturity increases from 6 to 7.5 percent, the price of the 8-year bond falls by about 9 percent (from $1000 to $911), but the price of the 32-year bond falls by almost 20 percent (from $1000 to $819.70). The price decline for the 16-year bond is more than for the 8-year bond but less than for the 32-year bond. This relationship also holds for periods of declining rates. The prices of all bonds rise, but the prices of long-term bonds rise more than the prices of short-term bonds. For example, if rates fall from 6 to 4 percent, the price of the 8-year bonds increases by about 13 percent (from $1000 to $1135.80) while the price of 32-year bonds rises more than 35 percent (from $1000 to $1359.20). Again the price rise of the 16-year bond is intermediate between the 8- and 32-year bonds.

THE LOANABLE FUNDS THEORY

Our discussion to this point has centered on the importance of the interest rate in allocating financial resources and on the relationships between the prices of fixed-income instruments and the interest rates on those instruments. However, to participants in the financial system—whether as individuals or as managers of business firms—it is vitally important to understand the *basic determinants of interest rate movements.* As the discussion of the impact of changes in interest rates on the prices of bonds made clear, the potential for gain or loss to investors in fixed-income instruments as the result of interest rate changes is substantial.

We now turn our attention to the underlying factors that produce interest rate increases or decreases. Although there are a number of different approaches to explaining the determinants of interest rate changes—each one emphasizing a different aspect of the process—our discussion is in terms of the *loanable funds theory,* in which the supply and demand for loanable funds (i.e., lending and borrowing) determines the interest rate. This explanation emphasizes the flow of funds by suppliers of loanable funds (lenders) and the flow of funds by the demanders of loanable funds (borrowers). It is a monetary theory of interest, since it focuses on the financial factors that influence interest rates (i.e., borrowing and lending). In addition, the loanable funds theory is a short-run, partial-equilibrium explanation, in which some factor or factors produce a change in the interest rate, but in which there is no analysis of the long-run impact of this change in the interest rate on the level of employment, income, and production or of the resulting impact of changes in employment, income, and production on the interest rate. Rather, the loanable funds theory focuses on the factors that underly the supply and demand schedules for loanable funds and on their interaction.

Supply of Loanable Funds

The supply of loanable funds provided to the marketplace is determined by two basic factors: (1) the amount of saving by households, businesses, and governments; and (2) the amount of new money created by the commercial banking system. We must therefore explain each of these different sources of loanable funds to provide an understanding of their influences on the interest rate.

In our explanation of the supply of loanable funds and also of the demand for loanable funds, we must keep in mind that we are dealing with supply and demand *schedules*. These schedules are "what if" relationships; that is, *if* the interest rate is at a certain level, then the quantity supplied or demanded is a certain amount. At a different interest rate, the *quantity supplied* (and *quantity demanded*) may be different, but we are moving along a given supply or demand curve, and the change in the quantities demanded and supplied result from the change in the rate of interest. In contrast, a change in supply or demand would involve a *shift in the schedule* whereby more or less would be supplied at all interest rate levels.

Saving

As discussed earlier, saving refers to the postponement of current consumption. The decision to save is the decision to forgo current consumption in order to have a larger quantity of consumption in the future. Households (individuals) save for a variety of reasons—the proverbial "rainy day," education of children, and other reasons—but there is little evidence to suggest that the quantity of loanable funds supplied through saving is markedly influenced by the level of the interest rate. A higher interest rate represents a greater reward to the saver for postponing current consumption and thus might be expected to produce a higher quantity of saving for some individuals. Yet for the individual who has a target level of desired wealth, the higher interest rate might lead to a reduction in saving. In the view of most observers, the quantity of savings supplied by individuals is principally determined by the level of income, and it is influenced to a lesser degree by the level of interest rates.[7]

This relatively small impact of changes in interest rates on the quantity of saving by individuals is probably equally true for businesses and governments. Business saving refers to the net income after taxes of the firm, less any cash dividends—i.e., retained earnings. Changes in business net income reflect changes in sales and costs, whereas the decision to

---

7. Of course, changes in the level of income will change the amount of desired saving at each level of interest rates.

distribute cash dividends reflects management judgment about internal investment opportunities, as well as management perceptions about the impact of dividend changes on the
stock price of the firm. There is little reason to believe that the volume of saving at business
firms is strongly influenced by the level of interest rates.

For governments, the volume of saving is defined as the difference between revenues
and expenditures, such that saving exists when revenues exceed expenditures (a budget
surplus). Completely separate from the fact that—at least at the federal level—
governmental units in the United States have seldom had budget surpluses in recent years,
there is again little reason to believe that the volume of saving is strongly influenced by the
interest rate. At the federal level, the budget surplus or deficit reflects the joint interaction of
fiscal policy—changes in tax and expenditure policies designed to achieve broad macroeconomic objectives—and the level of economic activity. At the state and local levels, the
budget surplus or deficit is influenced by the demand for services by local residents, as well
as by the strength of the local economy.

To summarize, saving (the postponement of current consumption) may be done by
households, businesses, and governments. The volume of saving of each of these units is
influenced by a variety of factors, of which the interest rate is only one. As a result, we might
expect that the relationship between the interest rate and the volume of saving would appear
as in Fig. 8.1—a mildly positive relationship between the interest rate and the volume of
saving. For example, at an interest rate of r, the volume of saving would be Q, whereas at the
higher interest rate of r', the volume of saving would be only a slightly higher Q'. The
responsiveness of saving to changes in interest rates is quite small. *Relatively large
increases in interest rates are required to produce modest increases in saving.*

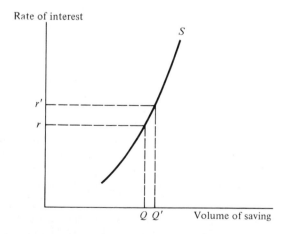

Fig. 8.1   The interest rate and the volume of saving

New Money

Although the volume of saving is the principal source of loanable funds in financial markets, the supply of loanable funds may be increased through the creation of new money beyond the amount made possible by current saving. The amount of money created is determined jointly by the actions of the commercial banking system and the central bank—the Federal Reserve System in the United States. Commercial banks use any excess reserves to make loans and purchase securities and create money (demand deposits) through the credit creation process. However, the ability of commercial banks to create money is limited by the Federal Reserve through the use of its monetary policy tools of open-market operations, reserve-requirement changes, and discount-rate changes.

Commercial banks are private, profit-seeking, business enterprises. In contrast, the Federal Reserve is a quasi-public organization, whose primary function is to control the supply and cost of money in order to achieve broad macroeconomic goals. There is little evidence that either the Fed or the commercial banks are substantially influenced in the money creation process by the level of interest rates. The principal factor that determines the volume of new money created by the banking system is the amount of reserves, and the principal factor that determines the amount of reserves is Federal Reserve monetary policy. Neither of these factors should be directly influenced by the level of interest rates.[8]

We may therefore draw the relationship between the amount of new money created and the interest rate as shown in Fig. 8.2. The volume of new money is thought to be completely unrelated to the interest rate level—at r the volume of new money supplied is Q, and at the higher interest rate r', the amount of new money created is the same Q. Essentially, changes in the money supply are determined by factors other than the interest rate.

In summary, the supply of loanable funds is the sum of the supply of savings and the amount of new money created.[9] The reader may imagine adding horizontally at every interest rate level the supply schedules in Figs. 8.1 and 8.2 in order to obtain the supply schedule in Fig. 8.3. This supply schedule of loanable funds (the amount of lending at each interest rate level) may be increased by either an increase in the desire to save by businesses, households, or governments or by the creation of more new money by the commercial banking system. Conversely, the supply of loanable funds may fall because of a reduction in the desire to save or a reduction in the amount of new money created.

---

8. This is something of an oversimplification. Higher interest rate levels encourage banks to use their reserves more fully, so there may be some positive relationship between the interest rate level and the quantity of money created on any given reserve base.

9. The amount of new money created is relatively insensitive to the level of interest rates, but the amount of these funds actually provided to the loanable funds market can be affected by the amount of hoarding or dishoarding. At relatively low rates, economic participants may hoard a portion of the new money (since the opportunity cost of holding money is low), whereas at high rates they may dishoard by reducing their existing money balances (since the opportunity cost of holding money is high). As a result, the supply of loanable funds may be less than the combined supply of savings and new money at low interest rates and more than the combined supply in periods of high interest rates.

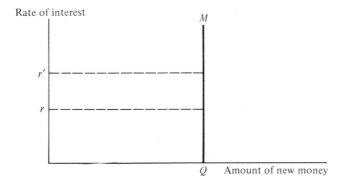

Fig. 8.2   The interest rate and new money creation

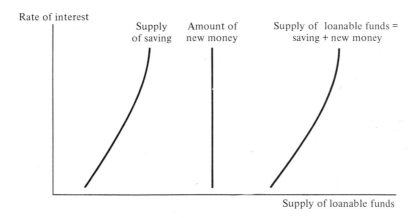

Fig. 8.3   The interest rate and the supply of loanable funds

The Demand For Loanable Funds

The demand for loanable funds is composed of the demand by individuals, businesses, and governments. We will discuss each of these separately and then put them together to form the demand function for loanable funds.

Consumer Demand

Individuals desire to borrow for a variety of reasons.[10] Perhaps the most significant reason is to acquire homes, automobiles, and consumer durable goods. The reliance of consumers on

---

10. Since households are the principal supply sector, it is also possible to subtract consumer borrowing from household saving and to talk about households only from a supply perspective.

funds borrowed through financial markets has become an accepted practice in the post–
World War II period. Indeed, there is little thought given by most consumers to the
possibility of accumulating enough savings before purchasing a home or a car. In the
inflationary environment of recent years, the emphasis has instead been on purchasing
goods before their price increases and financing such purchases with borrowed funds, which
can be repaid in depreciated dollars. In view of these strong motivating factors, the
responsiveness of the quantity demanded of loanable funds by consumers to interest rate
changes is generally thought to be relatively small. At the range of interest rate levels
historically experienced in the United States, higher interest rates appear to produce only a
modest reduction in the quantity demanded of loanable funds by consumers.[11]

Business Demand

Business demand for loanable funds is influenced by a variety of factors but principally
reflects investment spending for inventory and plant and equipment. Business investment in
inventory holdings is highly volatile—rising by billions of dollars in some periods and
falling by billions of dollars in others—and it is primarily determined by the differences
between expected (planned) sales and actual (realized) sales. In periods when actual sales
are greater than expected sales, inventory holdings fall. In periods when actual sales fall
short of planned or expected sales, inventory holdings rise. These undesired movements in
inventory holdings must be financed, and it is usual to finance them by tapping the market
for loanable funds (generally short-term funds). Not surprisingly, given the fact that many
of these changes in inventory holdings do not reflect the plans of business management, the
demand for loanable funds to finance changes in inventory levels is thought to respond only
slightly to changes in the interest rate.

   The other major determinant of business demand for loanable funds—expenditures for
plant and equipment purchases—reflects more significantly the long-run planning function.
Decisions to add to a plant or to install labor-saving equipment or other such plant and
equipment decisions are important for the success or failure of most business organizations.
Yet the profitability projections necessary to evaluate these potential purchases are subject
to wide margins of error. As a result, the required return on investment used by many firms
to justify the commitment of funds for plant expansion or other major investments is often
quite high, substantially higher than the cost of borrowed funds. As a result, movements in
the interest rate are likely to produce only relatively small changes in the quantity of
loanable funds demanded.

Government Demand

The demand for loanable funds by governmental units is usually divided for discussion
purposes into the demand by the federal government and the demand by state and local

---

11. There was some evidence, however, that consumer demand for loanable funds was more sensitive to
interest rates, particularly for housing credit, in early 1980, when rates reached then unprecedented levels.

governments. This distinction is an important one since the motives for state and local government borrowing tend to be similar to those of the private sector, whereas the motives underlying federal government borrowing decisions tend to be quite different from those of the private sector. The demand for loanable funds by state and local governments is basically a function of population growth in the local area, which expands demand for local government services. For example, the growth in population requires expansion of roads and sewage facilities. These expenditures, which are usually financed with borrowings from the loanable funds market, may be temporarily postponed if conditions in the credit markets are unfavorable, but they must be undertaken within a reasonably short period of the increased demand. As a result, even though there does appear to be responsiveness in the quantity of loanable funds demanded by state and local governments to changes in the interest rate, the impact of rising or falling interest rates is thought to be quite small.

Federal government demand for loanable funds is thought to be *completely* insensitive to changes in the interest rate. The amount of funds the federal government must borrow is determined by the overall balance of the federal budget, which in turn reflects the fiscal policy of the nation. Fiscal policy itself is designed to achieve broad macroeconomic goals and is not thought to be affected in any direct way by the level of interest rates. In short, Congress determines the budget surplus or deficit (almost always *deficit* in recent years), and the Treasury department must finance that deficit, regardless of the level of interest rates.

To summarize, the demand for loanable funds is made up of the separate demands by consumers, businesses, and governments. Although the interest sensitivity of each of these basic components of the demand for loanable funds varies, it is generally accepted that the overall responsiveness of the quantity of loanable funds demanded to changes in interest rates is relatively small. This is shown in Fig. 8.4, where the demand for loanable funds is drawn as downward sloping, indicating that there is an increase in the demand for loanable funds as the interest rate declines, but the demand curve is drawn as relatively inelastic, indicating that the responsiveness of the quantity of loanable funds demanded to interest rate movements is fairly limited.

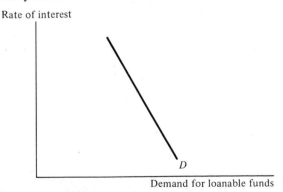

Fig. 8.4 Demand for loanable funds

Two other features of the demand of loanable funds should be discussed: the *volatility of the demand schedule* and the *importance of availability*. The quantity of loanable funds demanded is relatively insensitive to changes in interest rates, but the *amount* of loanable funds used by consumers, businesses, and governments varies widely. These large fluctuations reflect sharp changes (shifts) in the demand function itself. For example, in a period of rising inflationary expectations, businesses and consumers may desire to sharply increase their borrowings at any interest rate. This tendency is shown by the shift of the demand function from D to D' in Fig. 8.5. In periods of pessimism about the future of the economy, on the other hand, businesses and consumers may sharply curtail their borrowings at any given interest rate, as shown by D'' in Fig. 8.5. This immense volatility of the demand function for loanable funds is of substantial importance in understanding movements in interest rates over the business cycle.

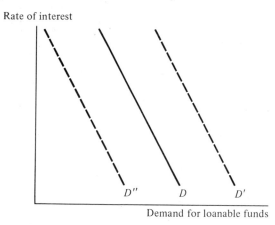

Fig. 8.5   Shifts in the demand for loanable funds

The second feature—the importance of availability—stems from the interest insensitivity of the demand function. If rising interest rates cannot be expected to curtail the demand for loanable funds, then the monetary authorities must supply some other means if monetary policy is to be used to counter inflationary booms. In the decades of the 1960s and 1970s the means chosen was availability, or nonprice rationing, rather than price (the interest rate). Instead of trying to curtail borrowing solely by increasing the price of money, the monetary authorities have concentrated during the post–World War II period primarily on reducing the availability of funds from financial intermediaries, which are, as discussed earlier, the principal purchasers of primary securities.

Supply and Demand for Loanable Funds

We are now in a position to show how the supply and demand functions for loanable funds jointly determine the interest rate. Within the loanable funds perspective, the interest rate (r) and the quantity of loanable funds bought and sold (Q) are determined by the interaction of the supply of loanable funds (lending) and the demand for loanable funds (borrowing). Given the demand and supply functions specified in Fig. 8.6, *r* and *Q* are equilibrium values. At an interest rate above *r*, the quantity of loanable funds supplied would exceed the quantity demanded. Lenders seeking to get rid of their excess funds would lower their price (the interest rate) until the quantity supplied and quantity demanded were equal. At an interest rate below *r*, the quantity of loanable funds demanded would exceed the quantity supplied. Borrowers competing for scarce loanable funds would then drive the interest rate higher. Only at *r* are the quantity supplied and the quantity demanded in balance.

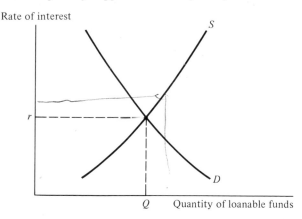

Fig. 8.6   Supply and demand of loanable funds

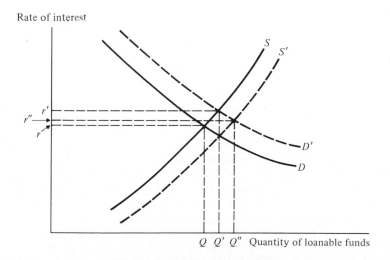

Fig. 8.7   Changes in the supply and demand for loanable funds

We can also explain *changes* in the interest rate through the loanable funds approach. For example, suppose that the demand for loanable funds shifted to D' in Fig. 8.7. This could occur because there was an increase in the demand for money at every interest rate level by consumers, businesses, or governments. In any case, the equilibrium interest rate would rise to r'. Conversely, suppose that the supply of loanable funds increased (a shift to the right of the supply schedule). This could result from a greater desire to save on the part of consumers, businesses, and governments, or an easy-money policy by the Federal Reserve, which allowed the banking system to expand the money supply. In this case, if the supply curve shifted to S', the interest rate would fall to r''. Using the loanable funds approach in this manner allows the financial analyst to predict and explain the impact of many diverse factors on the interest rate.

EXPLAINING AN INTEREST RATE CYCLE USING THE LOANABLE FUNDS THEORY

As discussed above, the loanable funds explanation of interest rates emphasizes the significance of three factors in leading to increases and decreases in "the" interest rate: (1) the volume of saving by individuals, businesses, and governments; (2) the amount of new money created; (3) the demand for funds by individuals, businesses, and governments. However, in any attempt to understand movements of interest rates over the business cycle, it is important to determine whether any of these factors is such as to be the major influence in bringing about changes in interest rates. Evaluating this issue with the use of actual financial data is difficult. The loanable funds theory, as with any theory, is an abstraction, since the theory deals with "what if" relationships, and since published financial data only approximate these abstractions. Yet it is often argued that the two dominant factors in explaining interest rate movements are changes in the demands for funds and changes in Federal Reserve monetary policy. We present below a brief discussion of interest rate movements in 1974 and 1975 and a basic explanation of rate movements during that period. We use 1974 and 1975 because those two years offer an illustration of an extremely rapid increase and decline in rates associated with a large change in the supply of and demand for loanable funds.

As indicated in Table 8.4, the period from the first quarter of 1973 through the last quarter of 1976 was one of sharp changes in rates. The interest rate on short-term government securities rose from 5.7 percent in the first quarter of 1973 to 8.2 percent in both the second and third quarters of 1974 and then receded to 4.7 percent in the fourth quarter of 1976. What caused these basic changes? The reasons are numerous, including a number of factors discussed in the following chapters, but two in particular are significant. First, there was a large change in the demand for funds, especially by business. Second, there were substantial changes in the supply of funds associated with changes in the money supply.

Demand and Supply of Funds

The demand for funds by business and other sectors increased sharply in the period of rising rates during 1973 and 1974. For example, total funds raised by nonfinancial sectors

Table 8.4   Interest rate on 3-month Treasury bill, 1973–1976

Period	Rate
1973	
I	5.7
II	6.6
III	8.3
IV	7.5
1974	
I	7.6
II	8.2
III	8.2
IV	7.4
1975	
I	5.7
II	5.4
III	6.3
IV	5.6
1976	
I	4.9
II	5.2
III	5.2
IV	4.7

Source: *Federal Reserve Bulletin*, vaious issues.

expanded from $151.0 billion in 1971 to $197.6 billion in 1973. A large portion of this growth in the demand for loanable funds represented a massive demand by businesses to finance large inventory accumulations, mostly accomplished by financing from commercial banks. Bank loans expanded by $34 billion in 1973, as compared with a growth of only $6 billion in 1971. Demand by consumers to finance the purchase of houses also expanded sharply. Home mortgage demand increased by $46 billion in 1973, as compared with only a $28 billion rise in 1971. Undoubtedly, these increases in the demand for loanable funds played a major role in the rise in interest rates in 1973 and 1974.

In contrast, both interest rates and the demand for loanable funds by businesses and consumers declined in 1975. For example, bank loans to businesses, which expanded by $34 billion in 1973, actually *declined* by $14 billion in 1975. This massive reduction in business demand for funds of almost $50 billion reflected the large inventory liquidation by businesses during the 1974–1975 recession. Demand for funds for mortgages also declined in 1975. Multifamily residential mortgages, which had expanded by $10 billion in 1973, showed no growth in 1975. Similarly, commercial mortgages, which grew $19 billion in 1973, increased by only $10 billion in 1975.

Increases in the money supply also play an important role in affecting the interest rate. In 1972, for example, the money supply expanded by a large $21.6 billion. Over the next two years, however, the money supply growth declined. Money increased only by $24.1

billion in 1973 and $8.5 billion in 1974, thereby curtailing the growth of the supply of loanable funds and contributing to an increase in the interest rate. However, beginning in 1975 and continuing through 1976, the growth rate of the money supply began to accelerate, thereby contributing to the declining rates of those two years.

It should be kept in mind, of course, that explaining these "real world" developments through the loanable funds approach ignores the influence of all the other factors that affect the relative pattern of yields in financial markets. For example, undoubtedly some of the interest rate movements in the 1973–1976 period reflect changes in inflationary expectations. For the first time in recent United States financial history, the rate of inflation reached the "double-digit" range in 1974. And of course, the largest economic decline since the depression of the 1930s undoubtedly affected the movements in yields during this period. In this as in the application of all simplified techniques, the financial analyst must recognize that there are numerous factors affecting financial development that are not accounted for in the basic models.

SUMMARY

"The" interest rate plays a vital role in the financial system in affecting the allocation of financial and real resources. Interest rates on fixed-income securities, such as bonds, may be measured either by the current yield or the yield to maturity. However measured, there exist certain basic relationships between interest rates and the prices of fixed-income securities. In particular, bond prices and interest rates or yields move inversely: when the general level of interest rates rises, the prices of existing bonds fall; when the general level of interest rates falls, the prices of existing bonds rise. Moreover, for a given change in interest rates, the prices of long-term bonds will change more than the prices of short-term bonds.

Of a number of ways of explaining interest rate movements, one approach commonly used by financial market analysts stresses borrowing and lending. This short-term, partial-equilibrium explanation focuses on the supply of saving as the basic determinant of the supply of loanable funds, the roles of the Federal Reserve and the commercial banking system in creating additional loanable funds, and the demand for borrowed funds by households, businesses, and governments. The interaction of the supply of loanable funds with the demand for them determines the equilibrium interest rate. Changes in interest rate levels, such as in the period from 1973 through 1976, may then be analyzed by looking at changes in the supply and demand for loanable funds.

Understanding the basic determinants of "the" interest rate and of movements in "the" interest rate over time is not easy. Yet such an understanding is vitally important to participants in financial markets, since the prices of financial assets are affected greatly by changes in the level of interest rates. The present chapter has presented a conceptual framework for organizing the various factors that influence interest rates. Yet this conceptual framework is necessarily abstract and simplified. We now turn our attention in the next two chapters to reducing the degree of abstraction in discussing the factors that influence interest rates. In Chapter 9 we explain how the time to maturity of a financial instrument affects the yield on the instrument, and in Chapter 10 we treat the influence of inflation, credit risk, and other factors.

QUESTIONS

1. Briefly explain how the interest rate may be viewed as an allocating device. In what ways do usury laws and regulations on rates paid for funds by financial institutions distort the role of interest rates as an allocating device?

2. Explain the relationship between interest rate changes and bond prices. If you expected interest rates to fall, would you want to hold bonds or money? Short-term or long-term bonds?

3. What is a premium bond? A discount bond? What causes the premium or discount?

4. In what way is the loanable funds theory a theory of borrowing and lending?

5. The interest elasticity of the demand for loanable funds is thought to be quite small. Of what significance is this for monetary policy?

6. Evaluate the interest sensitivity of each of the following.
  a) The supply of savings
  b) The supply of new money
  c) The demand for loanable funds

7. Using the loanable funds theory, explain the impact of each of the following on the interest rate.
  a) A decrease in the desire to save
  b) A shift to an "easy" money policy on the part of the Federal Reserve
  c) Increased profit opportunities on business investments

REFERENCES

Conard, Joseph, *An Introduction to the Theory of Interest* (Berkeley: University of California Press, 1959).

Culbertson, John M., *Money and Banking* (New York: McGraw Hill, 1972), Ch. 14.

Fisher, Irving, *The Theory of Interest Rates* (New York: Macmillan, 1930).

Homer, Sidney, *A History of Interest Rates* (New Brunswick, N.J.: Rutgers University Press, 1962).

Homer, Sidney, and Richard I. Johanneson, *The Price of Money* (New Brunswick, N.J.: Rutgers University Press, 1969).

Lutz, Frederick A., *The Theory of Interest,* 2nd ed. (New York: Aldine Press, 1960).

APPENDIX

THE LIQUIDITY PREFERENCE THEORY OF INTEREST RATE DETERMINATION

The "loanable funds" approach to interest rate determination focuses on supply and demand for loanable funds. An alternative approach, the "liquidity preference" view, focuses instead on the supply and demand for *money*. It is assumed that individuals inherently prefer money among all financial assets, since money can be used to make payments and is thus the most liquid of assets. Wealth holders are persuaded to hold financial assets other than money only because these nonmoney assets offer an interest return greater than that yielded by money (with both explicit and implicit returns on cash holdings being considered). Further, the greater the spread between the yields on nonmoney financial assets and money, the less the demand for money holdings and the greater the demand for other financial assets, and vice versa. The demand schedule for money can thus be depicted as a function of the rate of interest, as shown in Fig. 8A.1.

The amount of money that people wish to hold is also a function of the level of their spending, since money is used for payments. In turn, spending is determined by income.

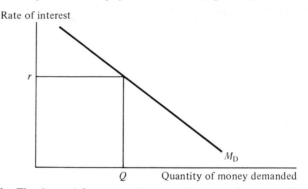

Fig. 8A.1   The demand for money (M_D) as a function of the rate of interest

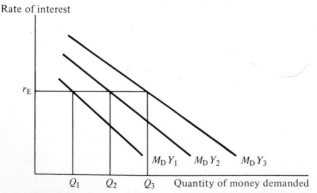

Fig. 8A.2   The demand for money as a function of the rate of interest and the level of income

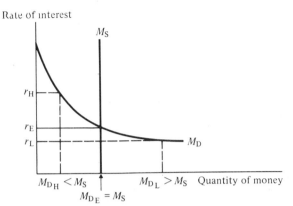

Fig. 8A.3   Interest rate determination according to the theory of liquidity preference

Thus the greater the income, the greater will be the quantity of money demanded at a given rate of interest, and vice versa. This relationship is depicted in Fig. 8A.2, where M_DY_1, M_DY_2, M_DY_3 represent the demand for money at the successively higher income levels Y_1, Y_2, and Y_3.

Thus for a given income level, say Y_2, and a given money supply, the rate of interest (r_E) is viewed as determined by the supply-demand equilibrium depicted in Fig. 8A.3, where M_s is the supply of money.[12]

The equilibrium interest rate, r_E, is obtained by actions of individuals seeking to maintain desired levels of cash balances. Since the amount of desired money holdings is a function of the rate of interest, there is only one rate of interest at which the demand for money balances is the same as the amount of the money supply. At a rate of interest *higher* than r_E, say r_H in Fig. 8A.3, individuals in the aggregate will be holding more money (M_s) than they desire (M_{D_H}) at that rate of interest (the total supply of money *must* be held by the public). To rid themselves of ''excess'' cash, individuals *purchase* interest-bearing financial assets, driving their prices up and their interest rates down. This occurs until the rate of interest falls to r_E, at which $M_{D_E}=M_s$.

The outcome, of course, is that the public still holds, in the aggregate, the same amount of money, but at the lower rate of interest, this is now the desired amount. On the other hand, if the interest rate is *lower* than r_E, say r_L in Fig. 8A.3, the public will be holding smaller money balances (M_s) than they desire (M_{D_L}) at that rate of interest. As a result, in order to obtain more cash in this situation, individuals *sell* interest-bearing securities, the aggregate effect of which is lower security prices and higher interest rates. The interest rate will thus rise to r_E, at which point desired cash holdings equal the supply of cash.

---

12. The *supply of* money, as well as the demand for money, can be viewed as responsive to the rate of interest. One reason for an interest-sensitive money supply function is the possibility that banks may hold smaller amounts of desired excess reserves as interest rates rise. However, the Fed can offset such a phenomenon (as it can do with any factor that induces money expansion) by use of its tools of monetary control.

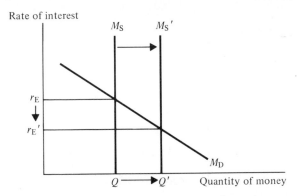

Fig. 8A.4   Effect of an increase in the money supply on the rate of interest

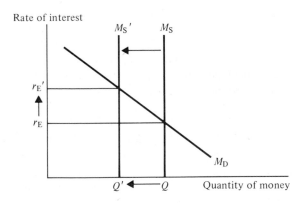

Fig. 8A.5   Effect of a decrease in the money supply on the rate of interest

A principal aspect of the liquidity preference model is that *changes in the money supply affect the rate of interest.* In the liquidity preference framework, with income and the price level assumed to be constant, an increase in the money supply will lower r_E, the equilibrium rate of interest (Fig. 8A.4), and a decrease in the money supply will raise r_E (Fig. 8A.5).

Figure 8A.6 serves as a summary depiction of interest rate determination according to the liquidity preference model. When the money supply is M_{S_1}, the rate of interest is r_1. As the money supply expands to M_{S_2} and M_{S_3}, the rate of interest falls to r_2 and r_3, respectively. The process by which interest rates fall as M_S expands can again be interpreted in terms of public preferences for money holdings relative to other financial assets, such as interest-bearing securities.[13] For example, as the money supply expands from M_{S_1} to M_{S_2}, individuals find themselves holding larger cash balances than they desire at interest rate r_1. As they seek to reduce money holdings by the purchase of securities, security prices rise and interest rates fall until a new equilibrium is established at interest rate r_2, where $M_D = M_{S_2}$.

---

13. Changes in interest rates also affect the level of desired holdings of *real* assets. Therefore individuals may increase their consumption and business firms may increase investment as interest rates decline, and vice versa.

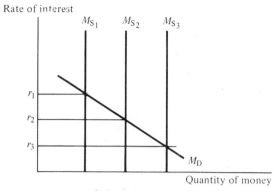

Figure 8A.6

This monetary view of interest rate determination, though having a measure of validity in the short run, ignores "feedback" from the real sector of the economy. Growth in the money supply has an impact on prices and production, although the *manner* and *degree* of impact are subjects of dispute. One "real" effect of lower interest rates due to an increased money supply is believed to be increased investment spending. The latter is likely to result in increased borrowing by investors (increase in *supply* of securities), which tends to *raise* interest rates. Further, if an increased money supply spurs inflation, inflationary pressures will cause interest rates to rise. Even more contrary to the liquidity preference model, if an increase in the money supply triggers expectations of inflationary pressures, an *anticipatory* rise in interest rates may result from a shift in the demand for money schedule.

Various limitations of the liquidity preference model stem from the fact that the demand-for-money schedule (M_D) is not constant:

1. It shifts with changes in income (and wealth) of the public. This complicates the analysis considerably, because changes in the rate of interest have a significant impact on income via its effect on saving and investment.

2. The demand for money is properly viewed as a demand for "real" money balances. It is a function of the quantity of goods and services that a given quantity of money will buy. Inflation reduces the purchasing power of money, and deflation increases it. Thus there is actually a different M_D schedule for every price level.

3. Further, *expectations* about the course of future price level changes, interest rate changes, and other economic events may cause shifts in the M_D schedule.

Finally, remember that although the monetary effect of interest rates in the discussion above has focused on the demand for money balances, the *velocity* of money varies inversely with the amount of money holdings. Thus interest elasticity of the demand for money necessarily implies interest elasticity of velocity.

How does the liquidity preference theory of interest rate determination compare with the loanable funds approach? In their general substance, the two approaches yield the same results. The principal difference between the two theories is one of methodology. The liquidity preference model is a "stock" theory, focusing on the rate of interest that will result in a given stock of money being held as a desired stock of cash balances. The loanable funds theory, on the other hand, focuses on the *flows* of funds in the financial system and the equilibrating action of the interest rate in equating the supply and demand of loanable funds. For the purpose of analyzing financial markets and institutions relative to the flow of funds in the financial system, the flow orientation and broader focus of the loanable funds approach make it a preferable framework.

Both approaches to interest rate determination are incomplete in the sense that they consider the financial sector without regard to changes in the real sector of the economy. In actuality, of course, events in the real sector are continuously impacting on the financial sector and thus on interest rates.[14]

Finally, we note that a great many empirical studies of "liquidity preference" (the demand for money) have been conducted by economists in recent years. The evidence from these studies indicates that the interest rate affects the demand for money but not much. (In technical terms, the demand for money is interest-inelastic.) Income and/or wealth are also significant variables, but the relationship is less elastic than might be expected. Until recent years, the demand for money has been a fairly stable function of income (wealth?) and interest rates. The relative instability of recent years is probably attributable to inflationary expectations and the emergence of N.O.W. and A.T.S. accounts (and the resulting definitional problems of what is "money").

REFERENCES

Ackley, Gardner, "Liquidity Preference and Loanable Funds Theories of Interest: Comment," *American Economic Review,* September 1957, pp. 662–673.

Conard, Joseph, *Introduction to the Theory of Interest* (Berkeley: University of California Press, 1959).

Lerner, Abba P., "Alternative Formulations of the Theory of Interest," in S. Harris (ed.), *The New Economics* (New York: Knopf, 1950).

Patinkin, Don, "Liquidity Preference and Loanable Funds: Stock and Flow Analysis," *Economica,* November 1958, pp. 300–318.

Tobin, James, "Liquidity Preference as Behavior toward Risk," *Review of Economic Studies,* February 1958, pp. 65–86.

Tsiang, S.C., "Liquidity Preference and Loanable Funds Theories, Multiplier and Velocity Analysis: A Synthesis," *American Economic Review,* September 1956, pp. 539–564.

---

14. *Expectations* regarding future changes in the price level and in interest rates also impact significantly on the demand for money. In the case of anticipated inflation, of course, wealth holders tend to reduce cash balances (and probably savings as well) in an effort to avoid the attendant loss of monetary purchasing power. When interest rates are expected to increase, money holdings may increase. This is a consequence of the incentive to "wait" for higher yields but, more significantly, to avoid capital losses on holdings of debt securities when interest rates rise (and prices of such securities fall).

Chapter 9

The Term Structure of Interest Rates

Our discussion in Chapter 8 of "the" interest rate was highly simplified and abstract. In reality, there are many thousands of different interest rates on many thousands of different financial contracts. The existence of numerous different interest rates naturally raises questions about what factors account for these variations in rates. Although the *relative level* of interest rates on different financial contracts is influenced by a large number of factors—such as maturity, differences in administrative costs, and the competitive state of the market—it is possible to explain most of the differences in rates on financial instruments traded in competitive markets by reference to only a few factors: *time to maturity, inflation, credit or default risk, taxability, callability,* and *marketability.* The present chapter deals with the influence of differences in the maturity of a financial instrument on the yield on that asset—the "term structure" of interest rates—and Chapter 10 discusses the impact of the other factors on the relative level of interest rates in financial markets.

Keep in mind throughout the discussion in these two chapters that we are focusing on the relationship between the yield on a financial asset and each one of the above-named factors while holding all the other determining factors constant. In this chapter, for example, we seek to identify the influence of time to maturity on yield while holding constant the influence on yield of inflation, credit risk, and the other important variables. Similarly, in the next chapter, we examine the influence of credit risk on yield while holding time to maturity and all other factors constant. Such a simplification is necessary to an understanding of the impact of each of these variables. Yet we must keep in mind that day-to-day movements in the relative structure of rates in the financial marketplace reflect the combined influence of all the factors.

MATURITY AND YIELD

Time to maturity appears to be one of the most pervasive influences on the relative structure of interest rates. Usually, though not always, yields to maturity on financial instruments increase as the time to maturity of the instruments increases. In some periods, however—generally when interest rates are extremely high—yields to maturity on financial instruments are lower, the longer the maturity of the instruments. In a few rare instances, yields to maturity neither decrease nor increase as the maturity lengthens.

The Yield Curve

The relationship between short- and long-term rates on a particular day on debt instruments that are alike in all characteristics except maturity is referred to as the *term structure of interest rates*. This relationship is usually presented graphically as a *yield curve*. For example, Fig. 9.1 presents two common types of yield curves. In that figure the yield to maturity (vertical axis) is related to the time to maturity (horizontal axis) for a group of securities that are the same in all respects except their time to maturity. In Fig. 9.1(a) the yield to maturity increases as the time to maturity increases. This positive relationship between yield and maturity is usually referred to as the "normal" yield curve, because it occurs most frequently.[1] In contrast, occasionally the yield curve is downward-sloping, as

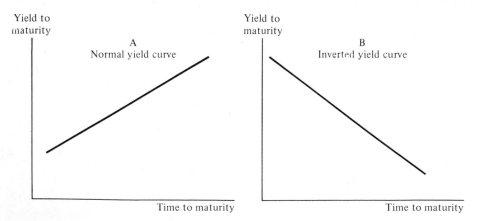

Figure 9.1

---

1. The yield curve in past years has been upward-sloping most of the time.

in Fig. 9.1(b). This downward-sloping yield curve is referred to as an "inverted" yield curve, because the "normal" relationship between maturity and time has been turned over or inverted.

The two yield curves in Fig. 9.1 provide a simplified view of the basic relationship between yield and maturity, but it is of course possible to have a yield curve that combines elements of each of these. For example, the yield curve may be upward-sloping for one portion of the maturity spectrum but downward-sloping for another maturity interval. Indeed, in some periods of increasing rates, the yield curve rises through the first year or two, then falls for a few years, and then becomes horizontal. This type of yield curve is referred to as "humped" for obvious reasons.

The Yield Curve and Borrowers and Lenders

The particular yield curve that exists at any moment of time has substantial importance for both lenders and borrowers in financial markets. For example, if the yield curve is upward-sloping, as it usually is, those who wish to borrow funds must pay a higher rate in order to "reach for maturity."[2] Although the borrower reduces liquidity pressures by borrowing long-term rather than short-term, that advantage of long-term borrowing must be balanced against the disadvantage of paying a higher rate to obtain the desired funds, which is associated with an upward-sloping yield curve. From the perspective of a lender, the upward-sloping yield curve indicates that higher yields to maturity may be obtained only by investing longer-term. However, as discussed in Chapter 8, the price variability of longer-term securities is greater than the price variability of shorter-term securities. Thus the investor or lender must balance the higher potential yield from the longer-term securities with the greater interest rate risk associated with those securities.

In those instances in which the yield curve is downward-sloping, the advantages and disadvantages to lenders and borrowers of short- versus long-term investments are altered. From the borrower's perspective, a downward-sloping yield curve indicates that the rate required to raise funds in the financial markets is lower for longer-term than for shorter-term securities. It seems then that the borrower would clearly choose to offer longer-term securities in this type of environment, since long maturity and lower rates can be obtained simultaneously. Yet this view ignores the fact that the inverted yield curve generally occurs in a period of high rates (the shape of the yield curve refers to the relationship between short- and long-term rates, *not the level of rates*). It may be preferable, if possible, for the borrower to postpone raising funds, or to borrow short-term today (despite the higher rates on short-term relative to long-term borrowing) in the hope of borrowing long-term in the future at lower rates. Moreover, as will be discussed below, the inverted yield curve generally occurs both when rates are high *and* when they are expected to fall in the future.

---

2. By "reaching for maturity," the borrower is seeking to reduce the immediate cash outflows associated with debt. From a financial-statements perspective, a policy of borrowing long-term rather than short-term improves the various liquidity ratios, such as the current ratio, although it has no impact on the total amount of debt or on leverage ratios such as the ratio of total debt to equity.

The inverted yield curve also has some important implications for the lender. Again it seems that the inverted yield curve represents the ideal situation for the investor—the lender can obtain the higher yield from shorter-term securities, as well as the lower price variability (risk) associated with these shorter-term securities. Yet, again, evaluation of the investment alternatives available is not that simple. Since interest rates are generally high when an inverted yield curve exists, the prices of all interest-bearing securities in the secondary market are low, and the prices of long-term securities are especially low. (Recall from Chapter 8 that, for any given increase in interest rates, the prices of all fixed-income instruments fall, but the prices of long-term securities fall more than the prices of short-term securities.) Moreover, if rates are high and expected to fall, then the prices of all fixed-income securities are expected to rise, but the prices of long-term securities are expected to rise more than the prices of short-term securities. In this type of environment, the investor might be better off to purchase long-term securities in order to capture the greater potential price appreciation associated with the securities. In this decision as in all others, lenders and borrowers must examine the yields and prices on securities today and expectations of the yields and prices tomorrow *before* making a decision today.

Examples of Yield Curves

A yield curve may be drawn for any group of securities—corporate, government, or municipals—that are identical in all respects except maturity. However, although yield curves for corporate and municipal securities are sometimes constructed for borrowing and lending purposes, the most widely used yield curve is drawn for U.S. government (Treasury) securities. Not only does the United States government have an enormous volume of debt outstanding—approaching $1 trillion—but that debt also offers a number of different maturity ranges, and it is homogeneous in credit risk. In contrast, the volume of debt outstanding from any one corporate or municipal issue is much smaller and usually does not offer a large number of different maturities.[3]

Normal Yield Curve

An upward-sloping or "normal" yield curve is presented in Fig. 9.2. This yield curve, drawn monthly by the U.S. Treasury, is published in the *Treasury Bulletin*.[4] As is typical for upward-sloping yield curves, the interest rate rises rapidly through the first few years of

---

3. Yield curves for corporate and municipal issues are often drawn for a number of different issuers with the same *presumed* credit quality. However, the usefulness of these yield curves is limited, since the actual credit quality of the issues often varies widely.

4. The yield curve as drawn by the Treasury is "fitted by eye" and has a number of securities that do not fall along the curve. Of course, if the yield curve held all factors that affect yield constant except time, then all the securities should fall along the curve. In fact, Treasury securities do differ in a number of respects (marketability and tax factors, for example), and these differences distort the yield curve.

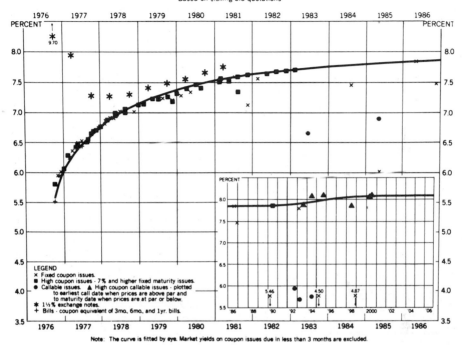

Figure 9.2

(Source: U.S. *Treasury Bulletin.*)

the maturity of the securities and then rises much more slowly thereafter. The yield curve as of June 30, 1976 (Fig. 9.2), reveals a marked increase in rates for maturities from mid-1976 through mid-1981. Hence, from the lender's perspective, a large increase in return could be obtained from extending the maturity of investments from one year to five years—one-year securities yielded about 6.5 percent whereas five-year securities yielded more than 7.5 percent. Similarly, from the borrower's perspective, small increases in desired maturity would cause large increases in the rates paid. Yet after five years, and particularly after ten years, there are only small increases in rates associated with lengthening maturities. For example, the yield on ten-year Treasury securities (those that would mature in 1986) was about 7.8 percent, but the yield on five-year Treasury securities (those that would mature in 1981) was about 7.6 percent. The yield on 30-year Treasury securities was about 8.05 percent. Hence lengthening maturity from one to five years as of June 30, 1976, would increase the yield to maturity by more than one full percentage point, but lengthening maturity by an additional five years would add only about 30 basis points (a *basis point* is 1/100 of a percentage point), and lengthening maturity by a further 20 years would add only another 25 basis points.

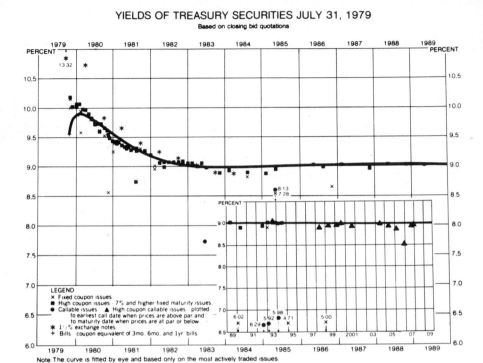

Figure 9.3

(Source: U.S. *Treasury Bulletin.*)

Inverted Yield Curve

A less common yield curve is presented in Fig. 9.3. In this yield curve, which is drawn for yields as of July 31, 1979, rates are downward-sloping (with the exception of a hump for the very short-term maturity issues), indicating an inverted yield curve—longer-term rates are lower than shorter-term rates. Note also that the *level* of rates as of July 31, 1979, was substantially higher than the level of rates on June 30, 1976. For example, the one-year rate was 6.5 percent on June 30, 1976, but it was 9.7 percent on July 31, 1979. And although the 20-year rate was 8 percent on June 30, 1976, it had increased only to about 9 percent by July 31, 1979; the implication is that between those two dates short-term rates advanced more than long-term rates. The greater increase in short- than in long-term rates during this period of rising rates is consistent with our discussion in Chapter 8.

The inverted yield curve shown in Fig. 9.3 is fairly "typical"—short-term rates are higher than long-term rates, and the sharp downward slope of the yield curve ceases after four or five years. For example, the one-year rate was above 9.5 percent, and the three-year rate was about 9 percent. Yet after two years the yield curve is essentially flat—the three-year rate was 9 percent and the 30-year rate was also 9 percent.

Figure 9.3 combined with Fig. 9.2 illustrates quite clearly the generalization that changes in the shape of the yield curve reflect primarily changes in short-term rates. All rates are generally increasing, but the increase in short-term rates is more pronounced than the increase in long-term rates. As a result, at some point in a rising interest rate cycle, short-term rates may exceed long-term rates, and the yield curve becomes inverted. In contrast, when rates begin to decline, all rates generally fall, but short-term rates fall more than long-term rates, and at some point the yield curve reverts to its "normal" shape.

To this point we have described only the various possible yield curves. Yet if one is to understand the shape of the yield curve, and especially if the lender or borrower is to make use of the yield curve, it is necessary to understand the factors that make it look as it does at any moment and to change from one moment to another. We now turn our attention to various theories that have been proposed to explain the shape of the yield curve.

EXPLAINING THE YIELD CURVE

There are three generally used though not mutually exclusive explanations of the shape of the yield curve at a particular point of time. These "theories of the yield curve" include the expectations hypothesis, the liquidity-premium theory, and the segmented-markets explanation. Each emphasizes a different aspect of borrower and lender behavior, and each focuses on a different element of the financial markets. The *expectations hypothesis* is quite abstract in nature and stresses the significance of investors' seeking to obtain the highest return on their investment over a given period. The *liquidity-premium theory* adds a further dimension to our understanding of the yield curve by introducing differences in the riskiness of different securities in explaining variations in the yield curve.[5] Finally, the *segmented-markets explanation* incorporates the importance of institutional factors, such as investor preference for specific-maturity assets, in explaining the yield curve (it is sometimes called the "preferred habitat" explanation). Most observers accept the expectations hypothesis, modified to incorporate the liquidity-premium concept, as at least a partial explanation of the yield curve. However, there is some disagreement over the importance of institutional factors that segment financial markets as influences on the shape of the yield curve. Nevertheless, many practicing financial analysts incorporate elements of each explanation in their work.

The Expectations Hypothesis

As the name indicates, the expectations explanation of the yield curve hypothesizes that the relationship between short- and long-term interest rates that exist at a point of time (i.e., the yield curve) is a function of investor expectations of interest rates in the future. Hence, if expectations are for rising interest rates in the future, the yield curve today will be upward-sloping; that is, long-term rates today will exceed short-term rates today. If

---

5. The liquidity-premium theory is sometimes treated as a modification of the expectations hypothesis.

expectations are that interest rates in the future will be the same as interest rates today, the yield curve will be horizontal. And if expectations are that interest rates in the future will be lower than interest rates today, then the yield curve today will be downward-sloping. The yield curve today is of course an observable fact, whereas *expectations of future interest rates are unobservable.* The expectations hypothesis connects expectations of future rates to the term structure of rates today by arguing that, under certain assumptions, the yield curve that exists today must reflect the expectations of market participants.

The expectations hypothesis assumes that investor behavior is influenced only by expected returns on investments, that is, that investors are return maximizers and risk-neutral (indifferent to risk). Given this assumption, investors are indifferent about the maturity of the securities in their portfolio and concerned only about their return. Hence an investor who had idle funds for three years (a three-year holding period) could invest in a six-year security and sell the security at the end of three years (the investor has purchased a security whose maturity is *longer* than the investor's holding period) or invest in a one-year security and reinvest in additional one-year securities for the full three-year period (the investor has purchased a security whose maturity is shorter than the investor's holding period). And of course, the investor could invest in a security with a three-year maturity, thereby matching precisely the maturity of the security and the holding period of the investor. According to the expectations hypothesis, in making this decision, the investor will be guided *solely by which security has the highest return over the investor's holding period.*

Given the basic assumptions of the expectations hypothesis—that investors are return maximizers, are risk-neutral, and have the same expectations, and that all securities are perfectly substitutable in investor portfolios—it may be shown that the structure of the yield curve today reflects expectations about the level of rates in the future. For example, assume that an investor has a two-year holding period. Further assume that the investor has only two investment alternatives: a one-year credit-risk-free security with a yield of 5 percent or a two-year credit-risk-free security. Assume also that investors believe that the interest rate one year from now on one-year securities will be 7 percent.

Given these conditions, what will be the interest rate today on the two-year security? Of course, once that interest rate is determined, the term structure of interest rates (the yield curve) is established. If investors are indeed return maximizers, risk-neutral, and indifferent about the maturity of their portfolios, the yield today on the two-year security must be 6 percent. Why? First, assume that the yield on the two-year security was 5 percent. In that situation, the investor could get 5 percent by purchasing the two-year security or 6 percent by purchasing a one-year security and then reinvesting in another one-year security at the expected return of 7 percent at the end of one year: $(5 + 7)/2 = 6\%$.[6] Obviously, a return-maximizing investor would not buy the two-year security. However, the lack of

---

6. This example ignores compounding. It also assumes that investor expectations are realized. However, for the expectations hypothesis to be valid, it is not necessary to assume that expectations are realized, only that investors act on their expectations of future rates.

demand for the two-year security would cause its price to fall and its yield to rise until the yield had increased to 6 percent, at which point the investor would be indifferent between the two-year security and the two one-year securities. Now assume that the two-year security offered a return of 7 percent. In that case, the investor would prefer the 7-percent yield on the two-year security to the 6-percent yield available by purchasing a one-year security today and reinvesting in another one-year security one year from now at the expected rate of 7 percent on that one-year security. But the demand for the two-year security would increase its price, and its yield would fall until the yield equaled that available from purchasing the one-year security and reinvesting at the end of one year. In *equilibrium, the holding-period return for an investor must be the same, according to the expectations hypothesis, regardless of the maturity of the securities held.*

In the example given above, where the investor expected future rates to exceed current rates, the yield curve was upward-sloping; i.e., long-term rates today exceeded short-term rates today. If investors act according to the assumptions of the expectations theory, their actions of buying and selling securities in order to maximize their holding-period returns would necessarily result in this term structure. If investors expected that interest rates would be lower in the future, their actions of buying and selling securities would produce a downward-sloping yield curve. If they expected rates to be unchanged in the future, the yield curve would be horizontal.

The expectations hypothesis, with its assumptions of highly competitive financial markets, has considerable appeal. Indeed, there are many observers who view the expectations hypothesis as the dominant (if not the only) basic explanation of the yield curve. Moreover, there is considerable empirical evidence to support the importance of expectations in affecting the shape of the yield curve. Yet there are a number of complexities concerning the behavior of investors and the institutional characteristics of the financial markets that add depth to our understanding of the yield curve and that make the yield curve more useful to analysts. The first of the complexities, as expressed by the *liquidity-premium theory,* assumes that investors have a two-dimensional preference pattern, reacting to both *return* and *risk.* The second complexity, as expressed in the segmented-markets explanation, incorporates the particular characteristics of financial institutions and other market participants in affecting the yield curve. We now discuss each of these in turn.

The Liquidity-Premium Theory

The liquidity-premium explanation of the yield curve assumes that investors not only react positively to return but also *react negatively to risk.* In other words, investors balance return with risk in making portfolio management decisions. This modification to the previous assumption about investor behavior—hence to the expectations hypothesis—is relevant when we recognize that the risk involved in purchasing securities of the same credit quality but with different maturities is not the same. As discussed earlier, the risk involved in purchasing securities varies with the maturity of the securities; i.e., longer-term securities have greater price variability than shorter-term securities. This *price* or *interest* or *market risk,* according to the liquidity-premium theory, must be incorporated into investor portfolio behavior and hence into the term structure of interest rate.

According to this explanation, investors have a preference for liquidity. This preference for the liquidity associated with short-term securities stems from their dislike of the risk involved in purchasing long-term securities. In order to induce investors to purchase long-term securities, then, the financial markets must offer a *liquidity* or *risk premium* on those securities with longer terms to maturity. Only the higher yields will induce investors to leave their ''safe harbor'' and purchase the longer-term issues.

Recognition of the need for a liquidity or risk premium in order to induce investors to purchase longer-term issues results in a substantial modification of the expectations hypothesis. For example, even if expectations are that interest rates in the future will be the same as interest rates today, the yield curve will be upward-sloping, as shown in Fig. 9.4. The solid line reflects the yield curve incorporating only expectations factors. But to these factors must be added the liquidity premium, which increases as the time to maturity increases, since risk rises with maturity. Hence the dashed line in Fig. 9.4(a) shows an upward-sloping yield curve, even though expectations are for interest rates in the future to remain unchanged from those today. A similar analysis could be used to incorporate liquidity preference into a yield curve that reflected rising or falling interest rates in the future. If the yield curve was upward-sloping because of expectations of rising rates, it would be more upward-sloping with the addition of the liquidity premium, as in Fig. 9.4(b). And if the yield curve was downward-sloping because of expectations of falling yields in the future, with the addition of the liquidity premium it could actually be *upward*-sloping, as in Fig. 9.4(c).

The liquidity-premium theory is attractive because it explicitly recognizes that investors balance risk and return in their portfolio management decisions. And our observations of financial markets indicate that investors *do* balance risk and return in making portfolio management decisions. Moreover, the assumptions of the liquidity-premium theory appear to be more consistent with the historical behavior of the yield curve than do those of the expectations hypothesis. With the liquidity-premium theory, the yield curve would be expected to be upward-sloping most of the time. A downward slope of the yield curve would occur *only* when expectations of sharply falling yields were sufficient to offset the liquidity premium. With the expectations hypothesis, it would be expected that rising and falling yield curves would exist with about the same frequency. In fact, as discussed earlier, the ''normal'' yield curve is upward-sloping, and downward-sloping yield curves occur much less frequently.

To this point our discussion of the shape of the yield curve has centered on the behavior of abstract economic units maximizing returns or balancing risk and return. Yet we must recognize that most securities are purchased by financial institutions, whose portfolio behavior is constrained by legal and other factors, and whose maturity distribution is often limited to a narrow range. It seems likely that these institutional factors influence the shape of the yield curve to a considerable extent. We now turn our discussion to the segmented-markets explanation, which incorporates these factors.

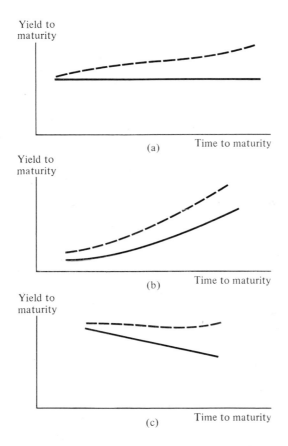

Fig. 9.4   The yield curve reflecting the liquidity premium

Segmented-Markets Explanation

The expectations theory, either with or without the modification introduced by the liquidity-premium concept, ignores the characteristics of the institutions that operate within the financial markets. In contrast, the segmented-market explanation ignores the role of expectations in influencing yield curves. This explanation emphasizes the behavior characteristics of the major financial institutions that dominate the financial market. By this explanation, it is principally the behavior of commercial banks and the Federal Reserve, in conjunction with changes in the demand for funds for inventory accumulation by businesses and changes in other types of demand, that causes increases or decreases in short-term interest rates. And it is changes in the supply of loanable funds by the major financial institutions, such as life insurance companies and pension funds, in connection with changes in the demand for loanable funds by businesses for capital expansion, by households for acquisition of homes, and by others, that cause changes in long-term interest rates. Following the logic of the argument, the financial markets are segmented into subdivisions based on the traditional maturity preferences of market participants. Within each of these subdivisions, changes in the supply and demand for loanable funds ultimately create a particular term structure. Each participant in the market has a preferred habitat, securities of different maturities are not perfectly substitutable in investor portfolios, and it would take extraordinarily large changes in the pattern of interest rates to induce investors to shift from one maturity group of securities to another. For example, commercial banks seek relatively short-term securities, given their relatively unstable sources of funds, whereas life insurance companies seek relatively long-term securities, given their relatively stable sources of funds.

According to the segmented-markets explanation of the yield curve, interest rate levels for short- and long-term financial markets are determined independently by supply and demand in each market. For example, in Fig. 9.5(a) the short-term rate (r_S) is below the long-term rate (r_L). This upward slope to the yield curve reflects the interaction of the supply and demand for loanable funds such that *relative demand pressure* in the short-term market is less than in the long-term market. For example, at any given interest rate, the demand gap (the difference between the quantity of loanable funds demanded and supplied) is smaller in the short-term market (where S_S is the supply schedule and D_S is the demand schedule) than in the long-term market (where S_L is the supply schedule and D_L is the demand schedule). And according to the segmented-markets explanation, these supply and demand schedules are independent and unrelated.

Changes in the yield curve reflect changes in these segmented supply and demand schedules. For example, in Fig. 9.5(b) short-term interest rates are higher than longer-term interest rates; i.e., the yield curve is inverted, or downward-sloping. According to the segmented-markets explanation, this inverted yield curve is the result of greater demand pressure in short-term markets than in long term markets. For example, the Federal Reserve may be following a "tight" money policy by restricting the availability of bank reserves. As a result, the supply of loanable funds from the banking system—*which is principally a short-term lender*—is constrained. At the same time, if business conditions are strong, business firms may have large inventory accumulation, *which is generally financed by short-term borrowing.* In contrast, the long-term supply of funds available from life insurance companies and pension funds and the capital spending plans of business firms will probably be much less affected by variations in Federal Reserve monetary policy and in the state of the economy.

Implicit in the segmented-markets explanation of the yield curve is an emphasis on changes in the supply and demand for loanable funds in the short-term markets. Although the supply and demand for loanable funds in the short-term (money) market are viewed as highly volatile, the supply and demand for funds in the long-term market are thought to be much more stable. Hence changes in the shape of the yield curve principally reflect shifts in short-term rather than long-term rates. For example, in the upswing of the business cycle,

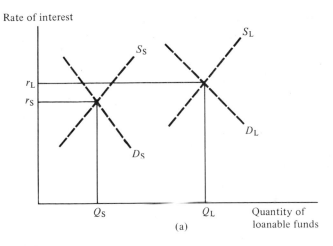

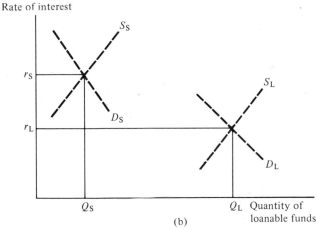

Fig. 9.5   Segmented markets and the yield curve

short-term rates rise rapidly (more rapidly than long-term rates), and the yield curve flattens. As the business cycle nears its peak, the supply of short-term funds is restricted by the Federal Reserve, whereas the demand for funds increases as businesses build inventory. As a result, short-term rates rise further, perhaps exceeding long-term rates and creating an inverted yield curve. However, as the economy slows, the Fed relaxes its monetary policy, business demand for inventory financing declines, and short-term rates fall rapidly. At some point, the upward-sloping yield curve is restored with short-term rates again lower than long-term rates.

Are Explanations Mutually Exclusive?

The question should perhaps be raised after this discussion of the various explanations of the yield curve—expectations, liquidity premium, and segmented markets—whether one is the "right" explanation and whether the others are "wrong." Although many observers consider the expectations hypothesis to be the principal (dominant) factor in shaping the yield curve, there is nothing mutually contradictory about any of the explanations. There is no reason why the yield curve may not reflect expectations about future rates modified by a liquidity premium and further modified by institutional rigidities that allow some substitution of securities with different maturities (though not perfect substitutions) in investor portfolios. Indeed, it appears quite likely that each one of these factors does play a role in determining the shape of the yield curve.

MATURITY VERSUS DURATION

Our discussion of the yield curve to this point has been in terms of the relationship between the yield on a financial asset and the maturity of that asset. In this analysis, maturity (i.e., the date on which the final payment of principal is made) is used as a measure of the length of life of the asset. Yet maturity is not the only measure of the life of a financial asset, nor is it necessarily the best. One other measure of the life of a financial asset that has received wide use in recent years is *duration*. In contrast to maturity, which indicates only when the final payment on a bond occurs, duration takes into account the timing of all payments on a bond. After discussing some of the limitations of the maturity concept, we will define duration and indicate its potential usefulness.

Let us assume that we have two securities that are identical in terms of credit risk. One security (call it low-coupon) has a zero coupon and matures in five years. The other security (call it high-coupon) has an eight-percent coupon and also matures in five years. Judged on the basis of maturity, these securities are identical, and their yields to maturity should be the same; that is, they should be at the same point on the yield curve.[7] Moreover, in the context of our previous discussion, the response of the price of these securities to interest rate changes should be the same. If interest rates fall by a given percentage, we should expect the price of both bonds to rise and by the same amount. But are these bonds identical? The answer is clearly no! On the low-coupon bond the investor receives no cash until the maturity of the bond, but on the high-coupon bond the investor receives $80 per year during the five years of the life of the bond. In terms of the life of the cash flow from the bond, the cash flow comes in earlier for the high-coupon than for the low-coupon bond. In short, the *duration*—the weighted average life of the bond's cash flow—is shorter for the high-coupon

---

7. As explained in the next chapter, because of tax factors (the differential and lower tax rate applied to capital gains), the low-coupon issue will sell at a lower yield to maturity than the high-coupon issue. However, our illustration abstracts from the tax issue.

bond than for the low-coupon bond. And *it can be shown that the price variability of a bond is a function of its duration rather than its maturity.* Duration can be calculated as follows:

$$d = \frac{\sum\limits_{t=1}^{n} \dfrac{C_t(t)}{(1+r)^t}}{\sum\limits_{t=1}^{n} \dfrac{C_t}{(1+r)^t}},$$

where d = duration, Σ = sum of or addition of, C_t = the cash flow from the bond (interest and/or principal), t = the time period for each cash flow, and r = the appropriate discount rate.

The denominator of the duration formula is the present value of the cash flows discounted at the appropriate rate. In other words, the denominator is the price of the bond. The numerator of the duration formula is the cash flow multiplied by the year in which the cash flow occurs. For a zero-coupon bond (our "low-coupon" issue), the duration and the maturity of the bond are identical. However, for any bond that has a positive coupon, the duration is shorter than the maturity of the bond. For example, the duration of the zero-coupon bond may be calculated as follows if the market return is 8 percent and the maturity is five years.

$$d \text{ (low-coupon)} = \frac{\dfrac{(1000)(5)}{(1.08)^5}}{\dfrac{1000}{(1.08)^5}} = 5 \text{ years}$$

In contrast, the duration of the high-coupon bond:

$$d \text{ (high-coupon)} = \frac{\dfrac{80(1)}{(1.08)} + \dfrac{80(2)}{(1.08)^2} + \dfrac{80(3)}{(1.08)^3} + \dfrac{80(4)}{(1.08)^4} + \dfrac{80(5)}{(1.08)^5} + \dfrac{1000(5)}{(1.08)^5}}{\dfrac{80}{(1.08)^1} + \dfrac{80}{(1.08)^2} + \dfrac{80}{(1.08)^3} + \dfrac{80}{(1.08)^4} + \dfrac{80}{(1.08)^5} + \dfrac{1000}{(1.08)^5}} = 4.3 \text{ years}$$

Hence these two securities have the same date on which the final payment is made (the same maturity), but they have different durations: 5 years for the low-coupon bond and 4.3 years for the high-coupon bond. As a result, for any given change in the general level of interest rates, the price of the low-coupon bond will change more than the price of the high-coupon bond. For this reason, it is often argued that in a determination of the association between time and yield to maturity, duration should be used rather than maturity.

USES OF THE YIELD CURVE

The yield curve is used by a wide variety of analysts for a number of different purposes. In this section we present a brief discussion of some of the different uses of the yield curve. The treatment is not exhaustive, but it should provide the observer with at least an introduction to the many ways in which financial analysts and students of the financial system use the yield curve.

Predicting Interest Rates.   One of the most widely used functions of the yield curve is the prediction of the future course of interest rates. As discussed earlier, changes in interest rates affect the price of fixed-income securities. Increases in rates are associated with declines in the value of fixed-income securities, and decreases in rates are associated with increases in their value These changes in rates and prices present the opportunity for large profits or risk of large losses to financial market participants. As a result, substantial resources are devoted to forecasting interest rate movements by financial institutions, such as commercial banks, and by others who hold fixed-income securities.

There are a number of approaches to forecasting interest rates. For example, some financial institutions use elaborate forecasts of the various elements of supply and demand for loanable funds in order to anticipate interest rate movements. Forecasts of the supply of loanable funds available from the major providers of funds in the financial marketplace—financial institutions—are prepared and compared with the demand for loanable funds emanating from households, businesses, and governments. As another alternative, elaborate econometric models of the economy, including the financial sector, are constructed by econometric forecasting services, such as Data Resources, Inc., Wharton Econometrics, and others. And of course, the interest rates on financial assets traded in the financial futures markets (such as Treasury bills) may be used to reflect market participants' expectations of future interest rates. For example, there are a number of financial assets in which trading occurs for delivery of securities at future periods. (These will be discussed in Chapter 18.)

The yield curve is one among the many approaches to forecasting interest rates. For those who accept the expectations hypothesis, either in its pure or modified form, the shape of the yield curve provides a forecast of future interest rate levels. Implicit in every yield curve is some *forward rate of interest.* For example, in the illustration of the yield curve provided earlier, if the yield on a one-year security is 5 percent, and the yield on a two-year security is 6 percent, then the forward rate for a one-year security one year from now is 7 percent. Since the expectations hypothesis argues that *the forward rate and the expected rate are identical,* those who follow the expectations hypothesis are provided with a forecasted rate for securities of different maturities at different points in the future.[8] Hence an upward-sloping yield curve would contain implicitly a forecast of higher rates in the

---

8. The forward rate may be calculated from a current yield curve for a one-year security for any period in the future, a two-year security for any period in the future, and for any other maturity for any period in the future.

future. Indeed, there is frequent reference to the shape of the yield curve in articles in financial publications devoted to a discussion of future interest rate developments. Of course, these predictions may not be realized.

Determining Borrowing and Lending Maturities.   The yield curve is of course useful in forecasting interest rates only to those who are willing to accept some form of the expectations hypothesis. But even though there may be some disagreement about whether the yield curve contains insight into future interest rates, there is no disagreement that the yield curve provides borrowers and lenders with vital information on the impact of alternative maturity choices on either the cost of funds or the potential yield on invested funds. For example, if the yield curve is upward-sloping, lenders are able to calculate precisely the impact of extending the maturity of their investment and to compare the extra yield with the higher risk associated with "reaching for yield." In many instances when the yield curve is upward-sloping, it tends to flatten out beyond the 10–15-year range. Hence investors have high incentive to lengthen the maturities of their portfolios up to the 10–15-year span but little incentive to increase maturities beyond that.

A similar analysis holds for borrowers facing an upward-sloping yield curve. Assume that borrowers wish to extend the maturity of their debt in order to reduce the liquidity management problems associated with large amounts of short-term debt. The existing yield curve tells such a borrower approximately what penalty, through higher costs, will be associated with lengthening the maturity of the borrowing. If the yield curve rises rapidly through the 10–15-year range but then flattens out, the borrower incurs a substantial penalty for extending maturity through the 10–15-year area but finds it relatively attractive to reach beyond that maturity range as the extra yield per year of extended maturity diminishes.

Selecting Individual Securities.   The yield curve may also be used as an investment device in the selection of individual securities for inclusion in a particular portfolio. In viewing the yield curve from this perspective, we must keep in mind how the yield curve is constructed—by taking a group of securities that are *identical in all respects* and examining the influences of varying times to maturity on the yield to maturity. Thus, if the yield curve is properly drawn and all factors except time to maturity have been held constant, all the securities should fall along the yield curve. Yet in the actual construction of yield curves, it may be found that some securities do not fall on the yield curve but are above or below it. For example, in Fig. 9.6, Security A falls above the yield curve, and Security B falls below it. There are two possible interpretations of this phenomenon, each with quite different implications for investment behavior. One interpretation is that the securities are mispriced by the market. For example, for Security A the yield to maturity is Y_A, but for a security with the characteristics of security A and maturity T, the yield should be Y. The yield on security A is too high (its price is too low), given its risk and maturity considerations.[9] This

---

9. Again, keep in mind the inverse relationship between price and yield on a fixed-income security.

interpretation suggests that the investor should purchase those securities that fall above the yield curve. Similarly, for Security B (its price is too high) the yield to maturity is too low for its risk and maturity characteristics. For example, the yield on Security B is Y_B but it should be Y. This interpretation suggests that the investor should eliminate Security B from the portfolio if it is already included in the existing portfolio and should avoid the security if it is not.[10] But there is a second interpretation for the existence of securities that lie off the yield curve: it may be that the analyst has not been successful in holding all other factors constant in drawing the yield curve. For example, Security A may have some undesirable characteristics (such as greater credit risk) that make its yield higher than the yield curve, and Security B may have some desirable characteristics that make its yield less than that expected from the time to maturity of the security.

Which of these explanations is correct? Unfortunately, there is no simple and universal answer. However, we note that for the first interpretation to be correct the financial markets must be inefficient—that is, it must be possible to earn higher than "normal" returns without taking higher than "normal" risks. Yet, as discussed in Chapter 1, the evidence of numerous studies is that the markets for securities are highly efficient. Moreover, we also know that market professionals—brokerage houses, large commercial banks, and other major purchasers of securities—are consistently engaged in seeking under- and overpriced securities. As a result, it seems likely that the opportunities for excess profit to the "nonprofessional" investor in finding securities that lie off the yield curve are probably quite limited.

Pricing New Issues.   For existing securities, coupon interest rates are fixed, but prices are variable, being determined by market movements in the general level of interest rates. However, for new securities the price is fixed (usually set by the issuer at or near par), and the coupon interest rate is variable. The issuer—either the issuing firm directly or the investment banking institution working for the issuer—seeks to determine the coupon rate that will make the securities attractive to the market. At or near the par price, too low a coupon rate will make it difficult or impossible to sell the issue, and too high a coupon rate will result in excessive interest costs to the issuing firm. In pricing the new issue—that is, setting the coupon rate—the investment banker may draw up a yield curve for securities of comparable risk. For example, we may imagine that Fig. 9.6 represents such a yield curve, and that the issuer wishes to sell securities with a maturity of T. In that case, the issuer wants to set the coupon around Y, perhaps a little above Y in order to offer some concession to the market for the purchase of a new issue. In any case, the issuer is using the yield curve as a guide in pricing the new issue.

---

10. A more aggressive strategy, which seeks to profit from the mispricing of the security, would be to sell Security B short; that is, borrow the security, sell it when it is overpriced, and buy it back later after its price has fallen in order to return the security to the lender.

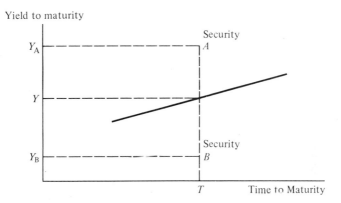

Yield to maturity

Fig. 9.6   Individual securities and the yield curve

Riding the Yield Curve.   One of the most interesting potential uses of the yield curve is what is known as "riding the yield curve." This practice, used by a variety of participants in the money market, consists of seeking to profit from an upward-sloping yield curve by investing in a security whose maturity is longer than the investor's holding period and selling the security prior to maturity. Its usefulness is based on the assumption that one investor's expectations of future interest rates may be more accurate than the average expectations of investors that are embodied in the yield curve. Under some conditions riding the yield curve may produce "holding period returns" that are greater than those possible through investing in securities whose maturities equal the investor's holding period. Although there is disagreement about the potential gains that are possible through riding the yield curve, we will present the conditions under which doing so *may* be profitable. First, however, we need to define the holding period return for a fixed-income security:

$$Y_h = Y_o + \frac{T_r(Y_o - Y_m)}{T_h} ,$$

where Y_h = the holding period return, Y_o = the original yield, Y_m = the market yield when sold, T_r = time remaining until maturity when the security is sold, and T_h = time held.

   Referring again to the example used in discussing the expectations hypothesis, suppose that the yield available on a one-year security was 5 percent and the yield available on a two-year security was 6 percent, and that the investor's holding period was one year. In that case, the holding period return involved in purchasing the one year security would clearly be 5 percent. What is the holding period return in purchasing the two-year security and selling it at the end of one year? As is apparent in the equation above for the holding period return, all the information needed to compute the holding period return is known at the time of the decision, except the market yield on the security at the time the security is sold. For the moment, let us make the unrealistic assumption that the yield curve remains unchanged, so the two-year security today is a one-year security one year from now, and its yield is 5 percent. In that case, the holding period yield from purchasing the two-year security today and selling it after one year is:

$$Y_h = \frac{6\% + 1 \text{ year } (6 - 5\%)}{1 \text{ year}} = 7\%.$$

The holding period yield is higher than that available from simply holding either the one- or the two-year security until maturity. The high yield results from the higher return obtained from "reaching for yield" by buying the two-year security plus a capital gain from selling the security at a price higher than its purchase price (since it was purchased to yield 6 percent and sold to yield 5 percent, it must be sold at a price higher than its purchase price). Note, however, that riding the yield curve would not be possible if the expectations hypothesis was entirely correct. In that case, the yield on the two-year security sold one year after purchase would be 5 percent:

$$Y_h = 6\% + \frac{1 \text{ year } (6 - 7\%)}{1 \text{ year}} = 5\%.$$

As explained earlier, if the expectations hypothesis is entirely valid, the holding period return for a given holding period is the same for securities of all maturities. Note also that the example did not include transactions costs. It may be that there are opportunities for higher holding period returns through riding the yield curve, but that these extra profits are reduced or eliminated by the transactions costs associated with the strategy.[11]

SUMMARY

The "term structure of interest rates" refers to the relationship between short- and long-term interest rates at a particular point of time on debt securities that are fundamentally similar in all characteristics except maturity. This relationship is usually presented graphically as a yield curve, generally with the use of U.S. government securities. It may also be presented by comparing the yields on securities with their duration. The yield curve is normally upward-sloping—long-term rates higher than short-term rates—but an inverted

---

11. The decade of the 1940s and until 1951 did provide the opportunity for riding the yield curve with very little risk. In that period, the Federal Reserve artificially pegged the structure of rates. Not only was the yield curve upward-sloping, but it was also unchanging. In that environment, riding the yield curve could be exceptionally profitable.

yield curve—short-term rates higher than long-term rates—also exists from time to time. There are three frequently used explanations of the shape of the curve: the expectations hypothesis, the liquidity-premium theory, and the segmented-markets explanation. These three concepts are not mutually exclusive but may all be integrated into yield curve analysis. The yield curve has many uses. They include predicting interest rates, determining borrowing and lending maturities, selecting individual securities, pricing new issues, and "riding the yield curve."

In the next chapters we turn our attention to other factors that influence the yields on financial instruments. Initially we discuss the influence of inflation on the term structure. Even if the expectations hypothesis is valid in that the relationship between short- and long-term interest rates is a function of expectations of future interest rate levels, the question remains as to why investors may hold expectations of increasing or decreasing rates in the future. One explanation involves inflation. If investors expect rising prices, they expect rising interest rates. As discussed in succeeding chapters, inflation has a profound impact on interest rates.

QUESTIONS

1. What is the term structure of interest rates? Why is it often referred to as the yield curve?

2. Discuss the meaning of the "normal," inverted, and humped yield curves. Under what economic conditions is each one of these yield curves likely to exist?

3. Discuss the meaning of each of the following explanations of the yield curve.
   a) Expectations
   b) Liquidity preference
   c) Segmented markets
Are these various explanations mutually compatible or contradictory? Why? Explain.

4. Assume that the rate today on one-year default-free securities is 5 percent, and the rate on one-year default-free securities one year from now is expected to be 7 percent. What should be the rate on two-year default-free securities today, according to the expectations hypothesis?

5. Why must investors be offered a premium to purchase long-term default-free securities? What does this assume about investor behavior? How does this assumption differ from that used in the expectations hypothesis?

6. Make a list of major financial institutions, and indicate which segments of the financial markets each one is active within.

7. What is duration? What is the relationship between duration and interest rate risk? Why is duration an alternative to maturity in the yield curve?

8. Explain the various ways that the yield curve can be used by financial analysts. Which is most relevant for borrowers? lenders?

REFERENCES

Conard, Joseph, *Introduction to the Theory of Interest* (Berkeley: University of California Press, 1959).

Culbertson, John, "The Term Structure of Interest Rates," *Quarterly Journal of Economics,* November 1957, pp. 485–517.

Kessel, Reuben, *The Cyclical Behavior of the Term Structure of Interest Rates,* Occasional Paper 91, National Bureau of Economic Research, 1965.

Malkiel, Burton, *The Term Structure of Interest Rates* (Princeton, N.J.: Princeton University Press, 1966).

Meiselman, David, *The Term Structure of Interest Rates* (Englewood Cliffs, N.J.: Prentice-Hall, 1962).

Modigliani, Franco, and Richard Sutch, "The Term Structure of Interest Rates: A Reexamination of the Evidence," *Journal of Money, Credit, and Banking,* February 1965.

Silber, William L., "The Term Structure of Interest Rates," in Murray E. Polokoff (ed.), *Financial Institutions and Markets* (Boston: Houghton Mifflin, 1970).

Van Horne, James, "Interest Rate Expectations, the Shape of the Yield Curve, and Monetary Policy," *The Review of Economics and Statistics,* May 1966, pp. 211–215.

APPENDIX

EMPIRICAL EVIDENCE ON THE TERM STRUCTURE

As discussed in Chapter 9, there are a number of differing though not necessarily contradictory explanations of the term structure of interest rates. The three most widely discussed explanations are the expectations, liquidity-premium, and segmented-markets hypotheses. Many analysts accept some form of the expectations hypothesis, but there is considerable disagreement about the relative importance of these three explanations. Fundamentally, of course, the validity of the three explanations is an empirical issue determined by factual evidence rather than by opinion. Fortunately, there is a substantial volume of empirical literature that has attempted to test the validity of these explanations, and a review of this literature is the purpose of this appendix. Unfortunately, however, even though empirical literature does provide some important information, there are substantial conflicts among the evidence that make definitive conclusions difficult to reach.

One of the major tests of the expectations hypothesis has centered on evaluating the extent to which the forward rate embodied in a yield curve as of a moment of time is an accurate predictor of future interest rates. In these types of studies, sometimes referred to as "perfect-foresight models," the yield on a particular maturity security, such as the three-month Treasury bill, for some future period (for example, one year from the date on which the prediction is made) is calculated from the existing yield curve. Then, after the fact, the forecasted yield is compared with the yield that actually existed on the particular financial instrument. In general, these studies have not found that forward rates embodied in the yield curve have any great ability to forecast future rates (see the studies of Hamburger and Platt and Culbertson referenced at the end of this appendix). However, keep in mind also that, at least in recent years, no other procedures have proved especially accurate in forecasting interest rates, either.

Although these perfect-foresight models have provided little support for the expectations hypothesis, one must recognize that the hypothesis itself does not require that expectations be realized; it requires only that expectations of future rates be important in determining the structure of rates today.[12] Testing the hypothesis by assuming that the forecasts are realized may impose excessive requirements on the validity of the theory. Recognizing this problem, other investigators (notably David Meiselman) have sought to determine whether reasonable models about the formation of expectations of future rates can be used to explain the current term structure.

Meiselman developed an error-learning model, in which expectations were assumed to reflect current and past observation of actual events, and in which expectations were adjusted in response to this "learning process." In this model, changes in one-year-forward

---

12. The basic problem, of course, in testing the expectations hypothesis is that the expectations themselves are not directly observable. Rather, indirect observable data must be used to infer those expectations. Some studies (the one by Malkiel and Kane, for example) have attempted to survey expectations directly with mixed results.

rates were assumed to be related to errors in forecasting the actual one-year rate. Hence the actual one-year rate would be compared with the one-year rate forecasted earlier, and expectations of future one-year rates would be revised to reflect any errors. Meiselman then computed the correlation coefficient between the forecast error and changes in forward rates, using data from the period 1900–1954. His principal finding was that the high correlation found between the forecast error and changes in forward rates provided substantial support for the expectations hypothesis.

Other indirect support for the expectations hypothesis has been provided by studies that have explored the timing of movements in short- and long-term interest rates. If the expectations hypothesis is valid, one would expect that long-term rates would move in advance of short-term rates. Although the evidence of this issue is by no means conclusive, Sargent found that long-term rates did lead rates on three-month Treasury bills in the 1951–1960 period.

Additional research has been conducted using the error-learning model in order to test for the presence of liquidity premiums. Meiselman found no evidence of liquidity premiums in his study, but Wood, using the same data series, found that the data were consistent with the existence of a liquidity premium. The conclusion was based on the finding that forward rates represented systematically high estimates of future rates. A similar conclusion was reached by Kessel in a separate study. In fact, there is substantial evidence supporting the existence of liquidity premiums, though there is less agreement on how these premiums change as the maturity of a financial instrument increases.

Tests of the hypothesis of market segmentation are also difficult to design and evaluate in a meaningful way. If the segmented-markets hypothesis is valid, one would expect that changes in the relative balance of supply and demand in particular segments of the market would produce changes in interest rates in those segments and thereby in the term structure of interest rates. Yet obtaining meaningful measures of supply and demand factors in subsectors of the financial markets is quite difficult. Modigliani and Sutch added supply variables to a model that also included expectations factors in attempting to explain the yield curve. In one study, published in 1966, they attempted to determine whether supply variables associated with "Operation Twist" (the attempt by the Federal Reserve in the early 1960s to alter the shape of the yield curve by changing the amount of short- and long-term government securities in the hands of the public) exerted any influence on the yield curve. They concluded that these supply factors had no more than a minor impact on the term structure. In another article, published in 1967, Modigliani and Sutch attempted to evaluate the segmented-markets hypothesis by evaluating the statistical significance of adding supply variables to their basic model. However, measures of the maturity distribution of outstanding debt did not appear to add additional explanatory power to the model.

Taking a different approach to testing the segmented-markets hypothesis, Malkiel looked at the portfolio of financial institutions in order to determine whether these institutions do indeed confine their purchases to a particular maturity. Using data from the period 1955–1965 for such financial institutions as commercial banks and insurance companies,

Malkiel could find no evidence that financial institutions appeared to alter the maturities of their portfolios in response to expected return and risk considerations.

Where does this leave us? Just what is the influence of expectations, liquidity-premium, and segmented-market considerations on the term structure of interest rates? On the basis of the evidence presented here and in recognition of the fact that there are conflicts in the relevant literature, it does appear that the yield curve incorporates expectations of future rates to some degree. Moreover, there do appear to be liquidity premiums in the yield curve. However, if there are segmented-markets supply/demand factors in particular markets affecting the yield curve, these factors appear to be relatively minor and transitory.

REFERENCES

Culbertson, John, "The Term Structure of Interest Rates," *Quarterly Journal of Economics,* November 1957, pp. 485–517.

Hamburger, Michael J., and Elliott Platt, "The Expectations Hypothesis and the Efficiency of the Treasury Bill Market," *Review of Economics and Statistics,* May 1975, pp. 190–197.

Kessel, Reuben, *The Cyclical Behavior of the Term Structure of Interest Rates,* National Bureau of Economic Research, 1965.

Malkiel, Burton, *The Structure of Interest Rates* (New York: McCalb-Seiler, 1970).

Malkiel, Burton, and Edward J. Kane, "Expectations and Interest Rates: A Cross-Sectional Test of the Error-Learning Hypothesis," *Journal of Political Economy,* July–August 1968, pp. 453–470.

Meiselman, David, *The Term Structure of Interest Rates* (Englewood Cliffs, N.J.: Prentice-Hall, 1962.)

Modigliani, Franco, and Richard Sutch, "Innovation in Interest Rate Policy," *American Economic Review,* May 1966, pp. 178–197.

————, "Debt Management and The Term Structure of Interest Rates: An Empirical Analysis," *Journal of Political Economy,* August 1967, pp. 569–589.

Sargent, Thomas J., "Interest Rates in the 1950's," *Review of Economics and Statistics,* May 1960, pp. 164–172.

Wood, John, "Expectations, Errors, and the Term Structure of Interest Rates," *Journal of Political Economy,* April 1963, pp. 165–166.

Chapter 10

Inflation and Other Influences on the Structure of Interest Rates

As discussed in Chapter 9, the structure, or pattern, of relative interest rates on various financial instruments is heavily influenced by differences in the time to maturity of these financial assets. Yet there are many other considerations besides maturity that affect interest rates. This chapter focuses on a number of them: *inflation, default risk, taxes, callability,* and *marketability*. These factors do not include all the influences on the pattern of rates found in financial markets, but they do encompass the major elements. In particular, many of the changes that occurred in interest rates in the decade of the 1970s can be attributed to changes in the rate of inflation. Given the pervasive influence of inflation on the financial system in recent years, it is important to provide some background information on inflation itself before we discuss the influence on rates of the high and accelerating rates of inflation that have characterized recent years.

INFLATION

Definition: Inflation is commonly defined as an increase in some general index of prices, such as the Consumer Price Index or the broad-based Implicit Gross National Product Deflator.[1] In understanding inflation, we should recognize the difference between an

---

1. The Implicit Gross National Product Deflator is sometimes referred to as the overall price index since it incorporates the prices on all subcomponents of the gross national product: consumption, investment, government spending, and exports.

increase in the price of one good or service, which does not necessarily represent inflation, and an increase in a general index of prices, which does represent inflation. In a market-oriented economy at any point of time some prices are rising and some prices are falling. These changes in *relative* prices serve as the basic mechanism by which resources are allocated; increases in the price of some particular good or service need have no particular inflationary significance for the overall economy. Yet when an average of all prices—expressed in a price index—rises, then the economic problem of inflation becomes a matter of concern. The general nature of price inflation and its significance for interest rates are the subjects of the following discussion.

Causes of Inflation.   There are a number of different though not necessarily contradictory explanations of the causes of inflation. The two most common are called *demand-pull* and *cost-push* inflation. Demand-pull inflation, often characterized as the classic type of inflation, occurs when an excessive demand for goods and services presses on the capacity of the economy to meet those demands. Demand-pull inflation is often described as a situation in which "too many dollars are chasing too few goods." Most episodes of so-called runaway inflation, or hyperinflation, in countries around the world have been of the demand-pull type.[2] In the United States, the recent inflationary period began with the acceleration of spending for the Vietnam War in 1966, and the origin of this inflation is an example of demand-pull inflation. In 1966 the economy was near full employment of labor and capital resources following a period of six years of expansion. Nevertheless, tremendous increases in war expenditures were added to the existing private demand; taxes were not increased to "pay for the war." The result was to create a situation where literally too many dollars did chase too few goods and services, and to start one of the most persistent and significant inflationary periods in the history of the United States.

Explanation of the other type of inflation—cost-push—emphasizes the importance of the supply side of the supply/demand relationship as the determining factor in producing inflation. In this view, the monopolistic elements of powerful labor unions and large businesses that administratively set prices are crucial in influencing the rate of inflation. Increases in wages negotiated by strong unions cause increases in the costs of producing goods and services. Unless the increased costs are offset by increases in productivity—an uncommon occurrence in recent years—the labor cost per unit of output rises. Business, seeking to restore profit margins, reacts by raising prices. The increase in prices then causes labor to seek higher wages in order to offset the decline in living standards, and the wage/price spiral has begun. Although this illustration started with the negotiation of higher wages by the unions, it could just as easily have begun with business increasing its prices. There is no easy way to "pin the blame" on one segment of the economy. Each segment—

---

2. The German experience in the 1920s provided an excellent illustration of demand-pull inflation fueled by the printing press. By 1923, prices in Germany were 34 billion times as high as in 1921, a phenomenal change in a period of only two years. In this type of environment, in which individual savings accumulated through a period of years become valueless in a period of minutes, there is little incentive for hard work and saving.

business and labor—acts in its own self-interest, and yet this action results in price behavior that is not in the national interest.[3]

Bear in mind that, in reality, the two different types of inflation are closely related, and that it is indeed often difficult to separate existing inflation into the part that is attributable to demand factors and the part attributable to the wage/price spiral. Inflation is frequently begun by excess demand. Once inflation starts, however, workers and businessmen react in such a way that costs rise and prices are increased, setting off a wage/price spiral. Yet the increases in costs and prices can be permanent only if there is sufficient demand to absorb the potential output at the higher price levels.[4] Hence the two types of inflation become intimately connected and frequently indistinguishable.

Recent Inflation. Figure 10.1 provides a historical perspective on the inflationary experience of the United States since World War II. Examine the annual rates of change of the Consumer Price Index and the overall price index (the GNP Deflator), as presented in Fig. 10.1. Note that, with the exception of a brief period after World War II and during the Korean War in the early 1950s, the United States economy was remarkably free of sustained inflation from the early 1950s until the mid-1960s. Prices did rise, though generally by less than 2 or 3 percent per year. Moreover, many observers feel that increases in the quality of goods during that period were sufficient to offset the advance in prices, so an index that fully adjusted for quality changes would show little or no price increases. Yet this period of relatively stable prices came to an end in the mid-1960s, initially from demand-pull sources associated with the Vietnam War and then through combinations of demand-pull and cost-push periods in the late 1960s and throughout the 1970s. The annual rate of change in consumer prices and the broader overall price index reached "double-digit" levels in 1974, following the sharp rise in the price of oil, and again in 1979 and 1980, with the combination of excess demand at full-employment resource levels and further increases in the price of oil by the Organization of Petroleum Exporting Countries (OPEC).

As we will discuss below, there is a strong connection both in concept and in practice between inflation and levels of interest rates. This connection becomes apparent from the data given in Fig. 10.2, which presents a historical picture of changes in the cost of short-term borrowed funds for high-quality corporations—the prime commercial paper rate—as well as the cost of long-term borrowed funds for these firms with the highest credit

---

3. Economic theory has traditionally argued that individuals acting in their own self-interest would further the interest of the community. However, this argument assumes the existence of competitive markets. The cost-push inflation argument, in contrast, incorporates the monopolistic power of labor unions and large business firms.

4. The United States reaction to the increased price of oil established by the OPEC countries in 1974 provides an example of the validation of higher prices through the action of the central bank. The Federal Reserve System accommodated the increase in the price of one commodity by increasing bank reserves and the money supply. As a result, all prices tended to rise. The "losers"—those who had their living standard lowered because of the higher price—were the individuals and groups who were unable to keep their prices and wages in line with the general price rise.

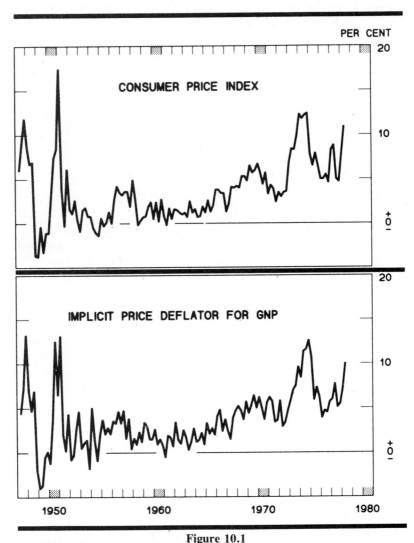

Figure 10.1
(Source: Board of Governors of the Federal Reserve System, *Historical Chart Book.*)

standing—the AAA corporate bond rate.[5] During the period from the early 1950s until the mid-1960s, both short- and long-term corporate rates were relatively low. For example, in 1964, AAA corporate bonds averaged not much more than 4 percent. Moreover, long-term rates were generally higher than short-term rates; in terms of the discussion in the previous

5. The rate on prime commercial paper should not be confused with the prime rate. The former is a rate on loans between large, high-quality businesses in which no financial institution plays a direct role. The latter is a rate on loans from a commercial bank to large, high-quality business firms. Chapters 13 and 14 provide more information on different money market rates.

LONG- AND SHORT-TERM INTEREST RATES

ANNUALLY

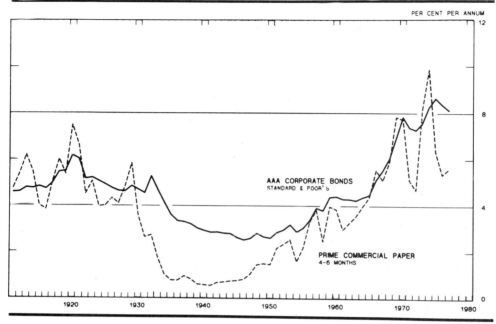

PER CENT PER ANNUM

AAA CORPORATE BONDS
STANDARD & POOR'S

PRIME COMMERCIAL PAPER
4-6 MONTHS

Figure 10.2
(Source: Board of Governors of the Federal Reserve System, *Historical Chart Book.*)

chapter, the yield curve was usually upward-sloping. Yet by the late 1970s, with high and rising inflation, interest rates had moved up sharply. The AAA corporate bond rate by 1979 exceeded 9 percent, and prime commercial paper rates exceeded 10 percent both in 1974 and in 1979. Moreover, short-term rates frequently exceeded long-term rates; thus an inverted yield curve existed. We now turn our attention to the basic reasons for this connection between inflation and interest rates.

Inflation and Interest Rates: An Explanation

The observed connection between changes in overall prices and the level of interest rates has a comparatively simple explanation. Perhaps the best way to provide this explanation is to discuss the impact of changing prices on the financial position of an individual. If interest rates were not related to changing prices, there would be a redistribution of wealth between lenders and borrowers as the result of changing prices. For example, a lender who extended a loan today of $1000 and was paid back tomorrow would receive only $500 worth of purchasing power if prices had doubled since the time the loan was made. A borrower would thus benefit from inflation if interest rates and changing prices were not related. In the example, the borrower would acquire $1000 of purchasing power at the time of the loan and would return to the lender only $500 of purchasing power. We would expect, then, that interest rates would reflect this potential loss to the lender and gain to the borrower such that the rate would adjust upward until there was no loss to the lender or gain to the borrower from the inflation.[6] At these rate levels, equilibrium would be established, and the inflation would not produce any redistribution of wealth between lenders and borrowers.

The Fisher Effect

This view of the relationship between price changes and interest rate levels may be visualized from the calculations in Fig. 10.3. Usually referred to as the *Fisher effect,* it is named for the economist Irving Fisher.[7] By this explanation, there is some basic and underlying *real* rate of interest, which is determined by the saving habits of the community and the productivity of capital investment[8] This "real" interest rate is thought to be relatively constant, at least in the short run. Although the precise level of the real rate is unknown, observation of interest rate levels in periods when inflation was not a problem suggests that the real rate is around 2 to 3 percent. Hence, in periods when inflation did not exist, we would expect that the rate lenders charged and borrowers paid—the *nominal* rate—would be 2 to 3 percent, the same as the real rate.

But how does this nominal rate change as the price level changes? We must recognize, of course, that it is the inflation rate *expected* to prevail over the life of the contract that is important, not the actual or past rate. A lender who contemplates making a loan for one year is concerned with the change in prices that will occur during that one-year period, and the lender is concerned with the current inflation rate only to the extent that it may serve as a predictor of future price change. But how does the nominal rate change as changes occur in the *expected* rate of inflation?

As discussed above and as illustrated in Example 1 of Fig. 10.3, in a period in which the expected rate of inflation is zero, the nominal rate and the real rate should be the same. If the real rate is 3 percent, then the nominal rate should also be 3 percent. But if expectations of inflation increased, we would expect that financial market rates would quickly adjust upward. As illustrated in Example 2 in Fig. 10.3, if prices were expected to rise by 10 percent during the duration of the financial contract, we would expect interest rates to adjust upward quickly to 13 percent. At the 13-percent level, neither borrower nor lender gains or loses from the expected inflation. For example, assume a one-year loan. The lender provides $1000 of purchasing power and receives back $1130 at the end of the year; if the $130 is the total return to the lender, $100 represents compensation for the loss of

---

6. There should be a very heavy demand for credit by borrowers in periods when the interest rate does not fully reflect inflation. The experience of the housing industry in the late 1970s provides illustration of this phenomenon. Individuals were quite willing to borrow to purchase houses since house prices were rising considerably more rapidly than the cost of money.

7. Irving Fisher, "Appreciation and Interest," *Publications of the American Economic Association,* August 1896, pp. 1–100.

8. See Chapter 8 for a more complete description of the determinant of the "real" rate.

Nominal rate = Real rate + Expected change in prices.

Examples:

1. Assume that expected increase in prices = 0%, real rate = 3%, and nominal rate = 3%.

    Nominal rate = Real rate + Expected change in prices.
            3% =   3%   + 0%.

2. Assume that expected increase in prices = 10%, real rate = 3%, and nominal rate = 13%.

    Nominal rate = Real rate + Expected change in prices.
           13% =   3%   + 10%.

3. Assume that expected increase in prices = 10%, real rate = 0%, and nominal rate = 10%.

    Nominal rate = Real rate + Expected change in prices.
           10% =   0%   + 10%.

Fig. 10.3 Price changes and interest rates

purchasing power and leaves the lender's inflation-adjusted financial position unchanged, whereas the $30 represents a "real" return to the lender.

Complications

One should recognize that the Fisher effect is something of an oversimplification of the workings of a complex financial world. In particular, the explanation does not take income taxes into account. The tax base for the application of the federal income tax is the nominal or total interest return, not the inflation-adjusted or real return.[9] In the example given above, the individual would be subject to federal income tax payments on the full $130 of interest, not just the $30 "real" return. Even if the financial markets adjusted fully to an expected inflation rate of 10 percent so that the nominal rate rose from 3 percent to 13 percent, the lender would still lose (if actual inflation proved to be 10 percent) because of the extra tax that would be required on the higher interest payments. This implies, of course, that once taxes are considered, an increase in expected inflation from 0 to 10 percent should result in a rise in the nominal rate of more than 10 percent.

Other complicating features of the connection between inflation and interest rates concern the stability of the real rate and the speed with which financial market rates adjust to changes in inflationary expectations. The "pure" Fisher effect basically assumes that the real rate is constant, and that financial markets adjust very quickly to changes in inflationary expectations. Neither of these assumptions may be completely valid. It may be that the real rate is variable, so changes in expected inflation impact partially or completely on the real rate as well as on the nominal rate. For example, refer again to Fig. 10.3. An increase in the

---

9. From the borrower's perspective, since interest expense is deductible for federal income tax purposes, the impact of higher interest rates on the borrower's position is reduced.

expected rate of inflation from 0 to 10 percent might be associated with a rise in the nominal rate to only 10 percent, in which case the real return to the investor (exclusive of tax considerations) would be 0 percent. Here, of course, the lender would lose as a result of the inflation, whereas the borrower would benefit. Moreover, if the financial markets adjusted slowly to inflation, the real rate of interest could be low or negative during the adjustment period. For example, if expectations of inflation went from 0 to 16 percent, the nominal rate might increase this year to 6 percent (implying a real rate of -10 percent), increase further to 10 percent in the second year (implying a real rate of -6 percent), and finally adjust to 19 percent in the third year (implying a real return of 3 percent). During the adjustment period, of course, lenders are harmed by the inflation while borrowers gain. Although few would argue that the connection between inflation and interest rates is perfectly described by the Fisher effect, most would agree that there is a strong relationship between the rate of inflation and the nominal interest rate.

Inflation and the Pattern of Rates

Up to this point our discussion of the impact of inflation has been in terms of "the" interest rate rather than the pattern of rates. However, changes in expected inflation should have a variety of effects on the structure of rates. Perhaps the most significant effect should be on the term structure of interest rates. For example, if the inflation rate was expected to increase at an accelerating rate—2 percent next year, 4 percent the year after, 6 percent in the third year, and so on—then the term structure should be greater in slope. Longer-term securities would have a higher rate than shorter-term securities. On the other hand, if inflation was quite strong in the current year but was expected to decline over time (for example, an expected rate of inflation of 9 percent in the current year, 6 percent in the second year, and 3 percent in the third year), then the term structure should be downward-sloping. Rates on three-year securities, for example, should be less than rates on one-year securities.

Changes in the expected rate of inflation might also produce a variety of effects in the structure of rates in more indirect ways. For example, expectations of increases in prices might cause rates on utility bonds to rise more than rates on industrial bonds. The logic behind this argument relates to the differences in pricing flexibility for the two segments of the economy. Utilities, which must obtain regulatory approval of rate increases, may find that inflation is increasing their costs more than their revenues, thereby reducing profitability and increasing the difficulty of repaying principal and interest on bonds outstanding. In contrast, industrial companies often have more flexibility in increasing prices and are able to maintain profit levels and their ability to meet their debt obligations. As another example, since inflation is frequently followed by recession, an increase in inflation may cause rates on lower-quality securities to rise more than rates on higher-quality securities. Lower-quality firms may have an especially difficult time in meeting their debt obligations in recessionary periods, but even a substantial decline in the economy need have no strong impact on the ability of "top-quality" firms to meet their debt obligations. However, since both of these arguments relate to the association between interest rates and credit risk, we will now explore that topic in some detail.

DEFAULT RISK

When credit is extended by a lender to a borrower, the expectation is—or at least should be—that the terms of the agreement will be fulfilled, interest will be paid as due, and principal will be repaid as scheduled. Unfortunately, it is not uncommon for events to occur during the life of the debt agreement that make it impossible for the borrower to meet the terms of the agreement. For a business, sales may decline because of changes in market taste or a recession in the economy. Or, costs may increase beyond expectations. For whatever reason, the borrower does not have the cash to make timely payment of principal and interest. It is this risk that is described as *default* or *credit* risk.

Default Risk Defined

Default risk refers to the probability that the borrower will be unable or unwilling to make the agreed-upon payments under a debt contract in a timely fashion. Default occurs whenever the borrower does not make a required payment or whenever the required payment is late. In either case, the lender has suffered a loss. If the payment is never made, the loss to the lender is obvious. If the payment is merely delayed, there is also loss, since the lender is unable to invest the funds and earn interest during the period of the delay. As a result, the interest return *actually realized* by the lender is less, in many cases substantially less, than the *rate agreed upon* in the loan contract.

Degrees of Default Risk

Default or credit risk exists on virtually all debt instruments. However, the degree of default risk varies widely. It is commonly accepted that U.S. government securities carry little or no default risk, since the U.S. government has the authority to meet its debt obligations by printing money. Indeed, the interest rate on U.S. government securities is often referred to as the "risk-free rate."[10] All other securities carry some degree of default risk. Securities issued by corporations obviously carry default risk. Changes in management, demand for products, costs, and other factors can produce default. We should also recognize that securities issued by state and local governments can carry substantial amounts of default risk, as the holders of New York City bonds unfortunately discovered in the mid-1970s. Although many state and local government securities are backed by the taxing power of the issuer, there is no guarantee that this taxing power will be used. Moreover, unlike the federal government, state and local governments do not have the ability to print money to pay their debts.

The Risk Premium

We would expect that financial market rates would adjust to compensate the lender for absorbing default risk. Rates on securities with large amounts of default risk should be

---

10. Like all debt securities, U.S. government securities bear "interest-rate" risk—the potential for unexpected changes in price due to changes in prevailing interest rates. For short-term U.S. government securities (such as three-month Treasury bills), this risk is minimal.

higher than rates on securities with low amounts of default risk. There should be a *risk structure* of interest rates. Not only should there be such a pattern, but indeed such relationships do exist and are among the most distinctive aspects of financial markets. The most common description of this relationship is provided by the concept of the *risk premium*. The risk premium is defined as the difference between the market rate on a security (yield to maturity at a point of time) and the risk-free rate for an equal maturity security.

$$\text{Risk premium} = \text{Yield to maturity} - \text{Risk-free rate}.$$

The risk premium describes the added return that the market requires over the risk-free rate in order for the investor to accept the default risk associated with a particular security. For example, if the risk-free rate is 5 percent, and if the market requires a 5-percent premium to accept the default risk on a high-risk security, then the yield to maturity on that security should be 10 percent. On a lower-risk security, where a 3-percent risk premium might be satisfactory, the yield to maturity would have to be only 8 percent. The entire spectrum of rates on corporate and state and local government securities of a particular maturity can be envisioned as a base "risk-free rate" plus a "risk premium."

Bond Ratings

There are a variety of ways to judge the default risk of various types of securities, but the approach most widely used, the one that is incorporated into the legal framework of regulation, is the bond-rating system of Moody's and Standard and Poor's. Both of these private organizations will provide, for a fee, a rating of any corporate or state or local government issue. The ratings range from the highest-quality issues through those that have some speculative characteristics and those that are principally speculative to those that are in default.

Figure 10.4 provides a brief explanation of the ratings for the various categories of securities. Note that the rating descriptions are essentially the same for the two agencies, although the symbols vary slightly. Moody's Aaa is "best quality," and Standard and Poor's AAA is "highest quality." When both agencies rate one bond, as they quite commonly do, the ratings are usually identical. As the ratings move from Aaa (AAA) to A and then into the B and C categories, the default risk increases, and we would expect that the risk premium would increase. The first four rating categories (Aaa to Baa or AAA to BBB) are especially significant. These categories collectively are referred to as "investment-grade" securities. They are particularly important since many financial institutions—including commercial banks—are limited in their security holdings to investment-grade issues.

The risk premium on differently rated corporate issues is graphically represented by Fig. 10.5. Note that, as expected, corporate issues have required higher rates than U.S. government issues (for the moment disregard the state and local securities). Financial

Rating	Description
Moody's	
Aaa	Best quality
Aa	High quality by all standards
A	Upper medium grade
Baa	Medium grade
Ba	Have speculative elements
B	Generally lack characteristics of the desirable investment
Caa	Poor standing; may be in default
Ca	Speculative in a high degree, often in default
C	Lowest grade; extremely poor prospects
Standard and Poor's	
AAA	Highest quality; extremely strong capacity
AA	High quality; very strong capacity
A	Strong capacity
BBB	Adequate capacity
BB	Low speculative
B	Speculative
CCC-CC	High speculation
C	Income bonds on which no interest is being paid
DDD-D	In default

Source: Moody's *Bond Record;* Standard and Poor's *Fixed Income Investor.*

Fig. 10.4   Bond-rating designations

markets do demand a higher return for placing funds in corporate securities, which carry default risk, than for investing in the "risk-free" U.S. government issues. Moreover, the risk premium on the lower-rated Baa issues is substantially greater than the risk premium on the Aaa issues. In fact, the risk premium on the Aaa issues is often very small, indicating that the financial markets expect a very low probability of default on the securities of the highest-quality corporations. Though not shown in Fig. 10.5, the risk premium on B-rated securities would be much larger than that for either Aaa or Baa securities.

One other aspect of the risk structure of rates that is brought out by Fig. 10.5 is the cyclical changes in risk premiums. Risk premiums on corporate issues appear to widen in periods of economic decline and to narrow in periods of economic expansion. This relationship is perhaps best illustrated by the difference between the risk premium in the 1930s and those in the 1950s, 1960s, and 1970s. But note also that the risk premiums in the post–World War II period have varied with the business cycle. For example, the risk premium on Baa securities became quite large in the recession of 1974–1975, as well as in the recession of 1969–1970. Declines in business activity associated with recession, especially sharp recession, appear to cause investors to take more seriously the prospect of default on debt securities, so such declines may be associated with greater risk aversion on the part of investors.

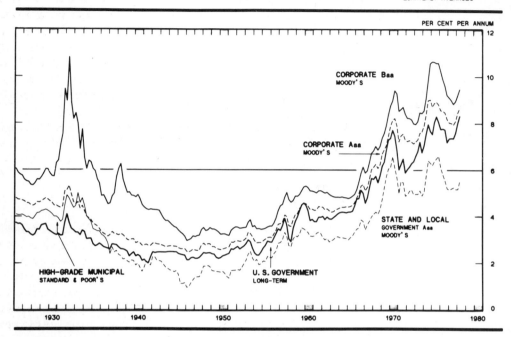

Figure 10.5
(Source: Board of Governors of the Federal Reserve System, *Historical Chart Book.*)

TAXABILITY

Differences in the way the returns to investors are treated under the tax laws are among the most significant factors influencing the pattern of interest rates in financial markets. Four considerations are especially relevant. First, the interest income on security issues of state governments and their subdivisions (commonly referred to as "municipal" securities) is exempt from the federal income tax. Moreover, interest income from municipal securities is usually exempt from the income taxes imposed by state and local governments in the state of issue. Second, the interest income on United States government securities is exempt from income taxes imposed by state and local governments. Although each of these two factors relates directly to the nature of the security, the third factor—the differential treatment of ordinary income and capital gains—has only an indirect impact on the relative structure of interest rates.[11] However, that impact is powerful. Fourth, some U.S. government securities may be used at par prior to maturity to settle estate tax liabilities (so-called flower bonds). We now turn to a discussion of the influence of each of these factors.

---

11. Long-term capital gains are taxed at a lower rate than ordinary income. Currently, 60 percent of any long-term capital gain is excluded from tax.

Exemption of Municipal Interest Income

The exemption of municipal interest income from federal income taxation and the further exemption of municipal interest income from some state and local income taxes should have a profound impact on the yield on municipal securities, as compared with the yield on corporate and U.S. government issues. For example, an investor in the 50-percent tax bracket, who could purchase a corporate bond with a yield of 10 percent, would be better off buying a municipal security, as long as the municipal yield exceeded 5 percent, since the after-tax return on the corporate bond is only 5 percent [(10%) (1 − tax rate)].[12] The tax advantage of municipal securities should then lead to a large demand for municipals, increasing their price and lowering their return. Indeed, examination of Fig. 10.5 does show that pretax interest rates on municipal securities are substantially below those on corporate and U.S. government securities. It also shows that the differential is larger in the post–World War II period than in the prewar era, reflecting the higher income tax rates in recent years.[13]

A further (though minor) influence on the pattern of rates is the exemption from income taxation of interest income on securities issued in the same state. This consideration is especially relevant in influencing the demand for securities from states with high state and local income taxes. For example, since both New York State and New York City have substantial income taxes, we would expect that residents of New York (both individuals and corporations) would have a special demand for New York securities. As a result, these securities could probably be sold to residents of New York State at a yield lower than those on municipal securities issued by other states and by local governments in states other than New York.

Exemption of U.S. Government Interest Income

The exemption of interest income on municipal securities from the federal income tax stems from the historical concept of the federal and state governments' both having sovereignty. Although the Civil War settled the issue of supremacy between federal and state governments, the exemption of interest income on municipal securities from the federal income tax currently serves as a means for the federal government to subsidize (through lower borrowing rates) state and local governments. However, the exemption of interest income on U.S. government securities from state and local income taxes is grounded in the U.S. Constitution and its interpretation by the Supreme Court. Since taxing authority conveys great power, state and local governments cannot tax the interest income from federal government securities.

12. In January 1981, Aaa municipal securities yielded 9.00 percent, and Aaa corporate bonds yielded 12.83 percent. This suggests that an investor in a tax bracket above 30 percent would obtain a higher after-tax return from the municipal than from the corporate issues.

13. We should note that the differentials in rates on municipals relative to corporate and U.S. government securities also reflect differences in credit risk, as well as differences in taxability. Municipal yields were actually *higher* than U.S. government yields in the 1920s, when there were considerable problems with defaults on state and local government issues.

One should understand that the interest income from U.S. government securities is exempt only from the income tax levies of state and local governments. The interest income from U.S. government securities is fully taxable by the federal government. Since state and local government income taxes are low as compared with the federal income tax, the impact on the relative structure of rates in the financial markets should be minimal. We would expect, however, that the rates on U.S. government securities would be lowered slightly as compared with corporate and other issues by the exemption of the interest income on these securities from state and local government income taxes.

Capital Gains versus Ordinary Income Taxes

Returns to investors on fixed-income securities may take the form of either interest income or capital gains. In a world without taxes, one would expect the investor to be indifferent between a dollar of interest return and a dollar of capital gains return. At present, however, capital gains returns are taxed at a lower rate than are interest returns, and investors thus prefer to take their returns in the form of capital gain rather than ordinary income. In fact, since returns on assets held more than one year are taxed at a rate less than one half of ordinary income, the tax-paying investor has substantial reason to prefer capital gains returns.

The differential tax treatment of ordinary income and capital gains has a profound impact on the yield to maturity on corporate and U.S. government bonds. Bonds that were issued in an earlier, lower-interest-rate period and that carry a lower coupon must sell at a price below par in order to offer a competitive yield to maturity. These so-called discount or deep discount bonds offer the investor a total return (interest return plus capital gains return) that is more heavily weighted toward capital gains than is true of bonds that sell near par. Investors (especially investors in high tax brackets) have a special demand for these issues, bidding up their price, and lowering the yield to maturity. As a result, deep discount corporate and U.S. government securities will sell at a lower yield to maturity than comparable bonds that have high coupon rates and sell at a price near par.

One must recognize that this relationship is valid only for taxable securities (corporate and U.S. government issues). For tax-free issues (municipals), the relationship is the reverse. Investors in municipal securities obtain a tax-free return from interest but incur tax liabilities or obligations on capital gains on these securities. Hence investors have reason to prefer municipal issues that sell at or near par and return primarily interest to those that sell at a discount and return substantial capital gains. As a result, deep discount *municipal* securities should sell at a yield that is *higher* than comparable high-coupon municipal issues.

Flower Bonds

The term "flower bonds" is applied to U.S. Treasury bonds that may be purchased at a discount and used at par value plus accrued interest to satisfy federal estate tax liabilities.

The name presumably derives from the connection between funeral flowers and estate tax liabilities; these bonds are also referred to as tombstone bonds—for equally obvious reasons. However, the provision allowing for the creation of flower bonds was repealed as of March 3, 1971. With no new flower bonds being issued and outstanding flower bonds being used to satisfy estate tax liabilities, the amount of flower bonds has gradually been decreasing. In 1980 there were roughly $15 billion of flower bonds outstanding.

Flower bonds represent a special group of discount bonds. Issued in an earlier period with coupons that are low compared with current interest rate levels, flower bonds must sell at prices below par to attract investors. Yet whereas other discount bonds can provide a capital gain only at maturity, flower bonds can provide a capital gain at the death of the holder and settlement of the estate tax liabilities. A special demand is thereby created for flower bonds from investors who have estate tax liabilities and who anticipate death in the near future. As a result of this special demand, flower bonds will offer lower yields than do comparable U.S. government bonds that do not carry the flower bond feature.[14]

CALLABILITY

Callability refers to the ability of the issuer of a security to call it away from the holder (retire it) prior to maturity. Most corporate bonds are callable, some municipal securities are callable, and only a few United States government securities are callable. The influence of the call feature on the pattern of yields in financial markets can perhaps best be understood by examining the conditions under which a security might be called and the impact of the call on the positions of borrower and lender.

The call feature is a characteristic attached to a security that is *advantageous to the borrower.* This feature allows the borrower to eliminate prior to maturity a security with excessively high interest rates or other undesirable features, such as a restriction on dividend payments. However, if the motive is to reduce interest expense (as it usually is), the bond will be called only if rates have declined since the original issue date. *From the lender's perspective, the call feature is undesirable.* A call of the security before maturity is most likely to occur when the opportunities for reinvestment available to the lender are limited and when the potential return available to the lender is low.

Since the call feature is advantageous to the borrower but unfavorable to the lender, callable bonds may be expected to carry a higher interest rate than comparable noncallable bonds. Lenders demand higher interest rates on callable bonds to protect them against the risk of having the bonds called when reinvestment rates are low. Borrowers, in turn, are willing to pay a higher rate for the call feature, since it provides an opportunity to obtain lower-interest financing over the life of the security and to eliminate any undesirable restrictions on management imposed under the terms of the security. As a general rule, in fact, callable bonds do carry higher interest rates than noncallable bonds. However, the

---

14. For example, flower bonds generally plot below the yield curve. Thus they offer a pretax yield to maturity that is less than would be expected, given the maturity of the issues (see Fig. 9.2).

interest rate differential appears to be directly related to the level of interest rates. When rates are high, the call feature adds a substantial amount to the return on the bond. When rates are high as compared with some past "normal" level of rates, they are expected to fall in the future. It is under these circumstances that lenders demand higher returns on callable bonds, and borrowers are willing to pay higher rates. When rates are low, callable bonds carry little or no extra return to investors. In periods when interest rates are low as compared with some past "normal" level of rates, there is no real expectation that rates will decline further. Lenders are not greatly concerned about the prospect of a call of the securities, nor are borrowers willing to pay a substantial amount to add a call feature to their securities.

MARKETABILITY

One influence on the pattern of interest rates that is difficult to quantify but nonetheless important is marketability. Although many investors purchase securities with the objective of holding the securities until maturity, their circumstances may change, and they may wish to sell the securities prior to maturity. There are also investors who *expect* to sell their securities prior to maturity. The latter group is especially important in the purchase and sale of relatively short-term securities. Since the ability to liquidate securities prior to maturity is a favorable characteristic to investors, we would expect that those securities with high marketability would carry interest rates that are lower than those of comparable securities with low marketability.

There are various dimensions to the marketability characteristic. First is the simple matter of whether a market exists for the securities in question. Is there trading in the security in which the free interplay of supply and demand determines the price of the security? For most corporate bonds there is no market in which existing bonds are traded. Second, if a market exists, how "good" is that market? Is it possible to buy or sell a large quantity of securities quickly and without substantial influence on price? For example, the market for existing U.S. government securities is strong, and it is possible for the buyer or seller to place large quantities of securities in this market without distorting the market price. One of the reasons for the relatively low rate on U.S. government securities is their high marketability, and one of the reasons for the relatively high rate on corporate bonds is their relatively low marketability. Unfortunately, however, it is very difficult to quantify the precise influence of marketability on relative yield.

SUMMARY

There are many factors that influence yields on securities. In recent years, inflation has been one of the most pervasive influences on interest rates. According to the Fisher effect, the rate of interest may be viewed as a constant real rate with an inflation premium that reflects expectations of future inflation. Given a constant real rate, the nominal rate will rise and fall exactly in response to changes in inflationary expectations. However, if there are different inflationary expectations for different periods in the future, the maturity or term structure of interest rates will be altered. In addition to being affected by inflation, interest rates on securities are affected by credit or default risk; differences in the taxability of the returns from particular securities; callability; and marketability features. These factors are not all those that affect interest rate movements, but taken together they explain a substantial portion of the changes that occur in interest rates on different securities.

The financial markets present an intricate network of rates on thousands of financial assets. The general level of interest rates may rise or fall or remain unchanged on a given day while the pattern of rates within the network is adjusting constantly. Yet disentangling the influences of *inflation, credit risk, taxability, callability,* and *marketability* on daily changes in interest rates on financial assets is not easy. At the least, however, we hope that the foregoing discussion serves to provide a logical framework within which students of financial market developments may organize their analyses. Without an understanding of the underlying forces that are continually influencing the pattern of rates, there is no way to see changes in financial markets as anything but a random process.

QUESTIONS

1. Why is it important to distinguish between a change in relative prices and a change in the general level of prices? Can this distinction be applied to the inflationary implications of the oil price increases in 1973 and again in 1979?

2. What has been the rate of inflation in the United States during the last year? Is this inflation caused by demand-pull or cost-push factors? Justify your argument.

3. Assume that prices are expected to increase by the same amount in the next year as in the past year. What is the "real" rate of interest consistent with this forecast? Does the market appear to have fully adjusted to the expected inflation?

4. Is the risk-free rate really risk-free? What element of risk might exist in the risk-free rate?

5. Carefully explain the potential impact on the interest rate on bonds issued by large commercial banks of the failure of five major United States banks.

6. What should happen to the interest rate on a bond whose rating was changed by Moody's from AAA to Aa? From Baa to Aa?

7. What is the probable effect on the interest rate on deep discount bonds of a large reduction in the capital gains tax rate? Explain.

8. How would an increase in the income tax rates affect the return on municipal securities? Why?

9. Compare interest rates on corporate, municipal, and U.S. government bonds today with those one year ago, and see if the changes in yield from one year to the next and between types of securities can be explained by the factors discussed in the chapter.

REFERENCES

Choate, G.M., and S.H. Archer, "Irving Fisher, Inflation, and the Nominal Rate of Interest," *Journal of Financial and Quantitative Analysis,* November 1975, pp. 675–685.

Cohan, Avery B., *The Risk Structure of Interest Rates* (Morristown, N.J.: General Learning Press, 1973).

Darst, David M., *The Complete Bond Book* (New York: McGraw-Hill, 1975).

Fisher, Irving, *The Theory of Interest* (New York: Macmillan, 1930).

Homer, Sidney, and Martin Leibowitz, *Inside the Yield Book* (Englewood Cliffs, N.J.: Prentice-Hall, 1972).

Jen, Frank C., and James E. Wert, "The Effect of Call Risk on Corporate Bond Yields," *Journal of Finance,* December 1967, pp. 637–651.

Sargent, Thomas J., "Interest Rates and Expected Inflation: A Selective Summary of Recent Research," *Explanations in Economic Research,* Summer 1976, pp. 303–325.

Van Horne, James, *Financial Market Rates and Flows* (Englewood Cliffs, N.J.: Prentice-Hall, 1978). Chs. 5–8.

Part IV
Financial Markets

Chapter 11

Risk, Return, and the Efficiency of Financial Markets

This chapter is the first of eight chapters that focus on the nature and role of financial markets in the financial system. The principal objective of these chapters is description and analysis of the instruments and operations of the financial marketplace, but they also fill another important need by providing an integrated view of the U.S. financial system. The latter objective is best achieved in this part of the book, for it is in financial markets that deficit and surplus economic units and financial intermediaries "come together" to exchange financial instruments. The financial marketplace is the "engine" of the financial system, the arena in which interest rates and security prices are established and where huge sums of funds flow among market agents.

Previous chapters of this book have served to introduce various important aspects of financial markets and to provide a description of the role they play in the financial system. The present chapter offers a more detailed treatment of certain of these topics. It is then followed by chapters that focus on the principal types of financial markets, the financial instruments traded in them, and the ways that the operations of financial institutions are influenced by events in the financial marketplace.

This chapter first offers an analysis of the asset-pricing function of financial markets and then provides an overview of the various types of financial markets.

PART 1: ASSET PRICING IN FINANCIAL MARKETS

The role of the financial system in the saving-investment process has been described in preceding chapters. Chapter 2 indicated the essential role of saving in economic growth, and it described how financial markets (and the other components of the financial system) serve to facilitate this expansion of an economy's productive capacity by providing a mechanism for external financing to economic units seeking funds to invest. Succeeding chapters described the saving and investment process in a "flow of funds" context (Chapter 3), the various financial intermediaries (Chapter 4), the role of government in the financial system (Chapter 5), interest rate determination (Chapter 8), and the significance of the level and structure of interest rates (Chapters 9 and 10).

The previous chapters focused primarily on *aggregate* saving and investment and the various factors that impact on their magnitudes. The discussion in those chapters was concerned with the quantity of saving by surplus economic units and with the reasons for such saving, not with what (or why) particular financial assets might be chosen as a repository for savings. Similarly, discussion of which financial instruments might be used by borrowers or of what decision criteria would be employed to select among alternative instruments was also deferred to the present chapter.

Underlying aggregate saving and investment, of course, are innumerable individual economic decisions made by participants in the financial marketplace, and the principal factors bearing on these decisions warrant additional discussion. Specifically, the determination of prices and yields of financial instruments traded in financial markets and thus the allocation of the funds of surplus economic units among deficit economic units hinge on the supply and demand for these instruments. The nature of the process underlying the pricing of securities is thus of considerable significance to an understanding of financial markets. In turn, an understanding of this process requires some attention to certain aspects of financial behavior, particularly those relating to *portfolio selection*—how surplus economic units allocate saved funds among the various financial instruments created by deficit units and intermediaries.

PORTFOLIO SELECTION AND DIVERSIFICATION

Risk, Return, and Expected Utility

Chapter 2 included an introductory discussion of the process by which prices of financial assets are determined. We indicated there that the price of a financial asset is a function of its *expected return* and the degree of *risk* associated with that expected return. The expected return is simply the weighted average of all possible returns, where the weights are the probabilities of each possible return. A common measure of the risk associated with the expected return is the variance (or the standard deviation, which is the square root of the variance) of the probability distribution of possible returns. Figure 11.1 shows a sample calculation of expected returns for two hypothetical securities, with possible returns and

Security A

Possible rate of return		Probability of possible rate of return		
0%	×	.3	=	0.0%
10%	×	.2	=	2.0%
18%	×	.4	=	7.2%
30%	×	.1	=	3.0%
		Expected rate of return	=	12.2%

Security B

Possible rate of return		Probability of possible rate of return		
5%	×	.3	=	1.5%
8%	×	.4	=	3.2%
10%	×	.3	=	3.0%
		Expected rate of return	=	7.7%

Fig. 11.1 Calculation of expected return

Security A

Possible rate of return	−	Expected rate of return	=	Variation of possible from expected rates of return	Variation squared	×	Probability of possible rates of return	=	
0%	−	12.2%	=	−12.2%	148.84	×	.3	−	44.65%
10%	−	12.2%	=	− 2.2%	4.84%	×	.2	=	.97%
18%	−	12.2%	=	5.8%	33.64%	×	.4	=	13.46%
30%	−	12.2%	=	17.8%	316.84%	×	.1	=	31.68%

Variance of returns = 90.76%

Standard deviation of returns = $\sqrt{90.76\ \%}$ = 9.5%

Security B

Possible rate of return	−	Expected rate of return	=	Variation of possible from expected rates	Variation squared	×	Probability of possible rates of return	=	
5%	−	7.7%	=	−2.7%	7.29%	×	.3	=	2.187%
8%	−	7.7%	=	.3%	.09%	×	.4	=	.036%
10%	−	7.7%	=	2.3%	5.29%	×	.3	=	1.587%

Variance of returns = 3.81 %

Standard deviation of returns = $\sqrt{3.81\ \%}$ = 1.95 %

Fig. 11.2 Calculation of variance of security returns

corresponding probabilities as shown. Figure 11.2 indicates how the variance (and standard deviation) of the return of each hypothetical security is calculated.

As indicated in Figs. 11.1 and 11.2, Security A and Security B offer expected returns of 12.2 percent and 7.7 percent, respectively. That "expected return" is a statistical artifact is evidenced by the fact that the calculated expected return for the two securities does not correspond to any of their particular possible returns. Nonetheless, to the extent that the identification of possible returns and their associated probabilities of occurrence reflect full and proper utilization of all available relevant information, the expected return calculation does offer an intuitively satisfying assessment of the likely profitability of a financial asset. The variance (and thus the standard deviation) measures the "spread" between the various possible rates of return and the expected return. The smaller the "spread," the greater the confidence one can attach to an expected return measure—the smaller the variance (standard deviation), the smaller is the degree of risk associated with realization of the expected return.

Although expected return and variance calculations are useful in security selection, they cannot alone necessarily resolve a choice among alternative securities. Consider, for example, a choice between Security A and Security B of the example above. Security A offers a 12.2 percent expected return versus a 7.7 percent expected return for Security B, but Security A's returns are subject to greater risk (a standard deviation of about 9.5 percent versus Security B's approximately 2 percent).[1] Does the higher expected return of Security A offset its greater variability in returns relative to Security B? The answer to this question depends on preferences regarding risk and return. Attitudes and behavior toward risk differ among individuals, and since risk is generally associated with security returns, risk-return preferences must be taken into account in security choices.

The concept of *expected utility* combines expected return, risk, and risk-return preferences.[2] Thus we will assume that investors (for the sake of brevity, we will now use the popular term for surplus economic units seeking to acquire financial assets with saved funds) are averse to risk and seek to maximize *expected utility* from their investments. (As the reader probably already knows, "utility" is the economist's label for happiness.) In other words, investors will select securities that offer the mix of expected return and associated risk that, given their risk-return preferences, makes them the most content.

To illustrate, suppose that Mr. Wary and Ms. Bold are two investors evaluating our Security A, with its expected return of 12.2 percent and standard deviation of 9.5 percent,

---

1. In effect, the standard deviation, as a risk measure, incorporates the degree to which possible returns differ from the expected return and the associated probability of such deviations. Thus positive deviations (possible returns *exceeding* the expected return), as well as negative deviations (possible returns *less than* expected returns), are reflected in the standard deviation calculation. Since investors are likely to be troubled by the latter possibility and not the former, it is important to remember that standard deviation measures reflect not only undesired variability in returns but also total variability.

2. The concept of expected utility, together with its relation to portfolio selection, is developed much more rigorously in several of the references cited at the end of this chapter. We choose to develop only an intuitive appreciation of the concept in this book.

and Security B, with expected return of 7.7 percent and standard deviation of 2 percent. Mr. Wary, who is very risk-averse, will maximize expected utility by investing in Security B; in his utility function, the lower risk (as measured by the standard deviation) compensates for the lower return, as compared with Security A. Ms. Bold, who is less risk-averse than Mr. Wary, will maximize expected utility by investing in Security A, with its higher expected return (and higher risk).

We have to know the degree of risk aversion that characterizes the risk-return preferences of an investor in order to predict the choice between securities (such as those in the example above), one of which offers a higher expected return than the other but also higher risk. We can confidently predict the (rational) choice, however, when the decision involves two securities with the same expected return but differing risk, or with the same risk but differing expected returns. In such cases, one investment possibility "dominates" the other. The risk-averse investor should select the security with the highest expected return for a given degree of risk, or the security with the lowest degree of risk for a given expected return. This "dominance" principle holds also for *portfolios*—collections of securities. An *efficient* portfolio is a collection of securities that offers the highest possible expected return for the level of portfolio risk or the lowest level of risk for a given expected portfolio return. We look now at some aspects of efficient portfolios that have considerable significance for security pricing.

Security Selection for Efficient Portfolios

It should be recalled that the purpose of the present discussion is to consider how investor selection of financial assets impacts on security pricing in financial markets. To this point we have considered only individual securities and have asserted that investors will select financial investments on the basis of securities' expected returns and risk according to each investor's own risk-return preferences. To the extent that investors are risk-averse, they will purchase riskier securities only if such securities offer expected returns commensurate with their additional risk. We can expect, then, that financial markets will "price" securities so that their expected returns and risk are commensurate.

The story does not end here, however, because investment in a single security, though not unheard of, is not representative of aggregate financial market behavior. Most security selection decisions are made in the context of adding (or not adding) a particular security to an existing portfolio of securities. Since an investor is concerned with the return and risk characteristics of the total *portfolio,* the relevant aspects of a potential addition to the portfolio are the change (if any) in portfolio expected return and risk resulting from acquisition of the security.

The expected rate of return for a portfolio is simply the weighted average of each constituent security's expected rate of return. The weights are the proportions of each security's invested value, relative to total portfolio value. Thus the effect of a potential new investment on portfolio expected return can be readily determined. The effect on portfolio risk (as measured by portfolio standard deviation), however, is much more complex. Except in the highly unlikely case that the possible returns of the security under consideration are "perfectly positively correlated" (they move in the same direction and in the same magnitude) with the possible returns of the portfolio as presently constituted, the standard deviation of the reconstituted portfolio will *not* be the weighted average of its constituent securities' standard deviation of returns. Indeed, a portfolio will never have a standard deviation of possible returns equal to the weighted average of the standard deviation of returns of its component securities unless returns of all these securities are perfectly positively correlated. This phenomenon is what makes possible the risk-reducing effects of diversification. It also causes the relevant risk measure of an individual security (the risk level reflected in the security's price) to be not the standard deviation of its returns but the *incremental risk* to a portfolio of the inclusion of the security in that portfolio.

Covariance

In mathematical terms, the returns of the various assets in a portfolio may be viewed as random variables. The *covariance* is the measure of the extent to which these random variables vary in the same way and to the same degree.[3] The mathematics of covariance calculation is rather complex, and we need not employ it here.[4] For our purposes, all that is necessary is an intuitive appreciation of how the covariance relationship among security returns may have the effect of lowering portfolio variance (and thus standard deviation) when securities are combined in portfolios. This effect is essentially due to the fact that, to the degree that the behavior of the returns of the various securities is independent (the returns are not perfectly positively correlated), unusually low returns on some securities are not likely to occur in the same periods when unusually low returns occur on other assets in the portfolio. The effect is a "balancing out" of returns among the various assets in the portfolio.

Suppose now that an investor holding a portfolio with equal amounts of investment in Security X and Security Y is considering adding another financial asset, Security Z, to the portfolio. What are the relevant decision variables? One key variable is the expected return of Security Z, since the new portfolio expected return would be the weighted average of the expected returns of Securities X, Y, and Z. The variance (or standard deviation) of Security Z *alone,* however, is *not* relevant to the investor's decision, except as it impacts on portfolio variance. The relevant measure of risk for Security Z is the *change* in the risk of the portfolio as the result of adding Security Z (in whatever amount) to the portfolio. The degree of

---

3. Covariance and correlation are obviously closely related concepts. The covariance measure for two securities is equal to the coefficient of correlation between the two securities multiplied by the standard deviations of the two securities.

4. Many investment and business finance textbooks offer a mathematical and graphical exposition of the risk-reducing effects of diversification in portfolio selection. See, for example, J. C. Francis, *Investments: Analysis and Management* (New York: McGraw-Hill, 1980, pp. 476–518) for an excellent development and discussion. The architect of modern portfolio theory is H. M. Markowitz, whose seminal work is cited in the references at the end of this chapter.

change in portfolio variance that will result is a function of the covariance of Security Z returns with those of Security X and Security Y, as well as Security Z's "own variance."

As more and more assets are added to a portfolio, the contribution of the incremental assets' "own variance" to portfolio variance becomes less and less. In a well-diversified portfolio, the incremental asset's "own variance" term is insignificant, and only the covariance of its returns with those of the other assets in the portfolio will have an impact on portfolio risk. Such a degree of diversification can be achieved with as few as 8 to 12 stocks (if selected from unrelated industries). Indeed, diversification becomes superfluous at some relatively small number of securities, because it becomes more and more difficult to identify securities that offer a pattern of possible returns that are *not* highly correlated with returns of securities already included in the portfolio. This is true whether the investor diversifies "naively" (by selecting cross-industry stocks at random) or "efficiently" (by assessing covariance relationships).

The covariance-calculation approach, unfortunately, requires such a huge number of inputs and computations that it is not practical to apply it to portfolio selection in the form outlined above. This approach requires an assessment of expected return, expected variance, and the covariance of returns for each security being considered for inclusion in a portfolio with all other securities presently or potentially included in the portfolio. For n securities, there are $n(n-1)/2$ covariances, so an analysis of only 25 securities would require 25 expected returns, 25 variances, and 300 covariances.

The key to a more operational approach to efficient portfolio selection lies in the distinction between two kinds of risk relating to security returns—systematic and unsystematic.

Systematic Versus Unsystematic Risk

Recall that the returns of most securities are positively correlated (tending to move in the same direction) but are not perfectly positively correlated (magnitudes and direction of movement not exactly equal). Why is this so often true? The answer is twofold. First, recognize that virtually all business enterprises are affected by economywide events, but not to the same degree. A recession, for example, will impact much more seriously on a firm in the recreation field than on one in the retail grocery business. An economic upswing, on the other hand, will be much more stimulating to recreation-related business firms than to food-related firms. Such broad economic developments affect returns on securities of virtually all firms in all industries, but they affect some much more than others.

The variability in returns of securities that is attributable to economywide trends and events is termed *systematic risk*. Because, by definition, this type of risk pertains to all firms (and thus returns of securities of all firms), it cannot be diversified out of a portfolio. Systematic risk is embodied in the positive covariance that exists among most security returns (in varying degrees).

Unsystematic risk is firm-specific and not the result of economywide developments. Successful new products, crippling strikes, discoveries of larcenous activities on the part of top management, cost-cutting new processes—these are examples of events in an enterprise's existence that are independent of those affecting other firms, and that give rise to positive or negative variability in returns. Such unsystematic variability in the returns of the securities of a given firm is unrelated to the variability in returns of other firms and thus can be eliminated from an efficiently diversified portfolio.

It is this distinction between systematic (undiversifiable) and unsystematic (diversifiable) risk that underlies an operational approach to portfolio selection and provides an important conceptual framework for understanding financial market behavior—the capital-asset pricing model.

THE CAPITAL-ASSET-PRICING MODEL

Suppose that an individual investor holds an efficient portfolio of financial assets. To qualify as "efficient," the portfolio must be characterized by the following factors.

1. No other collection of financial assets could offer a greater expected return at the same level of risk or could offer a lower level of risk without some decrease in expected return.

2. All unsystematic risk has been eliminated by diversification. (This second aspect of the portfolio is actually implicit in the first.)

The risk-return trade-off is now a *systematic risk* versus expected return trade-off, and it will be determined by the investor's risk-return preferences. The more risk-averse the investor, the lower the level of systematic risk(s) he or she will be willing to assume, and thus the lower the level of expected return(s) the investor can anticipate. How may systematic risk be measured in order to allow investors to efficiently construct portfolios to satisfy their preferences?

The basis for development of a measure of systematic risk is a *market index*—an available measure of returns for a collection of financial assets. For the stock market, for example, the Standard and Poor's 500 Stock Composite Index offers a measure of average returns for a broad sample of equity securities. The returns for a given security can then be compared with this index of returns in order to develop a measure of variability in this security's returns relative to "market" returns. This measure can be developed from the covariance of the individual security's returns with market returns, and it serves as an index of a security's systematic risk.

The *beta coefficient* (which statistically is the covariance between a security's returns and market returns, divided by the variance of market returns) provides an index of systematic risk. If a security has a beta of 1, its degree of systematic variability in returns corresponds to that of overall market returns. A beta greater than 1 indicates a degree of systematic variability exceeding that of the "market portfolio," and a beta less than 1 indicates a less systematically variable pattern of returns than that of the overall market. A beta of 0 indicates an absence of systematic variation in returns relative to the market—a (systematic) risk-free security.

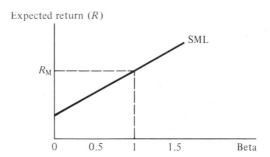

Fig. 11.3 The security market line (SML)

Given the prevalence of risk aversion, one would expect securities with high betas to be priced so as to offer higher expected rates of return than low-beta securities offer. Figure 11.3, the "security market line," shows this expected relationship. (Note that at a beta equal to 1, the expected return is that of the overall market portfolio, R_M.) The beta of a portfolio is the weighted average of the betas of the various securities in the portfolio. An investor can thus "tailor" a portfolio with the degree of systematic risk (and expected return) consistent with his or her preferences.

The body of portfolio theory underlying the "market model" suggests that there is a single portfolio of *risky* securities that is optimal for all investors—the market portfolio itself. This optimal combination, in theory, consists of *all* risky securities in existence in the proportions in which they are outstanding in the securities markets.

If a particular security was not included in this optional portfolio or was held in less than its proportionate value relative to all securities, its price would fall, and its expected return would increase. The rise in the expected return of the security would prompt its purchase by investors, which would result in its inclusion in the optimal portfolio in the proportion of its relative value in the securities market. On the other hand, holdings of a security in excess of its proportionate value would trigger its sale by investors, driving down its price and lowering its aggregate value. Security prices are thus the "adjustment variable" for optimal portfolio composition. As previously indicated, the market portfolio has a beta of 1. Does this imply that a beta of 1 is optimal for all investors? The answer is no, because a very risk-averse investor can mix risky security holdings with riskless securities (beta of 0) in whatever proportions fit that investor's risk-return preferences (a weighted average beta perhaps somewhere between 0 and 1). A less risk-averse investor, on the other hand, can borrow (in theory, though not in practice, at the risk-free rate of interest) and invest the proceeds in the market portfolio of risky assets. This "leveraging," as the use of low-interest borrowed funds to acquire high-interest assets is called, allows the investor to increase the expected rate of return, but only with a commensurate increase in risk.

Figure 11.4 shows the foregoing relationship, the "capital market line." All points along the line *RM* represent combinations of expected rates of return and standard deviation of return corresponding to mixtures of investments in riskless securities and the market portfolio of risky securities. (At *R* the investor holds only riskless securities and at *M* only

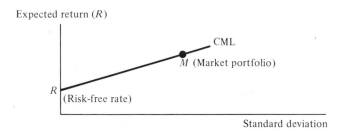

Fig. 11.4   The capital market line (CML)

risky securities.) Combinations of expected return and risk on the line to the right of *M* correspond to investments in the market portfolio that include the use of borrowed funds (As the capital market line, CML, is drawn here, borrowing at the risk-free rate is assumed to be possible. Differential borrowing and lending rates simply change the intercept and slope of the CML).

In practice, of course, one can only approximate the requirements of this theoretical construct, but close approximation is possible. In terms of market-related variability of returns, U.S. Treasury bills are a reasonable proxy as a "riskless" asset. And although one can hardly include holdings of all risky securities in a portfolio, a market-index mutual fund offers a readily available investment medium that will exhibit much the same behavior as would characterize such a portfolio.

To the extent that investors do construct portfolios in the foregoing manner, the implications for the behavior of financial markets is profound and to some extent startling.

Financial Asset Pricing in an Efficient Market

The portfolio theory sketched in this chapter is a normative theory: it does not necessarily describe what investors do; rather, it describes what they should do to achieve certain presumed objectives in the context of an investment environment assumed to exhibit certain key characteristics. Whether or not and to what extent investors do behave in accordance with the theory of portfolio selection is an empirical question, and the evidence in this regard is somewhat mixed. Before assessing the results of these empirical studies, however, let us consider the implications of portfolio theory for financial asset pricing in the financial markets.

The theory suggests that investors will seek to hold diversified portfolios in which unsystematic risk is minimal or nonexistent. These portfolios should be *efficient*—no other possible portfolio can offer a greater expected return without some increase in risk or a lower level of risk without some decrease in return. Further, to the extent that these efficient portfolios include holdings of risky assets, this collection of risky assets should be a microcosm of all market securities, both in type and proportions held.

Now suppose that all investors do behave this way. Securities are priced according to their expected returns and *relevant* risk. The relevant risk to our diversified investors is not total risk but only systematic risk. Unsystematic risk does not matter, because it will not impact on portfolio risk. *Thus unsystematic risk plays no role in the pricing of financial assets.* Indeed, securities are priced according to investor demand on the basis of their existence as part of the universe of securities (the market portfolio). If the total market value of Security X, for example, was 1 percent of the market value of all securities, each investor would seek to buy the amount of Security X that would make its proportion of the total market value of that investor's portfolio equal to 1 percent. Demand and supply would equilibrate to maintain a price for Security X that would maintain that same proportion (1 percent) of total (and individual portfolio) market value. Variations from that equilibrium price would result in market actions to restore it, since such price variations would alter Security X's proportion of total market value. An increase in price, for example, would cause that proportion to become greater than 1 percent. Investors would consequently reduce (sell) their holdings of Security X in an effort to restore the original proportion. As a result of this increased selling of Security X, the price of Security X would fall until the equilibrium price was reached. The reverse process would hold if, in the opposite kind of disturbance to equilibrium, the price of Security X fell below the equilibrium price. Similar equilibrating forces keep the risk-free rate of interest at (or moving toward) an equilibrium level.

Evaluation of Portfolio Theory and the Capital-Asset-Pricing Model

In assessing the foregoing theoretical structure regarding portfolio selection and the pricing of financial assets, the reader should recognize that much of this material must be viewed with a certain degree of caution. In our view, this advice is particularly pertinent for the capital-asset-pricing model (CAPM) and holds to a lesser degree for the theory of portfolio selection from which the CAPM is developed.

One should recognize that portfolio-choice models are rooted in expectations— expected return and expected variance. The probability distributions from which these variables are computed are subjective assessments of the likelihood of possible future outcomes. Although knowledge of current conditions combined with knowledge of past associations of given and subsequent conditions can offer a useful and meaningful basis for constructing such subjective probability distribution, the future remains unknowable.

Further, much of the theoretical basis of these models rests on highly artificial assumptions about the investment environment and investor behavior. (Relaxation of these assumptions has been shown to do very little damage to the theory of the CAPM.) Such assumptions are often necessary—and always helpful—in theory construction, and they often result in valuable insights into the functioning of a complex world, but their use quite properly gives rise to caution. It is unlikely, for example, that unsystematic risk is completely irrelevant for security pricing. Investor diversification is not likely to be so perfect as to lead to that result. Another example is the CAPM's assumption regarding borrowing for the purpose of investing in risky securities. Not only is borrowing at the risk-free rate infeasible in practice, but there are a great many legal, institutional, and psychological barriers to such leveraging of investments in securities.

Numerous empirical studies have aimed at testing the validity of the CAPM, even though the statistical difficulties of such investigations are formidable. The evidence is sufficiently mixed, and the adequacy of the methodologies employed is sufficiently uncertain, that no definitive conclusion can be drawn about the extent of the model's validity in the real world. The studies do suggest, however, that systematic risk (beta) is the only valid risk measure and confirm that the relationship between risk and return is indeed a positive one. At worst, the CAPM remains the best available conceptual framework for evaluating risk in the investment decision.

FINANCIAL MARKET EFFICIENCY

Chapter 2 introduced the notion of the relationship of risk, returns, information, and the efficiency of financial markets. Financial markets maximize their contribution to the efficient allocation of resources in an economy when financial assets are priced to reflect their levels of expected return and risk. The first part of this chapter has sketched the process by which an individual investor may select a portfolio that offers maximum expected return for a given level of risk or minimum risk for a given expected rate of return. To the extent that holdings of such efficient portfolios characterize investor choice, the aggregate economic effect will be a set of security prices that properly channel invested funds to the most productive uses. To better grasp this concept, visualize the saving-investment process for the entire economy as an aggregate portfolio selection process, in which countless individual portfolios are combined to direct the flow of saved funds into investment uses. If all these individual portfolios are efficient, this "aggregate" portfolio is efficient, and the funds are made available to finance the most promising investments, the related risk of which is consistent with societal preferences.

Although the reach of the foregoing concept may, in practice, exceed our grasp, the considerable degree to which such resource-allocative efficiency is possible is due to the existence of financial markets. Efficient investor choice among financial assets is made possible by the wide array of available instruments and by the various institutions and mechanisms that exist to facilitate portfolio selection. Efficient investor assessment of expected returns and risk is made possible by the vast information-gathering, analysis, and dissemination network that financial markets provide. Empirical studies indicate that publicly available information items relating to security returns and risk are impounded into security prices virtually concurrently with their generation—an attestation to the remarkable efficiency of this nation's financial markets.

We turn now to an overview of these financial markets in the second part of this chapter, followed by a more detailed examination of their nature in the seven succeeding chapters.

PART 2: TYPES OF FINANCIAL MARKETS

A "market" is simply a place where sales and purchases of some items are made. Financial markets are the markets in which financial instruments are traded. The prices of the traded financial instruments are determined in the financial markets by supply and demand. Certain characteristics of financial markets result in a highly competitive marketplace. These include a large number of participants and an extensive communications network capable of rapid gathering and dissemination of information. (As noted earlier, the principal anticompetitive influence in the financial system is the prevalence of government regulation.)

As indicated in Chapter 1, financial markets can be categorized in a number of ways. Perhaps the more useful distinctions are money versus capital markets and primary versus secondary markets. The trading of financial instruments having a maturity of one year or less constitutes the *money markets;* the trading of securities having a term to maturity exceeding one year makes up the *capital markets.* New issues of securities are sold (and purchased) in *primary markets;* previously issued securities are bought and sold in *secondary markets.* These categories obviously overlap. There are primary and secondary money markets and primary and secondary capital markets. Further categorizing is possible in terms of the origin (bank versus nonbank) of the financial instrument in the money market and the type of obligation (debt versus equity) in the capital market.

The Money Market

Money markets provide the means for short-term lending and borrowing and thus play a key role in the management of liquidity by business, governmental, and household economic units. Money market instruments are generally characterized by high degrees of marketability and capital certainty (predictability of expected market value at future dates), and they are thus highly liquid. The purchase of such instruments is a convenient means of temporary employment of excess cash, and their issue is a convenient means of financing a temporary excess of cash outflow over cash inflow.

The reader perhaps has noted that both singular (money market) and plural (money markets) terms are employed in this book for this particular component of the financial system. Both usages are correct, in that the money market is a single system for the short-term exchange of funds for a financial asset, but it is also composed of numerous segments that differ both in the nature of instruments used and in the types of participants. One of the most useful distinctions among these various components of the money market is between the direct, or customers' ("retail"), money market and the central, or "open," money market.

The customers' money market is encountered everywhere, for it involves the transactions between local financial institutions and their customers. The central money market is geographically centered in this country in New York City, and it typically involves "wholesale" transactions of very large amounts (frequently millions of dollars). The central money market, however, is connected to the rest of the country by an extensive communications network (telephone, teletype, and computer facilities) that permits widespread participation.

As might be expected, commercial banks are very active participants in central money market transactions. As net suppliers of money market instruments, commercial banks are surpassed only by the federal government. But the money market banks (the large banks located in New York City and other major financial centers) also supply funds to the central market as liquidity management actions and, in the case of the largest New York banks, as *dealers* in money market instruments. (The role of commercial banks in the money markets will be described in much greater detail in the next chapter.)

The federal government is one of the most active participants and a principal borrower of funds in the money market. This is evidenced, for example, by the fact that the dollar magnitude of U.S. Treasury bills outstanding at the end of 1979 approximated that of all other money market instruments combined. In the course of conducting its open-market operations, the Federal Reserve System deals continuously in money market instruments, mostly Treasury bills. (As described in Chapter 7, Fed purchases of Treasury bills supply reserves to the banking system, and sales withdraw reserves—with corresponding impact on the money supply.)

Foreign governments and institutions are major net suppliers of funds to U.S. money markets, mostly as a result of this country's trade deficits in its balance of payments. These deficits mean that more dollars are supplied to the rest of the world than are used to buy U.S. goods and services, and many of these "excess" dollars are used to buy money market instruments. The governments of oil-exporting (OPEC) nations are the most important group of foreign participants in the money market (they capture the most excess dollars).

Other important lenders in the money markets are state and local governments and nonbank financial intermediaries. Cash flows for state and local governments typically follow a "lumpy" pattern: large inflows tend to occur at periodic intervals, but outflows are generally continuous. This results in holdings of temporarily idle cash, which these governmental units often use to purchase money market assets. The emphasis of nonbank financial institutions on long-term lending results in temporary holdings of idle funds when demand for long-term credit slows, and these funds may be placed in the money market.

Perhaps no component of the money market more clearly illustrates its liquidity-management function than the market for federal funds. "Federal funds" are reserve balances at Federal Reserve banks, and the market for them is primarily their purchase (borrowing) and sale (lending) among financial institutions in order to adjust liquidity on reserve positions. Trading in federal funds is generally accomplished by telephone. Transactions in federal funds are typically single-day loans, with the sale effective on the contract day and payment due the following day.

Treatment of the various instruments of the money market and further description of the participants and workings of the domestic money market are offered in Chapters 13 and 14. The international money market is the subject of Chapter 20.

The Capital Market

The framework for the borrowing and lending of funds for periods longer than a year is called the capital market. Some observers view the capital market as composed of markets for intermediate (not more than ten years to maturity) and long-term (more than ten years to maturity) funds. And of course, the capital market has both a primary and a secondary component. A further categorization of the capital market is possible in terms of the market for equity instruments and the market for debt instruments.

Types of capital market instruments include federal government notes and bonds, state and local government securities, mortgages, corporate bonds, and corporate equities. Federal government borrowing, though quite large in amount, does not dominate the capital market to nearly the same degree that it dominates the money market. Corporations are the principal demanders of capital market funds (suppliers of capital market instruments). Equity instruments (common and preferred stock) constitute the largest portion of corporate obligations in the capital market, but corporate bond and mortgage debts are also very large amounts. Residential (as opposed to commercial) mortgages, however, dominate the mortgage market. State and local government securities, which offer the lure of nontaxable interest, are also a major factor in the capital market.

Individuals, both as lenders and borrowers, play a much more significant role in the capital market than in the money market. More than half of household investment in debt and equity capital market instruments is channeled through intermediaries, and the remainder is invested directly. The total amount of direct and intermediated investment in the capital market by the household sector greatly exceeds that of the government and business sectors. In terms of the total amount of capital market *borrowing,* the household sector ranks second to the business sector, with the government sector placing a close third.

Commercial banks play a very significant role in the capital market, though not to the same extent as in the money market. The capital market activities of commercial banks include mortgage lending, considerable equity and bond investment (through trust departments), intermediate-term lending to business and consumers, and the financing of other capital market institutions and agents. These agents and institutions include brokers, dealers, and investment banks.

The underwriting role of investment banks in primary security issues is examined in Chapters 15 and 17, and Chapter 20 describes the international dimensions of investment banking. In addition to underwriting security issues, investment banks are involved in real estate mortgage financing, project financing, and various other capital market activities.

Brokers and dealers perform an essential "middleman" function in the capital market. Brokers, of course, facilitate the buying and selling of financial instruments by others, and they are compensated by a fee or commission for their efforts. Dealers, on the other hand, assume risk by buying and selling securities for their own account, and their compensation must come in the form of the "spread" between the prices at which they sell (the "ask" price) and buy (the "bid" price) securities. More than 5000 firms in this country are registered with the Securities and Exchange Commission as brokers and dealers in securities.

The organized securities exchange and the "over-the-counter" (OTC) securities market, the arenas in which dealers and brokers ply their trade, are institutions of considerable importance in the capital markets. (The OTC also plays a significant role in the money market, with a huge amount of trading in short-term debt instruments taking place through its facilities.) The organized exchanges are essentially secondary markets for outstanding long-term debt and equity instruments. Primary issues of these securities, even if subsequently listed on organized exchanges, are generally channeled through the OTC market, although new issues that constitute additions to outstanding issues are sometimes distributed through organized exchanges.

With this overview of the money and capital markets—characteristics and participants—now complete, we can briefly consider some interrelationships between these two types of financial markets.

Linkages Between the Money and Capital Markets

The money and capital markets are highly interrelated. Many suppliers and demanders of funds use both markets, their degree of activity in either market shifting over time as their own situations and financial conditions change. A firm may tap the money market for temporary funding of long-term capital needs while waiting for more favorable capital market conditions. As already noted, a number of types of financial intermediaries and "middlemen" (i.e., commercial banks, brokers, and dealers) operate in both markets. Funds are constantly being "rolled over" from one market to the other; collections of long-term obligations may be plowed into short-term ones, or vice versa. Further, a borrower may pay a short-term obligation while concurrently borrowing long-term, or vice versa.

As discussed in Chapter 9, the term structure of interest rates is closely linked, although money market interest rates tend to be more sensitive (and variable) and capital market instrument prices (particularly equity securities) more volatile. In general, these two components of financial markets are so interrelated as to really amount to one market, but a market in which time to maturity and various other factors result in differing characteristics among the instruments traded.

Future Markets

To this point, we have discussed only "spot" markets for financial assets, characterized by the purchase or sale of financial instruments for immediate delivery. Of growing importance in the financial system are financial *futures markets*, which are concerned with the purchase or sale of financial assets for future delivery. A futures market is essentially an organized market in which forward (or futures) contracts are traded. A forward contract provides for delivery of a prescribed amount of a particular asset at a certain date.

The economic value of futures markets is in their provision of a means of risk avoidance to individuals or business firms. By entering into a futures contract, the transacting party "locks in" a certain price for an item, the market price of which may fluctuate in random fashion. Sale of an asset through the vehicle of a futures contract allows the seller to avoid the potential loss that would result from a price decrease, but it also obliges him to forego the potential gain that would result from a price increase. In effect, such a seller is willing to forego the possibility of the gain in order to avoid the possibility of a loss.

The use of the futures market to avoid the risk of price changes is called *hedging*. Farmers, for example, often sell futures contracts to ensure a certain price for the sale of crops or livestock, and food processors often buy such futures contracts to "lock in" a purchase price. This particular type of forward contracting is carried on in the *commodity* futures market. The *financial* futures markets serve a similar function by providing participants the means of ensuring a given security price (yield on a future investment or borrowing).

In addition to *hedgers,* who use futures markets to avoid risk, participants in these markets include *speculators,* who take risk positions in an attempt to turn profits on price changes. Though often maligned, speculators help "make the market" and, by their willingness to accept risk, perform a legitimate and necessary economic function.

Chapter 18 explores futures markets in detail, describing their modes of operation, and the ways they can be used to avoid risk and seek profits, and it analyzes their economic significance.

SUMMARY

The primary function of financial markets is the efficient allocation of the saved funds of surplus economic units for the use of deficit economic units. Transfers of saved funds from savers to their ultimate users is accomplished by the exchange of these funds for financial instruments issued either by the ultimate users or by intermediaries (which also purchase the financial instruments issued by ultimate users). The supply and demand for these various types of financial assets determine their prices (and yields).

The demand for a particular financial asset is a function of market perceptions regarding its likely returns and the degree of risk associated with those returns. Thus financial assets are priced in financial markets according to expectations regarding their future returns and risk. Over time, the extent to which these market expectations correspond to subsequent realities is a function of the quality and quantity of *information* provided to the marketplace, and of the speed with which relevant information relating to risk and returns of securities is impounded in security prices.

Resources made available by saving will be allocated to their most productive possible uses (consistent with society's preferences) only if the securities that serve as a vehicle for their transfer to ultimate users are priced according to their expected returns and risk. In turn, such expectations must reflect prompt and proper analysis of all available information pertaining to future security returns and associated risk. The financial markets are said to be *efficient* when these conditions are met.

Financial markets can be efficient *in the aggregate* only to the extent that the countless decisions of market participants relating to portfolio choice constitute efficient selection of financial assets. Aggregate market efficiency will prevail to the degree that the markets are dominated by holders of *efficient portfolios*—no other possible portfolio offers a higher expected return for a given degree of risk or a lower degree of risk for a given level of expected return. In theory, such an efficient portfolio can be constructed for any investor by a combination of risk-free assets and the risky market portfolio of assets that satisfies the risk-return preferences of the investor. Thus to the extent such an approach to portfolio selection characterizes financial market behavior, securities will be priced according to their expected return and their *systematic risk*—the degree of the security's variability in returns relative to the market portfolio's variability in returns. The operational measure of systematic risk (beta) can be estimated empirically.

The financial markets can be divided, somewhat arbitrarily, into the *money market* and the *capital market*. Financial instruments having a year or less to maturity are traded in the money markets. All other securities are traded in the capital markets. Both money and capital markets have a *primary* component (for new issues of securities) and a *secondary* component (for the trading of previously issued securities). Both debt and equity (ownership claims) instruments are traded in the capital market, but only debt securities are traded in the money market. The two markets are closely linked by funds flows and by yield structure.

QUESTIONS

1. What is an "efficient portfolio"? Is holding a *single* direct security likely to be efficient? Indirect security holdings?

2. Explain the relationship among expected return, risk, and expected utility. Will maximization of expected return necessarily maximize an investor's expected utility?

3. Why is diversification of security holdings likely to reduce risk more than expected return?

4. Define systematic and unsystematic risk, and explain their significance for efficient portfolio selection.

5. Explain and compare the "security market line" and the "capital market line."

6. What is meant by the "efficiency" of financial markets? What conditions are necessary for financial market efficiency?

7. Describe the various ways in which financial markets can be categorized.

8. What are some major differences in the characteristics of the money market and the capital market? Similarities? Linkages?

9. What are futures markets? What economic function do they perform?

REFERENCES

Bellemore, D., H. Phillips, and J. Ritchie, *Investment Analysis and Portfolio Selection: An Integrated Approach* (Cincinnati, Ohio: Southwestern, 1979).

Fama, E., "Efficient Capital Markets: A Review of Theory and Empirical Work," *Journal of Finance,* May 1970, pp. 383–417.

Fama, E., and A. Laffer, "Information and Capital Markets," *Journal of Business,* July 1971, pp. 289–298.

Jensen, M., "The Foundations and Current State of Capital Market Theory," in Jensen (ed.), *Studies in the Theory of Capital Markets* (New York: Praeger, 1972).

Lorie, J., and M. Hamilton, *The Stock Market: Theories and Evidence* (Homewood, Ill.: Irwin, 1973).

Markowitz, H., *Portfolio Selection* (New Haven: Yale University Press, 1959).

Sharpe, W., *Portfolio Theory and Capital Markets (New York: McGraw-Hill, 1970).*

Chapter 12

Operations of Financial Institutions in the Financial Markets

Understanding the financial markets—changes in interest rate levels, relative patterns of interest rates, and the flows of funds within financial markets—requires an understanding of the operations of financial institutions. As discussed earlier in this book, financial institutions dominate the flow of funds in the United States and other developed countries. Moreover, pressures on financial markets are usually transmitted through financial institutions. For example, monetary policy initially operates on bank reserve and liquidity positions and then affects the real sector of the economy largely through the portfolio adjustments commercial banks make in their financial asset positions in response to changing risk-return opportunities. Similarly, pressures on the mortgage markets produced by monetary policy and other economic and financial developments are usually transmitted through portfolio adjustments made by savings and loan associations, the principal lenders on single-family real estate. An understanding of why some markets are highly volatile while others are quite stable requires an understanding of the behavior and roles of different financial institutions.

The present chapter attempts to illustrate a few basic characteristics of the operations of financial institutions and to assess their contribution to an understanding of financial markets. Chapters 3 and 4, of course, provided some insight into the sources and uses of funds at major financial institutions. There are substantial differences in the operations of different financial institutions. Nonetheless, there are basic similarities that should be highlighted if we are to fit the pieces of the financial-markets puzzle together. We present initially an overview of the role of financial institutions and then concentrate on how different financial institutions use the financial markets in controlling both interest rate (or term structure) risk and credit risk, two of the principal determinants of their successful operations.

THE BASIC ROLE OF FINANCIAL INSTITUTIONS

Financial institutions sell financial services for which they receive payment. This payment usually results in a financial institution having funds to manage and invest, as well as obligations or liabilities to its customers. Moreover, the sale of services frequently involves the creation of financial instruments of considerable importance to financial markets. The motivation for the activity of financial institutions is usually profit, as it is for that of nonfinancial profit-seeking enterprises, but the motivation is more complex for financial institutions than for most nonfinancial organizations. For example, the fact that some financial institutions are mutual rather than stock associations raises important questions about the motivation of management.[1] Further, many financial institutions—especially commercial banks and other depository institutions—are involved with the public interest and are thus subject to intensive regulatory pressures (as discussed in Chapter 5). As a result, although predictions of the portfolio behavior of financial institutions using the risk-return framework developed in Chapter 11 are useful, other factors must also be considered. A few examples may help to explain the role of financial institutions in financial markets.

Commercial Banks

The commercial bank may be viewed as selling both deposit and credit services.[2] In exchange for funds placed in a demand deposit account, the bank offers convenient transfer of funds to a third party. In exchange for funds placed in a savings and/or time deposit account, the bank offers interest payments. As discussed earlier, banks also offer non-deposit liabilities, such as federal funds purchased, repurchase agreements, and Eurodollar liabilities, for which interest is paid. Many of these types of deposit and nondeposit liabilities are money market instruments. For example, as we will discuss later, the large negotiable certificate of deposit is one of the major instruments of the money market. Once

---

1. Mutual organizations are owned by their customers—depositors, borrowers, policyholders—rather than by shareholders. The mutual form of organization (along with traditional stock ownership) exists in the savings and loan industry and the insurance industry. All credit unions are ''owned'' by member depositors and borrowers.

2. Banks do, of course, offer other services not related to either deposit taking or credit creation. For example, banks offer trust services, cash management, and data processing services, to name only a few. However, the essence of commercial banking involves taking deposits and extending credit.

the funds have been obtained through services offered, the management of a bank faces the problem of purchasing income-earning assets that provide sufficient return to pay for the services offered (the costs are labor and equipment costs for demand deposits and interest for time and savings deposits) and to earn a "satisfactory" return on invested capital.

The invested funds may be committed either to loans, in which a personal relationship exists between the lender and the borrower, or to securities, in which the commitment is impersonal in nature.[3] In the former case, the bank provides loanable funds but does not become directly involved in the money or capital markets. This *customer's market,* though extremely important in providing loanable funds, is not generally viewed as a part of the money and capital markets. In the latter case, the bank both provides loanable funds and acquires a money market instrument, such as a Treasury security (bill, note, or bond) or a municipal security.

In its credit extension—either through making loans in the customer's market or purchasing securities in the money or capital market—the management of the bank must make basic portfolio management decisions. These decisions, which encompass both asset management and liability management, are referred to collectively as funds management. For example, decisions must be made about the maturity structure of assets as compared with the maturity structure of liabilities (the interest rate risk of the portfolio), as well as about the credit risk structure of assets. Management may match closely the maturities of assets and liabilities, or it may have assets whose maturity may greatly exceed the maturity of its liabilities. Management may concentrate in the customer's market with short- or long-term fixed-rate loans or may make only variable-rate loans. In terms of credit risk, management may accept large amounts of credit risk in the portfolio or may pursue a very cautious posture and make only extremely high-quality loans and purchase only the highest-quality securities in the money and capital markets. In both decisions, management will presumably be guided by the desire to increase the risk-adjusted profits of the organization—subject, of course, to legal and regulatory constraints on portfolio management.

Bank management has considerable flexibility in making the interest-rate–risk and credit-risk decisions. Moreover, the flexibility has increased in recent years.[4] At one time, bank management was essentially constrained to adjusting the interest-rate risk of its total portfolio by altering assets alone (i.e., asset management). But with the development of the markets for large CDs, federal funds, repurchase agreements, and Eurodollars, bank management is able to both buy and sell financial instruments in the money and capital markets in order to obtain the desired portfolio maturity. Moreover, through credit extensions in the customer's market and to a lesser extent through security purchases, management is able to alter the credit-risk dimensions of the portfolio in order to achieve a desired position.

---

3. Banks, of course, must keep reserve requirements set by the regulatory authorities and must also meet minimum liquidity needs established by management.

4. Yet there remain considerable limitations on bank portfolio management. Commercial banks may not generally hold equity securities in their portfolios or issue time deposits with a maturity of less than 14 days.

Other Depository Institutions

The role of the other depository financial institutions—savings and loans, mutual savings banks, and credit unions—may be analyzed in a similar fashion. Each offers deposit and credit services. Traditionally these deposit services have consisted primarily of passbook savings accounts, but in recent years each type of institution has achieved considerable portfolio flexibility by offering a large variety of certificate accounts. In addition, under the Depository Institutions Deregulation and Monetary Control Act of 1980, each has now achieved the legal authority to offer third-party-payment devices to individuals through negotiable order of withdrawal accounts for savings and loan associations and mutual savings banks and share drafts for credit unions. From the asset side of the balance sheet, each institution offers credit accommodation through its loan portfolio in the customer's market, and each participates in the money and capital markets through the purchase of such securities as U.S. government bills, notes, and bonds, corporate issues, and to a minor extent, municipal bonds.

These other depository financial institutions also must arrange the maturity and credit-risk dimensions of their portfolios to meet their desired positions. Most assets held by savings and loans are mortgages, and most assets held by credit unions are consumer installment loans. Savings deposits and certificates of deposit (mostly under $100,000) represent the principal sources of funds of these institutions. As a general rule, they have less flexibility in adjusting their portfolios than commercial banks have. Access to the money and capital markets through the issuance of new securities is more restricted for savings and loans, mutual savings banks, and credit unions than it is for commercial banks. However, these institutions have been innovative in gaining access to the money market through the sale of large CDs and to the capital market (at least for savings and loans) through the sale of mortgage-backed bonds. On the asset as well as the liability side of the balance sheet, these various nonbank depository institutions have less flexibility. Tradition and legal constraints are more significant in determining the average maturity of the portfolios of savings and loans, mutual savings banks, and credit unions than for the more diversified commercial banks (though there is considerable flexibility in altering the risk structure of the assets of these institutions). Moreover, analyzing the goals of these institutions is complicated, since most are mutual organizations.

Contractual Institutions

When we turn to the contractual institutions—life and property and casualty insurance companies and private and public pension funds—the analysis of function and motivation becomes even more complex. These institutions do not sell deposit services. The service offered by insurance companies is protection, and the service offered by pension funds is a change in the time distribution of cash inflows to individuals who sacrifice current consumption for greater future consumption. These institutions obtain funds to manage as a result of the difference between the time that cash is received through premiums (insurance companies) and contributions (pension funds) and the time that cash is paid out in the form of benefits. Consequently, although these types of financial institutions do have some flexibility in altering the maturity structure of their liabilities through borrowing in the money and capital markets, the flexibility stems principally from borrowings not associated with their basic services. These basic services give rise to a maturity structure of liabilities that is quite inflexible and is determined essentially by the nature of the service itself.

On the asset side of the balance sheet, the flexibility of contractual financial institutions in performing their credit-accommodation function is much greater. Moreover, contractual-type financial institutions provide a much larger portion of their credit through the money and capital markets (as compared with the customer's market) than do the depository financial institutions.[5] Although insurance companies are subject to state regulation of the types of securities placed in their portfolios, the maturity and credit characteristics of the mortgages and bonds acquired are determined to a very considerable degree by management judgment. Similarly, pension funds (especially private pension funds) are able to acquire equity and debt securities of different credit and maturity characteristics subject only to the "prudent man" rule.[6]

The form of organization of these contractual-type institutions, however, presents additional complications. Most life insurance companies are stock associations, but most of the *assets held* by life insurance companies are held by the larger mutual organizations. Similarly, a substantial proportion of the assets of property and casualty insurance companies is held by mutual organizations. For pension funds the motivation of management (i.e., the trustees of the fund) is even more complex. Not only do the beneficiaries of the pension plan usually have no influence on the portfolio management policies of the fund, but there are pressures from the sponsoring companies in private pension programs, since to these companies, contributions to the fund represent expenses of doing business.

All financial institutions provide financial services. These services result in financial institutions' managing funds and having obligations or liabilities to customers. To a considerable extent, the management of a financial institution has the flexibility to alter the maturity and credit-risk dimensions of its portfolio as it draws funds from the money and capital markets and as it invests funds in the markets. The decisions made by the managements of individual financial institutions with regard to the interest-rate and credit-risk dimensions of the institutions' portfolios have enormous implications for the structure of yields in the money and capital markets. Financial institutions make portfolio adjustments in response to changes in relative yields in the financial markets, but these portfolio adjustments in turn produce additional changes in relative yields. We now turn to a discussion of each of these considerations and evaluate in more detail how financial institutions may vary the maturity and credit-risk dimensions of their portfolios in the attempt to achieve their objectives.

---

5. This implies that on the asset side of the balance sheet the relationship between the contractual financial institution and its customers is less personal than is the relationship of commercial banks and its customers.

6. The "prudent man" rule, which has long been embodied in case or common law, states that an individual who manages the funds of others in a fiduciary capacity should make investment decisions as a prudent man would do. The investment manager can then be held liable for loss only if he behaved in an imprudent manner.

MATURITY MANAGEMENT

Most financial institutions are involved in maturity intermediation, whereby the average maturity of their liabilities is less than the average maturity of their assets. Indeed, as pointed out earlier in this book, one of the basic functions of financial institutions is to purchase assets whose maturity is longer than the maturity of their liabilities. Moreover, most credit extension by financial institutions has traditionally involved the acquisition of fixed-rate financial assets, either in the customer's market or in the money and capital markets. Yet in a world in which both the level of interest rates and the relationship between short- and long-term rates (the term structure) change dramatically over time, the profitability and indeed the viability of financial institutions may be substantially affected by maturity management. We now initially present a discussion of the movement of interest rates over the business cycle and then discuss various strategies financial institutions may use to achieve desired risk-return portfolios through maturity management.

Interest Rates and the Business Cycle

Both the level of interest rates and the relationship between short- and long-term rates are closely related to the various stages of the business cycle. Figure 12.1 provides a simplified view of these relationships. The business cycle is often divided into four periods: the *expansion* phase, when real income, production, and employment are rising; the *peak,* when the economy reaches its productive capacity; the *contraction,* when real income, production, and employment are falling; and the *trough,* at which point the decline ceases and the economy is poised for another expansion. Although no two business cycles exactly repeat themselves and there are distinctive elements to each phase of the cycle, there are sufficient similarities to permit the cycle to be divided into recurring patterns.

In the *expansion phase* of the cycle, interest rates are generally rising. The demand for loanable funds by businesses, households, and governments strengthens, and the supply of loanable funds is restrained by Federal Reserve monetary policy. Reflecting segmented-markets and/or expectations factors, the yield curve is moderately upward-sloping with long-term rates higher than short-term rates. However, the yield curve is shifting as short-term rates generally rise more than long-term rates, producing a flattening of the yield curve, so the difference between long- and short-term rates narrows. As the economy approaches its peak, interest rates continue to rise, peaking at about the same time as general business conditions do.[7] At or near the peak in general business conditions, the term structure of interest rates may change dramatically. Market participants may expect a fall in rates in the future, and the Federal Reserve may induce exceptional pressures in the money market. As short-term rates continue to increase more than long-term rates, the yield curve continues to flatten until at some point short-term rates exceed long-term rates. At this point,

---

7. Interest rates may be viewed as a "coincident" indicator, in that movements in open-market rates coincide with movements in the general economy. However, in earlier periods in American financial history, interest rates were viewed as a *lagging* indicator, moving behind changes in general business conditions.

Stage of the business cycle	Level of interest rates	Term structure
Expansion	Rising	Moderately upward-sloping
Peak	High	Flat or downward-sloping
Contraction	Falling	Slightly upward-sloping
Trough	Low	Strongly upward-sloping

Fig. 12.1   The business cycle and the interest rate cycle

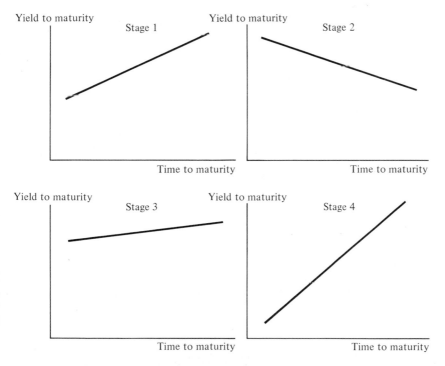

Fig. 12.2   The yield curve at different stages of the business cycle

the yield curve becomes downward-sloping or inverted. This shift in the yield curve is shown in Fig. 12.2 as a move from the yield curve in stage 1 to the yield curve in stage 2.

As the economy passes its peak and moves from stage 2 into stage 3 (declining general business conditions), interest rates begin to fall. The demand for loanable funds declines as businesses reduce inventory levels and curtail plant and equipment expenditures, consumers reduce their purchases, and governments retrench. The supply of loanable funds is stimulated by an easing of monetary policy, and perhaps the anticipated rate of inflation declines. Short-term rates usually fall more rapidly than long-term rates, reflecting both expectations and segmented-markets considerations. As a result, the yield curve begins to return to its "normal" shape, indicating that short-term rates are lower than long-term rates. Finally, as the economy approaches bottom at the depths of the recession, the yield curve becomes sharply upward-sloping, as shown in stage 4 of Fig. 12.2.

Financial Institutions' Operations and the Interest Rate Cycle

The recurring relationship between the business cycle and movements in the level and term structure of interest rates clearly has important implications for the operations of financial institutions in the money and capital markets. However, the impact of the interest rate cycle on the financial institution will be different if the financial institution follows a *passive* portfolio management policy as opposed to an *active* strategy. Under a passive policy, the management of the financial institution establishes portfolio management policy within a long-term perspective, recognizing that the profitability of the institution will be affected substantially over the cycle. No attempt is made to alter the maturity distribution of the portfolio in response to changes in expected interest rates. Profits in some periods will be higher than "normal" and in other periods lower than "normal." Under an active strategy, management seeks to structure the portfolio in order to achieve benefits from the interest rate cycle. If properly done, the profit from an active portfolio-management strategy can substantially exceed the profits from a passive maturity-management program. A brief discussion of each of these policies and their applications to different financial institutions follows.

Passive Portfolio Management

Since financial institutions practice maturity intermediation—borrowing shorter-term then lending—the impact of the interest rate cycle on the institution will be substantial as the term structure changes over the cycle. The impact will also vary considerably from one financial institution to another. For example, the difference in the maturity of assets and liabilities (the amount of maturity intermediation) for savings and loans is much greater than the amount of maturity intermediation for pension funds and life insurance companies. Savings and loan associations generally have long-term fixed-rate assets and short-term interest-rate–sensitive liabilities. Their profits will tend to widen in periods of falling rates and fall in periods of rising rates. In contrast, the average maturity of the liabilities of some contractual institutions, such as pension funds, is generally matched quite closely with the average maturity of their assets, so they are less substantially affected by interest rate movements.

Stage 1 will generally prove to be quite profitable for financial institutions, especially for those, such as savings and loans, that are short-term borrowers and long-term lenders. Not only is there a large gap between the rates paid to attract short-term funds and the rates charged on long-term credit advances, but there is usually a strong demand for credit as the pace of business activity quickens.[8] However, as the economy expands and moves into

---

8. The profitability of a financial institution is of course the result of both the spread (the difference between the interest earned on assets and the interest paid on liabilities) and the volume of earning assets.

stage 2, the profitability of the financial institutions often diminishes. Short-term rates rise more than long-term rates, thereby reducing the spread on earning assets. Moreover, the higher rates to be earned on assets are available only on new commitments if the institution has acquired fixed-rate assets (bonds or loans), whereas the higher rates to be paid to acquire funds may apply to most of the liabilities of the institution.

The problems faced by the savings and loan industry in 1980 and early 1981 provide examples of the impact of changing yield patterns on the financial position of a financial institution. Interest rates rose to record levels, and the yield curve became negative and remained negative for a long period. The cost of money to savings and loans increased dramatically as short-term certificate accounts were sold with high open-market interest rates. However, since the savings and loan has traditionally been a fixed-rate lender, the increase in the average rate earned on its portfolio was very small. As a result, the spread between rates earned and rates paid narrowed dramatically, and for some savings and loans it became negative.[9]

A financial institution that followed a passive portfolio-management policy would accept these interest rate fluctuations as an inevitable part of its business. It would seek to plan for variations in credit demand over the business cycle by maintaining a liquid asset reserve. For example, it might hold a portfolio of securities that was staggered in terms of maturity and automatically roll over excess funds into this portfolio, regardless of the interest rate outlook. However, it would not attempt to forecast interest rates, nor would it vary the composition of its portfolio on the basis of expected future interest rates.

The extreme fluctuations in interest rates that have occurred in recent years have made it increasingly difficult for financial institutions to maintain a completely passive portfolio-management policy. Yet many institutions are reluctant to change the maturity structure of their portfolios on the basis of forecasts of interest rates, most of which have been quite unreliable. Increasingly, though, financial institutions have moved to reduce risk by emphasizing *variable-rate earning assets.* This emphasis has been especially important for the savings and loan industry, where variable-rate mortgages have become common. The stress on variable-rate lending stems from the recognition that the liabilities of many financial institutions must fluctuate in cost with general market rates. With fixed-rate lending, the spread narrows in periods of rising rates and widens in periods of falling rates. The variability of the spread can be reduced (though probably not eliminated) by variable-rate lending, in which the rate on earning assets rises and falls with the rate paid on liabilities.

Active Portfolio Management

In active portfolio management, the financial institution attempts to alter the maturity of the portfolio in response to changes in interest rate expectations. A brief summary of this

9. The few savings and loans that were able to maintain their profitability in this environment were those that abandoned their traditional emphasis on mortgage lending and instead invested directly in the money markets.

Expectation of interest rate movements	Portfolio-management strategy		
	Maturity of liabilities	Maturity of assets	Variable rate
Rising	Lengthen	Shorten	Yes
Falling	Shorten	Lengthen	No

Fig. 12.3 Active portfolio management

strategy is provided in Fig. 12.3. In periods of rising rates, as in stage 1, the institution would attempt to lengthen the maturity of its liabilities and shorten the maturity of its assets. In addition, in its credit extension in the customer's market, where the institution has considerable discretion over the terms of the contract, there would be emphasis on acquiring variable-rate assets. For example, a commercial bank might reduce its borrowings in the one-day federal funds market and increase its borrowings in the longer-term CD market, thereby lengthening the average maturity of its liabilities. It could shorten the maturity of its loans and also reduce the maturity of its security holdings. In addition, the bank could emphasize variable-rate loans and discourage fixed-rate lending. By following these strategies, the bank could reduce the degree of its maturity intermediation and stabilize its spreads. In contrast, if interest rates were expected to fall, the bank would follow the opposite maturity-management policy. It would shorten the maturity of its liabilities, lengthen the maturity of its assets, and encourage fixed-rate lending. If its interest rate expectations were correct, the bank would be able to roll over its CDs at lower rates and would benefit from the fixed-rate longer-term loans.

As with most strategies that seek to increase profits, an active portfolio-management policy has considerable risk. For example, if the expectation of falling interest rates was not realized and, in fact, interest rates rose sharply, the individual institution would be subject to large losses. Indeed, many financial institutions—including some major banks—faced such a situation in early 1980. In late 1979, many market participants expected rates to fall in early 1980. Reflecting this expectation, many financial institutions increased the maturity structure of their assets and shortened the maturity of their liabilities. However, interest rates in early 1980 exploded upward and surpassed by a large margin previous historical peaks. In this environment, banks and many other lenders were locked into low-yielding assets that had to be financed with very costly short-term funds.

Perhaps the best recent example of such a problem is that of First Pennsylvania National Bank. Locked into a fixed-rate, low-yielding asset portfolio, which had been financed with short-term purchased funds, the bank suffered massive losses in late 1979 and early 1980, when money market rates reached record levels. Rumors of the failure of the bank were common among financial market participants. Finally, the Federal Deposit Insurance Corporation, along with a number of large banking organizations, "bailed out" the bank by making longer-term funds available, though at a substantial cost to the bank in terms of management discretionary power.

One should recognize that the extent to which financial institutions can use active portfolio-management policies varies from one type of institution to another. As a general rule, depository financial institutions have the greatest flexibility in following active portfolio-management policies. For example, many banks, particularly the larger ones, have considerable discretionary power over the maturity of their assets and liabilities. They draw large amounts of their funds from the money market, and many alter the maturity of those funds by changing the rates they pay. However, contractual-type financial institutions—such as life insurance companies and pension funds—have less discretion in the maturity of their liabilities. By the very nature of their operations, these organizations create long-term liabilities over which they have limited maturity control. As a result, these types of financial institutions vary the maturity structure of their total portfolio primarily by altering the maturity of their *assets*.

Interest Rate Volatility and the National Bank Surveillance System

We can examine the impact of changing interest rate levels on the profitability of a financial institution by looking at the operation of the National Bank Surveillance System, established by the Comptroller of the Currency to monitor the financial position of national banks through the use of financial ratios. As a part of that system, the Office of the Comptroller of the Currency calculates the "net position in market rate assets" and the "net position in market rate assets as a percentage of total assets." Each of these numbers provides this bank supervisory agency, as well as bank management, with an estimate of the impact of fluctuating interest rates on the profitability of the financial institution. The calculations involved in this analysis are illustrated in Table 12.1.

Table 12.1   Calculation of net position in market rate assets (millions of dollars)

	Bank A	Bank B
Market rate assets	$140	$230
Interest-bearing bank balances	10	20
One-year and less securities	30	60
Federal funds sold	20	30
Variable-rate loans	60	80
Fixed-rate loans (1 year or less)	20	40
Market rate liabilities	220	140
Federal funds purchased	20	10
Borrowed money (1 year or less)	60	50
CDs over $100,000	40	20
Other time deposits over $100,000	80	50
Money market time deposits	20	10
Net position in market rate assets	−80	90
Net position as a percentage of total assets	−8.6%	12.6%

A calculation is initially made of the amount of assets that are sensitive to interest rate movements. For example, as shown in Table 12.1, the Comptroller of the Currency includes as interest-sensitive the following assets: interest-bearing bank balances, securities with one year or less maturity, federal funds sold, variable-rate loans, and fixed-rate loans with a maturity of one year or less. Obviously not all these assets are equally sensitive to interest rate movements. Moreover, other assets not included in these calculations may have some degree of interest rate sensitivity.

Another calculation is made of those liabilities that are sensitive to interest rate movements. As shown in Table 12.1, the Comptroller includes the following as interest-sensitive liabilities: federal funds purchased, borrowed money with a maturity of one year or less, certificates of deposit with a denomination of $100,000 or more, other time deposits over $100,000, and money market time deposits (time deposits whose maximum rates are tied to the rates on Treasury securities). Again, bear in mind that not all these sources of funds are equally sensitive to interest rate movements, and that other sources may show interest rate sensitivity.

The final step in the calculation is to determine a net position in market rate assets by subtracting market rate funds from market rate assets. This net position provides information on the interest rate–risk exposure of the institution. However, as with most such numbers, it is difficult to interpret without relating to the size of the institution. Hence the net position in market rate assets is usually expressed as a percentage of the assets of the bank.

A bank that has an even balance between market rate assets and market rate funds and hence a low net position in market rate assets has limited exposure to interest rate movements. In contrast, a bank with a large net position in market rate assets has a substantial risk exposure to interest rate movements. For example, Bank A in Table 12.1 has a net position in market rate assets of −8.6 percent. Hence a large increase in interest rate levels would sharply reduce the earnings of the institution, because interest expense would increase more rapidly than interest revenue. Conversely, Bank B has a net position in market rate assets of 12.6 percent. Hence a sharp increase in interest rate levels would tend to increase the profits of the organization, because interest revenue would rise more than interest expense. The impact on the profitability of the banks would be exactly the opposite if rates fell.

CREDIT-RISK MANAGEMENT

The operations of financial institutions in the money and capital markets may also be viewed in terms of management control over the credit risk embodied in the asset side of the portfolio. This process may be subdivided into three components: step 1, determination of the desired level of credit risk; step 2, evaluation of the credit risk of alternative financial assets; and step 3, variation of the degree of credit risk over the business cycle. Taken together, these three steps, which are shown in Fig. 12.4, constitute the credit policy of a financial institution.

Step 1:   Determination of desired level of credit risk

Step 2:   Evaluation of credit risk of alternative financial assets

Step 3:   Variation of credit risk over business cycle

Fig. 12.4   The credit-risk management process

Thus the first step in formulating a credit policy is to determine the desired level of credit risk in the portfolio. To some extent, the regulatory authorities have already done this for many financial institutions. For example, banks (with few exceptions) are prohibited from acquiring equity securities and may purchase only debt securities that are nonspeculative in nature. Many other financial institutions may acquire only securities that are on a "legal list," which usually means securities that contain relatively low risk.

Despite these legal restrictions, the management of financial institutions still has some discretion in determining the degree of credit risk. And this discretion is usually greater for contractual financial institutions than for depository institutions, which are more intimately involved in the payments system. In lending operations, management may restrict lending to loans of very high quality or may make loans of lower quality. It can also purchase Aaa or lower-rated bonds. Naturally, different degrees of risk should be associated with different degrees of return. In making this decision, management should examine its risk preferences, as well as the desires of shareholders.

Once the desired degree of credit risk is specified, the financial institution must select securities and structure its portfolio in such a way as to meet its objectives. In the customer's market, in which there is a personal relationship between the lender and the borrower, the financial institution must perform a credit analysis. This analysis evaluates the probability of default by looking at the *character* of the borrower, the *capacity* of the borrower to generate income to repay the loan, and the *collateral* that can be pledged in order to reduce the risk exposure of the lender. The importance of these factors—known as the "C's of credit"—varies widely from lender to lender and with different types of loans. Yet they form the basis of the credit-risk evaluation process for most financial institutions.

In purchasing money- and capital-market instruments, the financial institution often has the option of using credit evaluation by the credit-rating agencies—Moody's and Standard and Poor's—either as substitutes for or supplements to its own credit analysis. These agencies have already analyzed the financial position of a given borrower and have issued a rating that summarizes the credit risk involved in the issue. Although these ratings are certainly not infallible, there is considerable evidence to indicate that they are reasonably accurate guides to differences in credit risk among securities.

Finally, the financial institution may wish to adjust the credit-risk posture of its assets over the business cycle as the risk-return relationship among different securities changes. For example, risk premiums between high- and lower-rated corporate bonds tend to widen in periods of recession and to narrow in periods of economic expansion. A similar though less pronounced movement seems to exist in the municipal market. This tendency might suggest a strategy of investing in lower-quality securities in recession and switching to higher-quality securities later in the expansion. Of course, such a policy would imply that the markets are inefficiently pricing risk over the business cycle, and that may not continue in the future. Moreover, a financial institution can achieve a desired credit-risk position for its entire portfolio by taking large risks in the loan portfolio and low risk in the securities portfolio, or by effecting some other mixture of risk in the two segments of the asset portfolios.

MATURITY MANAGEMENT, CREDIT-RISK MANAGEMENT, AND THE BASIC FUNCTIONS OF FINANCIAL INSTITUTIONS: A SYNTHESIS

As discussed in Chapter 4, the present functions of the major financial institutions are heavily influenced by the historical evolutions of the institutions. Custom and tradition, partially incorporated into law and regulation, have shaped the services offered by individual financial institutions and thereby their sources and uses of funds. Yet within these limits the managements of financial institutions have considerable discretion in their participations in the money and capital markets. They alter the maturity and credit-risk dimensions of their portfolios in response to changes in the level and term structure of interest rates and to changes in credit-risk premiums among different types of financial market instruments. Through their reaction, they in turn produce additional changes in the patterns of yields in financial markets.

Savings and loans, for example, are by tradition and regulation long-term lenders on single-family properties. Yet in periods of high interest rates, some savings and loans may become heavy investors in money market instruments, as an inverted yield curve makes long-term fixed-rate mortgages unattractive. Mutual savings banks, which have more discretionary power in asset selection, may shift their asset structure toward corporate bonds and away from mortgages if relative returns on corporate bonds are particularly attractive. Commercial banks may seek to sell large amounts of longer-term CDs in anticipation of rising interest rates, and they may seek to place these funds in variable-rate commercial loans.

Numerous additional examples could be presented of the behavior of financial institutions and the implications of their behavior for the money and capital markets. For our purposes it is sufficient to recognize that portfolio adjustments by financial institutions with the use of money- and capital-market instruments are profoundly important. Financial institutions acquire most of the instruments of the money and capital markets; indeed, many of the instruments of the financial markets, particularly the money market, are the liabilities of financial institutions. Their purchases and sales of Treasury bills, federal funds, CDs, and other money market instruments, as well as corporate, municipal, and U.S. government bonds and mortgages are so important to the financial markets that it is impossible to understand how financial markets operate without also understanding how financial institutions operate. In fact, the determination of equilibrium in financial market rates and in the portfolios of financial institutions should be viewed as a simultaneous or joint solution.

SUMMARY

Financial institutions play a key role in the financial system, simultaneously issuing and acquiring financial instruments, the "raw material" of the financial markets. An understanding of the financial markets—both the money market and the capital market—is impossible without an understanding of the way financial institutions behave.

A financial institution faces both *asset-* and *liability-management* problems in the financial management of its entire portfolio. In short, it faces numerous *funds-management* decisions. These decisions include the maturity-management decision, which is concerned with the average maturity of assets and liabilities. In making this decision, the financial institution must recognize the relationship between the business cycle and the interest rate cycle and must also adopt either a passive or an active portfolio-management strategy. Management decisions also encompass credit-risk considerations, in which the management of the financial institution must determine a desired level of credit risk, evaluate the credit risk of alternative financial assets (both loans and securities), and decide whether the level of credit risk should be varied over the business cycle.

We have attempted to explain financial institution behavior within a context of the management of maturity and credit risk and to explain briefly how these concepts relate to the strategies of some specific institutions. It is impossible to convey the full depths and complexities of the behavior of financial institutions within such a brief space, but we have tried to fit the financial institution into a financial markets framework through the material presented in this chapter.

QUESTIONS

1. In what sense are all financial institutions alike? In what sense are all financial institutions different?

2. What is the customer's market? How does it differ from the money and capital markets?

3. Compare the flexibility in credit and maturity management of depository and non-depository financial institutions.

4. What are the four stages of the interest rate cycle? How do the levels of interest rates and the term structure of interest rates change in these four stages?

5. Compare a passive with an active maturity-management strategy.

6. Assume a period of rising interest rates. How would an actively managed maturity portfolio be adjusted? A passively managed maturity portfolio?

7. Explain how the spread will be affected by changing interest rates with a fixed-rate–asset portfolio. With a floating-rate–asset portfolio?

8. What is meant by the term ''net position in market rate assets''? How does it relate to the impact of interest rate movements on the profitability of an organization?

9. Explain the three steps involved in credit-risk management.

REFERENCES

Edmister, Robert O., *Financial Institutions: Markets and Management* (New York: McGraw-Hill, 1980).

Gup, Benton E., *Financial Intermediaries* (Boston: Houghton Mifflin, 1980).

Kroos, Herman E., and Martin R. Blyn, *A History of Financial Intermediaries* (New York: Random House, 1971).

Rose, Peter S., and Donald R. Fraser, *Financial Institutions* (Dallas: Business Publications, 1980).

Silber, William L., *Portfolio Behavior of Financial Institutions* (New York: Holt, Rinehart and Winston, 1970).

Smith, Paul F., *Economics of Financial Institutions and Markets* (Homewood, Ill.: Irwin, 1971).

Chapter 13

The Money Market: Part 1

In this chapter we begin an extensive discussion of the various instruments of the money market and the different characteristics of the money market itself. We initially concentrate on the bank-related money market instruments—the federal funds market, large certificates of deposit, Eurodollars, and bankers acceptances. Our treatment of the instruments of the money market concludes in Chapter 14 with a discussion of other (nonbank) money market instruments—especially Treasury securities (such as Treasury bills), agency issues, and commercial paper. In each case, we present the characteristics of the instruments and the markets, discuss the major participants in the market, and evaluate the significance of the markets for the participants and for the financial system. Before looking at the details of the markets, however, we provide an overview of the money market and of the role of security dealers in that market.

THE MONEY MARKET: AN OVERVIEW

Nature of the Market

As discussed briefly in Chapter 11, the money market provides a place where financial market participants may adjust their liquidity positions. Those with a temporary liquidity surplus may dispose of their excess funds by purchasing money market instruments. Those with temporary liquidity deficiencies may eliminate them by selling money market instruments held in their portfolios (asset management) or by borrowing—that is, by issuing new money market instruments (liability management). The money market is often analyzed as an indicator of the degree of financial pressure in the economy and of the current posture of monetary policy. It serves to mirror the liquidity pressures on commercial banks, the largest group of financial institutions in the nation. Moreover, the Federal Reserve injects reserves into the banking system and withdraws reserves through its operations in the money market.

Money Market Instruments

There are a number of differences among the individual instruments of the money market, but there are certain basic characteristics that all money market instruments share. These similarities reflect the basic liquidity-adjustment function of all of the instruments of the market. For example, all money market instruments must be, by definition, *short-term,* and they are characterized by minimal credit risk. These two features guarantee substantial price stability to the purchaser. In addition, a money market instrument should have a high degree of marketability in the event that the holder wishes to dispose of the asset prior to its maturity.

These basic similarities among money market instruments imply that the money market is a very homogeneous market, in which substitution among the different instruments of the market occurs in the portfolios of market participants based on risk-return considerations. In fact, interest rates on most money market instruments rise and fall together and generally by a similar amount. It is indeed meaningful to discuss increases or decreases in interest rates in the money market generally, apart from changes in rates on individual money market instruments.

This similarity in rates is reflected in Table 13.1, which presents interest rates over time on a number of money market instruments.[1] These instruments are federal funds (short-term loans between commercial banks), Eurodollar deposits (dollar-denominated deposits at foreign banks), certificates of deposit (large, business-oriented certificates issued by major commercial banks), bankers acceptances (time drafts drawn on major banks in which the bank has guaranteed payment), Treasury bills (short-term U.S. Treasury securities), and commercial paper (short-term unsecured promissory notes issued by large businesses). Two important generalizations can be made on the basis of this information. (1) At any one time there is a fairly low spread among the rates on these instruments. For example, in December 1980 the spread was only 398 basis points (3.98%). (2) The rates on these instruments tend to move up or down by similar amounts. For example, between December 1979 and December 1980 the three-month CD rate increased by 526 points, and the commercial paper rate rose 483 basis points. Both of these relationships reflect the similarity among the money market instruments and the homogeneity of the market.

---

1. The rates in Table 13.1 are not fully comparable, because some rates (those of Treasury bills, for example) are calculated on a bank discount basis. See Chapter 14 for a discussion of the bank discount basis method.

Table 13.1 Money market rates, %

	Dec. 1974	Dec. 1975	Dec. 1976	Dec. 1977	Dec. 1978	Dec. 1979	Dec. 1980
Federal funds	8.53	5.20	4.65	6.56	10.03	13.78	18.90
3-month CD	9.23	6.01	4.66	6.72	10.72	13.39	18.65
3-month Eurodollar deposit	10.28	6.47	5.01	7.15	11.62	14.51	19.47
90-day bankers acceptance	9.19	5.72	4.62	6.60	10.55	13.15	17.96
3-month Treasury bill	7.15	5.44	4.35	6.07	9.08	12.04	15.49
90–119-day commercial paper	9.18	5.88	4.66	6.61	10.37	13.24	18.07

Sources: Board of Governors of the Federal Reserve System, *Annual Statistical Digest, 1974–1978*, pp. 85-89; Federal Reserve *Bulletin*, February 1980, A25; Federal Reserve *Bulletin*, January 1981, A 25.

Although there are important similarities among money market instruments, there are also important differences. These differences reflect the various factors, discussed in Chapter 10, that produce differences in yields on financial instruments. For example, the yield on Treasury bills is generally the lowest of all money market rates, reflecting their freedom from default risk. In fact, the Treasury bill rate is frequently used as a proxy for the "risk-free" rate. In addition, the interest rate on the Treasury bill is reduced relative to other money market rates by the existence of an excellent secondary market and by the fact that the interest income on Treasury securities is exempt from state and local government income tax. Reflecting these factors, the three-month Treasury bill rate was more than two full percentage points below all other money market rates in December 1980.

The whole structure of relative rates in the money market may be explained by reference to these same factors. Throughout these two chapters, as we discuss the nature of the various money market instruments, we will also point out the relevant characteristics that influence their relative interest rates in the market.

SECURITY DEALERS

Role of Dealers

As mentioned in Chapter 11, the money market is not limited to any one place (though activity in New York City is very important). Rather, the money market is an over-the-counter (or over-the-telephone) market, whereby trading for securities is carried on by private business firms that hold inventories of securities and stand ready to buy and sell securities at posted rates. These businesses are security dealers (commonly called "government security dealers" because of the importance of government securities to their operation), and their function is of crucial importance to the effective operation of the financial markets. These security dealers also play an important role in the operation of monetary policy, since some of them (the accredited U.S. government security dealers) engage in purchases and sales of securities with the Federal Reserve Bank of New York trading desk for the Federal Open Market Account.

How Dealers Make a Profit

Security dealers seek to make a profit in three ways. First, they attempt to profit by selling their inventory of securities for a higher price than the price at which the securities were purchased. Like any business firm with an inventory, the dealer seeks to mark up the inventory over cost in order to earn a return on invested capital. A dealer that holds an inventory of Treasury bills, CDs, bankers acceptances, or other money market instruments will offer to sell each of the securities (ask) at a price higher than the price at which it is willing to buy that security (bid). This potential profit is known as the "spread." In addition, dealers seek to earn a return from the "carry," from earning more on their securities portfolios than they pay to obtain the funds to finance the purchase of their various security holdings. This can be done if the maturity of their securities portfolios exceeds the maturity of their liabilities and if the yield curve is upward-sloping. Finally, dealers may seek to increase their profit by varying the size and average maturity of their portfolios with changes in expectations of future interest rate levels. For example, expectations of falling interest rates would lead dealers to expand the size and lengthen the maturity of their portfolios, whereas expectations of increasing interest rates would lead dealers to reduce the size and shorten the maturity of their portfolios.

Dealer Financing

Dealers operate on a very narrow capital base with enormous amounts of borrowed funds, most of which are very short-term, frequently overnight. Financing is provided by commercial banks, nonfinancial corporations, state and local governments, insurance companies, and other institutional investors. Repurchase agreements are frequently used as the mechanism for accomplishing the financing. However, with a low capital position and large amounts of short-term borrowing, there is little margin for error. Incorrect estimates of interest rate movements and financing needs can prove devastating to the dealer. In periods of rapidly rising interest rates, dealer losses can be substantial. When existing dealers withdraw from the market because of excessively high risk levels, the efficiency of the financial markets is reduced considerably.

FEDERAL FUNDS

Definition of Federal Funds

The term *federal funds* refers to overnight loans in immediately available (i.e., collected) funds, and the term *federal funds market* refers to the buying (borrowing) and selling (lending) of these immediately available funds. Traditionally, federal funds transactions have involved member bank reserves; however, the term "immediately available" is really the crucial one in defining a federal funds transaction.[2] In contrast with the settlement of a

---

2. The traditional definition of the federal funds market as the market for excess reserves at commercial banks is no longer valid. As discussed below, the federal funds market includes trading in bank reserves, but it also includes a large amount of other types of transactions. For an excellent discussion of the federal funds market, see the article by Lucas, Jones, and Thurston in the references at the end of this chapter.

transaction by check, in which the borrower does not have use of the funds for at least one business day and in which the lender does not surrender use of the funds for at least one business day, a federal funds transaction provides immediately usable funds to the borrower and takes immediately usable funds from the lender at the time of the transaction. Large institutions—both financial and nonfinancial—manage their cash positions carefully, particularly in periods of high interest rates, and prefer to avoid the delays associated with the normal check-clearing mechanism. They prefer trading in these immediately available (federal) funds to using delayed-availability checking or "clearinghouse" funds.[3]

Role in Financial System

The federal funds market plays an important role in the financial system. It has become the principal device whereby major commercial banks and large nonfinancial corporations adjust their liquidity positions. In seeking to dispose of temporarily idle funds, market participants compare the yield available on federal funds with the yields offered on other highly liquid money market instruments. In covering a temporary shortfall in liquidity, market participants compare the cost of federal funds borrowing with the cost of other types of short-term funds. Further, the federal funds market is closely related to Federal Reserve monetary policy. As the most liquid of all the various parts of the money market, the federal funds market is quickly affected by Federal Reserve actions to expand or contract the volume of bank reserves. Therefore, the federal funds rate has been closely observed by market participants as an indicator of monetary policy.[4]

Our discussion of the federal funds market in this section concentrates on the role of the commercial bank, this market's major participant. In addition, we include a treatment of the closely related market for repurchase agreements. Because government security dealers and large nonfinancial corporations now play an active role in the federal funds market, their role is also briefly described. The federal funds market is one of the most dynamic and rapidly changing parts of the entire money market. We hope to provide a flavor of this dynamism as we discuss the nature of the market.

Commercial Banks and the Federal Funds Market

The federal funds market began in the 1920s as an interbank market in which one bank with excess reserves and another bank with deficient reserves would trade reserve balances. For example, as illustrated in Fig. 13.1(I), Bank A has excess reserves, and Bank B has

---

3. The term "clearinghouse" comes from the fact that traditionally checks are settled among banks in clearinghouses, at which representatives of the banks physically exchange checks drawn on each bank.

4. The degree of usefulness of the funds rate as a guide to Fed policy is a function of the Fed's operating procedures. As discussed later in this chapter and in Chapter 21, during the 1970s the Fed used the funds rate as a target variable, but the apparent October 1979 shift to a reserves-based operating procedure reduced the usefulness of the funds rate as an indicator of Fed actions.

Bank A				I	Bank B			
Reserves	$ 15	Deposits	$100		Reserves	$ 5	Deposits	$100
Other assets	95	Capital	10		Other assets	105	Capital	10
Total assets	$110	Total liabilities and capital	$110		Total assets	$110	Total liabilities and capital	$110

Bank A				II	Bank B			
Reserves	$ 10	Deposits	$100		Reserves	$ 10	Deposits	$100
Federal funds sold	5	Capital	10		Other assets	105	Federal funds borrowed	5
Other assets	95						Capital	10
Total assets	$110	Total liabilities and capital	$110		Total assets	$115	Total liabilities and capital	$115

Fig. 13.1 Federal funds transactions

deficient reserves (we assume a 10% reserve requirement). If Bank B were to end the reserve computation period with this deficiency, it would be assessed a penalty, and if Bank A were to end with a reserve surplus, it would incur an opportunity cost through the loss of income from the funds it could have invested in earning assets. In this type of situation, the needs of both banks could be satisfied through the sale of federal funds by Bank A to Bank B.

As illustrated in Fig. 13.1(II), if Bank A sells $5 to Bank B, the reserve needs of both banks are satisfied. Bank A gets rid of an excess of cash (a nonearning asset) and has an interest-earning asset—loans to domestic commercial banks or federal funds sold. Bank B has eliminated its reserve deficiency by purchasing $5 in the federal funds market and thus has incurred a $5 liability—federal funds borrowed—which it must repay at the termination of the borrowing agreement (generally one day). Although there are a number of ways in which the transaction can be handled, traditionally a federal funds purchase and sale of this nature is consummated through the Federal Reserve System, and the ownership of reserves at the Fed changes as the result of the transaction.

Important Aspects

Certain aspects of federal funds transactions should be highlighted. From a monetary policy perspective, it is important to note that federal funds transactions do not create any new bank reserves, but they do result in greater use of existing reserves. One can easily see, by looking at Fig. 13.1(I and II), that the total amount of bank reserves before and after the federal funds transaction is $20. Thus federal funds transactions do not create any new reserves. Their significance for monetary policy is that a banking system with an effective federal funds market can support a larger volume of bank credit on a given reserve base than can one that does not have a well-developed federal funds market.

From the perspective of the lending and borrowing banks, the federal funds transaction represents a short-term, generally unsecured loan. The federal funds sale appears on the books of the lender as a loan to a bank, and it appears on the books of the borrower as a nondeposit liability. As a nondeposit liability it is not subject to reserve requirements or to F.D.I.C. assessment.[5] If the borrowing bank fails, however, the nondeposit liability (federal funds purchased) is subordinated to the claims of depositors. Therefore access to the federal funds market may be eliminated quickly for banks that are perceived as having financial difficulties.

Some Recent Developments

The federal funds market has undergone enormous change and phenomenal growth in recent years. These developments include a substantial change in the purpose for which participating institutions use the federal funds market, a broadening in the types of institutions that use it, and a lengthening in the maturity of many federal funds transactions. Reflecting these developments, the volume of federal funds transactions has soared. As Fig. 13.2 indicates, daily average federal funds borrowings at 46 large commercial banks grew from well under $5 billion in 1967 to over $20 billion in 1977.

One of the most significant changes in the federal funds market has been the more aggressive use of the market as a source of funds, primarily by the larger banks of the nation. Whereas originally the federal funds market was used as a temporary device to cover reserve shortfalls or excesses, the market has increasingly been used as a more permanent source or use of reserves. For larger banks, the federal funds market has become a major part of their *liability-management* program. Instead of maintaining large amounts of funds in short-term, highly liquid assets, such as Treasury bills, many commercial banks have minimized holdings of liquid assets and purchased federal funds in the open market when they needed additional liquidity. In addition, many commercial banks have used the federal funds market as a means of expanding their earning-asset portfolios beyond the size made possible through ordinary deposit sources of funds. For example, consider a bank that has demand, savings, and time deposits of $800 million. It may buy another $400 million in the federal funds market and thereby expand its lending ability well beyond the level that is possible with its $800 million deposit base.

These uses of the federal funds market give rise to the buying of funds, but there is also a more permanent use of the federal funds market that gives rise to the selling of funds. Many small banks now use the federal funds market as a means of placing otherwise idle funds rather than buying Treasury securities or other money market instruments. Such a use of the federal funds market as a means to adjust "secondary reserves" is quite different from the traditional use of the one-day reserve adjustment discussed above.

An important part of the changing nature of the federal funds market involves the development of repurchase agreements and the increasing participation by nonbank finan-

---

5. The absence of reserve requirements on federal funds borrowings must be qualified, since occasionally (as in the fall of 1979) the Fed attaches reserve requirements on federal funds borrowings that exceed some base level.

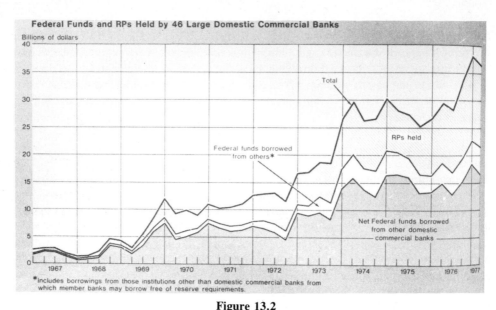

Figure 13.2
(Source: "Federal Funds and Repurchase Agreement," FRBNY *Quarterly Review,*
Summer 1977, p. 40.)

cial institutions and by nonfinancial corporations. Repurchase agreements (RPs) involve transactions in which securities are sold and paid for in immediately available funds and a simultaneous commitment is made to repurchase the securities at a later date, generally the following day. Banks sell their U.S. government and agency securities subject to a repurchase commitment in order to obtain immediately available funds.[6] These RPs are generally made with large corporations, and the development of the RP market has allowed access to the federal funds market to large nonfinancial corporations. As shown in Fig. 13.2, the use of RPs by major banks has become extensive in recent years.

There is also at present a substantial amount of activity in the market for immediately available (federal) funds by nonbank financial institutions. Savings and loans, in particular, have become active suppliers of federal funds, though not generally through repurchase agreements. This development has allowed the banking system to draw funds from a new source, and it has contributed to a more fully integrated financial system.

Monetary Policy, the Federal Reserve, and the Federal Funds Market

The federal funds market plays an important role in the monetary policy process. Throughout the 1970s the Fed implemented monetary policy by establishing a *target* federal funds rate. If the Fed wished to ease monetary conditions, it would reduce the target federal

---

6. Government security dealers also make RPs.

funds rate (with the expectation that this move would be consistent with a faster growth rate in money supply). If it wished to tighten monetary conditions, the Fed would raise the target federal funds rate (with the expectation that this move would be consistent with a slower growth rate in the money supply). Thus the federal funds rate was watched intently by outsiders for indirect evidence on the posture of monetary policy.

The expectation that control over the growth rate of the money supply could be achieved through setting a desired federal funds rate was not realized during the 1970s. Evidence has shown that, although the Fed was highly successful in achieving its desired federal-funds-rate target, it was quite unsuccessful in achieving its money-supply-growth-rate target.[7] As a result, beginning in October 1979, the Fed began to place more emphasis on achieving its money supply targets and less on achieving a narrow band in the federal funds rate. This appears to mean not that the federal funds rate has become insignificant in the monetary policy process but rather that it has been deemphasized. If this policy is continued, however, it implies that the federal funds rate (and other money market rates) in the future will be more volatile than in the past. This, in turn, has important implications for financial market participants.

Interest Rates on Federal Funds

Prevailing interest rates on federal funds are highly volatile. Since the federal funds market is intimately related to bank reserve adjustments, the rate on federal funds on any given day will fluctuate widely, up and down, as bank reserve conditions shift. Moreover, Federal Reserve action to change bank reserve positions will frequently produce large but short-term movements in the federal funds rate. Indeed, on a daily basis the federal funds rate is by far the most volatile of all money market rates. And even over a longer-term perspective, the volatility of the federal funds rate is noticeable. When rates are generally falling, the funds rate will often fall more than other money market rates do. When rates are rising, the funds rate will often rise more than other money market rates.

CERTIFICATES OF DEPOSIT

A certificate of deposit (CD) is a receipt indicating that a depositor has placed a particular amount of funds at a bank for a particular period of time, and in return the bank has agreed to pay a certain rate of interest over the life of the deposit. There are numerous types of certificates of deposit of different sizes, and CDs are issued by different kinds of depository financial institutions, but the certificate that is considered to be a money market instrument is one issued by a major bank in large denomination ($100,000 is considered the minimum amount, but units of $1,000,000 or more are common) and traded in a secondary market. The CD as a money market instrument is a relatively recent development, dating back to the

---

7. It can be shown that the Fed can control either the price of money (the interest rate) or the quantity of money, but not both at the same time.

early 1960s. Yet the CD has become one of the major money market instruments (in terms of volume outstanding) in a very short period. The existence and growth of CDs are an important example of the innovative characteristics of our financial markets.[8]

Origin of the CD

The large, negotiable, business-oriented CD was the product of a changing financial environment and the response of large banks to that changing environment. The change was the increase in interest rates that has occurred in the post–World War II era, particularly since the early 1950s. The response was the action by First National City Bank of New York (now Citibank) and other large banks to maintain their share of the flow of credit.

Large New York banks traditionally have been wholesale financial institutions, obtaining deposits from businesses and lending to businesses. In obtaining deposit funds, these banks (like all banks) were prohibited from paying interest on demand deposits. Moreover, they were generally unwilling to pay competitive interest rates on time deposits. Consequently, as interest rates increased in the post–World War II period, corporate treasurers began to look for ways to earn interest on their temporarily idle funds and began to reduce their balances at commercial banks in order to commit funds to Treasury bills and other money market instruments. Responding to this reduction in their sources of funds, Citibank designed the large CD with characteristics similar to other money market instruments and arranged with a government securities dealer to create a secondary market in these financial instruments. Not only did the creation of the CD allow the major banks to offer to their customers a financial instrument fully competitive with existing money market instruments, but it also allowed the major banks for the first time to manage their liabilities beyond one-day adjustments through the federal funds market. With CDs the major banks could meet unexpected loan demand by buying money rather than by turning down loan requests or by liquidating assets. To a very considerable extent the creation of the large CD was the beginning of extensive liability management by the nation's major banks.

The introduction of the CD proved a great success with corporate treasurers and other investors. The volume of the large CDs outstanding moved upward sharply to more than $20 billion in the mid-1960s, to more than $90 billion by 1974, and to well over $100 billion by 1981. Around this trend line of rapid growth, however, there were periods of substantial retrenchment. In 1966 and again in 1969 the magnitude of CDs shrank as Regulation Q rate ceilings made the CDs unattractive relative to other money market instruments. However, in the early 1970s Regulation Q ceilings were removed from the large CDs. As a result, fluctuations in the amount of CDs outstanding in recent years have principally reflected the demand for funds by large banks, which in turn is a function of the strength of loan demand at these banks.

---

8. For an excellent review of recent developments in the CD market, see the article by Melton in the list of references at the end of this chapter.

Characteristics of CDs

As with any time deposit, a large CD must have a minimum maturity of at least 14 days.[9] In fact, the *average* maturity of most CDs is very short. There is no maximum maturity, but most CDs are issued for periods of well under one year. As shown in Fig. 13.3, the average maturity of the large CDs issued by the major banks in the country generally varied between two and four months in the period from 1964 through 1977. In terms of denomination, the minimum size to escape Regulation Q ceilings is $100,000. However, most CDs are issued in much larger denominations, and a round lot in the secondary market is usually $1,000,000. Interest on CDs is computed on the basis of par (a nondiscount instrument) and on the basis of a 360-day rather than a 365-day year. Payment is normally made in immediately available (federal) funds.[10]

Average Maturity of Outstanding Large Negotiable Certificates of Deposit
Weekly reporting banks; not seasonally adjusted

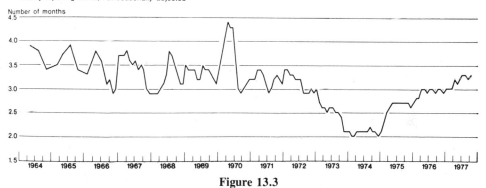

Figure 13.3
(Source: William C. Melton, "The Market for Large Negotiable CDs," FRBNY *Quarterly Review,* Winter 1977–1978, p. 29).

Buyers and Sellers

There is relatively little information available about the characteristics of buyers of the large CDs. Given the origin of the market, it is likely that most buyers are nonfinancial corporations, and scattered bits of evidence support this assumption. About two thirds of all CDs sold by the larger banks (and about 90 percent of all CDs issued are sold by the larger banks) are sold to individuals, partnerships, and corporations (IPCs). Most of the sales to IPCs are to business, but it also appears that smaller banks sell a larger percentage of their CDs to individuals than larger banks do—a not unexpected finding.

---

9. Foreign branches of U.S. banks do not have to observe this limitation. A corporate treasurer who wishes to invest for less than 14 days can purchase a Eurodollar CD from the London branch of a U.S. bank.

10. Reserve requirements must be held against certificates of deposit. That fact increases their cost as a source of funds, whereas federal funds borrowings do not increase required reserves.

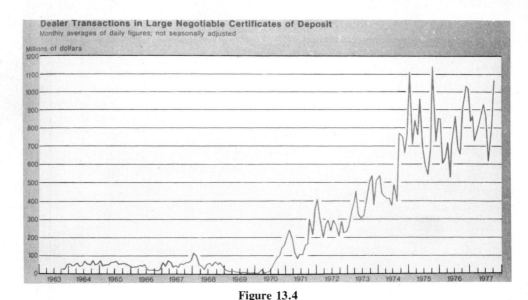

Figure 13.4
(Source: William C. Melton, ''The Market for Large Negotiable CDs,'' FRBNY *Quarterly Review,* Winter 1977–1978, p. 27.)

The major banks of the nation use the CD market both as a means of liquidity adjustment and as a means of raising additional funds to meet loan demand. With an active CD market, the bank has the alternative of either liquidating short-term assets or issuing CDs to meet liquidity needs. Presumably the bank makes that choice in light of the relative cost of funds from asset versus liability management. In addition, the bank may use the CDs to provide funds to support a loan portfolio larger than would be possible through its other deposit sources.

There is a well-developed secondary market for CDs. Indeed, the existence of a strong secondary market has been one of the major reasons for the growth of the CD market. As shown in Fig. 13.4, dealer trading in large negotiable CDs has averaged close to $1 billion per day in recent years. Though large both in absolute magnitude and as a fraction of the volume of CDs outstanding, this amount of trading is still much smaller than that in federal funds or Treasury bills. Moreover, the CD market is not homogeneous, since the CDs of different banks carry different degrees of credit risk.

Interest Rates on CDs

As shown in Table 13.1, interest rates on the large CDs are higher than on Treasury bills of comparable maturity. This differential reflects the greater degree of credit risk on CDs, the thinner secondary market for them, and the greater tax exposure for holders of CDs (interest on CDs is taxable at all levels, but interest on T-bills is not taxable at the state and local level). There are now also differences in rates that reflect the banks of issue. In the early years of CD market development, there was relatively little differentiation of CDs, one from another, by credit risk (except for the very crude distinction between prime and nonprime banks). Increasingly, however, purchasers of CDs are now making important distinctions among different banks. These distinctions have become built into the relative yield structure on CDs, a process known as *tiering*.

EURODOLLARS

The markets we have discussed to this point are bank-related and essentially domestic in nature. Yet increasingly the money market (as well as the capital market) is becoming international in character. The internationalization of these markets is nowhere more evident than in the phenomenal growth of the Eurodollar market in recent years. We present here only a brief discussion of Eurodollars. More extensive treatments are included in Chapters 19 and 20.

Eurodollars are liabilities of commercial banks outside the United States—including the foreign branches of U.S. banks—that are denominated in dollars. Actually, the Eurodollar market may exist anywhere in the world, but its focal point is in London. The origin and growth of the Eurodollar market is partially attributable to the large deficits in the United States balance of payments of the 1960s and 1970s. However, the expansion of the Eurodollar market reflects the ability of European banks to offer dollar deposits that pay a higher return than is available on domestic U.S. dollar deposits, and yet to offer loans at rates that are lower than those offered by domestic commercial banks. This is possible because the Eurodollar market is predominantly a "wholesale" market, characterized by large-volume loans and deposits, where there are substantial economies of scale. Most important, the Eurodollar banks are not subject to reserve requirements on their dollar-denominated liabilities. The Eurodollar banks may offer deposits of any maturity, whereas domestic banks are prohibited from paying interest on time deposits of less than 14 days, and most Eurodollar deposits are time deposits.

Interest rates on Eurodollar deposits tend to fluctuate in line with domestic money market rates. For example, as shown in Table 13.1, both domestic money market rates and three-month Eurodollar rates fell between 1974 and 1976, and both increased in the period from 1976 to 1980. These common movements reflect the potential and actual substitution of different money market instruments in the portfolio adjustments of major commercial banks and other large businesses. In addition, the three-month Eurodollar deposit rate is usually higher than the domestic money market rates, reflecting higher perceived risk, as well as other factors that are discussed in Chapter 20.

BANKERS ACCEPTANCES

One of the oldest and yet one of the least common of all money market instruments is the bankers acceptance. Its long history reflects its use in financing international commerce, whereas the relatively small quantity of acceptances outstanding stems from the specialized nature of this financial instrument. Yet in recent years the volume of acceptances outstanding has increased substantially.

A bankers acceptance is a time draft drawn on a commercial bank ordering the bank to pay a particular amount to the holder of the draft at the time of its maturity. This draft becomes an acceptance when the bank accepts responsibility for making payment on it and stamps ''accepted'' on the face of the draft. Once the bank—generally a large well-known bank—has guaranteed payment at maturity, the draft (now a bankers acceptance) becomes a money market instrument. With the backing of the bank, investors are willing to buy and sell the acceptance in the secondary market for liquidity-adjustment purposes.

Creation of a Bankers Acceptance

A bankers acceptance is usually created in the process of financing international commerce. A simple example may serve to illustrate the process by which acceptances are created. Assume that an American wholesaler wishes to import computers from a German manufacturer. In domestic commerce, this transaction would generally be financed with the use of open-book, trade credit. Yet the German exporter—lacking knowledge of the American importer and/or the existence of different laws between the two countries and perhaps for other reasons—will probably be unwilling to ship the goods on open account. But the American importer may not have adequate funds to pay cash for the merchandise. With the creation of a bankers acceptance, however, this problem can be solved, particularly if its creation is part of a *letter of credit* arrangement.

This financing arrangement requires the American importer to obtain from a U.S. bank a *letter of credit* in favor of the exporter. This letter of credit allows the exporter to draw a time draft against the U.S. bank. (In effect, the bank's credit standing is interposed between the importer and the exporter.) Confident of payment for the goods, the exporter can ship the merchandise and turn the letter of credit over to his bank in Germany. The German bank then draws a draft on the U.S. bank and sends the draft to the United States. The U.S. bank, after making sure that all supporting documents are in order, stamps ''accepted'' on the face of the draft, creating a bankers acceptance.[11]

Financing in the Bankers Acceptance Transaction

Note that the U.S. bank is only guaranteeing payment of the draft at maturity. It is not necessarily financing the transaction. The transaction is financed by whichever party holds the acceptance. For example, Fig. 13.5 presents three different versions of the financing of the transaction. In alternative 1, we first note that the German exporter has exchanged its inventory for money (a demand deposit at a German bank). The U.S. importer has obtained the inventory and has a short-term liability in favor of the bank. And the U.S. bank has both

---

11. Sight drafts are sometimes employed in settlement of international obligations, in which case payment (rather than ''acceptance'') is immediate, once the process of document verification and approval is complete.

a new asset (customer's liability on acceptance) and a new liability (bankers acceptance), and the items are of identical magnitude. But who has financed the transaction? In this case, the financing has been done by the German bank that holds the acceptance. Indeed, *whoever holds the acceptance is financing the transaction.* In alternative 2, the German bank has sold the acceptance to a security dealer and received payment in the form of a check drawn on a U.S. bank. In this case, the security dealer holds the acceptance and is doing the financing. In alternative 3, the German bank has sold the acceptance to the American bank. The American bank in this case is doing the financing, and the bankers acceptance is referred to as an "own bill" (since the bank has purchased its own acceptance).

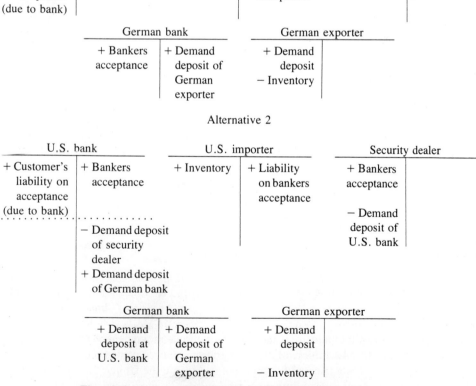

Fig. 13.5 Impact of bankers acceptance financing on participants
(continued)

Fig. 13.5   (continued)

Alternative 3

U.S. bank		U.S. importer		Security dealer	
+ Customer's liability on acceptance	+ Bankers acceptance	+ Inventory	+ Liability on bankers acceptance		
+ Bankers acceptance (own bill)	+ Demand deposit of German bank				

German bank		German exporter	
+ Demand deposit at U.S. bank	+Demand deposit of German exporter	+ Demand deposit	
		− Inventory	

Table 13.2   Acceptances outstanding, November 1980 (millions of dollars)

Total		$55,226
Holder		
Accepting banks		10,236
Own bills	8,837	
Bills bought	1,399	
Federal Reserve Banks		2,375
Own account	523	
Foreign correspondents	1,852	
Others		42,615
Basis		
Imports into United States		11,774
Exports from United States		13,670
All other		29,782

Source: Federal Reserve *Bulletin*, January 1981, A23.

Uses of Acceptances

Acceptances are used principally to finance the international movement of goods. As shown in Table 13.2, almost $12 billion of the $55 billion of acceptances outstanding as of November 1980 were associated with imports of goods into the United States, and almost $14 billion of acceptances outstanding were associated with the financing of exports from the United States. The "others" category includes acceptances used to finance the transfer of goods between countries outside the United States (called third-country bills), the shipment of goods within the United States, and a variety of other purposes.

Characteristics of Acceptances

Acceptances are money market instruments that have exceptionally low credit risk for a private instrument. The credit risk is low because the acceptance is guaranteed by both the drawer and a major commercial bank (two-name paper). The acceptance is also secured by the goods that are being financed. In addition, the secondary market for acceptances is quite good. However, the denomination of an acceptance is established by the amount of goods financed, and its maturity is frequently established by the amount of time involved in the shipment of the goods. Either of these—or both—may be inconvenient to the investor. Most acceptances have maturities of 90 days or less. In addition, the market for acceptances is composed of a fairly narrow set of buyers. As a result of the interaction of all these factors, acceptances tend to sell at a rate premium relative to Treasury bills, as shown in Table 13.1.

Participants in the Acceptance Market

Acceptances are attractive to a variety of businesses. From the importer's perspective, arranging a letter of credit and creating a bankers acceptance is a relatively inexpensive way to finance a purchase. The acceptance rate is generally well under the prime rate, although the borrower must usually pay a fee of 1.0 to 1.5 percentage points to the accepting bank. From the perspective of the accepting bank, it can serve the needs of its customers and earn a fee without commiting any of its own funds. Furthermore, if it wishes, the bank can invest in its own acceptances (own bills) as a part of its liquidity management. Indeed, as Table 13.2 shows, most acceptances held by banks are own bills. There are also a number of other investors who find the risk-return characteristics of acceptances attractive. In addition, the Federal Reserve holds a substantial amount of acceptances. However, most acceptances are held by other investors, principally foreign banks and nonbank firms.

SUMMARY

The money market plays a vital role in the efficient functioning of the financial system by providing vehicles for liquidity adjustment. A financial market participant with a temporary liquidity surplus may dispose of that surplus by purchasing money market instruments, and one with a temporary liquidity deficiency may eliminate that shortfall by selling money market instruments held in its asset portfolio or (where possible) issuing new money market instruments. Major participants in the money market include commercial banks, the Federal Reserve, security dealers, and a large number of financial and nonfinancial businesses. Purchases and sales of money market instruments are based on risk-return considerations, and market participants engage in frequent substitution of one instrument for another. This substitution tends to create a relative similarity (though not equality) among rates on different money market instruments.

In this chapter, we have taken a general overview of the money market, looked at the importance of security dealers in the market, and examined some of the detailed characteristics of the markets for federal funds, CDs, Eurodollars, and bankers acceptances. In all these markets the commercial bank plays an especially important role. Indeed, the commercial banking system is integral to the operation of the entire money market. In the next chapter, we will examine the characteristics of three other subcomponents of the money market, the markets for Treasury securities, agency securities, and commercial paper.

QUESTIONS

1. The money market is sometimes viewed as a homogeneous entity. What evidence would you give to support this view? What are the reasons behind this argument?

2. What functions do security dealers play in a financial market? How do they seek to earn a profit?

3. What are federal funds? How have participants in the federal funds market changed in recent years?

4. Discuss the use of the federal funds market, CDs, and Eurodollars by large commercial banks.

5. It is sometimes argued that the CD market has matured, and that growth will be slower in the future, though more steady. What factors have produced the rapid growth in the CD market? Why might growth be slower but more steady in the future?

6. Compare the credit risk of the bankers acceptances of a bank with the CDs of that same bank. Are the degrees of credit risk the same? If not, why not?

REFERENCES

Cook, Timothy Q. (ed.), *Instruments of the Money Market,* Federal Reserve Bank of Richmond, 1977.

Fraser, Donald R., and Peter S. Rose (eds.), *Financial Institutions and Markets in a Changing World* (Dallas: Business Publications, 1980).

Helfrich, R.T., "Trading in Bankers Acceptances," Federal Reserve Bank of New York *Monthly Review,* February 1976, pp. 51–57.

Lucas, Charles M., Marcus T. Jones, and Thomas B. Thurston, "Federal Funds and Repurchase Agreements," Federal Reserve Bank of New York *Quarterly Review,* Summer 1977, pp. 33–48.

Melton, William C., "The Market for Large Negotiable CD's," Federal Reserve Bank of New York *Quarterly Review,* Winter 1977–1978, pp. 22–34.

Securities of the United States Government and Federal Agencies and Related Money Market Instruments (New York: First Boston Corporation, 1978).

Stigum, Marcia, *The Money Market* (Homewood, Ill.: Dow Jones-Irwin, 1978).

Chapter 14

The Money Market: Part 2

In the previous chapter we described the basic functions of the money market, the homogeneity of instruments traded in that market, and the crucial role of security dealers in its workings. In addition, we discussed four instruments that play important roles in the money market: federal funds, large certificates of deposit, Eurodollars, and bankers acceptances. As we pointed out, each of these financial instruments is closely related to the operations of commercial banks. In the present chapter, we continue our discussion of money market instruments by examining the role of U.S. government securities, government agency securities, and commercial paper. It is important to keep in mind that all the various subcomponents of the money market are highly interrelated. Changes in the federal funds rate, for example, produce portfolio adjustments on the part of market participants that are likely to bring about changes in the prices and yields of commercial paper and other money market instruments.

U.S. GOVERNMENT SECURITIES

The debt of the United States government is massive—approximately $1 trillion at last count. Moreover, this debt—the cumulative result of all deficits during past years—is very short-term in average maturity. Therefore Treasury securities have played (and continue to play) a vital role in the financial markets, especially in the money market.

Types of U.S. Government Securities

Government securities (or "governments," as they are frequently called) are usually divided into three separate groups: bills, notes, and bonds.[1] The differences among these types of securities include maturity, minimum denomination, and method of payment of interest. Bills are issued with an original maturity of one year or less in a minimum denomination of $10,000, and they are discount instruments (the original purchase price is less than par value). Notes are issued with an original maturity of one to ten years, usually in a minimum denomination of $1000, and they are generally sold at par and carry a specific coupon rate. Bonds, by far the smallest portion of the U.S. government debt, are usually sold in maturities of more than 10 years, are generally sold in minimum denominations of $1000, and, like notes, are coupon instruments.[2]

Composition of the U.S. Treasury debt is shown in Tables 14.1 and 14.2. As shown in Table 14.1, roughly two-thirds of the U.S. debt consists of marketable securities, and of these marketable debt instruments, notes are the largest category ($311.9 billion) and bills ($202.3 billion) are by far the second largest group. This particular mix of bills, notes, and bonds suggests that the maturity of the federal debt is fairly short. Indeed, in recent years, the average maturity of the U.S. debt has generally ranged between two and three years. Information on the ownership of the federal debt is also presented in these tables. Table 14.1 gives the ownership of all (marketable and nonmarketable) U.S. government debt, and Table 14.2 provides information on the ownership characteristics of marketable government debt.[3] As shown in these tables, the U.S. government itself—through its agencies, trust funds, and the Federal Reserve—is a major investor in federal securities. U.S. Government agencies and trust funds held $193.4 billion as of October 1980 (most of which were nonmarketable issues), and the Federal Reserve held $121.5 billion (entirely in marketable issues.) Commercial banks were also major investors in U.S. government securities, holding over $100 billion. And individuals, principally through nonmarketable savings bonds, held large amounts of federal government securities.

Yield Calculations

Calculation of the yield to the investor on coupon issues (notes and bonds) is relatively straightforward. As discussed in an earlier chapter, the yield may be expressed either as the current yield or the yield to maturity, but the latter represents the "true" yield on the

---

1. Our discussion deals only with *marketable* government securities. A substantial part (about ⅓) of the U.S. debt is nonmarketable savings bonds, debt sold to U.S. government trust funds, debt sold to foreign central banks, and other types of nonmarketable issues. These nonmarketable securities play no direct role in the financial markets.

2. See Chapter 22 for further discussion of government securities within a perspective of fiscal policy and debt management.

3. Inconsistencies in the ownership groups revealed in Tables 14.1 and 14.2 are due to differences in the samples on which the tables are constructed.

Table 14.1 Interest-bearing government debt by type and ownership, October 1980

	Amount (billions of dollars)
Total	$906.9
By type	
Marketable	599.4
Bills	202.3
Notes	311.9
Bonds	85.2
Nonmarketable	307.5
By holder	
U.S. government agencies and trust funds	193.4
Federal Reserve Banks	121.5
Private investors	593.3
Commercial banks	103.4
Mutual savings banks	5.5
Insurance companies	15.3
Other companies	25.3
State and local governments	73.1
Individuals	122.9
Foreign and international	127.6
Other	120.2

Note: Classification by holder includes $1.3 billion of noninterest-bearing debt.

Source: *Federal Reserve Bulletin*, January 1981, A30.

security. However, for discount instruments, such as Treasury bills (also bankers acceptances and commercial paper), yields are generally presented on the bank discount basis, a method of yield calculation that is not comparable to the yield to maturity method.

The bank discount yield on a Treasury bill may be calculated by subtracting the purchase price of the bill from par, dividing by par, and then annualizing the yield by multiplying by 360 days divided by the maturity of the bill. For example, the bank discount yield for a 91-day bill that sells at a price of 98 (98% of par value of 100) is calculated as

$$\frac{100 - 98}{100} \times \frac{360}{91} \times 100 = 7.9 \text{ percent.}$$

The bank discount yield is not comparable to yields in the money market on nondiscount instruments. The bank discount yield is lower than the "true" yield, both because the

Table 14.2 Ownership of U.S. government marketable debt securities, October 1980

Type of holder	Amount (billions of dollars)
All holders	$599.4
U.S. government agencies and trust funds	10.1
Federal Reserve Banks	121.5
Private investors	467.8
Commercial banks	76.9
Mutual savings banks	3.8
Insurance companies	12.0
Nonfinancial corporations	8.1
Savings and loan associations	4.0
State and local governments	20.4
All others	342.6

Source: *Federal Reserve Bulletin*, January 1981, A31

discount is divided by par rather than price, and because the yield is computed on a 360-day rather than a 365-day year. However, the bank discount yield may be converted to a coupon-equivalent yield by the use of the following formula.[4]

$$\text{Coupon-equivalent yield} = \frac{365 \times \text{Discount basis}}{360 - (\text{Discount basis} \times \text{Days to maturity})} = 8.2 \text{ percent.}$$

In this instance, the coupon-equivalent yield, which is useful for comparing with yields on other nondiscount money market instruments, is 8.2 percent.

Primary and Secondary Markets

The market for government securities, like the market for other financial instruments, may be conveniently divided into the market for new issues (the primary market) and the market for existing issues (the secondary market). Although there is considerable overlap among the major participants in these two parts of the government security market, the Federal Reserve plays an especially important role in the primary market, and security dealers play a vital role in the secondary market.

The Federal Reserve acts as an agent for the Treasury in the sale of new U.S. government securities. Since new U.S. government securities with a maximum maturity of one year (which qualify as money market securities) consist of Treasury bills only, our discussion in this chapter of the primary market for government securities will be limited to bills.

---

4. For a more complete discussion, see *Securities of the United States Government and Federal Agencies*, 28th edition, 1978, First Boston Corporation.

Table 14.3 Positions of U.S. government securities dealers, October 1980 (millions of dollars)

U.S. government securities	2701
Bills	2557
Other within 1 year	− 1082
1–5 years	755
5–10 years	− 221
Over 10 years	692

Note: Includes securities that have been sold under repurchase agreements.

Source: *Federal Reserve Bulletin*, January 1981, A32.

Table 14.4 Transactions of U.S. government securities dealers, averages of daily figures, October 1980 (millions of dollars)

U.S. government securities	$17,464
Bills	11,543
Others within 1 year	350
1–5 years	2,745
5–10 years	1,060
Over 10 years	1,766

Source: *Federal Reserve Bulletin*, January 1981, A32

All bills are sold through an auction technique. Each week 91-day and 182-day bills are auctioned. In addition, nine-month and one-year bills are auctioned monthly. Bids may be submitted to any Federal Reserve Bank and to any branch of a Federal Reserve Bank. These bids may be competitive (both a price and a quantity are specified by the bidder) or noncompetitive (only a quantity is specified). The competitive bidder may receive the entire amount desired, part, or none. The noncompetitive bidder receives the amount bid for at the average price established by the competitive "tenders." Anyone may offer a competitive tender, but most such tenders are made by professionals—security dealers and major banks. Noncompetitive tenders are generally made by smaller investors, often individuals. The amount of noncompetitive tenders is usually small relative to the amount of competitive tenders, although the volume of noncompetitive tenders usually increases sharply in periods of high and rising interest rates.

As discussed in Chapter 13, security dealers play an important—indeed, a crucial—role in the money market.[5] This is especially true in the secondary market for government securities. Government security dealers play a vital role in establishing and maintaining the "depth, breadth, and resiliency" of the government securities market.[6] Dealers hold an inventory of government securities and stand ready to buy and sell these securities at posted prices. As shown in Table 14.3, as of October 1980, government security dealers held a position of almost $3 billion in these issues. The dominance of bills is evident—more than 90 percent of the net position was in bills. Similar conclusions are reached by examining the transactions data in Table 14.4. Total transactions averaged more than $17 billion per day during the month of October 1980.

---

5. For an excellent discussion of the role of dealers in the U.S. government securities market, see the article by McCurdy listed in the references at the end of the chapter.

6. A market that has "depth, breadth, and resiliency" is one that can absorb a large volume of securities or purchase orders with minimal impact on existing market prices.

Table 14.5   Ownership of Treasury bills, October 1979 (millions of dollars)

All holders	$161,692
U.S. government accounts and Federal Reserve Banks	44,072
Private investors	117,620
Commercial banks	5,138
Mutual savings banks	167
Insurance companies	455
Nonfinancial corporations	2,562
Savings and loan associations	202
State and local governments	3,241
All other	105,855

Source: U.S. Treasury *Bulletin,* December 1979, p. 73.

Participants in the Short-Term Government Security Market

Treasury bills and other short-term government securities are bought and sold for liquidity-adjustment purposes by a wide range of financial market participants. These investors, who value high liquidity and low risk, are especially attracted to Treasury bills. As shown in Table 14.5, major investors in Treasury bills include the Federal Reserve and commercial banks. The Fed uses bills for most of its open-market operations, since it can buy and sell large amounts of securities in the bill market with minimum disruption of the market. At one time, the Fed's open-market operations were characterized as "bills only," although now the term "bills preferably" would be more accurate. Commercial banks use bills for liquidity adjustment, as well as for collateral (public deposits at banks must be secured by "pledging" specific assets, such as government securities). In fact, banks have traditionally used T-bills as a major asset for liquidity adjustment. In addition, as shown in Table 14.5, other financial institutions, nonfinancial corporations, state and local governments, and a diverse group of other investors hold Treasury bills.

Interest Rates on Treasury Bills

As we saw in Table 13.1, interest rates on Treasury bills are the lowest of the rates on money market instruments. This pattern reflects three important factors. First, the Treasury bill is assumed to have no credit risk; in fact, the risk-free rate is often proxied with the Treasury bill rate. Second, the marketability of Treasury bills is very high. Since bills are short-term, they have little interest-rate or market risk, as well as being free of credit risk. And as already noted, there is an exceptionally good secondary market for bills, reflecting the position of dealers in the market. Finally, the interest return on Treasury bills (as on all Treasury securities) is exempt from taxation by state and local governments.

U.S. GOVERNMENT AGENCY SECURITIES

The United States government not only impacts on the credit markets through its direct borrowings but also has a substantial effect through the borrowings of its agencies. In fact, in recent years, borrowings by federal agencies have grown at a much faster rate than have borrowings by the U.S. Treasury itself. For example, in the period from 1966 through 1978, Treasury borrowing expanded by 137 percent whereas borrowings of U.S. government-sponsored agencies and mortgage pools expanded by 895 percent. Government agency borrowings have grown so rapidly in recent years and have become so large absolutely that they now play a major role in both money and capital markets.[7]

Federal agencies encompass a diverse group of institutions established to accomplish some public purpose. Included are agencies designed to foster the flow of credit to agriculture and housing, to finance international commerce, and to provide greater availability of credit at lower cost for a number of other purposes. And not only do the functions of the different agencies vary, but the methods of financing the agencies also differ. Most agency securities are sold with original maturities of from one to ten years, but there are also agency securities with extremely short and extremely long maturities. In this chapter, we will describe the different functions of the major agencies, concentrating on those agencies whose financing is essentially short-term. Additional discussion of the market for longer-term agency issues is offered in Chapter 15.

Types of Federal Agencies

Federal agencies are usually grouped into two basic categories: federally sponsored agencies and federally "owned" agencies. Federally sponsored agencies are privately owned, do not receive any direct federal funding, and yet carry an implicit promise of financial support from the federal government because of their particular social function. Their securities, however, do not carry any guarantee by the federal government. The federally owned agencies are merely subcomponents of the federal government, from which they receive all or a large portion of their funds. Their securities are generally guaranteed by the federal government.

The major federally sponsored agencies and federally owned agencies are listed in Fig. 14.1. The sponsored agencies, which are the major factors in the financial markets, are principally associated with agriculture (Banks for Cooperatives, Federal Intermediate Credit Banks, and Federal Land Banks[8]) and housing (Federal Home Loan Banks, the Federal Home Loan Mortgage Corporation, and the Federal National Mortgage Association). In contrast, the federally owned agencies are involved in a more diverse set of activities. More borrowing has been done by the federally sponsored agencies than by federally owned agencies. Therefore most of our discussion of the characteristics of federal agency debt as instruments of the money and capital markets will be confined to federally sponsored agencies.

Functions of Federal Agencies

Federal agencies exist in order to increase the availability of credit and/or lower its cost for portions of the economy that are assumed to have some special social role. It has been

---

7. For a review of the agency market, see the article by Banks listed in the references at the end of the chapter.

8. These three agriculturally related agencies are collectively known as the Federal Farm Credit System, and sell joint obligations as a part of the Federal Farm Credit Banks.

Name of Agency	Designation
Federally sponsored agencies:	
Banks for Cooperatives	BCs or Coops
Federal Farm Credit Banks	FFCBs
Federal Home Loan Banks	FHLBs
Federal Home Loan Mortgage Corporation	FHLMC or Freddie MAC
Federal Intermediate Credit Banks	FICBs
Federal Land Banks	FLBs
Federal National Mortgage Association	FNMA or Fannie Mae
Federal Agencies	
Export-Import Bank	EXIM
Farmers Home Administration	FmHAd
Government National Mortgage Association	GNMA or Ginnie Mae
Postal Service	PS
Tennessee Valley Authority	TVA

Fig. 14.1   Federal agencies

argued, for example, that it is socially desirable for the United States to be a country of "homeowners" rather than renters. Similarly, the concept of the "yeoman farmer" has deep roots in American history. The federally sponsored agricultural agencies contribute to these goals by borrowing funds in the nation's financial markets and lending them to farmers and farm organizations at rates below those available from other credit sources. For example, the Bank for Cooperatives lends to farm cooperatives, the Federal Intermediate Credit Banks provide funds to production credit associations, which in turn make short-term production loans to farmers, and the Federal Land Banks make long-term loans to farmers. Since these agencies are able to borrow at rates that are almost the same as those available on direct federal debt, they can provide relatively low-cost funds to their customers.

The other two major federally sponsored agencies, the Federal Home Loan Banks and The Federal National Mortgage Association, are housing-related agencies. The FHLBs borrow in the financial markets and lend these funds to savings and loan associations, which have most of their loans in home mortgages. Their lending rises in periods of high interest rates, when the savings and loan industry is having a difficult time raising funds, and falls in periods of low interest rates, when funds flows at the savings and loans are more ample. In contrast, both the Federal Home Loan Mortgage Corporation and the Federal National Mortgage Association exist to purchase mortgages in the secondary market from principal mortgage lenders, such as savings and loan associations, mortgage bankers, and others. By purchasing these mortgages, the FHLMC and the FNMA not only add to the liquidity of mortgages generally but also provide funds to mortgage lenders to acquire additional mortgages.

Information on the three major agencies in terms of dollar volume of lending and borrowing—the Farm Credit Banks, the Federal National Mortgage Association, and the Federal Home Loan Banks—is provided in Tables 14.6, 14.7, and 14.8. As of the end of

Table 14.6 Combined balance sheet of the Farm Credit Banks, December 31, 1979 (thousands of dollars)

	Federal Land Banks	Federal Intermediate Credit Banks	Banks for Cooperatives	Combined
Assets				
Loans	$31,916,803	$17,543,667	$8,379,459	$57,839,929
Cash	92,376	98,536	34,760	225,672
Investment securities	696,401	588,882	306,342	1,591,625
Interbank notes receivable	52,399	26,013	191,039	—
Bank premises and equipment	21,774	21,802	14,561	58,137
Other assets	66,885	30,227	30,062	127,174
Total assets	32,846,638	18,309,127	8,956,223	59,842,537
Liabilities and capital				
Consolidated bank and other bonds	16,006,172	2,676,288	591,471	19,273,931
Consolidated systemwide bonds	10,886,556	12,570,912	6,499,198	29,956,666
Consolidated systemwide notes	1,417,561	1,188,609	626,693	3,232,863
Notes payable to farm credit associations, commercial banks, and other financial institutions	303,727	15,397	51,703	370,827
Accrued interest	756,073	560,832	220,451	1,537,356
Interbank notes payable	71,385	119,659	78,407	—
Miscellaneous trust accounts	237,010	—	11,459	248,469
Other liabilities	71,009	61,756	30,055	162,820
Total liabilities	29,749,493	17,193,453	8,109,437	54,782,936
Total capital	3,097,145	1,115,674	846,786	5,059,605
Total liabilities and capital	32,846,638	18,309,127	8,956,223	59,842,537

Source: Farm Credit Banks, *Report to Investors*, 1980.

Table 14.7   Balance sheet of Federal National Mortgage Association, March 1980 (thousands of dollars)

Assets	
Mortgages	$52,452,786
Cash, U.S. government securities, and federal agency securities	1,139,767
Other assets	915,195
Total assets	54,507,748
Liabilities and stockholders' equity	
Liabilities	
Bonds, notes, and debentures	
Due within 1 year	15,775,415
Due after 1 year	35,749,421
Other liabilities	1,476,799
Total liabilities	53,001,635
Stockholders' equity	1,506,113
Total liabilities and stockholders' equity	54,507,748

Source: Federal National Mortgage Association.

Table 14.8   Maturity distribution of obligations of the Federal Home Loan Bank, April 1, 1980 (millions of dollars)

Maturity	Amount	Percent
0–6 months	$ 7,866.5	24.4
7–12 months	5,203.2	16.2
1–2 years	6,350.0	19.7
2–5 years	10,460.7	32.5
5+ years	2,310.0	7.2
Total	$32,190.3	100.0

Source: Federal Home Loan Banks

1979, the Farm Credit Banks had total assets of almost $33 billion, most of which consisted of loans to farmers and ranchers. In addition, the total assets of the Federal National Mortgage Association exceeded $50 billion in early 1980, and the total assets of the Federal Home Loan Banks were in excess of $37 billion. The size of these organizations, together with their ability to raise funds even in periods of high interest rates and intense credit restraint, makes them a potent force in the financial markets.

Characteristics of Agency Securities and of the Agency Market

Agency securities come in a variety of "shapes, sizes, and forms," reflecting the existence of different agencies with different purposes. Short-term agency securities, which fall within the money market, are usually sold in large denominations of $50,000 or more, whereas intermediate- and longer-term agency securities are generally sold in much smaller denominations. The maturity of agency securities is generally quite short. As of April 1980, for example, 40.6 percent of Federal Home Loan Bank securities matured in one year or less, and 42.2 percent matured in one to five years. However, the maturity distribution varied widely among the agencies.

New agency securities are generally sold through fiscal agents on a subscription basis. Secondary markets in agency securities, maintained by security dealers, are quite good, but they are much less well-developed than markets for direct Treasury debt reflecting the smaller positions of dealers in these securities, as well as the smaller volume of transactions.

Purchasers of Agency Securities

Agency securities are purchased by a number of different investors. The largest single investor group comprises the commercial banks, which hold about 20 percent of agency issues. Banks find agency issues attractive, because they have many of the same desirable characteristics as Treasuries but carry slightly higher yields. Other investors include U.S. government accounts and Federal Reserve Banks, with about 10 percent of the market, and a diverse group of individuals, nonfinancial businesses, and others.

Interest Rates on Agency Issues

Interest rates on agency issues are generally very close to those offered on comparable-maturity Treasury securities. The smallness of the premium reflects market perceptions that the issues of these agencies carry the implied guarantee of the United States government. That there is a premium reflects the reduced marketability of agency issues as compared with direct federal debt, as well as the fact that the interest income on agency securities is usually fully taxable at all levels, whereas the interest income on direct federal debt is tax-exempt for state and local income tax purposes.

There is some evidence that the yield spread between agency and Treasury issues has widened in recent years. This increase appears to reflect the extraordinarily rapid rate of growth in agency debt. In addition, the yield spread is highly variable over the business cycle, apparently reflecting changing risk perceptions, as well as relative supply factors.

COMMERCIAL PAPER

The last type of money market instrument we will discuss here is commercial paper, one of the most rapidly growing segments of the financial markets. Commercial paper consists of the short-term note issues of very large, "blue chip" quality business firms. We will discuss the basic characteristics of commercial paper, the nature of its buyers and sellers, and the relationship between interest rates on commercial paper and interest rates on other money market instruments.

Characteristics of Commercial Paper

Commercial paper issues are short-term, unsecured notes of large business firms having high credit ratings. Maturity is always 270 days or less (in order to avoid registration with the Securities and Exchange Commission). Denominations range widely, although most commercial paper (to qualify as a money market instrument) must carry a minimum denomination of at least $250,000. Most commercial paper is sold at a discount without an explicit coupon rate, and interest is figured on the bank discount basis in the same manner as for Treasury bills.[9]

Amount Outstanding

As shown in Table 14.9, commercial paper outstanding exceeds $120 billion; thus commercial paper is one of the largest of all the money market instruments. Moreover, the volume of commercial paper outstanding has grown at an exceptional rate, especially since the late 1960s. For example, commercial paper outstanding amounted to less than $10 billion until 1966, but it expanded to more than $30 billion by 1970 and to more than $50 billion by 1975. In fact, the rapid growth of commercial paper has caused concern among commercial banks that a large portion of the business sector—very large and high-quality businesses—were bypassing the banking system and engaging in self-financing. Although the growth of commercial paper has been explosive, however, it has also been unstable. In particular, the volume of commercial paper has tended to fall during periods when risk premiums on corporate debt issues rise. For example, the volume of commercial paper contracted in 1970 following the bankruptcy of the Penn Central Corporation. And the volume of commercial paper declined again in 1975 as the severe 1974–1975 recession produced concern on the part of buyers of commercial paper about the credit worthiness of some of the issues in the market.

Table 14.9   Volume of commercial paper outstanding November 1980 (millions of dollars)

All issuers	$124,776
Financial companies	
Dealer-placed paper	
Total	19,556
Bank-related	3,436
Directly placed paper	
Total	67,345
Bank-related	21,939
Nonfinancial companies	37,875

Source: *Federal Reserve Bulletin*, January 1981, A23.

---

9. For a useful review of commercial paper, see the article by Hurley listed in the references at the end of this chapter.

Nature of Issues

The principal reason for the high volume of commercial paper is cost. The cost of commercial paper is frequently—indeed, usually—below the cost of short-term borrowing from banks, particularly when the cost of bank borrowing is adjusted to include the cost involved in compensating balance requirements. (However, the "true" cost of commercial paper must include issuing costs and costs associated with maintaining a backup line of credit at a commercial bank.) In fact, although there has been a substantial upward trend in the volume of commercial paper outstanding, there has also been a marked change in the growth rate of commercial paper, reflecting differences in the commercial paper rate and the prime rate.

Commercial paper is usually divided into groups on the basis of the nature of the issues and method of sale. By nature of issues, commercial paper may be classed as financial-company paper and as nonfinancial-company paper. By this distinction, as shown in Table 14.9, most commercial paper is issued by finance-related firms. In fact, about 70 percent of all commercial paper is issued by finance-related businesses. By method of sale, commercial paper may be classed as dealer-placed or directly placed. In the former group are those firms that sell their paper with the aid of security dealers, generally paying ⅛ to ¼ of one percent commission to dealers. In the latter group are the businesses that sell their paper directly to the ultimate investors.[10]

As shown in Table 14.9, most financial-company paper is sold directly to ultimate buyers. This type of paper is usually sold by very large financial firms, such as General Motors Acceptance Corporation, and major bank holding companies, such as Citicorp. These firms regularly issue commercial paper (in fact, Citicorp has a regular auction of commercial paper) and find it cost-efficient to maintain their own staffs in order to market their notes. Moreover, the firms usually rely on commercial paper for the bulk of their short-term borrowing. Smaller financial companies rely less heavily on commercial paper for their short-term funds and use commercial banks more heavily. These smaller financial companies find it unattractive to market their securities directly and instead use dealers to find buyers. Although Table 14.9 does not classify the issues of nonfinancial companies by method of sale, most of these issues are placed through dealers. In fact, dealer-placed paper has grown more rapidly than directly placed paper in recent years primarily because of the entry into the commercial paper market of nonfinancial issuers.

Nature of Investors

Major buyers of commercial paper include large commercial banks (which frequently purchase commercial paper for their trust departments or for their customers), nonfinancial corporations, insurance companies, private pension funds, state and local governments,

---

10. There are actually only a small number of issuers of commercial paper, around 700 to 800. And most commercial paper is issued by fewer than 100 business firms.

investment companies, and others. Although complete data are not available, it appears that about 20 percent of all commercial paper is held by corporations engaged in manufacturing, mining, and wholesale or retail trade. Another 10 percent is held by life insurance companies. Commercial banks themselves appear to hold very little commercial paper for their own accounts. Individuals, who have traditionally held only small amounts of commercial paper, have become more active in investing in this financial instrument as the minimum denominations have been reduced in recent years.

Table 14.10   Ownership of commercial paper and bankers acceptances, 1979 (billions of dollars)

Sector	Amount
Households	$40.6
Nonfinancial corporate business	33.2
Rest of the world	30.2
Sponsored credit agencies	0.3
Monetary authorities	0.7
Commercial banks	15.2
Savings and loan associations	3.4
Mutual savings banks	2.4
Life insurance companies	7.3
Investment companies	3.8
Money market funds	19.3
Total	$156.4

Source: Board of Governors of the Federal Reserve System, *Flow of Funds Accounts, Assets and Liabilities Outstanding 1969–1979*, p. 800.

More information on the ownership of commercial paper is provided by Table 14.10, which includes the ownership of both commercial paper *and* bankers acceptances. However, one can make a rough estimate of commercial paper ownership, since bankers acceptances are held principally by commercial banks and foreign investors. The data in Table 14.10 suggest that large investments are made by nonfinancial businesses and industry and smaller investments by financial institutions. Money market mutual funds have been especially important as investors in commercial paper in recent years.

Nature of the Market

The market for commercial paper is essentially a primary market. No established secondary market exists for either dealer-placed or directly placed paper. However, the impact on the liquidity of commercial paper of the lack of an established secondary market is reduced by two considerations. First, the maturity of most commercial paper is very short. The average maturity of most directly placed paper is usually 20 to 40 days, and the average maturity of dealer-placed paper is usually 30 to 45 days. Second, most issuers—of both dealer-placed and directly placed paper—are ready to buy back the paper prior to maturity in the event of severe liquidity pressure on the investor.

Interest Rates on Commercial Paper

As shown in Chapter 13, interest rates on commercial paper generally exceed rates on Treasury bills by a substantial margin. The difference reflects the interaction of credit risk, marketability, and tax considerations. Commercial paper clearly carries greater risk than Treasury bills, and this higher credit risk is reflected in a risk premium in the interest rate structure. Interest rates on different issues of commercial paper also vary. Commercial paper sold by the very largest financial companies (generally directly) usually carries a lower rate than directly placed paper sold by less well-known companies. In addition, most commercial paper is rated by Moody's and/or Standard and Poor's, and rates vary with the ratings of these agencies.

Interest rate differences between commercial paper and T-bills also reflect marketability and tax considerations. There is no established secondary market for commercial paper, but there is an excellent secondary market for Treasury bills. In addition, the return on commercial paper is taxable at all levels of government, whereas the return on T-bills is taxable only at the federal level. Both of these considerations tend to increase the yield on commercial paper, as compared with Treasury bills.

The commercial paper rate also has an important association with the bank prime rate—the rate charged by commercial banks for loans to their best business customers. For large, well-established, high-quality firms, short-term funds are available either through bank borrowings at or near the prime rate or through the issuance of commercial paper. If the commercial paper rate falls relative to the prime, borrowers will substitute commercial paper as a source of funds for short-term bank borrowings, and that action will tend to raise the commercial paper rate and lower the bank prime rate until the normal relationship between these two sources of funds is restored. Conversely, if the commercial paper rate rises relative to the bank prime rate, borrowers will substitute bank borrowing for the issuance of commercial paper, and that will tend to raise the prime rate and lower the commercial paper rate until the normal rate relationship is restored.

There is one fundamental and important difference between the commercial paper rate and the prime rate. Although the commercial paper rate (indeed, all other money market rates discussed in Chapters 13 and 14) is determined by the free interplay of supply and demand in a competitive market, the prime rate is an administered rate set by commercial bank management. The bank prime rate has traditionally been viewed as a base rate, which sets a floor on bank loan rates, with other rates established as some multiple of the prime. However, the prime has diminished in importance in recent years as banks have devised innovative lending devices in order to compete more effectively with open-market rates. As a result, they have frequently been able to provide funds to their customers at rates below prime.

SUMMARY

The debt of the U.S. government plays a crucial role in the money market. Government securities include bills, notes, and bonds. Although bills are the core of the government securities traded in the money market, previously issued notes and bonds that are near maturity are also an important part of the money market. Reflecting considerations of credit risk, liquidity, and taxability, yields on Treasury securities are lower than yields on other money market instruments. However, since the yield on Treasury bills is calculated on a discount basis, it is not fully comparable to yields on money market instruments, such as certificates of deposit, which are sold initially at par.

Other money market instruments include agency securities, which are issues of a diverse group of government-owned and government-sponsored organizations. Of these, the issues of the Farm Credit Banks, the Federal National Mortgage Association, and Federal Home Loan Banks are the most important. Commercial paper also plays a significant role in the money market, particularly for large firms, which rely heavily on the commercial paper market as a short-term source of funds. The interest rate on commercial paper is also important in its relationship to the bank prime rate.

The money market is not static but ever-changing and dynamic. New instruments are created, new participants enter the market, and some existing participants leave the market. Some existing financial instruments become more important, and others decline in relative significance. Once dominated by Treasury securities, the money market has broadened to encompass a number of new financial instruments, such as certificates of deposit. Moreover, there has been growth and broadening of the numbers of participants, both as issuers of money market instruments and as investors in them. Such dynamic change will undoubtedly continue in the future.

In this chapter and in the preceding one, we have attempted to provide information and insight into the workings of the money market. The effectiveness of this market in providing liquidity adjustment vehicles for individuals, businesses, and governments is remarkable. Though basically homogeneous, the money market is composed of a number of separate subcomponents. Thus the nature of one instrument may overlap but is not identical to other financial instruments. And a similar overlapping occurs as we move out along the maturity spectrum to longer-term financial instruments. As we increase the maturity of the financial assets we are examining, the nature and function of the instruments change. Liquidity becomes less significant, and potential return becomes more so. However, as we turn our attention in the next chapter to these instruments of the capital market, we should not lose sight of the fact that all financial markets are interrelated (and all financial assets are substitutable to a degree) through the portfolio decisions made by market participants.

QUESTIONS

1. Compare the different securities issued by the United States government in terms of each of the following.
  a) Maturity
  b) Denomination
  c) Method of payment
  d) Marketability

2. Calculate the bank discount basis on a 182-day T-bill selling at 96. What is the coupon-equivalent yield?

3. What is a competitive tender? A noncompetitive tender? Who are most likely to make these different types of tender?

4. Differentiate between a government-sponsored agency and a government-"owned" agency. Give examples of each. Why do government-sponsored agencies exist?

5. Look up the yield on the security of one government-sponsored agency, and compare it with the yield on a Treasury security of comparable maturity. What accounts for the difference?

6. What is commercial paper? Why do businesses sell commercial paper? If cost is a principal reason, why don't all businesses sell commercial paper?

7. What explains the differences in yields between commercial paper and T-bills?

REFERENCES

Banks, Lois, "The Market for Agency Securities," Federal Reserve Bank of New York *Quarterly Review,* Spring 1978, pp. 7–21.

Cook, Timothy Q. (ed.), *Instruments of the Money Market,* Federal Reserve Bank of Richmond, 1977.

Fraser, Donald R., and Peter S. Rose (eds.), *Financial Institutions and Markets in a Changing World* (Dallas: Business Publications, 1980).

Hurley, Evelyn, "The Commercial Paper Market," *Federal Reserve Bulletin,* June 1977, pp. 526–536.

McCurdy, Christopher, "The Dealer Market for United States Government Securities," Federal Reserve Bank of New York *Quarterly Review,* Winter 1977–78, pp. 35–47.

Schadrack, Fred, "Demand and Supply in the Commercial Paper Market," *Journal of Finance,* September 1970, pp. 837–852.

Stigum, Marcia, *The Money Market* (Homewood, Ill.: Dow Jones-Irwin, 1978).

Chapter 15

The Capital Market: Bonds

The previous two chapters concentrated on financial instruments that are highly liquid and carry minimal risk. As we pointed out earlier, these market instruments are very homogeneous, serving market participants—individuals, businesses, and governments—as liquidity-adjustment vehicles.

Financial instruments of the capital market are much less homogeneous. Indeed, the capital market may be viewed as composed of a number of different subcomponents (separate capital markets) loosely integrated through substitution by market participants of one type of instrument for another through portfolio adjustments. In the present chapter and the following two, we will discuss financial instruments that are "long-term" in nature. These capital market instruments vary widely in terms of credit risk, market or interest-rate risk, marketability, and other characteristics. And they are used by market participants for a variety of purposes. They include *bonds* issued by corporations, state and local governments, and the federal government, *mortgages* issued by individuals, businesses, and governments, and common and preferred *stocks*.

The present chapter concentrates on bonds and leaves the treatment of mortgages and equity securities to the next two chapters. A discussion of the general characteristics of the capital market is presented initially. This is followed by a discussion of the market for corporate, municipal, and U.S. government debt. In each instance, the discussion not only provides the basic details of the market but also brings out the enormous changes that have been occurring in these markets in recent years. Rapid inflation has placed great strain on the functioning of the capital market generally and the debt portion of the capital market in particular. In fact, the question of whether the bond market was dead was a subject of serious discussion following the peak in interest rates that was reached in the spring of 1981.

DIMENSIONS OF THE CAPITAL MARKET

The capital market is massive, exceeding $3 trillion. Mortgages—home, multifamily, commercial, and farm—represent the largest component of the capital market, amounting to more than $1.3 trillion, with corporate equities holding second place in total amount outstanding at more than $1.2 trillion.[1] Moreover, the total volume of bonds outstanding—corporate, municipal, and government—exceeds $1 trillion. Yet the growth of the major components of the capital market has been quite different in recent years. Total mortgage credit has virtually exploded, more than doubling in the short period from 1971 to 1978. The bond market has also experienced rapid growth particularly in the corporate and municipal segments (U.S. government debt has grown rapidly with the large government deficits, but most of the debt has been financed short-term). In contrast, new sales of equity securities by the nation's corporations have been minimal. Explanations for these different phenomena will be provided as we discuss the detailed characteristics of these components of the capital market later in this section.[2]

Not only is the capital market large, but it is quite diverse. Characteristics of the major instruments of the capital market differ widely in terms of credit risk, market risk, marketability, taxability, and the other factors that influence relative yields. This diversity is reflected in the wide range of yields shown in Table 15.1. For example, as of December 1980, yields on state and local government securities (municipals) were substantially below yields on U.S. Treasury and corporate issues, primarily reflecting the tax-free status (at the federal government level) of interest income on these securities. Yields on Treasury securities were below yields on corporate bonds in response to the higher credit risk associated with corporates as compared with governments. Moreover, Baa-rated corporate or state and local issues carried higher rates than Aaa-rated securities because of the higher credit risk. It is also interesting to note that as of December 1980, the yield curve was downward-sloping, since longer-term governments yielded less than shorter-term issues.

---

1. Equities are valued at market price.

2. There are also a number of bonds issued by foreign organizations in the U.S. capital market. These include issues of foreign corporations and foreign governments and their agencies. They are generally compared with and competitive with domestic corporate bonds. The volume sold in the United States principally reflects interest rates in the United States as compared with other capital markets of the world.

Table 15.1   Yields on capital market instruments, December 1980 (percentages)

Instrument	Yield, %
U.S. Treasury notes and bonds	
5-year	13.25
10-year	12.84
30-year	12.40
State and local notes and bonds	
Aaa	9.44
Baa	10.64
Corporate bonds	
Aaa	13.21
Baa	15.14
Dividend/price ratio	
Preferred stocks	11.94
Common stocks	4.74
Mortgage*	14.70

*Mortgage rate is for November 1980.

Source: *Federal Reserve Bulletin.*, January 1981, A25 and A38.

CORPORATE BONDS[3]

Characteristics of Corporate Bonds

A corporate bond represents a contract whereby the issuer (the corporation) agrees to pay interest at specified times and to repay principal, usually $1000, at the maturity date of the bond.[4] The bond itself may have a number of different characteristics. Some bonds have claims on specific assets of the issuer (usually land and buildings, in which case the bonds are referred to as mortgage bonds). Other bonds have claims not on specific assets of the company but only on the general credit worthiness of the issuer (in which case the bond is referred to as a debenture bond). Increasingly, bond issues are debenture rather than mortgage bonds. The security for the bond, as well as other aspects of the issue, is specified in the *indenture*. This agreement states the rights of the lenders and the obligations of the borrower. Enforcement of the indenture is under the control of a trustee (generally the trust department of a commercial bank) acting under the general guidelines of the Trust Indenture Act of 1939.

---

3. For an excellent review of the corporate bond market, see the article by Zwick listed in the references at the end of this chapter.

4. Corporate bonds vary substantially in maturity, but maturities have been reduced in recent years as investors have been reluctant to commit funds for long periods in a world of high inflation and unstable conditions.

Corporate bonds differ in a number of ways other than security. Some bond issues have their claim on assets or income subordinated to other issues. These junior or subordinated bonds obviously carry greater risk to the purchaser than do the senior bond issues of the same corporation. Some indentures require that the issuer establish a "sinking fund" to retire the bond issue. Sinking fund specifications usually require that the issuer provide a trustee with funds sufficient to retire a portion of the issue at specified times prior to maturity. For example, assume a $1 million bond issue with a 10-year maturity. The sinking fund may require that the issuer provide the trustee with funds sufficient to retire $100,000 (face amount) of bonds each year. Hence, at the end of the ninth year there will be only $100,000 (face value) of bonds outstanding. The trustee may retire the bonds either by purchasing them in the open market (if the bonds have a secondary market) or by calling the bonds by a random call process.

Many—indeed, most—corporate bond issues also have *call provisions* under which the issuer may choose to retire the entire bond issue prior to maturity. It is important to distinguish this call feature from the sinking-fund provision. With the sinking fund the issuer must retire a portion of the bonds prior to maturity, but only a portion is retired during the life of the issue. With the call provision the issuer may or may not retire the issue prior to maturity; the decision is usually determined by whether rates have fallen since the bond was originally sold. But, if and when the bonds are called, all of the issue must be retired at one time.

The influence of the call provision on the yield on a corporate bond was discussed in Chapter 10. As pointed out there, the call feature is viewed as undesirable by purchasers of bonds. Not only do these long-term investors generally not want to get their cash back before they had planned, but the call usually occurs in periods of relatively low interest rates, when reinvestment opportunities are limited. As a result, corporate bonds that are callable generally must carry a higher yield than comparable bonds that are not callable, especially in periods when interest rates are high and are expected to fall.

Some bonds are also sold with a conversion feature. These *convertible bonds* allow the holder, at his or her option, to convert the bond into another financial instrument, generally common stock. The conversion terms—the number of shares of common stock into which one bond may be converted—are specified in the indenture, and they usually remain fixed during the life of the bonds. Convertible bonds are frequently sold by industrial corporations, often by relatively lower-quality industrial firms. Treasurers of many corporations attach the conversion feature to their bond issues in order to reduce the interest cost. Moreover, issuers hope that if the price of their stock rises, the bonds will be converted to common stock at a price that is higher than the current common stock price.[5] By this logic, the convertible bond allows the issuer to sell common stock indirectly at a price higher than the current price. From the buyer's perspective the convertible bond is attractive because it offers the opportunity to obtain the potentially large return associated with stock but with the safety of a bond.

---

5. The conversion price—the price at which common stock may be purchased by exercising the conversion right on a bond—is usually set at some premium above the price of the common stock at the time the bond is sold.

Supply of Corporate Bonds

The corporate decision to issue bonds depends on the rate of expansion of assets, particularly fixed assets, and the availability and cost of alternative sources of funds. The rate of expansion of assets determines the need for funds. In periods when dollar amounts of assets are growing rapidly, either because of a rapid expansion of assets measured on a constant dollar basis or because of rapid price inflation, corporations need large amounts of funds. Although some of the needed funds may be available internally through the retention of earnings, the growth of assets usually requires the injection of external funds, either debt or equity. Corporate treasurers must determine the proportion of funds to be provided by short-term debt, long-term debt, and equity.

In recent years, most of the external funds raised by corporations have taken the form of debt capital. In 1979, for example, corporate nonfinancial business raised over $100 billion in the credit market. Yet less than $4 billion of this amount was equity. There are many reasons for this reliance on debt as an external financing source, but two in particular stand out. First, interest payments on debt are tax-deductible, whereas dividend payments on equity (either preferred stock or common stock) are not. This difference sharply reduces the cost of debt as compared with the cost of equity. For example, assume that both debt and equity have a pretax cost of 10 percent, and that the corporation's marginal tax rate is 46 percent. The after-tax cost of debt is then only 5.4 percent, whereas the after-tax cost of equity is 10 percent.[6] The second reason for the dominance of debt financing relates to inflation. With debt, corporations take on the commitment to repay a fixed amount of dollars. These fixed nominal dollar payments become a smaller quantity of real dollars with inflation. (Dividend payments, on the other hand, generally tend to be set at a roughly constant proportion of total earnings.)

Although there has been a strong upward trend in the ratio of debt to total assets on corporate balance sheets, the mix of financing between short- and long-term debt has been less stable and predictable. The mix of short- versus long-term financing is very much dependent on the business cycle and the availability and cost of short-term versus long-term funds. Larger firms with access to the commercial paper market and to other short-term sources are likely to have greater flexibility in their financing mix than small firms that are totally dependent on commercial bank credit.

Leasing also provides a meaningful alternative to bond financing for many corporations. Instead of borrowing to obtain the funds to purchase a capital asset, such as a plant or a piece of new equipment, a corporation may sign a long-term, noncancelable lease in order to obtain the use of the capital asset for its economic life. Although such alternatives are available only for assets that are inherently "leasable," there has been rapid expansion in the volume of such "finance" leases in recent years. Comparisons of the relative advantages of leasing versus bond financing are complex, involving tax considerations and the impact of the decision on the financial statements of the borrower.

---

6. Actually, since investors view equity instruments as riskier than debt instruments, the pretax cost of equity should exceed the pretax cost of debt, making the comparison even more striking.

Table 15.2 Holdings of corporate and foreign bonds classified by investors, 1979 (billions of dollars)

Holder	Amount outstanding	Percentage of total
Total	$455.7	100.0
Household	$ 71.6	15.7
Foreign	10.2	2.2
Commercial banking	7.7	1.7
Mutual savings banks	20.8	4.6
Life insurance companies	173.1	38.0
Private pension funds	55.2	12.1
State and local government retirement funds	86.2	18.9
Other insurance companies	22.2	4.9
Open-end investment companies	6.5	1.4
Brokers and dealers	2.2	0.5

Note: The data include a small amount of dollar-denominated bonds issued by foreign corporations.

Source: Board of Governors of the Federal Reserve System, *Flow of Funds Accounts, Assets and Liabilities Outstanding, 1969–1979*, p. 740.

Buyers of Corporate Bonds

As shown in Table 15.2, the principal buyers of corporate bonds are contractual-type financial institutions. Life insurance companies and private and public pension funds account for almost 70 percent of the total volume outstanding of these types of bonds. However, households, mutual savings banks, and property and casualty insurance companies (shown as other insurance companies in Table 15.2) are also major buyers of corporate bonds.

As discussed in Chapter 4, life insurance companies seek stability of cash flow and invest primarily in corporate bonds and mortgages. However, their investments in corporate bonds are concentrated in issues that are noncallable or that have limited prospect of call. Although life insurance companies are the principal investors in corporate bonds, their relative share of the corporate bond market has diminished in recent years. This trend principally reflects the relatively slow growth in total assets at life insurance companies; the importance of corporate bonds in their portfolios has changed very little since 1950.

Pension funds have increased dramatically as important buyers of corporate bonds. For private pension funds, this increase reflects their explosive growth in total assets (the share of total portfolio devoted to corporate bonds has actually diminished as they have purchased more equity securities). In the case of public pension funds, not only have they had a rapid growth in total assets, but the share of total portfolio devoted to corporate bonds has increased. The importance of households as holders of corporate bonds has also increased, not only directly but also indirectly through their ownership of shares in open-end investment companies (mutual funds).

The Market For Corporate Bonds

The Primary Market.   The primary market for corporate bonds—the market for newly issued corporates—may be divided into two components: private placements and public offerings. With a private placement the seller of the issue places the entire bond offering with an institutional investor, such as a life insurance company or a pension fund. The terms of the issue are determined through negotiation between the seller and the buyer. Most private placements are made by industrial firms. Sellers of bond issues frequently find a private offering attractive because of the speed with which the offering can be consummated (the time-consuming process of registration with the Securities and Exchange Commission is not required). Further, buyers like being able to tailor the terms of the issue specifically to their needs and often obtain higher interest rates on private placement. The share of total new bond issues that are made through private offerings has trended downward to well under 50 percent, although there are great cyclical fluctuations in the ratio of private to public offerings, principally reflecting the availability of funds at life insurance companies, the major buyers of bonds through private placements.

Public issues of bonds are generally made through an underwriter, and the bonds are sold to a large number of investors, individual as well as institutional. The underwriters—investment banking companies—purchase the bonds from the corporate issuer and then resell them to investors at a higher price. This purchase may either be done through open competitive bidding (the laws of most states require that public utility issues be sold through competitive bidding) or through negotiation between the issuer and the underwriter. The underwriter assumes the risk that the bonds may not be saleable at the expected price. The underwriter also has the responsibility of finding buyers for the issue. Many underwriters have large regional and national sales representatives, who make placement of the issue easier.

Secondary Market.   Corporate bond issues have traditionally been purchased by long-term investors—generally financial institutions—with the expectation of holding the securities until maturity. Consequently, there has been relatively little need for a well-developed secondary market. In recent years, however, there has been more emphasis by institutional investors on improving the performance of their portfolios by trading their bonds. As a result, the secondary market for corporate bonds has expanded. However, even though a small quantity of bonds are traded on the New York Exchange, virtually all trading in existing corporate bonds takes place in the over-the-counter market. As discussed earlier, investment banking firms hold an inventory of bonds and post bid (buy) and ask (sell) quotes for selected issues. Through this process these security dealers make the secondary market in corporate bonds.

Yields on Corporate Bonds

Corporate bond yields vary widely, reflecting the credit-risk characteristics of the issuer, the maturity of the issue, and other relevant characteristics of the issue, such as the call feature.

As shown in Table 15.1, corporate Aaa bond rates exceeded rates on long-term U.S. government issues by more than 50 basis points as of December 1980. This difference may be attributable to the higher credit risk on corporate issues, as well as to the fact that interest income on corporate bonds is subject to income tax at both the federal and local levels of government, whereas interest income on U.S. Treasury securities is exempt from state and local income taxes. Another factor is that most corporate issues are callable, but most U.S. Treasury issues are not. The difference between yields on corporate issues and yields on municipals (state and local government bonds) is also affected by these factors, but especially by the tax exemption of interest income on municipals at the federal level.

There are also striking differences in the yields on different-quality corporate bonds, reflecting risk considerations as well as other factors. As shown in Table 15.1, yields on Baa corporate issues (the lowest group of investment-grade issues) exceeded yields on Aaa corporate issues by 193 basis points as of December 1980, indicating the higher credit risk of the Baa issues. Lower-quality corporate issues would of course carry even higher risk premiums. Also of considerable significance, the risk premium between the high- and low-grade corporate issues tends to vary over the business cycle, increasing during recession and narrowing during expansion, as both the actual riskiness of the securities and the market's reaction to risk changes over the cycle.

STATE AND LOCAL GOVERNMENT BONDS

State and local government bonds comprise all issues of state governments and their political subdivisions, including cities, counties, school districts, and a variety of special-purpose governmental units.[7] The volume of state and local government bonds outstanding is smaller than the volume outstanding of other major securities traded in the capital market. Yet the amount of municipals outstanding has grown very rapidly in recent years as a result of intense pressure on state and local governments to provide new services (and higher levels of existing services) to their constituents, joined with a reluctance on the part of these constituents to pay higher taxes to pay for the services.

Characteristics of Municipal Bonds

Municipal bonds differ markedly in their characteristics. Perhaps the most important distinction is between general obligation (G.O.) bonds and revenue bonds. The governmental unit that issues general obligation bonds pledges the taxing power of the government to pay interest and repay principal at maturity. These "full faith and credit" bonds, as they are called, are generally used to provide such basic government services as education and police and fire protection, for which either explicit fees are not charged or the fees that are charged provide only a small portion of the total cost of the service. General obligation bonds have

---

7. This section draws heavily on the article by Rosenbloom listed in the references to this chapter.

been the slowest-growing portion of the total debt issues of state and local governments in the post–World War II period.

Most of the growth in municipals has been among the revenue bonds. These bonds are sold to finance some specific revenue-raising service, such as a toll highway, a sewer treatment and delivery system, or a university dormitory. As a general rule, the governmental unit that originates the bond issue *does not* guarantee payment of principal and interest; such payment is strictly dependent on the revenue generated by the project being financed. However, there is frequently an implied promise that the governmental unit will bail out a revenue bond project if it experiences financial difficulties. Thus the riskiness of revenue bonds varies widely. Yet many revenue bonds have extremely low credit risk. For example, a revenue bond issued by a municipal utility district to provide electric generating facilities for a community experiencing rapid and stable growth would generally be viewed as relatively low-risk. An example of such a low-risk issue would be pollution-control revenue bonds in which the funds were used to install pollution control equipment on an Exxon oil refinery, with bond payments based on receipts from a long-term lease signed by Exxon.

Whether they are general obligation or revenue bonds, however, municipal securities have a number of characteristics that are quite different from those of corporate bonds. Two in particular should be mentioned: denomination and maturity. Most municipal bonds are sold with minimum denominations of $5000, whereas most corporate bonds carry $1000 minimum denominations. Partly this higher minimum for municipals reflects the attraction of the tax-free municipals to wealthier investors. However, the second characteristic— maturity—is at present of more significance. Corporate bonds are usually sold with a single maturity—so-called term bonds—but municipal securities usually carry multiple maturities, and they are referred to as *serial bonds*. These bonds, which mature in series, will have a portion maturing at the end of one year from the date of issue, another portion maturing at the end of the second year, and so on, through the last maturity date of the issue.[8] The serial nature of the municipal bond issue makes the sale of the security more complex. Since some investors want short-term securities, others want intermediate-term securities, and still others want long-term securities, it is usually not possible to place an entire municipal issue with one investor. Moreover, the serial nature of municipal securities makes their sale slower and thereby increases the risk exposure of underwriters.[9]

The Supply of Municipal Securities

Municipal securities are principally offered to finance capital expenditures by state and local governments. Therefore the major determinants of the growth of municipal debt are the growth rate of the population and the regional migration of population. Periods of rapid

---

8. In a sense, a serial bond is similar to a term bond with a sinking fund. However, the investor in a serial bond knows exactly when the bond held will be retired, whereas the investor in the term bond with a sinking fund does not know whether his portion of the issue will be retired prior to maturity.

9. Serial bonds became common in municipal finance after it was found that term bonds with sinking-fund provisions frequently were associated with fraudulent manipulation of the sinking fund.

growth in population and/or sharp changes in the regional distribution of the population are periods of rapid expansion in municipal debt as citizens increase their demands for governmental services. This association between population growth and migration and the growth of municipal debt is especially strong for general obligation bonds.

Another factor associated with the growth of municipal debt is the expansion of state and local governments into nontraditional and frequently controversial functions. Many municipal governments are heavily involved in providing basic utility services, such as electricity and water. As previously mentioned, governmental pollution-control districts have been created in order to purchase pollution-control equipment and lease it to private industry. In recent periods of high interest rates, local government has also become deeply involved in financing housing. Tax-free bonds have been sold for the purpose of constructing public housing or for providing lower-cost funds to individuals to purchase houses. As a result of these activities and others, revenue bonds have accounted for a sharply increasing share of total municipals, rising from about 25 percent in the 1950s to more than 40 percent of municipals issued in 1980.

Demand for Municipal Bonds

As Table 15.3 shows, the municipal market is dominated by a few buyers. In fact, municipal securities are of interest only to buyers that are exposed to relatively high marginal tax rates.[10] The three types of investor that have traditionally dominated the municipal market are commercial banks, property and casualty insurance companies, and individuals.

Commercial banks have found municipals attractive both for tax-planning and for portfolio-management reasons. As a result, commercial banks have been the largest single category of investor in municipal securities. However, the nature of the demand by banks for municipals causes problems for the municipal market. Bank demand for municipals is a residual demand within the portfolio-management policies of the banking industry. Commercial banks satisfy their loan demand with available funds, and they tend to commit large amounts of funds to municipals when loan demand is relatively weak. In periods when loan demand is strong, banks reduce their purchases in the municipal market and sometimes actually sell municipals from their portfolios. As a result of this unstable demand for municipals, interest rates on these securities tend to be more volatile than interest rates on other securities, especially in the short- and intermediate-term segment of the market.

A second major buyer of municipals is the property and casualty insurance industry. The motivation is the same as that for commercial banks: tax avoidance. The demand of property and casualty insurance companies for municipals is also quite volatile. Although municipals do not represent a residual use of funds for these investors, the profits of property

---

10. The tax rate at which the investor would be indifferent between municipal and corporate bonds may be calculated as

$$R_m = R_c(1-t),$$

where R_m = rate on municipal, R_c = rate on corporate, and t = tax rate.

Table 15.3   Ownership of municipal securites, 1979 (billions of dollars)

		Percentage of total
Total outstanding	312.7	100
Held by:		
Commercial banks	135.9	43.5
Household	74.3	23.7
Life insurance companies	6.4	2.1
Other insurance companies	74.7	23.9
Other investors	21.4	6.8

Source: Board of Governors of the Federal Reserve System, *Flow of Funds Accounts, Assets and Liabilities Outstanding, 1969–1979*, p. 740.

and casualty insurance companies are highly volatile, and thus their interest in municipals is cyclical. In periods of high profitability, property and casualty insurance companies find municipals extremely attractive, but in periods of reduced or negative profits returns on municipals are unattractive relative to the returns on other securities.

Individuals are also major buyers of municipals, either directly or through investment trusts, such as mutual funds. Naturally, upper-income individuals in high income tax brackets find municipals desirable investments. However, rapid inflation in recent years has caused "bracket creep," so the number of individuals in marginal tax brackets, where municipals are a desirable investment, has greatly increased. Unlike the demand for municipals by banks and property and casualty insurance companies, which is quite unstable, the demand by individuals is very stable. There is some evidence, however, that an inverse relationship exists between individual demand for municipals and the level of stock prices. When stock prices are rising, the demand for municipals frequently is reduced, whereas the demand for municipals is often high when stock prices are falling.

The Market for Municipals

Primary Market.   The primary market (the market for new issues of state and local governments) is subject to more regulation than is the primary market for corporate issues. New municipal securities are usually sold on a competitive bid basis (almost always so for general obligation bonds) and with a great deal of publicity. The issuer must provide advance notice of the issue and of the terms of the offering. Bids must be made by potential buyers according to a specified format, and there is a specified method for selecting the lowest bidder. Until recently, the low bid was determined by the Net Interest Cost method, which does not adjust for the time value of money, but awards are now increasingly made on the basis of "true" or time-adjusted interest. Commercial banks play a major role in the primary market for general obligation bonds. However, commercial banks are proscribed by law from underwriting revenue bonds—a restriction the banking industry has sought to eliminate for many years.

Secondary Market.   The secondary market for municipal securities is quite similar to the secondary market for corporate bonds.[11] The market is primarily over-the-counter. Most investors purchase the securities to hold for some time rather than to trade. However, there is some evidence that the market is more active relative to its size than is true for corporate bonds. As discussed earlier, banks view municipals as a residual use of funds and are not reluctant to sell municipals from their portfolios when loan demand increases. Moreover, property and casualty insurance companies will liquidate their municipals during unprofitable years.

Yields on Municipals

As we saw in Table 15.1, yields on municipals are lower than yields on corporate or government issues of comparable quality. A principal reason is the tax-exemption feature of interest income on the issues of state and local governments. However, this differential varies widely over the course of the business cycle. In periods of high and rising rates, the differential tends to narrow, and it usually widens in periods of falling rates. In addition, there is a risk-premium differential between high- and low-grade municipals. This differential is quite high, larger than for corporate issues, though it appears to be less cyclically sensitive than the risk premium for corporate issues.

U.S. GOVERNMENT AND GOVERNMENT AGENCY SECURITIES

Since most of the characteristics of direct U.S. government debt and of the debt of government agencies have already been discussed, we will comment only briefly here on a few important dimensions of the role of governments in the capital market. Though once the dominant instrument of the capital market (with the exception of mortgages), the U.S. government security has become less significant in recent years. One reason is the increasingly short maturity of the debt; most of the federal debt matures in a very small number of years. For example, the average maturity of the marketable interest-bearing U.S. government debt as of February 1980 was only three years and 10 months. And less than 20 percent of the debt in private hands had a maturity of five years or more. Another reason is the growing efficiency of the market for corporate and state and local government bonds. At one time, liquidity in the capital market was reserved for U.S. government securities. However, the liquidity of corporate and state and local government bonds has so improved that increasingly this role of U.S. government securities has diminished. Yet as the role of government direct debt has declined in the capital market, the role of agency debt—either direct agency debt or mortgage-backed but government-guaranteed debt—has expanded. It may be that in the future the marketable debt of the U.S. government will increasingly be viewed within a money market context.

---

11. The serial nature of municipal bond issues reduces the liquidity of the secondary market.

Table 15.4 Ownership of interest-bearing U.S. government marketable debt with maturities of one year or more, February 20, 1980 (millions of dollars)

Final maturity	Total	U.S. government accounts and Federal Reserve Banks	5375 Commercial banks	460 Mutual savings banks	288 Life insurance companies	436 Fire, casualty, and marine insurance companies	482 Savings and loans	420 Corporations	State and local governments	All other investors
1–5 years	168,993	31,549	39,612	1,524	689	3,560	1,745	2,471	4,050	83,732
5–10 years	51,132	13,539	7,333	467	631	2,486	92	326	1,877	24,379
10 15 years	21,745	4,235	1,106	115	341	587	34	410	1,462	13,454
15–20 years	7,583	3,299	242	65	149	116	10	28	540	3,128
20 years and over	33,130	11,005	1,434	83	587	306	14	0	3,288	15,993

Source: *U.S. Treasury Bulletin*, March 1980.

Note: Subcomponents may not add to totals because of rounding.

It is Treasury coupon issues—notes and bonds—that play a role in the capital market.[12] These securities are widely held (Table 15.4). Besides being held by the United States government and the Federal Reserve, Treasury notes and bonds are held by commercial banks; life insurance companies; fire, casualty, and marine insurance companies; mutual savings banks; state and local governments; nonfinancial corporations; individuals; and other investors. With its absence of credit risk and relatively good secondary market, the intermediate- and long-term Treasury issue appeals to a number of investors. However, the ownership of governments tends to vary with the maturity of the security, as shown in Table 15.4. Commercial banks are more heavily invested in coupon issues with maturities of less than 10 years. State and local governments are heavy investors in long-term government securities of 20 years or more to maturity, principally through their retirement funds, although they are also heavily invested in securities with 1–5 year maturities.

The primary and secondary markets for coupon issues are very similar to those for bills. New issues may be purchased from the Federal Reserve and are usually sold at auction. New issues are often offered to the public in exchange for existing issues that are about to mature (a refunding offer) or in exchange for issues that will mature at some future date (an advance refunding offer). The investor may submit either a competitive or a noncompetitive tender, as in the bill auctions. Existing U.S. government coupon issues may also be purchased in the secondary market through U.S. government security dealers.

As shown in Table 15.1, the yield on U.S. government security issues is lower than on corporate bonds, although the yield varies with the maturity of the issue, reflecting the shape of the yield curve. This reduced yield stems from the lower credit risk on governments than on corporates, the greater liquidity due to a deeper secondary market, and the freedom from tax on the interest income on governments by state and local governments. However, the yield on governments is higher than the yield on municipals, reflecting the exemption from federal income tax of the interest income on municipals.

Although most agency securities—with the exception of mortgage-related issues—are short-term in nature and more properly considered as part of the money market, there are some agencies that offer longer-term securities. For example, the Federal Intermediate Credit Banks offer securities with a maximum maturity of 5 years and with a minimum denomination of $5000. And the Federal Land Banks offer securities with a maximum maturity of 15 years and a minimum denomination of $1000. As a general rule, agency issues offer yields that are similar to, though slightly higher than, those available on U.S. government securities of comparable maturity.

SUMMARY

The capital market encompasses a diverse group of securities—bonds, mortgage, and equities—issued by economic units. In contrast to the money market, which is very homogeneous in nature, the capital market is quite fragmented. Its securities have consider-

---

12. The U.S. government in some past years also issued certificates that were coupon issues and that had an original maturity of up to one year.

able differences in credit risk, interest-rate risk, marketability, and other characteristics. The substantial differences in relative yields on capital market instruments reflect these underlying differences in the characteristics of the instruments themselves.

One of the most important subcomponents of the capital market is the bond market. The bond market comprises corporate, municipal, and U.S. government debt. The volume of new corporate bonds is principally determined by the growth rate of corporate assets, as well as by the relative cost of bonds versus other sources of funds. Most corporate bonds are purchased by contractual financial institutions that pay little or no taxes, such as pension funds. The primary market for corporate bonds includes large numbers of both private and public placements. The secondary market for corporate bonds has not been well developed, although the volume of trading in recent years has expanded as institutional investors have sought to improve the performance of their portfolios.

The volume of new municipal bonds reflects the demands of population growth, as well as the expansion of municipal financing into nontraditional areas. Municipal bonds include both general obligation and revenue bonds, but recently the most rapid growth has occurred in revenue bond issues. The principal distinguishing feature of municipal bonds is the exemption of their interest income from the federal income tax. This tax feature means that municipals are attractive to investors that are exposed to a potentially high federal income tax rate, particularly commercial banks, property and casualty insurance companies, and high-income individuals. It also means that the demand for municipals is relatively narrow, such that rates are subject to wider fluctuations than is true for corporate and government bonds.

Increasingly the market for U.S. government securities (as well as the market for government agency securities) is developing characteristics that are more like those of the money market than of the capital market. In particular, the maturity of government debt has become very short. U.S. government debt in the capital market includes both notes and bonds. The supply of new U.S. government debt in the capital market principally reflects the size of the government deficit and Treasury maturity management decisions. Purchasers of government debt include most major economic and financial institutions.

The bond portion of the capital market, as well as the mortgage and equity markets, is constantly in the process of evolution. Bond characteristics are modified to make them more relevant to changing market conditions, and the relative importance of different purchasers of bonds alters over time. Moreover, recent periods of high inflation and unstable conditions, as well as high and unstable interest rates, have caused major problems for the bond market and for the markets for all fixed-income instruments. There is a serious question whether the bond market as discussed in this chapter can continue to exist if the inflation rate is not controlled. Therefore, we must recognize that this "snapshot" of the bond market as of the early 1980s may become increasingly unrepresentative over time.

QUESTIONS

1. What are the major instruments of the capital market? Which are most important? Which are growing the fastest?

2. Referring to Table 15.1, explain the differences in yield among the capital market instruments.

3. Describe the different characteristics of corporate bonds and the impact of these characteristics on the yields on the bonds.

4. Why have corporations used debt rather than equity as their principal source of external funds?

5. Who are the principal buyers of corporate bonds? Explain their motivation.

6. Who are the principal buyers of state and local government bonds? Explain their motivation.

7. Explain how you might determine—from the perspective of after-tax yield—whether you would find it desirable to buy municipal bonds.

8. Distinguish between a revenue bond and a general obligation bond. Would you expect the yield on a revenue bond to exceed the yield on a general obligation bond? Explain.

9. It is sometimes said that the demand for municipal securities is unstable. Do you agree? Explain.

REFERENCES

Cohan, Avery, *Yields on Corporate Debt Directly Placed,* National Bureau of Economic Research, 1967.

Hempel, George, *The Postwar Quality of State and Local Government Debt,* National Bureau of Economic Research, 1971.

Homer, Sidney, and Martin Leibowitz, *Inside the Yield Book* (Englewood Cliffs, N.J.: Prentice-Hall, 1972).

Robinson, Roland I., and Dwayne Wrightsman, *Financial Markets,* 2nd ed. (New York: McGraw-Hill, 1980).

Rosenbloom, Richard H., ''A Review of the Municipal Bond Market,'' Federal Reserve Bank of Richmond *Economic Review,* March–April 1976.

Sherwood, H.C., *How Corporate and Municipal Debt Is Rated,* (New York: Wiley, 1976).

Zwick, Burton, ''The Market for Corporate Bonds,'' Federal Reserve Bank of New York *Quarterly Review,* Autumn 1977, pp. 27–36.

Chapter 16

The Capital Market: Mortgage Instruments

In the previous chapter we discussed the nature of the financial instruments traded in the bond market and the characteristics of the bond market itself. Discussion focused on the nature of corporate, municipal, and U.S. government and government agency securities. In the present chapter, we analyze the nature of another fixed-income security—the mortgage—and the characteristics of the mortgage market. Although we could have incorporated this analysis into the discussion of the bond market (and in fact mortgage bonds are generally included in a treatment of the bond market), we have chosen to treat the mortgage market separately. This special treatment reflects the specialized nature of mortgage instruments, the traditional social concern afforded to mortgages, and the enormous size of the mortgage market itself. Moreover, the mortgage market has changed markedly in recent years.

Mortgage debt represents the largest component of the capital market, exceeding $1 trillion at the end of 1980. Furthermore, mortgage debt outstanding has grown very rapidly in recent years. For example, total mortgage debt amounted to only $209 billion in 1960 and less than $500 billion in 1970. To a considerable extent, the rise in mortgage debt outstanding reflects the increase in construction costs in an inflationary environment. However, a substantial part of the recent increase in mortgage debt is attributable to the increase in prices for single-family housing in the late 1970s.

A mortgage is a debt instrument secured by real property—land and/or buildings.[1] Within the classification used by the Federal Reserve's flow of funds accounts, mortgages are subdivided into four categories: home (one- to four-family dwellings), multifamily residential (apartment houses), commercial (office buildings and industrial buildings), and farm. Of this group, home mortgages represent the largest component, accounting for about 65 percent of all mortgages outstanding as of the end of 1979. Commercial mortgages were a distant second, accounting for about 18 percent of the total. The amount of mortgages and the composition of total mortgages outstanding for selected years since 1970 are shown in Table 16.1.

The mortgage market is important not only because it is large but also because there is great public interest in the flow of funds to mortgages, especially to mortgages on single-family dwellings. The idea that each American family should have the opportunity to own its own home has deep roots in public policy discussion. There is intense interest in the availability of mortgage credit for single-family housing, and there is great concern whenever the availability is restricted, as it was in 1966, 1969, 1974, 1980, and early 1981. Moreover, the mortgage market has been one of the most dynamic portions of the capital market. Innovations in the mortgage market have become commonplace in recent years.[2]

CHARACTERISTICS OF MORTGAGES

A mortgage is a debt contract in which real property—land and/or buildings—serves as security for the contract. The traditional mortgage has been long-term—20 to 30 years—for residential properties, though somewhat shorter-term for commercial properties. The traditional mortgage has had a fixed rate; that is, the lender and borrower have agreed on a rate that remains fixed during the entire life of the contract. Most mortgages, particularly single-family home mortgages, have had relatively small penalties for prepayments.

Types of Mortgages

Claims of the mortgagor on the real property involved in the debt contract vary widely. The first-mortgage contract is by far the most common for both residential and commercial properties. With this contract the lender has first claim on the real property pledged to secure the contract. Many properties—both residential and commercial—are further financed with mortgages whose interests are subordinate to those of the first-mortgage holder. Since these "junior" or second mortgages carry a greater amount of risk to the lender, they are usually

---

1. There are also chattel mortgages, which use other types of property—inventories, autos, etc.—as collateral and which are frequently used in short-term lending. The discussion of the mortgage market in this chapter does not include chattel mortgages.

2. For some important developments in the mortgage market, see the article by Cook listed in the references to this chapter.

Table 16.1 Volume of mortgages outstanding, classified by type of mortgage, 1970–1979 (billions of dollars)

	1970	1975	1979
Total	473.1	801.5	1333.7
Home	297.7	490.8	868.3
Multifamily residential	60.1	100.6	132.0
Commercial	85.5	159.3	240.0
Farm	29.8	50.9	93.4

Source: Board of Governors of the Federal Reserve System, *Flow of Funds Accounts, Assets and Liabilities Outstanding, 1969–1979*, p. 760.

placed at a higher interest rate. Junior mortgages have become increasingly common in recent years as rapid escalation of property values has made it difficult for buyers to make the cash down payments associated with the purchase of real property. As a result, sellers have been forced to accept a second or junior mortgage in order to be able to complete the sale.

Increases in interest rates in recent years and the periodic episodes of diminished credit availability have produced a number of innovations in mortgage contracts. Increasingly, lenders on income-producing properties have sought to obtain a share of the inflation-induced increases in the value of the property being financed. Life insurance companies and other traditional lenders on apartment houses and office buildings have frequently required various types of ''equity kickers'' in order to justify the loan. These arrangements provide the lender with, in addition to the interest return, a share in any increases in gross rentals from the property that presumably may occur with rising prices. The ''wraparound'' feature has also become common in both residential and commercial mortgages. By this arrangement the lender (the seller of the property) gives the borrower (the buyer of the property) a mortgage for the full amount of the property (less a standard down payment), but the lender retains liability for the existing mortgage. The new mortgage, in effect, is wrapped around the old mortgage. From the buyer's perspective, the wraparound provides complete financing for the purchase of the property without resort to a junior mortgage. From the seller's perspective, since the wraparound is usually at a higher rate than that of the original mortgage, there is the prospect of a gain equal to the spread between interest expense on the old mortgage and interest income on the new mortgage.

Insured Versus Conventional Mortgages

As we pointed out earlier, the United States government has played a major role in the mortgage market for many decades. One of the most visible aspects of the attempts to improve the flow of credit to mortgages stems from the government mortgage insurance and guarantee program. Begun in the early 1930s, the mortgage insurance program of the Federal Housing Administration (FHA) has had an enormous impact on the availability of housing. Financed by a mortgage insurance fee, the FHA program has reduced the risk exposure of lenders. Moreover, it has encouraged the growth of amortized loans and contributed to the maintenance of quality in the construction of residential units. There currently exists a Veterans Administration guarantee program that performs functions similar to those of the FHA insurance program. The growth and acceptance of these types of federally sponsored programs has resulted in the split of the mortgage market into two subcomponents: insured (FHA or VA) and conventional (not FHA or VA).[3]

New Types of Mortgage Contracts

The mortgage market has been seriously strained in recent years by periodic episodes of inflation and reduced credit availability from the major mortgage lenders, such as savings and loan associations and life insurance companies. Rapidly rising interest rates have produced large losses in the capital value of fixed-rate mortgages held by financial institutions. And, financial institutions that have been "locked into" low-yielding fixed-rate mortgages in periods of rising interest rates have found it difficult to offer competitive rates to attract funds.

As a result, new types of mortgage contracts have been developed that allow the rate paid by the borrower and the rate received by the lender to adjust upward or downward as interest rate levels change. The most common of these arrangements is the *variable-rate mortgage (VRM),* which maintains the traditional long-term nature of the mortgage contract but allows the rate and/or the maturity of the instrument to vary with changes in open-market rates in the capital market. For example, an increase in interest rates in the capital market would lead to an increase in the interest rate on the loan or to a lengthening of the maturity of the loan or to some combination of the two. On the other hand, a reduction in interest rates in the capital markets would lead to a decrease in the interest rate on the loan or to a reduction in its maturity or some combination or the two.

Another new type of mortgage contract—the *renegotiated-rate mortgage*—is similar to the Canadian rollover mortgage, which has been used for a number of years. With this type of contract, the maturity of the mortgage is quite short (generally three to five years), and the rate on the mortgage is subject to renegotiation at the end of that period. The Federal Home Loan Bank Board granted all federally chartered savings and loan associations the right to offer these types of mortgage beginning in 1981.[4]

Note that the variable-rate mortgage and the renegotiated-rate mortgage substantially change the division of interest-rate risk between borrower and lender. With the traditional fixed-rate mortgage (particularly with small prepayment penalties), the interest-rate risk

---

3. There also exist a number of private firms that will insure a conventional mortgage for a fee.

4. Another new type of contract is the graduated-payment mortgage (GPM). This contract was devised to cope with the fact that young families were finding it increasingly difficult to purchase houses in periods of sharply rising prices. With the GPM the payments are low in the early life of the mortgage and then increase over time, presumably in line with the ability of the family to meet mortgage payments. See the article by Melton in the references at the end of this chapter.

was held by the lender. If rates increased, the lender was locked into a low-yielding asset. Yet if rates fell, the borrower could prepay the mortgage, and the lender would then be able to reinvest only at lower rates. With variable-rate mortgages and to a lesser extent with renegotiated-rate mortgages, much of the interest-rate risk has shifted to the borrower.

THE DEMAND FOR MORTGAGE FUNDS

The demand for mortgage funds stems from underlying economic factors associated with the growth and mobility of population. Increases in population and rapid geographic shifts in population will produce large demands for housing, office buildings, commercial structures, and other types of properties. Since real-property acquisition is usually accomplished with borrowed funds, any increases in the demand for real property will lead to an increase in the demand for mortgage funds. In addition, inflation in construction costs or the belief that real property (either residential or commercial) is an effective inflation hedge will also contribute to an increase in the demand for mortgage funds.

In understanding the demand for mortgages, it is important to distinguish the different types of mortgages, one from another. Expansion of the population in an area, of course, will increase the demand for mortgages. So will increases in the mobility of a given population. In addition, the demand for mortgages to finance office buildings and apartment houses may be explained within an investment decision-making framework that is similar to the analysis made for a new project or a new piece of business equipment. The demand for the office space or rental units must be estimated, vacancy rates and operating costs must be forecasted, and a rate of return on the investment must be calculated. This investment rate of return can then be compared with the cost of funds in determining the demand for funds. But the demand for farm mortgages, particularly mortgages on farm and ranch land, is perhaps the most complex portion of the total demand for mortgage funds. Although a portion of this demand may be explained by rate-of-return considerations, it must also be recognized that farming and ranching in many areas retain individual family-ownership characteristics that make the demand for mortgage funds more complex to understand and anticipate.

THE SUPPLY OF MORTGAGE FUNDS

Information on the ownership of home, multifamily residential, commercial, and farm mortgages is provided in Tables 16.2 through 16.5. Examination of these data suggests a number of important generalizations about the supply of mortgage funds. First, as is true for most financial instruments, the supply stems principally from financial institutions. Second, most mortgages are held by thrift institutions and contractual-type financial institutions. Savings and loans dominate the home mortgage market, and they are also the most important lenders on multifamily residential properties; savings and loans, life insurance companies, and commercial banks are the principal suppliers of commercial mortgage

Table 16.2 Ownership of home mortgages, 1979 (billions of dollars)

Amount outstanding	$868.3
Held by	
Households	65.1
U.S. government and government-sponsored credit agencies	52.9
Mortgage pools	104.4
Commercial banking	146.1
Savings and loans	393.4
Mutual savings banks	64.7
Life insurance companies	15.4
Finance companies	8.6
Other	17.7

Source: Board of Governors of the Federal Reserve System, *Flow of Funds Accounts, Assets and Liabilities Outstanding, 1969–1979*, p. 760.

Table 16.3 Ownership of multifamily residential mortgages, 1979 (billions of dollars)

Amount outstanding	$132.0
Held by	
Households	$ 7.8
U.S. government and government-sponsored credit agenices	14.0
Mortgage pools	6.8
Commercial banks	12.6
Savings and loan associations	38.5
Mutual savings banks	17.2
Life insurance companies	19.4
Other	15.7

Source: Board of Governors of the Federal Reserve System, *Flow of Funds Accounts, Assets and Liabilities Outstanding, 1969–1979*, p. 761

Table 16.4 Ownership of commercial mortgages, 1979 (billions of dollars)

Amount outstanding	$240.0
Held by	
Households	17.4
U.S. government	0.3
Commercial banking	77.7
Savings and loan associations	43.8
Mutual savings bank	16.9
Life insurance companies	72.1
State and local government retirement funds	3.3
Other	8.5

Source: Board of Governors of the Federal Reserve System, *Flow of Funds Accounts, Assets and Liabilities Outstanding, 1969–1979*, p. 761.

Table 16.5 Ownership of farm mortgages, 1979 (billions of dollars)

Amount outstanding	93.4
Held by	
Households	32.6
State and local governments	0.8
U.S. government and government-sponsored credit agencies	30.5
Mortgage pools	6.8
Commercial banks	10.4
Life insurance companies	12.3

Source: Board of Governors of the Federal Reserve System, *Flow of Funds Accounts, Assets and Liabilities Outstanding, 1969–1979*, p. 761.

funds.[5] Households and government-sponsored agencies are the principal investors in farm mortgages. The importance of government activity in the mortgage market is also evident in these tables. Mortgage pools and government-sponsored agencies accounted for almost 20 percent of total home mortgages, over 10 percent of multifamily residential mortgages, and over 30 percent of farm mortgages.

In the early 1970s, Real Estate Investment Trusts (REITs) were significant suppliers of mortgage funds, especially for income-producing property, such as office buildings and apartment houses. These REITs included short-term lenders, long-term lenders, and equity investors. Many were sponsored by large commercial banks. However, many REITs experienced massive loan losses on their investments, and by the late 1970s that instrument had ceased to be used as a significant supplier of mortgage funds.

One of the most significant factors affecting the supply of mortgages in recent years is the growth of mortgage-backed securities.[6] Until recently, the mortgage market was predominantly local, reflecting the heterogeneous nature of the mortgage contract and the great variety of different laws relating to real property. Creating a pool of mortgages and offering securities that are standardized and that represent an interest in the mortgage pool has transformed the mortgage market.

Three government agencies are responsible for the explosive growth of mortgage-backed securities: Federal National Mortgage Association (FNMA), Government National Mortgage Association (GNMA), and the Federal Home Loan Mortgage Corporation (FHLMC). The FNMA purchases government-insured and -guaranteed mortgages in the secondary market and finances these purchases by selling short- and intermediate-term notes. GNMA guarantees the timely payment of principal and interest on securities issued by private mortgage lenders that are backed by pools of government-insured or -guaranteed mortgages. These GNMA pass-through securities (so called because they pass through principal and interest payments from the underlying mortgages to the certificate holder)

5. The large amount of commercial mortgages held by commercial banks is somewhat misleading, because a substantial fraction of these mortgages represents property in the stage of construction. Upon completion, the permanent lending will generally be done by a life insurance company or savings and loan.

6. For an extensive discussion of this development, see the article by Severind listed in the references at the end of this chapter.

have revolutionized the secondary mortgage market. Performing a similar function, the FHLMC purchases conventional mortgages from savings and loans and other lenders and sells mortgage-participation certificates and guaranteed-mortgage certificates representing interests in these portfolios of mortgages. These various types of mortgage pools have grown enormously in recent years, exceeding $100 billion by the end of 1979.

A growing factor in the supply of mortgage funds is the real estate limited partnership. Generally sponsored by a real estate firm or a security brokerage firm, the real estate limited partnership has provided large amounts of funds in the income-producing property market. In this arrangement, there exist one or more general partners (usually real estate firms) and numerous limited partners. The limited partners, who have no management responsibility and whose liability is limited, provide most of the funds. The attraction to the limited partners is the opportunity to gain the tax benefits associated with real-property ownership (especially accelerated depreciation and large interest deduction from borrowed money used in the partnership), as well as the potential capital gain that is associated with the appreciation of a real asset in an inflationary environment. Of course, these limited partnerships provide the basic equity (rather than mortgage) money for real estate ventures. But by providing the equity funds, they provide a base for an additional flow of borrowed funds into the mortgage markets.

The Mortgages Market

Primary Market.   The primary market for mortgages (the market for newly created mortgages) has traditionally been a very local one involving local financial institutions, such as savings and loan associations. The initial lender is known as the *originator* of the mortgage. The originator may either retain the mortgage for its own portfolio or dispose of the mortgage in the secondary market if one exists. In a variant of this pattern, the mortgage bank, which has traditionally served as agent for such permanent lenders as pension funds and insurance companies, originates a mortgage loan and for a fee provides the necessary services during the life of the loan, such as maintaining records, accepting payments, and paying taxes and insurance on the property. Although most mortgage lenders other than mortgage banks have held the mortgages they originated, there has been a growing tendency to originate and dispose of mortgages in the secondary market.

Increasingly, the primary market for mortgages has broadened with the development of mortgage-backed securities. Indeed, these mortgage-backed securities have changed the mortgage market so greatly that in many respects it is now similar to the corporate bond market. These securities include the Government National Mortgage Association pass-through certificates, as well as private pass-through certificates and various types of mortgage backed bonds. More will be said about these securities in the following discussion of the secondary market in mortgages.

Secondary Market.   Traditionally the secondary mortgage market has been very weak, and mortgages have been viewed as highly illiquid financial instruments. But with the development of the various government agencies and the existence of mortgage-backed securities, the secondary market for mortgages has improved greatly. The Federal National Mortgage Association has strengthened the secondary market for both conventional and FHA and VA mortgages by conducting regular purchase auctions, and the Federal Home Loan Mortgage Corporation has created a secondary market for mortgages held by savings and loan associations. Moreover, GNMA pass-through securities have a secondary market that is quite good.

The secondary market for mortgages, especially home mortgages, involves both individual mortgages and mortgage pools.[7] The mortgage pools may be either federally insured or conventional. Each passes through to the holder of the security both interest and principal payments, whether regularly scheduled principal payments or repayments. Mortgage bankers have been very active in the creation of mortgage pools. In contrast, with a mortgage-backed bond, only interest payments are made to the holder of the security prior to the maturity of that security. Savings and loan associations have been active in the sale of mortgage-backed bonds as a means of obtaining additional sources of funds. (Technically, mortgage-backed bonds are not pools, since the securities holder does not have a joint interest in the mortgages, and since the issuer continues to record the mortgages on its balance sheet).

There are a variety of participants in the secondary market. They include federal agencies involved in mortgage credit, such as the Federal National Mortgage Association, the Government National Mortgage Association, and the Federal Home Loan Mortgage Corporation. They also include federally sponsored pools, in which a federal agency guarantees timely payment of principal and interest to the investors in the pool. Finally, a large number of private financial institutions, such as mortgage banks and savings and loan associations, are active in buying and selling individual mortgages in the secondary market.

Yields on Mortgages

Calculation of the yield on mortgages, including the yield on the various types of pools, is complicated by a number of factors. Initially many home mortgages are written with the requirement that the borrower pay the lender "points" (a point is one percent of the value of the loan) as a means of increasing the yield to the lender. The impact of these points is to raise the true yield above the contract rate. Moreover, the true yield to maturity on a mortgage is not known to the investor at the time of purchase, because the extent of prepayment is not known and can only be estimated. For example, estimates of yields on GNMA pass-through securities are based on the assumption of a 12-year average life. However, individual GNMA pass-throughs may be prepaid faster or slower than this assumed term, and thus the yield would differ from that initially calculated.

Since the credit characteristics of individual mortgages vary widely, it is not surprising that the yields on mortgage instruments also vary widely. Yet some generalizations can be made. Yields on insured mortgages tend to move with corporate bond rates, though with a

7. For a detailed discussion of the secondary market for home mortgages, see the article by Brockschmidt in the references at the end of this chapter.

lag. In the period from 1950 to 1965, yields on FHA mortgages averaged about 150 basis points above the yield on Aaa corporate bonds. In recent years, however, the yield spread appears to have narrowed, and the lag has diminished. Increasingly, mortgage rates are moving in line with corporate bond rates as the bond market and the mortgage market become more interrelated. Naturally, the yield on conventional mortgages will exceed the yield on FHA mortgages, generally by ¼ to ½ a percentage point.

THE TROUBLED MORTGAGE MARKET

The mortgage market, especially the single-family mortgage market, has experienced significant difficulties in recent years in fulfilling its necessary social function. This difficulty reflects a variety of interrelated causes, but fundamentally it stems from the existence and acceleration of inflation in the period beginning with the mid-1960s. A financial structure consisting of specialized financial institutions providing long-term fixed-rate mortgage funds has found it very difficult to deal with high inflation and high and variable interest rates. Indeed, to a considerable extent the innovations that have occurred in the mortgage market since the mid-1960s are attributable to the problems associated with the economic and financial environment.

The fixed-rate mortgage has traditionally served as the basic instrument in the mortgage market. Yet many investors have found that in periods of rising interest rates and inflation, the "real" return on these fixed-rate mortgages has been negative. Moreover, with rising rates the market value of fixed-rate mortgages diminishes, as is true for any fixed-income instrument, resulting in a loss of liquidity for the lender unless that lender is willing to accept a large capital loss on the liquidation of the mortgage. Although this problem exists for any fixed-income instrument, including all types of bonds, it is especially important for mortgage lenders, who are often specialized in very long-term mortgages. Lenders have devised various new types of mortgage contracts—including the variable-rate mortgage—in order to protect themselves from this problem. However, the long-term viability of these types of mortgage contracts is still unknown.

A second and related problem that has troubled the mortgage market in recent years arises from certain other difficulties experienced by the major lenders on residential mortgages, especially the savings and loan associations and mutual savings banks. At the same time that these institutions have been locked into long-term fixed-rate mortgages, they have been limited by Regulation Q ceilings on the maximum rates they can pay for funds, despite the fact that interest rates have increased substantially in response to inflationary pressures. In periods of high interest rates, such as in 1966, 1969, 1977, and 1980–1981, these financial institutions have suffered *disintermediation,* as funds have flowed directly to higher-yielding open-market instruments. Moreover, the growth of money market funds has substantially affected the availability and cost of funds to mortgage lenders. During periods of high interest rates, traditional mortgage lenders do not have funds to lend and are unable to perform their usual financial services.

As discussed earlier in this book, one of the principal purposes of the Depository Institutions Deregulation and Monetary Control Act of 1980 was to stabilize the flow of funds into savings and loans and mutual savings banks. Both were given the authority nationwide to offer transactions accounts, such as N.O.W. accounts, which provide additional sources of funds. Moreover, both were given the authority to broaden their lending to include other types of loans with maturities shorter than those of mortgage loans. Yet the ultimate impact of these changes on the availability and cost of mortgage credit from the traditional mortgage lenders is very much an open question.

SUMMARY

Mortgages are fixed-income instruments secured by real property. Taken as a group, mortgages are the largest component of the capital market, and home mortgages are the largest component of the mortgage market. Mortgages vary in their claims on the pledged property; they include first mortgages and various types of junior mortgages. The mortgage has traditionally had a fixed rate, though increasingly, various types of mortgages have been devised that carry variable rates. Mortgages may also be characterized as insured (or guaranteed) if protected by the FHA or VA or as conventional if not.

The demand for mortgages reflects the demand for real property, since most purchases of real property are financed with borrowed funds. Recent inflation, which has increased the price of real property, particularly residential property, has substantially increased the demand for mortgage funds. The supply of mortgage funds stems primarily from financial institutions, such as savings and loan associations, mutual savings banks, pension funds, and life insurance companies. However, government agencies are playing a growing role in the mortgage market. Both the primary and secondary mortgage markets have grown, but the secondary market has experienced tremendous expansion, particularly because of the growth of mortgage pools, such as those represented by GNMA pass-through certificates. The mortgage market has a number of significant problems that are forcing rapid changes in the mortgage industry.

QUESTIONS

1. What is a mortgage? What is the difference between a mortgage and a bond?
2. Distinguish between a first mortgage and a junior mortgage.
3. What is an "equity kicker"? A "wraparound" mortgage?
4. What is a variable-rate mortgage? Has it tended to replace the fixed-rate mortgage?
5. What is a mortgage pool? Explain the characteristics of GNMA pass-through certificates.
6. Why is it said that the mortgage market is in trouble? What might solve the problems?

REFERENCES

Brockschmidt, Peggy, ''The Secondary Market for Home Mortgages,'' Federal Reserve Bank of Kansas City *Monthly Review,* September–October 1977, pp. 11–20.

Cook, Timothy, ''The Residential Mortgage Market in Recent Years,'' Federal Reserve Bank of Richmond *Economic Review,* September/October 1974.

Dougall, Herbert E., and Jack E. Gaumnitz, *Capital Markets and Institutions,* 4th ed. (Englewood Cliffs, N.J.: Prentice-Hall, 1980).

Light, J.O., and W.L. White, *The Financial System* (Homewood, Ill.: Irwin, 1980).

Melton, William, ''Graduated Payment Mortgages,'' Federal Reserve Bank of New York *Quarterly Review,* Spring 1980.

Severind, Charles, ''Mortgage Backed Securities,'' Federal Reserve Bank of New York *Quarterly Review,* August 1979.

Chapter 17

The Capital Market: Equity Securities

Equity means an ownership claim, and equity securities evidence ownership in incorporated enterprises. Equity securities are thus an institutional aspect of a private enterprise economy—a means of holding wealth and a source of new capital funds for corporations. Many observers would rank the significant aspects of equity securities in that order. The use of equity securities as a means of transferring saved funds from surplus to deficit economic units, unlike the use of debt securities, has been largely an almost incidental aspect of their function in the financial system in recent years. Trading in equity securities is predominantly a secondary market; most corporations rarely issue new equity shares. (An exception is regulated firms, such as public utilities, which generally are required to maintain certain debt-equity ratios in their capital structure.)

Why, then, are equity securities of such importance to the saving-investment process? Table 17.1 offers a guide to the answer. For the years shown, new equity issues accounted for only about 5 percent of total funds obtained by nonfinancial corporations, whereas retained earnings accounted for 22 percent, depreciation and depletion charges provided about 49 percent, and debt accounted for the remainder. Thus corporate retained earnings are a very important means of investment financing. Bear in mind, however, that although retained earnings represent "corporate saving," the corporation is only an organizational framework—retained earnings are really *shareholder saving*. To better understand this relationship between equity securities and retained earnings, it is useful to review the sources and uses of corporate funds.

Table 17.1 Sources of funds for nonfarm, nonfinancial corporations, 1970–1978 (billions of dollars)

	1970	1971	1972	1973	1974	1975	1976	1977	1978
Internal sources									
Retained earnings	$ 9.7	$15.3	$22.5	$32.5	$39.1	$35.1	$47.9	$50.5	$58.6
Depreciation and depletion	54.3	58.4	64.9	69.9	77.0	84.0	91.4	99.7	107.5
Inventory valuation adjustment	−5.1	−5.0	−6.6	−18.6	−40.4	−12.4	−14.5	−14.9	−24.3
	$58.9	$68.6	$80.8	$83.8	$75.7	$106.7	$124.7	$135.3	$141.9
External sources									
Bonds	$19.8	$18.9	$12.7	$11.0	$21.3	$29.8	$25.3	$24.5	$23.3
Bank term loans (est.)	2.0	2.0	6.4	8.4	11.0	1.3	−1.1	5.2	10.5
Mortgages	6.7	10.2	17.0	18.2	13.7	9.5	12.9	19.0	23.2
Stocks	5.7	11.4	10.9	7.9	4.1	9.4	10.5	2.7	2.6
Bank and other debt (mainly short-term)	6.6	2.0	11.3	27.2	31.6	−13.5	10.6	27.3	29.9
	$40.8	$44.5	$58.3	$72.7	$81.7	$37.0	$58.2	$78.7	$89.5
Total sources	$99.7	$113.1	$139.1	$156.5	$157.4	$143.7	$182.9	$214.0	$231.4

Sources: *Survey of Current Business*; Federal Reserve Board of Governors, *Flow of Funds Accounts*; term loan data from Bankers Trust Company, *Credit and Capital Markets* (annual).

BUSINESS CORPORATION EQUITY FINANCING

The nature of the flow of funds for a nonfinancial business corporation can be readily assessed by considering the structure of a representative balance sheet for such a firm. In the exhibit below, the various groups of assets, liabilities, and equity items are listed in the conventional format, where "current" means an asset or liability of maturity of one year or less.

Assets	Liabilities and stockholder equity
Current assets	Current liabilities
Cash and short-term financial assets	Trade payables
	Other short-term debt
Trade receivables (credit extended to customers)	
	Noncurrent liabilities
Inventories	Bonds payable
	Other long-term debt
Noncurrent Assets	
Plant and equipment	Stockholder equity
Buildings	
Land	Equity shares outstanding
	Retained earnings

Business assets are "financed" with liabilities and stockholder equity. Such financing needs are often characterized as a need for "working capital"—current assets minus current liabilities—and "plant" (all noncurrent assets). Such a framework focuses on the firm's long-term financing structure. In equation form:

$$WC + NCA = NCL + SE,$$

where WC = working capital, NCA = noncurrent assets, NCL = noncurrent liabilities, and SE = stockholder equity.

The firm's financing needs and sources can now be seen in terms of changes (Δ) in these various balance sheet components:

$$\Delta WC + \Delta NCA = \Delta NCL + \Delta SE.$$

Thus a business corporation has only two means of financing its working capital needs (essentially inventories plus any excess of short-term trade credit extended over trade credit utilized) and plant and equipment expansion and replacement: an increase in long-term debt or an increase in stockholder equity. (Recognize that, in this context, *short-term* funds are *part of* working capital and thus do not finance it.) Chapter 15 focused on how firms rely on the use of bonded indebtedness for their financial needs and on the great extent of that reliance. The subject of this chapter, the equity component of corporate financial structure, has two parts: retained earnings and equity shares of stockholders. A firm can thus use equity financing either by increasing retained earnings (*internal* equity financing) or by issuing new stock (*external* equity financing).[1]

Internal Financing

Business corporations generate their own financing to the extent that their cash inflows for a period exceed the sum of all cash outflows for that period, including taxes and dividends. A convenient measure of this amount is obtained by adding depreciation for a period to the amount of after-tax earnings not distributed to shareholders in dividend payments (retained earnings). Table 17.2 shows corporate profits and their distribution in recent years. [Note that "net cash flow" is the sum of "undistributed profits" (retained earnings) and "capital consumption allowances" (depreciation).]

Table 17.2   Corporate profits and their distribution (billions of dollars)

Items	1974	1975	1976	1977	1978	1979
1. Profits before tax	126.9	120.4	156.0	177.1	206.0	236.6
2. Profits tax liability	52.4	49.8	63.8	72.6	84.5	92.5
3. Profits after tax	74.5	70.6	92.2	104.5	121.5	144.1
4. Dividends	31.0	28.9	37.5	42.1	47.2	52.7
5. Undistributed profits	43.5	41.7	54.7	62.4	74.3	91.4
6. Capital consumption allowances	81.6	89.3	97.1	109.3	119.8	131.0
7. Net cash flow	125.1	131.0	151.8	171.7	194.1	222.3

Source: *Federal Reserve Bulletin*, various issues.

Fluctuations in both the absolute amount of internally generated funds and its proportion of total business funding can be attributed largely to cyclical swings in business activity. The amount of internal funds generated is of course a direct function of earnings—rising markedly during upswings in business activity and dipping in periods of business recession.[2] Because of the sluggishness of the U.S. economy in the late 1960s and early 1970s,

---

1. Internally generated funds of business firms also include the amount of depreciation and various other items of operating expenses that do not involve an actual cash outlay. (These expenses are subtracted from corporate revenues in computing earnings but do not reduce corporate cash.) In the absence of price changes, the amounts of such items (in cost-based accounting) would provide for "capital maintenance"—the replacement of depreciating items as they are consumed in operations. With increasing prices, the funds needed to replace buildings and equipment have to be financed, just as do expansions in plant.

2. Retained earnings constitute the portion of total earnings not paid to stockholders as dividends. Thus changes in the amount of retained earnings can result from changes in dividend policy of corporations (increases or decreases in dividend payout as a percentage of earnings), as well as from changes in overall earnings. As a practical matter, corporations are generally very reluctant to reduce dividends, and they increase dividends only when it appears quite likely that the higher dividend can be easily sustained.

for example, the percentage of total business financing accounted for by internally generated funds dipped from more than 75 percent to less than 60 percent. Much of the increase in external funding is new debt. In recent years, corporations have in general reacted to disappointing amounts of internally generated funds by reducing their holdings of short-term liquid assets and substantially increasing the degree of leverage (ratio of debt to equity financing) in their financial structure.

External Equity Financing

Table 17.3 shows the amount of net new securities issued in recent years. As previously indicated, the amount of equity issues is quite small relative to total corporate financial flows

Table 17.3   New security issues of corporations, 1974–1979 (millions of dollars)

Type of issue or issuer, or use	1974	1975	1976	1977	1978	1979
All issues	38,311	53,617	53,488	53,792	47,230	51,464
BONDS	32,066	42,756	42,380	42,015	36,872	40,139
Type of offering						
Public	25,903	32,583	26,453	24,072	19,815	25,814
Private placement	6,160	10,172	15,927	17,943	17,057	14,325
Industry group						
Manufacturing	9,867	16,980	13,264	12,204	9,572	9,667
Commercial and miscellaneous	1,845	2,750	4,372	6,234	5,246	3,941
Transportation	1,550	3,439	4,387	1,996	2,007	3,102
Public utility	8,873	9,658	8,297	8,262	7,092	8,118
Communication	3,710	3,464	2,787	3,063	3,373	4,219
Real estate and financial	6,218	6,469	9,274	10,258	9,586	11,095
STOCKS	6,247	10,863	11,018	11,770	10,358	11,325
Type						
Preferred	2,253	3,458	2,803	3,916	2,832	3,574
Common	3,994	7,405	8,305	7,861	7,526	7,751
Industry group						
Manufacturing	544	1,670	2,237	1,189	1,241	1,679
Commercial and miscellaneous	940	1,470	1,183	1,834	1,816	2,623
Transporation	22	1	24	456	263	255
Public utility	3,964	6,235	6,121	5,865	5,140	5,171
Communication	217	1,002	776	1,379	264	303
Real estate and financial	562	488	771	1,049	1,631	1,293

Source: *Federal Reserve Bulletin*, various issues.

of funds. The decision by a firm to issue new equity securities is determined by both financial and nonfinancial factors. The fact that control of the corporation may be altered by the sale of such securities is the principal nonfinancial factor for nonregulated firms. Financial factors include (for given financing requirements) the following.

1. The degree of availability of internal financing relative to total financing needs
2. Cost of alternative external financing sources, specifically the interest rate
3. Current market price of the firm's stock (which governs the cost of equity financing)

Thus the use of external equity financing is likely to be significant only during periods of relatively high stock prices, especially if interest rates are concurrently high and total business financing needs are great. The U.S. tax structure is biased against external equity financing, relative to debt financing, since unlike interest payments, dividend payments are not deductible expenses for income tax purposes. Further, new issues of equity shares tend to dilute earnings per share, although the projects financed from the funds provided should generate sufficient future earnings to make such dilution temporary. Finally, external equity financing is unfavorable relative to internal financing because the former necessitates a costly and time-consuming registration process with the Securities and Exchange Commission. Also, shareholders view internal financing as making capital gains more likely (at the cost of forgoing dividends), and income from capital gains is subject to a lower tax rate than dividend income.

CHARACTERISTICS OF EQUITY SECURITIES

For the investor, equity securities are riskier than debt securities but offer the possibility of higher returns. For the issuing firm, equity securities are a less risky means of financing than debt, because there is no fixed commitment for payments to the holder of the stock. There are two types of equity securities: preferred stock and common stock.

Preferred Stock.   Preferred stock offers a fixed dividend per share, which must be paid to preferred stockholders before any dividends can be paid to common stockholders. Preferred stock usually carries a *cumulative* feature, which means that preferred dividends that are not paid in a given period or periods "accumulate" and must be paid in total before any common stock dividends are paid. The other major "preference" of this class of stock is a priority claim (relative to common shareholders) against corporate assets in the event of corporate liquidation.

Use of preferred stock issues is relatively infrequent in this country. Preferred stock is similar to bonds but with one very significant difference—unlike interest, preferred stock dividends are not a tax-deductible expense. As a result, preferred stock is a relatively expensive means of raising funds. To the issuing corporation, the only significant advantage of preferred stock, relative to bonds, is that preferred dividends may be "passed" (not paid) without the threat of bankruptcy that nonpayment of bond interest would invoke. However, there is a significant advantage to a corporation's investing in the preferred (and common) stock of another corporation—85 percent of dividends received are nontaxable.

Common Stock.   Unlike ownership of bonds or preferred stock, common stock ownership carries no corporate commitment to a fixed periodic return or payment of principal. Ultimate ownership rights to corporate assets are held by common stockholders, and the right to vote for members of the corporation's board of directors is inherent in common stock (although some corporations, generally those that are family-controlled, have nonvoting classes of common stock). Though occasionally important (as in so-called takeovers), this right to participate in corporate control is usually of minor significance to investors. They tend to value instead the right to unlimited participation in the fruits of company growth and profitability—dividends and capital gains—that common stock ownership brings.

Other Features of Equity Securities

Many preferred stocks have *convertible* provisions that enable their holders to convert them into common stock at a stated ratio of common shares for each preferred share presented for conversion. Issuers often sell convertible preferred stock because this feature's attractiveness to investors results in a lower cost relative to straight preferred stock. In addition, preferred stock is sometimes issued without a conversion feature but with attached purchase option warrants that can be used to acquire common stock at a privileged subscription price. The effect of such warrants on the preferred stock price, of course, is determined by the value of the warrants. The value of the warrants, in turn, is a function of the stated subscription price relative to the market price of the common stock.

Most preferred stock is *callable,* which means that the issuer has the right to redeem the preferred shares at a stated *call price.* Although the call price will always exceed the investor's purchase price for the preferred stock and thus result in an investor gain if exercised, the callable feature is still a disadvantage for the investor. The reason is that the issuing firm is likely to exercise the callable provision only when market yields have fallen (and security prices have risen) to the point where refunding the preferred stock issue is attractive. Thus investors who are obliged to sell back their preferred stock will have relatively less attractive investment opportunities in which to place the proceeds.

OWNERSHIP OF EQUITY SECURITIES

The distribution of ownership of outstanding equity securities for 1975–1979 is shown in Table 17.4. As we indicated in Chapter 11, households constitute the largest holders of equity securities. Holdings by institutions, particularly by pension funds, have become much more important in recent years. Private pension funds are the largest institutional holders of common stocks, followed by insurance companies (all types) and mutual funds.

Table 17.4   Total holdings of corporate equity securities by sector and selected institutions, 1975–1979 (end of calendar year; billions of dollars)

	1975	1976	1977	1978	1979
Households	660	827	777	808	907
Foreign	35	43	40	42	50
Mutual savings banks	4	4	5	5	6
Life insurance companies	28	34	33	36	40
Other insurance companies	14	17	17	19	26
Private pension funds	89	110	102	108	136
State and local government retirement funds	24	30	30	33	44
Mutual funds	34	37	32	31	34
Brokers and dealers	3	4	4	3	3

Source: Board of Governors of the Federal Reserve System, *Flow of Funds Accounts, Assets and Liabilities Outstanding, 1969–1979.*

Increased holdings by both life and property insurance companies are largely the result of relaxation of restrictions on the scope of their investments that began in the 1960s.

The generally stagnant nature of the stock market during the decade of the 1970s, together with a change in brokerage commission structure that increased the transactions costs of security investments to individuals, resulted in households' being net sellers of equities during that period. Household disenchantment with equities also impacted on household holdings of mutual funds specializing in stocks. This divestment of equities by households was absorbed by institutional investors, particularly pension funds. Thus the net effect was to shift households from direct to indirect ownership of equities.

Commercial bank trust departments account for ownership of more than $200 billion in common stocks, approximately evenly split between personal accounts and pension trusts managed for individuals.

Intercorporate holdings of preferred and common equity securities amounted to more than $125 billion in 1979. Some of these holdings of common stock represent a means of exercising a measure of control over other firms, but a considerable amount of the common stock holdings and all the preferred holdings are for investment income. To avoid "double taxation," 85 percent of dividend income received by corporations from other corporations is excluded from income tax, so the after-tax return on such intercorporate equity investments is greatly increased.

THE PRIMARY MARKET FOR EQUITIES

New issues of corporate stock may be sold directly to investors by the issuing firm or indirectly through investment banking institutions and dealers. Four significant means of direct issue of equity securities are:

1. Sale of a new issue of common stock to current stockholders at a "privileged subscription price"

2. Sale of new shares of stock to current stockholders as part of a "dividend reinvestment" plan

3. Direct placement of a new stock issue with institutional investors

4. Sale of new shares to employees via some company saving or incentive plan of stock purchase

The initial offering of new common shares of stock to current stockholders (the *preemptive right* of shareholders to maintain their proportionate share of ownership) may be required by the law of the state of incorporation or by the corporate charter. Even if not required, such a *rights offering* may be advantageous to the issuing corporation. The term "rights offering" stems from the issuance to present shareholders of rights that entitle them to buy new shares of common stock (or sometimes convertible bonds or convertible preferred stock) at a discount from current market price. Each shareholder is entitled to purchase the proportion of the new issue that corresponds to the proportion of his or her holdings of stock already outstanding. For example, suppose a corporation with 1,000,000 shares of outstanding common stock issues a rights offering of 100,000 shares. Each shareholder will receive one right for each share held, but 10 rights must be exercised for each new share purchased at the subscription price.[3] These rights have a value corresponding to the difference between the market price of the stock and the privileged subscription price, adjusted for the increase in the number of shares that the issue entails. To ensure complete distribution of the new securities, the issuing firm may engage an investment banker (or bankers) in a standby arrangement that obligates the latter to acquire any shares not purchased by stockholders.

Dividend reinvestment plans, as a means of issuing new equity shares, are of relatively recent vintage. These plans simply require agreement by a current stockholder that the dividends declared by the firm will be applied to the purchase of new securities instead of being distributed in cash. The advantage to the shareholder of such plans is the avoidance of the reinvestment costs that might otherwise be incurred.

Neither private placement nor employee purchase plans account for particularly large sales of new equity shares. Private placement is generally limited to issues of high-grade preferred stocks of public utility firms and to issues of small, financially sound firms for which use of an investment banker is either infeasible or unattractive because of the relatively small size of the new issue. Overall, direct issue by all these various means accounts for less than 15 percent of new common stock issues and less than 5 percent of new preferred stock issues.

Most new equity issues are thus distributed to investors through investment bankers via underwriting or agency selling arrangements. The role of investment bankers in the issue of

---

3. For the reader who is curious as to how share holdings that are not a multiple of 10 are handled, the answer is simple. The issuing firm generally acts as a clearinghouse for exchange of rights, facilitating the sale of rights by shareholders to other shareholders. Thus, in the example above, a shareholder currently holding 12 shares might buy one new share and sell two "rights" to another shareholder, who holds 18 shares, enabling the other shareholder to acquire two new shares.

new equity securities parallels their role in the issue of new corporate bonds, as described in Chapter 15. New public issues of equity securities are subject to the regulations and disclosure requirements of the Securities Act of 1933, as administered by the Securities and Exchange Commission (SEC).

The SEC also regulates the secondary markets for securities under the statutory authority of the Securities Act of 1934. In addition to imposing disclosure requirements on publicly owned corporations, this statute charges the SEC with regulatory purview over the organized security exchanges, the over-the-counter market, investment banking firms, brokers, dealers, and investment companies. Security trading is also subject to state regulation and to "private sector regulation" by the organized security exchanges and the National Association of Security Dealers (NASD).

THE SECONDARY MARKET FOR EQUITY SECURITIES

Secondary markets exist for many financial instruments, but the secondary market for corporate stocks is the largest in dollar volume and number of trades. Trading in the *organized exchanges* is dominated by equities in both dollar volume and number of trades. In the *over-the-counter* market, the total dollar volume of bond trading exceeds that of equities, but more trades involve equities than bonds. Such secondary market dominance is not surprising in view of the fact that the estimated market value of outstanding equities exceeds $1 trillion.

The Security Exchanges.   There are two national organized security exchanges, the New York Stock Exchange (NYSE) and the American Stock Exchange (AMEX), accounting for about 80 percent and 10 percent, respectively, of all organized exchange trading (in terms of number of shares traded). The other 10 percent is accounted for by the eleven regional organized exchanges, with the bulk of the trading occurring on the Midwest, Pacific, and Philadelphia-Baltimore-Washington exchanges.

To have its securities *listed* on an organized exchange, a firm must meet the trading volume and disclosure requirements of that particular exchange. The most stringent requirements are those of the NYSE, followed by the AMEX. The largest corporations are listed on the "Big Board" (the NYSE), and smaller (but national) firms are generally listed on the AMEX. The regional exchanges list securities of mostly regional firms, but they also list some NYSE and AMEX stocks ("multiple listing" cases), and trading volume in the latter category generally exceeds that in the former.

Organized security exchanges have the following characteristics.

1. Trading of securities takes place at a particular physical site—the "floor" of the exchange.
2. Trading is conducted among members of the exchange.

3. Trading is conducted according to the rules of the exchange, which dictate the manner in which trades are to be carried out by the exchange members and govern the conduct of the members, forbidding practices relating to manipulation of security prices.

Particular securities are traded at a designated *post,* a location on the floor of the exchange. At each post all trades are orally voiced (loudly) and recorded. Exchange members trade in a variety of capacities. Some act as *specialists* in a particular security or securities. (The specialist is charged with the responsibility for "making a market" in a security—selling when others will not sell and buying when others will not buy.) Some members trade for their own accounts, and some trade for accounts of other members. Most members, however, trade for commission brokerage firms and thus perform a pure *broker* function.

The OTC Market.   The trading of securities not listed on organized exchanges is conducted in the over-the-counter market (which is really mostly an "over-the-telephone" market). The OTC market is essentially a network of dealers who "make the market" in the various OTC securities. Dealers stand ready to buy any reasonable quantity of the security (or securities) in which they deal at the *bid* price, and to sell at the *asked* price. The dealer's gross profit margin stems from the *spread* between the bid and asked prices.

It is estimated that more than 14,000 various stock issues are actively traded in the OTC market. Such broad activity is made possible by an extensive and sophisticated communications network. Telephone and teletype facilities connect dealer trading rooms throughout the country. The National Association of Security Dealers Automatic Quotation (NASDAQ) system provides current bid and asked prices on a continuous basis for more than 3000 stocks. These quotations are made possible by having dealers in regularly quoted securities input any change in bid and asked prices into a central computer. Dealers seeking current quotations on these stocks are readily able to access the computer memory, and all bids and offers (and names of dealers) for a given stock can be instantly displayed on a video device.

The principal equity securities traded in the OTC market include bank stocks, insurance company stocks, and stocks of small, regional, and closely held corporations. There is also a great deal of OTC trading in stocks listed on organized exchanges. The trading of stocks listed on exchanges is referred to as the "third market" (organized exchange and OTC trading being the other two), and indeed, the dollar volume of such trading is about 10 percent of NYSE volume. There is also a "fourth market," in which institutions exchange securities directly without involving brokers or dealers, but it is of minor importance at present.

Trading in equity securities in the secondary market is dominated by financial institutions, especially on the NYSE. It is estimated that institutions currently account for about two-thirds of total trading (in dollar volume) on the NYSE. The growth in institutional dominance of the equities secondary market is a consequence of increased institutional ownership of equities, more frequent trading, and the fact that trades generally involve large *blocks* of stock. It is likely that the ability of the institutions to employ considerable analytical and information resources for purposes of security analysis has contributed to secondary market efficiency—the pricing of securities in accordance with informed perceptions of risk and expected return.

VALUATION OF EQUITY SECURITIES

The nature of returns on investment in equity securities differs in a number of respects from an investment in debt securities, including the following.

1. Equities have no fixed date of maturity; rather, they constitute perpetual-life investments.
2. Returns are more variable, since there is no contractual commitment to pay dividends each period as there is for the payment of interest.
3. The potential for capital gains and losses is generally much greater, as compared with debt security investments.

The periodic percentage return (r_t) on an equity investment is the algebraic sum of the dividend paid for the period (D_t) and the difference between the price at the end of the period (P_t) and the price at the beginning of the period (P_0), divided by the beginning price, or

$$r_t = \frac{D_t + (P_t - P_0)}{P_0}.$$

Since there is no "payment of principal at the maturity date," the basis of equity security value is expected dividends. Although capital gains (and losses) affect periodic returns on equity securities, these price changes can be attributed to changes in market expectations regarding the magnitude of future dividends and to changes in market perceptions of the riskiness of the security or other factors affecting the *market rate of discount* applied to the expected future dividends to be paid. The price of an equity security can thus be viewed as the present value of all expected future dividends, discounted at an appropriate market rate of interest.

The market rate of discount is largely determined by the market's assessment of the variability of future dividend payments; the greater that perceived variability is, the greater the discount rate will be. The discount rate represents the required market rate of return— what the security must yield to investors. An equity security will be priced (in equilibrium) to yield the required rate of return to investors.

The risk-return framework described in Chapter 11 indicates that equity securities, like all financial assets, will be priced according to expected return and their degree of "systematic" risk. (Recall that systematic risk is the incremental risk that a security poses for a portfolio—the portion of total risk that cannot be diversified away.) Thus, for a given stream of expected future returns, the greater the variability of this stream relative to expected overall market returns, the lower will be a stock's price, and vice versa. In practice, this measure of market-related variability in returns is calculated as the stock's beta, as indicated in Chapter 11. A beta of 1 implies that a stock's systematic variability in returns will correspond to overall market returns. A beta greater than 1 indicates that the systematic variability of a stock's returns exceeds the degree of variability in market returns, and vice versa for a beta less than 1.

Capital market theory thus suggests that the greater the magnitude of a stock's beta, the greater will be its expected return (the lower will be stock price for a given pattern and amount of expected future receipts). The theory also suggests that a stock's diversifiable, unsystematic risk is unrelated to its price (and expected returns).

Considerable empirical research has been conducted to test these postulated risk-return relationships for equity securities. Of course, empirical tests cannot include actual measures of investor expectations; rather, they focus on average returns over long time periods. It is supposed that such long-run average returns will approximate expected returns. These various studies indicate that, indeed, higher returns have generally resulted from holdings of higher-beta portfolios, but not to the degree predicted by capital market theory. Similarly, lower-beta portfolios are associated with returns that are somewhat higher than would be expected from the theoretical framework but smaller than returns of higher-beta portfolios. Thus the statistical evidence is somewhat clouded, although it offers general support for the theory.

Stock Market Efficiency

How *quickly* security prices adjust to reflect the "proper" risk-return relationship is a function of *capital market efficiency.* As indicated in Chapter 11, a financial market is characterized as efficient when financial asset prices continuously reflect all available information relevant to security values as analyzed and assessed by knowledgeable individuals who buy and sell securities according to this analysis and assessment. Three forms of stock market efficiency are postulated—*weak, semistrong,* and *strong.*

In its weak form, market efficiency exists when all information pertaining to *future* security price behavior that can be gleaned from *past* price movements is continuously reflected in *current* stock prices. (An implication of this is that "abnormal" profits—profits exceeding those commensurate with a security's risk—cannot be earned by "charting" stock prices.) In its semistrong form, stock market efficiency exists when all *publicly* available information is impounded in stock prices at all times. Much information relevant to security prices is of course *not* publicly available but is known only to "insiders." The strong form of stock market efficiency suggests that *all* relevant information, including "inside information," is immediately impounded into stock prices.[4]

---

4. Stock market behavior has been characterized as a "random walk" and postulation regarding its efficiency as "random walk theory." The term stems from the fact that information flows occur in random fashion, and if security prices continuously reflect all information (changing as *new* information becomes available), the path of stock prices will be a "random walk." For an excellent (and highly readable) account of random walk theory and related empirical studies, see Richard Brealey, *An Introduction to Risk and Return from Common Stocks* (MIT Press, 1969). A rather entertaining treatment of this subject can be found in Burton G. Malkiel, *A Random Walk Down Wall Street* (Norton, 1975).

The evidence from empirical studies strongly supports the weak and semistrong forms of stock market efficiency, but evidence is somewhat mixed regarding the strong form. Some of the most impressive supporting evidence has been gathered from studies of mutual fund performance. Mutual funds are of course professionally managed and well diversified, but the various studies indicate that they produce not "abnormal" returns but rather returns (after deduction of management costs) that are consistent with the risk profiles of their portfolios.

In summary, it appears that stock prices are established in the capital market according to investor expectations regarding future returns from the stocks and the volatility (risk) associated with these returns. It further appears that the information underlying the formation of investor expectations is impounded very quickly into security prices. This apparent high level of security market efficiency augurs well for the process of resource allocation in the economy.

STOCK AND BOND YIELDS

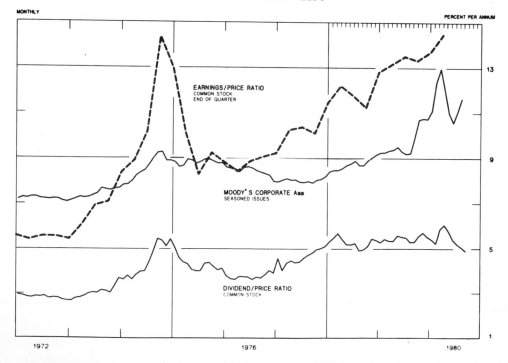

Figure 17.1
(Source: Board of Governors of the Federal Reserve System, *Historical Chart Book.*)

THE RECORD OF EQUITY RETURNS

Few aspects of financial behavior have been the subject of as much intense scrutiny as have yields on stocks. A thorough evaluation and assessment of stock returns is best left to books on investment, but a brief mention of the historical pattern of yields may be useful. (The interested reader will find additional suggestions in the references at the end of this chapter.)

Figure 17.1 shows the dividend yield and earnings-price ratio of common stock for the 1972–1980 period and, for comparative purposes, the yields on high-grade industrial bonds. The figure indicates the performance of bonds during this period—a pattern of returns closely correlated with that of preferred stock. In the case of common-stock dividend yields and earnings-price ratios, it should be recognized that the level of stock prices greatly influences these rough measures of equity returns.

The conventional wisdom of finance long held that common stock investment offered a hedge against inflation. More precisely, common stock returns were perceived as being less subject to purchasing power risk than were the fixed dollar returns offered by bonds and preferred stocks. The relatively low yields of common stocks in the 1960s and early 1970s were a serious blow to this notion for many investors, because stock yields sagged as inflation soared in the late 1960s and early 1970s. Yields improved in the late 1970s, however, and the equity market strengthened significantly at the beginning of the 1980s.

SUMMARY

The market for equity securities is primarily a secondary market. Although equity issues thus account for only a relatively small part of the flow of capital funds from surplus economic units to deficit economic units, the equity market is an important component of the financial system of any predominantly private enterprise economy. In such an economic system, ultimate ownership of corporate business is held by common stockholders—an aspect of considerable economic significance in a variety of ways. In terms of business financing, the very significant role played by internally generated funds (depreciation and retained earnings) can be viewed as possible only by acquiescence of shareholders (who forgo dividends to the extent of earnings retention). A capital base of equity ownership is also necessary for business borrowing.

The decision to use new issues of equity securities to raise capital funds is governed by a number of factors. One is the availability of internally generated funds relative to total financing needs. Such availability, in turn, is a function of a firm's profitability and dividend policy. Another key factor is the current market price of the firm's stock, which determines the cost of equity financing. Further, the cost of alternative external sources of funds (i.e., interest rates) is of critical importance. The cost of borrowed funds, relative to equity funds, is significantly lowered by the deductibility of interest payments (but not of dividends) for federal income tax purposes.

Both theory and empirical evidence suggest that the equities market is a highly efficient market, in which expectations relating to stock returns and associated risk determine stock prices, and in which information relevant to such expectation is quickly put to use. At the time of the present writing, the performance of equity returns (relative to bonds) shows some evidence of resurgence, but it is likely that sustained strength must await major shifts in the nation's tax structure.

QUESTIONS

1. In view of the relatively small proportion of the economy's flow of funds that is accounted for by new equity issues, why is the equities market considered to be such an important component of the financial system? Why are new equity issues relatively infrequent?

2. Define and compare "internal" and "external" equity financing. Is the existence of a well-developed equities market significant for the internal financing of business firms? Why?

3. Explain the following terms.
   a) Preferences of preferred stock
   b) Convertibility features of securities
   c) Callable securities
   d) Stock options

4. Discuss the nature of and procedures relating to a new issue of equity stock. What factors determine a choice between direct issue and use of an investment banking arrangement?

5. Describe the process by which an equity security price is determined in the stock market.

6. What is "stock market efficiency"? Why is it important to the economy?

REFERENCES

Brealey, Richard A., *An Introduction to Risk and Return from Common Stocks* (Cambridge, Mass.: MIT Press, 1969).

Eiteman, Wilford J., Charles A. Dice, and David K. Eiteman, *The Stock Market,* 4th ed. (New York: McGraw-Hill, 1966).

Jensen, Michael (ed.), *Studies in the Theory of Capital Markets* (New York: Praeger, 1972).

Lorie, James H., and L. Fisher, "Rates of Return on Investment in Common Stock," *Journal of Business,* July 1968, pp. 291–316.

Lorie, James H., and M. Hamilton, *The Stock Market: Theory and Evidence* (Homewood, Ill.: Irwin, 1973).

Malkiel, B.G. *A Random Walk Down Wall Street* (New York: Norton, 1975).

APPENDIX

THE OPTIONS MARKET

Trading in *stock options* has become increasingly popular in recent years. A buyer of a stock option contract obtains the right to buy (*call*) or sell (*put*) a specified number of shares (usually 100) of a particular stock (the "underlying security") at a specified price (the exercise price) on or before a specified date. A stock option is thus not a financial instrument but an agreement between contracting parties, which will result in the exchange of a financial instrument if exercised. The seller (or "writer") of a stock option is compensated in the form of a "stock price premium" paid by the buyer.[5] This premium is retained by the option writer, whether or not the option is exercised.

The market for stock options consists largely of the trading of standardized contracts listed on an organized exchange.[6] Of these various organized exchanges, all are general stock exchanges except the Chicago Board of Options Exchange. Options contracts listed with these exchanges pertain to listed, widely held, and actively traded securities. There is also an over-the-counter option market, which is made by about two dozen firms that are members of the Put and Call Brokers and Dealers Association (PCBDA). Still other options trading is conducted by put and call dealers who are not affiliated with the PCBDA. The SEC has statutory authority to regulate trading in options, and it monitors the options activities of both the organized exchanges and the OTC market.

The Chicago Board of Options Exchange (CBOE), which began operation in 1973, dominates options trading. By 1980 there were options on more than 100 stocks listed with the CBOE. The CBOE is part of the Chicago Board of Trade (CBT), and its success is due in large part to its access to CBT experience, prestige, resources, and facilities. For example, the CBOE utilizes the CBT's trade-handling procedures for its own transactions.

Buyers and sellers of put and call options are paired through the options marketplace— the OTC or an organized exchange. When the premium is paid by the option buyer to the option writer (seller), the contractual obligation of the buyer and seller *to each other* is replaced as a result of the intermediary role played by the Options Clearing Corporation (OCC). The OCC takes the place of the seller relative to the buyer and that of the buyer relative to the seller. For example, when a buyer exercises an option, the OCC will randomly select a seller of an option in that security with an open position and *assign* the exercise notice. The OCC's role allows buyers and sellers of options to act independently of one another. Since the OCC, in effect, acts as a guarantor of option commitments, stock options are quite marketable and may change ownership a number of times before expiration or exercise. Thus there is a ready secondary market in options as well as a primary market.

5. An option writer may or may not own the shares for which the option is written. Option writers who are "uncovered" by ownership or other means are generally required by dealers to put up a "good faith" cash deposit, usually about 50 percent of share value.

6. At the present time, options are traded on the Chicago Board of Options Exchange, the American Stock Exchange, the Philadelphia Stock Exchange, and the Pacific Stock Exchange.

In addition to facilitating a secondary market, the listing of options on organized exchanges greatly simplifies, standardizes, and regularizes options trading and thus lowers its costs to market participants. The exchanges bring forth a new set of options for trading on a periodic basis. In general, options have a life of about nine months before expiration, and the exercise (or striking) price is set approximately equal to the price of the underlying security (but rounded to the nearest multiple of $5). Expiration dates are set as the last Monday of an expiration month, and there are four such months in each option cycle. When significant price movements in an option's underlying security occur, movements that in effect "outdate" the exercise price of outstanding options, a new option series for the same security may be opened for trading. The new series will have a different striking price but may have the same expiration month or months as the previous option.

The Nature of Options Trading

Call options are the most popular type of stock option. The buyer of a call option obtains the right (but not the obligation) to buy 100 shares of a particular security at a specified price on or before a designated date.[7] The seller of a call option is obligated to sell to the buyer the securities at the specified price if the option is exercised. The buyer of a call option will gain if the market price of the underlying security exceeds the exercise price by more than the cost of the option (premium paid to seller) at the time of exercise. Unless the market price exceeds the exercise price, the option will not be exercised—the fate of about half of all options written.

Put options, which have been increasing in popularity relative to the dominant call options, obligate the writer to purchase 100 shares from the buyer of the option if it is exercised. The option buyer will profit by "putting" the shares to the option seller if the market value of the underlying security falls below the exercise price by an amount exceeding the premium.

As a reward for writing an option, the seller receives from the buyer a premium that may range from 5 to 30 percent of the market value of the underlying security. The amount of the premium is primarily a function of the spread between the current and exercise price of the security, the duration of the option contract, and the expectations of the contracting parties regarding the future price behavior of the security.

An option seller (in the absence of any other action relating to the underlying security) realizes maximum return when the option expires unexercised. The seller's maximum possible return is the amount of the option premium, but possible losses are bounded only by the limits of an adverse (to the seller) price movement in the security. The option buyer, on the other hand, confronts a maximum possible loss equal to the premium and a maximum possible gain limited only by the largest possible favorable price change in the underlying security.

---

7. A "European" call option may be exercised *only* on the designated date. An "American" call option is subject to exercise on or before the expiration date. In practice, option "positions" are often liquidated (by an offsetting option transaction or a secondary market transaction) prior to the exercise date.

Various combinations of put and call options are possible. A *straddle,* the most common of the possible combinations, is the purchase of both a put option and a call option of identical duration and exercise price on the same security. Thus sufficient price movement in either direction will be profitable to the buyer. Descriptions of more elaborate combinations (spreads, straps, and strips) may be found in most textbooks on investment, including those referenced below.

Options may provide fun and occasional profit to traders, but what, if any, contribution do options markets make to the economy? The charge can be (and often is) made that options trading is a sterile form of endeavor that may "crowd out" more fertile utilization of investor funds. The purchase of an option provides no funds to the business sector for the purpose of capital formation, nor does the exercise of an option, which involves only a change in ownership of outstanding stock. (This argument can also be aimed at the various kinds of futures contracts discussed in the next chapter.)

One of the most erudite examinations of the economic role of options (and similar financial claims) has been made by Nobel Prize winning economist Kenneth Arrow.[8] Arrow demonstrates that the existence of options and other contingent claims on assets serves to improve resource allocation in an economy. The lure of potential profits in options trading leads participants in the market to directly and indirectly cause increases in the production, dissemination, and analysis of information about securities. Increased production and analysis of security-related information results from the fact that the values of options stem directly from the values of the underlying securities. The resulting improvement in the information market contributes to the proper pricing of securities in the capital market and thus to improved allocation of resources.

REFERENCES

Black, Fisher, "Fact and Fantasy in the Use of Options," *Financial Analysts Journal,* July–August, 1979, pp. 36–41.

Clasing, Henry, *The Dow Jones-Irwin Guide to Put and Call Options* (Homewood, Ill.: Dow Jones-Irwin, 1979).

Francis, Jack Clark, *Investment: Analysis and Management* (New York: McGraw-Hill, 1980), pp. 405–418.

Gastineau, Gary L., *The Stock Options Manual* (New York: McGraw-Hill, 1975), Chs. 1–6.

Hettenhouse, G.W., and D.J. Puglisi, "Investor Experience with Put and Call Options," *Financial Analysts Journal,* July–August, 1975, pp. 53–58.

Malkiel, Burton G., and Richard Quandt, *Strategies and Rational Decisions in the Securities Option Market* (Cambridge, Mass.: MIT Press, 1969).

---

8. Kenneth Arrow, "The Role of Securities in the Optimal Allocation of Risk-Bearing," *Review of Economic Studies,* April 1964, pp. 91–96.

Chapter 18

Financial Futures Markets

Financial markets have been characterized by a significant degree of innovation in recent years. New financial instruments or variants of existing financial instruments have been developed at a rapid pace, especially in the last decade. In part, the speed of innovation reflects aggressive profit-seeking behavior on the part of financial market participants in pursuing opportunities to gain from the creation of new financial instruments. Another contributing factor to the rapid pace of innovation in financial markets is the enormous pressure and strain that have been placed on financial markets by the prevalence of inflation both at home and abroad, high and unstable interest rates, and the adjustments associated with increases in the price of oil and other energy sources. The explosive growth of the Eurodollar market, the development of a variety of financial instruments designed to provide access to the capital market for mortgage lenders, and the profound changes in the structure of the commercial paper market are but a few illustrations of recent innovative developments in financial markets and instruments. It is interesting to observe that, in a period when there has been great concern about declining innovation and competitiveness in the U.S. industrial sector, there has been such a burst of innovation in the financial sector.

One of the most significant of these innovations in financial markets in the decade of the 1970s was the development of the financial futures markets.[1] In this chapter we discuss the nature and significance of the financial futures markets. We begin by outlining the role of

---

1. By 1981, trading volume in the financial futures markets exceeded $10 billion on a typical day.

futures markets in general and financial futures markets in particular. The discussion encompasses the futures markets both for interest-bearing financial assets and for foreign currencies. We then present an explanation of the way in which participants may use the financial futures market. The chapter closes with a treatment of some of the issues raised by the explosive growth of these markets and some speculations as to the future of the financial futures markets.[2]

THE NATURE OF FINANCIAL FUTURES MARKETS

A futures markets is one in which the purchase or sale of a standardized contract on an organized market is accomplished now and in which delivery takes place at some future date. For example, an investor who contracts through the Chicago Board of Trade on March 25 to purchase a futures contract in Government National Mortgage Association pass-through certificates for delivery on June 24 is participating in the futures market.[3] Similarly, an individual who contracts on March 25 to sell such a contract on June 24 has entered into a futures contract. Note that the price at which the item is traded is set at the time of purchase and sale (March 25), not at the time of delivery (June 24). As another example, through the International Monetary Market an individual might purchase or sell a contract for British pounds for delivery at some future date.

These futures markets are used for two basic though different purposes. First, market participants who are exposed to the risk of significant price movements because of the nature of their business (grain dealers, for example) may use the futures markets to reduce their risk exposure. This use of the futures market is referred to as *hedging*. Second, other market participants who are seeking large returns (and accepting large risks) will use the futures market to gamble on favorable price movements. The latter use of the futures market is referred to as *speculation*. In essence, the futures market allows investors who incur the risk of price fluctuation as a by-product of their business to shift this risk to other investors who are willing to accept it in the hope of large potential return.[4] Of course, the workings of the futures market require the participation of speculators as well as hedgers.

It is important to distinguish between the *futures* markets and the forward markets. In purpose, these markets are quite similar in that they are both used by hedgers to reduce risk and by speculators to take risk in order to obtain large potential return. However, the futures markets are organized markets in which trading in a *standardized* contract takes place under rules prescribed by the futures exchange. Since trading is actually done with the "clearing-house" of the exchange, there is less possibility that the other party to the contract will

---

2. For an excellent review of the financial futures markets, see the article by Arak and McCurdy in the references at the end of the chapter.

3. See Chapter 16 for a discussion of GNMA pass-through certificates.

4. Futures markets have also been used to reduce tax liability. However, the Internal Revenue Service has made tax avoidance through sophisticated use of the futures market increasingly difficult.

default. Moreover, most participants in the futures markets do not plan to take delivery of the item purchased. In contrast, forward market trading involves a much less formal set of rules and does not take place on an organized exchange. A forward contract is tailored to the needs of the participants and is an agreement between the participants directly. And it is much more likely that the buyer will take delivery. Prior to the development of the organized financial futures markets, there was very little forward trading in interest-bearing financial assets. However, there was (and still is) a great deal of forward trading of foreign currencies among the participants in the foreign exchange market. Indeed, major multinational corporations still use the forward exchange market to hedge their foreign currency risks.

Futures markets have existed in agricultural commodities for decades. At present trading takes place on organized commodities markets for a wide variety of agricultural products. For example, trading of corn, oats, soybeans, soybean meal, soybean oil, wheat, barley, flaxseed, and rapeseed occurs among the grain products. In livestock and meat products, trading currently occurs in feeder cattle, live cattle, hogs, and pork bellies. In the food and fiber group, cocoa, coffee, cotton, orange juice, and citrus fruits are traded.[5] Hedgers in the markets are primarily the producers and dealers in the commodity, whereas speculators include a variety of individuals and institutions seeking large returns. Indeed, in the decade of the 1970s the commodities futures markets attracted a number of investors from the equity markets because of the relatively poor performance of equities. Reflecting this increased investor interest, as well as greater price variability in commodities generally, the number and volume of commodity futures traded have increased substantially in recent years.

The development of organized trading in *financial futures* is an especially recent development. Trading in major foreign currency futures was started by the International Monetary Market in the early 1970s. Today organized foreign currency futures markets exist for the British pound, German mark, Japanese yen, and a variety of other currencies. The first organized market for interest-bearing financial assets was established by the Chicago Board of Trade in 1975 for the purchase and sale of futures contracts in Government National Mortgage Association (GNMA) pass-through certificates. Shortly thereafter the International Monetary Market originated trading in three-month Treasury bills. Today, in addition to these financial instruments, trading of futures contracts occurs in long-term Treasury bonds, one-year Treasury bills, four-year Treasury notes, and commercial paper.[6] In terms of volume, these financial futures markets have been a great success. Participation now includes major financial institutions, as well as a number of nonfinancial institutions, and the volume of trading has been substantial. As shown in Table 18.1, trading in foreign

---

5. Futures trading also occurs in both precious and nonprecious metals, including copper, gold, platinum, and silver, as well as in lumber and plywood. In addition, a large variety of other commodities are traded on a less active basis than those listed in the text.

6. There also have been proposals for a large number of other futures contracts: debt instruments of varying types and maturities, equity securities, and even the Dow-Jones average.

Table 18.1   Volume of trading in financial futures, 1976–1979 (number of contracts)

Year	Financial Instruments	Currencies
1976	108,550	201,804
1977	604,622	393,234
1978	1,595,363	1,345,527
1979	4,570,694	2,003,746

Source: Commodity Futures Trading Commission, *1979 Annual Report*, p. 71.

currency futures markets exceeded two million contracts in 1979, and trading in the futures market for interest-bearing financial instruments totaled more than 4.5 million contracts in the same year.

Financial futures markets are used for the same reason as other futures markets. Any individual or institution who is exposed to risk associated with fluctuating interest rates of financial assets or changes in the value of foreign currencies is a potential hedger in the market. And since many (perhaps most) individuals and institutions are exposed to such risk, the potential number of participants is especially broad. Certainly the nation's major financial institutions offer a potentially fertile source of hedgers. And with the increasing importance of international commerce and the growth of the multinational corporation, the exposure to foreign currency risk has increased. Since many more people are familar with interest rates and foreign currencies than with pork bellies, it seems that the potential group of speculators in the financial futures market, as compared with the commodities market, should also be large. Given the wide spectrum of individuals and institutions with a potential interest in financial futures markets, it is not surprising that they have expanded rapidly and received considerable publicity in the financial press.

It is important to note that the financial futures markets have been created and have prospered in a period of great instability in interest rates and foreign currency values. Interest rate movements in the decade of the 1970s were sharp, both upward and downward, especially in the money market. It is no coincidence that these marked changes in interest rates and currency values produced a wish by some market participants for a means to hedge risk and by other market participants a wish for a means to speculate.[7] These substantial price changes create the potential for great losses for financial institutions and others and hence a desire to hedge against risk. At the same time, they create a great opportunity for others to speculate on the future of interest rate and foreign currency values in the hope of achieving large gains.

Tables 18.2 and 18.3 present information on selected futures markets. For example, Table 18.2 presents market prices for trading in the British pound, Canadian dollar, and

---

7. Sharp changes in interest rates, of course, mean sharp changes in the prices of financial investments, especially long-term financial investments. Moreover, the decade of the 1970s marked the end of the fixed exchange rate system, a substantial depreciation of the dollar, and marked changes in the relative value of many foreign currencies.

Table 18.2 Prices of foreign currency futures, March 12, 1981

British pound	
Delivery date	Price
June	$2.2235
September	2.2510
December	2.2605
Canadian dollar	
June	.8334
September	.8330
December	.8330
West German mark	
June	.4763
September	.4814
December	.4850

Source: *Wall Street Journal*, March 13, 1981, p. 34.

Table 18.3 Prices and yields of selected financial futures contracts, March 12, 1981

GNMA 8% (Chicago Board of Trade)		
Settlement date	Price ($100,000 principal)	Yield, %
June	67-26	13.647
September	68-03	13.581
December	68-09	13.537
March 1982	68-12	13.516
June	68-11	13.523
Three-month Treasury bills (International Monetary Market)		
Settlement date	Price ($1 million principal)	Yield, %
June	$88.46	11.54
September	89.12	10.88
December	89.27	10.73
March 1982	89.22	10.78
June	89.05	10.95

Note: Prices are per 100 dollars. GNMA fractions are expressed as 32nds.

Source: *Wall Street Journal*, March 13, 1981, p. 34.

West German mark in the foreign currency futures markets as of March 12, 1981. On that day, an individual or business firm could have purchased/sold a contract for delivery of the British pound in June, September, or December of 1981. The price per pound established by the free interplay of supply and demand was $2.2235 in June and $2.2605 in December, indicating the expectation by market participants that the pound would strengthen relative to the dollar during that period. Similar interpretations can be placed on the prices in the futures markets for the Canadian dollar and the German mark. However, note that the expectation was for a slight fall in the value of the Canadian dollar relative to the U.S. dollar.

In contrast to the foreign currency futures market, where only prices are quoted, the futures market for interest-bearing financial assets usually quotes both price and yield, although trading usually takes place in terms of price. For example, in Table 18.3, the price of the GNMA pass-through certificates for future delivery up to June 1982 is specified as of March 12, 1981. A GNMA futures contract for delivery in March 1982 could have been purchased or sold for 68 and 12/32 per $100 value as of that date; that is, a GNMA contract with a principal value of $100,000 could have been bought or sold for $68,375. Given certain assumptions about the repayment of the underlying mortgages in the pass-throughs, the yield on these pass-throughs for March 1982 delivery was 13.516 percent. Note that the prices established in the futures markets indicate that market participants in March of 1981 were expecting a small decline in interest rates. A similar explanation holds for the futures market in three-month Treasury bills, but price quotation is in terms of hundredths rather than thirty-seconds. It is interesting to note that investors were anticipating that short-term rates would fall through March 1982, as revealed by the prices and yields on the T-bills.

We now turn our attention to the ways in which hedgers and speculators can use the financial futures markets. Our discussion is initially in terms of the financial instrument futures markets. A shorter discussion of the foreign currency futures market follows.

BUYING AND SELLING FINANCIAL FUTURES CONTRACTS

Participants in the financial futures markets place either a buy or a sell order for a standardized contract. The dimensions of the contract vary with the nature of the financial instruments traded. An International Monetary Market contract for three-month Treasury bills (one of the most widely traded of all the instruments of the financial futures market), for example, consists of $1 million par value of Treasury bills. The Chicago Board of Trade contract for the Government National Mortgage Association contract consists of $100,000 principal balance of GNMAs. Delivery dates also vary with the type of financial instrument. The three-month Treasury bills contract traded on the International Monetary Market provides for eight different delivery dates extending over a two-year period at quarterly intervals.

Purchases or sales of contracts in financial futures markets are made on the floor of the relevant exchange through a futures commission merchant who is registered with the

Commodity Futures Trading Commission.[8] The actual transaction is accomplished by members of the exchange at the "trading pit" through an "open outcry" system, in which potential buyers and sellers shout their offers. As we stated above in making a distinction between a futures market and a forward market, the seller's contract is not with the buyer nor is the buyer's contract with the seller; rather, both contracts are with the exchange clearinghouse. In order to maintain the financial viability of the clearinghouse and thereby to allow buyers and sellers to participate in the market without fear of loss, the members of the clearinghouse must provide a margin (in effect a performance bond) for each contract, and their customers must in turn provide a margin. The size of these margins varies with the nature of the contract and the specific exchange. On the IMM, the initial customer margin for a $1 million Treasury bill contract is $1500.[9]

Most futures contracts are settled prior to the delivery date of the contract. Indeed, most participants in the markets do not intend either to take delivery or to make delivery at maturity. Rather, the market participant—either buyer or seller—terminates the contract when its speculative or hedging objective has been met (or when it is clear that the objective will not be met) by taking an offsetting position. For example, an individual who had bought a contract on June 14, 1981, in three-month Treasury bills for delivery on November 18, 1981, could eliminate the obligation to accept delivery of the bills (on June 18, 1981, e.g.) by selling a contract for delivery of the November 18, 1981, three-month Treasury bills.

Reflecting the pervasive existence of interest-rate risk among individuals and borrowers, there are a large number of different participants in the financial futures markets. A survey made by the Commodity Futures Trading Commission revealed that in March 1979 most contracts were held by nonfinancial businesses and individuals. For example, as shown in Table 18.4, individual traders held 34.8 percent of the contracts for three-month Treasury bills and 27.7 percent of the contracts for GNMA pass-through securities as of March 30, 1979. Depository financial institutions have thus far played a minor role in the financial futures markets. For example, as of March 30, 1979, commercial banks and savings and loan associations held only 3.8 percent of the contracts in three-month Treasury bills and 5.3 percent of the contracts in GNMA pass-throughs. It appears likely, however, that the participation of depository financial institutions will grow as they achieve regulatory permission to participate in the financial futures markets.

USES OF THE FINANCIAL FUTURES MARKETS: INTEREST-BEARING SECURITIES

As discussed above, the financial futures markets are used by two different groups for two different reasons. Hedgers use the financial futures markets to shift risk, and speculators use

---

8. The Commodity Futures Trading Commission has regulatory authority over trading in both commodity futures and financial futures.

9. The ability to obtain future delivery of $1 million par value of Treasury bills with such a low "investment" provides enormous leverage and potential for gain or loss to those speculating in financial futures markets.

Table 18.4   Participants in the financial futures market, March 30, 1979 (contracts)

	GNMA (percent of total)	Three-month Treasury bill (percent of total)
Securities dealers	7.2	12.5
Commercial banks	1.1	3.5
Savings and loan associations	4.2	0.3
Mortgage bankers	2.5	2.2
Other	3.4	15.0
Futures industry	35.4	18.9
Commodity pools	18.6	12.6
Individual traders	27.7	34.8

Note: Commodity pools are funds that purchase and sell futures contracts.
Source: Commodity Futures Trading Commission Survey.

them to accept risk in their search for high returns. The ways in which each of these groups uses the markets is discussed in this section. Since hedging in these markets is a more complex process than speculating, however, our treatment of hedging is necessarily much more detailed.[10]

Hedging

There are two basic types of hedges, the *short* (sell) *hedge* and the *long* (buy) *hedge*.[11] The short hedge involves the *sale* of a futures contract and provides protection against interest rate increases. The long hedge involves the *purchase* of a futures contract and provides protection against falling interest rates. Both the short hedge and the long hedge are generally conducted in the financial instrument held by the investor and giving rise to the risk being hedged. For example, if the investor held three-month Treasury bills (the cash or spot market position), the short hedge would be conducted in the three-month Treasury bill futures market.

We will now provide a brief example of each type of hedge. Our examples are in terms of the GNMA futures markets, but the principles would apply to futures trading in any financial instrument. Moreover, for purposes of illustration only, our examples are of "perfect" hedges, in which risk reduction is complete. In fact, although hedging will generally reduce risk, it will seldom eliminate it.

---

10. Our discussion omits transactions costs. Naturally, any gains would be reduced by the amount of the transactions costs and any losses would be increased. However, transactions costs represent a minor consideration for most activity in the financial futures market. Moreover, our purpose in this chapter is only to illustrate the uses of the market, not to calculate the exact gains and losses involved in individual transactions.

11. A cross hedge also exists. This type of hedge occurs when the hedger purchases or sells in the futures market a security that is different from the cash asset held. For example, an investor may hold bankers acceptances for which there is no futures market. In order to hedge against rising interest rates, the investor may execute a short cross hedge in the Treasury bill market and rely on the usual high correlation among money market rates to reduce risk. Naturally, a cross hedge may be either short or long.

The Short Hedge

Assume that a mortgage banker makes a commitment to lend $1 million for an FHA/VA mortgage pool in January of the coming year. At the time of the commitment (June) the interest rate on the mortgage pool is set. The risk to the lender is that interest rates will rise between the time of the commitment (June) and the closing of the loan (January). If rates do rise between June and January, the mortgage banker will have to accept less than $1 million for the mortgages if the mortgage banker wishes to sell the mortgage to a permanent investor (as is usually done). However, with the existence of the GNMA futures market, the mortgage banker can sell a short hedge in the futures market for March of the following year, thereby reducing (though not necessarily eliminating) the risk of rising interest rates.

Table 18.5 illustrates this short hedge. The mortgage banker makes a commitment in June for a $1 million mortgage pool with interest rates such that GNMA 8-percent coupon-rate issues are selling at a price of 97-16 (97 and 16/32 per $1000, or $97,500 per $100,000 contract).[12] Hence current interest rates are slightly above 8 percent (8.301 percent). In order to reduce the risk associated with rising rates, the mortgage banker sells 10 March GNMA futures contracts at 95-16, the current price for GNMA futures deliverable in March. In January, when the mortgage banker makes good on the commitment and takes the mortgages into the bank's portfolio, any sale of the mortgages will produce a loss if interest rates have increased. In the illustration provided in Table 18.5, we assume that the $1 million face value amount of GNMAs can be sold at a price of 95-00. If so, the investor incurs a loss of $25,000 on the transaction (2 and 16/32 percent of $1 million). If interest rates had increased more, of course, the loss to the mortgage banker would have been greater. However, the same rising interest rates that cause a reduction in value and a loss on the mortgage banker's commitment produce a gain on the short position in the futures market. In the illustration in Table 18.5, the mortgage banker "closes" the hedge by buying 10 March futures contracts for 93-00. The gain on the purchase of the March contract of $25,000 exactly offsets the loss on the mortgage commitment.[13] It is the offsetting of the gain and loss in the two markets that creates the opportunity for risk reduction.

One should of course note that the chance of loss is reduced, but that the chance of gain is also reduced. For example, if the price of the futures contract increased between June and January (that is, interest rates declined), the mortgage banker would have a gain on the commitment but would have a loss on the short hedge. The mortgage banker forgoes a potential gain in order to avoid a potential loss and thus preserve the "normal" profit.

The short hedge can be used in a variety of other ways. The most common is to protect an investor who currently holds an inventory of financial assets (in the cash or spot market)

---

12. Trading in GNMA pass-through futures is done with a uniform 8-percent coupon issue. Other coupon issues can of course be adjusted to provide the same yield as the standardized 8-percent issue. All issues are quoted in 32nds.

13. This so-called perfect hedge occurs only if the basis remains unchanged during the life of the contract; this is generally not so. The basis is defined as the difference between the cash price of a financial instrument and the price of a futures contract. In the illustration in Table 18.5 the basis was 2-00 in June (97-16 less 95-16) and remained 2-00 in January (95-00 less 93-00).

Table 18.5 The short hedge

Cash market	Futures market
June	June
Commitment of $1 million mortgage pool based on current GNMA 8's—cash price of 97-16	Sale of 10 March GNMA futures contracts at 95-16
January	January
Sale of $1 million of GNMA 8's at 95-00 Loss: $25,000	Purchase of 10 March GNMA contracts at 93-00 Gain: $25,000

from loss due to rising interest rates. For example, a U.S. government bond dealer could exercise a short hedge in order to reduce the risk of price depreciation. Similarly, a commercial bank with a large investment in U.S. Government securities could protect the value of its portfolio by exercising a short hedge. Indeed, any investor in financial assets could reduce risk through using a short hedge. However, we must emphasize again that the hedge not only reduces *risk* but also reduces potential *return*.

The Long Hedge

The long hedge is generally used in order to reduce the risk of falling interest rates and thereby to "lock in" the currently high rates. For example, assume that a savings and loan, mutual savings bank, commercial bank, or other institutional lender anticipates a large inflow of funds in the near future, but that it also anticipates that when those funds become available, rates will be below current levels. The investor can lock in the currently high rates on the GNMA pass-through securities by executing a long hedge. The mechanics of this long hedge are illustrated in Table 18.6.

Assume that the investor wishes to commit $1 million to GNMA pass-throughs in April, at which time interest rates are expected to have fallen. To lock in the current high yield, the investor can buy 10 June GNMA futures contracts at 96-00. In April, when the funds become available, the investor uses the $1 million to purchase the GNMA 8's at the then price of 97-00. Note that the investor's expectations have been realized; rates have fallen from their January levels. At the same time that the investor purchases the $1 million of GNMA 8's, 10 June futures contracts are sold at 99-00. As a result, the investor has a gain of $30,000 on the futures transaction (the futures contract was purchased at 96-00 and sold at 99-00). This gain offsets the opportunity loss of $30,000 (the difference between the price of 97-00 paid for the GNMAs bought in April and the price that would have been paid if the investor had had the funds to buy the GNMAs in January at a price of 94-00). As a result, the investor has locked in the higher yield available at the time the decision was made to purchase the GNMAs, instead of having to accept the lower yields available at the time the funds become available. We should of course again stress that the investor has reduced the

Table 18.6 The long hedge

Cash market	Futures market
January	January
Decision to lock in high yield on $1 million principal balance of GNMA 8's at 94-00	Purchase of 10 June GNMA futures contracts at 96-00
April	April
Purchase of $1 million principal balance GNMA 8's at 97-00 Opportunity loss: $30,000	Sale of 10 June GNMA futures contracts at 99-00 Gain: $30,000

risk that the yields will be lower when the funds become available but has also eliminated the potentially higher yield that would be possible if rates increased from January to April. In that case, the investor would have an opportunity gain on the cash market transaction but a loss on the futures market transaction.

Speculation

For the financial futures markets to work effectively, market participants must include *both* hedgers and speculators. If the hedgers are to use the financial futures markets to shift risk, that risk must be assumed by someone. From this perspective, the existence and active participation of speculators (despite the popular perception of speculators as troublemakers) is absolutely essential for the workings of these markets. And in the financial futures markets (as in all futures markets) there is ample opportunity for gain (or loss). We now turn to a brief example of the ways in which speculators may seek to gain from participation in the financial futures markets.

Speculators may gain through trading in the financial futures markets "by knowing better than the market what the future will be." Market expectations of future interest rates are embodied in the prices and yields established in the financial futures markets. If the speculator believes that the actual prices and yields will be different from market expectations, then an opportunity for gain exists if the speculator is correct and the market wrong. This opportunity for gain exists, regardless of whether the speculator believes that prices will be above *or* below what the market expects. It is necessary only that prices vary from expectations, not that they rise, in order to create the opportunity for gain for the speculator. This is illustrated by the following two examples drawn from the GNMA futures markets.[14]

---

14. The illustrations are in terms of speculation about changes in the level of rates. However, speculators may also concentrate on expected changes in the relative pattern of interest rates. This speculation takes the form of a spread, in which the participant buys one contract (a three-month Treasury bill contract, for example) and sells another contract (a commercial paper contract, for example).

Referring again to Table 18.3, suppose that the speculator believed that interest rates would fall substantially from June 1981 to December 1981, whereas the market apparently believed that rates would decline only slightly from June to December—the price on June 8-percent GNMAs is 67-26 (13.647 percent) and on the December GNMAs 68-09 (13.537 percent). In this situation the speculator could purchase a December contract in the hope that the market expectation was incorrect. If rates did fall substantially and prices did rise substantially, the speculator would of course have a gain. But the real possibility for gain (as well as loss) would occur from the leverage that is possible in the financial futures market. Since the contract in the GNMA futures market was for $100,000 of 8-percent coupon-rate securities, the speculator was paying $68,281 for the contract (68 09/32 × 100,000). But the margin—the minimum down payment that the speculator had to commit in order to purchase the contract—was only $2000. The result was an *enormous* change in the value of the speculator's investment as the result of *small* changes in the value of the contract. Leverage does of course permit large potential returns, but is also the source of large risk.

Suppose that after one day the market had revised downward its expectations of interest rates and thereby revised upward its expectation of the prices of securities. Suppose further that the price on the December contract had increased to 68-25 (an increase of less than one percent). The decrease in expected rates could result from a more expansive Federal Reserve monetary policy, a decline in the economy, or a variety of other factors. In this situation, the speculator could sell the December contract at the price of 68-25 and have a gain of $68,781 less $68,281, or $500. This gain would represent a 25-percent profit on the original investment, an annual rate of increase (excluding commission costs) of more than 8000 percent. And of course, the gain would be even larger if rates fell further. For example, if the price of the futures contract increased to 69 09/32, the gain to the investor excluding commission would be $1000 ($69,281 − $68,281), or 50 percent in one day. Of course, the speculator could incur large losses if rates moved up rather than down. For example, if the price fell to 67-09, the speculator would incur a loss of $1000 ($68,281 − $67,281), or a loss of 50 percent in one day. In fact, it is quite easy for the speculator to lose the entire investment in one day.

As mentioned earlier, the speculator can profit from the expectation of falling prices and rising rates, as well as of rising prices and falling rates. In the former instance, the speculator would sell the futures contract (take a short position) rather than buy the contract (take a long position). Again ignoring commission costs, the investor could sell the December contract at 68-09, or $68,281 on the $100,000 contract. The speculator would do so on the expectation that prices would fall and rates would rise. For example, if the contract price fell to 67-09, the investor would gain $1000 (the contract was sold for $68,281 and bought back at $67,281). However, if the expectations of the speculator were incorrect and market prices rose (yields fell), the contract would have to be purchased at a price higher than its selling price. If the price rose to 69-09, the investor would lose (ignoring commission costs) $1000. Speculating in the financial futures market is not for the timid.

USES OF THE FINANCIAL FUTURES MARKETS: FOREIGN CURRENCIES

Hedging

Hedging in the foreign currency futures market serves the same purpose as hedging in the interest rate futures market—the reduction of risk. In the interest rate futures market, the investor hedges to protect against the risk associated with fluctuations in interest rates. In the foreign currency futures market, one hedges to protect against the risk associated with *fluctuations in the value of currencies.* Naturally, hedging in the foreign currency futures market is most necessary for businesses—financial and nonfinancial—that operate internationally. Such hedging may take the form of a short (selling) hedge or a long (buying) hedge.

Short Hedge

Suppose that a bank in New York has excess funds to invest in short-term securities. Suppose further that the interest rates on 90-day British government securities are attractive relative to the interest rates on 90-day U.S. government securities—19 percent versus 6 percent, for example. There is no *interest rate risk* if the investor buys 90-day British government securities and holds them for 90 days. However, the interest is paid in British pounds, not U.S. dollars, so the investor is taking the risk that the value of the pound may fall during the 90-day holding period (exchange rate risk). Such a reduction in the value of the pound may reduce or eliminate the interest rate advantage from the purchase of the British security. In order to reduce such foreign exchange risk exposure, the investor may engage in a short hedge.

Details of the short hedge are illustrated in Table 18.7. The investor, the New York bank, bought 100,000 British pounds in June (cash or spot market) in order to purchase 90-day British government securities. At the same time, the investor sold 100,000 British pounds for September delivery. Note that the futures price of the British pound was below the current price ($1.95 per pound for September delivery versus $2 per pound, a discount of 2.5%), indicating that the market was expecting the pound to depreciate against the dollar.[15] If the bank had not hedged against the decline in the value of the pound, it would have incurred a loss in September at the time the British securities matured and the pounds were converted into dollars. This loss of $10,000 would have more than offset the interest rate advantage of purchasing the British securities. With the hedge, however, the investor made a gain of $10,000 on the futures transactions, so the currency risk was eliminated. Note again that the hedge of course reduced the potential return on the investment as well as reducing the risk. For example, if the bank had not hedged its position and if the pound had *appreciated* rather than depreciated as expected, the bank would have had the higher interest

---

15. In practice, the interest-rate difference between similar U.S. and British securities and the percentage difference between the cash or spot rate of exchange and the future rate of exchange should be quite similar.

return plus the gain on the currency transaction. However, with the hedge that possible gain was eliminated.

Table 18.7 Short hedge in foreign currencies futures market

Cash market	Futures market
June 1	
Buy 100,000 British pounds at $2 per pound = $200,000	Sell 100,000 British pounds for September delivery at $1.95 per pound = $195,000
September 1	
Sell 100,000 British pounds at $1.90 per pound = $190,000 Loss = $10,000	Buy 100,000 British pounds (September delivery) at $1.85 = $185,000 Gain = $10,000

Table 18.8 Long hedge

Cash market	Futures market
June 1	
Sell 100,000 pounds at $2 per pound = $200,000	Buy 100,000 pounds for October delivery at $2.05 per pound = $205,000
September 1	
Buy 100,000 pounds at $2.05 per pound = $205,000 Loss = $5000	Sell 100,000 pounds for October delivery at $2.10 per pound = $210,000 Gain = $5000

Long Hedge

A long or buying hedge occurs when the currency is bought in the futures market and sold in the cash market. Table 18.8 provides an illustration of a situation that would be appropriate for a long hedge. In this case, we assume a multinational firm with a manufacturing facility in the United States and in Britain. We further assume that the British firm has excess funds for a period of three months, and the U.S. plant has a deficiency of cash for operating expenses. Management would like to transfer funds from the British to the U.S. plant but is concerned about the foreign currency risk. In this instance, the currency risk could be reduced by a long hedge—the British pound would be sold in the cash or spot market in order to make the transfer, and the British pound would be bought in the futures market.

As illustrated in Table 18.8, the multinational firm would sell 100,000 pounds at $2 per pound, obtaining $200,000 to transfer from its British to its U.S. manufacturing subsidiary. At the same time, it would execute the purchase of 100,000 pounds for October delivery at

$2.05 per pound. In September, when it was necessary to transfer the funds back to the British subsidiary, the multinational firm would buy 100,000 pounds in the cash or spot market at the now higher price of $2.05. It would thus have a loss of $5000 on its cash transaction. However, it would sell 100,000 pounds for the futures market for $2.10 and would have a gain of $5000. The gain and the loss would thus offset each other, and the firm would have accomplished its operating purpose without gain or loss from the currency transaction.

Speculation

As with the interest futures markets, the efficient operation of the foreign exchange futures markets depends on the participation of both speculators and hedgers. Speculators take risk in order to reap large gains from betting that the market expectations will be incorrect. For example, suppose that the speculator observed that the price for delivery of the British pound three months hence was $2.10 per pound, and further suppose that the speculator believed that the pound would be worth more than $2.10 at that time. The speculator could purchase a contract for delivery of pounds three months hence. Since the contract size on the International Monetary Market is 25,000 pounds, the investor would pay $52,500 for the contract. However, the initial margin for the contract—the amount the investor must commit at the time of the purchase—would be only $1500. If the three-month pound futures contract rose to $2.15 on the day after the transaction, the speculator would have a gain of $1250 ($53,750 selling price less $52,500 buying price), or almost 100 percent in a one-day period. Conversely, if the price of the contract fell to $2.05, the speculator would lose $1250, or almost 100 percent of the original investment.

If the expectation was for a decline in the value of the pound, the speculator could execute a sell order on the futures contract. In this instance, if the price declined to $2.05, the investor would gain $1250. Conversely, if the price advanced to $2.15, the investor would lose $1250. Again, as in the illustration with the interest rate futures, the speculator can make a profit whether prices rise or fall.

ISSUES RAISED BY THE GROWTH OF FINANCIAL FUTURES MARKETS

The explosive growth of trading in financial futures has raised a number of issues and concerns. Questions have been raised about the potential impact on the behavior of the nation's major businesses. Other questions have been raised about the implications of intense speculation in the futures markets. Since the questions relate separately to the role of the markets as hedging vehicles, as contrasted with the participation of speculators in these markets, we shall deal in turn with each of these two distinct functions.

From the perspective of the markets as providing vehicles for holders of financial instruments and foreign currencies to hedge against interest rate and currency risk, the potential advantages of the financial futures markets are substantial. It might be expected, for example, that hedging interest-rate risk by major financial institutions would reduce the variability of earnings and further reduce the risk of failure. For many financial institutions, interest-rate risk is one of the most significant types of risk they face, whereas for many multinational businesses the risk associated with currency fluctuations is also substantial. The reduction of these types of risk may have profound implications for the management policies of the institution. Reduction in interest-rate risk may allow the financial institution to increase its lending or reduce the rates charged on its loans. It may also encourage lenders to the institution to provide more funds at lower rates. Furthermore, any risk reduction brought about by hedging may make it easier and cheaper for financial institutions to raise equity capital. For multinational corporations the development of the financial futures market may allow risk reductions beyond those traditionally available in the forward market, further encouraging the efficient use of resources internationally. For these potential benefits it seems that the transactions cost involved in the hedging operation are quite small. However, as pointed out earlier in this chapter, the participation by financial institutions in the financial futures market has so far been relatively limited. Moreover, most participants appear to be involved in speculation rather than hedging.

Most of the concern about the financial futures market is focused on the role of speculators. Yet the speculator is an absolutely essential part of an effective financial futures market. Two issues in particular have been raised. First, it has been argued that employees of the institution involved in the financial futures market might engage in speculation without the authorization of senior management. Losses from such speculation might seriously reduce the viability of the organization. This is certainly a possibility, but the problem is one of adequate internal controls on the activities of the employees of an organization. It is not a problem inherent in the workings of the financial futures markets. The second concern is more basic. It has been argued that speculative activity in the financial futures markets increases the volatility of interest rates and foreign currency values in the cash or spot market. By this argument, speculation in GNMA futures would destabilize the price of GNMA certificates, speculation in T-bill futures would destabilize the price of T-bills, and speculation in pound futures would destabilize the price of pounds. Such activity would make securities less attractive to investors and would force rates on securities upward. In the case of the GNMA certificates, the greater instability in the price of GNMAs would reduce the liquidity of the mortgage market and would have undesirable effects on the flow of credit to housing. Though perhaps an appealing argument to some, there is little actual evidence to support this view. Studies by the Federal Reserve and the Treasury, as well as by private economists, have not revealed any significant evidence that trading in financial futures has destabilized the cash price of the asset. There appears to be no greater volatility for Treasury bills for which there are futures contracts than for those for which there are no futures contracts.[16] To this point, at least, there seem to be few substantive negative aspects resulting from the growth of the markets for financial futures.

---

16. It must be admitted, however, that the evidence on the impact of futures markets in a financial instrument on the volatility of price and interest rates in the cash market is not complete. For example, one study did find that futures-market activity in GNMA pass-through certificates did increase the price variability of these financial instruments in the cash market. See the article by Figlewski listed in the references at the end of the chapter.

SUMMARY

A financial futures market is an organized exchange in which standardized contracts for delivery of a financial instrument at a future date are bought and sold. The financial futures market is used by individuals, financial institutions, and nonfinancial businesses to hedge (reduce) interest-rate and currency risk, as well as to speculate about future movements in interest rates and the values of foreign currencies. Although futures markets have existed in agricultural markets for many years, the development of futures markets in Treasury bills and other money and capital market instruments, as well as in foreign currencies, is a relatively recent phenomenon, dating back only to the early 1970s.

A hedger in interest-bearing securities may use either a short or a long hedge. A short hedge involves the sale of a futures contract, and the long hedge involves the purchase of a futures contract. For example, an investor with a cash or spot position in Treasury bills can reduce the risk of loss through rising interest rates by selling a futures contract in Treasury bills. Similarly, an investor who expects to commit funds to the purchase of Treasury bills in the future but wishes protection against the possibility that rates will decline by the time the funds are available, can buy a futures contract (the long hedge). As for speculators, those who expect rates to be higher than the consensus of the market as revealed in the price of futures contracts can sell a futures contract. On the other hand, those who expect rates to be lower than the consensus of the market can buy a futures contract.

Trading in the foreign currency futures market is done for similar purposes. Participants seeking to hedge against currency movements can execute either short or long hedges. Speculators may seek to profit by knowing better than the market what the future values of currencies will be.

The growth of trading in futures markets for interest-bearing securities and for foreign currencies has been a phenomenal development in the financial system of the United States and of the world. Participants in the financial system have substantially greater alternative vehicles for structuring financial portfolios with the development of these futures markets. All current indications are that the futures markets will continue to expand in volume of trading in existing markets, and particularly in the development of new trading vehicles. To a considerable extent, however, the speed of development will depend on the amount of instability in interest rates and foreign currencies. The more uncertainty there is in the financial system, the greater is the need for futures markets. Unless the world's financial system quickly returns to a placid state (an unlikely prospect), the decade of the 1980s is likely to see even more development of such sophisticated financial markets as those discussed in this chapter.

QUESTIONS

1. What is a futures market? How does a futures market differ from a forward market?
2. Does hedging in the futures market eliminate risk? Explain.

3. If the Federal Reserve "pegged" interest rate levels as it did in the 1940s, and if the world returned to fixed exchange rates, what would be the implications of these developments for the financial futures markets?

4. Imagine that you are an exporter of shoes to England and have sold shoes today on 90-day open account. How would you use the financial futures market to hedge your currency risk?

5. Imagine that you managed the investment portfolio of a large commercial bank. Explain how you would use the financial futures market to hedge your interest-rate risk in your municipal securities portfolio. What kind of hedge would be indicated?

6. What costs (both explicit and implicit) are associated with hedging?

REFERENCES

Arak, Marcelle, and Christopher J. McCurdy, "Interest Rate Futures," Federal Reserve Bank of New York *Quarterly Review,* Winter 1979–1980.

Bacon, Peter W., and Richard E. Williams, "Interest Rate Futures: New Tools for the Financial Manager," *Financial Management,* Spring 1976, pp. 32–38.

Burger, Albert E., Richard W. Long, and Robert H. Rasche, "The Treasury Bill Futures Market and Market Expectations of Interest Rates," Federal Reserve Bank of St. Louis *Monthly Review,* June 1977, pp. 2–9.

Chicago Board of Trade, *Hedging Interest Rate Risks,* August 1977.

————, *An Introduction to the Interest Rate Futures Market,* February 1978.

Duncan, Wallace H., "Treasury Bill Futures—Opportunities and Pitfalls," Federal Reserve Bank of Dallas *Business Review,* July 1977, pp. 1–15.

Figlewski, Stephen, "Futures Trading and Volatility in the GNMA Market," Working Paper 217, Salomon Brothers Center for the Study of Financial Institutions, New York University, July 1980.

Froewiss, Kenneth C., "GNMA Futures: Stabilizing or Destabilizing?" Federal Reserve Bank of San Francisco *Economic Review,* Spring 1978, pp. 20–29.

International Monetary Market, *T-Bill Futures,* February 1976.

————, *Understanding Futures in Foreign Exchange,* October 1975.

Poole, William, "Using T-Bill Futures to Gauge Interest-Rate Expectation," Federal Reserve Bank of San Francisco *Economic Review,* Spring 1978, pp. 7–19.

Stevens, Neil A., "A Mortgage Futures Market: Its Development, Uses, Benefits, and Costs," Federal Reserve Bank of St. Louis *Monthly Review,* April 1976, pp. 12–19.

Part V

The International Financial System

Chapter 19

The International Monetary System

The scope and volume of international financial transactions have grown at a remarkable rate in recent decades, paralleling the huge increase in international trade and investment that has occurred since World War II. Such international financial transactions include payments for goods and services sold to and bought from foreign buyers and financial investing and borrowing across national borders. International financial intermediation has become a phenomenon of considerable significance to the world economy, and the international money and capital markets in which such external intermediation is accomplished have grown enormously in the postwar period.[1]

This chapter offers a survey of the international monetary-financial system. Considered initially are the essentials of the international payments system and the foreign exchange market. Key elements of the international money and capital markets and international banking are identified, although more detailed discussion is deferred to Chapter 20.

---

1. International financial intermediation differs from domestic financial intermediation only in the fact that the economic entities having "surplus" funds (savers) and economic entities in a "deficit" position (borrowers) are residents of different nations. (And of course, different currencies are generally involved.)

FUNDAMENTALS OF THE INTERNATIONAL PAYMENTS SYSTEM

The fact that different nations have different currencies is the basic source of distinction between domestic payments systems and the international payments system. International trade and international borrowing and lending thus generally involve an exchange of currencies, as well as an exchange of goods, services, or financial instruments.[2] For example, if a Japanese firm exports goods to the United States, either the U.S. buyer must convert dollars to (sell dollars for) Japanese yen in order to make payment, or the Japanese seller must accept dollars and subsequently convert them to yen. Similarly, a Japanese investor wishing to acquire U.S. Treasury bills must first obtain dollars (in exchange for yen) in order to purchase the securities.

The Foreign Exchange Market

International markets for foreign exchange exist for the purpose of buying and selling various national currencies. The buying and selling of foreign exchange (i.e., foreign currencies) by governments, individuals, and firms is done for various reasons, including international trade, overseas travel by tourists, foreign investments, and speculation. The foreign exchange market is conducted primarily by foreign exchange brokers and banks acting as foreign exchange dealers through an extensive international telephone and cable communications network. There are two basic types of foreign exchange transactions (and rates)—"spot" and "forward." A spot transaction involves immediate (or within one or two days) delivery of the currencies being traded, and the rate of exchange is the *spot rate*. A forward transaction involves a forward exchange contract calling for delivery of the currencies being exchanged at a fixed future date at a specified exchange rate. The latter is the *forward rate* of exchange. Forward contracts generally involve periods of one, three, or six months, but contracts in major currencies for other periods are available.

Exchange rates are commonly quoted in a given country as the amount of that nation's currency (referred to as *local* or *home* currency) required to buy *one* unit of another nation's currency. The exchange rate between the U.S. dollar and the French franc, for example, may be expressed as $.25/FF in the United States and as FF4/$ in France. When the French franc *depreciates* relative to the U.S. dollar, it becomes cheaper in U.S. dollars; for example, it might depreciate from $.25/FF (FF4/$) to $.22/FF (FF4.545/$) over some time period. When the franc *appreciates,* it becomes more expensive relative to the dollar; an example would be an increase in the exchange rate from $.25/FF (FF4/$) to $.27/FF (FF3.7/$). Note that the currencies involved move in opposite directions; the value of the U.S. dollar relative to the French franc *appreciates* when the franc *depreciates,* and vice versa. Depreciation and appreciation of home currency relative to a foreign currency thus mean that the foreign currency becomes more expensive or cheaper, respectively, in terms of home currency.

---

2. Currency conversion is not always necessary for transactions among residents of different countries. The U.S. dollar, for example, has "vehicle currency" status; in effect, it is an international currency often used for international trade and investment transactions without currency exchange taking place.

An exchange rate is thus simply a price of a currency expressed in terms of another currency. A foreign exchange trader (usually a bank) will quote two "prices" for a given currency, a price at which the bank is willing to buy (bid) and a price at which the bank is willing to sell (the *ask* or *offer* price). The "spread" between bid and offer rates is the trader's compensation for "making a market" in the currency (analogous to the dealers' margin in the domestic OTC market for securities, as described in earlier chapters).

Forward exchange rates for a given currency frequently differ from that currency's spot rate of exchange. If the forward rate exceeds the spot rate, the difference is called a *premium* on the currency. If the forward rate is less than the spot rate, the difference is called a *discount* on the currency. For example, if the spot rate of the French franc is $.2505/FF, and the forward rate for French francs to be delivered in three months is $.2530, then a forward premium of $.0025/FF (approximately one percent) exists for three month francs in the forward market. Why might francs be trading at a premium in the forward market? The answer is that, although forward rates (like spot rates) are determined by supply and demand, the "market" apparently expects the spot rate of exchange of the franc relative to the dollar to appreciate.[3] If the market's expectation was that the franc was likely to depreciate relative to the dollar, forward francs would trade at a discount. As indicated in a subsequent discussion in this chapter, relative interest rates on currencies play a central role in the determination of premiums and discount on currencies.

Sources and Uses of Foreign Exchange

What causes exchange rates of currencies to depreciate or appreciate relative to other currencies? The answer to this question is implicit in the fact that an exchange rate is a price. Like the price of any item (in a free market), the exchange rate for a currency is determined by supply and demand for that currency. With demand unchanged, an increase in supply will lower the price, and a decrease in supply will result in a higher price. Similarly, with supply unchanged, an increase in demand will push the price higher, and a decrease in demand will lower the price. Understanding exchange rate determination thus amounts to recognition of the various transactions that give rise to the supply of and demand for a given currency.

International trade is of paramount importance in exchange rate determination. When a country *exports* goods and services, this gives rise to *demand* for that nation's currency. U.S. exporters, for example, want to be paid ultimately in dollars, and foreign importers must exchange their own currencies for dollars. (Note that the *demand for dollars* is the supply of *foreign currencies* exchanged for dollars.) When a country *imports* goods and services, the foreign exporters wish to be paid in their own currencies. Thus U.S. importers must *supply* dollars to the foreign exchange market (their contribution to the demand for the particular foreign currency). When a country's exports of goods and services are not equal

---

3. Future spot rates, like stock prices, can only be predicted; they cannot be "known." Thus the forward rate is only a predictor of future spot rates, but it is likely to incorporate all publicly available information pertinent to a currency's value as analyzed and assessed by knowledgeable individuals.

to its imports, this aspect of international currency flows will tend to raise (if exports > imports) or to lower (if exports < imports) the exchange of its currency relative to the currencies of its trading partners.

However, transactions other than foreign trade also give rise to supply and demand for a nation's currency. These include expenditures of tourists, military expenditures abroad, gifts and grants to foreign governments or residents, payments of interest and dividends to foreign investors, and international investment. Investment in a country by foreign investors has the same effect as an export of that nation's merchandise; the demand for the country's currency is increased. On the other hand, investment in a foreign country increases the supply of the investors' home currency in the foreign exchange market, just as does a home import of merchandise. The effect is the same for foreign *direct investment* (to the extent that foreign ownership amounts to control of a productive facility) or foreign *portfolio investment* (purchase of domestic securities by a foreign national or purchase of foreign securities by a resident). Demand and time deposits held abroad by residents have the same effect as do direct and portfolio investments held abroad by residents. Demand and time deposits held in a country by foreign residents constitute demand for that country's currency, just as does foreign investment in that country.

Table 19.1 summarizes the principal items giving rise to the supply and demand for a nation's currency in the foreign exchange market.

Table 19.1   Home currency supply-demand effects of international transactions

Uses of foreign exchange	Sources of foreign exchange
The supply of home currency to the foreign exchange market is increased (or decreased) by increases (or decreases) in	The demand for home currency in the foreign exchange market is increased (or decreased) by increases (or decreases) in
Imports of goods and services	Exports of goods and services
Purchases of residents traveling abroad	Purchases of foreign tourists
Investment abroad	Investment in home country by foreign residents
Remittances of interest and dividends to foreign investors	Receipts of interest and dividends from foreign investments
Gifts and grants to foreign governments and residents	Gifts and grants received from foreign residents

In addition to the items listed in Table 19.1, the supply and demand for a nation's currency (and thus its exchange rate) are also affected by speculators' transactions in that currency and by "hedging" transactions by business firms and banks.[4] The magnitudes of these amounts (and thus their influence on exchange rates) have increased substantially in recent years. The net of supply and demand from these many and varied transactions constitutes a nation's *balance of payments*.

Measures of Balance of Payments Deficit and Surplus

In technical terms, a country's balance of payments always "balances," because it is accounted for with the conventional double-entry bookkeeping model in which the sum of the debits (uses of foreign exchange) always equals the sum of the credits (sources of foreign exchange). This accounting equality corresponds to the economic identity of *realized* demand and supply (what is bought is identical to what is sold). These accounting and economic identities, however, are not useful for evaluating demand and supply conditions for a currency and thus for forecasting increases or decreases in the exchange rate for a currency.

Useful measures of a country's balance of payments can be developed by separating transactions that reflect fundamental economic uses and sources of foreign exchange (so-called *autonomous* items) and those currency flows that merely facilitate autonomous transaction items (so-called financing, accommodating, or compensating transactions). An example of an autonomous flow is merchandise imports, whereas the payment for the goods is an accommodating transaction. Although there is sometimes disagreement as to whether certain items are accommodating or autonomous, many foreign exchange transactions fall clearly into one category or the other. A "balance" in the balance of payments is computed as the receipts and payments of foreign exchange among some group of accounts considered to be autonomous in nature.

Table 19.2 shows how certain widely used measures of the balance of payments are calculated. (Table 19.3 shows the format and figures published for the United States in 1977–1979 but does not indicate all the "balances" included in Table 19.2.) The *balance of trade* is simply the difference between exports and imports of merchandise. There is certainly no argument that these transactions are autonomous, since they reflect both a nation's appetite for foreign goods and its capacity to earn foreign exchange by selling merchandise to other nations. A *deficit* in the trade balance reflects an excess of merchandise imports over exports and a *surplus* an excess of exports over imports.

The *balance on goods and services* adds to the trade balance the net payments of interest and dividends to foreign investors and receipts of interest and dividends from

---

4. Hedging is discussed extensively in Chapter 18 in the context of futures markets. Hedging techniques involve various means of balancing potential foreign exchange gains and losses and usually incorporate both spot and forward market transactions.

Table 19.2 Various balance of payments accounts measures

Accounts/items

Current account
  Trade account
    Exports
    Imports
      Balance of trade

  Service account
    Receipts for interest and dividends, travel, and financial charges
    Payments for interest and dividends, travel, and financial charges
    Balance in invisibles (services)

  Unilateral transfers (gifts and grants)

  Current account balance (sum of the above items)

Capital account
  Long-term capital flows
  Direct investment
    Sale of financial assets (net)
    Purchase of financial assets (net)

Portfolio investment
  Sale of financial assets (net)
  Purchase of financial assets (net)

    Balance on long-term capital account

Basic balance

Private short-term capital flows
  Sale of financial assets
  Purchase of financial assets

    Balance on short-term private capital account

  Capital account balance (sum of long-term and short-term capital accounts)

Overall balance (sum of the current account balance and the capital account balance)

Official accounts

  Changes in liabilities to foreign official holders
  Changes in reserve assets
    Gold
    Foreign currencies
    Special Drawing Rights

foreign investment, receipts and payments relating to international tourism, certain military-related transactions, and various other "services." Including government and private gifts and grants ("unilateral transfers") produces the *balance on current account.*

To this point, there is general agreement that these current account items are autonomous (rather than accommodating). However, considerable disagreement emerges in the *capital account* category, which includes changes in items relating to foreign ownership of domestic assets and domestic ownership of foreign assets (international capital movements). The *basic balance,* which adds net changes in *long-term* (but not short-term) capital movements to the current account balance, is one view of a nation's fundamental balance of payments. The basic balance excludes short-term capital movements (a large portion of which are changes in ownership of demand and time deposits) on the grounds that these transactions largely constitute financing of autonomous flows. (For example, an oil-exporting nation may deposit dollars received from a sale to a U.S. importer in a time deposit in a New York bank. The autonomous transaction is the U.S. oil import, and the increase in foreign ownership of U.S. bank deposits is accommodating. Some short-term capital movements, however, are not accommodating; rather they result from current or expected economic developments (interest rate or exchange rate changes). To the extent the latter types of short-term capital transactions exist in significant magnitude, the basic balance is suspect.

The *balance on capital account* does not include current account items; it includes only short-term and long-term capital movements. If both private *and* government capital flows are included in the capital account balance, this balance will equal the current account balance (except for statistical discrepancy) but will have the opposite "sign" (a capital account surplus will correspond to a current account deficit, or vice versa). If private and official capital movements are segregated (as in Table 19.2), an "overall balance" can be determined that is the algebraic sum of the basic balance and *private* short-term capital flows.

Such an overall balance corresponds to the amount of the change in "official liabilities" (obligations to foreign official institutions, such as central banks) and "official reserves" of a nation—its holdings of gold and convertible foreign exchange (currencies that can be converted into other currencies).[5] If a country has a *deficit* in its overall balance, its official liabilities must increase, and/or its official reserves must *decrease* (the deficit must be "financed"); a *surplus* will correspond to an *increase* in official reserves and/or a decrease in official liabilities.

---

5. This does not mean that a nation holds foreign currencies in bank vaults. Indeed, such holdings amount to entries on books of accounts, and they are generally invested in interest-earning assets. The Japanese central bank, for example, may keep all its U.S. dollar reserves invested in U.S. Treasury bills. Note also that the holdings of foreign currencies that are reserves of the holding nation are *official obligations* of the nations whose currencies are so held.

One comparatively minor component of international reserves (about 2 percent) consists of Special Drawing Rights (SDRs) created (by bookkeeping entry) by the International Monetary Fund (IMF) for all member nations. SDRs are not used as a means of payment in private international transactions; they are used only to settle obligations among governments.

Table 19.3 U.S. international transactions, 1977–1979 (millions of dollars)

Item credits or debits[1]	1977	1978	1979
1 Balance on current account	−14,068	−14,259	−788
2 Not seasonally adjusted			
3 Merchandise trade balance[2]	−30,873	−33,759	−29,469
4 Merchandise exports	120,816	142,054	182,055
5 Merchandise imports	−151,689	−175,813	−211,524
6 Military transactions, net	1,628	886	−1,274
7 Investment income, net[3]	17,988	20,899	32,509
8 Other service transactions, net	1,794	2,769	3,112
9 MEMO: Balance on goods and services[3, 4]	−9,464	−9,204	4,878
10 Remittances, pensions, and other transfers	−1,830	−1,884	−2,142
11 U.S. government grants (excluding military)	−2,775	−3,171	−3,524
12 Change in U.S. government assets, other than official reserve assets, net (increase, −)	−3,693	−4,644	−3,783
13 Change in U.S. official reserve assets (increase, −)	−375	732	−1,132
14 Gold	−118	−65	−65
15 Special drawing rights (SDRs)	−121	1,249	−1,136
16 Reserve position in International Monetary Fund	−294	4,231	−189
17 Foreign currencies	158	−4,683	257
18 Change in U.S. private assets abroad (increase, −)[3]	−31,725	−57,279	−56,858
19 Bank-reported claims	−11,427	−33,631	−25,868
20 Nonbank-reported claims	−1,940	−3,853	−2,029
21 U.S. purchase of foreign securities, net	−5,460	−3,450	−4,643
22 U.S. direct investments abroad, net[3]	−12,898	−16,345	−24,318
23 Change in foreign official assets in the United States (increase, +)	36,574	33,292	−14,270
24 U.S. Treasury securities	30,230	23,523	−22,356
25 Other U.S. government obligations	2,308	666	465
26 Other U.S. government liabilities[5]	1,159	2,220	−714
27 Other U.S. liabilities reported by U.S. banks	773	5,488	7,219
28 Other foreign official assets[6]	2,105	1,395	1,116
29 Change in foreign private assets in the United States (increase, +)[3]	14,167	30,804	51,845
30 U.S. bank-reported liabilities	6,719	16,259	32,668
31 U.S. nonbank-reported liabilities	473	1,640	1,692

Table 19.3   (continued)

Item credits or debits[1]	1977	1978	1979
32 Foreign private purchases of U.S. Treasury securities, net	534	2,197	4,830
33 Foreign purchases of other U.S. securities, net	2,713	2,811	2,942
34 Foreign direct investments in the United States, net[3]	3,728	7,896	9,713
35 Allocation of SDRs	0	0	1,139
36 Discrepancy	−880	11,354	22,848
37 Owing to seasonal adjustments	—	—	—
38 Statistical discrepancy in recorded data before seasonal adjustment	−880	11,354	23,848
MEMO:			
Changes in official assets			
39 U.S. official reserve assets (increase, −)	−375	732	−1,132
40 Foreign official assets in the United States (increase +)	35,416	31,072	−13,556
41 Change in Organization of Petroleum Exporting Countries official assets in the United States (part of line 23 above)	6,351	−1,137	5,508
42 Transfers under military grant programs (excluded from lines 4, 6, and 11 above)	204	2	305

1. Seasonal factors are no longer calculated for lines 13 through 42.
2. Data are on an international accounts (IA) basis. Differs from the census basis primarily because the IA basis includes imports into the U.S. Virgin Islands, and it excludes military exports, which are part of line 6.
3. Includes reinvested earnings of incorporated affiliates.
4. Differs from the definition of "net exports of goods and services" in the national income and product (GNP) account. The GNP definition makes various adjustments to merchandise trade and service transactions.
5. Primarily associated with military sales contracts and other transactions arranged with or through foreign official agencies.
6. Consists of investments in U.S. corporate stocks and in debt securities of private corporations and state and local governments.

NOTE: Data are from Bureau of Economic Analysis, *Survey of Current Business* (U.S. Department of Commerce)

Source: *Federal Reserve Bulletin*, January 1981, A52.

Thus there are two "lines of defense" for a nation that is experiencing a deficit in its current account transactions—private capital account transactions and official liabilities and reserves. In effect, a country can, for a time, finance a current account deficit by increasing its liabilities to foreigners (decreasing financial claims on foreigners) or by decreasing foreign investment. There are limits to all these actions, however, and correction of the current account deficit will eventually require increasing merchandise exports relative to imports or some other action or combination of actions that will increase current account sources of foreign exchange relative to current account uses.

The nature of the adjustment process for imbalances in the balance of payments differs, depending on whether the affected nation is on a "fixed" or "flexible" exchange rate regimen. Analysis of the balance of payments position also varies according to the exchange rate system. Thus a discussion of the difference between fixed and flexible exchange rate systems is now appropriate, and the following section offers such description in a historical context.

MODERN EXCHANGE RATE SYSTEMS

A *fixed* exchange rate system exists when nations seek to keep exchange rates for currencies approximately constant. During the era of the international gold standard (approximately 1870–1914), currencies were convertible into gold, and gold flowed freely across international boundaries. The result was a system in which exchange rates were kept fixed (within boundaries termed as the "gold export" point and the "gold import" point), because each currency unit was defined in terms of gold, and international gold flows kept exchange rates among currencies in line with their relative gold equivalents. Balance of payments "equilibrium" was supposed to prevail because of the following scenario. Nations having trade surpluses gained gold, and their money supply increased. The increase in the money supply resulted in higher prices for the nation's goods and services, thus reducing exports and increasing imports until the surplus was eliminated. The reverse held for nations experiencing trade deficits. (This "equilibrating specie flow price mechanism" obviously presumes totally flexible prices, or else a high tolerance for unemployment.)

World War I destroyed the international gold standard, and the Great Depression of the 1930s aborted attempts to restore it. The scope of this book does not warrant an analysis of this turbulent period in international finance, but the effect was to make the world's nations eager for an orderly system of fixed rates after World War II. A structure aimed at achieving such a system was developed in an international conference held at Bretton Woods, New Hampshire, in 1944. The "Bretton Woods system" was a *gold exchange standard,* in which currency values were defined in terms of gold (a par, or "parity," value), but gold flows were limited to official (central bank) transactions.

The Bretton Woods agreement, in addition to establishing exchange rates among currencies in terms of "parity values," provided for the International Monetary Fund (IMF) to assist nations in their efforts to maintain the parity value of their currencies, and provided for an "orderly" approach to devaluation or revaluation of currencies when parity values could not be maintained. The principal role of the IMF was to provide convertible currency loans to nations experiencing "temporary" balance of payments problems. Such a nation used the funds to protect the values of its currency. The U.S. dollar played a central role in the Bretton Woods system. It was a "reserve currency"—dollars became the most important part of official reserves—and the values of the currencies of IMF member nation were defined in dollars as well as gold.

Under this fixed exchange rate regime, a nation's central bank held amounts of monetary gold and currencies of other nations (especially U.S. dollars) as "official reserves" in order to be able to defend the parity value of its own currency. Such defense is accomplished by the exchange of these reserves for home currency when the home currency's value in the foreign exchange market would otherwise drop below the parity value; the increased demand for home currency raises its "price" relative to other currencies.[6] (The Bretton Woods agreement allowed for a "parity band" of ±1 percent in which a currency's value could fluctuate.) In addition to such foreign exchange market intervention, a nation could seek to protect the parity value of its currency by pursuing economic policies aimed at achieving balance of payments equilibrium. Indeed, IMF loans were (and still are) conditioned on the adoption of such policies.

Until 1971, the U.S. dollar was literally "as good as gold" as a reserve currency; foreign central banks could convert holdings of dollars to gold at $35 per ounce. For reasons discussed below, such convertibility was halted in August 1971, but the dollar has continued to be a major reserve currency for most of the world's nations, with about 75 percent of official reserves around the world being held in dollars. The end of convertibility (and the subsequent devaluation of the dollar) marked the beginning of the end of the Bretton Woods system of fixed exchange rates and set the stage for a new system of predominantly *flexible* exchange rates. The currencies of many major trading nations, including the United States, are now allowed to "float" in the foreign exchange market; the free forces of supply and demand generally determine the values of these currencies—with occasional intervention by central banks to maintain an "orderly" foreign exchange market.[7]

The Bretton Woods system of "stable but adjustable" exchange rates, which served the world economy quite well during the 1946–1971 period, collapsed essentially because the value of one currency—the U.S. dollar—was not adjustable. Further, because of the dollar's significance as a reserve (and vehicle) currency, it was necessary for the United States to run continuous balance of payments deficits in order to satisfy world liquidity

---

6. A nation *gains* official reserves by operations to keep its currency value from rising *above* parity. In this case, its central bank exchanges home currency for other currencies, and the increased supply of home currency in the foreign exchange market depresses its "price."

7. The degree of central bank intervention has been characterized in terms of "freely floating" currencies (nominal intervention) and "dirty floating" (frequent intervention to support or restrain its currency's exchange rate). Central bank "management" of the exchange rate is accomplished by the buying and selling of home currency in the foreign exchange market, as is done in the maintenance of fixed exchange-rate parity values.

needs, but these deficits in turn eroded confidence in the dollar. Diminished confidence in the dollar resulted in presentation of dollars for U.S. gold reserves in magnitudes that led to increased concern among U.S. officials. Finally, in August 1971, the U.S. government ended convertibility of dollars into gold and allowed the dollar to "float" in the foreign exchange market, where it promptly declined substantially in value relative to most major currencies.

During the 1971–1973 period, a new mixed system of world exchange rates supplanted that of the Bretton Woods agreement. At the time of this writing, of the countries that are members of the International Monetary Fund, 35 nations allow their currencies to float in the foreign exchange market and 87 nations peg their currencies' value to some other currency (the U.S. dollar, British pound, French franc, etc.). Eight of the ten nations of the European Economic Community (Common Market) constitute a special case; as members of the European Monetary System (EMS), they fix the value of their currencies relative to one another but allow exchange rates relative to the currencies of nations outside the EMS to float. (As of this writing, Britain and Greece are the only EEC members outside the EMS.)

Balance of Payments Adjustment: Fixed Versus Flexible Exchange Rates

Under a fixed exchange rate regime, a deficit in a nation's balance of payments creates downward pressure on the exchange rate of its currency. When the nation no longer has adequate reserves for the market intervention necessary to maintain the currency's fixed value, it must *devalue* the currency. A devaluation amounts to increasing the quantity of home currency units that are exchanged per foreign currency unit. (A continuous surplus warrants *revaluation,* or "up-valuation.") Because devaluation makes home currency cheaper to nonresidents and foreign currency more expensive to residents, devaluation results in making the nation's exports cheaper (in other currencies) and its imports more expensive (in home currency)—thus serving to correct the deficit.[8] Various domestic economic developments, both "automatic" and government-initiated, can also operate to reduce a deficit. These economic developments are discussed in Chapter 21, since they relate to economic policy formation and execution.

Under flexible (floating) exchange rates, correction of a deficit or surplus in the balance of payments is—at least theoretically—accomplished by the effects of supply and demand on a currency's value in the foreign exchange market. A deficit implies that the supply of the currency in the foreign exchange market exceeds demand; the resulting depreciation in the currency's exchange rate will result in cheaper exports (thus increasing them) and more expensive imports (thus decreasing them) and eventual elimination of the deficit. A surplus will cause a currency to appreciate in value and thus result in an increase in imports (now

---

8. The nature of this correction and the necessary conditions for devaluation to correct balance of payments deficits are described in any international economics or international finance textbook (such as those cited in the references at the end of this chapter). Implications of balance of payments problems for monetary and fiscal policy are discussed in Chapters 21 and 22.

cheaper in home currency) relative to exports (now more expensive in foreign currencies).

In practice, balance of payments adjustments are considerably more painful and otherwise much more difficult than the foregoing scenario suggests. Under the Bretton Woods system, countries were reluctant to revalue their currencies because of the injury this action inflicted on export industries.[9] Devaluation impacts on import-export relationships with a long and painful lag, because *quantities* of goods imported and exported change only slowly, whereas the effect on *currency* receipts and payments is immediate. With flexible rates, most governments still seek to "manage" the exchange rate to some degree to avoid the disruptive effects of sharply appreciating or depreciating currencies.

Balance of payments analysis has been significantly affected by the post-1971 shift to flexible exchange rates among the world's major trading nations. (Even countries that still employ fixed exchange rates have been affected, since they usually "fix" their currencies' value in terms of "floating" monetary units, such as the U.S. dollar.) Government transactions and official reserve holdings are much less important under a flexible rate regime. Greater emphasis is placed on current account transactions, for they offer a better guide to a nation's fundamental tendency for foreign exchange use. Relative interest rates are also of enhanced importance because of their influence on capital movements among nations. Whether exchange rates are fixed or flexible, balance of payments analysis must be meshed with a variety of economic information if meaningful assessments of likely future trends of currency value are to be made.

THE ROLE OF COMMERCIAL BANKS IN INTERNATIONAL PAYMENTS

Commercial banks play a key role in the international financial system. The importance of banks for international trade is apparent when one recognizes that payment for internationally traded goods is accomplished essentially by changes in the ownership of bank deposits. Banks also dominate the foreign exchange market, and they are primarily responsible for the worldwide efficiency of that market. Many banks are multinational organizations, and through their global operations they facilitate international investment as well as world trade. The first two of these aspects of international banking are examined below; the third is discussed in the next chapter.

Financing International Trade: The Payments Mechanism

The banking system of a nation contributes to the operation of the international payments mechanism simply by maintaining deposits in banks abroad, by accepting deposits of foreign banks, and by debiting and crediting these accounts as payments are made across

---

9. In the 1970s, rapidly rising dollar prices of OPEC oil (invoiced in U.S. dollars) made oil-importing nations much more willing to see their currencies appreciating relative to the dollar. A cheaper dollar meant cheaper oil for these nations (valued in their currencies), since oil prices were set in dollar terms.

international borders. Banks reduce the risk of international transactions by traders and investors by, in effect, interposing their credit for that of individual and institutional debtors via *letters of credit*. By helping maintain orderly and efficient spot and forward foreign exchange markets, banks reduce the foreign exchange risk associated with international financial obligations. Banks expedite international commerce by lending to both exporters and importers, and by making international financial intermediation possible, they facilitate global capital mobility.

The mechanics of international payments are relatively simple. Consider a resident making payment to a nonresident, i.e., a U.S. firm remitting to a foreign firm. The U.S. firm may ask its bank (Bank A) to make payment by debiting its demand deposit account. If Bank A does not have a correspondent bank in the country in which the foreign firm is resident, it will ask a domestic correspondent bank (Bank B), which has such a foreign correspondent (or a foreign affiliate), to make the payment. Bank B debits Bank A's account and then makes payment by one of two basic approaches. In the first, Bank B will credit its foreign correspondent's account and then mail or cable a remittance advice to the foreign bank, giving instructions for payment to the foreign firm (in local currency).

In the second approach, Bank B (the domestic correspondent bank) converts currency. It may do so by selling (for dollars) a foreign currency draft on its account (in local currency) with the foreign correspondent bank to the remitting U.S. firm. The U.S. firm then makes payment directly to its foreign creditor with the foreign currency draft on Bank B. When the draft is paid by Bank B, it will debit Bank A's account and advise the latter of the transaction; Bank A then credits Bank B's account. Alternatively, Bank B may write or cable its foreign correspondent to debit its local currency account and make payment to the foreign firm.[10]

Remittances *received* by residents from nonresidents are handled in the same fashion. For U.S. recipients, remittances may be made in dollars (foreign bank performs currency conversion) or in foreign currency. Payment may be accomplished through a U.S. bank, or a foreign currency draft on an overseas bank may be mailed to the U.S. creditor. In the former case, the paying U.S. bank will have its account with the foreign correspondent bank credited for the amount remitted. In the latter, the U.S. recipient may sell the draft to his bank for dollars. This bank then sends the draft to the named foreign bank for collection. Such collection may involve intermediate correspondent banks, but it will ultimately involve either a credit to a U.S. bank's account with a foreign bank or a debit to a foreign bank's dollar-denominated account with a U.S. bank.

Regardless of what channel international remittances may take, note that they ultimately involve (as do most domestic payments) only a change in ownership of a bank deposit in the designated amount.

---

10. Such local currency accounts held abroad in correspondent banks are called *nostro* accounts. Smaller banks, which may find it too expensive to maintain nostro accounts, use nostro accounts of large domestic correspondent banks.

Bankers Acceptances

The use of drafts (also called bills of exchange) is common to effect payment for internationally traded goods. In international transactions, an importer (or the importer's bank) often must "accept" (agree to pay) a *time draft* or make payment on a *sight draft* drawn by the exporter on the exporter's firm or bank before the importer can take possession of the merchandise. A sight draft requires immediate payment; a time draft becomes a *trade acceptance* if accepted by a business firm (the importer) or a *bankers acceptance* if accepted by a bank. Trade acceptances are generally not marketable and are likely to be held by the exporter until due. Bankers acceptances, on the other hand, are readily marketable and are often sold by exporters wishing to obtain immediate cash.

Since bankers acceptances, as short-term investments, have the same quality as bank certificates of deposit, there is a large and active market for these instruments. (See Chapter 13 for a more complete discussion.) In the United States, about a dozen New York acceptance dealers buy and sell bankers acceptances at a spread ranging from $\frac{1}{8}$ percent to $\frac{1}{4}$ percent. Purchasers of acceptances from these dealers include banks, insurance firms, corporations, and the Federal Reserve System (as part of its open-market operations). Foreign investors find acceptances attractive because interest on them is not subject to withholding tax. Further, bankers acceptances originating from international transactions are not subject to state usury laws, which prescribe interest rate ceilings—an attractive aspect during high interest-rate periods.

Letters of Credit

Letters of credit issued by banks are of considerable importance to international trade. A letter of credit amounts to a written promise by an importer's bank to make payment to the exporter in the event of default by the importer. For the exporter, a letter of credit minimizes credit risk (provided that a strong and reputable bank is the issuer), reduces political risk (governments are loath to jeopardize their banking system's reputation), reduces the need for credit checking, facilitates financing, and provides for immediate payment on delivery of the goods to the importer. The importer benefits by the issuing bank's becoming party to the transaction, for it provides a source of expert assistance in monitoring and ensuring exporter performance.

Foreign Exchange Trading

The role of commercial banks in foreign exchange trading is of considerable significance in the maintenance of efficient and orderly foreign exchange markets. Bank profit on the buying and selling of foreign exchange is realized by the spread between the "bid" (buying) and "offer" (selling) prices for a given currency. Although banks sometimes speculate in foreign currencies, they generally prefer to maintain a hedged position that minimizes their exposure to foreign exchange risk.

Bank trading in foreign exchange includes transactions with nonbank customers, domestic banks, and foreign banks. Trading occurs in both the spot and forward markets. One or more individuals are designated as foreign exchange traders for a given bank. Such traders must be highly skilled, because they must make rapid judgments (most major trades are accomplished by telephone or telex) about the buying and selling of frequently volatile currencies.

Until the emergence of the U.S. multinational corporation as a worldwide phenomenon in its rate of growth and economic significance, most U.S. banks could meet their customers' needs for international banking services by maintaining international banking departments. These departments handle foreign exchange trading, international payments, and trade financing (including letters of credit). But as more and more bank customers launched extensive foreign operations, their needs for the provision of bank services in their foreign locations increased. As a result, U.S. banks were led to greatly increase their overseas operations. The next chapter sketches selected aspects of U.S. banks' foreign operations.

INTEREST RATE AND EXCHANGE RATE RELATIONSHIPS

An important aspect of the international financial system is the relationship among interest rates, exchange rates, and the rate of inflation. Chapter 10 includes a discussion of the so-called Fisher effect, the view that the observed interest rate is the sum of a "real" rate and the expected rate of inflation. An extension of the Fisher effect to the international realm ("Fisher open") holds that interest rates in different nations reflect differences in their relative rates of inflation. If real rates of interest are approximately equal among nations, nominal interest rates will differ only by differences in expected rates of inflation. As with "Fisher closed," observed reality will not adhere exactly to this theory because of market "imperfections," but the concept is nonetheless a useful one.

"Fisher open" ties in rather nicely with a similar concept regarding the behavior of relative exchange rates. The so-called purchasing-power parity theorem postulates that, like relative interest rates, exchange rates will change so as to adjust for differential inflation rates among nations. For example, if the inflation rate in France for the next year was expected to exceed that of the United States by 5 percent, one would expect per-annum interest rates in France to exceed those of the United States by 5 percent, and one would also expect the French franc to depreciate by 5 percent relative to the U.S. dollar over that time period. If this was not so, a practice called "interest rate arbitrage" would become profitable, as described below.

When interest rate differentials are equal to rates of change in exchange rates, an investor gains nothing by borrowing in a low-interest currency and investing in a high-interest currency; the decline in exchange rate value offsets the additional interest earnings. Opportunities for gain arise when a significant difference develops between the interest rate differential and the expected percentage change in the exchange rate. Suppose, for example, that the difference in French and U.S. interest rates in the instance cited above was 6 percent instead of 5 percent. The investor could then gain approximately 1 percent (interest rate differential less the expected exchange rate change) by investing in French francs as compared with dollars. It would also be cheaper to borrow in U.S. dollars than in French francs; indeed, one could perhaps turn a profit by borrowing dollars and investing in francs. As more and more investors exploited these opportunities, the difference between the expected rate of change in the exchange rate and the interest differential would shrink for the following reasons.

1. Increased borrowing of U.S. dollars would tend to raise U.S. interest rates.

2. Increased investment in francs would tend to lower French interest rates.

3. Increased demand for French francs in the foreign exchange market would tend to *raise* the value of the franc relative to the dollar in the spot market, thus increasing the expected *future* decline in the franc's exchange rate relative to the dollar.

The eventual result of these developments would be approximate equality of the United States–France interest rate differential and the expected rate of depreciation of the franc relative to the dollar, and thus there would be an end to the profit incentive for interest rate arbitrage.

The existence of the forward market for foreign exchange facilitates interest rate arbitrage. An investor can "cover" the investment by selling the invested currency forward, thus protecting the potential profit from unexpected changes in the exchange rate. An example of covered interest arbitrage follows.

Assume the following data for pounds sterling (£) and U.S. dollars ($):

Spot rate	$2.00/£
1-year forward rate	$1.98/£
Interest rates:	
United Kingdom(£)	10%
United States($)	8%

The forward discount on the £ is

$$\frac{\$1.98 - \$2.00}{\$2.00} = -1 \text{ percent.}$$

An arbitrageur could profit by the following sequence of actions.

1. Borrow $200,000 for one year at 8 percent and convert loan proceeds to £100,000 at spot rate of $2.00.

2. Invest £100,000 at 10 percent for one year.

3. Execute a one-year forward contract for delivery of £110,000 (principal of £100,000 and interest of £10,000 on the above investment) at the forward rate of $1.98/£, or $217,800.

4. One year later, collect principal and interest totaling £110,000, deliver the £110,000, and collect $217,800 on the forward contract.

5. Pay the principal ($200,000) and interest ($16,000) on the loan, realizing a net profit of $1800.

The use of the forward market for "covering" interest rate arbitrage introduces an additional factor that helps bring interest rate differentials into approximate equality with discounts and premiums on currencies. The forward selling of pounds, which increases the supply of forward pounds, tends to lower the forward rate for the pound, thus increasing its discount. In the foreign exchange market, this decrease in the forward rate, in conjunction with the increase in the spot rate that results from an increased demand for spot pounds, tends to increase the discount on the pound above the initial 1 percent. In the money market, increased borrowing of dollars is tending to raise U.S. interest rates, and increased lending in pounds sterling is tending to lower U.K. interest rates; the net effect is a reduction in the interest differential between the two nations. As the interest differential narrows and the discount on the pound (premium on the dollar relative to the pound) rises, the profit to be gained by covered interest rate arbitrage approaches zero. In a relatively free market, interest rate parity will be attained by this scenario.

The international money market for major currencies is a relatively free market, and interest rate parity generally holds for these currencies. Thus when considering alternative currencies for borrowing or investment purposes, one must adjust the stated interest rate for any premium or discount on the currency. *A premium should be added to the interest rate and a discount subtracted from it.* Thus nominal rates can be misleading in terms of the ultimate cost of debt or the return on an investment. Many corporate financial managers, attracted by low interest rates, borrowed heavily in Swiss francs in the 1960s. When the value of the Swiss franc soared in the 1970s, these same managers discovered that it took far more of their home country currencies to pay the Swiss franc debt than had been anticipated; for many, the effective rate of interest was five or six times the nominal rate.

The foreign exchange market offers fertile ground for speculators. As described in Chapter 18, one means of speculating on the future value of a currency is offered by the futures market in the Chicago Mercantile Exchange, the International Monetary Market. The IMM presently deals in eight currencies: pounds sterling, Canadian dollars, Mexican pesos, French francs, Swiss francs, German marks, Dutch guilders, and Japanese yen. Trading in currency futures is similar to forward market transactions in foreign exchange.

The international money and capital markets and the foreign exchange market are closely intertwined. Interest rates in the money and capital markets and forward exchange rates are jointly determined by the interaction of transactions in these markets.

INTERNATIONAL FINANCIAL MARKETS

International financial centers have existed for many years. The City of London, for example, was the focus of international trade financing in the nineteenth century. But only after the Second World War did international financial *markets* (markets for financial assets external to the countries in whose currency the assets are denominated) develop to any significant extent. Reflecting the U.S. dollar's dominant role in the world after World War II, the first international *money* market was in dollars. It became known as the *Eurodollar market,* because European banks began the practice of accepting deposits and making loans in U.S. dollars in the early 1950s. That period was also characterized by rapid development of international *capital* markets, particularly the *Eurobond market* (bonds denominated in a currency other than that of the country in which they are sold).

The Eurodollar Market

As indicated in Chapter 13, a *Eurodollar* is simply a dollar-denominated time deposit in a bank outside the United States. The *Eurodollar market* is the intermediation of these offshore dollars. It is a huge market, amounting to an estimated one trillion dollars in 1980 (a very large part of this amount is interbank deposits), and it is primarily a market for short-term funds. Eurodollar deposits are accepted and lent by *Eurobanks,* which are simply banks that perform this function. Many Eurobanks are branches of U.S. banks.

The existence and rapid growth of the Eurodollar market is largely attributable to differences in regulatory constraints between the United States and other countries, particularly interest-rate restrictions and reserve requirements. Domestic banking regulation, in conjunction with the freedom allowed foreign-currency banking activities by most European nations, is thus the principal reason why Eurobanks can successfully compete with their U.S. counterparts for dollar deposits and loans.

The ''spread'' between deposit interest rates and loan interest rates is smaller in the Eurodollar market than in the United States. This feature, which is due to several aspects of the Eurodollar market, serves to attract both depositors and borrowers. The absence abroad of U.S. regulations on deposit yields and such deposit costs as Federal Deposit Insurance Corporation assessments, as well as the absence of reserve requirements, serves to make deposit rates higher. With the exception of single-maturity time deposits of $100,000 or more, interest rates on savings and time deposits in the United States are limited by Regulation Q. Further, various economies exist in the Eurodollar market that allow Eurobanks to offer both more attractive yields to depositors and more attractive lending rates to borrowers. The Eurodollar market is largely an ''interbank'' market, with more than 85 percent of Eurodollar liabilities being owed to other banks. Ultimate borrowers tend to be large corporations or governmental entities with very low credit risk. Both deposits and loans tend to be in very large denominations. These features, characteristic of a ''wholesale'' market, result in significant operating cost reductions to banks participating in the Eurodollar market.

Eurodollar lending rates are based on the London Interbank Offered Rate (LIBOR), which, as the name suggests, is the prevailing interbank deposit rate. A borrower of Eurodollars will pay the current LIBOR plus a premium based on the term of the loan and the lending bank's assessment of the borrower's credit standing. A frequent arrangement is the Eurocredit floating rate, with interest being paid every six months as the loan "rolls over" and a new, current interest rate is assessed. For example, such a loan arrangement may involve a rate established at six-month intervals until maturity of LIBOR plus 1 percent.

The next chapter offers a more detailed assessment of the nature and significance of the Eurodollar market, including an exposition of the process of Eurodollar creation. Other international money markets are also discussed.

The International Bond Market

In addition to the active market in intermediate-term financing via the various Eurocurrencies (and Eurobanks), large amounts of international capital market funds flows are accomplished by bond issues. There are two types of international bonds: foreign bonds and Eurobonds.

Foreign bonds are sold to investors in a foreign capital market; the bonds are denominated in the currency of the country in which they are issued. For example, a U.S. firm may issue bonds in the London capital market, but the securities are underwritten by British banks and denominated in pounds sterling. A frequent disadvantage of foreign bonds is that governments often subject such issues to close scrutiny and tight control. Long-term borrowers in international markets may avoid such controls by the issuance of *Eurobonds,* securities denominated in a currency other than that of the country of issue. The individuals and institutions purchasing the bonds may be residents of various nations. Table 19.4 indicates the magnitudes of new international bond issues in recent years.

Eurobond issues are generally managed by a syndicate of European banks and U.S. investment banking firms. (U.S. banks are not permitted to underwrite securities issues, but the prohibition does not hold for European banks or nonbranch European affiliates of U.S. banks.) Eurobonds are marketed by the managing syndicate in a number of capital market cities in different countries. The expertise of the investment houses that typically underwrite Eurobond issues has contributed to the success of this market.

As with the Eurocurrency market, a major reason for the emergence of the Eurobond market is its freedom relative to most domestic securities markets. Whereas most governments tightly regulate issues denominated in their own currencies, Eurobond issues are allowed a great deal more flexibility. Costs of issuance thus tend to be smaller and disclosure requirements much less stringent than for domestic and foreign bond issues. Eurobonds also offer tax advantages to the investor. Eurobond interest is generally not subject to a withholding tax, and the fact that Eurobonds are usually in bearer form means that neither owner's identity nor country of residence need be a matter of public record.

Table 19.4   Dollar amounts of new Eurobond and foreign bond issues, 1968–1977 (millions of U.S. dollars)

Year	Eurobonds	Foreign bonds (Outside U.S.)
1968	$ 3,573	$1,135
1969	3,156	827
1970	2,966	378
1971	3,642	1,538
1972	6,335	2,060
1973	4,193	2,626
1974	2,134	1,432
1975	8,567	4,884
1976	14,328	7,586
1977	17,735	7,185

Source: Morgan Guaranty Trust Company, *World Financial Markets*, New York, various issues.

The Eurobond market is not dependent on the existence of the Eurodollar market (or vice versa). However, the availability of large amounts of offshore U.S. dollars, in conjunction with several factors discouraging foreign bonds from being marketed in the United States (discussed in the next chapter), probably gave impetus to the development of the Eurobond market.

A FRAGILE INTERNATIONAL MONETARY SYSTEM?

To this point in this chapter, we have discussed various aspects of the international financial system in an attempt to convey an overview of this rather complex subject. In this concluding section, we offer an assessment of the recent origins and some present problems of the world monetary system. As indicated earlier, the present system was shaped in the 1971–1973 period and thus can hardly be said to have stood the test of time. Events of the decade of the 1980s will determine whether the present system will endure or, like the Bretton Woods system, be replaced by another framework or (perish the thought) slide into the semichaos that characterized international finance in the 1930s.

The early-1970s collapse of the international system of fixed exchange rates forged at Bretton Woods in 1944 seems, in retrospect, to have been inevitable. The system was based not only on the U.S. dollar (and gold) but on a *paramount position* of the dollar. The Bretton Woods system simply did not adequately provide for a weakening of the dollar relative to other currencies, even though a waning of relative dollar strength was inevitable as the economies of Western Europe and Japan recovered from the Second World War. Since the Bretton Woods agreement did not allow for systematic adjustment of the dollar's international value, it was quite predictable that the United States, to protect its economy and its gold reserves, would eventually force dollar devaluation by letting the dollar "float" in foreign exchange markets.

The United States could have prolonged the life of the Bretton Woods system by taking stronger measures to reduce its balance-of-payments deficits and by being less concerned about its "gold drain." However, the economic measures needed to "defend the dollar" (particularly a very tight monetary policy) entailed even slower economic growth and more unemployment for an already sluggish economy. Further, the loss of U.S. gold was quite alarming to those observers who, rightly or wrongly, viewed U.S. gold holdings as an important element in this nation's world economic strength. Under a fixed exchange rate system, a country must either devalue its currency or deflate its economy to correct continuing balance-of-payments deficits. In 1971, the United States chose devaluation, and although it was not the intention of the U.S. government, this action resulted in the emergence of the present system of predominantly flexible exchange rates.[11]

The Impact of OPEC

The first great test of the new system came very early in its life. In 1973, the Organization of Petroleum-Exporting Countries (OPEC) assumed control of world oil prices and began arbitrarily to drive them upward. The profound economic and political implications of OPEC's actions included a major challenge to the world monetary system. (Indeed, if the Bretton Woods system had not already been defunct, it would probably have collapsed as a result.) Oil-exporting nations began to run enormous balance of payments surpluses on current account as their dollar receipts (OPEC oil was priced and invoiced in U.S. dollars) for exports grew dramatically. Correspondingly, oil-importing nations began to experience large balance-of-payments deficits on current account as the price of oil skyrocketed (initially quadrupling and thereafter rising rapidly). Since the economies of most of the oil-exporting nations were neither sufficiently large nor sufficiently developed to utilize fully their huge oil export receipts via imports or other current account transactions, the burden of financing international oil shipments fell on the capital account and official settlements account. The magnitudes were enormous; in the 1974–1977 period alone, an estimated $70 billion of OPEC funds was channeled through the international banking system—the private sector's contribution to the so-called recycling of petrodollars by, in effect, returning them to deficit nations.

One can perhaps best appreciate the importance of "recycling" OPEC receipts by considering the alternative. The situation is simply that OPEC's huge current account surplus is matched with a huge rest-of-the-world current account deficit, which must be

11. The transition was not immediate. The Smithsonian Agreement of December 1971, the outcome of a United States–initiated effort to save fixed exchange rates, established a new structure of currency values. The new structure began to fall apart within a few months, and by early 1973 it had evaporated entirely. However, it was not until the 1976 Jamaica Agreement that the IMF put its official seal of approval on floating exchange rates.

financed. The alternative to such financing would be a degree of deflation (economic retrenchment) in the oil-importing nations that would shrink the *volume* of oil imports to the extent of the price increases. Such retrenchment would amount to a worldwide depression that would be likely to make the Great Depression of the 1930s look like a boom period. In other words, conventional balance-of-payments adjustment was not a feasible reaction to the OPEC-mandated oil price hikes. However, the recycling of many billions of OPEC dollars through the world financial system was no easy matter.

Lending by the International Monetary Fund has constituted the major *official* response to the financial challenge posed by OPEC's actions. The IMF instituted an "oil facility" lending program (1974–1976) by which OPEC deposits were used for loans to oil-importing nations, and it increased its various general lending programs considerably. Total IMF credit reached record levels (the "oil facility" alone accounted for $7 billion), but many nations found the various conditions imposed by the IMF objectionable. The dominant role in the recycling of petrodollars has thus been played by the *private* sector of the international monetary system—particularly the Eurobanks that hold extensive Eurodollar deposits. These banks obtain deposits of the OPEC states and lend the funds to the deficit nations, thus serving as intermediaries between the oil-exporting and oil-importing nations.

The continuing buildup in the balance-of-payments surpluses (and thus reserves) of the OPEC nations poses a threat to world financial stability in a number of interrelated ways. The high price of imported oil has served to increase the amount of *excess* U.S. dollars held abroad (the difference between foreign holdings of dollars and U.S. holdings of reserve assets)—the so-called dollar overhang—by more than double the 1971 magnitude. This result stems from the impact both of expensive imported oil on the U.S. balance of payments and of the massive flow of dollars to OPEC nations in payment for oil. A related effect is the disturbing growth in the volume of international liquidity—now approaching $300 billion in foreign exchange reserves alone (about 75 percent of which are in U.S. dollars). Much of this increase in liquidity is attributable to the widespread balance-of-payments deficits triggered by OPEC oil price hikes. These deficits have caused oil-importing countries to greatly increase their borrowing both from official institutions (such as the IMF) and from private financial institutions to finance their balance-of-payments shortfalls. This sharp rise in international liquidity is augmented and stimulated by the fact that the OPEC nations prefer to hold their huge surpluses in highly liquid assets.

Rapidly increasing international liquidity poses a number of concerns. The increase in liquid assets, of course, has a counterpart in increased liquid liabilities of institutions and in increased external indebtedness of nations, thus increasing both the likelihood of default and the severity of the consequences of such default. These enormous pools of liquid capital tend to slosh around the world in a manner that is quite unsettling for exchange rates. Economists who had advocated a worldwide system of flexible exchange rates were both disappointed and perplexed by the volatility that floating rates displayed in the 1970s. The frequency of large international capital movements, at least in part, is responsible for this exchange rate volatility.

Still another disturbing consequence of the OPEC nations' huge surpluses is the strain they have placed on the international banking system. OPEC nations have been generally unwilling to lend directly to deficit countries. Since the OPEC states' surpluses had to be somehow recycled back to the deficit nations, it fell largely on international banks to serve the intermediating function. Although the usual advantages of intermediation—reduction of risk via diversification and matching of asset maturity preferences—are present, there are also substantial risks to world financial order in the degree of participation of international banks in the recycling process. The world banking system has locked itself into a degree of exposure in its lending to less-developed countries (LDCs) that is alarming to many observers. The external debt of LDCs grew enormously in the 1970s, largely as the result of oil price hikes and the resulting need to finance balance-of-payments deficits. According to estimates of the World Bank, LDC external public debt grew from about $51 billion in 1967 (of which less than 6 percent was owed to banks) to about $273 billion in 1977 (of which more than 23 percent was owed to banks). Aside from the issue of the propriety of banks' involvement in pure balance-of-payments financing, there is concern about the repayment ability of the LDCs. Further, many banks are approaching their "country limits" (the maximum percentage of a loan portfolio to be held in a single country) for many LDCs. These concerns are interrelated. Pure balance-of-payments financing largely amounts to funding consumption, not economic development. Without economic growth and development, LDC capacity to service mounting debt will diminish, and cessation of lending by only a few banks could trigger widespread default.[12] Although the international financial system could probably survive the shock, no one wants an empirical test.

Finally and perhaps most notably, the concentration of enormous financial power in the hand of a few OPEC states is a matter of great concern. To engage in understatement, many of these nations are not models of political stability—Iran and Libya being cases in point. It is quite apparent that, among other things, OPEC states could jeopardize the future of certain banks (which have extended long-term credit on the basis of short-term OPEC deposits) by withdrawing their deposits. Further, OPEC could substantially alter the world exchange rate structure by changing the currencies in which they hold their considerable funds. On the other hand, it is argued that the OPEC nations have a very high stake in international financial stability, since they hold such huge amounts of financial assets outside their borders and thus are unlikely to endanger the world financial order.

A Floating Dollar Standard?

The continued dominant role of the U.S. dollar in an international monetary system of flexible exchange rates has led some observers to label the present system the "floating dollar standard." About 75 percent of reserve assets held by IMF member nations are in

---

12. Debt service commitments of LDCs are already so high that most of the countries are dependent on "rollovers" of private bank debt. It has been estimated that without debt rollover, debt servicing would have consumed more than 25 percent of LDC gross receipts from exports in 1979.

U.S. dollars (current efforts to "diversify" reserves are likely to reduce this percentage somewhat). The dollar continues to be the world's principal "vehicle" currency in international trade and investment, used widely in international payments by traders and investors of all nations. The dollar is also the currency used most often by monetary authorities of the world's nations to intervene in the foreign exchange market.

The continuing key role played by the U.S. dollar in the international monetary system is, unfortunately, a source of potential instability. The viability of the world payments system is inextricably linked with the strength of the dollar. Because both high rates of U.S. inflation and persistent U.S. trade deficits weaken the dollar, this country is viewed as bearing a special responsibility in its conduct of economic policy. During periods of dollar weakness, the U.S. government has frequently pressed the governments of Japan and western Europe to ease the burden on the U.S. economy by "reflating" (inflating) their economies and reducing their trade surpluses relative to their trade with the United States. The dollar's value relative to the currencies of these nations is largely a function of the *differential* between their inflation rates and the U.S. rate and their balance-of-payments positions relative to that of the United States. Thus the economic policies of these nations also bear directly on the strength of the dollar. The issue of how responsibility for the dollar's destiny is to be shared among the United States and its allies is likely to be a source of controversy for the foreseeable future.

One of the greatest threats to the value of the U.S. dollar, and thus to international financial stability, is the huge amount of holdings of dollars abroad. Some proportion of these holdings stems directly from the dollar's role as a reserve and vehicle currency. But the remainder—the dollar "overhang"—is a serious element in the international financial scheme. The dollar overhang makes a "run on the bank" phenomenon (mass dumping of vast amounts of dollars in the foreign exchange market) a perennial possibility, with potentially disastrous consequences for the world's financial system. Various plans have been proposed to "sop up" these excess dollars. One such proposal is the opening of an interest-earning *substitution account* with the IMF, into which central banks could pay in dollars and obtain, say, Special Drawing Rights as a substitute asset. The plan has run afoul of various technical difficulties (such as determination of who is to bear any losses resulting from depreciation of the dollar), as well as political objections. The latter include U.S. concern about IMF "monitoring" of U.S. economic policy and European concern about a weakening of U.S. resolve to control its trade deficit.

Thus there are grounds for pessimism about the future of the world monetary system. One measure of the perceived fragility of the international financial order is the price of gold—the "ultimate store of value." The remarkable rise in the price of gold in the late 1970s reflects a peaking of concern for the future of the world monetary system and a resulting flight from all currencies into holdings of the precious metal. The ebbing of gold's phenomenal price rise in the early 1980s perhaps reflects a renewal of confidence in the ability of the international financial system to weather the various economic and political storms that threaten it. Certainly there are grounds for such optimism, as well as concern. For example, the system of floating exchange rates and the international banking community have coped quite well with the problem of the massive funds flows to OPEC states since 1973. World commerce continues to grow, and international capital movements have never flowed more freely. A number of LDC economies show signs of a "take-off into sustained growth" (economist Walt Rostow's phrase). Finally—and perhaps most important—the strengthening of the U.S. balance-of-payments position in recent years is a good omen for the future. In 1979, the U.S. deficit on current account shrank to less than $800 million, after amounting to about $14 billion in each of the two previous years. In 1980, for the first time in many years, the United States ran a surplus on current account. The sharp improvement in the U.S. current account position was largely due to high levels of earnings on U.S. investments abroad, but it also reflected a narrowing of the U.S. trade deficit. These various encouraging developments suggest that the advocates of a return to fixed exchange rates and the proponents of a "remonetization" of gold will not prevail, at least for a time.

SUMMARY

International funds flows, whether for the exchange of real or financial assets, are complicated by the existence of different currencies in different countries. The trading of currencies in the foreign exchange market is a derivative of the trading of real and financial assets among residents of different nations. When a trader, investor, or traveler must make payments in a currency other than his or her home currency, the foreign currency must be obtained in the foreign exchange market in exchange for home currency. Similarly, foreign currencies received by international traders and investors will generally be converted into home currency in the foreign exchange market.

International commercial and financial transactions thus result in the purchase and sale of currencies in the foreign exchange market. When governments do not intervene, as in a system of flexible (or "floating") exchange rates, the supply and demand for a currency determine its "price" (rate of exchange) in other currencies. Thus when a country develops a trade deficit (its imports exceed its exports) that is not offset by other currency flows, the supply of its currency to the foreign exchange market will exceed demand, and the currency's exchange rate will fall (depreciate). Such depreciation results in the country's exports being cheaper (in terms of foreign currency prices) and its imports being more expensive (in home currency prices). These relative price shifts should serve to boost exports, curb imports, and thus currect the deficit. (The reverse will hold for a balance-of-payments surplus.)

When a government attempts to maintain a fixed rate for its currency, it (through its central bank) is obliged to intervene in the foreign exchange markets when the exchange rate threatens to move above or below some percentage of the pegged rate. Government intervention involves buying home currency in the foreign exchange market when its exchange rate weakens, thus buoying it up with increased demand. Such purchases of home currency are accomplished with "official reserves"—currencies of other nations held by the central bank. When the exchange rate moves excessively upward, the central bank will sell home currency in the foreign exchange market for other currencies, adding them to official reserves. In this case, the increased supply of home currency serves to lower its exchange rate.

Since the 1971–1973 collapse of the world fixed exchange rate system established by the 1944 Bretton Woods agreement, the United States, Japan, and most of the major Western nations have allowed their currencies to float in foreign exchange markets. Most "Third World" nations, however, still have fixed exchange rates for their currencies, although they are fixed relative to floating currencies. The nations belonging to the European Monetary System maintain a fixed rate regime among themselves but let their currencies float against those of nations outside the EMS.

Commercial banks play a vital role in the international financial system, facilitating both world trade and foreign investment. Most international payments are accomplished by a change in ownership of bank deposits from a resident to a nonresident, or vice versa. Banks facilitate foreign trade not only by providing the payments mechanism but also by financing the trade; for this purpose letters of credit are of special importance. Banks also dominate the foreign exchange market and contribute greatly to the efficiency of that market.

International financial markets have increased greatly in size and importance since the Second World War. The Eurodollar market is the largest of these markets, although the offshore market for other major currencies is growing rapidly. There are a number of reasons for the Eurodollar market's growth to enormous proportions, but U.S. regulatory restrictions and reserve requirements, which impact on domestic but not on offshore dollar deposits, are most responsible. The international capital market—Eurocredit lending, foreign bonds, and Eurobonds—also benefits from the comparative freedom that offshore operations provide.

The apparent fragility of the international financial system stems from a number of developments of the last decade. They include the collapse of the Bretton Woods agreement (and the troubled transition to a floating exchange rate system), the continued buildup of excess offshore holdings of U.S. dollars, and the dramatic shift of financial power to the OPEC states. Although the international banking system has performed laudably in the necessary recycling of OPEC trade surplus funds, this role has also placed a great deal of strain on the participating banks. At best, there are grounds for only cautious optimism for the continued stability of the world financial system.

QUESTIONS

1. What is meant by "spot" exchange rates versus "forward" exchange rates? What market forecast is implied by a difference in these rates for a given currency at a point in time? What implication is there for a nation's interest rate structure when the spot and forward exchange rates for its currency diverge?

2. Exchange rates of currencies in the foreign exchange market are determined by supply and demand. What are the principal determinants of quantities demanded and supplied?

3. Name and define four "balances" of the balance of payments. How does each compare to the overall balance of payments?

4. How does a nation attempt to maintain the par value of its currency under a fixed exchange rate system? When is devaluation necessary, and when should revaluation be effected?

5. How is devaluation (with fixed exchange rates) or depreciation (with flexible exchange rates) likely to correct a deficit in the balance of payments?

6. What is the role of commercial banks in the world payments system?

7. What is "interest rate parity"? What is the implication of interest rate parity for the *effective* rate of interest in cross-currency borrowing and lending?

8. Define Eurodollars and Eurobonds (relative to foreign bonds).

9. Why do some observers view the present state of the international financial system as "fragile"?

10. What is meant by the phrase "recycling of petrodollars"?

REFERENCES

Bame, Jack J., "Analyzing U.S. International Transactions," *Columbia Journal of World Business,* Fall 1976, pp. 72–84.

Coombs, Charles A., *The Arena of International Finance* (New York: Wiley, 1976).

Eiteman, David K., and Arthur I. Stonehill, *Multinational Business Finance,* (Reading, Mass.: Addison-Wesley, 1978), Chs. 1–2.

Henning, Charles N., William Pigott, and Robert H. Scott, *International Financial Management,* (New York: McGraw-Hill, 1978).

Kemp, Donald S., "Balance of Payments Concepts—What Do They Really Mean?" Federal Reserve Bank of St. Louis *Review,* July 1975, pp. 14–23.

Riehl, Heinz, and Rita Rodriquez, *Foreign Exchange Markets,* (New York: McGraw-Hill, 1977).

Solomon, Robert, *The International Monetary System, 1945–1976,* (New York: Harper & Row, 1977).

Chapter 20

International Financial Markets and Institutions

The title of this chapter is perhaps unduly ambitious. Entire books can be (and frequently have been) written about each of this chapter's principal topics—international financial markets and international aspects of financial institutions. What we have attempted, however, is not exhaustive treatment of these topics but, rather, a more detailed look than was possible in the previous chapter. We hope this chapter will facilitate the student's understanding of linkages between the domestic and international financial systems. Such linkage is important, for international financial markets complement, supplement, and compete with domestic markets, continuously both affecting and being affected by their domestic counterparts.

Multinational firms—both financial and nonfinancial—play a vital role in international financial markets. To a considerable degree, international financial markets are independent of the regulatory frameworks that govern national financial markets. This independence permits participants in the international financial markets—borrowers, lenders, and intermediaries—to exercise a measure of freedom that is seldom available to them in their respective domestic financial markets. The international financial activities of these various multinational institutions—particularly multinational corporations and international banks—account for much of the efficiency that characterizes the linkage between national and international financial markets.

In the first part of this chapter we describe the nature and significance of the international money markets (particularly the Eurodollar market) and the international capital markets (with emphasis on the Eurobond market). The second part of the chapter focuses on international financial institutions, principally those of special significance for the U.S. financial system.

INTERNATIONAL MONEY MARKETS

The huge growth and development of the international financial markets since World War II was both a consequence of and a necessary condition for the enormous expansion in international trade and investment that characterized this period. In money markets, the provision of worldwide liquidity and trade financing that the emergence of the Eurodollar market entailed constitutes one of the most important private-sector financial developments of this century.

In the capital markets, the Eurobond instrument provided a vital source of international long-term capital to business firms and governments. The postwar founding and growth of such international financial institutions as the World Bank, the International Monetary Fund, and the Inter-American Development Bank have helped to meet the special financial needs of developing nations and otherwise to strengthen the world financial system. In the 1970s, the international financial system showed surprising strength and resiliency in the relative ease with which it adjusted to accommodate, first, a shift from a fixed to a flexible exchange rate system, and then the channeling of enormous flows of funds to and from OPEC nations as a result of the soaring price of oil. Indeed, the most rapid growth of the Eurocurrency market occurred during the 1970s, and this remarkable expansion doubtless reflects, in part, the world financial community's response to the monetary turmoil of the period.

Many observers, especially public officials concerned with national economic policy, feel that the Eurocurrency market poses certain dangers to world economic health. Much of the innovation in financial instruments and arrangements that has characterized international financial markets has been a response to (and a means of circumventing) national financial regulatory policies. Since the international money markets are essentially extensions of national money markets (and thus include the same participants, currencies, and instruments), but they escape the jurisdiction of regulatory authorities, this concern can be understood, if not necessarily shared. The concluding section of this chapter considers some of the issues and recent developments regarding regulation of the international money markets. We turn our attention now to a description of the origins and nature of the largest component of these markets, the Eurodollar market.

Nature and Origins of the Eurodollar Market

Recall that Eurodollars are dollar deposits in banks outside the United States. Such a bank may be a foreign bank, an offshore subsidiary of a U.S. bank, or an overseas branch of a

U.S. bank. Eurodollars have existed for many decades, but only since the late 1950s has the Eurodollar market been of sufficient size to play a significant role in the international financial system.

The stage was set for the Eurodollar market by the Bretton Woods agreement, because the emphasis on the U.S. dollar as a key reserve and vehicle currency made it virtually an international currency. As the various western European economies recovered during the 1950s, dollar deposits began to accumulate in banks in those nations, particularly Britain and France. Some of the dollar deposits were Russian, for the Soviets feared confiscation or "freezing" of their dollars if their holdings were in U.S. banks. British banks, proscribed in 1957 from financing nonresident trade transactions with domestic currency, were eager to obtain dollar deposits for this purpose. The fact that British banks and other Eurobanks were able and willing to offer attractive deposit rates for Eurodollars attracted dollars from U.S. residents (then confronted with Regulation Q interest rate ceilings), as well as European holdings of dollars. The U.S. balance-of-payments deficits of the 1960s, though not a necessary condition for the Eurodollar market's existence, contributed to its growth.

The absence of reserve requirements on Eurodollar deposits makes them a cheaper source of funds for Eurobonds than domestic deposits, on which reserve requirements are generally imposed.[1] Competition for these deposits results in the passing on of most of their cost advantage to depositors in the form of higher deposit yields. The cost advantage can also be reflected in lower interest rates on Eurodollar loans, but borrowers tend to be much more responsive to rate differentials than depositors, and domestic and offshore lending rate differences (except for those reflecting differential *risk*) tend to be quickly "arbitraged" away. (A comparison of domestic and offshore rate structures is offered in a subsequent section of this chapter, including a discussion of the significant role of the risk associated with offshore depositing and lending.)

The amount of offshore dollar *demand* deposits is minimal; Eurodollar deposits are essentially *time* deposits for a specified period (sometimes as short as a single day) and at a specified rate of interest. Thus Eurodollar deposits cannot be used as a means of payment. They must first be converted into a demand deposit of a U.S. bank.

Size of the Eurodollar Market

The Eurodollar market is largely an interbank, "wholesale" market for short-term funds—an aspect that creates some difficulty in assessing its size. In 1979, approximately 900 billion of U.S. dollars were held in deposits offshore, i.e., in countries other than the United States. About $360 billion were interbank deposits (deposits of banks held by other

---

1. Reserve requirement ratios differ considerably among nations, and the central banks of some countries (such as the United Kingdom and the Netherlands) pay interest on reserves. Few major countries, however, have higher average reserve requirements than the United States, and interest is not presently paid on reserves of U.S. banks.

banks). Deposits of central banks and official international institutions accounted for roughly $200 billion of these offshore deposits.

The extensiveness of interbank transactions involving offshore deposits is due to several factors. In Europe, the Eurodollar market serves much the same function as does the market for federal funds in the United States. Very large banks perceived to be very strong financially can attract offshore dollar deposits at relatively low interest rates and lend them (at some small but attractive "spread") to banks not enjoying such status. Further, interbank lending reflects attempts by offshore banks to diversify their assets by countries and currencies as well as maturities. Finally, many interbank transactions are among affiliates, so tax considerations and certain regulatory requirements are also factors contributing to their high volume. Interbank transactions do not reflect a final extension of credit and thus have little or no monetary impact. During the 1977–1979 period, however, changes in offshore dollar deposits of nonbanks and official institutions, a rough measure of *new* offshore dollar credit creation, averaged more than $20 billion a year—a very significant amount, approximating new M-1 creation in the United States during this period.

Offshore dollars are generally not subject to reserve requirements, and Eurobanks typically hold only nominal reserves against Eurodollar deposits. Thus the "money multiplier" effect described in Chapter 6 appears to be very large for Eurodollars. Recall, however, that whereas low reserve-deposit ratios boost the money multiplier, "leakages" (borrowed funds that are spent and not redeposited by recipients) lower the multiplier. These leakages are very large in the case of offshore deposits because of the wide range of alternative financial instruments (and currencies) into which they can be converted.[2]

A more useful concept for assessing the size and growth rate of the Eurodollar market is to view it as a segment of an overall market for dollar intermediation—a market segment that has certain differentiating characteristics relating to risk and returns.[3] Thus the growth of the Eurodollar market relative to the domestic dollar market, in this view, becomes a function of the relative risks and returns of these two competing markets. This concept also suggests that growth of the offshore market comes at the expense of (and not in addition to) growth in the domestic market.

An assessment of the issues pertaining to the size and growth of the Eurodollar market is facilitated by an understanding of the process by which Eurodollars come into existence.

---

2. The money-multiplier concept is much more meaningful in a closed domestic economy, where "currency drain" and shifts into time deposits have historically been the only significant leakages. Even there, however—at least, in the U.S. financial system—money-multiplier analysis has been rendered less useful by various payments innovations in recent years such as N.O.W. and A.T.S. accounts, money-market-fund check writing, etc.

3. See Jurg Niehans and John Hewson, "The Eurodollar Market and Monetary Theory," *Journal of Money, Credit, and Banking* (February 1976), pp. 1–27., for a rigorous statement of this concept. For a very readable variant of this argument, see Ian Giddy, "Why Eurodollars Grow," *Columbia Journal of World Business* (Fall 1979), pp. 54–60.

Creation of Eurodollars

A Eurodollar comes into existence when a deposit in a U.S. bank is transferred to a Eurobank. For example, suppose that a firm holding a dollar time deposit in a New York bank, in order to earn a slightly higher yield, elects to shift the deposit to a bank in London. It can obtain a demand deposit from the New York bank at maturity of the time deposit and then transfer ownership of the demand deposit to the London bank in exchange for a time deposit there. At this point, a Eurodollar deposit has been created.

The London bank, which now holds a demand deposit in the New York bank, is unlikely to leave these funds idle. Instead, the bank will lend the acquired funds to a commercial firm or governmental entity, or it will "place" them in the Eurodollar interbank market. In the former transaction, the borrower obtains ownership of the demand deposit in the New York bank, and credit extension has occurred. In the latter transaction, another bank (assume a Paris bank) acquires the funds in the U.S. bank, and there is no final extension of credit. Such interbank lending of the funds may involve many banks before credit is extended to an ultimate borrower.[4] In turn, this borrower's expending of the funds sets the stage for another potential iteration of revolving ownership of the demand deposit in the New York bank. At some point, however, a non-U.S. recipient of the Eurodollar deposit will wish to convert the funds to his own currency. Such currency conversion transfers ownership of the deposit to the supplier of the local currency and may result in its withdrawal from the Eurodollar market. In general, Eurodollar deposits have the *potential* to generate any of the following.

1. An increase in world lending as the credit-granting capacity of Eurobanks is increased by Eurodollar deposits, but the lending capacity of the U.S. bank that holds the original deposit is not decreased.

2. An increase in the *world* volume of U.S. dollar deposits.

3. A multiple increase in credit to the extent that loaned Eurodollars are redeposited in the Eurodollar market.

4. A shift in the location of credit-granting from U.S. banks to Eurobanks.

Although these potential effects are of consequence, it is also important to recognize what Eurodollar creation does not do. It does not change the U.S. money supply, because only the ownership, not the quantity, of U.S. bank deposits is involved. And even though a multiple expansion of world credit due to Eurodollar creation is possible, such a multiplier effect requires at least the passive assent of European central banks—allowing Eurodollars exchanged for their currencies to be redeposited in the Eurodollar market. Note further that the extension of credit that occurs because of Eurodollar creation is no different than if the

---

4. For an excellent discussion of Eurodollar creation, expansion, and contraction, see Rita Rodriquez and Eugene Carter, *International Financial Management* (Englewood Cliffs, N.J.: Prentice-Hall, 1979), pp. 522–527.

demand deposits in the U.S. bank had never been exchanged for a Eurodollar deposit but had been loaned by the U.S. bank to the borrower (who instead acquired the funds in the Eurodollar market). Note also that the time deposit in the London bank plays a passive role; it is not "money" in the strict sense of a means of payment.

In sum, economists generally agree that the Eurodollar market does not significantly increase the capacity of the financial system to create money and credit.[5] European banks cannot create Eurodollars in the process of making loans (as is possible in their own currencies); they can instead only lend U.S. bank deposits that they own as a result of Eurodollar creation by a previous owner of those deposits. As noted above, a shift of U.S. demand deposit ownership from a U.S. resident to a foreign resident does not change the U.S. money supply.

U.S. and Eurodollar Money Market Interest Rates

As previously indicated, interest rates on Eurodollar deposits are higher than U.S. interest rates on deposits, and Eurodollar lending rates tend to be somewhat lower than U.S. lending rates. This "spread" advantage allows Eurobanks to compete effectively with domestic U.S. banks for deposits and loans. Eurobanks can operate profitably on this leaner margin, because, unlike the deposits of U.S. banks, their dollar deposits do not have the costs associated with statutory reserve requirements, deposit insurance fees, interest rate ceilings, and other regulatory constraints.

Although Eurodollar deposit rates are generally somewhat higher and loan rates consistently slightly lower than U.S. rates, the magnitude of the differences between domestic and external rates often varies, as shown in Fig. 20.1. What may be some reasons for this variation?

In the formative years of the Eurodollar market, differences in the degree of liquidity between it and the domestic market might have been properly viewed as a significant factor in the size of differentials between interest rates in the two respective-markets and in changes in yields between the markets. Given the present size of the Eurodollar market and its apparent efficiency, however, it is difficult to ascribe much significance to this factor.

The most important factor explaining the size of interest-rate differentials and changes in the differentials is relative risk in the two markets.[6] Market imperfections, particularly those relating to differences in the institutional and regulatory structure of domestic and external markets, also play a significant role. In the external-domestic market rate comparison, there is no foreign exchange risk; a Eurodollar differs from a U.S. dollar only in its

---

5. See Gunter Dufey and Ian H. Giddy, *The International Money Market* (Englewood Cliffs, N.J.: Prentice-Hall, 1978), pp. 107–154, for a complete conceptual discussion of this issue and a description of empirical research regarding the "Eurodollar multiplier."

6. Various controls employed by the United States during the 1963–1974 period to control capital outflows almost certainly had a significant effect on external-domestic money market rate differentials. However, no such controls exist at the time this book is being written.

EURODOLLAR AND U. S. MONEY MARKET RATES

AVERAGES FOR WEEK ENDING WEDNESDAY

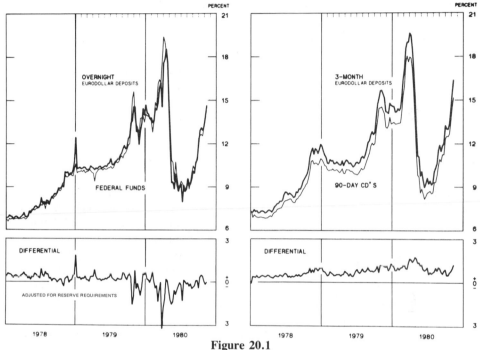

Figure 20.1

(Source: Board of Governors of the Federal Reserve System, *Historical Chart Book.*)

location, not in its value relative to other currencies. However, there is greater risk attached to Eurodollars in the strict sense of the degree of assurance that an obligation will be honored on the basis of agreed terms—credit risk. This risk is not associated only with potential developments in the country in which external borrowing occurs, for the possibility always exists that the home country will take actions that restrict or impair obligations in the external money market. Finally, since the perceived degree of the risk attached to Eurodollars varies over time, interest-rate differentials also vary over time.

Currency Composition of the Eurocurrency Market

The foregoing discussion has focused on the Eurodollar market, but the dollar is only one of the currencies (though the dominant one) in the Eurocurrency market. Other significant Eurocurrencies include the German mark (Deutschemark), the Swiss franc, the French franc, and the British pound. Eurodollars, however, still constitute about three fourths of Eurocurrency deposits.

A factor contributing to the continued dominance of the U.S. dollar among offshore deposits since 1973 has been the emergence of the so-called petrodollar. The invoicing in dollars of oil exports of the OPEC countries gave new significance to the dollar as a "vehicle currency." Many of the dollars flowing to OPEC nations in payment for oil found their way into Eurodollar deposits in Eurobanks. As indicated in the previous chapter, the Eurobanks have played the major role in the "recycling" of OPEC surpluses to oil-importing countries. If the OPEC nations shift away from dollar invoicing to SDRs or to some other composite-currency basis (as they periodically threaten to do), there is likely to be some diminution in the relative importance of the dollar in the Eurocurrency market.

Other Offshore Currency Markets

Offshore currency markets have evolved not only in Europe but also in Asia, the Caribbean area, and the Middle East in recent years. Though still quite small relative to the Eurocurrency market, these markets are likely to increase in significance in the future if Third World economic development accelerates.

The Asian currency market is centered in the city-state of Singapore. It originated in 1969, when Singapore eliminated a tax on interest payments on foreign currency deposits in Singapore banks. Like the much larger Eurocurrency market, the Singapore market is primarily an interbank market, and the bulk of deposits are U.S. dollars. Most ultimate borrowers are located in Asia, but American and European banks account for about 70 percent of all loans. Banks outside Singapore supply about three fourths of Asian currency deposits. As might be expected, interest rates are generally quite close to those prevailing in the Eurocurrency market.

The beginnings of a potential new offshore currency market can be discerned in the Middle East, particularly in Bahrain and Kuwait. Billions of dollars of surplus cash from oil revenues are being generated in this part of the world, and these funds offer the potential for considerable financial development in the region. Increased interest of the region's oil-rich states in direct lending of their surplus receipts would be a major spur to such development. At present, however, most of these "petrodollars" are placed in the Eurodollar and Eurobond markets.

A minor offshore currency market, which is really an offshoot of the Eurocurrency market, is centered in the Caribbean. The Bahamas, the Cayman Islands, and the Netherlands Antilles have attracted financial operations because of their favorable tax climate. Many U.S. banks have Caribbean branches, which serve as a center for their offshore operations.

Major Participants and Financial Instruments in International Money Markets

Given the diversity of borrowers and lenders in the external financial intermediation process, one of the more remarkable features of international money markets is the uniformity of treatment of these participants. Operating in a framework relatively free of government regulation, these markets have not developed the kind of segmentation that characterizes most domestic money markets. The only significant distinctions among borrowers and lenders are standard economic criteria relating to risk and volume.

Banks from around the world participate in the Eurocurrency and other international money markets as both suppliers and users of funds, and they are the nucleus of the external financial intermediation process. External and domestic financial market linkage is largely accomplished by the continual flow of bank funds between domestic markets and international markets.

Large *multinational corporations,* which also play a dominant role in international money markets, are the principal group of ultimate borrowers. The international money market offers two major related advantages to corporate borrowers—availability of funds, even when domestic credit is tight, and a minimum of restrictions on the use of the funds. And external credit is often less expensive than domestic credit. For the multinationals, the fluidity, breadth, and relative freedom of international money markets make them an ideal medium for moving funds around the world. These characteristics, along with generally higher deposit yields, also result in corporations being principal suppliers of funds to the Eurocurrency and other external money markets, as well as users of those funds.

Governments and governmental entities are becoming increasingly important participants in international money markets. As suppliers of funds to these markets, the OPEC states are notable, accounting for deposits of many billions of dollars per year. For political as well as economic reasons, the OPEC states find these markets attractive depositories for the huge surplus of funds generated by their sales of oil. In addition to yield and liquidity advantages, international markets offer anonymity and a separation of jurisdiction over funds from the country in whose currency the funds are denominated.

Governmental entities of considerable importance in the Euromarkets are various central banks. Central banks supply funds directly to the Eurocurrency market via deposits of dollars in Eurobanks and holdings of dollars and other currencies with commercial banks in their countries, which subsequently deposit the funds in Eurobanks. Central banks are also borrowers in international money markets, along with various other governmental entities.

Eurodollar *borrowers* include U.S. banks, especially during periods of monetary stringency in the United States. Branches of U.S. banks located abroad may lend dollar deposits to the parent bank. Until 1969 there were no reserve requirements on such borrowings by the home office of Eurodollars from a foreign branch, but in that year reserve requirements of 10 percent (subsequently 20 percent) were instituted. These reserve requirements remained in effect until August 1978, when they were eliminated.[7] They were reimposed in 1980 as part of a 10-percent reserve requirement on so-called managed liabilities of banks, but they were eliminated again in the same year. The Depository

---

7. The 1978 elimination of reserve requirements on Eurodollar borrowings by U.S. banks was part of an effort by the Carter administration to bolster the strength of the dollar in the foreign exchange market. It was anticipated that ending reserve requirements would result in increased borrowing by U.S. banks of Eurodollars, and that this increase in demand for offshore dollars would raise the exchange rate of the U.S. dollar.

Institutions Deregulation and Monetary Control Act of 1980, as part of its overhaul of the reserve-requirement structure described in Chapter 7, established a reserve requirement of 3 percent on Eurocurrency liabilities of U.S. banks.

Eurocurrency market loans are usually short-term, although the proportion in intermediate-term financing has grown appreciably in recent years. (See the discussion of Eurocredit lending in the following section.) Approximately one fourth of total lending is related to the financing of international trade, and this generally involves short-term loans. In recent years, Eurocurrency loans (other than interbank) with maturities of more than six months have frequently featured the Eurocredit floating rate (LIBOR plus a premium) mentioned in the preceding chapter. Such Eurocredit arrangements generally involve maturities from five to eight years, with interest being paid every six months as the credit is rolled over and a new, current interest rate is assessed. This feature permits banks to borrow short and lend long with a minimum of interest-rate risk.

Most (85–90%) Eurocurrency deposits with banks are in time deposits of fixed maturity and rate. The remainder are in negotiable certificates of deposit (CDs). So-called tap CDs are issued in maturities ranging from a few days to five years, with three- and six-month maturities the most popular. ''Tranche'' CDs (from the French word for ''slice'') are actually a series of certificates identical in interest rates, interest payment dates, and maturities but differing in denominated amount. The advantage to an investor is that ''slices'' of the tranche CD can be sold without liquidating the entire CD, as is necessary with a single-certificate CD.

THE INTERNATIONAL CAPITAL MARKET

The volume of lending since 1958 in the international capital market is depicted in Fig. 20.2 for the three component instruments of this market—Eurocredit lending, Eurobonds, and foreign bonds. The remarkable growth in this market since the mid-1960s is apparent. The impetus for this huge surge in volume came first from the 1963–1974 U.S. capital controls programs (discussed below) and then from the quadrupling of world oil prices in 1973 (discussed in the previous chapter). The former served to close the U.S. capital market to many foreign borrowers, who were then obliged to turn to Eurocredit or Eurobond financing. The latter resulted in the huge petrodollar surpluses that had to be recycled back to oil-importing nations through the international financial system. Many of the latter nations were obliged to finance their balance-of-payments deficits (on current account) by borrowing in the Eurocurrency market.

Eurocredit Lending

Eurocredits are intermediate-term, generally unsecured loans provided by international banking syndicates. Maturities range from one to fifteen years, but most are from five to eight years. (Technically, Eurocredits are six-month renewable loans, stretching out to the designated maturity.) Eurobank margins on such loans are fixed. The use of a floating

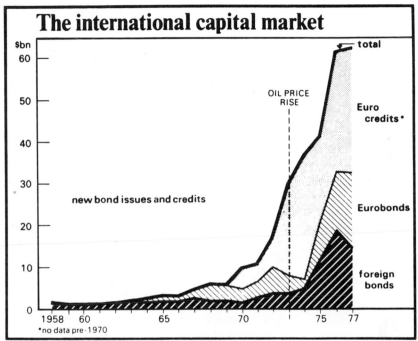

Figure 20.2

(Source: M.S. Mendelsohn, *Money on the Move* (New York: McGraw-Hill, 1980) p. 3. Reprinted by permission.)

interest rate serves to maintain the "spread" between deposit cost and the interest received on the Eurocredits. Though quite disadvantageous to the borrower, the floating rate feature certainly contributed greatly to the availability of Eurocredit loans in the large amounts demanded in the 1970s (more than $200 billion by some estimates). Most large-scale official borrowing, especially by developing and Communist nations, is accomplished by means of Eurocredits.

The banking syndicates that usually provide Eurocredit loans are not permanently affiliated; rather, they are formed by banks willing to participate in a particular loan. The borrower engages a *managing bank* (or banks) to put together a syndicate of participating banks and draw up a loan agreement. The managing bank receives a management fee (a percentage of the loan) for its efforts. *Lead banks* in the syndicate (those providing most of the funds) will receive from the managing bank a *participation* fee (a share of the management fee). A relatively small number of banks dominate Eurocredit lending—the largest U.S. and European banks.

Consortium banks also play a significant role in syndicated Eurocredit lending. These multinational banking consortia are joint ventures of two or more banks of different nations, and unlike the banking syndicates, they are permanently affiliated. These consortia both channel business to their parent banks and undertake their own projects. Projects conducive to consortium handling, in addition to syndicated loans, include Eurobond issues, multicurrency loans, and merger or acquisition efforts across international borders.

International Bonds

There are two types of international bond issues: foreign bonds and Eurobonds. The Eurobond market is a relatively recent phenomenon, but foreign bond issues have been in existence for many years. The distinction between foreign bonds and Eurobonds was made in Chapter 19. A foreign bond issue differs from a domestic issue only in the fact that the issuer is not a resident of the country in which the bonds are sold. A foreign bond issue is denominated in the currency of the country of issue, and it is subject to all the laws and regulations governing securities in that country. Eurobonds, on the other hand, are truly international bond issues. They are typically underwritten and marketed by a multinational group of financial institutions, and they are sold to investors in a number of countries. Eurobonds may be denominated in any of one or several major currencies. They may even offer the investor certain options regarding currencies (described later in this chapter).

Effect of U.S. Capital Controls (1963–1974)

In the absence of government controls and restrictions and other market imperfections in the flow of international capital funds, the Eurobond market would not exist. Capital movements among nations would be effected by foreign bond issues in national markets. Further, if such unrestricted capital flows across national borders existed, interest rate differentials would tend to shrink to magnitudes reflecting only present and anticipated premiums and discounts on currencies.

Most of the restrictions on international capital flows reflect differences in the institutional and economic structure of nations—both in kind and degree of development—and in efforts of governments to control capital inflows and outflows for economic policy reasons. A striking example of the nature and impact of the latter type of restriction is the 1963–1974 program of the United States to control capital outflows.

Until 1963, the New York foreign bond market was the principal source of foreign capital for the world's nations, although the German, Swiss, and London markets were significant. New York offered a broad, deep, and efficient market characterized by relatively low interest rates and issuance costs. However, U.S. government concern over this country's balance-of-payments deficits prompted a series of actions, beginning in 1963, that were intended to sharply reduce the outflow of U.S. dollars to borrowers in other nations. (In the 1960–1964 period, private outflows of long-term and short-term capital increased from about $4 billion to almost $6.5 billion.)

In mid-1963, the United States imposed an *interest equalization tax* (IET) on the value of foreign securities purchased by U.S. residents. Except for the various exempted securities (those of Canada, developing nations, and international financial institutions), the IET had the effect of sharply curtailing the U.S. market for new foreign bonds. Predictably, foreign borrowers turned next to U.S. banks for direct loans. In 1965, such bank lending was brought under the purview of the capital-outflow controls program, and steps were also taken to curb direct foreign investment by U.S. business firms.

The U.S. capital-outflow controls program was an enormous stimulus for the Euro-credit and Eurobond markets (and to a lesser extent the Eurodollar market). Foreign borrowers who were shut out of the New York foreign bond market turned to Eurobond issues, as did many U.S. firms seeking long-term funds for their foreign operations. Dollar-denominated Eurobonds served as a means of tapping the large pool of offshore dollar deposits in Europe and elsewhere, since access to the domestic U.S. capital market was impeded by the IET and related measures. The volume of Eurobond issues rose from only $150 million in 1963 to $557 million in 1964, to more than a billion dollars by 1966, and to more than two billion dollars in 1967. Eurocredit lending also increased greatly (see Fig. 20.2).

Recent Developments in the Eurobond Market

Table 20.1 indicates the dollar amounts of Eurobond issues in recent years by the currency of denomination and by category of borrower. As shown in this table, non-U.S. companies have been the largest borrowers in the Eurobond market. Participation by U.S. companies dropped off sharply after the termination of the U.S. foreign investments control program in 1974, but it has recently resumed a great deal of its previous momentum.[8] Governments and various governmental entities have recently become major participants in the Eurobond market, accounting for more than 40 percent of new issues in 1978. International financial institutions, such as the World Bank, also account for a significant amount of Eurobond issues, although these organizations tend to favor foreign bond issues.

The U.S. dollar has been the dominant currency of denomination for Eurobonds, as shown in Table 20.1, followed by the German mark. The key factor in selecting a currency of denomination is its relative degree of exchange rate stability. The U.S. dollar's reputation in this regard has weakened somewhat in recent years, but it continues to command sufficient confidence (along with its continuing role as a vehicle and reserve currency) to be the favorite Eurobond currency.

Multiple Currency Bonds

Eurobonds either may be "straight" (denominated in a single currency) or may be denominated in multiple currencies. Although straight Eurobonds have been dominant, the volatility of exchange rates in recent years has made multicurrency bonds more popular. Outstanding multiple-currency issues amounted to almost a billion dollars by 1977.

---

8. The degree of interest of U.S. firms in the Eurobond market is largely a function of the U.S. dollar's strength in foreign exchange markets. A factor contributing to recent increased use of Eurobonds by U.S. firms is strong European interest in "Euroconvertibles" (Eurobonds ultimately convertible into common stock of the issuing firm), especially those of energy and energy-related companies.

Table 20.1 Dollar amounts of new Eurobond issues by borrower category and currency of denomination, 1968–1977 (millions of U.S. dollars)

	1966	1967	1968	1969	1970	1971	1972	1973	1974	1975	1976	1977
Eurobonds, total	$1142	$2002	$3573	$3156	$2966	$3642	$6335	$4193	$2134	$8567	$14,328	$17,735
By category of borrower												
U.S. companies	439	562	2096	1005	741	1098	1992	874	110	268	435	1,130
Other companies	376	575	603	817	1065	1119	1759	1309	640	2903	5,323	7,284
State enterprises	118	442	349	682	594	848	1170	947	542	3123	4,138	4,707
Governments	108	303	500	584	351	479	1019	659	482	1658	2,239	2,936
International organizations	101	120	25	68	215	98	395	404	360	615	2,193	1,678
By currency of denomination												
U.S. dollar	921	1780	2554	1723	1775	2221	3908	2447	996	3738	9,125	11,628
German mark	147	171	914	1338	688	786	1129	1025	344	2278	2,713	4,109
Dutch guilder	—	—	—	17	391	298	393	194	381	719	502	361
Other	74	51	105	78	112	337	905	262	179	610	443	935
Canadian dollar								0	60	558	1,407	674
French franc								166	0	293	39	0
European unit of account								99	174	371	99	28

Source: Morgan Guaranty Trust Company, *World Financial Markets*, New York, various issues.

Multiple currency bonds have two basic forms: option issues and composite-currency denomination issues. The former allows a bondholder to request payment of interest and principal in any of several currencies, not just in the currency of the loan. This option reduces exchange rate risk for the bondholder.

Suppose, for example, that a British investor buys such a bond with three currency options: Swiss francs, German marks, and U.S. dollars. If any or all of these currencies appreciate against the British pound, the investor will gain, and the amount of the gain will be determined by the currency that appreciates the *most*. The investor will suffer an exchange rate loss only if *all* the currencies depreciate relative to the British pound, and then the loss will be limited to that related to the currency that depreciates the *least*. This option obviously shifts most of the exchange rate risk of international bonds to the borrower.[9] One would thus expect such bonds to be issued by less-than-prime credit risks or, if issued by financially strong borrowers, to offer a lower yield relative to single-currency bonds.

Eurobonds denominated in a weighted-average composite of several different currencies (a so-called currency cocktail) generally share exchange rate risk between borrower and lender. The borrower gains if his or her home currency appreciates relative to the composite unit of account and loses if depreciation occurs. The reverse holds for the lender, in terms of his or her currency. For both the borrower and lender, exchange rate risk is dampened as compared with the case where only the borrower's currency and the lender's currency are involved. Several composite-currency units of account exist, but the European Unit of Account (based on nine European currencies) is the one that has been used most often in the past to denominate composite-currency Eurobonds. Special Drawing Rights (SDRs) also serve a composite-currency denominating function.[10]

In 1977, a number of non-U.S. firms began issuing convertible bonds that combined the usual feature of convertibility into shares of stock with an alternative-currency election for exercise of convertible rights. For example, a Swiss firm may issue dollar-denominated bonds convertible into a fixed number of shares with a stock price expressed in Swiss francs. If the Swiss franc appreciates against the dollar, the shares into which the bonds can be converted become more valuable in terms of dollars. (The opposite holds if the Swiss franc depreciates relative to the dollar.) Whether or not such conversion is profitable to the lender depends, of course, on market interest rates and stock price performance, as well as relative exchange rates. If the bonds are not converted, as they are unlikely to be unless the dollar

---

9. Exchange rate risk on international bonds is very significant. Consider the purchase of a U.S. dollar-denominated Eurobond paying 9 percent per annum at par value of $1000 by a foreign national when the exchange rate is two units of his or her currency per U.S. dollar (2LC/$). Suppose that the exchange rate one year later is 1.5LC/$. The per annum interest of $90, which was equivalent at the time of purchase to LC180, is now convertible to only LC135. Further, the bond's maturity value of $1000, equivalent to LC2000 when the investor acquired it, is now only LC1500. Although the bond's market price at the latter date will reflect many influences other than the local currency's appreciation relative to the dollar, the dollar's decline in value will surely have a dampening effect.

10. In 1980, the calculation of SDR value was changed by the IMF from a 16-currency base to a trade-weighted average of the world's major currencies—the U.S. dollar, British pound, German mark, Japanese yen, and French franc.

depreciates relative to the Swiss franc, the Swiss borrower will bear an exchange rate loss when the bonds are redeemed to the extent that the dollar appreciates relative to the Swiss franc.

At the time of the present writing, dual-currency convertible bonds appear to be winning wide acceptance. They are often denominated in such strong currencies as the German mark and the Swiss franc (because of the relatively low interest rates on borrowings in these currencies), as well as in U.S. dollars, Japanese firms have been the most active issuers of such bonds, but European firms are also using this new borrowing instrument.

Interest Rates on International Bonds

Interest rates on foreign bonds and Eurobonds generally approximate those of domestic bonds of the country in whose currency they are denominated. Exceptions to this general paralleling of domestic and international bond rates occur when a country imposes capital controls for balance of payments or other reasons. For example, the interest equalization tax included in the 1963–1974 U.S. program to curtail capital outflows significantly increased the effective interest cost of foreign bond issues in this country. On the other hand, Switzerland, which has had persistent surpluses in its balance of payments (and thus a strong currency), has often encouraged international borrowers to borrow Swiss francs.

In addition to home country interest rates and the effects of home government policies, international bond rates are directly related to bond rates in other currencies and prevailing Eurocurrency money market rates. As in the case of the Eurocurrency loans previously discussed, effective interest rates on Eurobonds are directly related to anticipated exchange rate changes. If the currency in which a Eurobond is denominated appreciates, the percentage increase in exchange rate value relative to an investor's home currency is an addition to his investment yield rate, and vice versa for depreciation.

The market for dollar-denominated Eurobonds and the Eurodollar market are closely linked. Eurodollar holders frequently shift into short-term holdings of Eurobonds when current or expected rate differentials make such a move attractive. Central banks in countries of Eurobond issue may prefer (and thus encourage) the purchase of dollar-denominated Eurobonds with Eurodollars, since this reduces use of domestic currency and thus minimizes exchange rate pressures. As Eurodollars are shifted into Eurobonds, rates on the former will tend to rise, and the rate differential between Eurodollar loans and Eurobond yields will narrow until such substitution ceases to be attractive to investors.

Institutional Aspects of Eurobond Issues

As indicated in Chapter 19, Eurobond issues are usually managed by multinational syndicates of European banks and U.S. investment banking firms. One or two of these participating institutions will manage the issue, and the other participants (often more than twenty) will subscribe for it. A second larger group of banks, securities firms, and dealers (perhaps as many as a hundred) acts as the selling group, placing the securities with clients or taking them for their own portfolios. This ''selling'' operation is more akin to a U.S. private placement than to a public issue.

The multinational nature of Eurobond issues epitomizes the internationalization of finance in recent decades. To a remarkable degree, the financial systems of the world's nations have become linked together in recent decades by the emergence of huge, efficient international financial markets and by the corresponding development of multinational financial institutions. We turn now to the latter aspects of the international financial system, focusing primarily on the international operations of this country's commercial banks.

U.S. COMMERCIAL BANKING ABROAD

During the past two decades, international banking operations have grown at a phenomenal rate. The highest rate of growth has been in multinational activities of U.S. banks. This country, particularly as compared with such European nations as Great Britain, is very much a newcomer to international banking. Only since the Second World War, when U.S. corporations began their great wave of overseas expansion, have U.S. banks moved abroad in significant fashion. In a sense, U.S. banks were following their largest customers abroad—customers they wished to retain. By 1977, more than 140 U.S. banks had foreign branches. There were more than 750 of these branches, with their total assets amounting to more than $250 billion. Table 20.2 indicates the growth of foreign branch assets of U.S. banks since 1970.

Table 20.2 Domestic and foreign branch assets of U.S. commercial banks, 1970–1979 (billions of dollars)

Assets as of December	Foreign branches	Domestic offices	Total	Foreign as percentage of total
1970	47.4	576.2	623.6	7.6
1971	61.3	640.3	701.6	8.7
1972	78.2	739.0	817.2	9.6
1973	121.9	835.2	957.1	12.7
1974	151.9	919.6	1071.5	14.2
1975	176.5	938.4	1134.9	15.6
1976	219.5	1010.8	1230.3	17.8
1977	258.9	1145.4	1402.9	18.4
1978	306.8	1268.6	1575.4	19.5
1979	364.2	1351.0	1715.2	21.2

Sources: *Federal Reserve Bulletin*, various issues.

Some of the most significant expansion in U.S. banks' international activities has taken place under the aegis of legislation passed early in this century. The 1919 Edge Act (an amendment to the Federal Reserve Act) authorized the Fed's Board of Governors to permit the establishment of corporations "for the purpose of engaging in international or foreign banking . . . either directly or through the ownership, or control of local institutions in foreign countries." U.S. banks were thus allowed to engage in international banking activities and acquire foreign banks by the establishment of federally chartered subsidiary "Edge Act corporations" (EACs).[11]

The Edge Act permitted U.S. banks to indirectly own foreign bank subsidiaries, although they were long prohibited from doing so directly. Further, the Edge Act permitted EACs to have U.S. offices, although such domestic offices can be used to engage only in activities directly related to foreign operations. Banks operating internationally through Edge Act subsidiaries use such U.S. offices (often located in Chicago, Los Angeles, Miami, San Francisco, and Houston) to service their multinational customers, to accept deposits related to foreign transactions, and to refer potential new customers to the parent bank. Such offices have permitted large U.S. banks to develop an interstate network of banking services, despite the legal prohibition of interstate branching. This development was expedited when, in 1979, the Federal Reserve System excluded EACs from the interstate branching rule. Edge Act corporations may now, subject to approval by the Fed, establish and operate branches in other states. The Fed took this action under the mandate of the International Banking Act of 1978, which includes a directive to the Fed for relaxation of restrictions on EACs in order to allow them to compete more effectively at home and abroad with foreign banks operating in the United States (which are allowed interstate branches).[12]

Edge Act overseas subsidiaries are generally allowed to engage in activities common to foreign banking practice in the host country, even though such activities may be prohibited in the United States (or even to the country's own resident banks). EACs are regulated by the Federal Reserve System; the Fed governs the scope of operations of both the domestic and the foreign offices and must approve all equity participations in foreign institutions.

Scope of Foreign Banking Operations

Although overseas operations of U.S. banks are notable in aggregate impact, only a relatively small proportion of this country's banking institutions (the largest banks) are involved. Only about one percent (approximately 140 of 14,500 banks) of U.S. banks have overseas branches or affiliates. Many of these 140 banks have only a few relatively small branches abroad or have only "shell" branches (essentially a set of accounts kept in a

---

11. "Agreement corporations," permitted under earlier legislation, are similar to EACs but of much less importance. In 1977 there were only six agreement corporations, as compared with 113 EACs.

12. Foreign bank branching was restricted by the International Banking Act of 1978. Interstate branching by foreign banks is still permitted, but only one branch can accept deposits. (Branches created before July 1978 are not affected.)

Caribbean-area or other such offshore office, where international transactions originating in the United States are recorded). Ownership of more than 80 percent of overseas branches and affiliates and 90 percent of all overseas banking assets is held by only 20 U.S. banks. As might be expected, these same banks also dominate domestic banking, holding more than 30 percent of U.S. bank assets.

Overseas branches and affiliates of U.S. banks are located throughout the world. Of the total, 30 percent are located in Latin America, 20 percent in Europe, and 20 percent in Asia. Most of the others are shell branches located in the Bahamas and the Cayman Islands. Because of London's special significance in international finance, U.S. banks are heavily represented in that city, with about 50 branches and affiliates in London in 1975.

Overseas operations have provided U.S. banks with both the means and the incentive to significantly deepen and broaden their international lending. Besides traditional export and import financing and lending to U.S. multinational firms and their foreign affiliates, U.S. banks' foreign assets now include extensive amounts of loans to foreign local firms, foreign banks, and foreign governments and their various entities.

In addition to increased amounts of overseas lending, a number of U.S. banks have undertaken extensive diversification programs abroad. To a large degree, such diversification was necessary for U.S. banks to compete effectively with their European counterparts, which have traditionally offered their customers a full range of financing services. A domestic base for worldwide diversification was provided in the late 1960s, as one-bank holding companies provided a means for involvement in such activities as leasing, factoring, cash management, and mortgage banking. The Federal Reserve Board has generally permitted such "finance-related" activities of Edge Act subsidiaries abroad. (Foreign branches are limited to the same activities permitted to their U.S. parent banks.) Such large U.S. banks as Bank of America, First National Bank of Chicago, and Manufacturers Hanover Trust have investment banking subsidiaries in Europe.

Expansion of foreign operations has been a very significant aspect of overall profitability for some U.S. banks in recent years. From 1970 to 1975, 95 percent of total earnings growth for 13 large U.S. banks were attributable to international operations, with foreign earnings accounting for almost half of total earnings. For these same banks, more than 20 percent of total assets were held abroad.[13]

FOREIGN BANKS IN THE UNITED STATES

As U.S. banks have greatly increased the scope and volume of their offshore operations, foreign banks have become much more visible and active in this country. Foreign bank assets in the U.S. grew from about $7 billion in 1965 to about $134 billion in 1979. (The composition of foreign bank assets and liabilities is shown in Table 20.3.) In 1977, there

---

13. Salomon Brothers, *United States Multinational Banking*, New York, 1976.

Table 20.3 Foreign bank assets and liabilities in U.S., September 30, 1977 (millions of dollars)

Assets	
Cash	$12.4
Investments	4.7
Loans	45.2
Customers' liabilities on acceptances and letters of credit	3.2
Due from directly related institutions	14.9
Other assets	1.8
Total assets	$82.2
Liabilities	
Demand deposits	$15.7
Time and savings deposits	17.2
Other borrowing	16.3
Liabilities on acceptances and letters of credit	3.4
Other liabilities	1.3
Due to directly related institutions	26.0
Reserves and capital accounts	2.3
Total liabilities	$82.2

Note: These data do not include assets and liabilities of U.S. financial institutions owned by nonresidents. Source: Federal Reserve Board of Governors, "Monthly Report of Condition for U.S. Agencies, Branches and Domestic Banking Subsidiaries of Foreign Banks as of Report Date in October 1977," Washington, D.C., 1977.

were 222 foreign banks with offices in the United States. These offices, which included foreign investment companies, representative offices, and agencies, as well as banks, totaled more than 400.[14] Foreign bank operations are presently being carried on in only 12 states, and they are concentrated in the cities of New York, Los Angeles, San Francisco, Chicago, and Houston.

The reasons for the rapid growth of foreign bank operations in the United States are similar to those accounting for the expanded overseas operations of U.S. banks. Just as U.S. banks followed multinational U.S. firms abroad, foreign banks have followed their customers into U.S. operations. Investments in the United States by foreign firms have grown enormously in recent years as a consequence of both the decline in value of the U.S. dollar (U.S. assets have become relatively cheaper in terms of many foreign currencies) and a higher rate of economic growth in this country as compared with most European countries. The latter factor also serves to make the United States an attractive arena for foreign banks to

---

14. An *agency* is similar to a branch, except that most countries do not allow agencies to accept public deposits. Agencies perform many functions relating to international finance, including trade financing, issuance of letters of credit, and foreign exchange operations. *Representative offices,* much more limited than agencies, amount essentially to an information and liaison office for the parent bank.

pursue new lending business. In addition to these factors, foreign banks have initiated or expanded U.S. operations in order to operate outside home country restrictions and regulatory constraints, to improve their access to U.S. money and capital markets, and to obtain a new source of dollars by competing for deposits.

U.S. Regulation of Foreign Banking

In October 1978, the U.S. Congress, by unanimous vote, enacted the International Banking Act. This legislation reflected congressional reaction to the rapid growth of foreign banking in the United States, in conjunction with concern about the lack of federal jurisdiction over foreign banks. Additional impetus came from several successful and attempted acquisitions of U.S. banks by foreign banks. (In 1979, at least 109 U.S. banks had more than 10 percent foreign ownerships.) The purpose of the Act was to establish a framework for Federal Reserve supervision and regulation of foreign banking and to put foreign banks operating in this country on the same footing as domestic banks insofar as governmental restrictions are concerned.

Foreign banks have expanded rapidly in this country for reasons that are similar to those for U.S. bank overseas expansion. They include both the wish to "follow" non-U.S. firms that have U.S. subsidiaries and the wish to operate outside various home country restrictions and regulatory constraints. Foreign banks also seek to improve their access to U.S. money and capital markets and to obtain a new source of dollars by competing for deposits.

U.S. regulation of foreign banking has been primarily a state responsibility. Almost all foreign banks are state-chartered, since national banks must belong to the Federal Reserve System, and all directors must be U.S. citizens. With the passage of the 1970 Bank Holding Company Act, the Federal Reserve System gained certain statutory authority over foreign bank *subsidiaries,* but not jurisdiction over foreign branches and agencies. Many observers have viewed the lack of federal control over foreign banks as at best something of an anomaly and at worst a serious problem. It has also been argued that foreign banks in the United States have certain advantages over U.S. banks, such as exemption from federal laws forbidding U.S. banks to branch across state lines or to engage in investment banking activities. Regardless of the merit of such arguments, the enactment of the International Banking Act of 1978 is evidence that they were taken seriously by legislators. The present level of concern in the U.S. Congress for these and other issues pertaining to U.S.-foreign banking relationships will probably result in other significant legislative action in the near future.

INTERNATIONAL BANKING AND FINANCIAL MARKETS: A NEED FOR CONTROLS?

The rapid growth of international banking and of international money and capital markets has, not unexpectedly, triggered concern about potential problems for domestic economic policy and for domestically oriented financial institutions. The first concern relates primarily to the impact that international markets may have on the efficiency of domestic monetary policy. The second concern focuses on possible inequities that may be present between, on the one hand, large banks having easy access to unregulated international money markets and foreign banks not subject to much domestic regulation and, on the other hand, small domestic financial institutions that lack either potential advantage. A truly international concern is that unregulated offshore currency markets have spawned a huge pool of "stateless" money that causes chronic instability in the foreign exchange market.

Whether or not these concerns are valid (or to what extent) is outside the purpose of this book. The advent of extensive international regulation of external financial markets, however, would have a pronounced impact on their size and the nature of their operations. The subject thus warrants some attention.

Concern about the lack of regulation of offshore currency markets is most evident among U.S. officials. In 1979, the Carter administration launched an unsuccessful worldwide diplomatic effort to persuade foreign governments to implement, through their central banks, reserve requirements for Eurocurrency deposits. United States proposals to establish a system of global governmental control over international markets and institutions included a plan for each major central bank to regulate foreign branches of its own banks. (This proposal would require the United States to relinquish its present system of foreign bank regulation.) Various other suggestions for restricting international banking and financial markets have been offered, including limits on bank loans to foreign nationals and other means of curbing such loans.

Predictably, banks heavily committed to offshore operations are fiercely opposed to the imposition of such restrictions. Their basic argument is that the existence of external financial intermediation poses no significant economic problems but rather contributes to international capital mobility and commerce. These and other opponents of international regulation perceive its threatened implementation as an outgrowth of an irresistible impulse among regulators to expand their control to the world's last free financial market. Such countries as Britain and Switzerland, whose banks secure a large share of their profits from Eurocurrency operations, are opposed to the U.S. and German push for restrictions.

Proponents of controls do not seek to destroy the Euromarket, but they do wish to check its growth. The rate of growth in Eurocurrency deposits during the 1974–1979 period averaged 22 percent a year. This rapid growth in international liquidity (much of it in this period due to deposits of petrodollars by OPEC nations) is seen as posing an increasingly potent barrier to effective monetary control in the United States and other nations. Further, the larger the Eurocurrency market becomes, the more vulnerable the world's financial and exchange rate system is to this pool of uncontrolled funds.

Such measures as the imposition of worldwide reserve requirements would certainly have a significant impact on offshore currency markets. The cost of funds in these markets would immediately rise, reducing (or eliminating) the present deposit and lending rate advantage of Eurobanks. Such a system of international reserve requirements, if a high degree of cooperation and coordination were achieved among the world's central banks, would be a formidable tool of global economic policy.

SUMMARY

International financial markets have been greatly broadened and deepened in recent decades by the emergence and rapid development of the Eurocurrency and Eurobond markets. Because these markets involve transactions in bank deposits located outside the nation of their currency of denomination, they offer participants the opportunity to engage in lending and borrowing outside the regulatory framework of any nation. Relative to domestic U.S. banks, the absence of reserve requirements and a minimum of restrictions allow Eurobanks to offer higher deposit yields and lower loan rates. The Eurobond market offers a similar means of avoiding regulatory constraints. The freedom that characterizes these markets is one of the principal reasons for their spectacular growth since their inception in the late 1950s.

The Eurodollar market is closely linked to domestic U.S. money markets because of the identical currency, the leading role of U.S. banks and U.S. multinational corporations in the Eurodollar market, and the relative ease with which participants in either the domestic or Euromarket can switch to the other. Thus rate-structure and funds-availability conditions in the two markets tend to move very closely together. The Eurodollar market continues to dominate the offshore deposit (Eurocurrency) market, with dollar deposits accounting for about 75 percent of total offshore bank deposits. The Eurocurrency market is dominated by interbank transactions in short-term deposits in very large amounts—essentially a "wholesale" market—but is also a significant credit source for nonbank borrowers.

The market for Eurobonds, bonds denominated in a currency other than that of the country of issue, and the Eurocredit market (intermediate-term lending of Eurocurrency) experienced dramatic growth as a result of the U.S. capital-outflows control program of the 1960s. The program effectively closed the New York capital market to many foreign and U.S. multinational firms, obliging them to turn to the Euromarket for capital funds. The U.S. dollar is the predominant currency of denomination for Eurobonds and the most frequently borrowed Eurocredit currency. Thus the Eurocurrency capital market is closely linked to the Eurodollar market and the domestic U.S. capital markets.

The huge increase in international trade and investment since the 1950s has spurred a corresponding expansion in international banking. Though relative latecomers to the international banking scene, U.S. banks have established an extensive worldwide network of overseas operations during this period. More recently, U.S. banks have been confronted with increasing foreign bank competition in their domestic markets.

The enormous economic influence of international banking and financial markets has generated a great deal of concern among national financial regulatory authorities, who fear that domestic monetary and financial policies will be outflanked by "stateless" money and financial arrangements. To this point in time, the concern has resulted in only relatively minor attempts to extend regulatory controls over international financial markets and institutions.

QUESTIONS

1. "Every Eurodollar deposit is linked to a domestic U.S. deposit." Explain why this statement is correct.

2. What were some of the principal reasons for the emergence and growth of the Eurodollar market?

3. Evaluate the following statement (from an 8/30/74 editorial in the *Wall Street Journal*): "In the Eurocurrency markets there are no reserve requirements at all, which means that $1 of reserve can be multiplied endlessly—theoretically, if the banks lost all prudence, into millions of dollars of bank deposits."

4. Compare interest rate structure and behavior in the domestic U.S. money markets and the Eurodollar market.

5. Discuss the major participants in the Eurodollar market. How does their participation serve to link the Eurodollar market and the domestic U.S. money market?

6. Why did the U.S. capital-outflows control program of 1963–1974 spur the development of the Eurobond and Eurocredit markets?

7. Describe "currency option" Eurobonds. Why is this feature attractive to investors?

8. Compare the development of U.S. overseas banking and foreign banking in the United States.

REFERENCES

Aliber, Robert Z., "International Banking: Growth and Regulation," *Columbia Journal of World Business,* Winter 1975, pp. 5–9.

Dufey, Gunter, and Ian H. Giddy, *The International Money Market* (Englewood Cliffs, N.J.: Prentice-Hall, 1978).

Hewson, John, and Eisuke Sakakibara, *The Eurocurrency Markets and Their Implications* (Lexington, Mass.: D.C. Heath, 1975).

Lees, Francis A., *International Banking and Finance* (New York: Wiley, 1974).

Lees, Francis A., and Maximo Eng, *International Financial Markets* (New York: Praeger, 1975).

Mendelsohn, M.S., *Money on the Move: The Modern International Capital Market* (New York: McGraw-Hill, 1980).

Ricks, David, and Jeffrey S. Arpan, "Foreign Banking in the United States," *Business Horizons,* February 1976, pp. 84–87.

United States Multinational Banking (New York: Salomon Brothers, 1976).

Part VI

Monetary, Fiscal, and Debt Management Policies

Chapter 21

Monetary Policy: Implementation and Impact

Chapter 7 of this book described the tools of monetary control available to the Federal Reserve and explained how the Fed uses these various instruments to implement monetary policy. The present chapter offers additional description and analysis of the Fed's policy instruments but focuses primarily on their economic effects. Monetary policy, the subject of this chapter, and fiscal policy, the subject of the next chapter, are the principal methods employed by the government in its attempts to achieve certain goals of economic policy. Thus the purpose of this chapter and Chapter 22 is to examine the nature of these policies and goals and the ways that policy actions impact on both the financial system and the real sector of the economy. We begin by describing the economic policy tools available to the government and explaining how they relate to economic activity. We then discuss policy objectives and some of the problems associated with their pursuit. The remainder of the chapter focuses on monetary policy.

ECONOMIC POLICY AND ECONOMIC ACTIVITY

The economic policy tools that may be employed in a market economy (such as that of this country) may be grouped into three types: monetary policy, fiscal policy, and incomes policy. The first two policy types generally impact broadly across the economy, although certain instruments of selective impact are included among the various measures of both monetary and fiscal policy. For example, monetary policy includes (presently or potentially) various consumer credit controls and margin requirements on security purchases.[1] Fiscal policy includes spending programs and tax measures that focus on relatively narrow segments of the economy. In general, however, monetary and fiscal policy are aimed at the aggregate level of spending in the economy, perhaps the broadest possible target for an economic policy tool.

Economic Policy and Aggregate Demand

Both fiscal and monetary policy are intended to impact on aggregate demand in the economy—the total spending for goods and services. Restraining an expansion of aggregate demand is the intent of an anti-inflationary policy, since a reduction in demand for goods and services presumably dampens the tendency for prices and wages to rise. On the other hand, the stimulation of aggregate demand by policy action is presumed to bring forth an increase in aggregate supply—the quantity of goods and services produced—thus expanding employment as well as output and income.

Aggregate demand has four components: consumption, investment, net exports, and government spending (see Fig. 21.1).[2] *Consumption demand* is the spending for durable goods (cars, furniture, appliances, etc.), nondurable goods (food, clothing, etc.), and for services (transportation, entertainment, medical care, etc.). Income is the principal determinant of consumption spending, but the ratio of consumption to income (percentage of income spent on consumption) is affected in varying degrees by such factors as wealth, expectations, and interest rates.

Investment demand is composed of business spending for plant and equipment (business fixed investment), changes in business inventories, and household-sector spending for residential housing. Changes in business inventories are determined, of course, by the difference between production and sales, and though important, they account for a relatively small part of total investment spending.[3] The amount of business fixed investment is

---

1. The Credit Control Act of 1969 permits the President to authorize the Fed to "regulate and control any and all extensions of credit" when deemed necessary to control inflation.

2. Aggregate demand—in total and in its various components—may be viewed as an *ex ante* (before the fact) schedule of potential amounts of aggregate spending, or as an *ex post* (after the fact) amount that was expended during some past period. *Ex ante* aggregate demand can thus be unequal to aggregate supply (*ex ante* and *ex post*), but *ex post* aggregate spending necessarily equals *ex post* aggregate supply—the amount sold must be equal to the amount bought.

Aggregate supply includes goods and services produced for *export* to the rest of the world, and aggregate domestic spending includes *imports* from the rest of the world. Thus exports increase the gross national product (GNP), but imports do not; i.e., GNP = consumption + investment + government spending + (exports − imports).

3. Changes in inventories constitute an "early warning" indicator of shifts in the level of economic activity. Businesses generally attempt to maintain stable inventory levels (harmonize production and sales), but their ability to do so is a function of the level of stability in the economy and/or their ability to forecast future sales. Unexpected surges in demand thus result in reduced inventories, and unexpected sales dips result in inventory buildup.

MAJOR COMPONENTS OF GROSS NATIONAL PRODUCT

SEASONALLY ADJUSTED ANNUAL RATES, QUARTERLY

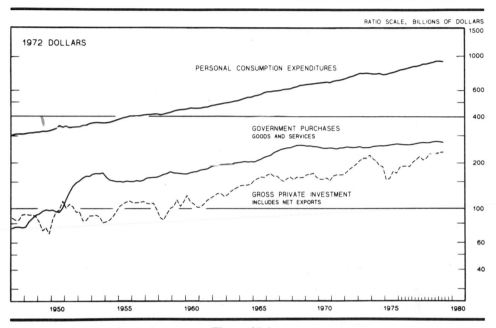

Figure 21.1

(Source: Board of Governors of the Federal Reserve System, *Historical Chart Book.*)

largely determined by business firms' expectations of future sales volume (and thus production volume) in relation to existing capacity and inventory levels. The availability and cost of funds to finance plant and equipment expansion are also significant. The degree of sensitivity of investment spending to the interest rate—the relationship of changes in investment spending to changes in the rate of interest—is termed the *interest elasticity* of investment demand.

The demand for residential housing is viewed as quite responsive to credit conditions. Higher interest rates for mortgage credit and reduced availability of mortgage lending curtail this component of investment spending, whereas eased credit conditions stimulate it. Various demographic factors outside the purview of economic policy, such as the age composition of the population, are also critical determinants of spending for residential housing.

Total *government spending* is the sum of the expenditures of the federal, state, and local governments. Although the spending of all government units has significant economic impact, only federal spending is considered to be a fiscal policy tool aimed at the management of aggregate demand in the economy.

Monetary and fiscal policy are thus intended to affect consumption, investment, and state and local government (not federal) spending. The presumed effectiveness of monetary policy as an instrument of economic stabilization is dependent on a relatively stable and systematic (and thus predictable) relationship between the money supply (and perhaps various other financial variables) and the various components of aggregate demand. Increases in the money supply should stimulate aggregate demand and thus result in expanded employment and production; and vice versa for decreases in the money stock.

Fiscal policy affects aggregate demand via the balance between government *tax collections* (which withdraw purchasing power from the economy) and government spending (which injects purchasing power into the economy). When expenditures exceed tax receipts, aggregate spending increases, rippling through the economy to create additional income in some multiple of the excess of spending over taxes. Output and employment rise concurrently. The reverse effect holds for an excess of tax collections over government spending.[4]

Incomes Policy

Incomes policy, essentially an anti-inflation policy, represents an attempt by government to restrain prices, profits, and wages directly rather than through the indirect mechanism of aggregate-demand restraint. Such a policy, both in its compulsory and "voluntary" variations, has been invoked on several occasions in recent decades. The perennial popularity and political appeal of incomes policy can be attributed to a number of things, including the following.

1. The fact that wage-price controls, unlike the esoteric workings of monetary and fiscal policy, are readily comprehensible to the lay public.

2. The belief that some inflationary bouts are due to "structural imperfections" in the economy that push up costs and prices in the absence of excessive aggregate demand.

3. The view of a number of professional economists that an incomes policy can restrain prices while monetary and fiscal policies (which obviously impact much more slowly on the price level) are taking hold and "wringing out" inflationary expectations.

Neither an analysis of the likely effectiveness of incomes policy nor an account of its use in this country is within the scope of this book. However, direct economic controls (of any sort) alter the pattern of resource allocation (relative to a market-determined path) to a much greater degree than do economic measures that impact more generally. Further, the "track record" of wage-price controls is rather dismal.

Economic Policy and Aggregate Supply

The point is often made that, since monetary and fiscal policy impact directly only on aggregate demand, changes in aggregate supply occur as a consequence of changes in

---

4. Whether or not these fiscal effects, independent of monetary expansion, result in sustainable increases or decreases in income is an issue of considerable debate and will be considered at a later point in this chapter.

aggregate demand. This aspect is of special significance for anti-inflation policies. So-called demand-pull inflation amounts to an excess of aggregate demand over aggregate supply at the existing price level; prices of goods and services rise to fill the "inflationary gap." Monetary and fiscal policies are aimed at closing the inflationary gap by *curbing aggregate demand*. Unfortunately, the impact of these policies is not only on inflationary "fat" but on real output "muscle." In effect, the price of an aggregate-demand-policy-induced reduction in the inflation rate is the goods and services forgone because of the policy's impact on output and employment.[5]

So-called supply-side economics is a response to this policy dilemma. This approach to curbing inflation emphasizes tax incentives and other policy measures to increase productivity and thus total output of goods and services. The objective is to close the inflationary gap by increasing aggregate supply rather than by decreasing aggregate demand. Discussion and analysis of supply-side economics would take us too far afield, but we will note here only that, irrespective of the extent that policymakers turn their attention to aggregate-supply stimulus measures, appropriate aggregate-demand policies remain important for economic stability.

GOALS OF ECONOMIC POLICY

The standard litany of economic goals is full employment, price stability, sustainable economic growth, and a "balanced" balance of payments. One of the many difficulties in "managing the economy" is the fact that monetary and fiscal measures appropriate for the achievement of one of these goals are often counterproductive to one or more of the other goals. For example, policies aimed at increasing employment and the rate of economic growth conventionally focus on monetary expansion and fiscal stimulus (increased government spending and/or a reduction in taxes). A resulting increase in economic activity may create both inflationary pressures and balance-of-payments problems. The threat to price stability emerges even before the economy reaches full employment, because various imperfections in the markets for productive resources cause scarcities that trigger price increases. (Once full employment of available resources is attained, any additional stimulus will result only in inflation—money income will rise but not real income.) A further potential difficulty with a policy of stimulus is that, since the volume of imports increases with income, a balance-of-payments problem may develop as imports expand more than exports. There are other difficulties in pursuing the various goals of economic policy, but prior to assessing some of these problems, we present a brief overview of the goals themselves.

---

5. According to the estimates of the late Arthur M. Okun ("Efficient Disinflationary Policies," *American Economic Review,* May 1978, pp. 348–352), it takes about a 1-percent increase in unemployment in a year to cut the inflation rate 0.3 percent, and a loss of real GNP (relative to potential) of about 10 percent to bring about a 1-percent decrease in the rate of inflation in a given year.

Full Employment

The worldwide Great Depression of the 1930s was characterized by massive and unprecedented unemployment. In addition to the human suffering and shocking waste of human and material potential that this economic crisis entailed, it contributed in large measure to the chain of events that culminated in the Second World War. Thus it is not surprising that full employment emerged as the paramount economic objective of this country (and most other countries) in the postwar period. Indeed, by act of Congress (the Employment Act of 1946), the promotion of ''maximum employment, production, and purchasing power'' was named as a goal of government.

Full employment does not mean a zero unemployment rate; rather, it means an employment level that allows for ''friction'' in the labor market, such as workers changing jobs and new entrants into the labor force finding jobs. The amount of friction is in turn affected by the composition of the labor force. There is disagreement as to what level of unemployment is acceptable in the pursuit of a full-employment goal. The term *natural rate of unemployment* has been given to that level of unemployment at which the demand and supply of *available* labor are equal and there is neither upward nor downward pressure on the real (price-level-adjusted) wage rate. There is no operational measure of the natural rate of unemployment (although some economists have estimated it to be about 6 or 7 percent for the United States). However, the concept does serve as a vehicle for the argument that government economic stimulus in the pursuit of ''full employment'' has frequently unleashed inflationary pressures. During the decade of the 1970s, this view won enough adherents to cause the ''acceptable'' rate of unemployment, among professional economists, to rise.[6] Many economists viewed the target for unemployment of the 1978 Full Employment and Balanced Growth Act (the Humphrey-Hawkins Act)—4 percent overall and 3 percent for workers over the age of 20—as inflationary at the time of enactment, despite the fact that a 4-percent unemployment rate had been the ''full employment'' benchmark for many years. As indicated in Fig. 21.2, this goal has been elusive since the early 1950s.

Inflation

The paramount economic problem of the U.S. economy since 1965 has been inflation. As indicated in Fig. 21.3, the purchasing power of the dollar greatly eroded in the 1966–1979 period. Indeed, the entire post–World War II era has been characterized by a rising price level.[7] As measured by the Consumer Price Index (CPI), the price level has declined in only

---

6. In the 1950s and 1960s, ''full employment'' was deemed to be achieved at a 4-percent unemployment rate. In the late 1960s, the latter rate was boosted to 4½ percent and then to 5 percent in the 1970s.

7. The U.S. economy was periodically plagued by inflation before World War II, but such inflationary periods were followed by periods of declining prices. It is estimated that the general price level in 1940 was approximately the same as in 1800.

LABOR FORCE, EMPLOYMENT, AND UNEMPLOYMENT

SEASONALLY ADJUSTED, QUARTERLY

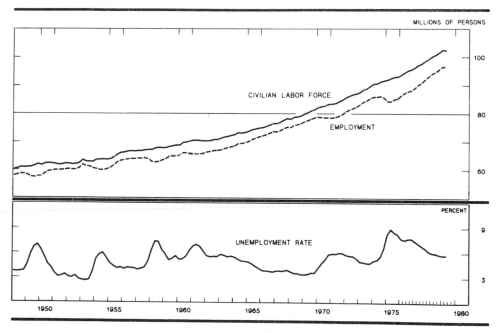

Figure 21.2
(Source: Board of Governors of the Federal Reserve System, *Historical Chart Book.*)

40|
119|

CONSUMER PRICES   ALL ITEMS

QUARTERLY AVERAGES, 1913–

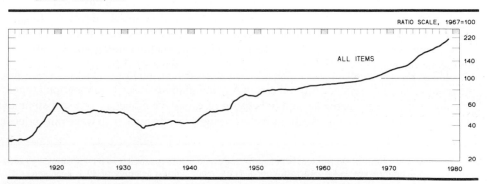

Figure 21.3
(Source: Board of Governors of the Federal Reserve System, *Historical Chart Book.*)

two periods since 1945 (the 1948–1949 and 1954–1955 periods), and these dips were very slight. Between 1948 and 1965, the CPI rose at an average annual rate of about 1.7 percent, but it increased at an average annual rate of 6.5 percent from 1966 to 1979. "Double-digit inflation" came in 1973 and returned again in 1979 and 1980.

Why has inflation been so persistent and severe in recent years? There are a great variety of explanations, and it may be of interest to list some of the most commonly cited ones.

1. *Excessive monetary growth.* There exists a close statistical relationship between growth of the money supply and changes in the price level. Although such association does not necessarily mean causation, many economists (so-called monetarists) consider excessive monetary growth to be the salient cause of inflation.

2. *Large and continuous deficit federal spending.* Since 1960, the federal budget has been balanced or in surplus only twice, resulting in a huge increase in the national debt. Although some observers emphasize the monetary aspects of deficit spending and others emphasize its direct stimulus to the economy (as discussed in the next chapter), there is general agreement that postwar fiscal policies have contributed to inflation.

3. *Externally imposed price "shocks."* The principal example here, of course, is the huge hike in oil prices since 1973. Because of the large and pervasive role of petroleum in the production of goods and services, the OPEC-mandated oil-price increases had to raise the general price level unless there were offsetting declines in other costs. Such price declines, in a modern industrialized economy, are likely only if employment and output decline sharply—perhaps to an unacceptable degree.[8]

4. *Wages, productivity, and expectations relationships.* Labor costs are the most significant component of the total costs of most goods and services. When wages rise more than productivity (output per hour of work), prices can be expected to rise. Workers have an incentive to press for such inflationary wage increases, either to increase their share of the "economic pie" or, if they *expect* inflation, to maintain the size of their current share. Thus *inflationary expectations* can be self-fulfilling as a "wage-price spiral" develops. Lagging productivity gains (an average annual increase of only about 1 percent since 1973 versus 2–3 percent average rates in previous years) exacerbate such an inflationary tendency.

There are a number of other possible causes of recent inflation, most of which (like those above) are interrelated. A usual dichotomy of inflation causes is demand-pull (aggregate demand exceeds aggregate supply because of excessive monetary or fiscal stimulus) and cost-push (structural imperfections in the economy tend to ratchet up wages and prices).

---

8. The *downward* rigidity of many prices in industrialized economies is apparent, and it is explained by various legal (i.e., minimum wage laws) and institutional (i.e., labor unions) features of such economies. This phenomenon has been labeled the "ratchet" effect—prices go up but not down. Perhaps the basic reason for the ratchet effect is the unwillingness of most modern governments to permit the kind of economic declines that, in previous eras, forced prices (and wages) down.

Rather than developing a more detailed assessment of the origins of inflation, we may accept the premise that its causes are complex and turn to an assessment of some of its ill effects.

Inflation is an economic problem because of its effects on the distribution of income, which pose equity concerns and create social and political tensions, and its effects on the allocation of resources, which pose a threat to economic growth.[9] During inflationary periods, real (inflation-adjusted) income tends to shift from groups that do not have the market power, institutional status, legal ability, and/or foresight to keep their money incomes increasing in step with the price level to those groups that do. A powerful union, for example, may impose an "escalator clause" (indexing wage rates to the CPI) on management and thus protect its members from inflation. The U.S. Congress may choose to protect certain groups of recipients of government paychecks in similar fashion, as it has done for Social Security beneficiaries, military retirees, and retired federal employees. On the other hand, such groups as professors at state colleges and universities can only hope that state legislators will choose to boost their salaries in keeping with inflation rates in a timely fashion—an action that has only rarely been taken.

Inflation also tends to shift income from taxpayers to government. With progressive-rate income taxes, rising money income (even if corresponding to falling real income) will move taxpayers into higher tax brackets and may result in a greater proportion of real as well as money income being paid in taxes. And corporate tax payments increase (even if profits are constant), because cost-based depreciation allowances lag behind real capital consumption.

Inflation is likely to be injurious to both saving and investment. Although it can be argued that efficient financial markets impound expectations about inflation (the risk-return implications) into security prices, inflation will still discourage the flow of saving into financial assets to the extent that savers do not believe in the existence of such efficiency.[10] Certainly surges of "unexpected" inflation, such as the early 1980 price-level spurt (which sent interest rates soaring and bond prices tumbling), persuade many individuals to plow their available funds into personal possessions (and perhaps precious stones and metals), rather than into purchases of financial assets or productive real assets.

Inflation not only jeopardizes the availability of funds for investment but also tends to make most potential investment projects less attractive to business managers. Business firms undertake investment projects according to much the same risk-return decision criteria that characterize the purchase of financial assets. The prospect of continuing inflation (at uncertain rates) has a significant, often pivotal, impact on the assessment of risk regarding proposed investment projects.

---

9. The point is often made that if all economic units in an economy correctly anticipated the rate of inflation and could adjust their factor receipts accordingly, the various ills of inflation would not result. This is true but hardly descriptive of actual economic behavior.

10. Debtors are generally viewed as "gainers" from inflation (and creditors as "losers"), since debts are repaid in depreciated dollars. Whether this is true for a particular debt, however, depends on the interest rate–inflation rate relationship.

Inflationary expectations thus may tend to distort the flow of funds in the economy, so money capital may be increasingly channeled into nonproductive uses. Efficiency in both the financial markets and the markets for goods and services may diminish as confidence in the future purchasing power of money wanes. Economic growth is inevitably and adversely affected by inflation when its occurrence and pace engender such behavior.

Economic Growth

Figure 21.4 indicates growth in the U.S. gross national product in recent years. Such growth is a measure of the rise in the material standard of living, which, if not ensuring a rise in the overall quality of life, does generally help. Economic growth is a consequence of an increase in the quantity of the factors of production and/or an increase in the productive capacity of these various factors.

Aggregate output may rise simply because labor, capital, or natural resources become more abundant. Output per worker, however, is likely to increase only if the latter two factors of production become more plentiful (cheaper). This aspect of economic growth is the reason for the importance of capital formation (and its necessary conditions, saving and investment). Economic growth is also made possible by an increase in the productive capacity of a given labor supply or stock of capital. Labor becomes more productive as skills are gained and improved by training and education. Capital becomes more productive as technological improvements in the use of capital occur, or as capital is used more intensively.

Economic growth is thus a more fundamental goal than either price stability or full employment. Economic growth is facilitated by both the full employment of resources and the appropriate degree of price change (not necessarily zero). Yet these conditions, though necessary for a maximum rate of economic growth, are not sufficient. The desire and capacity of people to save, invest, innovate, and simply "work hard" are the basic determinants of economic growth. An efficient financial system and a rational tax system can contribute to capital formation, but the necessary ingredients include social, cultural, and political factors as well as economic conditions.

Balance-of-Payments "Equilibrium"

As described in Chapter 19, the U.S. transition to a floating exchange rate regime reduced the direct role of the Federal Reserve in maintaining the value of the dollar in the foreign exchange market. However, the Fed still intervenes periodically to avoid violent fluctuations in the dollar's value, and the Fed's interest rate targets are surely influenced by international economic considerations. Further, the Fed acts as fiscal agent for the Treasury in its various international transactions.

The level of interest rates in the United States relative to other countries affects the capital-account-balance component of the balance of payments. If U.S. rates are relatively

GROSS NATIONAL PRODUCT

SEASONALLY ADJUSTED ANNUAL RATES, QUARTERLY

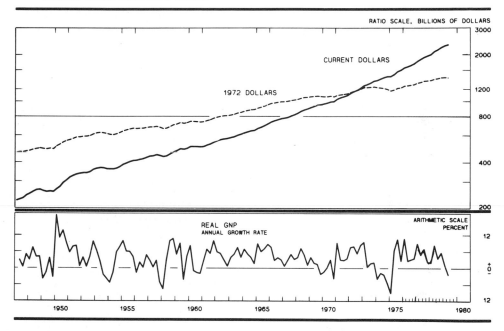

Figure 21.4
(Source: Board of Governors of the Federal Reserve System, *Historical Chart Book.*)

lower than those prevailing in other major countries, foreign private and official holders of U.S. money market instruments may sell them and invest the dollar proceeds in other countries. The resulting inflow of dollars (increased supply) to the foreign exchange market may depress the value of the dollar. On the other hand, high U.S. interest rates tend to attract foreign investment in U.S. money market instruments. As foreign investors obtain U.S. dollars for such investments, the increased demand for dollars tends to raise the dollar's value.

Of critical importance to currency values in the long run is a country's *balance of trade*—its exports relative to its imports. Paradoxically, rapid growth of the domestic economy can create problems for a country's trade balance. Rising income tends to expand imports but creates no corresponding incentive for the boosting of exports (unless the economies of trading partners are expanding at a commensurate or more rapid pace).

Expansionary monetary policy may result in balance-of-payments problems for two reasons. As the money supply increases, interest rates tend to fall, and spending (as well as income) tends to rise. When fiscal policy measures are employed to stimulate the economy, only the resulting income increase is a potential source of a balance-of-payments problem, for interest rates tend to rise in this case. (The reverse holds for anti-inflationary monetary and fiscal policies.)

We turn now to an analysis of the pattern of economic impacts that is characteristic of the use of monetary policy to pursue these various economic goals. The next chapter will focus on the corresponding aspects of fiscal policy.

EFFECTS OF MONETARY POLICY

Chapter 7 described the various means by which the Federal Reserve exercises control of the level of depository institution reserves and thus the money supply. Recall that the Fed relies primarily on the flexible (but potent) tool of *open-market operations,* which is the buying and selling of securities by the Fed. When the Fed is seeking to *expand* reserves and monetary aggregates, the System Open Account Manager (an officer of the Federal Reserve Bank of New York) is instructed by the Federal Open Market Committee (FOMC) to *buy* securities from government securities dealer firms. Such purchases by the Fed serve to supply new reserves to the depository system, and these new reserves serve as a base for monetary expansion in some multiple of the Fed's injection of reserves. *Sales* of securities by the Fed *reduce* reserves, thus setting in motion a contraction of monetary aggregates.

In addition to open-market operations, the Fed can impact on credit and monetary aggregates by changing reserve requirements and/or the cost and availability of discount-window lending to depository institutions. The discount window, however, is less a tool of monetary policy than a "safety valve" when other instruments are being employed to impact sharply on reserves. As for reserve requirements, the Fed has made comparatively little use of this powerful tool for monetary policy purposes. Prior to the enactment of the Depository Institutions Deregulation and Monetary Control Act of 1980, the Fed's apparent hesitancy to *raise* reserve requirements perhaps reflected, in part, concern over declining Fed membership (see Chapter 7). Since this act applies Fed reserve requirements to nonmember banks as well as member banks (and indeed, to all institutions holding transactions-type deposits), concern that an increase in reserve requirements will cause member banks to leave the system is no longer a factor in the Fed's choice of policy instruments. The reserve requirements section of the 1980 act also supplies the Fed with the means of *immediately* impacting on all depository institutions (as well as immediately impacting on the quantity of reserves), whereas the effects of open-market operations must work their way (with some time lag) through the financial system.

The Credit Control Act of 1969 gives the Fed broad powers to control lending, although it stipulates presidential authorization for the exercise of such powers. These powers have been invoked on several occasions, most notably in March 1980, when, among other actions, the Fed imposed "special deposit requirements" (required reserves) on increases in certain managed liabilities of nonmember banks (the levy had been imposed on *member* banks six months earlier), on credit-card and various other unsecured consumer loans, and on money market mutual funds. (These credit controls were in place only about five months.)

In addition to these various tools of money and credit control, the Fed can in some measure affect the behavior of financial institutions via "moral suasion" and voluntary guidelines. This "moral authority" is of course related to the Fed's very real statutory authority to regulate and administer the banking system.

The Transmission of Monetary Policy

How are the measures taken by the Fed to increase or reduce the level of bank reserves transmitted to the economy? There is more agreement on the ultimate economic effects of monetary policy than on how monetary measures bring about such effects. We will offer here an account of the various elements of the transmission process, while recognizing that there is difference of opinion as to the relative importance of these various elements. Our scenario considers open-market operations, but the effects of any policy-induced change in reserves will be essentially the same.

The chain of events triggered by open-market operations begins when the trading desk of the New York Federal Reserve Bank, acting on instructions from the Manager of the Open Market Account (who is in turn acting on much less specific instructions from the Federal Open Market Committee), executes an order. If the Fed sells securities, bank reserves will contract; if the Fed buys securities, bank reserves will expand. What happens next? The subsequent effects of a monetary policy action may be grouped into three interrelated transmission elements: (1) credit (price and availability) effects, (2) portfolio-adjustment effects, and (3) wealth effects. (Again, these effects can be expected to ensue for any Fed policy move impacting on bank reserves, although our discussion here focuses on open-market operations.)

Credit Effects

The buying and selling of securities by the Federal Reserve has an immediate effect on security prices and thus on interest rates. When the Fed buys, say, Treasury bills, their prices rise and their yields fall. Security holders are induced to sell their holdings of T-bills and acquire other securities. The prices and yields of these various other securities thus rise and fall, respectively, and the dampening effects on interest rates of the Fed's purchase spread quickly.[11] When the Fed sells securities, interest rates will tend to rise by corresponding actions in the reverse direction.

Concurrently, reserves of depository institutions are impacted by the Fed's actions. A Fed purchase of securities injects new reserves into the depository system, providing a

---

11. The process by which the Fed action's impact on security prices and yields is disseminated across all financial assets is one of the "portfolio effects" described in the next section.

means for banks and other institutions to acquire new loans and securities. The new lending and security purchases by financial institutions augments the downward pressures on interest rates that the Fed purchase initiated. A Fed sale of securities, on the other hand, reduces reserves while tending to boost interest rates. As institutions curtail lending and sell securities to restore their reserve positions, additional upward pressure on interest rates develops.

Note that, up to this point, the presumed effects of a Fed action are limited to the *financial* sector. But as consumers and business firms find the price and availability of credit altered, their borrowing and spending are affected. If interest rates have fallen and credit is more easily obtained, borrowing and spending are stimulated. If interest rates are rising and credit is tightening, consumers and business firms may curtail, cancel, or defer planned spending.

Because of various institutional limitations and financial market "imperfections," the impact of more expensive (and less available) credit on the economy is rather uneven. For example, state and local governments may face statutory limitations on the level of interest rates they are permitted to pay. To the extent that lenders "ration" credit, borrowers viewed as less credit-worthy (often small business firms) are more likely to be denied credit. Depending on the degree of increase in interest rates, the mortgage market (and thus the construction industry) may experience particular difficulty because of legal restrictions on rates.[12]

Portfolio Effects

The portfolio effects of the Fed's monetary policy actions stem from the kind of equilibrating portfolio-selection process, as described in Chapter 11, that is presumed to characterize wealth holders' behavior. A Fed policy action changes the supply of securities held in the private sector, the quantity of money, security prices, and interest rates, and thus it disturbs the equilibrium position of wealth holders. Wealth holders respond by taking action to restore their risk-return equilibrium position.[13] These actions include the sale or purchase of securities and spending for real (as well as financial) assets. (Note the universality of these presumed portfolio effects—all economic units hold asset portfolios, the size and composition of which are viewed as affected by monetary policy actions.)

---

12. The Depository Institutions Deregulation and Monetary Control Act of 1980 mandated a "phase-out" of some particularly bothersome interest rate restrictions. The act provided for the phased elimination (by 1986) of rate ceilings on savings deposits at commercial banks, savings banks, savings and loan associations, and credit unions. The legislation also set aside state-enacted ceiling rates on mortgages and commercial lending, although state legislatures could reimpose them. (None have done so as of this writing.)

13. Fed actions also affect *expectations* regarding future interest-rate and price-level changes, and portfolio rearrangement may result from these shifts in expectations as well as from the actual Fed maneuver. Further, the impact of changes in expectations may be *counter* to the Fed's intentions. For example, instances can be cited when an announced *increase* in the rate of growth of the money supply corresponded to an increase, rather than a decrease, in interest rates. In such cases, the "expectations effect" (of increased inflation and/or offsetting tight money in the future) outweighed the "liquidity effect."

Consider, for example, the portfolio effects of a Fed open-market *sale* of Treasury bills, which drains reserves from the depository system. The purchasers of these T-bills alter the composition of their portfolios by exchanging bank deposits for the securities, and their portfolio rearrangement is unlikely to end here. Depository institutions, of course, experience immediate disturbance of their portfolio positions by the shrinkage of their deposits and reserves. They will act to restore portfolio balance by selling securities and curtailing lending. As these actions reverberate through the economy, security prices tend to fall and interest rates tend to rise, triggering more portfolio effects. Declining values of financial asset holdings and higher available yields on prospective financial-asset acquisitions tend to reduce spending for real assets—business firms curtail investment spending and consumers reduce consumption spending.

A reverse pattern of events follows a Fed open-market *purchase*. In this case, banks experience increased deposits and reserves, and their portfolio rearrangements involve new lending and security purchases. Throughout the economy, portfolio effects both result from and result in rising security prices and falling interest rates. Spending for real assets is stimulated as an integral part of the total pattern of portfolio adjustments.

Credit effects and portfolio effects are thus closely intertwined. The former focus primarily on interest rate changes on borrowing and spending, whereas the latter focus on a broader framework of economic decision. Both point to similar economic effects of Fed actions, however. When the Fed reduces depository institution reserves by open-market sales of securities, an increase in reserve requirements, or reduction of its lending to depository institutions (or some combination thereof), the money supply will fall, interest rates will rise, and spending for real assets will be reduced. When the Fed increases reserves by purchasing in the open market, by reducing reserve requirements, or by increasing its lending to depository institutions (or some combination thereof), the money supply will expand, interest rates will fall, and borrowing and spending will increase.

Wealth Effects

Spending (as well as other aspects of economic behavior) is influenced by *wealth,* which is defined as the present value of all future income flows, discounted (capitalized) by some rate of interest. Income is generated by capital assets, including "human capital" (providing one's services is the means of generating income from this particular asset), other real assets, and financial assets. Since monetary policy measures can impact on wealth, it is postulated that such induced changes in wealth can subsequently affect spending and engender various other economic effects.

Expansionary monetary policy can conceivably increase *apparent* wealth in several ways. The stock of financial assets of private wealth holders is increased. Debt security prices increase (and perhaps market values of equities as well) as interest rates decline, raising the market value of financial portfolios. To the extent that current interest rates affect the long-run capitalization rate for future income flows, the present value of these expected future flows (which is wealth) increases. The apparent increase in wealth may induce increased consumption and investment spending.

Again, the reverse is postulated for contractionary monetary policy measures. In this case, the rise of interest rates impacts adversely on security prices and the present value of expected future income. The decline in wealth is presumed to result in reduced consumption and investment spending.

UNSETTLED ISSUES OF MONETARY POLICY

The Monetarist View

The fact that there exists considerable disagreement about the transmission process by which monetary policy impacts on spending for real assets was mentioned above. Much of this disagreement is between "monetarist" economists and "Neo-Keynesian" economists. *Monetarists* emphasize the portfolio-adjustment pattern of monetary-policy effects, whereas *Neo-Keynesians* attach more significance to credit effects. The underlying technical argument between these camps, which is also of significance for the relative effectiveness of monetary and fiscal policy, is addressed in the next chapter. This argument concerns how responsive the behavior of economic agents is to changes in the rate of interest in terms of demand for cash balances and spending for real assets. (As discussed in the next chapter, monetarists regard the demand for money as relatively insensitive to changes in the rate of interest and real spending as very sensitive; Neo-Keynesians hold that the reverse is true.)

Some monetarists paint a rather ambivalent picture of monetary policy. The money stock is viewed as a crucial economic variable, but *discretionary* management of its growth is deemed to be of dubious merit. The potency of the quantity of money, in the monetarist framework, stems from a perception that the rate of turnover of the money supply (monetary velocity) is a stable function of certain economic variables (including wealth, price level expectations, and rates of interest). Since total spending is necessarily the product of the money stock used for transactions and the number of times that stock "turns over" (is used for transactions purposes), it follows that the amount of the money supply determines the amount of aggregate spending if the number of "turnovers" (velocity) does not shift to a significant degree.[14] (Figure 21.5 shows the historical pattern of the income velocity of money for three different measures of money.) To a large degree, however, monetarists point to *empirical evidence* of the economic significance of the money stock, rather than to a theoretical framework. Such evidence shows a close relationship between the money supply, GNP, and the price level.

All monetarists believe that changes in the money supply impact significantly on the economy, but not all monetarists favor the use of discretionary monetary policy to stabilize the economy. Milton Friedman, the best-known monetarist, contends that the historical

---

14. See Chapter 6 for a discussion of the "equation of exchange" that defines this argument. The Quantity Theory of Money, the monetarist credo, is a derivative of this equation. This theory holds that velocity is a function of a number of variables but is determined largely by behavioral patterns that are slow to change. Further, the usual preference of monetarists for a measure of "money" is M-2, not M-1.

INCOME VELOCITY OF MONEY

ANNUALLY, 1910-46; SEASONALLY ADJUSTED, QUARTERLY, 1947-

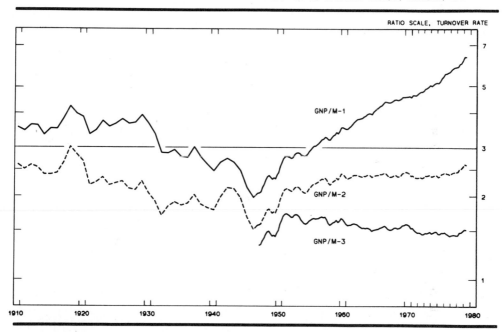

Figure 21.5
(Source: Board of Governors of the Federal Reserve System, *Historical Chart Book.*)

record shows that, in the long run, changes in the quantity of money affect only the price level, not real income.[15] Friedman (together with many other monetarists) believes that nonmonetary factors determine real income, that the economy has great "built-in" inherent stability, and that discretionary monetary policy is destabilizing. Friedman's view that discretionary monetary management does more harm than good is based on the results of his empirical investigations of lags in the effect of monetary policy—results, it should be noted, that are not consistent with those of other investigators.

Lags in the Effects of Monetary Policy

The amount of time required for monetary policy to impact on such key economic variables as employment, output, and the price level is of crucial importance to its usefulness as an

---

15. See Milton Friedman, "A Theoretical Framework for Monetary Analysis," *Journal of Political Economy* (March 1970), for an account of this view, which is also described in several of the references at the end of this chapter.

instrument of economic stabilization. If the lag in the economic effects of monetary policy is either unduly long or unduly variable in length, discretionary monetary policy may be destabilizing rather than stabilizing. Economic conditions can change very rapidly, and economic policymakers have often been surprised by how suddenly the current economic problem shifts from recession to inflation, or vice versa.

The total time lag involved in the use of monetary policy to pursue economic objectives is often separated into the "inside lag" and the "outside lag." The inside lag is the amount of time it takes for the Fed to recognize the need for policy action (or change in policy), to decide what the particulars of its response will be, and to put the policy measure into effect. (The inside lag is thus sometimes divided into recognition, decision, and implementation lags.) The outside lag is the time period required for the policy action, working through the various transmission channels, to impact significantly on economic activity.

Both the inside and outside lags are generally assessed as being matters of *months* (not days or weeks, unfortunately), although how many months is a matter of disagreement. The inside lag is probably about three to six months and the outside lag about six to nine months, but not all observers would accept even these wide ranges.

Milton Friedman has argued for many years that the monetary policy lag is both *long* and *variable*. For this reason, he views discretionary monetary policy as being more apt to destabilize the economy than to stabilize it. Friedman argues that discretionary monetary policy, which necessarily involves Fed-engineered changes in the rate of growth of the money supply, should be replaced by a steady, unchanging rate of monetary growth. Such constant growth in the money supply would be at a rate sufficient to accommodate long-run economic growth. In effect, Friedman has more faith in the economy's inherent capacity for self-stabilization than in the ability of government policymakers to stabilize it.

It does not appear likely that Friedman's "rule" for monetary management will be adopted—unless the future holds some spectacular lag-related failures of monetary policy. The Fed will doubtless continue its efforts to shorten the inside lag by improving its administrative, information-gathering, and analysis procedures. Perhaps future research will also improve our understanding of the outside lag, thus permitting the Fed to better predict the time path and extent of monetary policy incidence. We turn now to description and analysis of the Fed's operating procedures in its implementation of monetary policy.

MONETARY POLICY TARGETS

The ultimate objective of monetary policy measures is to impact in some desired fashion on the price level, employment and production, and/or (via its impact on these economic variables) the balance of payments. However, as discussed above, monetary policy inevitably involves time lags before such impacts can be assessed. In order to adopt, conduct, and adapt the exercise of policy instruments in an appropriate and *timely* fashion, the Fed is obliged to employ *intermediate* targets. Potential target variables include interest rates, bank reserves, the monetary base (bank reserves plus currency in circulation), and one or more of the various monetary aggregates (measures of the money stock) described in Chapter 6.[16] Needless to say, changes in such intermediate economic variables should be closely linked to ultimate changes in output, employment, and the price level. If they are, the Fed can adjust its policies according to changes in target variables.

The Fed's present emphasis (as of this writing) on bank reserves received a great deal of media attention when it was adopted in October 1979, but it can be viewed as the outcome of an evolutionary process over the decade of the 1970s.

Before 1970, the Fed's policy procedures were essentially focused on a constellation of target variables summarized as "conditions in the money market." Such money market conditions included interest rates, the level of bank reserves, and the operating positions of securities dealers (including their financing costs and inventory holdings). Beginning in 1970, the Fed began to focus more attention on monetary aggregates—bank credit and the various measures of the money stock. Evidence of this shift includes the Federal Open Market Committee's adoption of explicit references to these various monetary aggregates in its instructions to the Manager of the Open Market Account. Further, the FOMC's instructions began to be more specific during this period, not only in regard to monetary aggregates but also in regard to their target variables, the federal funds rate and bank reserves.

The Federal Funds Rate as a Policy Target

In sum, the operating-target policy for the 1970–1979 period can be characterized as one that focused on monetary aggregates, but that sought to use the federal funds rate as a means of gauging "appropriate" changes in the money stock.[17] The role of the federal funds rate as an "operating target" stemmed from its apparent ability to serve as an "indicator" of emerging trends in the growth of monetary aggregates. The funds rate is viewed as a very sensitive indicator of the degree of ease or tightness in bank reserves. The policy linkage

---

16. The literature on this subject is made somewhat confusing by the plethora of terms—goals, objectives, targets, indicators, guides, etc.—that are used to describe the Fed's various benchmarks of results. In this chapter, the terms "goals" and "objectives," which are used synonymously, refer to ultimate contributions to the economic goals cited in the chapter. The term "targets" is used to refer to economic variables that constitute intermediate impact goals. The term "operating targets" is used to denote economic variables the Fed uses to gauge its impact on "policy target" variables.

17. There were variations in emphasis among target variables and changes in Fed procedures during this period. However, the charge made by some observers that *interest rate levels* were the Fed's *policy* targets at any time during this period is denied by Fed officials. The official position of the Fed is that bank reserves and monetary aggregates were the policy targets throughout this period, and the Fed's deliberate influencing of interest rate levels was only a means of pursuing these policy targets.

was viewed as follows:

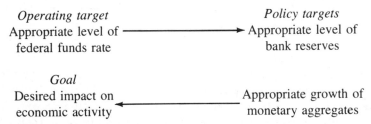

Operating target   *Policy targets*
Appropriate level of ————————→ Appropriate level of
federal funds rate   bank reserves

Goal
Desired impact on   Appropriate growth of
economic activity ←————————   monetary aggregates

The use of the funds rate as an operating target in implementing monetary policy had a number of advantages. One was relative simplicity. The Fed sought to supply or withdraw bank reserves so as to set the federal funds rate at a level consistent with the desired rate of growth in monetary aggregates. To do so requires, among other things, an estimate of the demand for money at different interest rates for a given level of income. Since the quantities of money demanded and supplied are equal in equilibrium, this estimate provides a means of identifying the funds rate consistent with the money supply target. This procedure does not require reliance on the monetary-multiplier link between bank reserves and the money supply and thus is not subject to its occasional shifts in magnitude. Further, money-supply disturbances, such as changes in float and currency in circulation, are readily accommodated by the stabilization of the funds rate.

Although the funds-rate procedure avoids money market disturbances by accommodating shocks to the supply side of monetary aggregates, it also accommodates shocks on the demand side—a source of serious potential problems. Shifts in the demand for money often signal the emergence of inflationary or deflationary economic pressures. Under the funds-rate approach, such shifts are not allowed to change interest rates. Thus the potential for rate changes to correct such trends is dissipated. This is particularly bothersome when the money demand shift is due to inflationary increases in money income, because the Fed's action in holding rates stable (supplying new reserves) "validates" inflation.[18] In general, to the extent that demand for money shifts occur when the Fed is focusing on the funds rate, the Fed will tend to overshoot or undershoot its monetary growth goals. Indeed, the record shows that the Fed had a great deal more success in achieving its targeted federal funds rate than in achieving its monetary aggregate goals.

The Fed's Shift to a Reserves-Based Policy Procedure

While focusing on the funds rate, the FOMC did not ignore bank reserves during the 1970–1979 period. Indeed, from early 1972 to early 1976, target growth rates were specified for "RPDs"—reserves available for private nonbank deposits—which consist of

---

18. The Fed's accommodation of shifts in the schedule of the demand for money is appropriate when a permanent change in the relation of money to income (velocity) occurs. Accommodation of a *temporary* change in this relation, however, will result in growth of monetary aggregates that may be undesirable.

total member bank reserves less legal reserves for Treasury and interbank deposits. (The RPD segment of total reserves was viewed as the one most significant to the economy.) The FOMC had little success in achieving targeted RPD growth rates during this period. This lack of success was largely due to the higher priority given the funds rate (the committee was unwilling to allow it to fluctuate to a major degree), but it was also due to an apparent instability in the relationship of RPDs to monetary aggregates. The "experiment," though resulting in some useful learning experience for the Fed, served mainly to reinforce the FOMC's preoccupation with the funds rate→money supply approach until 1979.

In October 1979, however, the Fed announced a change in operating procedures from the funds rate to a reserves-based approach. Part of the reason was technical—the Fed's mounting dissatisfaction with the tendency of the funds-rate procedure to lead to the overshooting of money supply targets. Perhaps more significant was the desire of Fed chairman Volcker, during a period of sharp decline in the dollar's value in the foreign exchange market, to regain international confidence in the Fed's ability and determination to control U.S. monetary growth.

The reserves-based operating procedure begins with the formulation of a targeted path for the money supply. The estimated demand for currency in circulation is then deducted from the money supply targets, resulting in a target growth path for deposits. The targeted deposit amounts in turn imply target levels of required reserves, which must be estimated for the various reserve requirement categories. In addition to required reserves, the Fed must also allow for excess reserves holdings by banks and required reserves for deposits that are not included in the money supply (interbank deposits, Treasury deposits, and foreign central and commercial bank deposits). The net result is a targeted growth path for total reserves. In the use of open-market operations to achieve these total-reserves targets, the Fed must—as always—consider the effects of such factors as changes in float, currency in circulation, and Treasury deposits in commercial banks.

Total reserves consist both of reserves borrowed from the Fed via the discount window and of nonborrowed reserves. The Fed must thus assume some level of borrowing in order to develop an estimate of the level of nonborrowed reserves that is to be achieved by open-market operations. The Fed's control of the discount rate provides a means of altering this "mix" of total reserves if it chooses to do so, since the volume of borrowing is largely a function of the level of the discount rate relative to the federal funds rate.

Note that the Fed's reserves-based procedure does not rely on an estimate of the monetary multiplier. A multiplier magnitude "falls out" of the process instead of being estimated as a means of projecting the level of reserves needed to attain money supply targets.

The duration of the new reserves-based procedure depends largely on its real and perceived contribution to the Fed's ability to hit its monetary aggregate targets and the extent to which the procedure disturbs the money markets. An inevitable consequence of a shift away from a focus on the federal funds rate is an increased tendency for the funds rate to fluctuate widely. To the extent that the Fed intervenes to dampen such fluctuations, its focus on managing the growth of total reserves tends to be compromised. At the same time, wide swings in the funds rate are a dysfunctional element in the money markets. At present, the Fed appears to have navigated an acceptable course under the new operating procedures, but it is much too soon to draw more than tentative conclusions about the future.

Announcing Federal Reserve Targets

Since 1975, the Fed has been required by Congress to announce publicly its target rates of growth in monetary aggregates for the ensuing 12-month period.[19] The Fed complies by announcing its monetary growth goals in terms of an *annual target range* (minimum and maximum) of money supply expansion. In 1980, for example, these target ranges were 3.5–6 percent for M-1A, 4–6.5 percent for M-1B, 6–9 percent for M-2, and 6.5–9.5 percent for M-3. (Actual monetary growth rates in 1980 were 5 percent for M-1A, 7.3 percent for M-1B, 9.8 percent for M-2, and 9.9 percent for M-3.) In addition, the *short-run* targets established by the FOMC in its monthly meetings are made public with about a one-month lag. For each meeting, the FOMC's directive to the System Open Market Account Manager, a condensed version of the minutes of the meeting, and various policy decision notes are published a month or so later as the "Record of Policy Actions of the Federal Open Market Committee" in the *Federal Reserve Bulletin.* (The reporting lag is meant to avoid any profiteering by individuals acting on the FOMC's policy decisions— probably a needless concern in efficient financial markets.)

THE FUTURE OF MONETARY POLICY

The impact of monetary stringency on aggregate supply was indicated in a previous section of this chapter. In addition to the short-run loss of output and increase in unemployment that anti-inflationary monetary policy necessarily entails, there are long-run consequences in both the financial and real sectors of the economy. Monetary stringency spurs innovation in the financial system as it squeezes out liquidity. Such innovation, both in domestic and international financial markets, has been amply treated in previous chapters of this book. Many of these changes are positive in terms of economic stability, but some are not. Some observers fear that the frequent rounds of "tight money" that have characterized recent decades have stretched the financial system rather thin, making both the domestic and international components vulnerable to a crisis of confidence.

   In the real sector, there is concern that anti-inflationary monetary policy impacts on *investment,* as well as on consumption spending. Although the argument can be readily accepted that the effects of high rates of inflation on capital formation are much more

---

19. The Full Employment and Balanced Growth Act of 1978 requires the Federal Reserve (in the person of the Chairman) to report to Congress its objectives for monetary growth and the ways in which they will contribute to the goals of the act.

insidious than those of monetary stringency, the fact remains that the cure inflicts some of the same damage as the disease.

The future of discretionary economic policy aimed at aggregate demand—both the monetary and fiscal varieties—probably hinges on its real and perceived performance in coping with these problems in coming years. In the next chapter, we describe and evaluate the other principal instrument of economic policy, fiscal policy. Further attention is also given to monetary policy in that chapter, particularly an assessment of "monetarism."

SUMMARY

Monetary policy is intended to impact on aggregate spending in the economy in a fashion that will contribute to the goals of full employment, price stability, sustainable economic growth, and balance-of-payments equilibrium. Monetary policy is conducted by the Federal Reserve primarily via its open-market operations, discount-window policies and rates, control of reserve requirements, various selective controls, and "moral suasion." These various instruments of monetary policy impact initially on monetary and credit aggregates, security prices, and interest rates. The effects of changes in these variables reach the real sector of the economy (impacting on investment and consumption) through various "transmission" channels. Such transmission channels include credit-price and availability effects, portfolio effects, and wealth effects.

Monetary policy affects economic activity only after some time lag, part of which is administrative (the "inside lag") and part of which relates to the time required for monetary measures to be transmitted to the real sector of the economy (the "outside lag"). Because of the lag in monetary policy impact, the Fed must rely on one or more intermediate "targets" to assess policy effects. At present, the Fed is focusing on monetary aggregates, using a targeted growth path of bank reserves as the intermediate policy objective. During the 1970s, the Fed focused on the federal funds rate as an "operating target" to indicate the pattern of monetary growth but shifted away from this procedure in 1979. The current reserves-based procedure has resulted in somewhat wider short-run fluctuations in the federal funds rate.

The record of monetary policy is somewhat mixed. As an economic policy instrument that impacts on aggregate demand, it influences aggregate supply indirectly and with a bothersome lag. When monetary policy is used to fight inflation, it depresses real as well as inflationary income, and the corresponding dampening of investment spending poses potential long-run problems for capital formation. In addition, the Fed must cope with a perennial inflation-unemployment trade-off and the tenuous but increasingly important role of expectations in its pursuit of monetary policy. These and other problems have led to a reemphasis on fiscal policy, increased interest in "supply-side economics," and the development of a "rational expectations" theory of policy effects that questions the usefulness of any instrument of economic stabilization focused on aggregate demand.

Despite these various developments, monetary policy is likely to continue its important role for the foreseeable future.

QUESTIONS

1. Discuss the concept of aggregate demand, its various components, and its relationship to aggregate supply.

2. Describe how monetary policy impacts on aggregate demand.

3. What are the principal goals of economic policy? In what way do they sometimes become conflicting goals?

4. Trace the presumed sequence of effects of a monetary policy measure in terms of credit, portfolio, and wealth effects.

5. Discuss lags in the effect of monetary policy. Why do such lags necessitate the use of "operating" and "policy" targets in the pursuit of monetary policy?

6. Compare the "funds-rate" and the "reserves-based" approaches to monetary policy, and discuss the advantages and disadvantages of each.

REFERENCES

Brunner, Karl (ed.), *Targets and Indicators of Monetary Policy* (San Francisco: Chandler, 1969).

Eastburn, David P., and W. Lee Hoskins, "The Influence of Monetary Policy on Commercial Banking," Federal Reserve Bank of Philadelphia *Business Review,* July/August 1978.

Federal Reserve Bank of Boston, *Controlling Monetary Aggregates,* 1969.

————, *Controlling Monetary Aggregates II: The Implementation,* 1973.

Fisher, Douglas, *Money, Banking, and Monetary Policy* (Homewood, Ill.: Irwin, 1980).

Friedman, Milton, "The Role of Monetary Policy," *American Economic Review,* March 1968, pp. 1–17.

Mann, Maurice, "How Does Monetary Policy Affect the Economy," *Journal of Money, Credit, and Banking,* August 1969, pp. 538–548.

Mayer, Thomas, *Elements of Monetary Policy* (New York: Random House, 1968).

Modigliani, Franco, "The Monetarist Controversy or, Should We Forsake Stabilization Policies," *American Economic Review,* March 1977, pp. 1–19.

Poole, William, "Interest Rate Stability as a Monetary Policy Goal," *New England Economic Review,* May/June, 1976.

Prager, Jones (ed.), *Monetary Economics: Controversies in Theory and Policy* (New York: Random House, 1971).

Ritter, Lawrence L., "The Role of Money in Keynesian Theory," in D. Carson (ed.), *Monetary and Banking Studies* (Homewood, Ill.: Irwin, 1963), pp. 134–148.

Uselton, Gene C., *The Lag in the Effect of Monetary Policy* (New York: Marcel Dekker, 1974).

Teigen, Ronald, *Readings in Money, National Income, and Stabilization Policy* (Homewood, Ill.: Irwin, 1978).

APPENDIX

EXPECTATIONS, ECONOMIC POLICY, AND THE PHILLIPS CURVE

In 1958, A.W. Phillips, an Australian economist, published results of a study he had made of unemployment levels and the rate of change in money wage rates in the United Kingdom from 1861 to 1957. The term "Phillips curve" was adopted for the inverse relationship between these variables that Phillips reported. Since the money wage rate is the principal component of the cost of goods and services, the Phillips curve has often been cited to indicate the apparent trade-off between inflation and unemployment that characterizes modern economies. According to the assumed dynamics of this trade-off, as economic activity accelerates and unemployment declines, labor markets tighten and money wages rise, creating upward pressure on the price level. The reverse holds for economic downturns.

Until about 1968, inflation and unemployment data for the United States and most industrialized Western nations fitted the Phillips curve fairly well. Then the "fit" dissolved, when rising unemployment and accelerating inflation began to occur together during the 1970s. As economists sought to "explain" the empirical breakdown in the Phillips-curve relationship between unemployment and inflation, the attention of many monetarists focused on the role of *inflationary expectations* as a potential stumbling block for economic stabilization policy.

In his 1967 presidential address to the American Economic Association, Milton Friedman implicitly (and correctly) forecasted the demise of the Phillips curve by labeling its demonstrated unemployment-inflation relationship as a purely transitory phenomenon. Phillips's oversight, Friedman charged, was in charting the *money* wage rate rather than the *real* wage rate (the money wage rate less the rate of increase in the price level). The money and real wage rates are equivalent only in the absence of inflation, and Phillips's good empirical fit merely reflected a past prevalence of price-stability expectations among workers, Friedman asserted.

If, as Friedman suggests, the correct "Phillips curve" relationship is one of real wages and unemployment, there will be, in effect, a Phillips curve for each possible price level when the money wage rate and unemployment rate are compared.[20] During periods in which workers expect the price level to rise (doubtless the state of affairs during the 1970s), the actual money wage–unemployment relationship will be on a Phillips curve *to the right*

---

20. Friedman and others argue that a "Phillips curve" depicting real wage and unemployment rates in the long run will not be a curve at all; it will be a vertical line at the so-called natural rate of unemployment—the "full employment" level of unemployment that allows for "frictional" unemployment. The argument negates any policy significance of the Phillips curve, since it indicates that (except temporarily) unemployment is not affected by the inflation rate, or vice versa. Deviations from the natural rate of unemployment occur only when employers or workers or both are fooled regarding the real wage level for the employment period, most likely because they have overestimated or underestimated the rate of inflation for the ensuing period.

of a Phillips curve for a period of anticipated relative price level stability. (This result is due to the necessity for money wages to increase at the same rate as the price level if the real wage is to be constant.) Thus the trade-off between two economic "bads"—inflation and unemployment—worsens during periods of inflationary expectations.

The inflation-unemployment trade-off has been called the "dilemma model" for economic policy makers. If the scenario above is accurate, it appears that inflationary expectations can exacerbate this dilemma. One possible implication for monetary policy is that monetary stringency must be applied longer and more vigorously to check inflation, for inflationary expectations must be wrung out of the economy before the dampening of aggregate demand can have a significant impact on the tendency for wages and prices to rise. This also implies that the "price" of price stability—the real output lost as a result of monetary restraint and ensuing unemployment—will be much higher when inflationary expectations have become ingrained in the economy. Public belief in the Fed's capacity and determination to curb inflation thus becomes a necessary element of monetary policy, and such credibility is attained by the application of monetary stringency "as long as it takes."

On the other hand, in regard to the public's perceptions and expectations of Fed policy, if anti-inflationary policy moves are credible, the belief that the inflation rate (and economic activity) will soon be slowed may result in *anticipatory* behavior that reinforces and speeds up the policy's effects. A plausible possibility in this instance is the observed tendency of business firms to curtail inventory growth and defer investment projects when the Fed signals that credit will be tightened as an anti-inflationary action. In this context, when the public is persuaded that the Fed will pursue a strong program of monetary restraint that *will* check inflation (or when recession is the problem, it is believed that a Fed program of monetary ease will stimulate recovery), expectations effects can be viewed as a channel for the transmission of monetary policy action to the real sector of the economy.[21] In the long run, according to this view, the proper anti-inflationary stance for the Fed is an *announced* policy of stable monetary growth to which the Fed religiously adheres.

Whether inflationary expectations must be slowly and painfully squeezed out of an economy or can instead be erased relatively quickly and painlessly depends on the process by which these expectations change. If the public's "forecast" of future inflation is based solely on *experienced* inflation (an "adaptive" process), there is no alternative to the slow and painful "wringing out" process. On the other hand, if the public is able and willing to use information *other than past price level changes* in forming its collective inflation forecast, inflationary expectations can shift very rapidly. Granting the public this degree of sophistication and wisdom has markedly interesting implications.

---

21. Indeed, at the present writing, the Conservative government of the United Kingdom is pursuing an anti-inflationary monetary policy based in large measure on this hypothesis. By announcing targets of monetary growth that constitute a sharp reduction from the pace of the preceding decade and pursuing them despite very high interest rates and mounting unemployment, the British government seeks to make the country's powerful trade unions accept smaller money wage increases and thus ease price pressures.

The Rational Expectations Hypothesis

The fact that the Fed's actions affect expectations regarding future economic developments and that such alterations in expectations influence the pattern of subsequent economic events is obvious. "Fed watching" is an everyday activity in the financial community, and the statements and actions (or absence thereof) by Federal Reserve officials are carefully monitored and widely reported. The significance of this phenomenon for economic policy, however, is not at all obvious.

Some of the theorizing concerning the relationship of expectations to economic policy is closely related to the efficient (financial) markets hypothesis described in Chapter 11. Recall that the concept of financial market efficiency pertains to the speed and nature of the process by which new information is incorporated into security prices. Also recall that most empirical studies indicate that a very high degree of efficiency prevails in the financial markets—information is impounded very quickly in security prices. Such efficiency can properly be attributed to the large number of knowledgeable participants in the financial system who have both the incentive and the capacity to continuously monitor, analyze, and act on pertinent information. If a similar process exists for the rapid adaptation of economic behavior to economic policy initiatives, what are the implications for the transmission of monetary policy and its ultimate economic effects?

One view is the rational expectations theory, which leads to the startling (and perhaps disturbing) conclusion that monetary policy (and perhaps *any* policy measure) cannot affect real income or employment; it can only alter the price level. This theory assumes that economic units possess the ability to assess economic policy actions and their implications very quickly and accurately and, further, that they have the capacity to immediately adapt their economic situations in accordance with their (presumed correct) forecasts. If these suppositions are generally valid, anticipated economic policy measures will be thwarted insofar as real sector impacts are concerned. That is, the expectation of a policy move neutralizes the potential policy effects, because all economic agents will have adjusted their positions by the time the policy measure is initiated. For example, consider the initiation of a fiscal policy measure, such as a faster tax write-off of new acquisitions of depreciable assets, that is intended to spur business investment. If fully anticipated, such a measure may serve primarily to *defer* business spending for fixed assets until the new depreciation schedule is enacted. To the extent that this view is valid, only "surprise" policy measures can have any real effect. The underlying assumptions of the rational expectations theory, however, are of dubious validity.[22] The immense complexity of modern economies is a

---

22. One may also question whether the implications of the rational expectations theory are really so devastating to economic stabilization policy. Most of the theorizing at the present time has emanated from the monetarist camp, so economic forces other than changes in the money supply have been given little attention. In a broader theoretical framework, the theory can be viewed as supportive of discretionary economic policy, for potentially destabilizing developments may be dampened by the likelihood of policy intervention. As developed by monetarist economists, the policy implications of the rational expectations hypothesis hinge largely on the presumed *neutrality* of money—the view that changes in the money supply do not affect (except temporarily) output and employment; they affect only the level of prices.

major problem for professional economists, as anyone who compares economic outcomes to economic forecasts can attest. Further, relatively few economic agents possess the degree of control over their economic situations that the theory in its extreme form presumes. Labor and management are often committed to long-term wage contracts, lessors and lessees to long-term leases, business firms to various long-term supply contracts, and so forth.

Nonetheless, the rational expectations theorists have contributed a great deal to the economic policy debate by their strong emphasis on the fact that the public is not "deaf, dumb, and blind" to pending economic change and will seek to protect its economic interests in anticipation of such change. Much of the macroeconomic theorizing before the 1970s was couched in terms of a passive and inert public responding, amoebalike, according to the prescription of economic policy makers. Further, much of the ill-founded euphoria concerning the efficacy of economic policy was rooted in this premise. Neither this knee-jerk view of economic response nor the related euphoria is likely to be revived in the foreseeable future.

REFERENCES

Alchian, Arman, "Information Costs, Pricing, and Resource Unemployment," in E. Phelps (ed.), *Microeconomic Foundation of Employment and Inflation Theory* (New York: Norton, 1970).

Friedman, Milton, "The Role of Monetary Policy," *The American Economic Review,* March 1968.

Smaistrla, Charles J., and Adrian W. Throop, "A New Inflation in the 1970's?" *Financial Analysts Journal,* March–April 1980, pp. 47–57.

Solow, Robert, *Price Expectations and the Behavior of the Price Level* (Manchester: Manchester University Press, 1969).

Chapter 22

Fiscal Policy and Federal Debt Management: Taxing, Spending, and Borrowing

This chapter offers description and analysis of the fiscal activities of government—taxation, expenditures, and management of the national debt—and the impact of these activities on the financial system and the economy. Various issues relating to the effectiveness of fiscal policy as a tool of economic stabilization are also assessed.

The economic and financial effects of government income, expenditures, and fiscal management are considerable. Such significant impacts are ensured, if for no other reason, by the sheer magnitude of government taxing, spending, and borrowing. The fiscal year 1980 budget for the federal government amounted to more than $520 billion in gross receipts, more than 20 percent of the gross national product. The national debt (federal government's debt) amounted to more than $900 billion at the end of 1980.[1] The size of the national debt, of course, reflects the federal government's propensity for deficit spending since the 1930s. In the past 20 years, the federal budget has been in balance or in surplus only twice. Table 22.1 indicates the amount of federal government receipts and expenditures and the corresponding surplus or deficit for fiscal years 1960–1980.

The management of the fiscal and financing operations of the federal government is the responsibility of the U.S. Treasury. Some aspects of Treasury activities have been discussed

---

1. A large portion of the *gross* amount of the federal debt (more than 20 percent) is held by federal agencies and trust funds. The *net* federal debt is held by the Federal Reserve, U.S. resident private investors, state and local governments, and foreign investors.

Table 22.1   Federal government receipts and expenditures (unified budget), 1960–1980 fiscal years (billions of dollars)

Fiscal year	Receipts	Expenditures	Surplus or deficit
1960	92.5	92.2	+ .3
1961	94.4	97.8	− 3.4
1962	99.7	106.8	− 7.1
1963	106.6	111.3	− 4.8
1964	112.7	118.6	− 5.9
1965	116.8	118.4	− 1.6
1966	130.9	134.7	− 3.8
1967	149.6	158.3	− 8.7
1968	153.7	178.8	−25.2
1969	187.8	184.5	+ 3.2
1970	193.7	196.6	− 2.8
1971	188.4	211.4	−23.0
1972	208.6	231.9	−23.2
1973	232.2	246.5	−14.3
1974	264.9	268.4	− 3.5
1975	281.0	324.6	−43.6
1976	300.0	365.6	−65.6
1977	378.5	402.1	−45.1
1978	402.0	450.8	−48.8
1979	465.9	493.7	−27.8
1980	520.1	579.0	−58.9

Source: *Federal Reserve Bulletin*, various issues.

in previous chapters, but a more detailed description of Treasury fiscal management activities will be useful prior to an assessment of the economic and financial effects of fiscal policy and debt management.

FISCAL MANAGEMENT ACTIVITIES OF THE U.S. TREASURY

The U.S. Treasury has the responsibility for collecting taxes and other federal revenues, handling federal disbursements, borrowing the amounts necessary to finance deficit spending (also temporary shortfalls in cash flow), and refunding the maturing portions of the federal debt. All these activities involve the Treasury's management of its tax and loan (T & L) accounts, held by more than 13,000 commercial banks and (since 1977) savings and loan associations and credit unions, as well as its account with the Federal Reserve System.

The purpose and workings of the tax and loan account system were mentioned in Chapter 6. Most of the Treasury's cash balances are held in T & L accounts. Transfers of funds from the T & L accounts to the Treasury's Federal Reserve account generally occur concomitantly with federal disbursements. Thus the flow of federal government payments into the recipients' bank accounts approximately corresponds to the decrease in T & L account balances with the banking system. The intended result is minimum disturbance of aggregate bank deposits and reserves.

The mechanics of the T & L accounts are designed to keep federal financing operations from resulting in large and irregular movements of deposits out of the banking system. Payments by check to the federal government are deposited in the T & L accounts of the banks on which the checks are drawn, thus avoiding abrupt *regional* (as well as aggregate) shifts of bank deposits. Further, banks acquiring new issues of federal government securities when the Treasury is borrowing can make payment by simply crediting the T & L accounts. This procedure allows banks to acquire federal securities without reducing total reserves (although excess reserves are reduced by the amount of reserves required against the increase in Treasury deposits).[2]

Treasury Borrowing

Even in years of balanced or surplus federal budgets (rare in recent U.S. financial history), the Treasury is obliged to borrow extensively. One reason is that cash inflows and outflows do not occur evenly throughout a fiscal year. As a result, the Treasury must sometimes borrow to cover temporary deficits during a year of a balanced budget. Further, maturing issues of outstanding federal government securities must be refunded by the Treasury (except on those rare occasions when the national debt is being reduced, and the Treasury has a large cash surplus with which to redeem maturing debt). An issue of Treasury bills, for example, matures each week. And of course, an excess of government spending over government revenues in a fiscal year increases the federal debt by the amount of this deficit, necessitating new Treasury borrowing in that amount.

As discussed in Chapter 14, Treasury securities include both marketable and nonmarketable issues. Nonmarketable securities, which amounted to about $306 billion on December 31, 1980, are held by individuals (savings bonds), various U.S. government trust funds (including the federal employee retirement and Social Security funds), foreign governments, and state and local governments. Nonmarketable securities may not be resold. Marketable Treasury securities, which amounted to about $623 billion as of December 31, 1980, include bills and coupon-bearing securities (notes and bonds), and they can be resold by their holders.

In refunding debt, the Treasury generally offers holders of the maturing securities either a new issue of the same type of security or some alternative issue in exchange. But whether

---

2. Until 1978 banks paid no interest on T & L deposits. This practice was long justified on the grounds that it constituted a means of compensating banks for their services to the Treasury. In 1978, however, congressional action resulted in new procedures whereby banks are directly compensated for services, and the Treasury is permitted to invest funds in interest-bearing notes of depository banks. The 1978 changes also caused most banks to begin paying for government securities by having their reserves with the Fed reduced, rather than by crediting T & L accounts.

the Treasury is issuing new securities for the purpose of refunding maturing debt or financing a deficit, the Treasury must make a determination regarding the *time to maturity* of the issue. It is in the choice of the maturity length of Treasury securities that the potential for discretionary policy action in federal debt management exists—a subject we will address at a later point in this chapter. Aside from any policy considerations, the Treasury is likely to consider the availability of funds in various segments of the financial markets. In the refunding of a maturing issue, the choice is generally dictated by the maturity of the particular issue. In general, the Treasury's principal goal appears to be the minimization of interest costs on the public debt.

The Treasury has used the auction method for Treasury bill issues for many years, and in recent years it has employed this method for notes and bonds as well. The alternative to the auction method (of which there are several variations) is a subscription approach, which obliges the Treasury (rather than the market) to determine an interest rate on the subscription issue. Use of the subscription method usually involves Federal Reserve System cooperation; the Fed acts to ensure a successful subscription issue by "stabilizing" financial market conditions. (In the absence of Fed assistance, a shift in market conditions could cause a subscription issue to fail.) As a practical matter, Fed intervention is also certain if the auction of Treasury issues encounters difficulties. In general, however, the auction method poses less interference with the Fed's pursuit of monetary policy.

The Treasury has contributed to the efficiency and smoothness of operation of the financial markets in recent years by offering many of its securities on a regularly scheduled basis. Three- and six-month Treasury bills are auctioned weekly, and one-year bills are auctioned monthly. The Treasury has also developed more regular cycles for its two-year, four-year, and five-year notes, as well as for its bond offerings. Such regularity in Treasury offerings minimizes market disturbances and facilitates inventory management. As discussed in Chapter 13, government security dealers play a very significant role in both the primary and secondary markets for Treasury securities.

Federal Lending Programs

A portion of total federal outlays (about $12 billion in 1979) is for lending programs rather than expenditures for goods and services.[3] However, these "off-budget" outlays affect the size of the federal deficit and impact on the allocation of economic resources in much the same way as any other federal government expenditure. There is thus little justification for not including these federal lending outlays in the total federal budget, as has been the practice in the past.

In an effort to make federal lending operations more efficient, the Federal Financing Bank (FFB) was created in 1973. The FFB is empowered to issue debt securities and lend

---

3. This distinction is not always clear-cut. Certain "loan" programs for agriculture and less-developed countries amount to outright grants, since repayment is made unlikely by various provisions of the loan agreements.

the proceeds to the various federal agencies that administer the government's credit programs, although in practice it generally obtains funds by borrowing from the Treasury.[4] FFB outlays amounted to almost $15 billion in 1980. Prior to the FFB's establishment, most federal credit agencies financed their lending operations by issuing their own securities. These agency securities, though fully backed by the federal government, lacked a well-developed secondary market and thus tended to carry greater interest costs than ordinary federal securities. The FFB's activities served to correct this problem. About 20 federal agencies use the services of the FFB, including the U.S. Postal Service, the Small Business Administration, Amtrak, the Export-Import Bank, and the Government National Mortgage Association. By 1980, FFB debt exceeded $80 billion.

Government-sponsored privately owned agencies are not eligible for FFB services, and they issue securities directly to the public. These agencies include the Federal Home Loan Banks, the Federal National Mortgage Association, and the Federal Land Banks. In 1980, the debt of these federally sponsored agencies was more than $150 billion. The FNMA had about $52 billion of outstanding securities, and Federal Home Loan Bank securities amounted to more than $35 billion. The market for federally sponsored agency securities is thus one of the largest financial markets in the United States.

It is difficult to evaluate the effects of these various lending programs. Many of the loans amount to subsidies in the sense that they support economic activities that would not otherwise take place. (Indeed, if the economic activity in question would otherwise be conducted, a low-interest federal loan amounts to a windfall gain for the borrower.) Such lending programs thus usually result in a reallocation of resources among the various sectors of the economy, just as federal taxing and spending do.

The policy pursued in managing the *composition* of the federal debt can have significant effects on the financial system and thus the overall economy, thought to a lesser extent than the taxing, spending, and lending that determine its size. These effects include potential impacts on the degree of liquidity in the economy and on the term structure of interest rates. Before assessing these potential effects of debt management policy, however, we will examine a much more powerful instrument of economic policy: fiscal policy.

FISCAL POLICY

The deliberate use of fiscal measures by governments to stimulate or restrain economic activity is a relatively recent phenomenon. Before the 1930s, belief in the capacity of government taxation and spending policies to affect aggregate economic activity was generally limited to individuals untrained in economics. The accepted view among professional economists was that government spending could displace private-sector spending but

---

4. In January 1980, the Treasury held about $112 billion in securities issued by government corporations and agencies. Of this total, FFB obligations amounted to approximately $69 billion. Such Treasury holdings amount to indirect borrowing from the public by these agencies.

could not enlarge total spending in the economy. (A modified variant of this view has enjoyed a renaissance in recent years.)

Fiscal policy was swiftly incorporated into conventional economic theory after the 1936 publication of John Maynard Keynes's monumental book, *The General Theory of Employment, Interest, and Money.* In this classic work, Keynes demonstrated a plausible scenario in which fiscal policy could impact significantly on the aggregate level of spending and employment in an economy.[5]

The Theory of Fiscal Policy

The great intellectual barrier to fiscal policy was the "equation of exchange," examined briefly in Chapter 6 of this book:

$$MV = PQ,$$

where M = the amount of the money supply, V = income velocity, or the number of times the money supply "turns over" (changes ownership in transactions that generate income in a given period of time), P = the price level for the period, and Q = real income for the period.

The potential for monetary policy to affect prices and income is quite apparent in the equation of exchange, but this is not so for fiscal policy. For a fixed and constant money supply, government taxation and spending can obviously impact on prices and income only if income velocity (V) changes *as a consequence of fiscal action.* In other words, fiscal measures could be credited with the potential for affecting aggregate economic activity in any predictable pattern only if such measures affected the velocity of money in some systematic fashion.

Keynes's great contribution in this regard was his "liquidity preference" theory, which plausibly postulates the "interest-elasticity" of the demand for "money." This means that individuals and institutions will economize on cash balances as interest rates rise and increase their money holdings as interest rates fall.[6] In this theoretical framework, money velocity is a function of the rate of interest (as well as income levels and established patterns of payments). Thus if fiscal-policy measures affect interest rates, they also affect velocity and prices and income.

How may fiscal measures affect interest rates, given a fixed money supply? Suppose the federal government increases its spending relative to revenues and borrows to finance the

5. Keynes had many predecessors (and indeed, many successors) in the economic theorizing that is labeled "Keynesianism," "Neo-Keynesianism," and "fiscalism," but an account of the development of the theory that would give them fair credit is beyond the scope of this book. Such an account is provided by several of the references at the end of this chapter.

6. Keynes postulated the demand for money in terms of transactions, precautionary, and speculative motives; in other words, cash balances are held for spending, possible spending, and investment reasons. The exposition here incorporates the modern view of cash balances as simply another financial asset holding, which is thus responsive to the usual portfolio-choice decision parameters of risk and return.

resulting deficit. The excess of expenditures over revenues is perhaps a deliberate attempt to stimulate an economy in recession. The increase in the supply of federal debt securities tends to lower the price of all debt securities and raise interest rate levels. As investors respond to the availability of higher yields on financial assets by reducing idle cash balances, money velocity increases. The monetary environment (MV) thus expands to accommodate the effects of government spending on money income in the economy—income rises by some multiple of the increase in government spending. The rise in interest rates will tend to reduce private spending, but the net effect is presumed to be an expansion in aggregate output and employment.

When the government seeks to dampen economic activity (perhaps to resist inflationary pressures), federal spending may be cut or federal taxes may be increased. Total spending in the economy will thus be reduced—public spending if the former approach is taken and private spending if the latter. The ultimate decrease in aggregate spending will be a multiple of the reduction in federal spending or the increase in taxes. In either case, the spending reduction reduces the (transactions) demand for money. As an increased amount of money balances is now available for purchase of financial assets, their prices tend to be bid up, and interest rates tend to fall. Money holdings increase (monetary velocity slows) as a consequence of lower interest rates. Again, the change in interest rates is likely to impact on private economic activity in a fashion counter to policy, but the net effect is viewed as one of restrained spending.

The Monetarist View

Keynesians and so-called Neo-Keynesians believe that fiscal policy is a powerful economic tool, because it directly impacts on spending (versus the indirect linkages of monetary policy). Although "fiscalists" would want and expect monetary policy to be properly coordinated with (and thus to "accommodate") fiscal policy, their belief in the interest-elasticity of demand for money causes this to be a secondary consideration. Further, the rise in interest rates that expansionary fiscal policy entails (in the absence of monetary expansion to stabilize or even lower interest rates) is not viewed as having a major dampening effect on private investment and consumption spending. (In technical terms, the relevant interest-elasticities are viewed as low.) Nor is the decline in interest rates that contractionary fiscal policy entails (again in the absence of counteracting monetary action) viewed as significantly stimulative to private consumption and investment spending.

The monetarist school of macroeconomic theory generally regards fiscal policy as an ineffective tool for economic stabilization. The monetarists view the interest-elasticity of the demand for money as quite low and the interest-elasticity of investment and consumption spending as quite high.[7] Thus monetary policy is viewed as having very powerful economic effects (though not necessarily as being a useful tool for economic *stabilization,*

---

7. Many monetarists would object to this statement. They view the transmission mechanism that links spending on goods and services to monetary change to be primarily a "portfolio effect" rather than a "credit effect." (See the discussion of the "transmission mechanism" of monetary policy in the previous chapter.)

for there may be long and variable lags in these effects), because such a pattern of elasticities augments monetary policy, just as it impedes fiscal policy. In the view of most monetarists, fiscal policy is seen as simply effecting a division of resources between the public and private sectors; high government spending and borrowing are believed to have the effect of "crowding out" private-sector economic activity.[8]

Monetary Effects of Fiscal Policy

Despite frequent assertions to the contrary by politicians and the media, federal government deficits need not result in an inflationary expansion of the money supply. When the Treasury sells securities to nonbank lenders, the effect is simply the transfer of money from these lenders to the recipients of federal outlays; no new money is created. When the Treasury sells securities to banks, the effects differ somewhat, depending on whether or not the banks are holding excess reserves. In either case, the *potential* for new money creation is unchanged unless the Fed injects reserves into the banking system.

If the banks acquiring new Treasury securities are holding excess reserves, the new debt holdings simply correspond to a reduction in these excess reserves and an increase in Treasury deposits. Ownership of the latter deposits then passes to the recipients of government outlays. The final outcome—decreased excess reserves and increased deposits—is no different from what the banks could have accomplished by any alternative use of their excess reserves. Nonetheless, the money supply does expand by the amount of new deposits.[9]

No significant degree of monetary expansion will occur if the banks acquiring the new Treasury securities hold only negligible amounts of excess reserves, as is the present norm. Under these circumstances, purchase of federal securities by banks necessarily involves the selling of other security holdings or the reduction of outstanding loans. The latter actions result initially in a reduction in deposits, but as government spending of the borrowed funds takes place, these deposits are restored.

A multiple expansion of the money supply *will* occur if the Fed injects reserves into the banking system to "support" the Treasury's borrowing operations. The same would be true if the Treasury sold securities to the Fed (an operation that is prohibited except in emergency situations). Such a purchase of new securities by the Fed—as with any purchase—would provide new reserves to the banking system in the amount of the purchase, and money creation would follow.

---

8. Economics is not a value-free discipline, and it appears that political and social beliefs often color one's perception of what is and is not economic wisdom. Thus it is not surprising that few monetarists are "liberals" (in the modern sense of government-activism advocacy), and relatively few Keynesians are conservatives. Thus perceptions as to the proper size and role of government and the inherent stability and health of the private sector are perhaps as significant in the monetarist-fiscalist debate as the magnitude of interest-elasticities.

9. The amount of new deposits will not necessarily be equal to the amount of new Treasury borrowing but may rather be some multiple thereof.

Do large federal budget deficits induce the Fed to "finance" the deficit via open-market purchases of securities? Table 22.2 shows the net change in federal debt held by the public and by the Fed, respectively, in recent years. It does not appear that the magnitude of deficits has influenced Fed policy in any identifiable and systematic fashion. In some years, the Fed has increased its holdings of federal securities by an amount exceeding the increase in the

Table 22.2 Changes in federal debt held by the public and by the Federal Reserve, fiscal years 1955–1978 (billions of dollars)

Fiscal year	Net change in federal debt held by public* (1)	Net change in federal debt held by Federal Reserve (2)	Ratio, col. 2 to col. 1 (percent) (3)
1955	2.1	− 1.4	− 66.2
1956	− 4.3	0.2	− 4.6
1957	− 2.8	− 0.8	28.5
1958	6.9	2.4	34.6
1959	8.6	0.6	6.9
1960	2.2	0.5	23.0
1961	1.4	0.8	56.1
1962	9.8	2.4	24.6
1963	6.1	2.3	38.2
1964	3.1	2.8	89.5
1965	4.1	4.3	106.0
1966	3.1	3.1	99.8
1967	2.8	4.6	160.3
1968	23.1	5.5	23.9
1969	−11.1	1.9	− 16.7
1970	5.4	3.6	67.1
1971	19.4	7.8	40.1
1972	19.4	5.9	30.4
1973	19.3	3.8	19.5
1974	3.0	5.5	181.7
1975	50.9	4.3	8.5
1976	83.4	9.7	11.7
1977	57.2†	8.2†	14.4
1978	59.1	10.0	16.9

* "Public" includes the Federal Reserve and all other holders except federal government agencies.
† Figures for fiscal year 1977 reflect an extra "transitional" quarter. Data have been adjusted by multiplying them by 4/5.
Sources: *Annual Report of the Secretary of the Treasury on the State of Finances*, various issues; *Economic Report of the President*, various issues.

net federal debt. In other years, the Fed has acquired only a small portion of the increase in the debt.[10]

Only if a budget deficit has any monetary effect will the deficit have any *short-run* effect on the economy. It is government spending and taxing that quickly affect the economy, not the financing of deficits. In the longer run, however, the magnitude of deficits—because they must be financed by new government borrowing—may adversely affect private-sector economic growth by "crowding out" private borrowing for investment purposes. This possibility has received considerable attention in recent years and warrants some discussion.

Do Deficits "Crowd Out" Private Borrowing?

Chapter 8 described the process by which loanable funds flow to financial markets. This process must be kept in mind when evaluating the "crowding out" argument. The supply of loanable funds is unlikely to be some fixed quantum. Rather, it is a flow of funds that is responsive to a number of economic variables (which may be in turn be affected by the quantity of loanable funds demanded). It is obvious that if available funds for lending are a fixed amount, every dollar of these funds that the government takes is one less available dollar to finance private spending. But this is a necessary (as well as sufficient) condition for government spending to result in a dollar-for-dollar displacement of private spending.

As indicated in Chapter 8, the quantity of loanable funds provided is determined by aggregate saving in the economy and the amount of new money creation. Thus the significant factors are the degree of slack in the economy, the level of interest rates, and the monetary policy being pursued by the Fed at the time the government borrowing occurs. Perennially significant economic variables include the interest-elasticity of private investment demand and saving and the marginal propensity to save (portion of income increases that is saved). Taking all these factors into consideration, one can postulate plausible scenarios along a spectrum from government borrowing that has little or no dampening effect on private sector borrowing to an exact substitution of government for private borrowing.

The "crowding out" issue should not be allowed to obscure a more fundamental aspect of fiscal policy—the fact that government *spending* uses resources that are thus rendered unavailable to the private sector. If the economy is at the point of full employment of resources, it makes no difference whether the government taxes or borrows to finance its spending—private spending will be supplanted in an amount approximately equal to government outlays. Further, unless offset by appropriate monetary policy (and unless dollar-for-dollar "crowding out" occurs), government *deficit* spending in a full-employment economy will be inflationary.

---

10. In recent years, foreign holdings of federal debt securities have increased enormously, from less than $20 billion in 1970 to more than $125 billion in 1979. The relative proportion of holdings by the Fed and U.S. investors has remained approximately the same for decades.

The High-Employment Budget

The degree of economic stimulus of fiscal policy is generally viewed as a function of the amount of the surplus or deficit. A surplus indicates that government taxation is removing more funds from the economy than are being provided by government outlays. A deficit indicates the reverse. However, the meaningfulness of the magnitude of the deficit or surplus as a measure of *appropriate* fiscal stimulus is a function of the level of economic activity. This is so because the amounts of most government receipts and some expenditures are determined by the level of economic activity. For example, income tax revenues decline and unemployment compensation payments increase during periods of recession. In this case, a deficit will probably result, but its magnitude may be inadequate to provide sufficient stimulus to economic recovery. On the other hand, economic booms swell tax revenues while transfer payments are declining. This "induced" surplus may be inadequate to provide a fiscal policy check to inflationary pressures.

The high-employment or "full-employment" (5-percent unemployment rate) budget is meant to deal with this difficulty by separating those budget amounts that are a function of economic conditions from those that are determined autonomously. This is accomplished by constructing a hypothetical budget for each fiscal year that incorporates estimates of revenues and expenditures at full employment. Actual budget expenditures are adjusted for additional unemployment compensation payments, and receipts are adjusted to reflect full-employment economic conditions. The amount of the deficit or surplus of the high-employment budget provides a benchmark for assessing the fiscal impact of the actual budget on the economy. When this hypothetical budget shows a surplus or is in balance, the corresponding actual budget is not providing any fiscal stimulus—even if the actual budget has a sizable deficit. Table 22.3 offers a comparison of the high-employment and national-income accounts (actual) budgets in recent years.

Coordination of Fiscal and Monetary Policy

The debate over the relative effectiveness of monetary and fiscal policy sometimes obscures the need for their integration and coordination. Effective economic policy surely requires their tandem utilization at joint-, not cross-purposes.[11]

When the economy is threatened by recession, the appropriate prescription is fiscal stimulus and monetary expansion. Whether the fiscal stimulus takes the form of increased government spending or a tax cut to spur private spending, the immediate effect will be to

---

11. Unfortunately, this has not always been so. The classic example is the 1968 income tax surcharge. This tax increase (a 10 percent add-on to 1968 tax liabilities) was intended to dampen inflation, but monetary expansion continued. (It appears that the Fed overestimated the contractionary impact of the surtax and thus chose not to slow monetary growth to a significant degree.) The apparent failure of the surtax to have any major impact on spending has been hailed by some monetarists as evidence of the greater relative potency of monetary policy, but this does not necessarily follow. The emphasis on the surtax as "temporary," for example, is likely to have contributed to its lack of impact.

Table 22.3 Comparison of the national income accounts budget and the high-employment budget, 1971–1979 (billions of dollars)

	1971	1972	1973	1974	1975	1976	1977	1978	1979
National Income Accounts Budget									
Receipts	198.6	227.5	258.3	288.6	286.2	331.4	375.4	432.1	473.9
Expenditures	220.6	244.7	265.0	299.3	356.8	385.1	421.7	459.8	508.6
Surplus or Deficit (−)	−22.0	−17.3	− 6.7	−10.6	−70.6	−53.7	−46.3	−27.7	−34.7
High-Employment Budget*									
Receipts	211.0	227.3	258.4	295.6	318.8	353.0	384.2	435.3	482.0
Expenditures	219.5	244.0	265.1	298.6	349.9	379.8	418.3	458.4	506.2
Surplus or Deficit (−)	− 8.5	−16.7	− 6.7	− 3.0	−31.1	−26.8	−34.1	−23.1	−24.2

*Data for the high-employment budget are on a national-income accounts basis.

Sources: Office of Management and Budget, U.S. Department of Commerce, and Federal Reserve Bank of St. Louis.

raise income. Monetary expansion serves to check the rise in interest rates that the fiscal measure would otherwise trigger, while concomitantly stimulating economic activity through the credit, portfolio, and wealth effects described in the previous chapter.

When inflation is the policy target, both fiscal and monetary restraints are in order. Again, fiscal policy can quickly impact on aggregate spending either by decreasing government outlays or by raising taxes (and thus curtailing private spending). The various effects of a tighter monetary policy will also act to reduce aggregate spending. Fiscal restraint alone would result in declining interest rates, which would be at cross-purposes with policy, but monetary restraint will check this tendency for rates to fall.

When a balance-of-payments problem (a persistent deficit) must also be confronted by economic policy, the appropriate mix of monetary and fiscal measures is affected by domestic economic conditions. Monetary restraint is more effective if inflation is the current domestic problem. This is true because anti-inflationary monetary policy entails higher interest rates, which help the balance-of-payments problem by attracting foreign capital. When both recession and a balance-of-payments deficit are to be combatted, expansionary fiscal policy is preferable, since it tends to raise interest rates while stimulating economic activity.

"AUTOMATIC" AND DISCRETIONARY FISCAL EFFECTS

The foregoing discussion in this chapter has focused on *discretionary* fiscal policy measures—deliberate tax and spending policies of the government to stimulate or restrain economic activity. There are also certain "built-in" features of the economy that "automatically" react to economic events in a stabilizing fashion.

The principal built-in stabilizer is the U.S. income tax system. Since income taxes are paid as a percentage of income, it necessarily follows that tax receipts increase when aggregate income is rising and decrease when aggregate income is falling. This effect is enhanced by the fact that income tax rates are "graduated," increasing as income levels increase. Thus a tendency for the economy to move into recession (declining incomes) is automatically countered by a reduction in tax payments. The reverse holds for inflationary tendencies in the economy. The U.S. system of transfer payments—unemployment, welfare, and retirement benefits—also plays a role as a built-in stabilizer.

Too much should not be made of these automatic stabilizers. Tax payments will increase for desired as well as undesired expansions in aggregate income, and they will decrease for desired as well as undesired contractions in aggregate income. Transfer payments reduce the human cost of policies of economic restraint (which increase unemployment) and provide a built-in check against undesired economic contraction. In the opinion of many observers, however, the growth in transfer payments in recent years (both new programs and increased payments in existing programs) has exacerbated the economic stabilization problem. For example, cost-of-living adjustments aggravate inflation, and generous unemployment benefits may necessitate a higher level of unemployment in order to achieve a desired degree of anti-inflationary contraction in spending. All these various aspects may result in a need for discretionary policy action.

Once implemented, fiscal policy impacts quickly on economic activity. The path to its implementation, however, is often long and tortuous, for fiscal policy measures require action by both the legislative and executive branches of the federal government. Even when both the President and the Congress agree on the need for a change in taxes or spending, agreeing on *which* taxes and *which* expenditures seldom comes easily or quickly. The fact that monetary policy must so often carry the brunt of the economic stabilization burden is less a triumph of monetarist theory than a reflection of this political reality.

Nonetheless, fiscal policy is not without a "track record." Proponents of fiscal policy point to the 1964 tax cut as evidence of its power to spur economic activity. That huge tax cut (the bill for which languished in the Congress for more than two years) did indeed mark the beginning of a long and vigorous economic expansion. (One should note, however, that monetary policy was also expansionary during that period, and Vietnam war expenditures provided additional fiscal stimulus.)

The 1964 tax reduction featured across-the-board income tax cuts and cuts in federal excise taxes. During the early 1960s, selective tax measures were enacted to stimulate business investment spending. These measures included an investment tax credit (which permits a firm to deduct from its income tax liability for a year a certain percentage of its outlays for plant and equipment during that year) and more liberal depreciation allowances for business depreciable assets.

More recent fiscal policy measures have apparently been much less successful than the 1964 tax cut. In 1968, for example, as a response to mounting inflationary pressures, the Congress (at the urging of President Lyndon Johnson) imposed a 10-percent surtax on 1968 income taxes payable. (A taxpayer who would otherwise have owed $1000 of income taxes on 1968 income then owed $1100.) The surtax apparently had little effect on inflation. The ratio of consumption spending to income fell somewhat, but the ratio of saving to income fell more. It is likely that, insofar as consumption spending was curtailed, the surtax did slow inflation, but the impact was simply inadequate. As mentioned previously, this is an excellent example of the need to harmonize monetary and fiscal policy, for monetary expansion continued in 1968 and thus did *not* support the surtax effort. It is also an example of the importance of accurate economic forecasting, since the Fed apparently "over-reacted" to the enactment of the surtax, overestimating its economic impact.

The lack of success of the surtax, along with a number of other developments, led to some disenchantment with fiscal policy as an anti-inflationary tool. More recently, as indicated in the previous chapter, similar disenchantment with monetary policy's ability to check inflation (in an acceptable time frame) has developed, and renewed interest in fiscal policy measures is surfacing.[12]

---

12. So-called supply-side economics is, to a large degree, a program of fiscal measures—cutting and restructuring of taxes to encourage productivity and capital formation. The huge federal spending and taxation cuts enacted in 1981 were in this vein.

DEBT MANAGEMENT AS A TOOL OF ECONOMIC POLICY

The sheer magnitude of the federal debt is the primary source of its potential as an economic policy tool, separate and apart from the fiscal policy actions that gave rise to its size. Because federal securities account for such a significant proportion of total financial asset holdings of the private sector, the composition of the national debt has implications for all securities. Specifically, the maturity structure of the federal debt may affect the term structure of interest rates in the economy. Also, the allocation of the national debt between marketable and nonmarketable securities, as well as the maturity structure, has implications for the liquidity of the financial system.[13]

Table 22.4 shows the maturity distribution of the federal debt (marketable securities) as of January 31, 1980. It is apparent that the "tilt" of debt management policy is toward relatively short-term debt instruments. In the case of outstanding securities, the impact on average maturity is the time *left* to maturity, not the original time to maturity. Thus the effect of continuously maturing outstanding securities is to shorten the average maturity of the debt. In the absence of new issues of long-term securities, the debt's average maturity would become progressively shorter.

The Treasury is continuously issuing securities, both for new debt and for the refunding of existing debt. Thus the opportunity for restructuring the debt's maturity composition is continually available and, to the extent that debt maturity "matters," is a potential countercyclical economic-policy instrument.

The possible economic consequences of the national debt's maturity composition stem from its potential influence on the term structure of interest rates (and security prices).[14] To some extent, it is possible that a lengthening of the debt's average maturity will lower the market prices on long-term securities and thus boost long-term interest rates (relative to short-term rates). Similarly, shortening the debt's average maturity should ease long-term interest rates while raising short-term rates. The economic significance of inducing such a "tilt" in interest-rate structure stems from the fact that long-term rates are likely to be more significant for business and household spending than short-term rates. Thus a countercyclical debt-management policy would involve the issue of long-term securities when rising aggregate spending threatens to trigger inflationary pressures. When economic recession looms, the appropriate measure would be the issuance of short-term securities by the Treasury in its new borrowing and debt refunding operations. The latter action, by keeping the Treasury from competing with other borrowers for long-term funds and increasing aggregate liquidity, would presumably serve as a stimulus to aggregate spending.

---

13. Nonmarketable Treasury issues must be held until maturity or redemption. These issues include savings bonds and notes, foreign issues, and various special issues. As of the end of 1979, the dollar amount of nonmarketable issues accounted for about 37 percent of the gross public debt.

14. The term structure of interest rates, as indicated in Chapter 9, is determined by a number of factors other than relative supplies of long- and short-term securities. For example, to the extent that *expectations* shape the yield curve, debt management policy is irrelevant for the term structure.

Table 22.4   Maturity distribution of marketable federal securities, January 31, 1980 (billions of dollars)

By type of security	
Issued by U.S. Government	
Treasury bills	175.5
Treasury notes	284.0
Treasury bonds	76.1
Total	535.6
By maturity distribution	
Call classes (due or first becoming callable)	
Within 1 year	259.6
1 to 5 years	164.3
5 to 10 years	55.1
10 to 15 years	19.7
15 to 20 years	12.7
20 years and over	24.2
Total	535.6
Maturity classes (final maturity)	
Within 1 year	257.4
1 to 5 years	165.5
5 to 10 years	50.4
10 to 15 years	22.2
15 to 20 years	6.8
20 years and over	33.3
Total	535.6

Source: *U.S. Treasury Bulletin*, March 1980, p. 73.

The Federal Reserve also has the ability to influence the average maturity of outstanding federal debt because of its large holdings of Treasury securities and the frequency of its open-market operations. The Fed can alter the debt's maturity structure by purchasing securities at one point in the maturity spectrum and selling securities of a different time to maturity. An example of such an effort by the Fed was "Operation Twist" of the early 1960s, when the U.S. economy was jointly plagued by slow growth and balance-of-payments deficits. The Fed attempted to "twist" the interest-rate structure toward lower long-term rates (to spur economic growth) and higher short-term rates (to attract inflows of foreign capital and thus alleviate the balance-of-payments problem). Operation Twist took the form of Fed purchases of long-term federal securities and sales of short-term securities. Unfortunately for the Fed's goal, the Treasury was *issuing* long-term securities during that period. Perhaps this factor and various others (the market for negotiable certificates of deposit emerged during that period) account for the relatively limited success of Operation Twist. However, the Fed's lack of success in achieving a major tilt in the yield structure adds credence to the generally accepted view that the potential for debt management to play a significant policy role is quite limited.

The capacity of debt management policy to serve as an economic stabilization tool depends on a number of economic variables that do not lend themselves to easy assessment. These include some of the factors mentioned in the previous discussion of the "crowding out" issue—such as the interest-elasticity of investment spending—in addition to the more fundamental issue of whether or not debt management policies can exert a significant influence (for a meaningful duration) on the term structure of interest rates. In any event, it does not appear that a countercyclical debt-management policy can accomplish anything that an "extra dose" of appropriate monetary/fiscal policy cannot.

The Treasury's apparent objective in debt management has generally been to minimize interest costs, not to contribute to economic stabilization. (This is not to imply that the Treasury is indifferent to economic stability; rather, it suggests that the Treasury does not view the pursuit of economic stability as one of its primary responsibilities.) Indeed, the approach to a policy of minimizing interest paid on the federal debt is exactly the reverse of a countercyclical policy. During periods of economic recession, long-term interest rates are generally low, and the Treasury thus has an incentive to issue long-term securities. When long-term rates are high during an economic boom, the Treasury minimizes long-run interest costs by issuing short-term securities. Such actions, of course, are exactly contrary to those dictated by countercyclical considerations. For this reason, few (if any) economists believe that minimization of interest costs should be the sole objective of debt management policy.[15]

SUMMARY

It is undisputed that federal government taxation and expenditures have an enormous impact on the financial system and the economy. The federal government's ability to command and allocate huge amounts of resources makes it a dominant participant in the financial markets and the market for goods and services. Less generally accepted is the view that the federal government can exercise its taxing, borrowing, spending, and lending powers to effectively ensure economic stability and growth.

Fiscal policy is the use of changes in federal taxes and spending as a tool of economic stabilization. Like monetary policy, it impacts on aggregate spending—expanding it to increase output and employment in the economy, and restraining it when inflationary forces emerge or accelerate. Its effectiveness as a stabilization tool, both in absolute terms and in terms relative to monetary policy, remains an unsettled issue among economists.

15. See Vance Roley, "Federal Debt Management: A Re-examination of the Issues," *Economic Review,* Federal Reserve Bank of Kansas City (February 1978), pp. 14–23.

The management of the national debt is the task of the Treasury. Although debt management is a potential economic-stabilization policy tool, the Treasury has generally focused on an interest-rate-minimization objective in its management of the debt's maturity composition, rather than the pursuit of countercyclical policies.

QUESTIONS

1. Evaluate and discuss the following statement: "Both in its operating procedures and in its choice of maturities for new security issues, the Treasury attempts to minimize the financial and economic impact of its operations, thus avoiding the exercise of discretionary economic policy measures."

2. What economic relationships must exist in a significant degree for fiscal policy to have the potential for a major impact on the level of economic activity?

3. Analyze and discuss the argument that deficit spending is inherently inflationary because it results in an expansion of the money supply.

4. What is meant by the term "crowding out"? When is this phenomenon likely to occur? Unlikely?

5. Why is coordination of monetary and fiscal policies so important to an effective program of economic stabilization?

6. What is a "high-employment budget"? What is it used for?

7. How and why could debt management be employed as an economic policy tool?

REFERENCES

Bedford, Margaret E., "Recent Developments in Treasury Financing Techniques," Federal Reserve Bank of Kansas City *Monthly Review,* July–August, 1977, pp. 12–24.

Board of Governors of the Federal Reserve System, "Fiscal Policy and Debt Management," *Federal Reserve Bulletin,* November 1965, pp. 1507–1517.

Dew, Kurt, "The Capital Market Crowding Out Problem in Perspective," Federal Reserve Bank of San Francisco *Economic Review,* December 1975, pp. 36–42.

Dornbusch, Rudiger, and Stanley Fischer, *Macroeconomics* (New York: McGraw-Hill, 1978), Chs. 10, 19.

Federal Reserve Bank of Boston, *Issues in Federal Debt Management,* Conference Series No. 10, June, 1973.

Federal Reserve Bank of Kansas City, *The Federal Budget and Economic Activity,* 1969.

Friedman, Milton, and Walter Heller, *Monetary vs. Fiscal Policy* (New York: Norton, 1969).

Keynes, John M., *The General Theory of Employment, Interest, and Money* (New York: Harcourt Brace and World, 1936).

Spencer, Roger W., and William P. Yohe, "The 'Crowding-Out' of Private Expenditures by Fiscal Policy Actions," Federal Reserve Bank of St. Louis *Review,* October 1970, pp. 12–24.

Stein, Herbert, *The Fiscal Revolution in America* (Chicago: University of Chicago Press, 1969).

Index

AAA corporate bond rate, 206, 207
Accounting, double-entry system of, 112
Aggregate demand, components of, 420–422
Aggregate market efficiency, 240
Aggregate spending, management of, 126
Agricultural commodities, futures markets in, 345
Agricultural production, and credit distribution, 54
Agricultural sector, government subsidy of, 91, 92
American Stock Exchange (AMEX), 332
Announcement effects, 143
Annual percentage rate (APR), 88
Anti-inflationary policy, 420–422
APR
  See Annual percentage rate
Arrow, K., 341
Asia, U.S. banks in, 409
Asset management, liability management as substitute for, 56
Asset pricing, capital-asset-pricing model, 230–234
  in efficient market, 232–233
  and financial market efficiency, 234
  portfolio selection and diversification, 224–230
Assets, on balance sheet, 30–31
  on commercial bank balance sheet, 112–115

of commercial banking industry, 51–52
of credit unions, 61
defined, 6
and expected returns, 25
of Federal Reserve, 117
of finance companies, 65
of foreign banks in U.S., 410
of insurance companies, 62, 63
of mutual savings banks, 60
for nonfinancial business corporations, 325
of pension funds, 64, 65
of savings and loan associations, 58
A.T.S. accounts, and interest-rate instability, 176
Auctioning, of Treasury bills, 452
Automated clearinghouses, 74
Automated teller machines (ATMs), 68, 69, 74
Automatic quotation, of National Association of Security Dealers (NASDAQ), 333
Average money holdings, 109

Bahamas, U.S. banks in, 409
Bahrain, offshore currency market in, 398
Balance on capital account, 369
Balance on current account, 369
Balance of payments, deficit in, 372

and dollar, 373–374
"equilibrium" in, 428
and fixed vs. flexible exchange rates, 374–375
impact of OPEC on, 385
measures of deficit and surplus for, 367–372
Balance sheet, commercial bank, 112–115
of Federal Reserve, 118
fundamental equalities in, 31–32
Balance of trade, 429
Bank of America, national scope of, 96
Bankers acceptances, 9, 271
characteristics of, 275
creation of, 272
financing, 272–273, 274
in international trade, 377
in open–market operations of Federal Reserve, 139, 140–141
ownership of, 290
uses of, 274
Bankers Trust Company, forecasts of flow of funds prepared by, 43
Bank Holding Company Act (1970), 96, 411
See also Holding companies
Banking, economies of scale in, 97
geographical scope of, 96
international, 411
national, 130–131
See also Interstate banking
Banking acts (1933, 1935), 132
Bank Merger Act (1960), 148
Bank reserves, quantity of, 116–120
Banks, central, 129
commercial, 79
balance sheet of, 113
in capital market, 237
common stocks held by, 330
commercial mortgage funds of, 315
compared with nonbanks, 49–50
credit-creation function of, 53
distribution of loans at, 53
Federal Reserve members, 132
flow of funds accounts for, 39
forecasting supply of funds for, 46–47
general obligation bonds of, 305
impact of interest rate cycle on, 256
in international financial system, 389
international operations of, 407–409
and international payments, 375–378
liquid assets of, 54
in money market, 236
municipal bonds of, 304
role of 7–8, 244–245
U.S. government securities of, 278, 307
consortium, 401–402
for cooperatives (BCs), 91, 285

Federal Reserve, 118, 132
excess reserves and borrowings of, 143
location of, 135
regulation and supervision of, 147–148
U.S. government and government agencies securities of, 307
as firms, assets and liabilities of, 51–55
functions of, 50–51
sources of funds, 55–56
and uses of funds, 56–57
foreign, 409–411
in international money market, 399
lead, 401
See also Institutions, financial
Bank wire systems, 73–74
Barter system, 4, 104
Basis points, 181
Beta coefficient, 230, 234, 235
"Big Board," 332
"Blue chip" firms, 287
Board of Governors of Federal Reserve, 132, 134
function of, 136, 149
policy powers of, 135
responsibility of, 147–148
Bond market, international, 382–383
Bonds, callable, 217
in capital market, 295
current yield, 155–157
deep discount, 216
defined, 154–155
flower, 216–217
international, 402, 406
long- vs. short-term, 158
mortgage, 297
multiple currency, 403–406
ratings for, 212–213
and relationship between yield and price, 157–159
U.S., 278, 279
yield to maturity of, 155–157
See also Corporate bonds; Municipal bonds
Book value, 31
See also Net worth
Borrowers, in capital market, 237
and callability, 217
of federal funds, 265
during inflation, 207
in international money market, 399
and yield curve, 179–180
See also Lenders
Borrowing, in commercial banking industry, 54–55
and "crowding out" argument, 458
regulation of, 86–90
Treasury, 451–452
"Bracket creep," 305

Branch banking, controversy over, 96
  regulation of, 82
Bretton Woods system, 389
  collapse of, 373
  established, 372
  and Eurodollar market, 393
  failure of, 383
  replacement of, 374
  revaluation under, 375
Britain, central bank of, 129
  "clearing banks" in, 95
  futures market in, 347, 348
Brokers, in capital markets, 237–238
Budget surplus, 6
Business cycle, expansion phase of, 248
  and interest rate cycle, 257
  and maturity management, 248–250
  risk premiums in, 213
Business sector, 5
  balance sheet for, 30, 40
  debt instruments of, 9
  and demand for loanable funds, 164
  flow of funds account for, 35–40
  forecasting saving behavior of, 43
  and inflation, 204
  saving in, 160
  and saving–investment process, 18

Callability, 217–218
Call options, 340
Call price, for preferred stock, 329
Call provisions, 298
Cambridge equation, 125, 126
Canada, central bank of, 129
  futures market in, 347, 348
Capital, on commercial bank balance sheet, 112–115
  in commercial banking industry, 54–55
Capital-asset-pricing model, 230–232
  in efficient market, 232–233
  evaluation of portfolio theory, 233–234
Capital market, bonds in, 295–309
  dimensions of, 296–297
  equity securities in, 322–341
  Federal Reserve in, 141
  financial instruments in, 22
  international, effect of U.S. capital controls in, 402–403
    Eurobonds in, 403
    Eurocredit lending in, 400–402
    interest rates in, 406
    multiple currency bonds in, 403–406
  linkages with money market, 238
  vs. money market, 21
  mortgage debt in, 311

mortgages in, 311–321
  nature of, 237–238
  primary and secondary components of, 240
  role of governments in, 306
Capital market line (CML), 231–232
Caribbean, offshore currency market in, 398
"Carry," 262
Carter administration, and international banking, 412
  and reserve requirements on Eurodollar borrowings, 399
Cash, of Federal Reserve, 117
Casualty insurance companies, corporate bonds held by, 300
  as financial institutions, 63
  U.S. government and government agencies securities of, 307
Cayman Islands, U.S. banks in, 409
CDs
  See Certificates of Deposit
Central money market, 235–236
Certificates of Deposit (CDs), 8, 9, 267–271
  buyers and sellers of, 269–270
  characteristics of, 269
  and Federal Reserve, 55
  and interest rates, 260–261, 270–271
  origin of, 268
  requirements for, 82
  secondary market for, 270
  tap, 400
  tranche, 400
Checkable deposits, and measurement of money supply, 107
Checking accounts, 7, 105–106.
  See also N.O.W. accounts
Chicago Board of Options Exchange, 339
Chicago Board of Trade (CBT), 339
Citicorp, and commercial paper, 289
  national scope of, 96
"Clearinghouse" funds, 263
Clearinghouses, automated, 68, 69
Coin, commercial bank holding of, 52
  as modern money, 104, 105
Commercial banking industry, outside U.S., 80
  See also Regulation
Commercial paper, 9, 287
  amount outstanding, 288
  characteristics of, 288
  and interest rates, 260–261, 291
  investors in, 289–290
  market for, 290–291
  nature of issues, 289
  ownership of, 290
Committee on Paperless Entries, 74
Commodity futures market, 239

See also Futures market
Commodity Futures Trading Commission, 348
Commodity money, 104
Common stock, 329, 337
Community Reinvestment Act, provisions of, 89
Competition, in commercial banking industry, 53, 55
  among financial institutions, 67–69
  and government regulation, 82, 83
  and Regulation Q, 86–87
Comptroller of the Currency, functions of, 85
  in National Bank Surveillance System, 253
  and national banks, 147, 149
Consortium banks, in syndicated Eurocredit lending, 401–402
Consumer loan market, commercial banks in, 67
Consumer Price Index (CPI), 203, 424
Consumer protection laws, 88–90
Consumers, and demand for loanable funds, 163–164
Consumption demand, 420
Continental bills, 105
Contracts, forward, 238
Contractual institutions, role of, 246–247
Convertible bonds, 298
Cooperatives, banks for, 91, 284, 285
Corporate bond market, flow of funds accounts in, 37
  forecasting supply of funds for, 47
Corporate bonds, 9
  buyers of, 300
  characteristics of, 297–298
  convertible, 298
  market for, 301
  supply of, 299
  yields on, 297, 301–302
Corporate stocks
  See Equity securities
Corporations, equity financing of, 325–328
  equity instruments of, 9–10
  financing between short- and long-term debt, 299
  new security issues of, 327
  nonfinancial sources of funds for, 324
  U.S. government and government agencies securities of, 307
Cost-push inflation, 204
Costs, search and transactions, 104
Coupon instruments, 278
Coupon rate, 155
Covariance, concept of, 228–229
Credit, on commercial bank balance sheet, 112–115
  in commercial banking industry, 53
  and Eurodollar creation, 395–396
  forecasting supply and demand for, 42–46

  impact of usury laws on, 88
  regulations of access to, 89–90
  and role of Federal Reserve, 138, 143, 145
  See also Default risk
Credit-card services, impact of 1980 legislation on, 70
Credit Control Act (1969), 145
"Credit crunch," cause of, 87
  1966, 143
Credit risk, of commercial paper, 291
  defined, 211
  in money market, 260
  of revenue bonds, 303
  See also Risk
Credit-risk management, process of, 254–256
Credit standard, 106
Credit unions, characteristics of, 60–61
  role of, 8, 246
"C's of credit," 255
Culbertson, J., 199
Currency, 104
  commercial bank holding of, 52
  devaluation of, 374
  exchange rate for, 365
  of Federal Reserve, 117
  public demand for, 116
Currency market, Asian, 398
Current yield (CY), calculating, 156
  explained, 155
Customer bank communications terminals (CBCT), 74
Customer's market, 235, 245

Dealers, in capital market, 237–238
Dealers, securities, financing of, 262
  and government securities, 281
  profit-making of, 262
  role of, 261
Debits, on commercial bank balance sheet, 112–115
Debt instruments, defined, 9
  government, 9
  private, 9
Debt management policy, 463–465
Default risk, and bond ratings, 212–213
  defined, 211
  degrees of, 211
  and government regulation, 80–81
Deficit, in balance of trade, 367
Deficit economic units, 6
Deficit sector, 34, 35
Deficit unit, on flow of funds statement, 32
Demand deposits (checking accounts), 7, 105–106
  expansion of, 112–115
  public demand for, 116

Demand deposit services, of commercial banking industry, 52–53
Demand–pull inflation, 204
Denominations, of indirect securities, 20
Depository Institutions Deregulation and Monetary Control Act (D.I.D.M.C.A.) (1980), 50
    effect on mutual savings banks, 60
    and Federal Reserve banks, 132–133
    and Federal Reserve lending, 142
    impact, on credit unions, 61
        on mortgage market, 321
        on payments system, 106
    and interest rate ceilings, 87, 145–146
    and interstate banking, 98
    and N.O.W. accounts, 246
    provisions of, 69–71
    and reserve requirements, 144, 400
    and state usury laws, 88
Deposit rate ceilings
    See Regulation Q
Deposits, checkable, 106
    derivative, 116
    interbank, 52
    interest-rate ceilings on, 69
    noncheckable, 106
    primary, 116
Deutschemark, 397, 404
Devaluation, of currency, 374
"Dilemma model," 445
Direct money market, 235
Discounting, of "commercial paper," 142
Discount-window policy, 142, 143, 145, 149
Disintermediation, 146
    in mortgage market, 320
    periods of, 59
    reduction of, 70
Dissaving, 6
Diversification, defined, 20
    systematic vs. unsystematic risk in, 230
Dividend reinvestment plans, 331
Dividends, defined, 6
Dollar, Canadian, Eurobond issues in, 404
Dollar, U.S. Eurobond issues in, 404
    vs. Eurodollar, 396
    paramount position of, 383
Dollar return, expected, 25
Duration, vs. maturity, 190–191

Economic policy, and aggregate demand, 420–422
    and aggregate supply, 422–423
    and balance-of-payments "equilibrium," 428–430
    debt management as tool of, 463–465
    and economic growth, 428, 429
    full employment in, 424, 425

goals of, 423–430
    inflation in, 424–428
    and Phillips curve, 444–445
    types of, 419
Economic units, surplus, 6
Economies of scale, 21, 97
Economy, financial system in, 4–6
    significance of money in, 108–111
Edge Act (1919), 408
Edge Act corporations (EACs), 408
Edge Act subsidiaries, 95
Efficiency, allocational, 23
    operational, 23
Elasticity, in money supply, 142
Electronic funds transfer systems (EFTS), implications of, 75–76
    movement toward, 68, 69
    and role of financial intermediaries, 73–76
    types of, 73–75
Employment, and economic policy, 424
    and money supply, 125–127
    unemployment, 424, 425, 444
Employment Act (1946), 424
Entry, regulation of, 82
Equal Credit Opportunity Act (1974), provisions of, 89
"Equilibrating specie flow price mechanism," 372
Equilibrium, determination of, 170
Equilibrium interest rate, determination of, 173–174.
    See also Interest rate, basic
Equities market, efficiency of, 338
Equity, definition of, 323
Equity financing, external, 327–328
    internal, 326
Equity instruments, in capital market, 237
    defined, 9
    types of, 9–10
"Equity kickers," 313
Equity returns, record of, 336, 337
Equity securities, characteristics of, 328–329
    definition of, 323
    market for, 337
    new issues of, 337
    OTC market for, 333–334
    ownership of, 329–330
    primary market for, 330–332
    secondary market for, 332
    valuation of, 334
"Escalator clause," 427
Eurobanks, 381
Eurobond market, recent developments in, 403
Eurobonds, 382–383, 402
    dollar amounts, 404
    institutional aspects of, 406

multiple-currency, 403–406
Eurocredit arrangements, 400
Eurocredit market, growth of, 413
Eurocredits, 400–402
Eurodollar deposits, and interest rates, 260–261
Eurodollar market, 381–382
  currency composition of, 397–398
  interest rates in, 396
  nature and origins of, 392–393
  size of, 394
Eurodollars, 271, 395–396
Europe, commercial banking industry in, 80
  U.S. banks in, 409
European Economic Community (Common
  Market), 374
European Monetary System (EMS), 374
Examinations, bank, 81–82
Exchange, equation of, 110–111
  money as medium of, 103–104
Exchange flows, in economic system, 5
  intermediated, 7
  nonintermediated, 7
  payment mechanism in, 23
Exchange rate risk, on international bonds, 405
Exchange rates, fixed vs. flexible, 374–375
  floating of, 374
  and interest-rate relationships, 380
  volatility in, 385
Exchange-rate systems, convertibility, 373
  fixed, 372
  modern, 372–375
Expansion phase, of business cycle, 248
Expectations, and Phillips curve, 444–445
  portfolio-choice models and, 233
  and rational expectations hypothesis, 446–447
  and velocity of money, 110
Expectations hypothesis, of yield curve, 183–185,
  199–200
Expected return, 224, 225
Expected utility, concept of, 226
Exporters, and bankers acceptances, 273, 274
Exports, and foreign exchange, 365–367

Fair Credit Billing Act, provisions of, 89
Fair Housing Act, provisions of, 89
Fannie Mae
  See Federal National Mortgage Association
Farm credit system, 91
Federal agencies, and FFB, 453
  functions of, 283–286
  interest rates on issues of, 287
  securities of, 286
  types of, 283, 284
Federal budget, and demand for loanable funds, 165
Federal debt, maturity distribution of, 463–464

Federal Deposit Insurance Corporation (F.D.I.C.)
  functions of, 85
  and interest-rate ceilings, 145
Federal Farm Credit Banks, 284
Federal Financing Bank (FFB), 452–453
Federal funds, changing nature of, 265–266
  and commercial banks, 263–265
  definition of, 262–267
  and Federal Reserve, 266–267
  and interest rates, 260–261, 267
  and monetary policy, 266–267
  in money market, 236
  role in financial system, 263
Federal government, in money market, 236
Federal Home Loan Bank Board, 85, 92
Federal Home Loan Banks, 284
  maturity distribution of obligations of, 286
  and savings and loan associations, 59
Federal Home Loan Mortgage Corporation
  (FHLMC), 284, 317–318
Federal Housing Administration (FHA), mortgage
  insurance program of, 313
  mutual savings bank insured mortgages of, 60
Federal Intermediate Credit Banks (FICB), 91
  assets and liabilities for, 285
  long-term securities of, 308
Federal Land Banks (FLBs), 91, 284
  assets and liabilities of, 285
  long-term securities of, 308
Federal National Mortgage Association (FNMA),
  92, 284
  balance sheets of, 286
  function of, 317–318
  purchase auctions of, 319
  in secondary market, 319
Federal Open Market Account, 261
Federal Open Market Committee (FOMC), 137
Federal Reserve Act (1913), 132
Federal Reserve float, 118
Federal Reserve notes, 119
Federal Reserve System, 3
  bank wire system established by, 73–74
  Board of Governors of, 132, 134, 135, 136,
    147–148, 149
  control over commercial banks, 50
  credit controls of, 145
  discount window policy of, 142, 143, 145, 149
  and federal debt, 457, 464
  and federal funds market, 266–267
  Federal Open Market Committee, 137
  as fiscal agent, 147
  flow of funds accounts published by, 34–40
  founding of, 130–132
  functions of, 84–85
  and government securities, 280–281

holding company provisions of, 96
lending of, 141–144
major components of, 148
measures of monetary aggregates of, 107
and money supply, 117–120, 122
and nonmember depository institutions, 134
open-market operations of, 137, 138–141, 149
organization of, 133
and problems of monetary control, 146
Regulation Q of, 55, 86–87
and reserve requirements, 149
source of revenues for, 135
structure of, 132–137
target rates of, 440
See also Regulation; Reserve requirements
Federal Savings and Loan Insurance Corporation,
    85
Fiat money, 104, 105
Finance, direct vs. indirect, 18
Finance companies, characteristics of, 65–66
Financial futures, potential advantages of, 357–358
Financial futures market, 239
Financial sevices industry, and government regula-
    tion, 79
Financial system, efficiency of, 23–26
  evolution of, 71
  functions of, 3
  role of, 4–7
First National City Bank of New York (Citibank),
    268
First Pennsylvania National Bank, FDIC "bail out"
    of, 252
Fiscal policy, 126, 419, 420
  coordinated with monetary policy, 459–461
  defined, 465
  discretionary effects of, 461
  and economic activity, 462
  and high-employment budget, 459
  monetarist view of, 455–456
  monetary effects of, 456–458
  theory of, 454
Fisher, I., 208
Fisher effect, 208–209, 378
Float, Federal Reserve, 118, 138
"Floating dollar standard," 386–388
Flower bonds, 216–217
Flow of funds, for forecasting financial market
    pressures, 42–47
  for nonfinancial business corporation, 325
  real vs. financial use of, 33
Flow of funds accounts, activities of, 32–34
  assets in, 30–31
  concept of, 29–40
  fundamental equalities in, 31–32
  liabilities in, 31

net worth in, 31
published by Federal Reserve, 34–40
FOMC
  See Federal Open Market Committee
Forecasting, of financial events, 25
Foreign banks, in United States, 409–411
Foreign bond market, New York, 402
Foreign bonds, 402
Foreign branches, approval for, 148
Foreign currencies futures market, hedging in,
    355–357
  speculation in, 357
Foreign exchange, sources of, 365–367
  uses of, 365–367
  See also Exchange rate
Foreign-exchange markets, and government inter-
    vention, 388
  nature of, 364–365
  supply and demand in, 366
Foreign governments, in U.S. money markets, 236
Forward transaction, in foreign-exchange market,
    364
"Fourth market," 333
Franc, French, 397, 404
Franc, Swiss, 397
France, central bank of, 129
Freddie MAC   *See* Federal Home Loan Mortgage
    Corporation
Friedman, M., 126, 127, 434, 444
Full employment, and economic policy, 424
  and fiscal policy, 459
Full Employment and Balanced Growth Act (1978),
    424
"Full faith and credit" bonds, 302
Funds managment, 245, 257
Futures market, buying and selling in, 348–349
  development of, 343
  foreign currencies
    hedging with, 355–357
    short hedge, 355–356
    speculation in, 357
  vs. forward market, 344–349
  growth of, 357–358, 359
  interest-bearing securities in, 349–354
    hedging with, 350
    long hedge, 352–353
    short hedge, 351
    speculation with, 353–354
  nature of, 238–239, 344–348
  participants in, 350

General Motors Acceptance Corporation, and
    commercial paper, 289
General obligations (G.O.) bonds, 302
General Theory of Employment, Interest, and

Money, The (Keynes), 454
Georgia Automated Clearinghouse, 74
Ginnie Mae
  See Government National Mortgage Associa-
    tion, 284
GNMA *See* Government National Mortgage As-
    sociation
"Gold drain," 384
"Gold export" point, 372
Gold holdings, of Federal Reserve, 117
"Gold import" point, 372
Gold standard, 104–105
  abandoned, 105
  and fixed exchange rates, 372
Government, as financial intermediary, 91–93
  fiscal activities of, 449
  fiscal policy of, 453–461
  in international money market, 399
  See also Government sector; Local governments;
    Regulation; State governments
Government agency securities, market for, 309
Government debt, interest-bearing, 279
Government National Mortgage Association
    (GNMA), 92, 317–318
  in futures market, 345, 347, 348, 351, 354
  in secondary market, 319
"Governments," 278
Government sector, 5
  balance sheet for, 30, 40
  debt instruments of, 9
  and demand for loanable funds, 164–166
  forecasting saving behavior of, 43
  saving in, 161
Government securities, market for, 309
Government spending, nature of, 421
Great Depression, cause of, 17
  impact on financial system, 372
  and money supply, 125
"Greenbacks, " 105
Gross national product (GNP), deflator, 203
  forecasting, 43
Growth, economic, impact of savings and invest-
    ment on, 17
Guilder, Dutch, Eurobond issues in, 404

Hamburger, M. L., 199
Hamilton, Alexander, 130
Hedgers, 239
Hedging, 239, 344
  cross hedge, 350
  in foreign currencies futures market, 355–357
  long hedge, 352
  nature of, 350
  short hedge, 351–352
Hoarding, 32

Holding companies, bank, controversy over, 97–98
  Fed's responsibility for, 148, 149
  growth of, 68
Home Mortgage Disclosure Act, provisions of, 89
Home mortgage market, flow of funds accounts for,
    38
Horvitz, P. M., 97
Households, corporate bonds held by, 300
  equity securities held by, 329
Household sector, 5
  balance sheet for, 30, 40
  and demands for loanable funds, 163–164
  flow of funds account for, 34–35
  forecasting saving behavior of, 43
  government subsidization of, 92–93
  net acquisition of financial assets by, 36
  and saving–investment process, 18, 160
Housing, single-family, 312
Housing starts, forecasting, 43
Humphrey–Hawkins Act (1978), 424
Hyperinflation, 204

IET *See* Interest equalization tax, 402
"Immediately available," use of term, 262
Implicit gross national product deflator, 203
Importers, and bankers acceptances, 273, 274
Imports, and foreign exchange, 365–367
Income, real vs. nominal, 109
Incomes policy, 419, 420, 422
Income tax, vs. capital gains, 216
  on corporate bond interest, 302
  and fiscal policy, 461
Incremental risk, 228
Indenture agreement, 297
Individuals, partnerships, and corporations (IPCs),
    269
Inflation, and aggregate demand policies, 423
  and bond market, 309
  causes of, 204, 426
  and construction costs, 311
  definition of, 203–204
  "double-digit," 170, 205
  and economic policy, 424–428
  fiscal remedy for, 126
  impact on capital market, 296
  impact on depository institutions, 8
  and interest rates, 207, 208
  monetary remedy for, 126
  and pattern of rates, 210
  recent, 205–207
  and stock yields, 337
  and troubled mortgage market, 320
  and unemployment, 444
Information market, and options, 341
Institutions, financial, 12

banks vs. nonbanks, 49–50
and competition, risk, and performance relation-
    ships, 83
and consumer protection laws, 89
contractual, 62
credit-risk management of, 254–256
credit unions, 60–61
defined, 3
depository, 57–58, 67
    expansion in competition of, 67
    and regulatory agencies, 84–85
finance companies, 65
growing competition among, 67–69
impact of interest-rate cycles on, 250
insurance companies, 62–63
maturity management of, 248–254
mutual savings banks, 59–60
nondepository, 85–86
private nonbank, 39
role of, 243–247
and saving–investment process, 19
savings and loan associations, 58–59
securities, 261–262
types of, 57–66
Instruments, financial, 12
bankers acceptances, 271–275
bonds, corporate, 297–302
    state and local government, 302–306
    U.S. government and government agency,
        306–308
in capital market, 237, 295
certificates of deposit, 267–271
commercial paper, 287–291
Eurodollar, 271
federal funds, 262–267
fixed-income, 154–159
    (See also Bonds)
in international money market, 400
in money market, 260–261
mortgages, 311, 321
types of, 9–10
U.S. government agency securities, 282–289
U.S. government securities, 277–282
Insurance companies, casualty, 63, 300
equity securities held by, 328–330
as financial institutions, 62–63
in financial markets, 246–247
life, 63, 300, 307, 315
property, 63, 300, 304–305
role of, 8, 246–247
Inter-American Development Bank, 392
Interest, defined, 6
Interest elasticity, of investment demand, 421
Interest equalization tax (IET), 402
Interest income, tax exemption for municipal, 215

tax exemption for U.S. government, 215–216
Interest rates, basic, 153
    as allocating device, 154
    and demand for loanable funds, 165
    liquidity preference theory of, 172–176
    and loanable fund theory, 159–168
    and volume of saving, 161
    yields and prices, 154
calculation of impact on profitability, 253–254
on CDs, 270–271
ceilings, and Regulation Q, 87
set by Federal Reserve, 145–146
on commercial paper, 291
cycle for, and funds management, 257
    impact on financial institutions, 250
    loanable funds theory applied to, 168–170
and exchange-rate relationships, 378–380
in futures market, 349, 358
and inflation, 203–210
    complications associated with, 209–210
    Fisher effect, 208–209
on international bonds, 406
and marketability, 218
and maturity management, 248–250
in money market, 261
predicting yield curve for, 192
relative level of, 177
risk, 157, 158, 355
and role of Federal Reserve, 138, 143
Salomon Brothers 1980 forecast for, 47
and taxability, 214
term structure of, 177, 178, 196
and time to maturity, 178
and troubled mortgage market, 320
unstable, and bond market, 309
    and futures markets, 346, 359
and velocity of money, 110
See also Yield curve
Intermediaries, financial, 6
government as, 91–93
impact of EFTS on, 73–76
types of, 7–9
Intermediation process, 6–7
explained, 6–7
international, 363
International Banking Act (1978), 95, 411
International capital market, 400–407
International financial system, fragility of, 389
Internationalization, of finance, 407
International Monetary Fund (IMF), 392
function of, 372–373
lending by, 385
International monetary system, dominant role of
        U.S. dollar in, 386–388
fragility of, 383–388

futures in, 344, 345–346
less-developed countries in, 386
OPEC in, 384–386
United States in, 370–371
International money markets, Eurodollar market, 392–398
  financial instruments of, 400
  major participants in, 398–400
International payments system, balance of payments in, 367–372
  foreign-exchange market in, 364–367
  fundamentals of, 364–372
  rate of commercial banks in, 375–378
International trade, bankers acceptances in, 377
  letters of credit in, 377
  payments mechanism for, 375–376
Interstate banking, and branch banking controversy, 96–97
  and holding-company controversy, 97–98
  impact of, 99
  and 1980 legislation, 98
  question of, 95–96
Investment, 32
  and anti-inflationary monetary policy, 440
  encouragement of, 6
  impact of inflation on, 427
  importance of, 17
  nature of, 16
  real vs. financial, 17
Investment companies, characteristics of, 66
Investment demand, 420
Investment portfolios, in commercial banking industry, 57
  See also Portfolio management; Portfolio theory
Investor behavior, and expectations hypothesis of yield curve, 184–185
  and theory, 232

Japan, commercial banking industry in, 80
  and floating dollar standard, 387
Johnson, Lyndon, 462

Kessel R., 200
Keynes, J. M., 454
Keynesianism, 126
Kohn, E., 97
Kuwait, offshore currency market in, 392

Latin America, U.S. banks in, 409
Lead banks, 401
Leasing, vs. bond financing, 299
"Legal tender," 105
Lenders, and callability, 217
  in capital market, 237
  of federal funds, 265

during inflation, 207
and yield curve, 179–180
See also Borrowers
Lending, 32
  federal, 452–453
  of Federal Reserve, 141
  regulation of, 86–90
Less-developed countries (LDCs), and world banking system, 386
Letters of credit, creating bankers acceptances, 272, 275
  in international trade, 376–377
Leveraging, 231
Liabilities, on balance sheet, 31
  on commercial bank balance sheet, 112–115
  of commercial banking industry, 51–52
  of credit unions, 61
  of Federal Reserve, 117
  of finance companies, 65
  of foreign banks in U.S., 410
  of insurance companies, 62, 63
  of mutual savings banks, 60
  for nonfinancial business corporation, 325
  of savings and loan associations, 58
Liability management, and federal funds in, 265
  as substitute for asset management, 56
LIBOR
  See London Interbank Offered Rate, 382
Life Insurance Association of America, forecasts of flow of funds prepared by, 43
Life insurance companies, commercial mortgage funds of, 315
  corporate bonds held by, 300
  as financial institutions, 63
  U.S. government and government agencies, securities of, 307
Liquidity, defined, 20
  of indirect securities, 21
Liquidity adjustments, short-term, 54
"Liquidity preference" theory, 454
  of interest-rate determination, 172–176
  liquidity-premium explanation of, 185–186
Loanable funds, demand for, 163–168
  and importance of availability, 166
  supply of, 160
  supply and demand for, 166–168
  and volatility of demand schedule, 166
Loanable funds theory, 159–160
Loan portfolios, in commercial banking industry, 57
  See also Portfolio management
Loans, in commercial banking industry, 53
  current trends for, 53
  of farm credit agencies, 91, 92
  real vs. financial aspect of, 4

Local governments, pension funds of, 64–65
  bond issues of, 302–306
  U.S. government and government agencies securities of, 307
  See also Municipal bonds
London, Eurodollar market in, 271
  U.S. banks in, 409

Macroeconomic theory, monetarist school of, 455
Malkiel, B., 200
Management, bank, 245
Manager of the System Open Market Account, 137, 139
Manufacturers Hanover Trust, national scope of, 96
Marine insurance companies, U.S. government and government agencies securities of, 307
Mark, German, 397, 404
Marketability, and interest rates, 218
Markets, financial, 22
  asset pricing in, capital-asset-pricing model, 230–234
    portfolio selection and diversification, 224–230
  defined, 3
  federal funds, 262
  forecasting pressures in flow of funds for, 42
  function of, 239
  government influence on, 93
  intermediated vs. nonintermediated, 22
  international, 271, 381–383
    bond, 382–383
    control over, 411–413
    Eurodollar market, 381
  loanable funds, 162
  participants and instruments in, 19
  role of, intermediation, 17–21
    investment, 15
    saving, 15
  types of, 21–22
    capital market, 237–238
    futures, 238–239
    money markets, 235–236
Market index, 230
Market segmentation, and yield curve, 187–190, 200–201
Matched sale–purchase transaction (reverse RP), in open–market operations of Federal Reserve, 139, 140–141
Maturity, defined, 9
  and yield on bonds, 155–156
Maturity management, and interest–rate cycle, 250
  interest rates and business cycle, 248–250
  and interest on volatility, 253–254
  and passive vs. active portfolio, 250–253
Maturity structure, acceptability of, 57

of banks vs. nonbanks, 50
maturity vs. duration in, 190–191
of municipal securities, 303
yield curve in, 178, 192–196
McFadden Act (1927), 95
Meiselman, D., 199
Mergers, jurisdiction over proposed, 148, 149
  regulation of, 82
Middle East, offshore currency market in, 398
Migration, and supply of municipal securities, 303
Military–related transactions, in balance of payments, 366, 369
Modigliani, F., 200
Monetarists, emergence of, 126–127
  and fiscal policy, 455–456
  and monetary control, 146
  vs. neo-Keynesians, 434
Monetary base, defined, 121–122
  and money supply, 123
  and role of Federal Reserve, 138
Monetary multiplier, 121–122
Monetary policy, 111, 419, 420
  credit effects of, 431–432
  discretionary, 126
  effects of, 430
  federal funds in, 264
  and federal funds market, 266–267
  and Federal Funds Rate, 437–438
  and Federal Reserve banks, 134
  fiscal policy coordinated with, 459–461
  future of, 440
  goals of, 436
  lags in effects of, 435–436
  monetarist view, 434–435
  portfolio effects of, 432–433
  problems of control, 146
  and rational expectations theory, 446
  and reserves-based policy procedure, 438–440
  stringency, 138–139
  transmission of, 431
  wealth effects of, 433–434
Money, creation of, 112–115
  demand deposit expansion, 112–115
  economic significance of, 108–111
  and equation of exchange, 110–111
  impact of EFTS on demand for, 76
  modern, 105–106
  nature of, 30, 103, 104
  price of, 154
  standards, 104–105
  and supply of loanable funds, 160, 162
  velocity of, 109–110
Money market, vs. capital market, 21
  central, 235–236
  defined, 6

expansion of, 293
financial instruments in, 22
instruments of, 260–261
international, currency composition in, 397–398
  Eurodollar market, 392–398
  major participants and financial instruments
   in, 392–400
linkages with capital market, 238
nature of, 235–236, 259–260
primary and secondary components of, 240
Money market fund, development of, 66
functions of, 67–68
Money market mutual funds, phenomenal growth
  of, 87
Money multiplier, and role of Federal Reserve, 138
Money-multiplier effect, for Eurodollars, 394–395
Money standards, 104–105
Money supply, Cambridge equation, 125, 126
changes in, 162
circular flow, 109
and economic performance, 105
elasticity in, 142
and Federal Reserve, 117
impact of changes in, 111
and interest-rate determination, 174
measurement of, 106–108
and real sector, 103
and role of Federal Reserve, 138
and treasury's borrowing operations, 456
Moody's, bond-rating system of, 212
credit evaluation by, 255
Mortgage bonds, 297
Mortgage credit, impact of government programs
  on, 93
Mortgage funds, demand for, 315
supply of, 315–320, 321
Mortgage loans, government-guaranteed, 60
of savings and loan associations, 58
Mortgage market, flow of funds accounts in, 38
Mortgage pools, federally sponsored, 93
Mortgages, 9
in capital market, 295
characteristics of, 312
classification of, 312, 316–317
definition of, 312
demand for, 321
insured vs. conventional, 313
market for, 318–319
new types of, 314–315
ownership of, 316–317
as primary security, 18
troubled market for, 320
types of, 312–313
volume of, 313
yields on, 319–320

Multinational corporations, 391
and international banking services, 378
in international money market, 399
Municipal bonds, 9
characteristics of, 302
demand for, 304–305
market for, 305–306
yields on, 306
Municipal securities, in bank portfolios, 57
supply of, 303–304
Mutual funds, efficiency of, 336
equity securities held by, 328–330
role of, 8
Mutual savings banks, characteristics of, 59–60
corporate bonds held by, 300
impact of interest rate cycle on, 256
impact of 1980 legislation on, 70
role of, 8, 246
U.S. government and government agencies, securities of, 307

National Association of Security Dealers (NASD),
  332
National Automated Clearinghouse Association, 74
National Bank Act (1863), 96, 130
National Bank Surveillance System, 253
National Banking System, 130–131
National Income Accounts, 29
National Monetary Commission, 131
Negotiable orders of withdrawal
  See N.O.W. accounts
Neo-Keynesians, 434, 455
Net creditor on flow of funds statement, 33
Net debtor on flow of funds statement, 33
Net interest cost method, of low-bid determination,
  305
Net worth, on balance sheet, 31
New York, central money market in, 236
relaxation of branching limitations in, 97
New York Stock Exchange (NYSE), 90, 332
Notes, U.S., 278, 279
N.O.W. (negotiable orders of withdrawal) ac-
  counts, and interest-rate instability, 176
nature of, 67
1980 legislation on, 69
and nonbank depository institutions, 68
of savings and loan associations, 59
spread of, 69, 87, 106

Obligation, financial, 6
Offshore currency markets, 398
Open-market operations, of Federal Reserve,
  138–141, 149
Open Market Trading Desk, 139
Open money market, 235–236

"Operation Twist," 200
Options Clearing Corporation (OCC), 339
Options market,339–341
Organization of Petroleum Exporting Countries
    (OPEC), 205
  and Eurodollar market, 398
  impact of, 384–386
  impact on balance of payments, 385
  and international banking, 412
  in international money markets, 399
  in money market, 236
Over-the-counter (OTC) market, 333–334
"Own bill,"273

Panics, financial, 131
"Parity band," 373
Paper money, 105, 119
  See also Commercial paper
"Passbook" savings accounts, 8
Pass-through certificates, of GNMA, 92
  in mortgage market, 318
Pass-through securities, GNMA, 319
Payments mechanism, checking-account system in,
    68
  in financial system, 23
  and velocity of money, 109
Payments system, impact of 1980 legislation on,
    106
  role of commercial banking in, 52
Penn Central Corporation, bankruptcy of, 143, 288
Pension funds, corporate bonds held by, 300
  equity securities held by, 329
  financial characteristics of, 63–65
  role of, 9
Personal identification number (P.I.N.), 74
"Petrodollars," 398
Phillips curve, defined, 444
Plant and equipment expenditures, forecasting, 43
Platt, E., 199
Point-of-sale systems, 74–75
Point-of-sale terminals, 68, 69
Pollution-control revenue bonds, 303
Population, and supply of municipal securities, 303
Portfolio management, active, 251–253
  passive, 250–251
  passive vs. active strategy of, 250
Portfolios, efficient, 230, 240
  of mutual funds, 336
Portfolio selection, covariance in, 228–229
  and diversification, 229
  and expected return, 224–226
  and expected utility, 226
  and incremental risk, 228
  and risk aversion, 227
  systematic vs. unsystematic risk in, 229–230

Portfolio theory, capital-asset-pricing model in,
    233–234
  for efficient market, 232–233
  market model in, 231
  monetary policy in, 432
Pound, British, 397
Predictions, informed, 25
Preemptive right, of shareholders, 331
Preferred stock, 328–329, 337
Price adjustment, in efficient market, 24
Prices, determining, 157–159
Price stability, and money supply, 125–127
Primary market, for corporate bonds, 301
  for equity securities, 330
  for government securities, 280
  for mortgages, 318
  for municipal securities, 305
Prime commercial paper rate, 205, 207
Prime rate, vs. commercial paper rate, 291
Profitability, impact of fluctuating interest rates on,
    253–254
Profits, "abnormal,"335
Property insurance companies, corporate bonds
    held by, 300
  as financial institutions, 63
  municipal bonds of, 304–305
"Prudent man" rule, 247
Public, and demand for currency, 116
Put and Call Brokers and Dealers Association
    (PCBDA), 339
Put options, 340

Q
  See Regulation Q
Quantity theory, of money, 111, 125

Rational expectations hypothesis, 446–447
"Real bills" doctrine, 142
Real Estate Investment Trusts (REITS), 317
Real-estate limited partnership, 319
Real-estate loans, current trends for, 53
  impact of 1980 legislation on, 70
  provisions of, 89
"Real" sector, money supply in, 103
Regulation, government, and allocation of credit,
    78
  consumer-protection laws, 88–90
  and degree of risk, 80–81
  and dual banking system, 85
  functions of, 84–86
  and individual institutions, 79
  influence of, 93
  limitations on function, 80
  of nondepository financial institutions, 82–83
  and outside examination, 81–82

Regulation Q, 86–87
and risk vs. performance, 83–84
Securities and Exchange Commission, 90
and structure of industry, 82
usury laws, 88
See also Federal Reserve System
Regulation Q, 55, 79, 86–87
impact on CDs, 268
and mortgage market, 320
Regulatory authorities, and credit-risk management, 255
Remote service units (RSU), 74
Renegotiated-rate mortgage, 314–315
Repurchase agreements (RPs), in open-market operations of Federal Reserve, 139, 140–141
in federal funds market, 266
overnight, 108
Reserve currency, 373
Reserve requirements, changes in, 149
and demand-deposit expansion, 120
and D.I.D.M.C.A., 133–134
1980 legislation on, 70
as policy tool, 144–145
See also Federal Reserve system
Resource allocation, impact of money on, 109
interest rate for, 154
Resource use, exchanges over time, 5
Retained earnings, 6
Returns, expected, 25
and financial markets efficiency, 24–26
Revaluation, of currency, 374
Revenue bonds, 302, 303
Rights offering, 331
Risk, and expected return, 224
and financial markets efficiency, 24–26
and government regulation, 80–81
of indirect securities, 20
interest rate, 157, 158
vs. performance, 83–84
with short-term borrowings, 56
systematic, 240
systematic vs. unsystematic, 229–230
See also Default risk
Risk aversion, 26
and portfolio selection, 227
and variable-rate earning assets, 251
Risk avoidance, in futures market, 239
Risk-free rate, 211
Risk premium, 186
concept of, 211–212
cyclical changes in, 213
Risk-return framework for equity securities, 334
Rollover mortgage, Canadian, 314
Rostow, W., 388
RPs. *See* Repurchase agreements

RPDs (reserves available for private nonbank deposits), 438–439

Salomon Brothers, forecasts of flow of funds prepared by, 43
forecast for 1980 of, 46, 47
Saving, encouragement of, 6
impact of inflation on, 427
importance of, 17
nature of, 16
and supply of loanable funds, 160–161
Saving-investment process, equity securities in, 323, 324
without financial institution, 19
intermediation in, 18, 19
operational efficiency of, 24
Savings account, as indirect security, 18
Savings bonds, and commercial banking industry, 54
Savings and loan associations, automated teller machines used by, 69
characteristics of, 58
commercial mortgage funds of, 315
in federal funds market, 266
in home mortgage market, 315
impact of interest-rate cycle on, 256
impact of 1980 legislation on, 70
and Regulation Q, 87
role of, 8, 246
tax-avoidance device for, 80
U.S. government and government agencies securities of, 307
traditional functions of, 79
SEC. *See* Securities and Exchange Commission
Secondary market, for corporate bonds, 301
for equity securities, 332–334
for government securities, 280
for mortgages, 318–319
for municipal securities, 306
Securities, of commercial banks, 8
dealers in, financing of, 262
profit-making of, 262
role of, 261
direct (or primary), 7
indirect, 7
monetary indirect, 50
mortgage-backed, 317
municipal, 214
nonmonetary indirect, 50
over-the-counter (OTC), 238
primary, disadvantages of, 20–21
vs. indirect, 18
of state governments, 214
U.S. government, 277
interest rate on, 211

primary and secondary markets for, 280–281
  short-term, 282
  types of, 278
  yield calculations for, 278–280
U.S. government agency, 282
  See also Bonds
Securities Act (1933), 332
Securities and Exchange Commission, 79
  disclosure goal of, 90
  and equity securities, 332
  functions of, 90
  impact of, 86
Security exchanges, characteristics of, 332–333
Security market line (SML), 231
Seller, option, 340
Services, bank, impact of branching on, 97
Shareholders, preemptive right of, 331
Shareholder saving, 323
Shares, of savings and loan association, 8
"Shell" branches, 408–409
"Shocks," price, 426
Sight draft, in international trade, 377
Singapore, Asian offshore currency market in, 398
Sinking fund, specifications for, 298
Small Business Administration (SBA), 91
Smithsonian Agreement (1971), 384
Special Drawing Rights (SDRs), calculation of, 405
Speculation, 344
  in foreign currencies futures market, 357
  nature of, 353–354
Speculators, 239
Spot transaction, in foreign-exchange market, 364
"Spread," 262
Stability, economic, impact of saving and invest-
    ment on, 17
Standard deviation, concept of, 226
  and covariance, 228
  See also Variance
Standard of deferred payment, money as, 104, 122
Standard of living, measure of, 428
Standard and Poor's, bond-rating system of, 212
  credit evaluation by, 255
  500 Stock Composite Index of, 230
Standard of value, money as, 104, 122
State Banking Commissions, functions of, 85
State governments, and bank chartering, 130
  bond issues of, 302–306
  pension funds of, 64–65
  regulation, 95
  U.S. government and government agencies secu-
    rities of, 307
  usury laws, 88
  See also Interstate banking
Stockholders, ownership rights of, 9–10
Stock market, efficiency of, 335

Stock options, trading in, 339–341
Stock prices, and demand for municipals, 305
Stocks, in capital market, 295
  common vs. preferred, 10
  OTC market for, 333
  yields on, 337
Store of value, money as, 104–122
Subscription approach, as alternative to auction
    method, 452
Subsidiaries, approval for, 148
Substitution account, with IMF, 387
Supply-side economics, and inflation, 204, 423
Surplus, in balance of trade, 367
Surplus economic units, 6
Surplus sector, 33–34, 35
Surplus unit, on flow of funds statement, 32
Surtax effort, 462
Surveillance system
  See National Bank Surveillance System
Sutch, R., 200
Switching and processing center (SPC), 75

Tax and Loan (T & L) accounts, 119, 450
Tax collections, 422
Technology, impact on financial system, 71
Teller machines, 74
"Third market," 333
"Third World" nations, and fixed exchange rates,
    389
Time deposits (savings accounts), 7–8
Time draft, in international trade, 377
Tourism, in balance of payments, 366, 369
Trade acceptance, in international trade, 377
Trading in foreign currency futures markets, 359
Tranche CDs, 400
Transactions, real vs. financial, 4
Transactions accounts, of commercial banking in-
    dustry, 51–53
Treasury, U.S., 3
  currency produced by, 120
  debt management policy of, 465
  Federal Reserve as fiscal agent for, 147
  fiscal management activities of, 450–453
Treasury bills, 9, 278, 279, 282
  auctioning of, 281
  vs. commercial paper, 291
  in futures market, 347, 348
  and interest rates, 169, 260–261, 282
  in open-market operations of Federal Reserve,
    139, 140–141
  ownership of, 282
Treasury bonds, 9
Treasury notes, 9
Treasury securities, in bank portfolios, 57
Trust Indenture Act (1939), 297

Truth-in-Lending Act (1969), 88

Unemployment, and economic policy, 424, 425
    and inflation, 444
Unilateral transfers, in balance of payments, 366,
    369
Unions, and inflation, 204
Unit of account, money as, 104, 122
United States, First Bank of, 130
    Second Bank of, 130
    international transactions of, 370–371
    See also Federal Reserve system; Treasury
Up-valuation, of currency, 374
Usury ceilings, elimination of, 70
Usury laws, function of, 88
    and government regulation, 79
Utilities, 226
    impact of inflation on, 210
    municipal provision of, 304

Variable-rate earning assets, 251
Variable-rate mortgage (VRM), 314–315
Variance, 224
    calculation of, 225
    and covariance, 228
Veterans Administration (VA), mutual savings
    bank insured mortgages of, 60
Vietnam War, impact on inflation, 204, 205
Virginia, relaxation of branching limitations in, 97
Volatility, of demand for loanable funds, 166
VRM

See Variable-rate mortgages, 314

Wage/price spiral, 204
Washington County study, 300
Wealth, and economic policy, 433–434
Western Europe, and floating dollar standard, 387
West Germany, futures market in, 347–348
Wire systems, 73–74
"Working capital," 325
World War I, impact on financial system, 372
World War II, impact on international financial
    markets, 389
"Wraparound" features, 313

"Yeoman farmer," concept of, 284
Yield curve, and borrowers and lenders, 179–180
    and business cycle, 249–250
    expectations hypothesis of, 183–185, 199–200
    explanation of, 178, 183–190
    "humped," 179
    individual securities and, 195
    inverted, 182–183
    liquidity-premium explanation of, 185–186
    "normal," 178, 180–181
    riding, 195
    segmented-markets explanation of, 187–190,
        200–201
    uses of, 192–196
Yield to maturity (YTM)
    calculating, 156
    explained, 155